& WORLD HISTORY

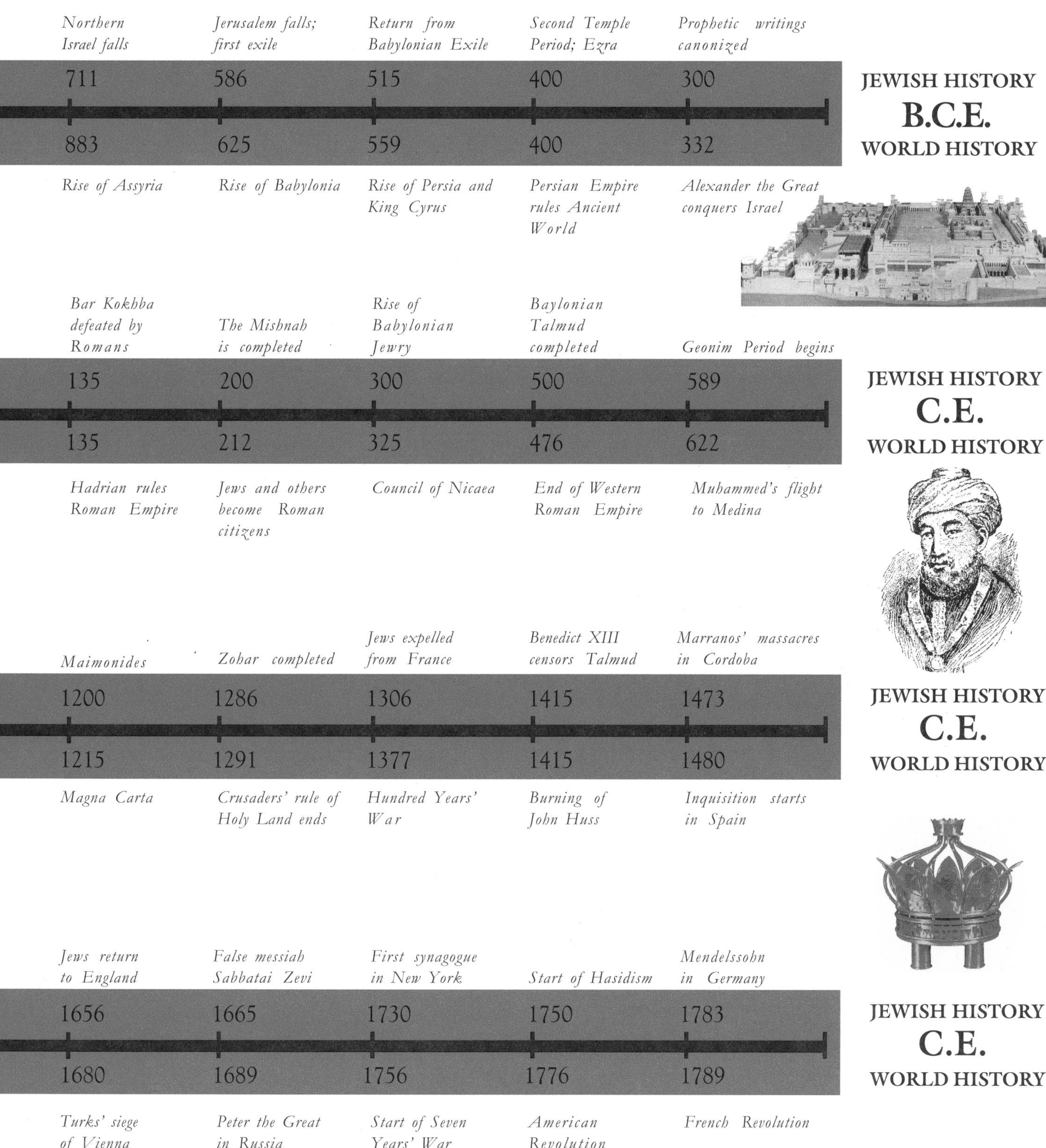

JEWISH HISTORY — B.C.E. — WORLD HISTORY

Northern Israel falls	*Jerusalem falls; first exile*	*Return from Babylonian Exile*	*Second Temple Period; Ezra*	*Prophetic writings canonized*
711	586	515	400	300
883	625	559	400	332
Rise of Assyria	*Rise of Babylonia*	*Rise of Persia and King Cyrus*	*Persian Empire rules Ancient World*	*Alexander the Great conquers Israel*

JEWISH HISTORY — C.E. — WORLD HISTORY

Bar Kokhba defeated by Romans	*The Mishnah is completed*	*Rise of Babylonian Jewry*	*Baylonian Talmud completed*	*Geonim Period begins*
135	200	300	500	589
135	212	325	476	622
Hadrian rules Roman Empire	*Jews and others become Roman citizens*	*Council of Nicaea*	*End of Western Roman Empire*	*Muhammed's flight to Medina*

JEWISH HISTORY — C.E. — WORLD HISTORY

Maimonides	*Zohar completed*	*Jews expelled from France*	*Benedict XIII censors Talmud*	*Marranos' massacres in Cordoba*
1200	1286	1306	1415	1473
1215	1291	1377	1415	1480
Magna Carta	*Crusaders' rule of Holy Land ends*	*Hundred Years' War*	*Burning of John Huss*	*Inquisition starts in Spain*

JEWISH HISTORY — C.E. — WORLD HISTORY

Jews return to England	*False messiah Sabbatai Zevi*	*First synagogue in New York*	*Start of Hasidism*	*Mendelssohn in Germany*
1656	1665	1730	1750	1783
1680	1689	1756	1776	1789
Turks' siege of Vienna	*Peter the Great in Russia*	*Start of Seven Years' War*	*American Revolution*	*French Revolution*

The Shengold

JEWISH ENCYCLOPEDIA

"But for learning,
Heaven and Earth
would not endure."

— TALMUD, PESAHIM

“For the earth shall be full of the knowledge of the Lord, as the waters cover the sea.”

— *Isaiah 11:9*

Printer’s mark used by Abraham Usque, sixteenth century Jewish printer of Ferrara, Italy.

The Shengold JEWISH ENCYCLOPEDIA

Edited by
Mordecai Schreiber

Alvin I. Schiff, Consulting Editor
Leon Klenicki, Consulting Editor

SCHREIBER PUBLISHING

Rockville, Maryland

The Shengold Jewish Encyclopedia
Second Edition

Published by:

Schreiber Publishing
Post Office Box 4193
Rockville, MD 20849 USA
www.schreiberpublishing.com

Second Edition

Library of Congress Cataloging-in-Publication Data

The Shengold Jewish Encyclopedia / edited by Mordecai Schreiber ; Alvin I. Schiff,
Leon Klenicki, consulting editor[s].-- 2nd ed.
p. cm.
ISBN 1-887563-66-0
1. Jews--Encyclopedias. 2. Judaism--Encyclopedias. I. Schreiber, Mordecai. II. Schiff,
Alvin I., 1926- III. Klenicki, Leon.

DS102.8 .S545 2001
909'.04924'003--dc21

200149002

Printed in the United States of America

Ma Nishtana...

Why Is This Encyclopedia Different?

In the beginning there was the *Junior Jewish Encyclopedia.* For nearly half a century, this one-volume Shengold sourcebook on everything Jewish was one of the most familiar books on the American Jewish scene and throughout the English-speaking Jewish world. It instructed and delighted two generations of Jews, and was reprinted and updated fourteen times. During that time Jewish life both in the Diaspora and in Israel changed radically. American Jewry has become thoroughly acculturated, yet many young Jewish adults have begun to look for their roots and their heritage. It became clear to the Publisher that the time had come to thoroughly update and rewrite the *Junior Encyclopedia* so that it could be used as a handy reference tool for all ages. Hence, the *Shengold Jewish Encyclopedia.* This new adaptation—rich in information, illustrations, charts, and maps—is accessible to the young and useful for adults. It does not lay any claims to full coverage of a culture and a history that require many volumes to even begin to touch on everything. Instead, the editors have carefully selected the essential, the most representative, and the most instructive, so that the reader may obtain some immediate information, use cross-references, and feel motivated to look for other sources of in-depth knowledge on any particular subject.

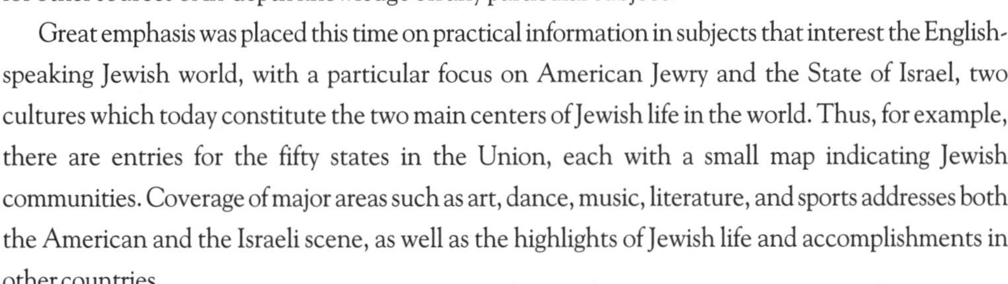

Great emphasis was placed this time on practical information in subjects that interest the English-speaking Jewish world, with a particular focus on American Jewry and the State of Israel, two cultures which today constitute the two main centers of Jewish life in the world. Thus, for example, there are entries for the fifty states in the Union, each with a small map indicating Jewish communities. Coverage of major areas such as art, dance, music, literature, and sports addresses both the American and the Israeli scene, as well as the highlights of Jewish life and accomplishments in other countries.

To make it easier to use this book, we have provided an introductory section on how to use the *Encyclopedia*, as well as a list of maps, tables, and color plates.

It has been argued that the world today is changing so rapidly and information travels so fast that there is no point in publishing a new encyclopedia, which will quickly become obsolete. This is not true in the case of the present volume. While some statistics do change daily, and some major world developments will occur by the time one reads these lines, most of the information in this book will still be useful in the new century, and much of it is timeless. This is, after all, the story of an ageless people, a people who saw the pyramids being built, who defied the Roman Empire, who shared in nearly every major event of the last two millennia, and, in our time, rose out of the ashes and reestablished itself in its ancestral land.

Many sources throughout the Jewish world have been drawn upon in preparing this volume—Jewish organizations in the United States, Israel, and around the world; government agencies; libraries and archives; museums and private collections; news agencies and newspapers; and many other information sources. Literally thousands of books and documents have been consulted, and countless photographs, drawings, engravings, maps, charts, and lists have been reviewed to find the best verbal and visual material for communicating the incredible cultural heritage of the people who originated the Bible at the dawn of civilization and continue to enrich every field of human endeavor to this day.

Acknowledgments

We wish to acknowledge the work of all those who contributed to the creation of this beautiful book. First, a special tribute is due to Moshe Sheinbaum, founder of Shengold Publishers and creator of the *Junior Jewish Encyclopedia*, whose invaluable advice has made the present volume possible, and to the editors and contributors of that award-winning volume.

Our deepest thanks to the editors of the present volume, to whom this has been a labor of love, and to the artists, who also made this project an affair of the heart, particularly Debra Valencia and Mark Sabatke. Rachel Schreiber and Sara Nevin of Indiana University helped restore many photos and images. A special thanks to Kimberly Craskey for her editorial assistance.

Jed Lyons and Miriam Bass at National Book Network provided the initial encouragement and the sustained moral support in undertaking this arduous task and completing it in record time.

Two "women of valor" without whose support this project would not have come to fruition are Hanita Schreiber, CEO of Capital Community Health Plan, and Marla Schulman, Vice President of Schreiber Translations, Inc.

In addition to all the many individuals and organizations who have contributed to this book in the past, added support was provided this time by the Embassy of Israel in Washington, DC; the *Washington Jewish Week*; Na'amat USA; the Anti-Defamation League; Tal Brody of Maccabi Tel Aviv; Yad Vashem in Jerusalem; the Diaspora Museum in Tel Aviv; the U.S. Holocaust Museum in Washington, DC; and the Library of Congress, Judaica Section, in Washington, DC.

All color plates are courtesy of the Embassy of Israel, Washington, DC.

How to Use the Shengold Jewish Encyclopedia

Entries. Most important personalities, places, events, institutions, organizations, customs, practices, and so on have individual entries. Some, however, appear within a larger article. For example, "Seder" appears under *Passover*. Hence, when you look up "Seder," you will find the reference "*See* **Passover**."

Cross references. In almost every entry you will find words in **bold** print, indicating that there is a separate entry under that particular word. If you are looking for further information on your subject, you may want to check those cross references which in most instances will provide either direct or related information on the subject in which you are interested.

Hebrew transliteration. Many entries are Anglicized renditions of original Hebrew words and terms. This creates a problem of transliteration, since there is no universal way of rendering Hebrew in English letters, and since some Hebrew letters, such as *het* and *khaf*, do not have English equivalents. The Hebrew word *Hanukkah*, for example, begins with the letter *het*, which is not pronounced like the English *h*. Hence, you may also see *Hanukkah* spelled as *Chanukah* or *Chanuka* (without the final *h*, since the Hebrew word ends with a silent *h*), where the initial *ch*, as in the Scottish word *loch*, imitates the Hebrew sound *het*.

To further compound the problem, Hebrew also lives within the Jewish dialect known as Yiddish, where a word like *Shalom* becomes *Sholom*.

All of this creates a serious problem for looking up Hebrew-based entries, and sometimes you may have to look in several places before you find the right term. This, unfortunately, cannot be helped, and one simply has to be patient.

Names. Jewish family names are less than 200 years old. Hence, personalities who lived more than 200 years ago are often known as "son of," as in the case of Simeon ben Shetah, or Simon, son of Shetah. In this case, the name appears under *Simeon*. Conversely, Jews who lived under Islam were often known by *Ibn*, Arabic for "son of." Thus, in the case of Abraham Ibn Ezra, the listing is under *Ibn Ezra*. In other instances, a personality may be known by a title or by a popular name, such as "Maimonides" for Moshe ben Maimon, in which case the entry is under the familiar name *Maimonides*.

Here again there are no set rules, and at times some searching is required.

Statistics. There is a great deal of population statistics in this book. However, one must keep in mind several things: (a) most Jews live in urban areas, and urban statistics are often misleading, since they may or may not cover certain suburbs or adjoining areas of a main urban center; (b) populations change daily, hence figures are never exact; (c) in the past ten years most of the Jews of Eastern Europe have left for Israel and the West, changing world Jewish demographics radically, and the end is not yet in sight. Thus, statistics should be seen as approximate, rather than absolute.

Maps and Lists. Your attention is drawn to the Time Line inside the covers of the book, which provides a bird's eye view of all of Jewish history. When you look up an entry in the book and wonder about the time frame of both Jewish and world events, you may want to check the Time Line to put that entry in its chronological context.

There are many useful tables and maps inside and in the back of the book, which offer easily accessible information on major Jewish subjects. A list is provided on the following page.

Maps

Lists

Color Plates

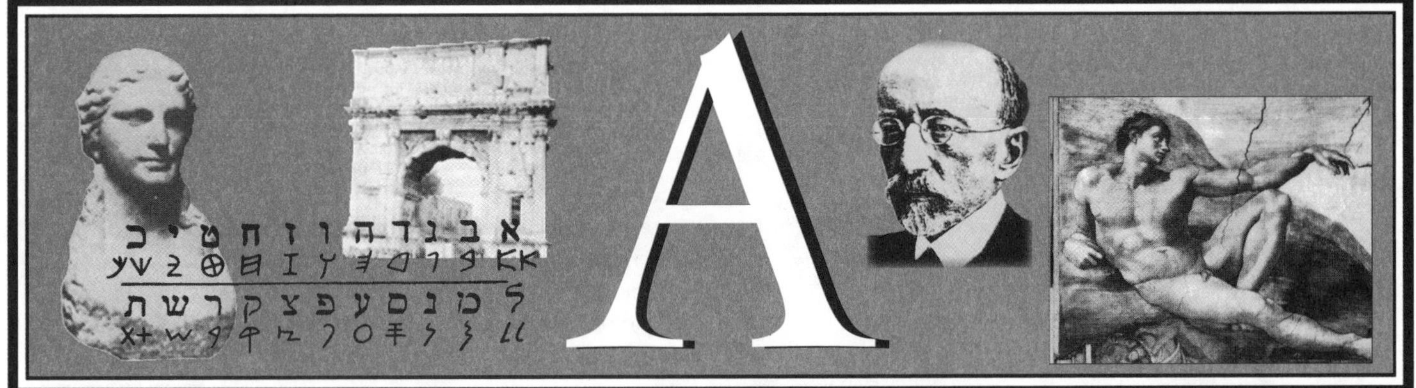

AARON (ca. 1300 B.C.E.). **Moses'** older brother and spokesman in Egypt. Together they appeared before Pharaoh when Aaron "cast down his staff before Pharaoh...and it became a serpent" (Exod. 7:10). Aaron is represented as the first high priest in Israel, having officiated in the **Tabernacle** built in the wilderness. He became the ancestor of all the priests and high priests, thus permanently dividing the tribe of **Levi** into two categories: the priests and the Levites, or servitors, both of whom served in the Sanctuary. (*See also* **Kohen**.)

Aaron and Moses before the Pharaoh, by Gustav Doré.

AARONSOHN, AARON (1876-1919). Agricultural expert and early Zionist leader in Palestine. He conducted valuable experiments to improve crops cultivated in Palestine, and discovered wild wheat, a special type of grain sought by botanists the world over. During World War I, with his brother Alexander, his sister Sarah, and close friends, he joined the NILI, a secret organization which sought to aid Britain in conquering Palestine, in order to realize a Jewish homeland. Sarah was captured by the Turks who tortured her to find out who NILI's members were. She refused to tell and finally shot herself. At the end of the war, Aaronsohn set out on a political mission to **England**. On May 15, 1919, on the way from **London** to **Paris** to the Peace Conference, his plane mysteriously disappeared. It is assumed that it fell into the English Channel. Aaronsohn left behind valuable botanical studies which were published after his untimely death. K'far Aaron, a village in **Israel**, as well as the Agricultural Institute of the **Hebrew University** in **Jerusalem**, are named in his honor.

Sarah Aaronsohn

Aaron Aaronsohn

ABBA SIKRA (SIKARA). Leader of extremist rebels in the Jewish uprising against **Rome** in 69-70 C.E. When his uncle, Rabbi **Johanan Ben Zakkai**, wanted to leave the beleaguered **Jerusalem** and establish a center of learning at **Yavneh** in southern Palestine, Abba Sikra saw to Rabbi Johanan's safe passage through one of the city gates.

ABEL. Son of **Adam** and **Eve**; a shepherd. When Abel's offering was accepted by God, his brother, Cain, grew jealous and slew him. Then the Lord asked Cain, "Where is Abel, thy brother?" Cain answered, "I know not; am I my brother's keeper?" As punishment, the Lord made Cain a "fugitive and a vagabond on the earth" (Gen. 4:1-4:16).

ABRAHAM (ca. 1940 B.C.E.). Founder of the Jewish people; first of the patriarchs, who discarded idol worship for belief in one God. The **Covenant** between God and Israel began with Abraham. His story is told in Genesis 11-25, from his birth in Ur of Chaldea in southern Mesopotamia to his death and burial in the cave of Machpelah near Hebron in the land of Canaan. Abraham was commanded by God to leave his birthplace between the Tigris and Euphrates Rivers and to settle in "the land that I will show you." He

> *"Be of the students of Aaron, who loves peace and pursues it, friendly to all people, and brings them closer to the Torah."*
>
> — PIRKE AVOT

Cain and Abel. Engraving After Titian. "And it came to pass, when they were in the field, that Cain rose up against Abel his brother, and slew him." — Genesis 4:8

obeyed and set out with his family on the long journey to Canaan. When he came to Sh'chem, "the Lord appeared to Abraham and said, 'Unto your seed will I give this land!'" (Gen. 12:7) Throughout Genesis 11:26-17:5, Abraham is called *Av-Ram*, "exalted father." Then his name is changed to *Av-Raham*, "father of multitudes"—"for the father of a multitude of nations have I made you...And I will establish my covenant between Me and you, and your seed after you in their generations for an everlasting covenant." As a sign of this everlasting contract, Abraham instituted circumcision of every eight-day-old male child.

The biblical account of Abraham brings new dignity to the story of humankind. Through the covenant of Abraham, each person becomes a partner in a contract with God, obligated to serve righteously and obediently, receiving in return the Promised Land as inheritance.

Sacrifice of Isaac. Ink Drawing by Franz Kirzinger, 1769.

As the story of Abraham unfolds, his love of peace, sense of justice, and compassion for suffering are revealed in his acts. With great patience, he settled the disputes between the sheep herders of Lot and his own men. With great daring, he pleaded with God not to destroy the wicked people of Sodom and Gomorrah, even if there were only ten righteous people among them. In the story of Isaac's sacrifice, Abraham's submission to God was tested. As commanded, Abraham placed his son upon the altar, preparing to offer him up. An angel of God restrained him: "Lay not your hand upon the lad... for now I know you fear God." Then Abraham lifted his eyes and saw a ram "caught up in a thicket by his horns." He sacrificed the ram instead of Isaac. In Abraham's time, sacrificing children to the gods was a common ritual among heathens, but the new religion of Abraham taught that God forbade child sacrifice and that human life was sacred.

ABRAMOWITZ, SHALOM JACOB. *See* **Mendele Mocher Sefarim.**

ABRAHAM, HAROLD. *See* **Sports.**

ABRAVANEL, DON ISAAC (1437-1508). Scholar, philosopher, and statesman. Don Isaac was an illustrious member of one of the most distinguished Sephardic Jewish families that traced its origin to King David. Born in Lisbon, Abravanel served as treasurer to King Alfonso V of **Portugal**. When Alfonso died, his successor accused Don Isaac of conspiring against the king, forcing Abravanel to flee to **Spain** in 1483. There he served King Ferdinand and Queen Isabella in state financial affairs. When a decree expelling Jews from Spain was issued in 1492, he and other influential Jews pleaded before the court for its withdrawal, but to no avail. Abravanel was offered personal exemption from the decree, but chose to flee to Naples, where he again entered royal service.

Abravanel. Courtesy Jewish National Fund.

Abravanel's Jewish scholarship is shown in his commentaries on the **Bible**. Despite his firm faith in the divine revelation of the Bible, he saw clearly the importance of historical background in biblical exposition. Stirred by Jewish suffering, he wrote three works to perpetuate belief in the coming of the Messiah (*see also* **Messianism**). As a philosopher, he supported the principle of free will, and opposed the influence of Aristotle and Plato on Jewish thought. Abravanel was survived by three distinguished sons: Joseph, a physician and scholar; Judah Leon, also a physician; and Samuel, scholar and patron of Jewish learning.

ABSALOM. Third son of **David** and his wife Maacha, the daughter of Talmai, King of Geshur. The Hebrew *Av-Shalom*,

"Father of Peace," is an ironic name for the son who stirred up a rebellion against his father in order to wrest the throne from him and who became a perennial symbol of a rebellious child. For four years Absalom secretly plotted and then openly set up military headquarters in Hebron. David withdrew from Jerusalem, a stratagem which proved successful, for it brought Absalom to "the forest of Ephraim," east of the **Jordan River**, where David, long skilled in guerilla fighting, had no difficulty in defeating his son. As Absalom fled from the battlefield on a mule, his long hair caught in the branches of an oak tree. His mule trotted on, leaving him helplessly trapped. He was killed by David's general, Joab. Hearing the news of this act which he had expressly forbidden, David the King uttered a cry that has become a classic expression of a father's grief: "O my son Absalom, my son...would I had died for thee..." (II Sam. 19:1).

The Death of Absalom, from an old engraving.

ABULAFIA, ABRAHAM. *See* **Kabbalah**.

ABORTION. *See* **Life, Sanctity of.**

ABZUG, BELLA (1920-1998). First Jewish woman to serve in the U.S. Congress (1971-76) and first person elected on a women's rights platform. Abzug was a peace activist, labor lawyer, lecturer, news commentator, and civil rights advocate. "Women," she once said, "have been trained to speak softly and carry a lipstick. Those days are over."

ACADEMIES, BABYLONIAN. *See* **Talmud**.

ACCENTS (t'amim, or trope). Signs above and underneath letters of the Scriptural texts, indicating how the text should be chanted to make the meaning clear and the reading pleasant. Thus, accents serve both as musical notes and as punctuation. The signs are the same in all books of the **Bible**, but are read differently in certain passages and sections. Jews of various countries have evolved different chants for them. This system of accents is said to date back to **Ezra the Scribe** (5th century B.C.E.) and the Great Assembly.

Notes for chanting the Torah (top) and the hattaran (bottom).

ACOSTA, URIEL (Gabriel da Costa) (1585-1640). Uriel Acosta was born in Oporto, **Portugal**, to an aristocratic **Marrano** family that had been forcibly converted to Christianity. He came to doubt the teachings of Catholicism, but having no contact with Judaism he formed a highly personal view through his reading of the **Bible**. After his father's death, he persuaded his family to move to **Amsterdam** and return to Judaism. There he began to express his ideas and wrote *Proposals Against Tradition*; in 1624 he developed these ideas further in *Comparison of Pharisaic Tradition with the Scriptures*. In this book Acosta expressed his rejection of the soul's immortality, resurrection, and reward and punishment. These views resulted in the public burning of his books. The Amsterdam Jewish community placed him under "the great ban" in 1618. Everyone, including his brothers, shunned him. In 1633, when he could no longer bear the isolation, Acosta publicly renounced his opinions, only to revert back to his controversial beliefs. Again excommunicated, he led a solitary life for seven years. When this existence became unbearable, he again recanted and submitted to a harrowing ceremony of repentance in the Amsterdam synagogue. Acosta could not bear to live after this public humiliation. He wrote a short autobiography defending his views, then in 1640, committed suicide.

ACRE (Akko). Seaport town on the northern hook of **Haifa** Bay. In Canaanite times it was a "strong-walled" Phoenician seaport allotted to the tribe of Asher (Judges 1:31), seized alternately by **Egypt** and Assyria. Since 800 B.C.E., it has served successively as a Greek and Roman port, Crusaders' fortress, Moslem battlefield, and French trading center. After being destroyed by the Turks, Acre was rebuilt in 1749, only to be besieged by Napoleon. It continued to change hands until it was acquired by the British. In 1948, Acre fell to the State of Israel, which built a new Jewish town outside the walls. Its population of 50,000 includes Moslem, Maronite, Quaker, Druze, and Bahai minorities. With the advent of steamships, Haifa replaced Acre as a major port.

Aqueduct near Acre

ADAM. Hebrew for "man; son of the earth." In the **Bible**, Adam is the first man, created "in the image of God" on the sixth day of Creation and given by the Lord "dominion over all the earth." (For the story of Creation, see the first chapter of Genesis.)

ADAR. Sixth month of the Jewish civil calendar. Traditionally known as a month of merriment since **Purim** falls on the 14th.

ADLER, CYRUS (1863-1940). Scholar of and authority on Far East civilizations and Semitic languages, and prominent leader in the American Jewish community. Adler was born in Van Buren, Ark., almost two years before the end of the Civil War. He played an important role in shaping the cultural life and in developing some of the great organizations of the American Jewish community as he watched it grow from a few thousand to five million during his lifetime. He was a founder and active member of the American Jewish

Historical Society and the **Jewish Publication Society of America**. He served as president of the **Jewish Theological Seminary of America** in **New York City** and of Dropsie College (*see* **Annenberg Research Institute**) in Philadelphia. As a young man, he taught Semitic languages at Johns Hopkins University in **Baltimore**. Between 1888 and 1909, he served as director of the Ancient East department of the Washington National Museum. At the Smithsonian Institution he served as librarian (1892-1905) and assistant secretary (1905-08). He edited publications of Jewish learning, including *Jews in the Diplomatic Correspondence of the U.S.* He was a founder and president of the **American Jewish Committee** and the National Jewish Welfare Board. He was active in forming the **Jewish Agency** for Palestine, and served as its non-Zionist co-chair. His autobiography, *I Have Considered the Days,* is an engaging profile of his era and its many noteworthy leaders.

Cyrus Adler

ADON OLAM. *See* **Siddur**.

AFGHANISTAN. Middle Eastern country lying between **India**, Pakistan, and **Russia.** Jews have lived in Afghanistan since before the destruction of the Second **Temple** in 70 B.C.E. There is a legend that they are descended from the **Ten Lost Tribes**. Little is known about the history of the Jewish community there, except that Jews have always been second-class citizens under the medieval despotism prevailing in Afghanistan. Until 1914, they were forced to live in sealed ghettos. After 1914, there was a brief period during which abuse was curtailed and their situation improved. However, in the early 1930's, largely under the influence of several hundred German technicians working in the country, discriminatory measures were renewed. Jews were required to obtain special permits for travel, forbidden to write letters abroad, excluded from the civil service and most of the professions, banned from commerce, expelled from rural areas, and confined to the cities of Kabul, Herat, and Balkh. By the end of World War II, the number of Jews in Afghanistan had been reduced from about 12,000 to 5,000, largely through illegal emigration.

In 1948, with the establishment of the State of Israel, the majority of Afghanistan Jewry expressed the desire to emigrate, but the government obstructed their emigration. Between 1949 and 1970, approximately 4,200 Afghan Jews reached Israel. In 1993, there were fewer than 100 Jews in the country.

To this day, there are wandering tribes on the borders between Afghanistan and Pakistan which can trace their origin to the twelve tribes of Israel. They are divided into twelve large families, each named after a son of **Jacob**. They retain some Jewish customs, such as lighting candles on Friday night and wearing **Tzitzit**, or fringes.

AFIKOMAN. *See* **Passover**.

AFTERLIFE. *See* **Heaven and Hell**.

AGAM, YAAKOV (1929-). Internationally renowned Israeli artist, known for his abstract, colorful painting which change colors when seen from different angles, known as kinetic and optical art. Agam has produced many works based on Jewish ritual objects and traditional Jewish themes.

AGGADAH. Part of the **Talmud** which, complementing the legal **Halakhah**, stresses its ethical and inspirational meaning. It sparkles with picturesque similes, proverbs, and epigrams, as well as wonderful tales. The origins of the Aggadah may be traced to biblical times, and it continued to be written throughout the Middle Ages. Beginning in Israel, it is saturated with the atmosphere of the Holy Land. The Aggadah collections of Reb Yaakov ben Habib in the 15th century, titled *Ein Yaakov*, became one of the most popular Jewish books.

AGNON, SAMUEL JOSEPH (1888-1970). Hebrew novelist. Born in Galicia, Agnon settled in Palestine in 1909, but lived in Germany from 1912 to 1923. His works are based chiefly upon traditional Jewish life in Europe. They are rich in Hasidic lore and legend, capturing the spirit and flavor of Jewish culture. Agnon's prose has a charm of its own. Although abundant in realistic detail, it often has a dreamlike quality.

Among Agnon's finest novels are *Hachnasat Kallah* (The Bridal Canopy), *Sippur Pashut* (A Simple Story), and *Oreah Natah La-lun* (Lodging for a Night). In *T'mol Shilshom* (Only Yesterday), he draws upon his experiences in Palestine to create a fascinating epic. In December 1966 he became the first Hebrew writer to receive the **Nobel Prize** for Literature, an award he shared with the German-Jewish poet Nelly **Sachs**.

Agnon receiving notice of the Nobel Prize in 1966.

AGRICULTURE. Now chiefly city dwellers, Jews spent the first two millennia of their history as shepherds and farmers. **Abraham** came to **Canaan** in search of grazing land for his flocks. For several centuries his descendants were semi-nomadic, settling down to farm only at the time of the conquest of Canaan around 1200 B.C.E. Under the **Judges** and during the First and Second Commonwealths, most Israelites were farmers, breeding livestock and raising wheat, barley, grapes, olives, and vegetables.

The dispersion of the Jews by the Romans in the 1st century C.E. led to their separation from the land. In **Babylonia**, most exiles settled in cities and into handicraft and trade occupations. Jews were removed further from agriculture in the Middle Ages when most Christian princes forbade Jews to own land. Thus, by the beginning of the 19th century, less than one percent of Jews in the world were farmers.

At that time, however, a movement had arisen to bring the Jews back to the soil. Pondering the problem of **anti-Semitism** and the economic distress of East European Jewry, many thinkers concluded that a return to the soil might provide a solution. In 1804, Tsar Alexander I of **Russia** founded seven colonies expressly for Jewish subjects, as part of a plan for their segregation as well as rehabilitation. In the following decades several Jewish colonies were established in the Americas; due to lack of funds and experience, most failed. Not until the 1880's and 1890's were small but successful colonies founded in Palestine, **Argentina**, and the U.S.

In 1900, the Jewish Agricultural Society was established in the U.S. by joint action of the **Jewish Colonization Association** and the Baron de **Hirsch** Fund. During the first forty years of the Society's existence, more than 13,000 Jewish farmers were assisted in land acquisition and development. Jewish agricultural communities are located in New Jersey, Pennsylvania, and other states. The National Farm school was established in Doylestown, Pa., in 1896. An agricultural magazine, *The Jewish Farmer*, established in 1908, provides agricultural information in both Yiddish and English.

During the 20th century, the number of Jewish farmers has steadily increased, swelled by refugees from Eastern and Central Europe. In Israel, where land settlement has been the first goal of the Zionist movement, the number of Jewish farmers has risen from several hundred in 1900 to about 83,000 in 1984 (in a total work force of 1.3 million.) The Jewish farm population of the U.S. has increased from about 300 families in 1900 to more than 10,000 in 1960. In 1979, there were about 30,000 Jewish farmers in Argentina. Colonization on a smaller scale has taken place in **Brazil**, **Australia**, **Poland,** and the Balkans.

AGRIPPA I (ca. 10 B.C.E -44 C.E.). King of Judea. Son of Aristobulus and grandson of **Herod** and Mariamne, at the age of six Agrippa was sent to **Rome** to be educated. He was a companion to the Roman crown prince Gaius Caligula and shared in the gay and frivolous court life. Accused of favoring the crown prince over the reigning Emperor Tiberius, he was thrown into prison. Upon Caligula's ascent to the throne, he was released and appointed king of **Galilee**.

The vineyards of Judea and Samaria provide grapes for Israel's wine industry.

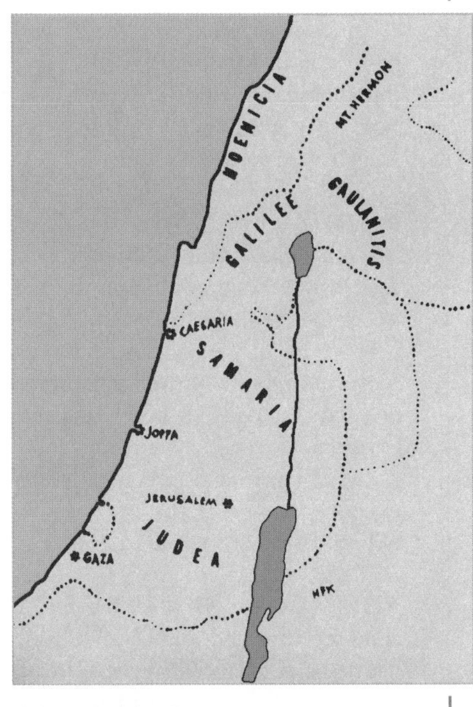

Palestine of Agrippa I

The Jews received Agrippa's appointment with great joy. Having been subjected to Roman rule for 45 years, the appointment of Agrippa I signified liberation from foreign dominion and oppression. (When at one time he deplored the fact that he was not of pure Jewish stock, the scholars consoled him, saying, "Fear not, Agrippa, you are our brother.") When Claudius replaced Caligula as emperor, Agrippa's rule was extended to Samaria and Judea. A brief era of peace began, which recalled the glories of the Hasmonean period.

Agrippa planned to strengthen Jewish rule and eventually free Palestine from Roman yoke. The great hopes of his people for full independence were shattered when he died suddenly in 44 C.E. while attending the Roman games in Caesarea. It is assumed that he was poisoned by enemies of the Jews.

AGRIPPA II (ca. 28-93 C.E.). Son of **Agrippa I**, he was the last king to rule Palestine before the destruction of the Second **Temple**. He was reared in the same corrupt Roman court atmosphere as his father; however, unlike his father, Agrippa II was completely alienated from his people. The Roman rulers appointed him king of the eastern provinces of Palestine and entrusted him with the care of the **Temple**. All of western Palestine remained under Roman rule.

When the Jewish revolt broke out against foreign dominion in 70 C.E., Agrippa urged unconditional submission to Rome. His cooperation with the hated enemy angered the people, and together with his sister, he was forced to flee Jerusalem. He remained in the Roman camp until his death.

AGUDATH ISRAEL. Worldwide organization of Orthodox Jews, founded in 1912 in Kattowitz, **Poland**. Before World War II, Agudath Israel was influential in many European countries, particularly in Poland, **Czechoslovakia**, and **Germany**. Its total membership was estimated at half a million. A rabbinical council of prominent Talmudical scholars, called Moetzet Gedolei HaTorah, was established to hand down decisions on Jewish law. Today, Agudah has headquarters in three world capitals: **London**, **Jerusalem**, and **New York City**.

Through a special fund, the Keren Ha-Torah, the movement has established and maintained many *yeshivot* and Talmud Torahs throughout the world. It has also promoted the Beth Jacob school system for girls in many countries, providing both religious and secular education for its students.

Agudath Israel is active in combating laws which interfere with traditional religious observance. It has opposed the passage of laws in Europe and the U.S. that prohibit ritual slaughter. It has also campaigned against changes in the calendar which would jeopardize the observance of Jewish holy days.

From its inception, Agudath Israel has opposed political **Zionism**. After the birth of Israel, however, the Agudah joined the first government of Israel and participated in subsequent government coalitions.

Prominent leaders of Agudath Israel included the late Jacob Rosenheim of Israel, the late Rabbi Aaron Kotler of Lakewood, N.J., and the late Rabbi Eliezer Silver of Cincinnati, Ohio.

AHAB (Ruled 876-853 B.C.E.). Seventh king of Israel; contemporary and ally of Jehoshaphat, King of Judah. Ahab married the Phoenician princess **Jezebel**, daughter of Ethbaal, King of Tyre. This alliance, by securing Israel's peace with a powerful neighbor, left Ahab free to resist an Assyrian attack successfully and win a victory over Ben Hadad II, King of Damascus. Three years later, Ahab was slain by a chance arrow in the battle for Ramot Gilead. **Elijah**'s prophecy had foretold Ahab's death as punishment for tolerating the **Baal** worship instituted by **Jezebel**, and for lawlessly executing Naboth, whose vineyard he desired.

"Ahab the Israelite" is mentioned in the "monolithic inscription" left by Shalmaneser III (858-825 B.C.E.) of Assyria. Here, Ahab is portrayed as a formidable foe commanding a force of 2,000 chariots and 10,000 soldiers.

AHAD HA-AM (Asher Ginzberg) (1856-1927). One of the foremost thinkers and essayists in Hebrew literature. Writing under the pseudonym Ahad Ha-Am, meaning "one of the people," he taught cultural or "spiritual Zionism." As "political Zionism" emerged under **Herzl**, Ahad Ha-Am argued in such essays as *Lo Zeh ha-derekh* (This Is Not the Way) that Israel must first become a spiritual and cultural center before it could develop into a viable Jewish state. His essays, collectively published as *Al Parashat Derakhim* (At the Crossroads) roused the Jewish public and stand as a landmark of Hebrew literature. His forceful, moral personality greatly influenced Zionism. Before World War I, Ahad Ha-am lived in England, where he played an important role in the events leading to the **Balfour Declaration**. At 66, he settled in Palestine, on a Tel Aviv street named in his honor.

Ahad Ha-am

AHASUERUS, KING OF PERSIA. *See* **Esther, Book of.**

AKDAMUT. *See* **Shavuot**.

AKEDAH. Meaning binding or preparing for sacrifice; Abraham's offering of Isaac as a sacrifice to God (Gen. 22).

AKIVA BEN JOSEPH (ca. 40-135 C.E.). Great Talmudic scholar and leader. It is told that until he was forty years of age, he was an ignorant shepherd. Rachel, the beautiful daughter of Kalba Sabbua, a rich Jerusalemite, fell in love with Akiva and secretly married him. Enraged that his daughter married beneath her station, her father immediately disinherited her. Rachel's ardent wish was that Akiva study Jewish law. Despite their poverty, Rachel encouraged Akiva as he studied for many years in the academy. When he finally returned home followed by thousands of pupils, Rachel came to meet him. When his students, not knowing who she was, wanted to turn her away, Rabbi Akiva rebuked them, saying, "Let her be. Your wisdom, as well as mine, are due to her."

Rabbi Akiva. Courtesy Jewish National Fund.

Akiva's brilliant and penetrating mind is revealed in his interpretation of Jewish law. He assembled and edited the teachings of previous scholars, and in arranging them by subject, laid the foundation for the editing of the Mishnah. A great Jewish patriot, he joined **Bar Kokhba** in inspiring the Jews to rebel against Roman rule, sixty years after the destruction of the Temple. Akiva saw the Messiah in Bar Kokhba (*see* **Messianism**), applying to him the biblical prediction of the coming of the Messianic redeemer of the Jews: "A star (*kokhav*) shall rise out of Jacob" (Num. 24:17). However, the rebellion failed, and the Roman Emperor Hadrian prohibited, under penalty of death, the observance and study of Jewish law. Having defied the Emperor's decree, Akiva was one of the ten martyrs sentenced to death by flaying. Accepting his fate to serve God with all his soul, he faced his end serenely. While the sage recited the traditional prayer of **Shema** ("Hear, O Israel, the Lord our God, the Lord is one"), he relinquished his spirit, setting a lasting example for the Jewish martyrs to come.

ALABAMA. Jewish merchants in Mobile, Ala., date back to 1777. Later in 1840, the congregation Shaare Shamayim was organized there. German Jews settled in Selma in the 1840's. In the 1960's, American Jewish leaders, such as **Heschel**, took part in the struggle for civil rights in this state. Today, Alabama has thriving Jewish communities in Birmingham (5,200), Mobile (1,100), Montgomery (1,300), and Huntsville (750).

ALASKA. Jews from California were instrumental in making this territory part of the United States and in establishing the Alaska Company which controlled the state's main industry, the fur trade. Records of Jewish life date back to the mid-19th century. Today, most Jews live in Anchorage (1,600), with a smaller community in Fairbanks (540).

ALBO, JOSEPH (1380-1435). Spanish-Jewish philosopher who encapsulated Jewish dogma in his book *Sefer Ha-Ikkarim* (Book of Principles.) He based this summary on God's existence and revelation, and on divine reward and punishment.

ALBRIGHT, WILLIAM FOXHALL (1889-1971). "Father of Biblical Archeology." Albright was the son of Christian missionaries. He paved the way for major Jewish archeologists like Glueck and **Yadin**. He directed the American School for Oriental Research in Jerusalem, and taught Semitic languages at Johns Hopkins University. Among his books is *The Archeology of Palestine*.

ALCOTT, AMY. *See* **Sports**.

ALEPH. First letter of the Hebrew alphabet; also, the number one.

ALEXANDER THE GREAT (356-323 B.C.E.). King of Macedonia; conqueror of the ancient world. In his defeated provinces, Alexander introduced Greek forms of government, encouraged intermarriage among his followers and his new subjects, and spread the Greek language and customs. As a result, a new civilization, **Hellenism**, spread throughout Alexander's empire. His attitude toward the Jews was friendly, and in Maccabean times, his name was used frequently among Jews. His many legends have been told in Talmudic literature. The Hellenism he introduced into **Syria** and **Egypt** had a deep influence on Judaism and its history.

ALEXANDER JANNAEUS (Hebrew name, Jonathan). Reigned 103-76 B.C.E. as king and high priest; son of Johanan **Hyrcanos**; first of the Hasmonean dynasty to be called king; and first to issue coins stamped in both Greek and Hebrew. He married Queen **Salome Alexandra**, sister of Simon ben Shetah, president of the **Sanhedrin**, or high court.

Jannaeus was a courageous warrior-king who extended Palestine's borders by conquering the Mediterranean coast as far as the Egyptian border. He reconquered the eastern area from Lake Huleh to the **Dead Sea** and captured a number of cities beyond the eastern regions of the Jordan. In their dispute with the **Pharisees**, he sided with the **Sadducees**. This quarrel brought on a civil war and served to detract from the honor of king and country. During his last battle against the king of Arabia, Jannaeus died from a severe attack of malaria. He was buried near the Damascus Gate in **Jerusalem**.

ALEXANDRIA. City in northern **Egypt** where a tributary of the Nile feeds into the Mediterranean. Founded in 331 B.C.E. by **Alexander the Great**, the city soon became a great metropolis. Alexander the Great was friendly to the Jews, and Alexandria was the first Greek city to give them citizenship. Under the rule of the Ptolemy kings who succeeded Alexander in Egypt, and under the rule of the Romans who defeated Cleopatra, the last of the Ptolemies, the Jewish community was autonomous and prosperous. Jews held civic office and served as soldiers. With their population fluctuating between half a million to a million, Alexandrian Jews spoke Greek. Their Greek version of the Bible, the **Septuagint**, was used in their synagogue in place of the Hebrew. The Great Synagogue of Alexandria was said to hold 100,000 worshipers. The reader had to wave a flag to indicate when the people, some of whom could not hear him, should say the responses. Such sages as **Philo** lectured on Hellenistic Judaism (*see* **Hellenism**) to multitudes of interested pagans. Nevertheless, such heathens as the priest Apion instigated hatred of Jews to the point of riots. This hatred increased after Egypt became Christian. When Christian mobs destroyed the Jewish quarter of Alexandria, Hellenistic Judaism was doomed. Under Arab and Turkish rule, some Jews returned to Alexandria, but the center of Egyptian Jewry gradually moved to Cairo. Before 1956, the year in which thousands of Jews left for Israel, Alexandria had a Jewish population of about 15,000. Today, there are practically none. (*See also* **Egypt**.)

ALFASI, ISAAC BEN JACOB (1013-1103). Known as the Rif; Talmudic scholar who lived and taught in Fez, North Africa. He was the forerunner of **Maimonides** in summarizing Jewish law.

ALGERIA. Jewish communities have existed in Algeria since the 1st century C.E., and have lived under Moslem rule since the 7th century. Refugees from the Spanish **Inquisition** swelled the Jewish population in the 15th century, making the country an important center of **Sephardic** Jewry. In 1830, when Algeria became a French colony, Jews were granted French citizenship by the Cremieux Decree of 1870. During the seven-year political struggle leading to Algeria's independence in July 1962, the Great Synagogue of Algiers was looted and many Jews were killed. Due to heavy emigration to **France** and some to **Israel**, the Jewish community declined from 135,000 in 1958 to 500 in 1998. Most live in the capital, Algiers.

ALHARIZI, JUDAH (1170-1235). Spanish-Hebrew poet and translator. His entertaining style of poetry shed light on Jewish life in his time, according him a special place in medieval Hebrew literature.

AL HET. *See* **Yom Kippur**.

ALIYAH. Literally, going up. In the synagogue service, *aliyah* is the act of going up to the reading desk of the synagogue to read a portion of the Torah. In the Bible, three aliyot, or pilgrimages, to the Temple in Jerusalem were appointed for **Passover**, **Shavuot**, and **Sukkot**. In modern times, the term *aliyah* has been used to denote immigration to Israel.

ALKABETZ, SOLOMON (ca. 1505-1584). Hebrew poet, **Kabbalist**, and biblical commentator. Alkabetz was born in **Turkey** but lived most of his life in **Safed**, Palestine, the 16th century center of mysticism. The best known of his poems, *Lekhah Dodi* (Come, My Beloved), is chanted in synagogues on Friday night. The poet expresses the love of the Jewish people for the Sabbath Bride and their longing for Zion to be rebuilt. Legend has it that every Friday afternoon, Alkabetz and his students, dressed in their **Sabbath** best, set out to welcome the Sabbath Queen. In the open field outside Safed they marched in procession at dusk, chanting psalms and *Lekhah Dodi*.

ALKALAI, YEHUDA BEN SOLOMON HAI (1798-1878). Serbian rabbi dedicated to the idea of establishing a Jewish state in Palestine 100 years before the rise of **Zionism**. A forerunner of political Zionism, he proposed that the Jews obtain Palestine from the Turks through the intervention of **England** and **France**. He maintained that the Jews' suffering was completely the result of their own passivity and inaction. Rabbi Alkalai also worked out a plan for redemption of Palestine that was similar to the plan adopted by the present **Jewish National Fund**, founded in 1901. Disappointed with the attitude of European Jewish leaders toward his ideas, he emigrated to Palestine at the age of 76, and there founded a society to resettle Jews on the land. He did not live to see his dream come true, dying in **Jerusalem** at the age of 80. A few days after Rabbi Alkalai's funeral, some of his devoted followers bought the land which later became the site of Petach Tikvah, the first Jewish agricultural colony in modern Palestine.

Rabbi Alkalai

ALLEN, WOODY. *See* **Stage and Screen**.

ALLENBY, VISCOUNT EDMUND HENRY HYNMAN (1861-1936). British field marshal and veteran of many campaigns. At the outbreak of World War I in 1914, he was given command of the cavalry in **France**. During 1917-1918, he served as commander-in-chief of the Egyptian-based expeditionary force of Great Britain. In his victorious battle in Samaria on September 18-21, 1918, he invaded Palestine and captured **Jerusalem**, ending Turkish resistance. Jewish Legion troops took an active part in Allenby's Palestine campaign.

ALLIANCE ISRAÉLITE UNIVERSELLE. French Jewish organization of international scope and influence; first to represent world Jewry on a political basis. Founded in 1860 by a group of seventeen Parisian Jews in protest against such anti-Semitic incidents as the **Damascus affair** and the **Mortara case**, the alliance expanded to world membership, becoming the Mediterranean area's central educational agency and a powerful medium for the interests of world Jewry. In 1862, the Alliance founded a network of schools in the lands of the Middle East and North Africa for the purpose of uniting Mediterrean Jews with a common identity. The first school was set up in Tetuan, Spanish Morocco.

In 1979, the schools founded by the Alliance had an enrollment of about 14,000. Many Jewish children from the Middle East and North Africa have been educated in schools founded by the Alliance. In these schools, the children receive a secular as well as a Jewish education from teachers specially trained in schools maintained by the Alliance in **Paris** and Casablanca. Alliance schools have successfully combated some of the dreaded childhood diseases prevalent in the Mediterranean area, improving children's overall health. In 1869, the alliance founded the first agricultural school in Palestine at **Mikveh Israel**. The Alliance maintains a vocational school and a school for deaf mutes in **Jerusalem**. To this day, the Alliance is a major educational force in the Jewish world.

Alliance Educational Publications

ALLON, YIGAL (1918-1980). Israeli army commander and Cabinet member. Born in Palestine, he was one of the founders and later commander-in-chief of the **Palmach**. He subsequently played a leading role in military operations during Israel's War of Independence. A leader in the **Labor Zionist** and **Kibbutz** organizations, he was first elected to the **Knesset** in 1955. He was appointed Minister of Labor in 1961 and Deputy Prime Minister in 1968. He served as Israel's Foreign Minister from 1974 to 1977.

ALPHABET, HEBREW. From the Greek letters *alpha* and *beta,* those based on the Hebrew *aleph* and *bet.* The Hebrew alphabet has 22 basic letters, five having special final forms. Through the use of points, or dots, the sounds of the following letters are changed: *bet, kaf, pe, shin, tav*. In Sephardic pronunciation, the *tav* is not changed by the dot.

According to the authorities, the Hebrew alphabet came into being around 1500 B.C.E. Before that, the Egyptians used hieroglyphics, or picture writing, to express ideas or objects. Then some of the hieroglyphics were adapted into 22 sound symbols; the earliest examples of such a script come from inscriptions found in the **Sinai peninsula**. It is thought, however, that the first true alphabet was developed in Palestine. The Semitic alphabets were quite similar to one another, the Phoenician being closest to the Hebrew. The Phoenicians, mostly seafaring merchants, carried this script to many lands just before the 9th century B.C.E. Various peoples took this alphabet and altered it to suit their own

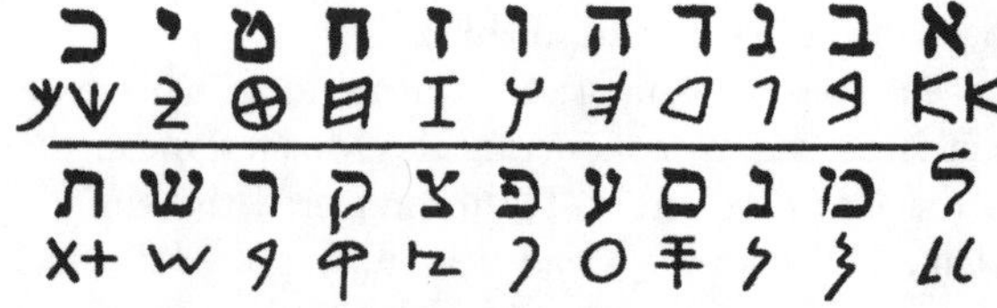

Hebrew square letters and the corresponding Canaanitic.

language. According to tradition, the Greeks received this Hebrew-Canaanite alphabet from Cadmus, the Phoenician who was considered the Greek *kadmi*, Hebrew for "Easterner." Like Hebrew, the oldest Greek inscriptions were written from right to left, using the 22 Hebrew letters in original order and with their original names, though these had no meaning in the Greek language. All European alphabets can be traced to this common origin. North of Canaan, in the territories which formerly belonged to **Assyria**, the alphabetic script developed a cursive and square form. Following the rapid diffusion of the Aramaic language, this square script, too, came into general use. According to tradition, the Jews came in contact with this "Assyrian" or Aramaic script during the Babylonian exile in the 6th century B.C.E.; over time they adopted it, and still use it today. The old Hebrew script was still being copied on the Maccabean as well as the **Bar Kokhba** coins.

THE HEBREW ALPHABET

Pronunciation	Script	Printed Letter	Pronunciation	Script	Printed Letter
m	מ	מ	(Silent letter)	א	א
m (used at the end of a word)	ם	ם	b, v	בּ, ב	בּ, ב
n	נ	נ	g (as in "good")	ג	ג
n (used at the end of a word)	ן	ן	d	ד	ד
s	ס	ס	h	ה	ה
(Silent letter)	ע	ע	v	ו	ו
p, f	פּ, פ	פּ, פ	z	ז	ז
f (used at the end of a word)	ף	ף	ch (as in "Pesach")	ח	ח
tz	צ	צ	t	ט	ט
ts (used at the end of a word)	ץ	ץ	y (as in "yes")	י	י
k	ק	ק	k, ch	כּ, כ	כּ, כ
r	ר	ר	kh (used at the end of a word)	ך	ך
sh, s	שׁ, שׂ	שׁ, שׂ	l	ל	ל
t	ת	ת			

ALROY, DAVID (12th century). Self-declared messiah to the Jews of **Babylonia** who led a revolt against Persia in 1160; born in Chaftan, **Kurdistan**. With his large following, he planned to capture **Jerusalem** as the first step to redeeming the Jewish people. He began his campaign with an attack on the citadel of his native town, was defeated and died, possibly at the hand of his own father-in-law. For a while his memory was kept alive by the Menahemites ("The Consolers"), a Jewish sect which greatly revered him. Folk stories endowed his personality with great beauty and valor. In the 19th century, this legend-encrusted figure became the hero of Benjamin **Disraeli**'s novel, *David Alroy*. (*See also* **Messianism**.)

ALTERMAN, NATHAN. *See* **Literature, Hebrew**.

AMALEKITES. Aborigines who tried to prevent the Israelites from entering Canaan and who continued to wage war against them up to the time of **David**. Because of their cruelty, and because Haman (*see* **Purim**) was thought to be one of them, the Amalekites were branded by tradition as enemies whose "memory is to be blotted out." (Told in Exod. 17:8, Deut. 25:17, and Esther 3:1.)

AMEN. "So be it" or "verily"; biblical word spoken to confirm the statement of another, or chanted in affirmation of a prayer. It first occurs in the Book of **Numbers**. Amen is nearly universal, being used by Jews, Christians, and Moslems.

AMERICA-ISRAEL CULTURAL FOUNDATION. Agency that promotes cultural exchanges between Israel and the U.S. It was originally founded in 1939 by Edward A. Norman to unify American-Jewish fundraising for educational, cultural, and social service institutions in Palestine.

AMERICA-ISRAEL FRIENDSHIP LEAGUE. Established by the Bnai Zion order, the league is dedicated to promoting friendship and understanding between Americans and Israelis through the interchange of cultural, educational, artistic, and scientific knowledge. Its program and activities are channeled through the American-Israel Friendship House in **New York City**. Membership is open to all who subscribe to its principles, irrespective of race, creed, or religion. One of its ongoing projects is the High School Students Exchange Program.

AMERICAN ASSOCIATION FOR JEWISH EDUCATION. *See* **Jewish Education Service of North America (Jesna)**.

AMERICAN COUNCIL FOR JUDAISM. Organization which defines Jews as members of a religious faith only, not as a people. It was founded in 1942 by Rabbi Louis Wolsey of **Philadelphia**. Its adherents were members of the Reform movement who were dissatisfied with the gradual acceptance of Zionism by the majority of Reform Jews. The Council waged a bitter campaign against the establishment of a Jewish state in Palestine. After the creation of the State of Israel they raised the issue of dual loyalties and dual citizenship. The Council has been charged with playing into the hands of hatemongers, as well as with encouraging assimilation. Following the **Six-Day War** of 1967, the Council all but ceased to exist.

AMERICAN ISRAEL PUBLIC AFFAIRS COMMITTEE (AIPAC). American lobby for **Israel** that works actively on legislation affecting the State of Israel; established in 1954 in Washington, DC. Widely supported among American Jews, it is considered one of the most effective lobbies in Washington.

AMERICAN JEWISH COMMITTEE. Nationwide American Jewish organization, founded in 1906. At present, more than 50,000 members are dispersed throughout eighty chapters. The committee's objectives, as stated in its charter of incorporation, are to prevent the violation of civil and religious rights of Jews everywhere; to take action when such violations occur; to "secure for Jews equality of economic, social, and educational opportunity"; and to relieve Jews who suffer from persecution and disasters.

Although the Committee initially opposed Jewish nationalism, a number of its leaders, particularly Louis **Marshall**, who served as president from 1912 to 1929, were instrumental in establishing the **Jewish Agency** for Palestine. In 1947, the AJC urged the U.S. to support the Palestine partition resolution in the UN.

With the cooperation of the **Jewish Publication Society of America** the Committee has published annually since 1909 the *American Jewish Yearbook*, a handbook of information on Jews around the world. It also publishes *Commentary*, a monthly opinion magazine on Jewish affairs.

AMERICAN JEWISH CONGRESS. Founded in 1916, the Congress sent a delegation to the **Versailles Peace Conference** in 1918 to help secure Jewish rights all over the world. Though the Congress adjourned "permanently" in 1920, it was felt that it needed to continue, and so it was revived in 1922. During the Nazi period, the American Jewish Congress worked militantly against Nazism. It also worked consistently for Zionism, both before and after the establishment of the State of Israel, actively pursuing issues of social justice for all people.

The total membership is approximately 50,000. Its presidents, following Nathan **Straus**, have included Stephen S. **Wise**, Israel Goldstein, Joachim Prinz, Arthur J. Lelyveld, and Arthur **Hertzberg**.

AMERICAN JEWISH JOINT DISTRIBUTION COMMITTEE. The JDC, or "Joint" as it is universally known, was founded on November 27, 1914, to serve as the overall distribution agency for funds collected by different American Jewish groups for overseas relief. By 1917, it was conducting its own centralized fundraising campaign. From 1939 on, it received the bulk of its funds from the **United Jewish Appeal**.

Since 1914, the JDC has spent more than $1.2 billion for the relief of Jews everywhere in the world. In 1979, the Committee aided more than 435,000 Jews in more than 25 countries, mainly in North Africa, the Middle East, Israel, and Europe. The first half century of its existence may be divided into six periods: World War I, when the Jewish refugees' status required urgent help in many parts of Europe; the postwar emergency period of 1918-1920, when food and clothing had to be distributed in huge quantities; the reconstruction period from 1921-1932, when JDC aided Jewish communities throughout the world to help themselves; the Nazi period, 1933-1945, when Jews had to be saved from death, moved to new countries, and fed and clothed until they were self-sufficient; and the emergency period after World War II, when the JDC bore its greatest burdens. Tens of thousands of Jewish displaced persons (DP's) had to be helped to rebuild their lives. DP camps in Europe needed food, clothing, teachers, social workers, medical personnel—every possible kind of help. Throughout 1947, the Committee served 224,000 rations daily in the DP camps. As thousands of Jews moved to Israel, they had to be rehabilitated, taught new trades, and settled in their new home. Later, emergencies developed in **Iraq**, **Yemen**, North Africa, and elsewhere. In each case, JDC was needed to help Jews emigrate when possible, to supply relief on the spot when necessary. Between 1945 and 1953, the JDC aided 621,206 Jewish emigrants, of whom 504,208 settled in Israel. In 1948, at the peak of DP period, JDC had hundreds of workers in Europe and the Middle East,

Some of the founders and leaders of the American Jewish Joint Distribution Committee, gathered at the 40th annual JDC meeting. Seated, l. to r.: Adolph Held, Bernard Semel, James N. Rosenberg, Herbert Lehman, and Paul Baerwald. Standing, l. to r.: Rabbi David de Sola Pool, Alexander Kahn, Dr. Bernard Kahn, Alex A. Landesco, Baruch Zuckerman, I. Edwin Goldwasser, and Rabbi Jonah B. Wise.

> *"And I will bring back my people Israel...and no longer will they be uprooted from their land."*
>
> AMOS 9:14-15

supplying relief on a previously unheard-of scale. In 1960, the JDC's aid was required by some 250,000 men, women, and children in 25 countries of Europe, North Africa, and the Near East. In Israel, JDC-Malben provided medical, welfare, and other care for aged, ill, and handicapped newcomers. In Moslem countries, the agency gave medical, feeding, relief, cultural, and religious assistance to some 100,000 Jews. The emphasis in Europe was on technical and reconstruction assistance to the local population, as well as to aid migrants and refugees. During the 1990's, the JDC developed a new intensive program in Jewish communities in the former Soviet Union as well as Eastern Europe.

AMERICAN RED MAGEN DAVID FOR ISRAEL. *See* **Magen David Adom.**

AM HA-ARETZ. Literally, country folk. It became a derogatory phrase, meaning one ignorant and uneducated in Jewish matters. The term originated in the biblical books of **Ezra** and **Nehemiah**. These two leaders urged those who returned from the Babylonian Exile with them to separate themselves from "the people of the earth," called *Ammei Ha-Aretz*. This separation was necessary to prevent Jews from assimilating and losing their identity. The **Talmud** has many definitions of an *Am Ha-Aretz*, such as: "One of the multitude which knows not the (Jewish) law," and "he who has children and does not educate them in the Law."

AMIDAH. *See* **Prayer** *and* **Siddur.**

AMNON OF MAYENCE. Hero of a legend first published around 1350 that reflected the bloody persecutions of the Jews during the **Crusades**. The Archbishop of Mayence continually pressed Amnon, a distinguished and learned man of wealth among the Jews of Mayence in **Germany**, to convert to Christianity. Finally, Amnon asked the archbishop for three days to come to a decision. At the end of this period, Amnon did not appear before the archbishop because he regretted having given the impression that he was considering changing his faith. As punishment, the archbishop commanded that Amnon's hands and feet be cut off. This happened just before the Jewish New Year, and Amnon, dying of his wounds, had himself carried into the synagogue on **Rosh Hashanah** during the services. As the cantor was about to recite the *Kedusha*, or Sanctification, Amnon stopped him, saying: "Pause that I may sanctify the most holy Name." He then began the hymn starting with the words *U'netaneh Tokef*, We will celebrate the mighty holiness of this day. When he reached the words "and our Name hast Thou linked with Thine own," Amnon died. The famous Rabbi Meshullam ben Kalonymus of Mayence (ca. 1000 C.E.) who published this poem, is considered its author. Since then, *U'netaneh Tokef* has been a part of Rosh Hashanah services.

AMORA. Hebrew and Aramaic, meaning speaker or interpreter. The title "Amora" was given to all teachers of Jewish law in Palestine from about 200 C.E. to 500 C.E. The Amoraim continued the work of the Tannaim, the creators of the Mishnah. After the Mishnah was edited, many new problems requiring clarification arose in Jewish law. To help solve these problems, the Amoraim explained the Mishnah, discussing its rulings and reinterpreting its decisions. Their work was eventually incorporated into what is today known as the Gemara, which, together with the Mishnah, forms the Palestinian and Babylonian **Talmud.** The names of more than 3,000 Amoraim are mentioned in the Talmud.

AMOS (ca. 750 B.C.E.). Third of the Minor Prophets in the **Bible**; first of the prophets known to have recorded their visions. Amos was a shepherd in the village of Tekoa nestling in the hills of the kingdom of Judah. He came to nearby Bethel, the principal religious center of the northern kingdom of Israel, to sell his sheep and fruits. There, Amos cried out against the injustice and poverty of the masses under Jeroboam II. In pity and sorrow, he predicted the punishment of Israel and its destruction by Assyria. Turning to **Samaria**, the political center of Israel, he accused the wrongdoers and warned them of the ruin they would bring on their nation. The main idea of Amos was justice for all humanity, not only for his own nation. He was the first to see God as the universal Lord of all the nations, not only of Israel. Israel must live up to a unique standard of righteousness, being the home of God's chosen people. Amos taught also that God required not sacrifices, but justice, purity, and truth. He dreamed of a future golden age of peace, when "the exiles of my people Israel" will return home, rebuild the wasted cities, replant the vineyards, and never be uprooted again.

Amos rebukes Israel's indulgence.

AMSTERDAM. The first Jews to settle in the **Netherlands**' capital were refugees from persecution in **Portugal** and of the Spanish expulsion of 1492. They were given religious freedom but were barred from all professions except medicine. They became active in commerce and industry and, during the 17th century, established synagogues and schools, including the great yeshiva,

Etz Hayim. The earliest waves of Ashkenazic Jews came from Poland in the wake of the Chmielniki pogroms in 1648. Shortly after, German Jews settled in Amsterdam. The entire community participated in the development of a rich cultural life. Outstanding among the many scholars of this period was Rabbi **Manasseh ben Israel**, the diplomat, author, and printer who set up the first printing press in Amsterdam. The community accorded great power to its rabbis, who opposed the study of the Kabbalah, as they did the Messianic movements. They excommunicated the religious rebel Uriel **Acosta** in 1640 and the philosopher Baruch **Spinoza** in 1656.

In 1796, in the wake of the French Revolution, Jews were granted equal rights, attaining complete emancipation during the 19th century. They continued to play an important role in the economic life of the city, until the outbreak of World War II.

Ashkenazic Synagogue in Amsterdam.

With the Nazi rise to power in **Germany** in 1933, a mass migration of Jewish refugees to the Netherlands began. When Hitler's armies entered the Netherlands, there were approximately 80,000 Jews in Amsterdam. The familiar Nazi pattern of mass deportation and atrocities against Jews destroyed 85 percent of Dutch Jewry. When the Allied armies of liberation entered Amsterdam in 1945, they found about 25,000 Jewish survivors of this once great Jewish community. The most famous victim of Naziism in Amsterdam is Anne **Frank**, author of *Diary of a Young Girl*.

Since then, Amsterdam Jewry, with the assistance of the Netherlands government, has slowly recovered and reestablished itself. In 1998, about 13,000 Jews lived in the city. Schools for children and synagogue services were serving the community. The Ashkenazi community of Amsterdam celebrated its 350th anniversary in April 1986.

ANAN BEN DAVID. Founder of the **Karaite** sect, which rejects the authority of the **Talmud** and bases its beliefs on the Bible only. A sharp quarrel broke out between Anan and his younger brother, Hananiah (Josiah), over the office of "Prince of Exile." The Jewish leaders supported Hananiah's appointment, and it was duly confirmed by the Caliph of Baghdad. When Anan protested he was arrested. While in prison he made the acquaintance of the prominent Moslem theologian Abu Hanifah, who advised him to declare himself leader of a new religious sect. Anan did so, and as a result he was freed.

In 770, Anan wrote the *Sefer ha-Mitzvot*, or "Book of Commandments," which became the basic text for the new sect. By recognizing Jesus and Mohammed as prophets he won the friendship of both Christians and Moslems. The members of his sect, originally called Ananites, came to be known as Karaites from the Hebrew *Karaim* or "[strict] readers of Scriptures." Anan died in 800, but his sect exists to this day. (*See also* **Karaites**.)

ANGEL. *Mal'ach* in Hebrew. The Bible mentions angels as spiritual beings, ministering to God and appearing to men on special missions. Angels came to **Abraham** to predict the birth of a son, and to Lot to warn him of the imminent destruction of Sodom. **Jacob** saw angels ascending and descending on a ladder "set up on the earth, and the top of it reached the heaven." Similarly, an angel appeared to **Moses** "in a flame of fire, out of the midst of a bush." Descriptions of angels are to be found in **Isaiah**, where they have six wings, and in Ezekiel. They are powerful, wise, and holy, but are subject to the will of God and obey His command. While the Book of **Daniel** names only the angels Michael and Gabriel, Talmudic and Midrashic literature mentions names of many angels, each one performing a specific task. In Jewish tradition a special place is occupied by the Angel of Death, the ministering angels who give praise to the Lord, and angels appointed to guard the nations of the world.

ANGLO-JEWISH ASSOCIATION. A philanthropic organization of English Jews, with branches throughout the British empire. Shortly after being founded in 1871 in conjunction with the **Alliance Israélite Universelle**, it dissociated itself from the French organization. The Association aims to help Jews everywhere to "obtain and preserve full civic rights," "to protect those who suffer for being Jews," "to foster education of Jews particularly in the Middle East," and "to support the upbuilding of Israel." The Anglo-Jewish Association has contributed greatly to the support of Jewish schools throughout the Middle East (including Palestine) and in Shanghai. It worked with the Board of Deputies of British Jews until 1946.

ANIELEWICZ, MORDECAI (1919-1943). Leader of **Warsaw** ghetto uprising. In 1943, at the height of Nazi terror, the Warsaw ghetto was populated by 40,000 Jews; 460,000 had been systematically exterminated. Unless drastic action was taken, the survivors would be led like sheep to slaughter. The Jewish underground resolved at that moment to rise in open rebellion against their murderers.

A 24-year-old member of the Labor Zionist movement, Anielewicz chose to stay in **Poland** after Nazi occupation. Traveling from ghetto to ghetto in fear of his life, he spent the first four years of the occupation training young men in self-defense units.

Under Anielewicz's able and inspiring command, the ghetto factions were welded into a single fighting force. During the Passover holiday of 1943, the ghetto fighters lashed out against their oppressors. For two weeks the poorly armed and heavily outnumbered "army" battled against the air and tank divisions that had been called in to quell the uprising. At the end of two weeks the ghetto stood no longer. Its defenders lay dead in the rubble. Among them was Anielewicz, and by his side as always was Mira, his wife.

The heroism of these defenders is commemorated in a massive monument erected at Yad Mordecai, a kibbutz in Israel named after Mordecai Anielewicz.

ANNENBERG, WALTER H. (1908-). Leading American publisher and philanthropist, who gave $365 million to four schools. Publisher of *TV Guide*, Annenberg served as U.S. ambassador to **England** from 1969 to 1975.

ANNENBERG RESEARCH INSTITUTE. Formerly Dropsie College, the Institute was founded in 1907 in **Philadelphia** by Moses Aaron Dropsie, and became one of the institutions of higher Jewish learning in America. It is a non-sectarian, non-theological postgraduate institution, specializing in the science of Judaism. It offers courses leading to degrees of Doctor of Philosophy, Doctor of Education, and Master of Arts. The Institute consists of three divisions: the interrelated Hebrew and Semitic studies in the Department of Hebrew and Cognate Learning; the School of Education, with parallel courses in **New York City**; and the Institute for Israel and the Middle East, which trains qualified personnel for government, social, and educational agencies in the U.S. and Israel. The Institute issues a number of scholarly publications, including the *Jewish Quarterly Review*. It was reorganized in 1986 and given its present name.

ANTI-DEFAMATION LEAGUE. One of the nation's oldest and largest human relations organizations, ADL was founded in 1913 to combat **anti-Semitism**. Its mandate was "to end the defamation of the Jewish people...to secure justice and fair treatment for all citizens alike." The agency has grown into an international organization, headquartered in **New York City** with 30 regional offices in this country, a European office in **Paris** and Vienna, an **Israel** office in **Jerusalem**, affiliated offices in **Latin America** and **Canada**, and a consultant in **Rome**.

Both at home and abroad, the agency combats anti-Semitism and other forms of bigotry and discrimination, counteracts anti-Israel propaganda; alerts government officials and the public to threats to the democratic process. strengthens intergroup and interfaith friendship and understanding; and works generally in behalf of Jewish concerns and interests.

In seeking "fair treatment for all citizens," the agency has fought successfully against quotas barring Jews and other minorities from schools, jobs, and housing. Today, still dedicated to a system of merit, ADL opposes the reverse discrimination inherent in the use of racial quotas as the criteria for access to employment and education.

ADL leaders Melvin Salberg and Abraham H. Foxman, with U.N. Secretary General Boutros Boutros-Gali.

ADL enlists the support of international public opinion in speaking out against oppression of Jews in the former Soviet Union, **Latin America**, and elsewhere, and condemns terrorist acts directed against Jewish communities in Western Europe. It also advocates the security of Israel and supports the peace process. It prepares annual audits of incidents of anti-Semitic vandalism and violence.

ANTIOCHUS. *See* **Maccabees.**

ANTI-SEMITISM. The hatred of Jews. The purpose of anti-Semitism in its active political phase is to degrade the Jews by removing their civil, political, social, economic, and religious rights, and finally, by exterminating them. The term appears to have been first used in **Germany** in 1879, in a pamphlet by Wilhelm Marr titled *The Victory of Judaism Over Germanism*. That same year, Marr founded the Anti-Semitic League. Of course, this first use of the term "anti-Semitism" was certainly not the first appearance of anti-Semitism. In the story of the biblical Book of **Esther**, Haman makes use of many of the classic techniques of anti-Semitism—libel, false accusations, and discrimination—to gain his ends. After the end of the **Bar Kokhba** revolt against **Rome** in 137 C.E., the new Christian religion rapidly developed strong anti-Semitic feelings. As **Christianity** came into power in the Roman Empire, the dark age of anti-Semitism began for the Jewish people. Increasingly, Jews lost their civil and other rights, and oppression became widespread.

The Middle Ages. The Middle Ages was a period of discrimination, violent persecution, and expulsions for Jewish people, acts anti-Semitic in origin. There were some relatively good periods, beginning in the 7th century when Pope Gregory the Great actively opposed anti-Semitic violence. From that time until the beginning of the Crusades in 1096, the situation of the Jews in Christian Europe was tolerable. But the Crusaders, on their way to the Holy Land, "revenged" themselves upon the Jews, killing thousands of men, women, and children in pogroms. Jews were blamed for having started the Black Death, a plague which killed off millions of people in Europe beginning in 1348. The result was more bloody backlash against Jews.

The Middle Ages did not end for the Jewish people until the end of the 18th century, when the spread of enlightenment, scientific knowledge, and democracy brought the breakdown of ghetto walls and the beginnings of more objective judgment and equal opportunity for Jews. Nevertheless, organized and individual anti-Semitism remained everywhere—less in **France**, **England**, and the **United States**, but more in Germany, **Austria**, and especially in **Poland** and **Russia**. The pogroms which erupted in Russia beginning in 1881 brought 2.1 million Jews to the New World by 1910.

The Protocols of the Elders of Zion. The most potent piece of anti-Semitic literature in the flood of hate-books and pamphlets which have appeared in the last century is undoubtedly the *Protocols of the Elders of Zion*. First produced in 1901 by Sergius Nilus, a Russian mystic, as an adaptation of a satire of Napolean III by Maurice Joly of France, it was rapidly printed and distributed in various languages in Europe and later

This adaptation by the Nazis of a Medieval German drawing of Jews murdering innocent Christian children in order to use their blood for ritual purposes is the culmination of centuries of anti-Semitism.

in the U.S. The Protocols claim to be the strategic plans made by the World Zionist Congress in 1897 for the Jewish conquest of the world. Despite repeated public proof that they were forgeries, the circulation of the Protocols continued on a large scale until the end of Nazism in 1945 and still continues to this day in some countries.

The most fateful outbreak of anti-Semitism in history occurred in Germany between 1933 and 1945. Adolf Hitler and his Nazi Party rose to absolute power in that country on a platform based on anti-Semitism. Since Jews were to blame for Germany's problems, Hitler argued, the only solution was to exterminate them. Hitler and his followers almost succeeded. During World War II, six million Jews were killed in crematoria and Nazi murder chambers. Poles, Hungarians, Romanians, and others joined the Nazis in this massacre.

Anti-Semitism in the United States. The history of anti-Semitism in the U.S. may be simply charted. The first overt case of anti-Semitism in the U.S. occurred in 1862, when General Ulysses S. Grant issued his notorious General Order No. 11, banning Jews from his army area. (This order was quickly revoked by President Abraham Lincoln.) The next major incident occurred in 1877, when it was learned that Jews were not welcome as guests at the largest hotel in Saratoga, N.Y. Through the years, until World War I, there was much subtle discrimination of Jews—in hotels, clubs, colleges, and jobs—but little organized anti-Semitism.

A Board of Delegates of American Israelites was formed in 1859 to fight for Jewish rights. It never achieved great prominence, and in 1878 merged with the **Union of American Hebrew Congregations**. The most active Jew in Washington during this period was Simon Wolf, who advised the Presidents on Jewish problems.

In 1906, the **American Jewish Committee** was formed to provide for the increasing need for activity to fight anti-Semitism and to secure equal rights for Jews. Later, other organizations joined this movement: the **American Jewish Congress**, the Jewish Labor Committee, the **Anti-Defamation League of B'nai B'rith,** local Jewish community councils, and the National Jewish Community Relations Advisory Council.

The most famous case of anti-Semitism in the interim between the World Wars involved automobile magnate Henry Ford and his infamous newspaper, the *Dearborn Independent*, which reprinted the *Protocols of the Elders of Zion* and carried on an active anti-Semitic campaign. After he was sued for libel in 1927, Ford apologized in a public letter to Louis **Marshall**, recalled all copies of the *Dearborn Independent*, and never again allowed himself to be involved in anti-Semitic activity.

During the Nazi period, the German government sponsored widespread anti-Semitic propaganda and activity in the U.S. Most vocal and vicious, the German-American Bund achieved a fairly large membership, at least in the Yorkville section of New York. It was joined by organizations and individuals like the Silver Shirts of William D. Pelley, Gerald Winrod's organization, Father Charles Coughlin of the Christian Front, Gerald L.K. Smith, and many others. They achieved a measure of success despite efforts by Jewish and non-Jewish organizations and persons until the outbreak of World War II, when anti-Semitism, associated with Hitler, was discredited.

Between 1945 and 1968, memories of the **Holocaust** limited organized anti-Semitism in the U.S. to a "lunatic fringe." Also, the rise and achievements of the State of **Israel** helped transform the image of the Jew in society. By the 1960's American Jewry felt sufficiently secure to take a leading role in various social and civil rights causes. Many Jews participated in "freedom marches" and similar demonstrations for Black rights.

Following the assassination of Rev. Martin Luther King, Jr., in 1968, part of the Black community became openly hostile to whites, especially Jews, who were accused of being slum landlords and ghetto store owners who created poor Blacks' credit problems. Moreover, the goal of the Black militant movement was "national liberation," and as such it allied with similar movements, including the so-called "Palestine Liberation" movement. Anti-Zionism became a convenient front for a new anti-Semitism, refusing to begin dying down until 1979.

Theories of Origin. There are many theories about the origin of anti-Semitism. One is religious conflict, the traditional Christian dislike for Jews because they rejected Jesus of Nazareth as the Messiah (*see* **Messianism**) and, some allege, were responsible for his crucifixion. Many persons consider this historic lie to be the chief source of anti-Semitism. Another theory maintains that this hostility is due to the fact that Jews have remained a minority refusing to lose its identity and community.

Neither of these theories provides a complete answer to this complicated question. Scientists have worked out some ideas to explain the basis of hatred and bigotry. They have found that unhappy, emotionally insecure people tend to be intolerant. Their feelings of inferiority breed hostility within them. They join groups through which they vent their feelings on other people, who serve them as scapegoats. Probably, anti-Semitism is the result of a combination of religious, social, and psychological reasons.

ANTOKOLSKI, MARK (1843-1902). Russian sculptor. Born in the city of **Vilna**, Antokolski chose the career of sculpture against the wishes of his orthodox parents. After studying in St. Petersburg and Berlin, he moved to **Paris**. His statue of Ivan the Terrible made him famous at the age of 28. He made life-size statues of such thinkers as Socrates and **Spinoza**, as well as fine portrait busts (among his sitters was the aged novelist Count Leo Tolstoy). Well known is his *Christ Before Pilate*: with bowed head and bare feet, Jesus, a Jewish peasant, stands before his unseen judge. For his earliest work, *The Jewish Tailor*, made in high-relief, he received a silver medal. It shows a lean old craftsman in cap and gabardine, sitting cross-legged in the window of his tiny shop, holding his needle against the light to thread it.

APIKOROS. Rabbinical term meaning skeptic or heretic, derived from the name of the Greek philosopher Epicurus, whose students argued against Judaism.

APOCALYPTIC LITERATURE. Books written during the time of the Second **Temple** and shortly after its destruction (ca. 200 B.C.E.-100 C.E.). These books describe future events through extraordinary and symbolic images and visions. Many parts of the **Bible**, such as the first chapters of **Ezekiel** and **Daniel**, contain apocalyptic references. Parts of the **Apocrypha** belong to this group, including the Book of Enoch, Book of Jubilees, Apocalypse of Baruch, Psalms of Solomon, Book of Adam and Eve, Assumption of Moses, and others. Most of these books were created in times of danger and stress. They are full of mystic visions, prophesying Judgment Day and the coming of the Messianic Age. (*See also* **Apocrypha**.)

APOCRYPHA. From the Greek *apokryphos*, meaning "hidden, not recognized"; a series of books written during the last centuries B.C.E. and excluded from the **Bible** when the **canon** was set up ca. 90 C.E. Several of the Apocrypha were written at a later date. Some of them were written in Greek, and all were generally modeled after a book in the Bible. They compromise wisdom books such as **Ben Sira**, poems, such as the *Wisdom of Solomon*, and prayers such as that of Manasseh. The two historical Books of the **Maccabees**, as well as such instructive stories as the books of Tobit, Judith, and Susanna, are a part of the Apocrypha. In the Book of Judith, the heroine rescues a whole city from a besieging Assyrian army by killing its general, Holofernes. Also among the Apocrypha are prophecies or revelations of the unknown, called Apocalyptic writings. None of these books equals the Bible's grandeur of ideas or beauty of writing, and many of them were lost and forgotten by Jews. Some survived only in Greek and were included by the early Church Fathers in the Catholic Bible.

APPELFELD, AHARON (1932-   ). Leading Israeli author who survived the **Holocaust** as a child. His novels, dealing with Holocaust themes, are considered the finest of their kind in Israeli literature.

ARAB INFLUENCE ON JEWISH HISTORY. The Arabs are peoples living throughout the Middle East and North Africa. They speak various Arabic dialects and are for the most part of the Islamic faith.

Jewish and Arab tradition hold that the Arabs are the descendants of Ishmael, son of **Abraham**. In ancient times there were several small but highly developed kingdoms in the Arabian peninsula. Most of the Arabs, however, were camel breeding nomads. Those mentioned in the **Bible** probably wandered northward from Arabia and lived on the fringe of the Jewish settlement in Palestine. The early Arab kingdoms fell into decay in the first centuries of the common era. It was only with the religious revolution of Mohammed in the 7th century that the Arabs emerged as a major force.

Scion of a wealthy merchant family, Mohammed declared himself the prophet of "the only true faith." Known as **Islam**, this religion centered around Allah, the "one true God," but accepted the religious writings of both Christians and Jews. Its prophets included **Abraham**, **Moses**, the biblical prophets, **Jesus**, and Mohammed. Mohammed believed it was his duty to convert humankind to Islam. To this end, he began a series of "Holy Wars." Leading an army of fierce desert warriors, he and his successors conquered the entire Middle East from **Egypt** to Central Asia. Later, North Africa and **Spain** were brought under Islamic rule. The pagan people of the conquered countries were converted to Islam, taught the Arabic language, and made subjects of a single Arab empire.

At that time most Jews lived within the Arab empire. When both persuasion and persecution failed to shake their faith, the Arab rulers were forced to evolve a policy of some tolerance. Jews were generally accepted as second-class citizens. But this legal definition of their status did not put an end to persecution. Fanatic Moslem sects led the occasional violent outbursts of hatred which often led to massacres. On the whole, however, Jews were much better off in the Islamic world than in Christian Europe. Though they continued to study Hebrew, Arabic became their spoken tongue. They came and went freely in the markets of the east.

By the 10th century, Jews were important in the international trade flourishing from **Spain** to **India**. There were Jewish bankers, ministers, generals, and doctors at most Moslem courts. In addition, the Jewish community remained fairly independent, and the community head had an honored place in the government of the Caliphs.

Golden Age of Judeo-Arabic Culture. Especially distinguished during this era was the cultural life of the Jews. Between the 7th and 10th centuries the Arabs evolved one of the greatest civilizations in history. In addition to the development and study of their own religion, Arab scholars had worked fruitfully in the fields of philosophy, poetry, language, history, geography, medicine, astronomy, and other branches of science. Speaking Arabic and mixing freely with Arab scholars, Jews contributed to all these fields of learning. More important, they developed a culture of their own, based on their ancient traditions and on the research of their Moslem neighbors. In **Babylonia**, the heads of great Talmudic academies continued the work of their predecessors in interpreting the Jewish law. Saadiah **Gaon**, head of the Jewish community in Babylonia during the 10th century, not only translated the Bible into Arabic, but also published studies in philosophy, poetry, religion, and law. In the following century, the center of Jewish life shifted to Spain, and a series of brilliant

Maimonides

figures participated there in creating the "Golden Age" of Jewish history. At this time, **Maimonides**, a physician by profession, was one of the great masters of philosophy. His great works include a codification of Jewish law and a justification of the Jewish religion in terms of ancient Greek philosophy. The greatest achievements of the Golden Age, however, were not in philosophy, but in poetry. Living in both Christian and Moslem Spain, such poets as Judah **Ha-Levi**, Solomon **Ibn Gabirol**, and Moses **Ibn Ezra** created some of the most beautiful poetry in the Hebrew language. Their poems treat religious and secular subjects in forms derived from classical Arabic verse. They were all learned in science and philosophy and masters of classic Arabic prose as well as Hebrew and Jewish lore. Other poets and scholars in Babylonia, North Africa, and Tunis contributed to the flowering of Jewish culture.

The Golden Age of Judeo-Arabic culture came to an end with the decline of the entire Arab civilization in the 13th and 14th centuries. At that time, barbarian rulers gained domination over most of the Islamic empire. In the course of that period, the center of Jewish life passed from the shores of the Mediterranean to Europe proper. Many Jews continued to live on the shores of the Mediterranean but ceased to play a vital role in Jewish life. Until the rise of Jewish nationalism at the end of the 19th century, Mediterranean Jews lived as a subject people among their Arab neighbors who were under the dominion of foreign powers.

The Modern Arab Revival. The 19th and 20th centuries, which have witnessed the return of the Jews to Palestine and the creation of a Jewish state there, have also seen a negative change in Arab-Jewish relations. The Arab states, which were created after the defeat of the Ottoman-Turkish Empire in World War I, have firmly opposed the return of the Jews to their homeland. This opposition flared into open warfare in 1948, when the armies of five Arab nations invaded the newly-declared State of **Israel**. Despite four successive defeats on the battlefield, the Arabs did not accept the legitimacy of the Jewish state for more than 30 years. **Egypt** in 1979 and **Jordan** in 1994 finally signed peace treaties with Israel.

ARAD, YAEL. *See* **Sports**.

ARAMAIC. A group of Semitic languages, known as Chaldaic in their most ancient form. The earliest surviving form of Aramaic dates ca. 900 B.C.E. The Assyro-Babylonian and Persian empires absorbed this language, and since Aramaic was closely related to Hebrew, it was picked up by the Jewish exiles in **Babylonia** in the 6th century B.C.E. When they returned to Judea, Jews brought the Aramaic tongue home with them. By 300 B.C.E. it was used in daily life, and many prayers were chanted in Aramaic. Aramaic was also the language of trade and diplomacy in the whole Middle East. Isolated portions of the Bible (Dan. 2:46, Ezra 4:8-6:18, 7:12-26, and Jer. 10:11) are written in a West Aramaic dialect. This is also the language of the Palestinian **Talmud** (except for the **Mishnah**, which is in Hebrew) and of the **Midrashim**. Aramaic is the language of the Babylonian Talmud and of an authorized translation of the **Bible** known as Targum **Onkelos**. Aramaic is the language of parts of the **Siddur**, or prayer book, of the **Kaddish**, and of a section of the **Passover** Haggadah, beginning with the words "This is the bread of affliction." The *Had Gadya* (One Little Goat), the popular song sung toward the end of the Passover Seder, is also in Aramaic.

ARARAT. Mountain in northern Armenia, landing place of Noah's ark in the biblical narrative (Gen. 8:4). Also a city planned on Grand Island, Niagara, N.Y., by **M.M. Noah** in 1825.

ARBA KANFOT. Literally, four corners. A rectangular vestlet covering the chest and back, with ritual fringes, or *tzitzit*, attached to its corners, in remembrance of the biblical command that Jewish males wear a fringed garment (Num. 15:37-41). It is also called a *tallit katan*, or little tallit.

ARCH OF TITUS. A triumphal arch overlooking the Roman Forum, built to celebrate the Roman victory over Judea after three years of bitter fighting from 67-70 C.E. On one of its inner panels the artist carved a scene from the triumphal procession of the victorious Roman legions. Soldiers crowned with laurel leaves are shown carrying the sacred objects they had plundered from the **Temple** in **Jerusalem** before destroying it. Their figures lean forward, straining against the weight of the golden table, the **holy ark**, the seven-branched menorah, and the musical instruments of the **Levites**. For centuries, Jews in Rome would walk long distances to avoid passing this memorial.

Above, the Arch of Titus in Rome. Left, a detail from the inside of the Arch depicting the Romans as they parade the religious objects they took from the Temple in Jerusalem (70 C.E.).

ARCHEOLOGY. The scientific study of the material remains of the past. Long before the time of the Greeks, who first coined this term, people had been digging up the past, unearthing hidden passages to burial chambers, and passing on the oral history of much earlier generations.

In the 7th century B.C.E., **Assurbanipal of Assyria** was proud of his ability to decipher writings on ancient clay tablets, and sent his scribes far and wide to collect copies of early records and documents for his wonderful library at Nineveh. Nabonidus, who ruled **Babylon** in the 6th century B.C.E., made exploratory excavations in the age-old *Ziggurat*, or temple tower, which loomed up at Ur, the birthplace of **Abraham**. He read the foundation records of its ancient builders, and carefully carried out restorations, as told in his own inscriptions. The daughter of Nabonidus shared her father's interest and maintained a small

Marble bust found in Caesarea.

museum in which objects of great importance were kept. Similarly, a royal commission was appointed by Rameses IX of **Egypt** to examine the physical condition of ancient tombs and pyramids. This interest has remained unabated through the ages.

Modern archeological research emerged a little more than 150 years ago, and has ingeniously awakened the ancient past. Buried for thousands of years in clay tablets, papyri, scrolls, and inscriptions, long forgotten tongues have now been deciphered and revived. Whole cities and settlements have been found arranged one atop the other, forming artificial mounds, or *tel* in Hebrew. These mounds have been carefully excavated, sliced down like a layer-cake to reveal as many as seventeen different levels of culture. Objects of all types, secular and religious, have been found in the ruins of each layer. Even shards of pottery have been picked up and carefully restored. The styles and shapes then provide clues for dating other objects found on the same level. Charts of pottery vessels of almost every age and geographical area are available and as indispensable for the archeologist as the stamp album for the stamp collector.

Archeology uses both strict scientific methods and the latest technology: electronics, aerial photography, X-rays, and radio carbon. For example, X-rays penetrate the wrappings of Egyptian mummies, locating the exact positions of jewelry and sometimes determining the cause of death. Radiocarbon is used to determine the exact age of all organic matter.

The development of archeology has been made possible through the teamwork of scholars and experts of many different nations and religious backgrounds. Each group, with its own motivation, enables us to see more vividly the world of the **Bible**, the text which the great prophets preached and from which sprang Judaism and **Christianity**. On the other hand, Israelis study the Bible and biblical archaeology to obtain new and important knowledge of the land which they are now reclaiming and on which they plan to build a great future.

Every child in modern **Israel** is an amateur archeologist. Knowing the Hebrew Bible almost by heart, and equipped with maps and archeological guide books, children hike the length and breadth of their historic land, identifying ancient places and ruins, and recognizing the flowers, plants, and animals natural to that region.

In 1948, the young Israeli general Yigael **Yadin** was able to surround an invading Egyptian army by following an old Roman road in the **Negev** known to him from his studies in biblical archeology. Nelson Glueck, a famous Jewish scholar conducting a series of explorations in the Negev, has proven that hundreds of towns and settlements thrived in antiquity in an area which has for many centuries been the great wasteland of southern Palestine. He likewise unearthed King **Solomon**'s copper mines and refineries near **Elat**, the port at the northern tip of the Red Sea. There he found that the ancient Israelites had anticipated some of our most modern methods for refining metals.

This Roman and Byzantine commerical thoroughfare, called The Cardo, has been uncovered and restored. Today, its vaulted recesses serve once again as shops.

Daring military archeologists have reopened the ancient fortress of **Masada**, high in the rocks of the wilderness of Judah. Until recently, this legendary stronghold, famed for the last stand of the Zealots in the desperate war against the Romans in 70 C.E., could be seen only by aerial photography. Now the labyrinth of underground passages has been laid bare, revealing implements and vessels of all types, with interesting inscriptions or graffiti on the walls. Masada has become one of the great national shrines of the State of Israel.

In 1965, Yigael Yadin reported the discovery of part of the Hebrew original of the Apocryphal Book of Jubilees in Masada.

At Wadi Muraba'at near the **Dead Sea**, several stratified grottoes were found to contain, amidst a mass of other relics, some coins and a number of dated personal documents from 2nd century C.E. Written on papyrus and crude leather in Hebrew, Aramaic, and Greek, these documents include a letter by **Bar Kokhba**, the leader of the last Jewish revolt against the Romans in 132-35 C.E. In this letter bearing the signature of Simeon ben Koseba, his authentic name, the rugged Jewish general warns his chief of staff, Joshua ben Galgola: if Galgola will not follow instructions regarding the prisoners of war and the requisitioning of private property, Bar Kokhba will fetter his legs with chains, as he has previously done to another disobedient subordinate. In 1959, an Israeli archeological expedition assisted

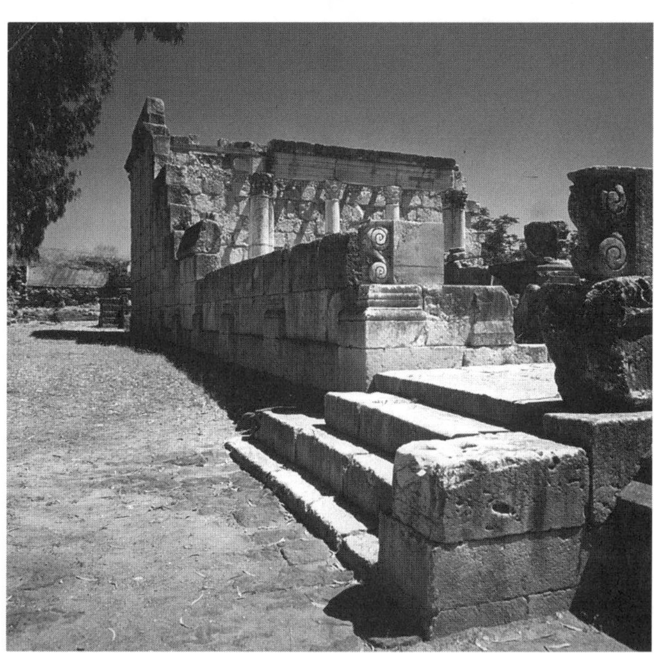

Synagogue at Capernaum. Courtesy Dr. Nelson Glueck.

Remains of Bet Shearim, seat of the Sanhedrin and the residence of Rabbi Judah the Prince (2nd century C.E.).

by army helicopters uncovered another Bar Koseba letter in a cave at Nahal Heber in the Judean Desert.

The archeological findings of Israel may not be as spectacular as the Pyramids of Egypt or some of the other great monuments of the past. They do, however, shed light on the greatest and most enduring spiritual monument ever created, the Hebrew Bible, and on the subsequent history of its creators.

After the **Six-Day War**, extensive excavations were begun in many parts of the country, especially in the vicinity of the **Western Wall** and the Old City of **Jerusalem**. The discoveries in Jerusalem have been breathtaking. Artifacts dating back to the First Temple were discovered. Entire streets, markets, and homes were found underground, revealing facets of life during the time of King **Solomon** and King **Herod**, as well as the Byzantine, Crusader, Mamluk and Turkish periods. One such spectacular discovery is the *Cardo*, the Roman and Byzantine "shopping mall," which has been reopened and once again features real-life shops. Another find is a scroll with the Priestly Benediction, dating back to the 7th century B.C.E., one of the oldest Hebrew biblical texts ever found. (*See also* **Dead Sea Scrolls**.)

ARENDT, HANNAH (1906-1975). German-American political thinker. An authority on totalitarianism and Nazism, her views on Jewish behavior during the Holocaust caused great controversy.

ARENS, MOSHE (1925-). MIT educated, Arens moved from the U.S. to **Israel** in 1948 to teach aeronautical engineering at the **Technion** in **Haifa**. A member of Likud, he served as ambassador to the U.S., and later as defense and foreign minister.

ARGENTINA. Republic in southeastern South America. The first Jews arrived with early Spanish settlers in the 16th century. They were **Marranos**, forced converts who practiced their religion in secret. By the time of Argentina's liberation from Spain in the early 19th century, the Marrano community had vanished. The earliest modern community was set up in 1868, but regular immigration did not begin until 1891. In that year Baron Maurice de **Hirsch** founded the **Jewish Colonization Association** (I.C.A.) to encourage the settlement of Jews upon the land. Swelled by waves of immigrants, the community grew from 1,000 in 1890 to 210,000 in 1998, more than half of Latin-American Jewry.

Most of Argentina's Jews live in Buenos Aires and other urban centers. About half are engaged in trade, with businesses ranging from tiny shops to huge commercial establishments. A large percentage are workers in the leather, furniture, and garment industries. Many have entered the professions. Jews have played an especially important role in the economic life of the country. Among the ideas introduced by Jewish merchants were installment and direct sales, and the organization of cooperatives for both buying and selling. Within the Jewish community there are many cooperative banks, as well as cooperative business undertakings.

Until recently, agriculture played an important part in the life of Argentinian Jewry. The first independent Jewish farm settlement was founded in 1899 by refugees from Russia. Other settlements were established and aided by the Jewish Colonization Association (I.C.A.). By 1940, there were 28,000 Jewish colonists on the pampas of Argentina, living in nineteen I.C.A. settlements, six non-I.C.A. settlements, and on private farms. This was one of the largest Jewish farm communities in the world. Owing to the decline of the farm economy under the dictatorship of Juan Peron and to the tendency for children of settlers to move to the cities, the farm community has dwindled to less than 5,000.

Buenos Aires, the capital of the country and home of most of its Jews, has been one of the world's leading centers of Yiddish culture. With Yiddish daily newspapers, weeklies, and numerous other periodicals, it has been a great center of Yiddish publishing. Hundreds of Yiddish writers, artists, musicians, and scholars lived in the city. To educate the young, the community maintains about seventy Jewish schools. Buenos Aires has an active Jewish theater as well.

The capital is also distinguished by the strength of its communal organization. The Argentine-Jewish Community of Buenos Aires, known as the Kehilla, is a truly unique organization. With a membership of about 50,000 families, it handles all aspects of communal life for the Jews of East European origins—cultural, educational, social, and religious. The Kehilla also maintains ties with the local non-Jewish communities, as well as with Jewish communities abroad. Two other organizations handle the affairs of the German and **Sephardic** Jews, but they tend not to merge with the other communities. On the national level, the Delegation of Argentine-Jewish Associations (D.A.I.A.) represents all local organizations on the national and international scenes.

Zionism has been an especially powerful force in Argentina. Most of the Jews in the country are either refugees or the children of refugees, and have been particularly concerned with assuring a homeland for Jews wherever they may be. Considerable sums are sent to **Israel** each year, and many Argentinian youths have settled there. However, in 1979, under the military dictatorship of Rafael Videla, there was a resurgence of anti-Semitism in Argentina and thousands of Jews were arrested. An investigation of anti-Semitism in

Argentina was conducted by various Jewish organizations. This situation has improved since 1983.

In July 1994, the D.A.I.A. building in Buenos Aires was bombed, resulting in some 100 deaths and the destruction of the communal archives. Two years earlier, the Israeli embassy was bombed, killing Israelis and Argentinians. These events have cast a shadow on the future of the community.

ARIZONA. There were few Jews in Arizona in the 19th and early 20th centuries. Only in recent decades has their number increased to nearly 50,000 in Phoenix, the capital, and 19,000 in Tucson. Those two communities have Jewish communal institutions. The *Arizona Jewish Post* is published in Tucson, the *Jewish News* in Phoenix.

ARK. *See* **Synagogue**.

ARK OF THE COVENANT. According to tradition, the Ark contained the tablets on which the **Ten Commandments** were inscribed. In ancient times, the Ark, carried by priests, led the people to battle. The **Bible** tells us that, when the Ark moved forward, **Moses** cried: "Rise up, O Lord, and let thine enemies be scattered." According to legend, the Ark was hidden under the Temple at the time of the Babylonian exile. The second Book of **Maccabees** relates that the prophet Jeremiah hid the Ark on Mount Nebo, where it would remain until the coming of the Messiah. A Holy Ark found in every synagogue contains the Torah scrolls used in the services. The Ark traditionally faces east, toward **Jerusalem**. It is opened on special occasions when certain solemn prayers are recited. Great attention has been given to the structural beauty of the Ark, usually the most decorative part of the synagogue.

"Ark of the Covenant," by Gustav Doré.

ARKANSAS. The Jewish community dates back to 1838. Only 2,000 Jews live in Arkansas, mostly in Little Rock. Among the distinguished native sons of Arkansas is Cyrus **Adler**.

ARLOSOROFF, VICTOR HAIM (1899-1933). Zionist political and labor leader. Born in the **Ukraine**, Arlosoroff spent his youth and received his education in **Germany**. In 1924, he settled in Palestine and plunged immediately into its Labor Zionist movement. He became the movement's political expert a year later at the age of 25. A brilliant young man, he was elected in 1931 to serve on the Executive of the **Jewish Agency** for Palestine where he assumed charge of the Agency's political work. When Hitler came to power in 1933, Arlosoroff was sent to **Germany** to negotiate with the Nazis. Since it was Nazi policy to expel Jews from Germany, Arlosoroff undertook to work out an agreement permitting as many Jews as possible to leave for Palestine, where the Jewish community was eager to receive them. After preliminary negotiations with Nazi leaders, Arlosoroff returned to Palestine where he reported to the Jewish leaders and to the British officials. But before he could resume negotiations, Arlosoroff was shot by an unknown assassin while walking with his wife on a **Tel Aviv** beach. The man convicted in the act was later released by a higher court, and it was never officially determined who fired the fatal shot on that June evening in 1933.

ART. While Jews are considered primarily the "People of the Book," Jewish artists, craftsmen, and architects abound throughout history. While the Second Commandment forbids the creation of graven images which can be worshiped in the pagan manner, its ban does not apply to architecture and so-called "applied arts." The Book of **Exodus** describes in glowing terms the beauty of the **Tabernacle**, fashioned by Bezalel and Oholiab, but no part of it has survived. Excavations in **Israel** have, however, unearthed the remains of lavishly decorated palaces and other buildings dating back to the time of the **Kings**. Nothing remains of the magnificent temple built by King **Solomon** in **Jerusalem**. Of the imposing temple erected by King **Herod** only a few fragments have been found. We can, however, see beautiful mosaic floors in ancient synagogues built after the destruction of Herod's Temple, and the superb frescoes in the ruins of a small synagogue at Dura Europos on the Euphrates river in **Syria**.

Jews were famous in antiquity for goldsmithery. In the Middle Ages, however, arts and crafts flourished among Jews who were free from oppression for long periods in **Spain**, **Italy**, **Greece**, **Poland**, and some Moslem countries in Asia and Africa. Jews were highly esteemed as dyers, lacemakers, bookbinders, and cartographers. They minted coins for Christian and Muslim rulers. Toward the end of the Middle Ages a pope forbade Jewish smiths to manufacture Christian ceremonial objects, such as goblets and crucifixes, and barred them from binding Christian religious books.

From the Middle Ages to the Emancipation, Jewish art was mainly ritual art for synagogues and home. The Torah Scroll was written—and sometimes illuminated, or ornamented—by special sofrim, or scribes. Some Hebrew Bibles had beautifully ornamented pages; others were provided with initials illuminated in gold and with full-page miniatures showing biblical figures such as **Adam**, **David**, and other heroes. The **Passover Haggadah** lent itself to illustration more than any other book, as it was used not in the synagogue but at home, and religious restrictions imposed on the artist were not so severe.

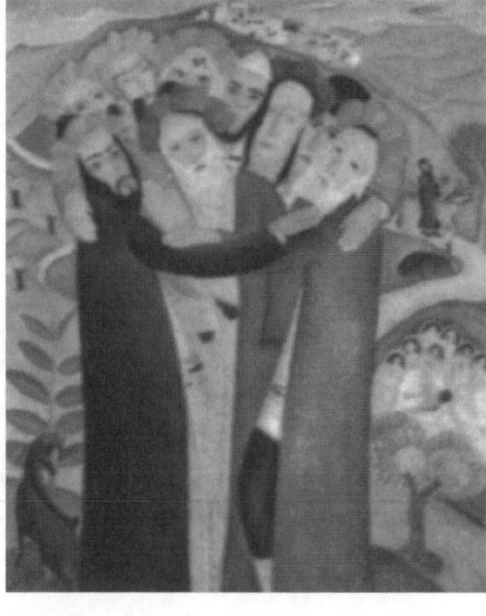
Reuven Rubin, early Israeli artist.

The Torah mantle, generally of silk or velvet, was skillfully embroidered by pious women. Little religious art older than 400 years has come down to us. Among the exceptions are some **Hanukkah** lamps of brass from North Africa and Italy, probably the work of Jews. As a rule, the Christian guilds of Europe had a monopoly only over the works in the precious metals, gold and silver. The superb ritual silver objects of the 17th and 18th centuries are the works of Gentiles. While the Jewish patron gave a general description to the Christian craftsman on the construction of a particular object, he did not mind if it was executed in the style of the period, whether

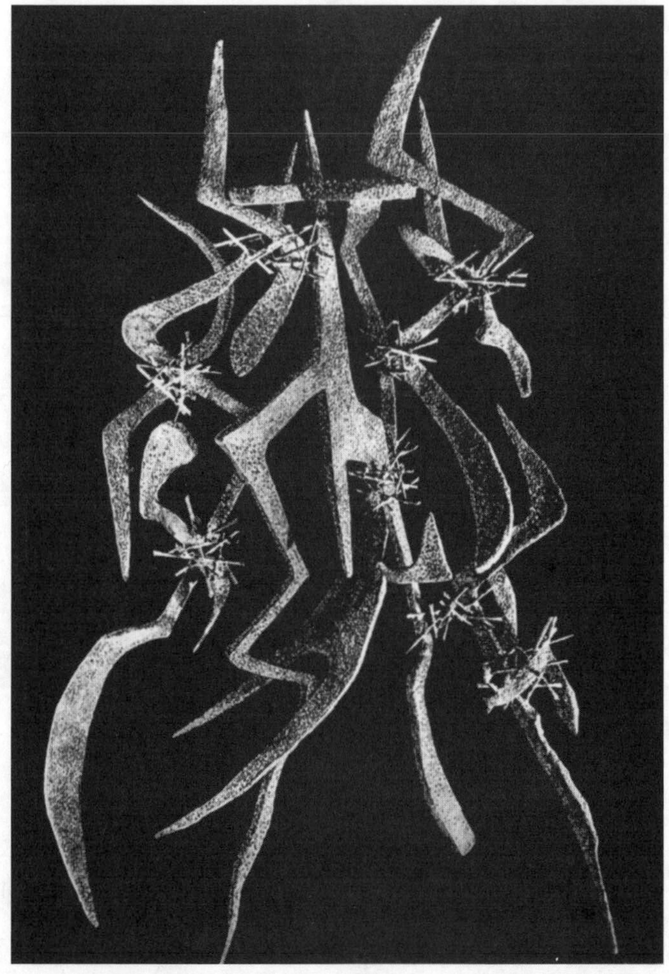
The Burning Bush, by Herbert Ferber (1951). Courtesy Congregation B'nai Israel, Milburn, New Jersey.

Ben Shahn, American Jewish artist.

Renaissance, Baroque, or Rococo.

Before the Emancipation, few Jews, mainly those converted to **Christianity**, became painters and sculptors. Things changed in the 19th century, when western European art schools and academies opened their doors to all willing students. Some Jewish artists gave up their ties to Judaism, making art their religion. Jews took the lead in the fight against the old romantic and historical schools, introducing realism, open-air painting, and an appreciation of art's social role.

These artists produced mainly portraits and landscapes, or worked in wood, metal, or stone like their Gentile colleagues. Until about 1900, it was rare to see Jewish artists occupied with themes related to Judaism. The Russian Jewish sculptor Mark **Antokolski** and the Dutch Jew Joseph **Israels** represent the dichotomy of pursuing Jewish and universal themes. The **Sephardic** Jewish artist Camille **Pissarro** greatly influenced impressionist and post-impressionist art. There were some, though, who tried to translate the messages of the Jewish faith, the spirit of the holidays, and the great historical traditions into pictorial terms. Maurycy **Gottlieb** became famous for his **Yom Kippur** painting.

Everything changed in the 20th century. Jewish art, as well as art created by Jewish artists, proliferated around the world. In **Paris**, the so-called *École Juive*, or Jewish School, of painters and sculptors produced world renowned artists such as Amedeo Modigliani, Marc **Chagall**, Chaim Soutine, and Jules Pascin. Of the great sculptors of the century, Sir Jacob **Epstein** of England, and Jacques **Lipschitz** of Europe, later the U.S., are among the best known.

Jewish artists in the U.S. have had a major influence on nearly all aspects of 20th century American art. Some, like Ben Shahn, pursued both Jewish and universal themes, particularly those related to social justice. Another example is Raphael Soyer, who depicted the downtrodden. Other leaders in innovative art were

A section of the mosaic floor of the synagogue at Bet Alpha. Courtesy Dr. Nelson Glueck.

Jackson Pollock, abstract American artist.

Jackson Pollock, the abstract expressionist; Alexander Calder, of mobile sculpture fame; Jim Dine, a leading pop artist; and Morris Hirshfield, a leading naive painter.

In Israel, art officially begins at the start of the 20th century with sculptor Boris **Schatz**, who founded the Bezalel School of Arts and Crafts in Jerusalem. In the pre-state era, artists such as Reuven Rubin and Nahum Gutman sought to create styles that reflected renewed Jewish life in the Middle East, laying the groundwork for Israeli art. Today, artistic activity in Israel, in nearly all forms, is vigorous and widespread. It encompasses not only painting and sculpture, but also ritual objects, original jewelry, posters, stamps, and other objects in fabric, metal, and stone. Artist colonies thrive in **Safed**, Ein Hod, **Jaffa**, and **Jerusalem**, to mention a few. Among world renowned Israeli artists are Yaakov **Agam**, known for his kinetic and optic art; Israeli-born Moshe **Safdie**, a world-class architect famous for his habitat; and Shalom of Safed (Moskovitz), whose biblical paintings are a leading example of naive art.

Among the most spectacular creations are synagogues. Until recently, architects' designs imitated churches of different styles. There is now a new trend to develop a style of architecture distinctively for synagogues, one that stresses both modernity and tradition, on the facade as well as the interior. The U.S., with the richest and largest Jewish community, leads this trend. However, some original and admirable architectural contributions have been made in **England**, **Canada**, **France**, and, of course, Israel.

ASARAH B'TEVET. *See* **Fast Days**.

ASCALON. *See* **Ashkelon**.

ASCETICISM. A regimen of self-denial to help one avoid temptations and distractions that hinder spiritual development. The **Nazirites** and Rechabites of the **Bible**, who abstained from wine, were ancient examples of asceticism. Rechabites also refrained from living in houses and dwelt in tents instead. In the time of the Second **Temple** there was an ascetic sect called the **Essenes**. Fasting frequently or eating very little, wearing rough clothing, avoiding company, doing without money, these were practices among the ascetics. The growing influence of the **Zohar** and the **Kabbalah** during and after the Middle Ages, plus the increasingly difficult conditions of Jewish life, furthered asceticism. A practice favored by many ascetics was "putting oneself in exile." The ascetic would leave home and family for a time, in order to appreciate more fully the exile of all Jewry. Jewish authorities such as **Maimonides** allowed limited asceticism for short periods, but opposed it as a way of life. A familiar ascetic figure was the *matmid*, one who devoted his days and nights to Torah study and allowed no other interests to distract him. The Mussar movement, which began in **Lithuania** about 1850, had ascetic leanings. But it placed less emphasis on self-inflicted suffering and more on the examination of the conscience as a means of self-improvement.

ASCH, SHOLOM (1880-1957). Outstanding Yiddish novelist and dramatist. Asch spent his early youth in the small town of Kutno, Poland, where he received a traditional education. At the turn of the century he dedicated himself to literary work in Yiddish and Hebrew. One of his idyllic novels of the Jewish small town, *Dos Shtetl*, attracted great attention. His later plays and novels revealed him as a keen observer and vivid portrayer of Jewish life. Almost all of his important works have been translated into English and other languages: *Motke the Thief*, *The Three Cities*, *Salvation*, *Uncle Moses*, *The Song of the Valley*, and many other contemporary and historical novels and stories.

Sholom Asch. Courtesy YIVO, New York City.

Asch has treated a wide range of subjects, including the saga of Jewish struggles and achievements in Europe, the U.S., and Palestine. He has caught the spirit of the revolutionary changes of our times; in his historical novels he has glorified Jewish martyrdom and piety. Some of his works based on New Testament figures, such as *The Nazarene*, are considered highly controversial. Two of his last novels portray the biblical figures of **Moses** and **Isaiah**. Asch lived for many years in the U.S., settled in Israel in 1956, and in October 1957, died while visiting London.

ASHDOD. 4,000-year-old port on coast of **Israel**. Neglected over the centuries, it now has a deep-water harbor, the largest in Israel. The town, now populated by about 123,000, is rapidly expanding through the growth of such industries as an electric power plant, a rayon factory, and an assembly plant for heavy vehicles.

ASHER. Literally, happy or blessed. Eighth son of **Jacob**. The tribe of Asher was allotted territory from the Carmel and the lower Kishon plain as far north as the Phoenician capital of Sidon. Asher never captured Acco and Sidon from the Phoenicians, but settled largely in the Plain of Jezreel. Isaiah called their territory *Galil ha-Goyim*, "the district inhabited by many nations"; hence, this area came to be called Galilee.

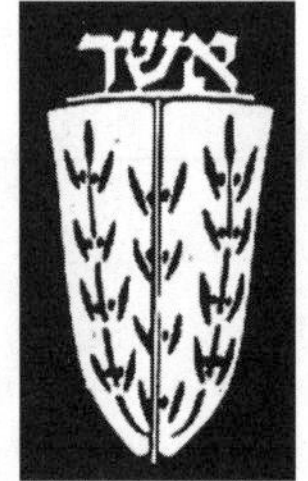

Emblem of the tribe of Asher

ASHKELON. Ancient Mediterranean port; one of the Five Towns of the Philistines. A modern Israeli city and resort area with about 80,000 residents, it has been developed with the aid of the South African Zionist Federation.

ASHKENAZI, VLADIMIR. *See* **Music**.

ASHKENAZIM. Literally, Germans. The name was applied to Jews of **Germany** and Northern **France** beginning in the 10th century. In the middle of the 16th century, the term Ashkenazim came to include Jews of Eastern Europe as well. The Ashkenazim have developed a set of distinctive customs and rituals, different from those of the **Sephardim**, that is, Jews from Spain, Portugal, Mediterranean countries, and North Africa.

ASIMOV, ISAAC (1920-1992). American scientist and author, considered to be the father of the science fiction genre. He wrote 100 books trying to become the first person to publish a book for every classification of the Dewey decimal system.

ASMODEUS. In rabbinical tradition, an evil spirit or demon.

ASSIMILATION. Throughout Jewish history, Jews have tended to "assimilate," adopting the language, manners, and customs of their neighbors, wherever they lived. At the same time, they continued to live a full Jewish life, producing great Jewish individuals and uniquely Jewish books. Individual Jews have left the Jewish community for other groups, but the bulk of the Jewish people has maintained its identity.

While the Jews lived in ghettos in medieval and post-medieval Europe, the **ghetto** walls protected them from assimilation. As the ghetto walls started to come down in the late 18th century, Jews began to discover a new world around them and soon learned that to achieve full equality they would have to conform to the general culture. A new movement, the **Haskalah**, or the Enlightenment, emerged, seeking to adapt to the European culture while remaining Jewish. During the French Revolution, French Jewish leaders agreed with the French liberals that the ultimate aim for Jews was to disappear completely as a national group. When Napoleon convened his Assembly of Jewish Notables, or French Sanhedrin, these Jewish leaders assured the emperor that first and last they were Frenchmen of Jewish descent.

In **Germany**, the Haskalah started when Moses **Medelssohn** translated the **Bible** into German. This translation introduced its Jewish readers to the German language, which opened the door to European culture. The generation that followed Mendelssohn used this culture to escape from the ghetto; in their headlong rush, large numbers were lost from Judaism altogether. Having adopted the German culture and way of life, they expected to be accepted into the "brotherhood of man." Instead, they discovered that full citizenship and social and economic advancement were possible for Jews only after baptism—the "ticket of admission to European civilization." Many took this step. Among those who explored this possibility was David Friedlaender of Berlin. He addressed an anonymous letter to Protestant clergymen, writing not only for himself but for a group of equally anonymous heads of Jewish families. These men were willing, the letter stated, to accept baptism if it were understood that they were rationalists for whom it was a mere formality. Would the Church be willing to accept them on this condition? Naturally, the Church was not willing, and the letter created an unhappy stir.

Yet Friedlaender's influence reached into **Poland** and **Russia**. The early Jewish Enlightenment movement in Poland and Russia had assimilationist tendencies and leaders, some of whom called themselves "Members of the Old Testament Persuasion in the Kingdom of Poland." In 1825, a rabbinical seminary aimed at the Polonization of Jews in Poland opened in **Warsaw** with the blessings of the Polish government. Its purpose becomes clear when one considers that the department of Hebrew and Bible was headed by Abraham Buchner, author of the pamphlet, *The Worthlessness of the Talmud*. In Russia, the Society for the Diffusion of Enlightenment was founded in 1867 in St. Petersburg. The aim of this society was most clearly expressed by its Odessa branch as "the enlightenment of the Jews through the Russian language and in the Russian spirit."

But reaction in **Germany**, pogroms in Russia, and anti-Semitic events like the **Dreyfus Affair** in France disillusioned the "enlighteners." Jews learned in the course of the 19th century that Europe was not ready to accept the Jews fully, whether or not they assimilated. This lesson was given its final and tragic validation during the **Holocaust**, when the official policy of the Nazi occupation of Europe was the physical extermination of all Jews, whether or not assimilated.

All of this changed in the second half of the 20th century. With the birth of Israel, and the coming of age of American Jewry, Jews are finally free to either live a full Jewish life or assimilate completely. Today, most Jews outside Israel assimilate by intermarriage and by lack of Jewish education. In the U.S., more Jews marry outside their faith than inside. The issue of assimilation has in recent years become a cause for alarm among American rabbis and community leaders.

ASSYRIA. The Asshur of the **Bible**. The North Mesopotamian empire of the city of Asshur stretched along the fertile plain on the upper Tigris River and included the towns of Kalchu and Nineveh. Assyria became a great empire after 1300 B.C.E. when it extended southward and ruled **Babylon** for a short period. Its drive westward continued for the next eight centuries until it controlled the whole Mediterranean coast and **Egypt**. The first direct conflict between Israel and Assyria occurred around 854 B.C.E., when King **Ahab** together with the ruler of **Damascus** fought King Shalmaneser III of Assyria at Karkar. Among the great rulers of this empire who figure disastrously during the next two and a half centuries in the history of Israel and Judah are Shalmaneser V, Sargon II, Sennacherib, Esarhaddon, and Assurbanipal. King Sargon defeated Israel, destroyed its capital, Samaria, and deported the flower of Israel's population to Mesopotamia and Media. The history of Assyria as an independent empire came to an end when the Babylonians and the Medes took Asshur in 616 B.C.E. and Nineveh in 612 B.C.E, destroying them both.

ASTRONOMY. The **Bible** contains a number of references to the heavenly bodies, their motions and appearance. God told **Abraham** to look toward the heavens and count the stars "if thou be able to count them...So shall thy seed be." Eclipses of the sun are described in the books of **Amos** and **Joel**. Some of the planets and constellations are mentioned in the Bible by name.

In Talmudic times, knowledge of astronomy was important in determining the Jewish **calendar**. Jewish scholars had some knowledge of the solar system. Mention is made of the Milky Way and comets. Rabbi Joshua was familiar with a star that appears once in 70 years, believed to be Halley's Comet. The Amora Rabbi Samuel was deeply interested in astronomy, and declared that the heavenly paths were as familiar to him as the streets of Nehardea, his hometown.

In the Middle Ages the science of astronomy was one of the favorite subjects of Jewish scholars. They translated the works of Greek astronomers, especially Ptolemy's *Amalgest*, and drew up astronomical tables. The physician, Sabbatai Donnolo of the 10th century, the poet Abraham **Ibn Ezra**, the great Talmudist and philosopher **Maimonides**, the commentator and philosopher, **Levi ben Gershon**, were some of the outstanding Jewish scholars who took an interest in astronomy in the 15th century. The cartographer Abraham **Zacuto**'s astronomical charts were used by **Columbus** and played their part in the discovery of America.

ASYLUM, TOWN OF. In the Bible (Ex. 21 and Num. 35), a place where an accidental killer could find refuge from the revenge of the deceased person's relatives.

ATHENS. This capital of **Greece** had Jewish residents by the 1st century C.E. Even before this time the Athenians had voted a gold crown to the high priest Hyrcanus, and later to the Herodian kings and to Princess Berenice, in gratitude for the kindly treatment of Athenians in Judea. There were many Athenian proselytes and semiproselytes. The **Talmud** has a number of stories about "the wise men of Athens." In Byzantine and Turkish times Athens decayed, and few Jews lived there. In 1830, when after Greece's liberation the first king was German, German Jews followed him to Athens. **Sephardim** from Greece and Syria, as well as Russian Jews after World War I, increased the Jewish community. During the persecution in World War II, many Athenian Gentiles hid Jews from the Germans. After the war, survivors and remnants from other Greek Jewish communities moved to Athens. In 1997, approximately 2,800 Jews, less than half of Greek Jewry, lived there.

ATONEMENT, DAY OF. *See* **Yom Kippur**.

AUERBACH, ARNOLD ("RED"). *See* **Sports**.

AUSCHWITZ. Town in southwestern **Poland** where the Germans in World War II maintained the most gruesome of all the concentration camps. Four million inmates, mostly Jews, were exterminated by gas, phenol injections, shooting, hanging, hunger, and disease. (*See also* **Holocaust**.)

AUSTRALIA. Organized Jewish life in Australia began in 1828, when Jews in Sydney formed a congregation. At that time, the Jewish population numbered 300. As the colonization and settlement of Australia continued, Jewish settlement proceeded apace, and soon there were organized congregations in the principal cities of Melbourne, Brisbane, Adelaide, and Perth in western Australia. Most of the early Jewish immigrants came directly from **England**. Jewish

On the left, former Prime Minister of Australia Bob Hawke, with Mark Liebler, Chairman of the Zionist Federation, and Uzi Narkiss, Chairman of the Information Department of the WZO.

immigration to Australia was spurred by the activities of the **Montefiore**, Levi, and Lazarus families, influential British Jews active in the economic development of the British dominion. Later, Australia was a haven for refugees fleeing Nazi tyranny, absorbing more Jewish immigrants in proportion to its pre-1938 Jewish population than any country except Israel. Jewish immigration peaked in 1954 and has been declining since. In 1998, there were about 95,000 Jews in Australia, most of whom lived in the six major cities, with 90 percent concentrated in Sydney and Melbourne. Organized in 1944, the Executive Council of Australian Jewry represents the entire Jewish community, serving as its mouthpiece on civil rights, welfare, and community status. Recent years have seen a reawakening of religious life, as well as increased interest in Jewish education. The Zionist movement is active and well organized, with close links among the various Zionist councils and local education boards of the Jewish schools. A number of Jews have played an active part in Australian life, including Sir Isaac Isaacs, the first Australian-born Governor General, and Sir John Monash, who commanded the Australian Expeditionary Force in World War I. Three Jewish weeklies in English and two in Yiddish are published in Australia, in addition to numerous monthlies and organizational publications.

AUSTRIA. Jews in Austria constituted an important community in Europe, with traces going back to the 9th century. Their history is a series of immigrations and expulsions and a constant struggle for existence. In 1421, about 210 Jews were burned to death by the order of the Vienna Edict, while the rest were driven out. Gradually, they returned, but in 1670 there was another expulsion. At that time, a number of individual Jews were permitted to return to Austria on the condition that they would not form any congregation. Among these "privileged Jews" was Samson Wertheimer, rabbi and banker to the court. In 1782, Emperor Joseph II issued his Edict of Toleration, which revoked many anti-Jewish regulations, but was opposed by Orthodox Jewry because of its interference in religious and cultural affairs and its hidden aim of compulsory assimilation.

Following their participation in the 1848 revolutions, the Jews enjoyed a short-lived period of liberty. In 1867, they attained equal political rights, which they enjoyed until the Germans occupied Austria in 1938.

Jews contributed greatly to the development of Austrian economics, science, art, literature, and media. In purely Jewish matters, they were influenced by eminent scholars whose books were accepted by Jewry throughout the world. Vienna had the largest Jewish community in Austria. Others were located in Graz, Salzburg, Innsbruck, Wiener-Neustadt and the Burgenland area.

The close of the 19th century witnessed the growth of the Zionist movement, due in no small measure to the fact that Theodor **Herzl** made his home in Vienna and served as literary editor and correspondent for the influential newspaper *Die Neue Freie Presse*. World War I brought many Jews to Austria from Galicia and **Hungary**; many remained after the war and exercised a strong influence on Jewish life in Austria. The *Anschluss* with **Germany** marked the beginning of the end for Austrian Jewry in March 1938. At that time, when Austria enthusiastically welcomed the German occupation, the Jewish population numbered 185,246. About 178,000 Jews lived in Vienna. By the end of World War II only 7,000 Jews remained: about 128,000 had fled the country, and about 50,000 were annihilated by the Austrians and Germans, many of them in the gas chambers of Auschwitz.

In 1998, there were 8,500 Jews living in Austria; a great majority of them live in Vienna and are registered with the Vienna Kultusgemeinde, central agency of the Austrian Jewish community. Postwar efforts of the community centered around negotiations for restitution and compensation of losses suffered under the Nazis. The Austrian Jewish community has had to contend with a resurgent **anti-Semitism.** Provisions for Jewish education have been lagging because of the dispersal of the children and their small numbers. Aided by the **American Jewish Joint Distribution Committee,** which is extremely active in relief and welfare work in Austria, the *Kultusgemeinde* maintains a Hebrew school, several Talmud Torahs, and a credit cooperative.

Ronald S. Lauder was appointed by President Ronald Reagan as Ambassador to Austria in April 1986 and served until October 1987. During his tenure, Lauder forged strong diplomatic bonds between the U.S. and Austria, while personally repudiating the Austrian President Kurt Waldheim.

AUTO-DA-FE (ca. 1481-1810). Portuguese, meaning act of faith. Tragic and justly infamous ceremony; climax of a heresy-hunting investigation by the Inquisition in **Spain** and **Portugal.**

A 15th-century woodcut portraying an auto-da-fe.

Those condemned as heretics were led to public penance or execution, the latter usually by being burned at the stake.

The auto-da-fe took the form of a procession through the main streets of the city to the public square, usually in front of a church. It was led by hooded monks who were followed by the hapless prisoners. Those condemned to death carried lit candles, wore a pointed cap on their heads and a tunic called the *san benito* upon which the "crimes" of the victims were inscribed and various diabolic symbols were painted. Priests, monks, and soldiers brought up the rear of the procession.

AV. Eleventh month of the Jewish civil calendar. (*See also* **Calendar** *and* **Fast Days**.)

AVERAH. A trespass or sinful act; opposite of *mitzvah*. The term does not include sin in general, but was applied to sins committed against one's friend or against God. Judaism believes that man is not born with original sin, but rather, possesses the power of free will: "I have set before you life and death...therefore choose life..." (Deut: 30:19). Human beings, however, are weak, and may tend to sin; God, therefore, provides an opportunity for repentance, and if done sincerely, he or she is forgiven. Although one may seek forgiveness at any time, it is on **Yom Kippur** that Israel as a whole prays to God to pardon its transgressions.

AVOT. *See* **Ethics of the Fathers**.

AYIN. Sixteenth letter of the Hebrew alphabet, numerically, seventy.

AZULAI, CHAIM JOSEPH DAVID (1724-1805). Scholar and author. Azulai, known by his initials as Hida, traveled extensively throughout Europe. He was sent by the Jewish community in **Jerusalem** to gather funds for the poor scholars in the Holy Land. Azulai had received a thorough training in **Talmud** and **Kabbalah** and was endowed with a keen historical sense. He utilized his travels to visit famous libraries and to gather valuable information for his most important work, *Shem Ha-Gedolim*, in which he listed 1,500 scholars and authors and more than 2,000 books written from Talmudic times to his own day.

Overleaf: Candelabrum sculpted in stone inside the catacombs of Bet Shearim. Courtesy Israel Office of Information.

BAAL. Literally, ruler, possessor. Pagan god of rain and fertility; foremost among Canaanite gods. Baal was not the name of one particular god, but the presiding deity of a given locality. He was killed each year by the hosts of Mot, the god of drought and death. Fertility and growth ceased until autumn, when Baal came to life, bringing back the rains. In spring, Baal married the goddess of fertility and war, returning fruitfulness to the land and its inhabitants. The Canaanites worshiped Baal with idolatry and fertility rites. The **Bible** records how judges and prophets opposed Baal worship among the people of Israel. (*See also* **Elijah**.)

BAAL SHEM TOV, ISRAEL BEN ELIEZER (ca. 1700-1760). Founder of **Hasidism**. The life of the pious Baal Shem (literally, "master of the name," or "miracle worker") has been the subject of so many legends and stories that it is often difficult to separate fact from myth. He left no written works, but his sayings were collected by disciples, especially Rabbi Baer of Mezhirich. Israel was orphaned at an early age and raised by the community. Though deeply religious, he was not an eager student, preferring solitary prayer and meditation. In his early life his occupations were varied: he was an assistant teacher in charge of **Heder** children, a synagogue helper, a ritual slaughterer, and even a charcoal burner. Upon his marriage to Anna Kuty, whose brother was the well-known scholar Rabbi Gershon Kutower, the Baal Shem moved to an isolated town in the Carpathian mountains. There he spent long hours with God and nature. Rabbi Gershon had given the couple a horse and wagon, and they made a bare livelihood by selling one wagonload of lime to the villagers every week. On his wedding day, Israel revealed to his bride that he was a divinely chosen *tzaddik*, or righteous man, but swore her to secrecy until the time was ripe for him to make himself known. He lived in obscurity until he was 36 years old. Then he began to travel through towns and villages, healing the sick and performing miracles.

An artist's rendition of Baal Shem Tov.

Israel's personality, piety, and imaginative expression gradually brought him fame. He became known as a man of deep religious feeling and enthusiasm, with a gift for communicating these emotions to the simplest and most ignorant person. His consideration and love for lowly people are illustrated by his comment to a disciple: "The lowliest person you can think of is dearer to me than your only son is to you." His followers' awe of him is apparent in legends. Rabbi Dov Baer of Mezhirich once asked Heaven to show him a man who was completely holy, and he was shown a fiery vision of the Baal Shem Tov. The image had no shred of matter; it was nothing but flame.

The Baal Shem yearned to go to the Holy Land, a longing which was never satisfied. In 1740, he settled in Podolia, a province in the Ukraine, where many scholars, rabbis, as well as common folk to form the nucleus of the Hasidic movement. Israel stressed devotion to God and dedicated prayer. He taught that joyful and enthusiastic worship, even that of an ignorant man, finds more favor in the eyes of the Maker than cold scholarship and dry knowledge of the Law. These teachings had great popular appeal and this new Hasidism which the Baal Shem had initiated spread like wildfire through East European Jewry.

BABEL, ISAAC (1894-1941). Russian author; one of the great short story writers of the 20th century. He served in the Soviet cavalry during the Russian Revolution. Accused of betrayal, he perished in a prison camp.

BABEL, TOWER OF. The Bible, after the story of creation, tells of a tower built in **Babylonia** that reached to heaven to defy God. Incurring divine fury, the tower was destroyed, and humankind, which until then only spoke one language, was now made to speak many different languages to prevent future rebellion against God.

BABYLONIA. Ancient Asiatic land lying between the Tigris and Euphrates Rivers, today southern Iraq, Babylonia was the cradle of ancient civilization and the seat of empires, occupying an important place in Jewish history. Ur, the capital of the Sumerian Empire—one of the earliest in the region—was the birthplace of the patriarch **Abraham**. Hammurabi, one of the most famous rulers of the region (ca. 1700 B.C.E.), is known for his code of law, parts of which

The Tower of Babel, by Gustav Doré.

parallel the biblical code. Hammurabi made the great city of Babylon the capital of his empire.

In the course of the 11th century B.C.E., the powerful empire of **Assyria** conquered Babylonia and destroyed Babylon, building its own capital, Nineveh. Three centuries later, the Assyrian kings, Tiglath-Pileser IV and Sargon II, conquered the northern kingdom of Israel, destroyed its capital, Samaria, and deported its inhabitants, the ten tribes of Israel.

A revival of Babylonian civilization was introduced by the Semitic Chaldeans, known in Hebrew as the *Kasdim* of the Bible. The Chaldean Empire peaked under King Nebuchadnezzar II, who captured Jerusalem in 597 B.C.E., destroyed it a decade later, and banished all the Jews to Babylonia.

In Babylonia, the exiles of Judah may have joined the lost ten tribes of Israel, who had been deported by the Assyrian kings two centuries earlier. The exiles developed their own traditions and institutions. The Babylonian kings gave them autonomy in religious and spiritual matters, at the same time allowing them to engage freely in agriculture and trade.

After the conquest of Babylonia by **Cyrus**, king of Persia (538 B.C.E.), the Jews were permitted to return to Zion. Many joyfully seized the opportunity to rebuild their homeland, but the majority of the exiles remained in their adopted land, Babylonia. During the succeeding centuries of Persian rule, Babylonia became one of the greatest Jewish centers, second only to **Palestine** in importance and influence. Communities sprang up throughout the land but kept close ties with Jews in Palestine. Many made the pilgrimage to the Second Temple in Jerusalem. Numerous schools provided basic education in Jewish law. More promising students went to Palestine to continue their studies, and later returned to spread Jewish learning throughout Babylonia.

In the year 312 B.C.E., shortly after the death of **Alexander the Great**, who had conquered Babylonia, this flourishing country came under the rule of the Syrian king Seleucus Nicator. In 160 B.C.E., Babylonia was conquered by Mithridates I, king of Parthia. The Parthians of Central Asia granted the Jews equal rights and full freedom of religion. Babylonian Jewry was headed by an **Exilarch**, a descendant of the House of David. The Exilarch had absolute authority on religious matters and was highly esteemed by Babylonian Jewry. As the official head of his people, he appeared at the court of the king dressed in stately robes, riding a golden chariot, and preceded by horsemen who announced his arrival. The Exilarch had varied powers: he collected taxes for the king's treasury from the Jewish population and acted as the supreme judge of Babylonian Jewry. He appointed officials and judges who were responsible for maintaining law and order in the Jewish communities.

Babylonian Jewry actively supported their Palestinian compatriots in the struggle for liberation from Syrian rule during the time of the Hasmoneans. Later in 69 C.E., when Jews in Palestine attempted to throw off the Roman yoke, thousands of Babylonian Jews joined their ranks. They supplied the fighters with funds and ammunition for their resistance to the enemy. After the destruction of Jerusalem, when the centers of learning were re-established in other parts of Palestine, many Babylonians came to the academies to study law. Among them were such great scholars as Abba Arikha, known as Rav, and Samuel Yarhinai. Upon their return to Babylonia, Rav founded the Academy of Sura and Samuel Yarhinai built the academy of Nehardea. Other great schools of learning were established later in the Jewish centers, Pumbeditha and Mahuza. Rav and Samuel were the first Babylonian **Amoraim**.

With the fall of the Parthian Empire (226 C.E.) and the rise of the new Persian rule, the Jews of Babylonia suffered great hardships. Their devotion to the study of the Law, however, did not diminish. During the period extending from the 3rd to 6th century, Babylonian scholars produced the great work known as the Babylonian **Talmud**.

At the beginning of the 5th century, the Byzantine empire abolished the last remnant of Jewish religious freedom in Palestine. Babylonia then became the spiritual center of all Jewry, cementing Jewish unity through intensive scholarly activity. This study continued despite frequent persecution by Persian rulers. At the

Bulls in relief on the ancient walls that surround the capital of Babylonia in the days of Nebuchadnezzar.

end of the 5th century, when Persian priests were making life intolerable for Jews, a young Exilarch, Mar Zutra II, rebelled against Persian rule and established a small, independent Jewish state at Mahuza. For seven years he succeeded in fighting off the enemy, until he was overpowered by superior Persian forces. Mar Zutra was captured and publicly executed.

In the 7th century a revival of Jewish life and learning took place in Babylonia after the Muslims conquered the land. The office of the Exilarch was restored to its full power and glory. A new period of Jewish scholarship, the period of the Geonim (*see* **Gaon**), emerged and endured for 400 years. The academies of Sura and Pumbeditha flourished again in the days of the Amoraim and their learned successors, the Saboraim. The Geonim stood at the head of the academies. Two months of the year, called the Kalla months, were devoted to popular study. Jews from all walks of life would flock to the **yeshivot** during this time to study the Law. Thus, knowledge of the Talmud became widespread and entrenched in Jewish life.

Jews from around the world, especially North Africa, gave financial support to the Babylonian academies. Whenever problems of law arose, they relied upon the decisions of the Babylonian Geonim. Though Palestinian scholarship experienced a similar revival under Muslim rule, it did not enjoy the prestige conferred on the Babylonian teachers. One of the greatest Babylonian Geonim was **Saadiah** Gaon, who successfully combated the **Karaite** sect which threatened traditional Judaism. After his death, the Babylonian Jewish centers began to decline. In 948, persecution, poverty, and a weakening of the Muslim empire forced the closing of the renowned academy Sura after 700 years of creative activity. The office of the Exilarch was abolished. Only the Pumbeditha academy still existed, headed by two of the foremost scholars, **Sherira** Gaon and his son, **Hai** Gaon. By the middle of the 11th century, Babylonian centers had dwindled considerably. Jewish life and scholarship now moved westward to **Spain**, **Italy**, and **Germany**.

BACALL, LAUREN. *See* **Stage and Screen**.

BADHAN. Aramaic; literally, to cheer up, to make laugh. A professional merrymaker, dating back to the Middle Ages, whose duty was to entertain the guests at weddings. A badhan was a sort of poet who spontaneously made up and sang appropriate rhymes to suit the important persons he met at the wedding. One of the last badhanim to become well known was Eliakim Zunser (1836-1913). Many of Zunser's lyrics were popular among Eastern European Jews.

BAECK, LEO (1873-1956). Leader of German Jewry before and during the **Holocaust**, Baeck was one of the great theologians of the **Reform** movement. He explained his views of Judaism in his book *Essence of Judaism*, and later in *This People Israel*, which grew out of his experience at the Theresienstadt concentration camp. After the war he taught at the **Hebrew Union College** in Cincinnati. A college in **England**, an institute in **New York**, and a high school in **Haifa**, **Israel** are named after him.

Leo Baeck

BAER, MAX. *See* **Sports**.

BALFOUR DECLARATION. In the midst of World War I, British Foreign Secretary Arthur James Balfour wrote the following letter to Lord Lionel Walter Rothschild, of the Zionist Federation in England:

Foreign Office
November 2nd, 1917

Dear Lord Rothschild,

I have much pleasure in conveying to you on behalf of His Majesty's Government the following declaration of sympathy with Jewish Zionist aspirations, which has been submitted to, and approved by, the Cabinet:

"His Majesty's Government view with favor the establishment in Palestine of a national home for the Jewish people, and will use their best endeavors to facilitate the achievement of this object, it being clearly understood that nothing shall be done which may prejudice the civil and religious rights of existing non-Jewish communities in Palestine or the rights and political status enjoyed by Jews in any other country."

I should be grateful if you would bring this Declaration to the knowledge of the Zionist Federation.

Yours sincerely,
Arthur James Balfour

Arthur James Balfour

The three sentences of this document giving international recognition to Zionist aims were the result of three years of diplomatic negotiations reaching out from London to **France**, **Italy**, and the U.S. The Balfour Declaration was issued with the support of the French government, and with the backing of Woodrow Wilson, then President of the U.S. Official approval came from France on February 14, 1918; from Italy on May 9, 1918; and from President Wilson in a letter to Stephen S. **Wise** on August 31, 1918. The U.S. Congress voted in its favor, and President Harding approved the declaration on September 21, 1922. The Balfour Declaration became the basis for a mandate for the creation of Palestine. This mandate was given to Britain by the League of Nations and affirmed on July 24, 1922. The news of the Declaration was received with waves of joy and spontaneous celebrations all over the Jewish world, and today, November 2nd is celebrated as Balfour Day. (*See also* **Zionism**.)

BALTIMORE. One of the most representative and historically significant Jewish communities in the U.S., dating back to the late 18th century. The first synagogue was founded in 1830. German Jews settled in the 1840's. During the Civil War, Baltimore Jewry was divided between North and South. Reform Rabbi David Einhorn supported the North, and had to flee the city, which was part of the South.

Campus of Bar-Ilan University in Israel.

In the late 19th and early 20th century, a large influx of east European Jews settled in Baltimore. The poet Israel Efros founded the Baltimore Hebrew College (later **Baltimore Hebrew University**), and the *Baltimore Jewish Times*, one of the finest Jewish weeklies in America, was started in 1919. Baltimore became a stronghold of Zionism, with leaders like Henrietta **Szold**, founder of **Hadassah**. In 1933, the Ner Israel Rabbinical College was founded, making Baltimore a center of Orthodox Judaism. American culture was enriched by such Baltimorean Jews as Gertrude **Stein,** who helped shape the literary style of writers like Ernest Hemingway, and the poet Karl Shapiro. The novel *Exodus*, by Baltimorean writer Leon **Uris**, had a positive impact on explaining the birth of the State of Israel to the world.

Today, Baltimore has a well organized and diversified Jewish community, with several day schools, and the full range of Jewish communal services.

BALTIMORE HEBREW UNIVERSITY AND TEACHERS TRAINING SCHOOL. Founded in 1919 in Baltimore; one of the first institutions in America to offer a full Hebrew teachers' training program. In addition to the Teachers' Training School, the college offers a four-year afternoon high school program and adult education courses.

BAMIDBAR. *See* **Numbers.**

BAR GIORA, SIMON. A leader of the Zealots, a party of extremists who were most responsible for the Judean rebellion against **Rome** from 67-70 C.E. Simon Bar Giora was a man of great physical strength, boundless courage, and ceaseless ambition. During the siege of **Jerusalem,** he fought ruthlessly not only against the Roman legions, but also against the moderate party in Jerusalem, until the commander of the garrison forced him to flee the city. Bar Giora fortified himself in **Masada**, a mountain fortress on the western shore of the **Dead Sea**. There he gathered a large army, and with the help of the Edomites, moved into Jerusalem and massacred many of his Zealot opponents. The incessant fighting among the Zealots stopped only when the Roman Emperor Titus surrounded Jerusalem in a bitter siege and Roman battering rams pounded down its walls. Then, Bar Giora fought the Romans with single-minded fury, but when the Temple was destroyed by Titus, he retreated to the Upper City. When that, too, was captured, Bar Giora hid in a cave and then tried to escape, but fell into the hands of the victorious Romans. As he was brought back to Rome with the other Judean captives, Bar Giora was forced to march in chains behind Titus's chariot at the head of the triumphal procession. Later, he was executed as a chief of the rebellion.

BAR ILAN, DAVID. *See* **Music.**

BAR-ILAN (BERLIN), MEYER (1880-1949). World **Mizrachi** leader. Born in Volozhin, **Russia**, Rabbi Bar-Ilan went to Berlin in 1910 where he served as general secretary of the world Mizrachi movement. In Berlin, he founded and edited the weekly *Ha-Ivri.*

Meyer Bar-Ilan

In 1913, he came to the United States where he developed local Mizrachi branches into a national organization of which he was president from 1916 to 1926. Afterward, he settled in Palestine. Bar-Ilan was a man of tremendous energy, with an erudition and attitude that embraced all Jewish life. In addition to playing a primary role in international **Zionism**, he edited Mizrachi's Hebrew daily *Ha-Tzofeh*, organized support for Israeli *Yeshivot*, or Talmudic academies, and worked on the publication of a new edition of the **Talmud**. When the First **Knesset**, or parliament, convened, he was a leading representative of the religious bloc. On April 18, 1949, while pleading against the internationalization of Jerusalem, Bar-Ilan died. In his honor are named the central World Mizrachi building in **Tel Aviv**, Bet Meir, the Berlin Forest, and the Mizrachi-sponsored **Bar-Ilan University** in **Israel**. His memoirs, *Fun Volozhin Bis Yerushalayim* (From Volozhin to Jerusalem), written in Yiddish, were first published in 1933.

BAR-ILAN UNIVERSITY, ISRAEL. Founded in 1955 as an "American University in Israel" with an initial class of eighty students; chartered by the Regents of the State of **New York**. Bar-Ilan is the only American-chartered university in Israel, being conducted and administrated in the manner of American universities. The essence and uniqueness of Bar-Ilan springs from the will of its founders to create in Israel a university espousing traditional teachings of Judaism. Secular training in liberal arts is blended with religious orientation, providing an environment in which the pursuit of knowledge is coupled with an understanding of heritage and a devotion to humanity. By 1996, the student body had grown to 20,000 men and women from **Israel**, the U.S., and nearly 35 other nations. In addition to baccalaureate programs, it now provides master's and doctoral degrees in 32 disciplines. The Jacov Herzog School of Law, opened in 1970, seeks to integrate Jewish law into the analytic study of each area of the law. A new post-high school program, *Tochnit Achat*, has been developed for American students living in Israel. The university awards a number of maintenance and tuition scholarships.

BARENBOIM, DANIEL. *See* **Music**.

BAR KOKHBA, SIMEON. Leader of the rebellion against the Romans (132-135 C.E.). His name, meaning "son of a star," is believed to be derived from the Messianic interpretation of the prophecy, "There shall step forth a star out of Jacob." Known also as Simeon ben Koziba, Bar Kokhba won numerous enthusiastic followers who believed in his mission to free Judea from the Roman empire. Among his supporters were famous scholars and his host of disciples. In particular, **Rabbi Akiva** considered him the Messiah and changed his name from Ben Koziba to Bar Kokhba. At first, Bar Kokhba and his heroic men conducted guerilla warfare against the powerful garrison in Palestine. His army grew steadily, attracting zealous fighters from all over Palestine and the Diaspora. According to legend, he tested the valor of his soldiers by requiring each to cut off one of his fingers. After the rabbis protested this needless mutilation, Bar Kokhba devised a less cruel test. Every prospective soldier was required to uproot a cedar tree while charging on horseback. Within a short time the army was strong enough to meet the Roman legions in open battle. Over the next two years, the Jews captured ninety forts and a thousand cities and villages, including Jerusalem.

The Roman emperor Hadrian, fearing that the Jewish revolt would encourage the uprising of more subject countries, dispatched his best legions to squash the revolt. At the head of his legions he placed Julius Severus, the general who had distinguished himself in the campaign against Britain. Severus recaptured all the fortresses, including Jerusalem, forcing Bar Kokhba to concentrate on the mountain stronghold of **Betar** in the Judean hills. The siege of Betar lasted a year. After a bitter struggle, the Roman legions entered the city on the ninth of Av, 135 C.E. Bar Kokhba and his men continued fighting to the end, dying with sword in hand. The number of Jewish dead reached half a million. Scores of Jews were sold as slaves. The rest hid in caves or fled to neighboring countries. Jerusalem was renamed Aelia Capitolina, in honor of Hadrian. The subjugation of Palestine was now complete, but the story of the Bar Kokhba revolt would become a living symbol of the Jewish desire for freedom and independence.

BAR MITZVAH. Literally, "son of the Commandment"; a boy who has reached the age of thirteen and is expected to accept adult religious responsibilities. The female equivalent of Bar Mitzvah is called Bat Mitzvah. This "coming of age" is the occasion for a ritual in the synagogue, where on the first Sabbath of his fourteenth year, the boy is called for the first time to read from the Torah and the prophets. It is a joyous occasion, accompanied by gifts for the bar mitzvah boy from friends and family. Traditionally, the Bar Mitzvah boy delivers a learned speech. Though the Bar Mitzvah is usually observed on the Sabbath, it may, in fact, take place any other day of the week when the Torah is read at the synagogue, i.e. Monday, Thursday, the New Moon. The beginnings of this ceremony are ancient. References to the custom are found as early as the 5th and 6th centuries. (*See also* **Confirmation**.)

A new immigrant to Israel celebrating his Bar Mitzvah. Courtesy Joint Distribution Committee.

BARAK, EHUD (1942-) Prime minister of Israel 1999-2001. Israel's most decorated soldier, Barak defeated **Netanyahu**, vowing to make peace with the Palestinians. He pulled Israeli troops out of Lebanon, and held extensive peace talks with Chairman Arafat and President Clinton. The talks failed, as the

Palestinians started rioting (the second Intifada). In early 2001, Barak lost his bid for reelection to Ariel **Sharon**.

BARUCH, BERNARD MANNES (1870-1965). American financier known as "advisor to Presidents." During World War I, President Wilson entrusted him with the task of heading various commissions to direct the war industries of the entire nation. At the end of the war, Baruch served as a member of the American Peace Commission. He served on the President's Agricultural Conference in 1922, and continued to give valued aid to American agriculture, helping to promote legislation for farm relief. Baruch was President Franklin D. Roosevelt's advisor on national problems, and is credited with planning the National Recovery Act of 1933. In World War II, Baruch acted as advisor to the war mobilization director, and in 1944 prepared a report for President Roosevelt on war and postwar plans. In 1946, he served as U.S. representative on the UN Atomic Energy Commission, and presented the American proposal for the international control of atomic energy on June 14, 1946. As a philanthropist, Baruch's interests led him to contribute large sums for the investigation of the causes of war and for possible means of preventing its outbreak. Baruch wrote articles and books on a variety of subjects. His autobiography, *My Own Story*, was published in 1957.

BEERSHEBA. Ancient town in **Israel** in the northern **Negev**, where **Abraham** dug a well and planted a tamarisk tree and where the biblical tribes of Israel gathered. Currently the site of Ben-Gurion University. In Roman and Byzantine times it was a prosperous station on the route from the Red Sea to the Mediterranean. Under Arab rule it declined, and during the 1948 Israeli War of Liberation it was a market town of about 3,000 Arabs, who fled after the Israeli occupation. Since then, it has developed into a bustling town of 150,000 residents, and has become the administrative center of the Negev. To this day, one can still see Bedouins riding their camels near Beersheba.

BEGIN, MENACHEM (1913-1992). Israeli statesman, born in **Russia**. He received a nationalist-religious education and studied law in **Warsaw**. As a teenager, he became a devoted follower of **Jabotin-sky** and an active member of the **Betar**, or Revisionist Zionist, youth movement. In 1939, on the eve of World War II, he was commander of Betar in **Poland**. In 1940, he was arrested by the Soviet secret police for his Zionist activities and sent to a Russian jail. Freed in 1942, he made his way to Palestine. A gifted orator, writer, and organizer, he became the commander of the **Irgun Z'vai L'umi** (IZL) in 1943, and led this underground organization in its fight against British rule. The IZL sought to sabotage British installations and speed up the termination of the British Mandate, without causing unnecessary loss of life.

Menachem Begin

After the establishment of Israel, Begin and his followers founded the Herut party (*see* **Revisionist Zionism**), a right-wing, strongly nationalist faction which he led in the **Knesset** for three decades. On the eve of the **Six-Day War** in 1967 he joined the National Unity Government as a minister without portfolio but left the cabinet in 1970 over a disagreement on foreign policy with Premier Golda **Meir.** In 1973, he became the leader of the Likud bloc which, led by Herut, opposed the Labor alignment. In May 1977, after almost 30 years in the opposition, Begin became Israel's first non-socialist prime minister. He was the first Israeli chief of state to make peace with an Arab leader when he invited Egyptian President Sadat to **Jerusalem** in November 1977. He subsequently participated in the Camp David talks with President Carter, which led to the peace treaty between Israel and Egypt in 1979, for which he was awarded the **Nobel Peace Prize**. In 1983, disappointed over the outcome of the Lebanon War, he resigned as prime minister and went into retirement. Until his death in 1992, he stayed away from public life.

BEILIS, MENDEL. Central figure in a notorious ritual murder trial in 1913 in Kiev, **Russia**. Beilis, a worker in a brick kiln, was accused of murdering a Russian boy whose body had been found near the kiln in March 1911. Although an investigation soon established that the boy had been murdered by non-Jewish thieves, the "Beilis Affair" dragged on for more than two years. The government of Czarist Russia stepped in and accused Beilis of committing this crime to use the boy's blood in the baking of matzos for **Passover**. To discredit the Jewish people, the anti-Semitic Russian government revived the centuries-old yet preposterous belief that Jews use Christian blood for such ritual purposes. The atmosphere surrounding the trial was charged with hate. Russian "experts" gave false testimony, and the judges and jury were prejudiced. Yet Beilis was acquitted thanks to his brilliant team of defense lawyers and because of international protests of the trial. Shortly after his acquittal, Beilis settled in Palestine, where he lived for eight years. He came to the U.S. in 1924 and lived there until his death in 1934 at Saratoga Springs.

BELGIUM. Jewish history in Belgium before and during the Middle Ages is not a happy one. In 1370, after the Black Death, the brutal Brussels Massacre wiped out the Belgian Jewish community. Jewish life did not flourish until the beginning of the 18th century, when Belgium became part of **Austria**, subsequently of **France** and the Netherlands. In 1830, when Belgium was granted independence, religious equality was established, and for first time Jews were able to have their own communal organization with a chief rabbinate in Brussels.

When the Allied armies entered Belgium in late 1944, they found 19,000 Jewish survivors. These were the remnants of a community numbering 100,000 before the Nazi occupation. Another 30,000 survived by escaping, being hidden by Belgian neighbors, or by having false documents. In 1998, there were about

David Ben-Gurion. Courtesy State of Israel Bonds.

32,000 Jews living in Belgium, mainly in Brussels and Antwerp. The majority of Antwerp Jews work in the diamond industry. It is the center of Orthodox Jewry, while Brussels Jewry is mostly non-Orthodox. The Zionist Federation of Belgium is the only organized Jewish body conducting cultural, educational, and social programs on a nationwide basis. The federation's biweekly paper is the *Tribune Sioniste*, the only Jewish publication in Belgium.

BELLOW, SAUL (1915-). Leading American novelist, born in **Canada**. Bellow's novels, mainly *The Adventures of Augie March* and *Herzog* (the main character, Moses Herzog, has strong Jewish roots), established him as one of the finest observers of the predicament of modern man, and won him the **Nobel Prize** in Literature.

BENEDICTIONS (B'rachot). Blessings addressed to God. Tradition ascribes them to the 120 elders of the Great Assembly in the time of **Ezra**. A total of 100 benedictions was to be recited daily. They are categorized into four groups: First, before sensory pleasures (tasting food or drink or enjoyment of a perfume); Second, for the privilege of fulfilling a **mitzvah**; Third, praising divine goodness upon hearing good or bad news, witnessing the wonders of nature, and giving thanks upon deliverance from sickness or danger (*birkat hagomel*), or upon joyous occasions and seasonal holidays (shehecheyanu); Fourth, during the daily prayers, such as the *Shmone Esre*, or 18 Benedictions, which include petitions for personal well-being and the welfare of the Jewish people in addition to blessings of praise and thanksgiving.

BEN-GURION, DAVID (1886-1973). Pioneer builder of the State of **Israel** and its first prime minister. Born David Gruen in **Poland**, he inherited from his father a strong love for Zion into which he blended his own socialist ideals. In 1903, at age 17, he was already one of the founders of the Socialist Zionist Party, *Poale Zion*, in Poland. Even as a youth, he manifested great determination to fulfill his ideals, and pursued his aims with unusual courage.

In 1906, at 20, Ben-Gurion went to Palestine where he worked as a common laborer, experiencing all the hardships of the young pioneer. He became active in the **Galilee**, which had scarcely been opened for Jewish colonization. Work was hard, and the danger of Arab attacks lurked everywhere. Ben-Gurion led in founding the Jewish self-defense movement, and took an active part in organizing the Socialist Zionist worker's movement. When **Turkey**, which then ruled over Palestine, entered World War I, Ben-Gurion was expelled from Palestine. He came to the U.S. where he helped found the **American Jewish Congress** and organized the **Jewish Legion**, which he joined as a private. In 1921, he returned to Palestine and became general secretary of the **Histadrut**, or General Federation of Labor, participating at the same time in other Zionist activities. In 1933, he was elected to the Executive of the World Zionist Organization, and from 1940 on he acted as chairman.

Ben-Gurion played a decisive role in the struggle for the establishment of the State of Israel. Despite heavy pressure from the U.S. Department of State to postpone the proclamation of independence for Israel, he was largely instrumental in bringing it off as scheduled on May 14, 1948. As prime minister and minister of defense during the formative years of the state, he may be credited with many of its achievements. His scholarly articles and orations served the movement for years in clarifying Zionist ideals and aims. During his pioneering days, he wrote, "A land is built only by pioneers who know how to give their lives to realize their ideals." He became the embodiment of this pioneering spirit. Ben-Gurion retired at age 67 to the isolation of the Negev, but returned to assume leadership in 1955. He initiated the Sinai Campaign. He retired from the premiership in 1963 and was succeeded by Levi **Eshkol**. In 1965, he broke away from Mapai and formed *Rafi*, or Israel Labor List. He resigned from the Knesset in 1970 and retired to his **kibbutz**, *S'de Boker*, where he engaged in study and writing until his death.

BENJAMIN. Literally, son of the right hand, of good fortune. **Jacob**'s twelfth and youngest son; **Rachel** died giving birth to him. Founder of the warlike tribe of Benjamin that settled on a stretch of land reaching up from the river **Jordan** toward the hills of **Jerusalem**. **Saul**, the first king of Israel, was a Benjaminite.

Emblem of the tribe of Benjamin.

BENJAMIN OF TUDELA (12th century). Merchant and traveler, often called the "Jewish Marco Polo." He started out from Saragossa, **Spain**, in 1160 and spent 13 years traveling around the then-known world. He kept a lively diary in Hebrew, recording detailed descriptions of Jewish life in Europe, Asia, and North Africa. The first English translation in 1840 of his journeys is highly esteemed for the historical and geographical light it sheds on the far away and little known Orient of that time. Benjamin's vivid descriptions are particularly valuable because they include information on several peoples that disappeared completely once conquered by the Tatars.

BEN SIRA (ca. 200 B.C.E.). Joshua ben Simeon ben Eliezer ben Sira or Sirach. Author of a book of proverbs, Ben Sira lived in Jerusalem. The Book of Ben Sira, part of the Hebrew Wisdom Literature, presents through its proverbs an interesting record of Jewish social life of that time. It includes praise of the high priest's function and of the **Temple** ritual. Originally written in Hebrew, the book was translated into Greek by a descendant of Ben Sira around 132 B.C.E. During the Middle Ages the Hebrew and Aramaic versions were lost. Finally in 1896, most of the original Hebrew text was discovered by Solomon **Schechter** among the fragments of the Cairo **Genizah**.

BEN YEHUDA, ELIEZER (1858-1922). Father of the modern Hebrew language, Ben Yehuda's life was an example of single-minded devotion to a cause: the revival of the ancient **Hebrew language**.

At the age of 19, Ben Yehuda left **Lithuania**, where he had been brought up in a traditional environment, to study medicine in Paris. At first he was attracted to socialism. Later, the struggle of the Balkan countries to gain their independence made him aware of the need for a Jewish national homeland.

In 1880, Ben Yehuda decided to settle in **Jerusalem** where he immediately set out to realize his cherished ideal of adapting the Hebrew language to daily use. He was subjected to ridicule by many people who considered the task impractical. It took Ben Yehuda many years of persistent work to convince the skeptics that Hebrew could be revived. His home was the first in Palestine in which Hebrew was the only language spoken.

Eliezer Ben Yehuda

Ben Yehuda concentrated all his efforts on his monumental lifework: *The Dictionary of the Hebrew Language, Old and New*, which appeared initially in fifteen volumes. The sixteenth and seventeenth volumes appeared in 1959. Numerous words for daily use were coined by Ben Yehuda and became part of modern Hebrew. Ben Yehuda also published newspapers, composed textbooks for Hebrew schools, and was one of the founders of the Committee for the Hebrew language, now the Academy for the Hebrew Language.

BEN-ZVI, YITZHAK (1885-1963). Second president of **Israel**, born in the **Ukraine**. At age 18 he went to Palestine. Upon his return to **Russia** in 1905, the year of widespread pogroms in many parts of Russia, he joined Ber **Borochov** in establishing the Socialist Zionist party, Poale Zion. The Tsarist government, troubled by revolutions, found the Jews a convenient scapegoat and in many cases actually encouraged attacks upon them. Ben-Zvi, along with his father and brother, helped organize Jewish self-defense units. The Russian police exiled the entire Ben-Zvi family to Siberia, but Yitzhak succeeded in eluding his captors and escaped from Russia. For about two years he engaged in intensive Zionist work in **Germany** and **Switzerland**. In 1907, he finally reached his destination Palestine. On his arrival, Ben-Zvi immediately became a spokesman for and leader of the Jewish workers in Palestine. He was among the founders of **Hashomer**, the earliest Jewish defense force in modern Palestine. During World War I he accompanied David **Ben-Gurion** to America, where he organized first the **Hehalutz**, or pioneer movement, and later the **Jewish Legion**, which fought with the British for the liberation of Palestine from Turkish rule. After the war, he returned to Palestine, where he participated in the establishment of the **Histadrut**, the Palestine Workers Union, and Knesset Yisrael, the organized Jewish community of Palestine. For fourteen years, from 1931 to 1945, Ben-Zvi was head of the *Vaad Leumi*, or National Council, the executive arm and official representative body of Palestine Jewry. With the establishment of Israel, Ben Zvi became a member of the **Knesset**, the state's parliament. In 1953, he succeeded Chaim **Weizmann** as the second President of the State of Israel.

Yitzhak Ben-Zvi

In addition to his political and communal activities, Ben-Zvi devoted a great deal of time to scholarly studies and writing. His books on the history of the Jews in the Holy Land and on the different ethnic groups that made up Palestine Jewry are regarded as authoritative and exhaustive studies. His wife, Rahel Yanait Ben Zvi (1884-1979), was a well-known Labor Zionist leader, pioneer, and educator in her own right.

BERDITCHEVSKY, MICAH JOSEPH (1865-1921). Hebrew novelist and essayist. Born in **Ukraine**, he studied at the Yeshiva of Volozin and later at the University of Berlin. He was critical of Jewish religious tradition, which he found stifling, and under the influence of the German philosopher Nietzsche, he advocated a new approach to Judaism, emphasizing life and nature. Under the pen name Micah Joseph Ben-Gorion, he published twenty volumes. In his novels and short stories, he deals chiefly with small-town people, describing their struggles and passions with a mixture of realism and fable. His Hasidic tales and collections of **Midrashic** legends constitute a rich contribution to Hebrew letters.

BERENSON, BERNARD (1865-1959). One of the world's leading art historians. He was born in **Lithuania**, educated in the U.S., and lived in **Italy** where he embraced the Christian faith. His work includes *Italian Painters of the Renaissance.*

BERESHIT. *See* **Genesis**.

BERGEN BELSEN. Nazi concentration camp near Hanover, **Germany**, established by the Nazis in July 1943. Originally intended for Jews whom the German government wished to exchange for Germans in Allied territories, it became one of the infamous death camps. Anne **Frank** was among the victims of Bergen Belsen. The camp was liberated by the British on April 15, 1945. (*See also* **Holocaust; World Federation of Bergen Belsen Associations.**)

BERGSON, HENRI (1859-1941). One of the great philosophers of the 20th century, Bergson was a French Jew removed from Judaism. His book *Creative Evolution* influenced many creative minds of his time. In 1927, he won the **Nobel Prize** for Literature. When the Nazis occupied **France**, he protested against the anti-Semitic legislation they introduced.

BERKOWITZ, MICKEY. *See* **Sports.**

BERLIN, IRVING (1888-1989). One of the leading American songwriters of the 20th century (*God Bless America, White Christmas*), Berlin was born in **Russia** to a Jewish cantor. Without formal musical education, he managed to write more than 1,000 melodies, many of which have become American classics.

Sarah Bernhardt.

BERNHARDT, SARAH (1844-1923). Known as the "Divine Sarah," Bernhardt was the most famous actress in **France** in her day, and is still considered one of the great actresses of all time.

BERNSTEIN, LEONARD (1918-1990). Composer, conductor, and pianist. Born in Lawrence, Mass., of middle-class Jewish parents, Bernstein was educated at Harvard University and embarked early on a musical career. At age 25 he became assistant conductor of the New York Philharmonic Orchestra. A year later he was named conductor of the New York City Symphony Orchestra. In 1948, he became musical director of the Israel Philharmonic Orchestra, conducting for soldiers at the front during Israel's War of Liberation.

Leonard Bernstein

Bernstein's numerous compositions, ranging from symphonies to scores for successful Broadway musicals (*West Side Story*), include a number of works based on traditional Jewish motifs. His first symphony, *Jeremiah*, is a moving score based on the cantillation for the Book of **Lamentations**; his synagogue music has similarly rendered age-old melodic material with modern techniques. He was professor of music at **Brandeis University**, head of the conducting department at the Berkshire Music Center, and conductor of the New York Philharmonic.

BERTINORO, OBADIAH (b.1470). A noted Talmudic scholar, Bertinoro served as rabbi in several Italian communities. At age 36 he decided to go to Palestine. In **Jerusalem** he organized about 70 Jewish families into a community. With the arrival of exiles from **Spain**, the community grew rapidly in numbers and prestige.

Tomb of Rachel in Bethlehem.

Bertinoro's letters describing conditions in Palestine are of great historic importance. He is, however, best known for his commentary on the **Mishnah**. Its clarity of language and style and its comprehensive presentation made it one of the most popular commentaries on that work.

BET. Second letter of the Hebrew alphabet; numerically, two.

BET DIN. Literally, "court of law." The term dates back to post-biblical times. Today it refers to a rabbinical court, where personal status matters, such as marriage, divorce, and conversion, are decided. Historically, Jews have voluntarily resorted to a bet din to settle financial and other disputes which they preferred not to bring before a state court. In Israel, the bet din or the rabbinical court handles personal issues, while the state legal system handles all other matters.

BET HAMIDRASH. Literally, House of Study. Used to designate study halls for Jewish learning, the term is also used to describe one of the functions of the **synagogue** in Jewish life.

BET HILLEL AND BET SHAMAI. The School of **Hillel** and the School of Shamai represented the followers of two contemporary *tannaim*, or sages of the 1st century. Hillel was moderate, seeking compromise and accommodation. Shamai was the strict interpreter of the law, who refused to compromise on many issues of Jewish law. In time, the views of Bet Hillel prevailed in most cases.

BETAR. *See* **Bar Kokhba.**

BETAR, BRITH TRUMPELDOR ORGANIZATION. *See* **Revisionist Zionism.**

BETHLEHEM. Town in the Judean hills south of **Jerusalem**. Bethlehem was the setting of the Book of **Ruth**, the home of **David**, and, according to New Testament tradition the birthplace of **Jesus** of **Nazareth**. The architectural beauty of the Basilica, the Church of the Nativity, built in the 4th century, is still preserved. As the most important Christian shrine, Bethlehem is visited by many thousands of pilgrims, especially at Christmas time. Its population of about 10,000 consists mainly of

Christian Arabs, in whose dress and features the influence of the Crusaders has been preserved. The holiest Jewish site in Bethlehem is the Tomb of Rachel. Under the **Oslo Agreement**, the town was put under Palestinian Authority rule.

BETTELHEIM, BRUNO (1903-1990). World-renowned American child psychologist and educator. Born in Vienna, he spent a year in a Nazi concentration camp before he was released to go to the U.S. He wrote about this experience, and in later writings dealt with many other areas of human experience. His book *Children of the Dream* is a study of kibbutz-raised Israeli children.

BEZALEL SCHOOL OF ARTS AND CRAFTS. School founded in **Jerusalem** in 1906 by the sculptor Boris **Schatz** for the development of the arts, home industry, and crafts in Palestine. It is named after Bezalel, chief architect of the **Tabernacle** (Exod. 31:1-6 and 35:30).

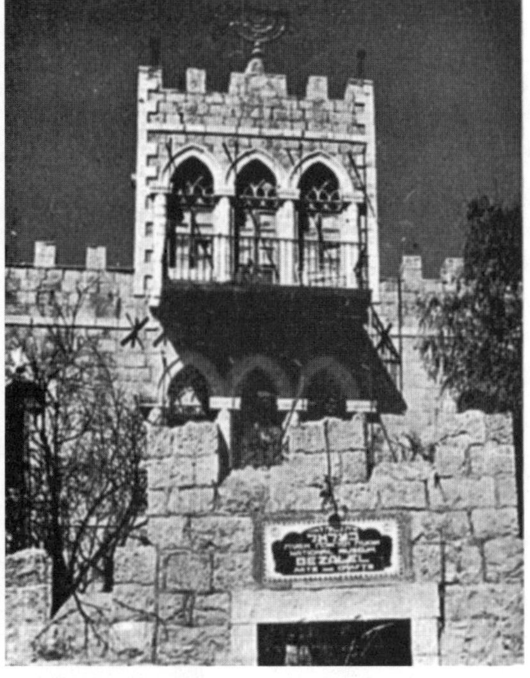

Bezalel National Museum and School of Arts and Crafts.

The school is closely associated with the Bezalel section of the Israel Museum, which contains a large selection of Jewish art objects and reproductions, many of which tour every corner of Israel. The Bezalel School is supported by the Women's International Zionist Organization (WIZO) and the American Fund for Israel Institutions. In international art competitions, Bezalel students have received an average of twenty prizes a year.

BIALIK, CHAIM NACHMAN (1873-1934). One of the greatest Hebrew poets of modern times, Bialik is considered the national poet of Israel. At age 11, he had already studied Jewish philosophic works, concentrating on the **Talmud**. At 16, he entered the famous Yeshiva of Volozhin in **Lithuania**. Later, in one of his poems he immortalized the yeshiva student, or *matmid*, who dedicated himself to study, excluding all worldly matters from his thoughts. During the year he spent in Volozhin, the young Bialik drew closer to **Zionism** and to modern **Hebrew literature**. When the Russian government closed the Volozhin Yeshiva in 1891, he went to **Odessa** in southern **Russia**, drawn by its flourishing Hebrew literary center. In an anthology called *Ha-Pardes*, Bialik published his first poem, *El Hatzipor*, or "To the Bird," expressing his boundless love for the old-new Zion. Other poems followed. His outstanding talent immediately impressed his readers. Here was poetry, deeply personal, yet touching the soul of the Jewish people. Like the ancient prophets, Bialik rebuked his people and exposed their weaknesses in fiery and sharp-edged verses. Yet the poet inspired the Jewish masses with hope, pride, and self-respect. His poem *The City of Slaughter*, written after the Kishinev **pogrom** in 1903, roused the younger generation to take up arms in self-defense. Bialik linked the past with the present in his poetic works. Drawing upon the rich sources of Jewish creativity, he gave new power and meaning to age-old traditions and ideals. He imparted unusual beauty and charm to folk themes, and created wonderful poems for children. In essays and stories, he was a master of Hebrew prose. He assumed a leading role in Jewish cultural life, a symbol of the national revival. At his magic touch, the Hebrew language became a vital cultural force. Together with his life-long friend J.C. Ravnitzky, Bialik popularized the rich treasury of the Talmudic and Midrashic legend, the **Aggadah**. In addition to poems, stories, and Talmudic legends he collected in *Sefer Ha-Aggadah*, Bialik wrote biblical legends in *Vayehi ha-Yom*, or "It Came to Pass," recapturing their ancient charm and humor. He translated into Hebrew such classics as Cervantes' *Don Quixote* and Schiller's *Wilhelm Tel*.

Chaim Nachman Bialik

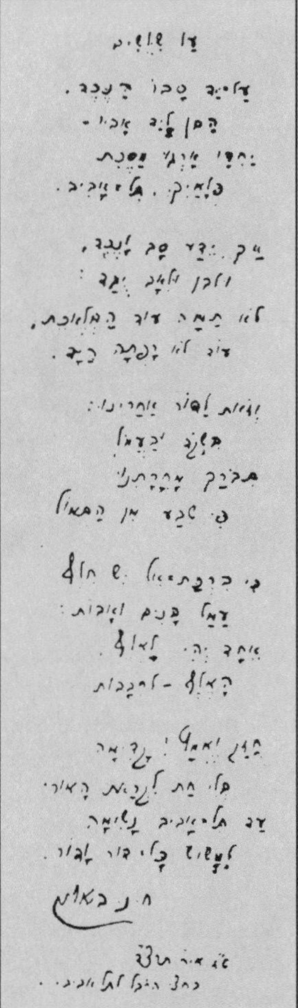

A poem by Bialik in his handwriting.

Bialik was beloved and revered while yet in Russia. After the Bolshevik Revolution, he was forced to leave the country and went to Germany. In 1924, he settled in Palestine. His home in **Tel Aviv** on a street now named after him became a place of pilgrimage for Hebrew writers. In 1929, Bialik visited America, and was received with acclaim. During the last years of his life, as editor, publisher, and critic, he became the guiding spirit of every Hebrew cultural and literary activity. He participated actively in the work of the **Hebrew University** in Jerusalem and the Committee for the Hebrew Language. The **Oneg Shabbat** gatherings in Tel Aviv, over which Bialik presided, became a celebrated institution. His home in Tel Aviv has been preserved as a cultural center. Mossad Bialik, one of the foremost publishing houses in Israel, and Bialik prizes for the best in Hebrew literature are symbolic monuments to his memory. The 21st day of Tammuz, the date of his death, is observed as a national memorial day in Israel.

BIBLE. From the Greek *biblia*, meaning books. In Hebrew TaNaKh, meaning Torah, Prophets, Writings. The Hebrew Bible came to have many names: the Holy Scriptures, the Book of Books, the Old Testament, Divine Revelation.

Canon. Sometime during the 1st century, the final decision was made as to which sacred books were to be considered part of the biblical canon, also known as the Holy Scriptures. The word "canon," meaning standard, that was applied by scholars to the holy books, comes from the Greek *kanones*, meaning models of excellence.

Influence of the Bible. For Jews, the Bible has been the source of life, growth, and survival. They read in it the record of their people's spiritual progress, from **Abraham**, the first to reject polytheism, to the prophets' momentous vision of God as the loving Father of all creation. When the Jews were expelled from Palestine and became wanderers, the Bible became a way of life and a Jewish "portable homeland."

The influence of the Bible was not limited to Judaism, but has extended to two other religions: **Christianity** and **Islam**. Mohammed, the creator of Islam, was so deeply influenced by the Bible that at first he thought of himself as a new prophet of Judaism. His mind was so filled with biblical stories that he traced his descent to **Ishmael**, son of **Abraham** and **Hagar**. The theology of the Koran, the sacred book of Islam, shows Mohammed's debt to the Bible and to Judaism. As Mohammedanism spread, the Bible influenced many people in the East.

Christianity took over the Hebrew Bible and added the New Testament. As Western civilization took shape, it absorbed the Hebrew Old Testament ideas. Biblical ideas—the common origin of man, the equality of men before God, the law of mercy, and the equal right to knowledge—filtered down only gradually to the common man in the Christian world. For at first the Bible was known only to priests and to those few who could read its ancient Greek and Latin translations. But the Renaissance movement, the invention of printing, and the religious Reformation spread learning

Micah exhorts Israel to repent, by Gustav Doré.

BOOKS OF THE BIBLE

Torah	Prophets	Writings
Genesis	*Joshua*	*Psalms*
Exodus	*Judges*	*Proverbs*
Leviticus	*Samuel I and II*	*Job*
Numbers	*Kings I and II*	*Song of Songs*
Deuteronomy	*Isaiah*	*Ruth*
	Jeremiah	*Lamentations*
	Ezekiel	*Ecclesiastes*
	Hosea	*Esther*
	Joel	*Daniel*
	Amos	*Ezra*
	Obadiah	*Nehemiah*
	Jonah	*Chronicles I and II*
	Micah	
	Nahum	
	Habakkuk	
	Haggai	
	Zephaniah	
	Zechariah	
	Malachi	

and knowledge of the Bible to increasing numbers of people. As they read the Bible, the people began to apply its ideas to their own lives.

When Adam delved and Eve span,
Who was then the gentleman?

John Ball used this old English rhyme in a speech to the rebels of the Wat Tyler Insurrections in 1381. His rough peasant worker audience understood well this Bible-inspired view of equality.

Bible Translations. The first translation of the Bible was the **Septuagint**, a Greek translation for the Jews of **Alexandria** begun in the middle of the 3rd century B.C.E. and continued until the end of the next century. During the 2nd century C.E., a series of new Greek translations was made by the Christian Church Fathers. The first great translation into a West European tongue, the Latin Vulgate version of 382, became the official Bible of the Roman Catholic Church. Each age produced Bible translations in hundreds of languages, all over the world. The Jews found the need to make translations: after the Septuagint came the **Aramaic** translations by **Onkelos** and by Jonathan Ben Uziel. In the 10th century, the great scholar **Saadiah Gaon** completed one of the most successful Arabic translations. A Persian translation appeared about 400 years later. By the middle of the 15th century, Europe saw the first Bible printed from wood blocks. It was an inexpensive illustrated Bible known as the *Poor Man's Bible*, and under its many pictures of biblical scenes were short explanations in Latin and the local vernacular. The Renaissance and the Reformation brought new translations to western Europe. Martin Luther's 1534 German translation exerted great influence. In **France**, Roman Catholic scholars published the important Douay Version in 1610. Perhaps the greatest and most influential translation is the English King James Version of 1611. The beauty of its language came close to the spirit of the Hebrew Bible. The King James version became an instrument that formed noble minds and inspired great works of music and literature. New translations, by Jews and non-Jews, are still being performed. To this day, scholars research the ancient Hebrew texts as they are discovered (*see* **Dead Sea Scrolls**), compare the translations with the originals, and correct errors. The Bible has been translated into 1,108 languages, and missionary linguists have initiated additional translations into 2,000 dialects for primitive peoples in the distant corners of New Guinea, Africa, Southeast Asia, and for South American Indians.

Bible in American History. The influence of the Bible in the early history of the **United States** cannot be overstated. The Puritans lived by the Bible. They looked upon themselves as God's chosen people, like the ancient Israelites, and in New England colonies they formed their "Holy Commonwealth." They felt their church to be a continuation of the **Covenant** between God and the Jews. For the early Protestants of New England, the Old Testament was the supreme authority, and in the colleges where their sons trained for the ministry, the Bible was studied in the original Hebrew. Records of births, deaths, and marriages were kept in the family Bible. Every day a chapter was read aloud to the household. American pioneers gave biblical names to their towns and villages: Jerusalem in the State of **Washington**, Jonah in **Texas**. New England settlers based the political laws governing their colonies on the Scriptures. Forty-six of the 48 laws in the Body of Liberties which they drew up in 1641 were based on the Hebrew Bible. It is no wonder that a verse from the Bible was engraved on the Liberty Bell when it rang out in July 1776 to announce the Declaration of Independence: "Proclaim liberty throughout the land unto all the inhabitants thereof" (Lev. 25:10).

The influence of the Bible on Western literature and art cannot be briefly put. From earliest times, storytellers and poets, sculptors, and painters have used biblical themes for their books and poems, for their statues and pictures. The libraries and museums of the Western World are filled with works of art inspired by the Bible. In great concert halls people listen to musical translations of the Bible, from Handel's oratorio *Israel in Egypt* to Ernest **Bloch**'s *Schelomo* rhapsody. Books, works of art, and music are only some ways in which people recognize the Bible as a great spiritual heritage for all humankind. (*See also* **Reading of the Law**.)

BILU. Movement formed after the pogroms of 1881 in **Russia**; composed mainly of university students who became the first pioneers to go to Palestine. The name "Bilu" is an abbreviation of the Hebrew words *Bet Yaakov Lechu Venelcha*—"O House of Jacob, come, and let us go forth" (Isaiah 2:5). These young people were infatuated with the idea of serving as the trailblazers of Jewish settlement. Their program

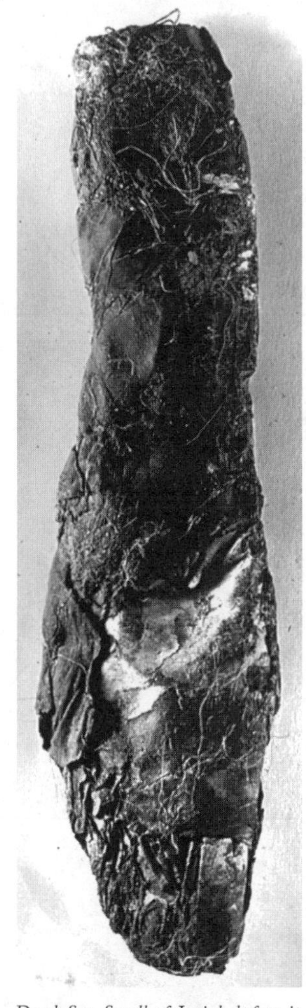

Dead Sea Scroll of Isaiah before it was unrolled.

Leah Hervet, one of the Biluim who founded Gedera, reminiscing with her granddaughter. Courtesy Zionist Archives and Library in New York.

called for the establishment of an agricultural colony built on cooperative social foundations. Their goal was the "politico-economic and national spiritual revival of the Jewish people in the Land of Israel."

The first Bilu group which came to Palestine in 1882 had 20 members. They endured hardships in a land that had been desolate for generations. They began their work at the agricultural school of **Mikveh Israel**. The director of the school tried to dissuade them from dedicating their life to a "hopeless cause." Most of the pioneers, however, preferred their spade and hoe to a professional career, and they founded one of the first colonies, **Rishon Le-Zion**, and later Gederah. The Bilu members endured hunger, poverty, and Arab hostility, serving as an inspiring example for the future builders of Israel.

BIMAH. Literally, elevated platform or stage; the *bimah* is situated in the front of the synagogue or temple (in the **Sephardic** synagogue, it is in the center) sanctuary, where the service is conducted and the Torah is read.

BIRKAT HAMAZON. *See* **Prayer.**

BIROBIDJAN. Far-Eastern province of the former Soviet Union, north of Manchukuo, bordering the Amur River. The region was set aside by the Soviet government for Jewish colonization on March 28, 1928. On May 7, 1934, Birobidjan was officially declared an autonomous Jewish region. Yiddish was to be the official language of the area in all educational, cultural, and legal institutions. Jewish communists and communist sympathizers around the world hailed the project as a great Soviet contribution to the solution of the Jewish problem. However, the experiment proved unsuccessful. In contrast to **Israel**, this desolate region held no national appeal to the masses of Jews. Information about Jewish life in Birobidjan is currently difficult to obtain. However, it is estimated that of the 40,000 original settlers, fewer than 7,000 Jews remain, a small minority of the total population. Since the end of World War II, the Soviet government has made no effort to reestablish a Jewish autonomous region in Birobidjan. The Yiddish schools have been liquidated and only one synagogue remains, without a rabbi.

BIUR HAMETZ. *See* **Passover.**

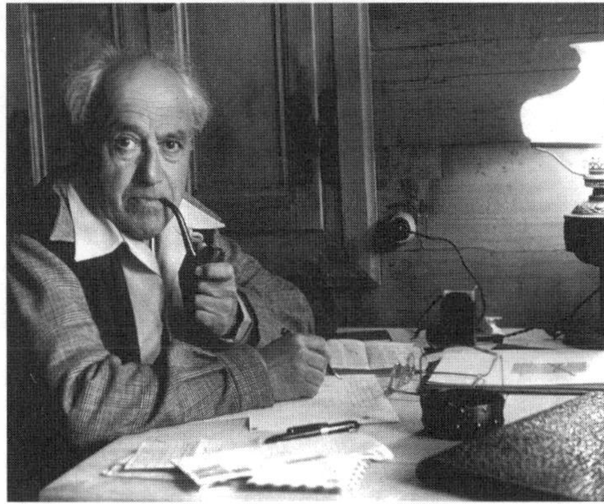

Ernest Bloch. Courtesy G. Schirmer, Music Publishers.

BLOCH, ERNEST (1880-1959). Composer. Son of a Geneva clockmaker, Ernest Bloch studied in his native **Switzerland** and in Germany. *Macbeth*, an opera performed in **Paris** in 1910, gained him immediate critical acclaim. In 1916, he came to the U.S. where he spent the rest of his life. A large part of Bloch's work, distinguished by passionate intensity of feeling and free play of melody, has been devoted to compositions on Jewish themes. These included *Israel*, a symphony; the *Baal Shem Suite*; *Schelomo*; and *Avodat Hakodesh* (Sacred Service), an oratorio based on the Sabbath synagogue service. Even his works with non-Jewish themes—such as *America, Helvetia,* and *Evocations*—have been said to be essentially Jewish in spirit.

BLOCK, HERBERT (1909-). Known as "Herblock." Leading American political cartoonist, whose cartoons have been appearing in the *Washington Post* since the end of World War II.

BLOOD ACCUSATION. The false charge that Jews use Gentile blood in connection with holiday rituals, particularly on **Passover**. This falsehood has been hurled at Jews in various places since the 12th century. Though popes, Christian scholars, and judges have denounced the suggestion of such an act, about 200 cases of this accusation exist on record. Often, Jews were tortured to make them "confess their guilt." As late as the 19th century, 39 such cases occurred in Europe and in the Near East. One of the most notorious cases of blood libel was the **Beilis** case in 1911. In 1928, this accusation turned up in the U.S., when a Christian child disappeared in Massena, N.Y. Some officials asked the rabbi whether ritual slaying was part of the **Yom Kippur** observance. This case so shocked the nation that the organization later to be known as the National Conference of Christians and Jews issued a statement declaring, "There is no custom...among Jews anywhere...which calls for the use of human blood." The Nazis tried to give the charge additional circulation, but in recent times it has died out. What makes the accusation especially absurd is the fact that the **Bible** (Lev. 17:10, Deut. 12:16, 1 Sam. 14:32-34) expressly forbids the consumption of blood, and the **dietary laws** are replete with rules about the scrupulous removal of blood from meat.

BLOOM, CLAIRE. *See* **Stage and Screen.**

BLUM, LEON (1872-1950). French statesman, three-time premier of **France**, socialist leader, and writer. Blum's father was a

Leon Blum.

wealthy Alsatian merchant whose four sons grew up with a good Jewish background. Young Leon studied law, and by the age of 22 was a distinguished poet and writer. The **Dreyfus** case stirred Blum deeply, and he became active in the defense of the Jewish officer accused of treason by the French Army. In the course of this work in 1896, he met Jean Jaures, famous leader of the French Socialists. Under his influence, Blum joined the Socialist movement, and by the end of World War I he had become the outstanding leader of the Socialist party. From 1919 onward, Blum served in the Chamber of Deputies almost continuously. From 1936 to June 1937 and again in 1938, he was premier of **France**.

Under the threat of the growing Nazi power in **Germany**, the French Socialist Party joined the Communists in a Popular Front coalition during the late 1930's. Blum successfully opposed all efforts at a merger with the Communists. During World War II, when Nazi Germany ruled France through the puppet Vichy government, Blum was imprisoned and brought to trial for treason in Riom. With remarkable courage, Leon Blum faced his accusers as "a Socialist among Fascists, a Jew among anti-Semites," and turned accuser himself. He showed so effectively that the appeasers were the real traitors of France that the Vichy government stopped the trial. Blum was transferred from the French prison to a German concentration camp; at the approach of the Allied armies, he was sent to a camp in **Italy**. Then in his seventies, he managed to stay alive until the Allied victory brought his freedom in 1945. France immediately put him into public service again, and in the spring of 1946, he came to the U.S. on a mission for his country. In December of that year, he again became premier of France. Leon Blum always identified himself closely with Jewish causes and repeatedly aided **Zionism**. In 1929 in Zurich, he participated in forming the enlarged Jewish Agency for Palestine. The **halutzim** of Palestine were grateful to Leon Blum. On November 10, 1943, while he was behind the barbed wire of a concentration camp, a **kibbutz** in northern **Galilee** was named after him: Kfar Blum.

BLUVSTEIN, RACHEL. *See* **Rachel**.

B'NAI B'RITH. On October 13, 1843, twelve German Jews living in **New York City** met together to form what they called a *Bundes Brüder*, or "Brothers of the Covenant." Patterned after other lodges of the day, it had ritual, regalia, and benefits in the form of insurance and mutual aid. It later became known as the Independent Order of B'nai B'rith, and finally, after 1930, as B'nai B'rith.

B'nai B'rith's membership in the U.S. stands at 550,000 people, in addition to the members of Aleph Zadik Aleph (AZA) and B'nai B'rith Girls (BBG), its junior affiliates. It is organized into somewhat autonomous local lodges, women's chapters, and district grand lodges. The supreme lodge establishes general policies for the order.

Over the years, B'nai B'rith has supported, in whole or in part, the following institutions: Bellefaire, an orphan home in Cleveland; the Jewish Children's Home of New Orleans; the Touro Infirmary of New Orleans; the Jewish Orphan Home of Atlanta; the Home for the Aged in Yonkers, N.Y.; the National Jewish Hospital in Denver; the Leo N. Levi Memorial Hospital in Hot Springs, Ark.; the B'nai B'rith Orphanage in Erie, Pa.; and the B'nai B'rith Home for the Aged in Memphis.

B'nai B'rith has always been interested in advancing the rights of Jews, and working with government and other groups to combat anti-Jewish agitation at home and abroad. Today these activities, together with B'nai B'rith's concern for the democratic rights of all people, center in the **Anti-Defamation League**, formed in 1913.

Cultural and educational activities are emphasized by B'nai B'rith, both in local lodges and on a national scale, through speakers, bureaus, cultural programs, and publications. The *National Jewish Monthly*, published under various names since 1886, has had the largest circulation of any Jewish journal in the English language. B'nai B'rith sponsors an extensive adult education program, featuring the annual Wildacres Institutes for adults, held at various camps in the U.S.

There are affiliates in 37 countries, including Israel.

Hillel: The Foundation for Jewish Campus Life. Formerly B'nai B'rith Hillel Foundation. A network of cultural, religious, and social centers for Jewish college youth. The first Hillel Foundation was set up at the University of Illinois in 1924 to make Jewish life and culture vital and meaningful to college students. Taken up as a national project by B'nai B'rith in 1925, the Foundation now maintains 120 foundations and affiliates on more than 300 campuses in the U.S., Canada, Latin America, Europe (including Russia), Israel, and Australia. In addition, it has professorships of Judaic studies in American universities. Hillel campus programs include cultural, religious, fellowship, community service, personal guidance, and interfaith activities. To stimulate discussion and understanding of Jewish life and thought, the foundation published a series of Hillel Little Books. *What is the Jewish Heritage*, by Ludwig **Lewisohn**, was the first.

B'nai B'rith Youth Organization. The first B'nai B'rith youth groups were founded in Omaha, Nebraska, in 1924. Known as Aleph Zadik Aleph, they quickly took root throughout the Midwest, and by 1925 were incorporated as a national branch of the adult organization. In 1927, the B'nai B'rith Girls (ages range from 15 to 21) were formed as a sister organization to the AZA. About fifteen years later, to satisfy the needs of college students and young war veterans, the B'nai B'rith Young Adults was founded. All three groups, joined in the overall Youth Organization since 1949, conducted programs designed to familiarize young Jews with their heritage and to prepare them for active participation in Jewish and general community life. In addition to discussions and study groups dealing with specifically Jewish affairs, the organization concerns itself with problems of social welfare and citizenship, and conducts a broad program of leisure-time sports and social activities. There are over 30,000 members in 1,200 units in fifteen countries.

BOARD OF DEPUTIES OF BRITISH JEWS. Founded in 1760 when, following the accession of George III in 1760, the Sephardic and Ashkenazic communities agreed upon the creation of a joint body to represent English Jewry at court. The board is organized on a synagogal basis and functions through committees. In addition to the administrative committees, specific committees deal with Israel affairs, charities, education, *Shehitah* (ritual slaughter), and defense against **anti-Semitism**.

BOARD OF JEWISH EDUCATION OF GREATER NEW YORK. The world's largest central agency for Jewish education, BJE conducts extensive and varied services for Jewish school teachers, principals, parents, and students from the early childhood level through high school. These services include a network of Jewish Teachers' Centers; guidance of schools' production of multimedia materials; *World Over* magazine; scholarship aid to students; nutrition education; family education; and art and music programs for children.

At one of the early childhood programs offered by the Board of Jewish Education of Greater New York, future doctors are examining their teddy bear.

BOHR, NIELS (1885-1962). Born in **Denmark**, Bohr was one of the originators of the modern atomic theory. For his research in this field, he was awarded the **Nobel Prize** in 1922. Bohr's investigations of the fission of uranium paved the way for the modern atom bomb and atomic energy. From 1943 to 1945, he took an active part in the preparation of the atomic bomb in Los Alamos.

BOKHARA. Region in central Asia, now part of Uzbekistan. Bokhara is the home of an ancient and colorful Jewish community, which believes itself descended from the Ten **Lost Tribes** of Israel. Its ancestors are known to have come from Samarkand and other areas in Persia, where the Jews have lived since the destruction of the First **Temple**. The early records of Jewish life in this tiny country were destroyed during the invasion of the Huns in the 13th century. The Bokharan community is still Judeo-Persian in culture. It possesses a considerable literature in Tadjik, a Persian dialect which its members still speak. Until the conquest of Bokhara by Russia in the 19th century, the community was completely cut off from the rest of the Jewish world. In 1893, to escape persecution by the Tsar, a number of Bokharans settled in Jerusalem. The settlement has grown, but the bulk of Bokharan Jews—20,000—remain in the former Soviet union, where they earn their livelihood in the production and sale of textiles.

BOLIVIA. Republic in South America. In 1998, total general population was 7.4 million; Jewish population, 700. Jews were active in exploiting Bolivia's rich silver mines during the early period of Spanish colonization in the 1500's. All of them were **Marranos**, Jews who had been forced to convert to Catholicism and who practiced Judaism in secret. This community was stifled by the **Inquisition**, which was established in 1570. From that time until the rise of Hitler, few Jews lived in Bolivia. Between 1933 and 1939, however, Bolivia was the only country which did not restrict the immigration of Jews. As a result, 10,000 German refugees settled there.

BONDS FOR ISRAEL. State of Israel Bonds is an international securities organization offering interest-bearing instruments issued by the government of **Israel**. The Israel Bonds organization was established in 1951 through the efforts of Israeli Prime Minister David **Ben-Gurion**, who recognized the opportunity to secure long-term investment capital through the sale of securities. Since its inception, the organization has secured more than $16 billion in investment capital for the development of every aspect of Israel's economy, including agriculture, commerce, and industry, transforming an underdeveloped country into a highly advanced industrialized nation in fewer than four decades. Recently, Bonds proceeds have supported the absorption of vast numbers of Jews immigrating to Israel from the former Soviet Union, Eastern Europe, and elsewhere.

Israel's steadily developing economy, its well-educated, highly-trained population, and its expanding role in world markets have led Israel Bonds to become firmly established in the North American, European, and Latin American investment communities. Israel Bonds are purchased by a broad spectrum of investors including corporations, banks, foundations, institutions, and individuals.

BOOK OF LIFE. The idea of a divine book of life dates back to the Bible (Ex. 32:32). In the Talmud we are told that every year on **Rosh Ha-shanah** a set of books of life is opened in heaven, and the fate of each person is set for the coming year. This concept has been incorporated into the High Holy Day service.

BORGE, VICTOR. *See* **Stage and Screen**.

BOROCHOV, DOV BER (1881-1917). Labor Zionist leader, writer, and Yiddish philologist. He became active in the Zionist movement, joining the **Poale Zion** in 1905. Because of his activities, Borochov was arrested by the Russian police and made his escape from the country in 1907. He came to the U.S. in 1914, where he continued to be active in the Labor Zionist movement. He edited *Der Yiddisher Kempfer* and other publications and wrote books on Yiddish philology. His important theories on Socialism and **Zionism** were published in 1937 in *Nationalism and the Class Struggle*, a Marxist approach to the Jewish problem. Borochov returned to **Russia** after the Revolution in 1917, and died there shortly afterward. Ber Borochov was one of the founders of the World Confederation of Poale Zion in 1907, and **Labor Zionism** owes much to him. He formulated theories fusing Zionism and Socialism, and his ideas served greatly to win the sympathy of many labor and socialist circles for the Jewish upbuilding of Israel.

BOSTON. One of the oldest cities in the U.S., Boston first saw Jews arrive in the mid-17th century, but a Jewish community did not start until the mid-19th century. The first synagogues were organized by German Jews. Around 1900, large Jewish immigration from Eastern Europe signaled the beginning of what is today one of the best organized and most representative and influential Jewish communities in the U.S.. The metropolitan area's Jewish population is 228,000.

Boston may be the American leader in Jewish literacy, with 80% of its Jews having received some form of Jewish education. It has important Reform, Conservative, Orthodox, and even Hasidic communities. It has a long tradition of producing rabbis, leaders, scholars, jurists, artists, and writers who have enriched both Jewish and general culture: Rabbi Louis Epstein, a leading Conservative scholar; Rabbi Ronald Gittelson, a leading Reform rabbi; Rabbi Joseph **Soloveitchik**, one of America's greatest Talmudists; Louis **Brandeis**, a great American jurist; Leonard **Bernstein**, conductor and composer; Mike Wallace, a leading television journalist.

Boston has many Jewish communal institutions, including a Hebrew Teachers College. It is one of the main centers of Jewish learning in the U.S., with Judaica chairs in schools like Harvard and Boston University, and especially with its full-fledged institution of higher learning, **Brandeis University**, the first non-sectarian Jewish university in America. A Jewish weekly, *The Jewish Advocate*, has been published in Boston since 1903.

BOXER, BARBARA (1940-). Democratic U.S. Senator from **California**. In 1993, Boxer was elected for a six-year term to the Senate. Boxer was hailed by the **Anti-Defamation League** as champion of human rights.

BRANDEIS, LOUIS DEMBITZ (1856-1941). American jurist and Zionist leader. Born in Louisville, Ky., he received his early

Students in Feldberg Lounge at Brandeis University.

Louis Brandeis. Courtesy Brandeis University.

education at a private school in Louisville and an academy in **Germany**. He had little formal Jewish training in his childhood.

In 1877, Brandeis, at the age of 20, was graduated from the Harvard Law School with its highest honors. He began his private law practice in St. Louis, but soon settled in **Boston** where he lived and practiced law for about forty years. In law, Brandeis distinguished himself as "the people's attorney." He defended the citizens of Boston against the monopolies and unethical practices of public utility companies.

Brandeis's defense of the common man against the encroachments of "big business" continued throughout his career. His book *Other People's Money* had such an effect on President Wilson that in 1916 he appointed Brandeis to the U.S. Supreme Court where he served for 23 years. His judicial opinions exerted a profound influence on American constitutional law. Brandeis often joined Justice Oliver Wendell Holmes in minority dissenting opinions. These historic opinions changed American thought on social problems. Brandeis's belief in the need for legal change to meet the new conditions of industrial society, and for public regulations to protect the public interest, foreshadowed the social legislation of the New Deal in the 1930's.

In 1910, Brandeis's interest in Jewish life was awakened by his contact with the Jewish garment workers of **New York**, when he served as mediator in a strike. His active participation in **Zionism** dates to the period closely preceding the World War I. As chairman of the Provisional Committee for General Zionist affairs from 1914 to 1918, he strengthened the World Zionist movement which had been disrupted by the war. He was influential in obtaining American approval of the **Balfour Declaration**. A businesslike Zionist, Brandeis stressed the practical aspects of the rebuilding of the Land of Israel. He helped found the Palestine Economic Corporation, and played an important part in the encouragement of the investment of private capital in Palestine. As a result of a disagreement with Chaim **Weizmann** on the proper methods to be employed in developing Palestine economically, he resigned from his Zionist offices in 1921. Brandeis remained, nevertheless, a devoted Zionist all his life, and was often consulted on important policy matters.

BRANDEIS UNIVERSITY. Founded in 1948 and located in Waltham, Mass., Brandeis University is the first Jewish-sponsored nonsectarian institution of higher learning in the Western Hemisphere. Named after the late Supreme Court Justice Louis Dembitz **Brandeis**, it admits students without regard to race, color, or religious affiliation. Its first president was Abram Sachar, a Jewish scholar and former national director of the Hillel Foundation of **B'nai B'rith**. In 1995, total university enrollment reached 4,192. The religious requirements of Christians and Jewish students are respected in planning the school calendar and in the dining hall. In October 1955, Brandeis University dedicated a modern group of three chapels, for students of the Catholic, Jewish, and Protestant faiths. This is a departure from the usual college practice of having a single non-denominational chapel.

BRAZIL. Federal republic; largest country in South America. Brazil, which was discovered by **Portugal** in 1500, was the home of the first organized Jewish community in the New World. Large numbers of **Marranos**, forced converts who observed their Jewish faith in secret, arrived early in the 16th century. They prospered in commerce and industry, but at the price of denying their Judaism publicly. Only when the Dutch conquered Pernambuco in 1630 were the Marranos able to declare their faith. Their congregations were enlarged by Jews from Holland, the West Indies, and North Africa. So extensive was their trade that Pernambuco came to be known as "the port of the Jews." This happy interlude ended when the Portuguese recaptured Dutch Brazil in 1654, and expelled the Jews from the country. Most of the Brazilian Jews fled to Holland. Small groups found refuge in Surinam and Curacao in the Dutch West Indies. Twenty-three boarded a ship which bore them to New Amsterdam, where they became the nucleus of the famous Portuguese-Jewish community of **New York**.

So effective was the Portuguese persecution that for the next 175 years there was no indication of Jewish life in Brazil. After Brazil achieved its independence from Portugal in 1824, however, a small community of Marranos revealed its Judaism in Belem, far from the capital. Later in the century, two other small communities were founded in Brazil. Yet it is only at the turn of the 20th century that the "modern" community may be said to begin. At that time, the **Jewish Colonization Association** began to encourage European Jews to emigrate to Brazil and settle on farms. The farm colonies were not very successful. Most of their members settled in cities and founded communities there. These communities were enlarged by new immigrants, especially after the U.S. began to restrict its own immigration in 1924. Because of the opportunities it offered to newcomers, Brazil became the home of the second largest Jewish community in **Latin America**. Totaling 100,000 in 1998, it is second only to the Argentinian settlement of 210,000. Between 1957 and 1959, Brazil received some 3,000 immigrants from Egypt and 700 from Hungary.

The Brazilian Jewish community is a prosperous one. Most of its members are merchants or manufacturers; the remainder are largely skilled craftsmen. The large majority live in Rio de Janeiro and Sao Paulo, but there are Jews in every major city in the country. Since 1951, all sectors of the Jewish community have been represented in the **World Jewish Congress** by the Confederation of the Jewish Societies of Brazil.

The cultural activities within the community are varied. There are Yiddish newspapers and many Jewish periodicals in Portuguese. The larger communities have Jewish school systems and elaborate community organizations. Zionist feeling has run high, especially since the creation of the State of **Israel**. Educators from Israel play a large part in running the Jewish schools in Rio and Sao Paulo, although non-Zionists have their own schools. In addition, teachers from most of the Jewish schools are regularly sent to Israel for training. In 1954, an Israel-Brazilian Cultural Institute was inaugurated under the chairmanship of Brazil's foreign minister. It grants scholarships to Brazil's students who wish to study in Israel, and has set itself the task of popularizing Brazilian literature in Israel and Israel literature in Brazil. Another cultural institution of note is the Jewish-Brazilian Institute of Historical Research, which studies the history of the Jewish community in Brazil.

BRENNER, JOSEPH CHAIM (1881-1921). Zionist pioneer and Hebrew novelist who first attracted attention with his stories of the grim life in poverty-stricken small towns of **Russia**. His larger novels, *Ba-Horef*, *Mi-Saviv La-Nekudah*, are stories of the futile strivings of Jewish youth to improve their situation in Czarist Russia. In his later novels, he describes life in Palestine. Brenner lived for several years in **London** and edited there a Hebrew monthly, *Ha-Meorer* (The Awakener). He settled in Palestine in 1909, and there, deeply influenced by A.D. **Gordon**, followed Gordon's ideas in advocating a just society and a life close to nature. Brenner advocated friendly relations with the Arabs, and lived and mingled freely with them. Ironically, he was killed in an Arab riot on May 1, 1921. One of the largest agricultural settlements, Givat Brenner, bears his name.

Joseph Chaim Brenner.

BRIT (BRIS). *See* **Circumcision** *and* **Covenant**.

BRISCOE, ROBERT (1894-1969). First Jew ever to serve as lord mayor of Dublin, **Ireland** (1956-57, 1961-62). Briscoe was active in the Irish Republican Movement during Ireland's struggle for independence. He was also an ardent Zionist who supported **Revisionist Zionism.** His son, Benjamin Briscoe, was lord mayor of Dublin in 1989-90.

BRODETSKY, SELIG (1888-1954). Mathematician, Zionist leader. Brought to **England** from **Russia** at the age of five, Brodetsky was a professor of mathematics at the Universities of Bristol and Leeds. In 1921, he attended his first Zionist Congress; he was elected to the World Zionist Executive in 1928. Brodetsky was president of the **Board of Deputies of British Jews** and of the Zionist Federation of Great Britain from 1940 to 1949, and served as president of the **Hebrew University** in **Jerusalem** from 1949 until 1951.

BRONFMAN, EDGAR (1929-). President of the **World Jewish Congress** since 1981, Bronfman is the son of Samuel Bronfman (1891-1971), one of **Canada**'s leading Jewish industrialists and communal leaders. Edgar Bronfman developed the

Seagram Company founded by his father, and became an international Jewish leader as president of the Congress. Under his leadership, the Congress exerted influence on Jewish affairs around the world, mostly notably the exposing of **Austria**'s president, Kurt Waldheim, as an ex-Nazi, and the discovery of bank accounts in **Switzerland** with funds belonging to Jewish victims of the Nazis.

BROOKNER, ANITA (1938-). Novelist and art historian. Brookner teaches art at Cambridge, **England**, and is considered a leading novelist, with books such as *Hotel du Lac.*

BRODY, TAL. *See* **Sports**.

BROOKS, MEL. *See* **Stage and Screen**.

BUBER, MARTIN (1878-1965). Jewish philosopher and scholar, who exerted great influence on Jewish and Zionist thought in Western Europe. He was born in Vienna. Most of his works are in German, some in Hebrew. From 1916 to 1924 he was the editor of *Der Jude*, a leading publication of Jewish thought, philosophy, and religion, published in Berlin. Buber's religious philosophy has its roots in an ethical and social approach to man's place in the world. Together with Franz **Rosenzweig**, he translated the **Bible** into German. Buber delved into Jewish mysticism and published collections of Hasidic tales, in which he brought to light the beauty and thought of **Hasidism**. After the rise of Nazism, Buber settled in Palestine. In 1938, he became a professor of social philosophy in the **Hebrew University** of **Jerusalem**. He was the recipient of many honors from postwar Germany, including the Honor Prize of the City of Munich in 1960. Other honors included the Albert Schweitzer Medal.

Martin Buber.

BUCHENWALD. Town in **Germany**. In 1937, the Nazis established a concentration camp there to provide slave labor for factories in central Germany. In November 1938, 10,000 German Jews arrived in Buchenwald; by 1944, the figure rose to nearly 100,000. Among the prominent political prisoners was the former French premier Leon **Blum**, who was liberated by American troops on April 11, 1945. Many inmates died of hunger, disease, and maltreatment. (*See also* **Holocaust**.)

BULGARIA. Jews lived in Bulgaria during the 2nd century C.E. By the end of the 12th century the Jews controlled Bulgarian trade with Venice. In 1335, King Ivan Alexander married the Jewess Sarah, who on her baptism took the name Theodora. Her son Ivan Sisman III came to the throne in 1346, and continued his mother's amiable attitude to the Jewish population. Bulgaria was conquered by **Turkey** in 1389, and soon became a haven for Jewish refugees from the **Spanish Inquisition**. Since then, the majority of Bulgarian Jews have been **Sephardim**. During World War II, the Nazis exterminated the majority of the Jews of Bulgaria. Of the few Jews who survived at the end of the war, the majority emigrated to Israel in the mass exodus of 1949. In 1998, there were about 3,200 Jews in Bulgaria.

BUND. Jewish Socialist Party, founded in **Russia** in 1897. A militant group, the Bund worked for the overthrow of the Russian Tsarist government, organizing demonstrations and strikes. Some Bundists escaped to the U.S. and became active in the Jewish social movement in America. After the Russian Revolution in 1917, a part of the Bund joined the Jewish section of the Communist party. It established schools, conducted cultural work in the **Yiddish language**, and organized youth groups and workers' cooperatives. Initially, the Bund bitterly opposed **Zionism** and considered it a "bourgeois utopia." It was equally antagonistic to Hebrew as the Jewish national tongue. Remnants of the Bund are still active in America, **Israel**, and some European countries.

BURIAL AND MOURNING. Burial customs date back to the stories of **Abraham** and **Sarah** in the **Bible.** In Jewish tradition, proper burial in the ground is one of the main life-cycle commandments. A corpse is to be treated with utmost respect, regardless who the person is, since, according to traditional belief, the soul is about to enter eternal rest, and the bones begin to wait for the eventual resurrection in the **messianic** age. Trained Jews (*see* **Hevra Kadisha**) purify the body and dress it in a simple white linen garment. A pious Jew stands by and recites **Psalms.** In **Israel,** no coffin is used, except for soldiers fallen in battle. In the Diaspora, a plain pine coffin is preferred, so as not to distinguish between rich and poor. Families often purchase a burial section in a Jewish cemetery for their members. A funeral service consists of prayers, a eulogy, and a Mourner's **Kaddish** recited at the grave side.

Mourning customs. Prior to the burial, the mourner tears an article of clothing (typically a shirt), as a sign of mourning. After the burial, the family gathers at the home of the closest of kin to start the seven-day mourning period known as "sitting *shiveh*." The mourners sit on low stools, take off their shoes, and cover the mirrors in the house. Friends and neighbors bring food and conduct services at the house of mourning. Men do not shave during the mourning period; women do not use makeup. All abstain from work. The mourning for relatives continues with less restriction for 30 days, and for parents for 12 months. Mourners continue to recite the Mourner's Kaddish at the **synagogue** during the rest of their mourning period.

A tombstone is prepared for the departed, and a special ceremony called "unveiling" (*gilui matzevah*) is held at the end of the mourning period in the cemetery to dedicate the stone.

Each year the anniversary of the death of a relative is observed by lighting a special *yahrzeit* (anniversary) candle and reciting the Kaddish. Memorial services for the dead are also held during the High Holy Days and the Festivals.

BURLA, YEHUDA. *See* **Hebrew Literature**.

CAESAREA. Town on Israel's coast, south of **Haifa**, dating back to the 4th century B.C.E. It was named Caesarea by King **Herod**, in honor of Augustus Caesar. Herod built a major port and town, the remains of which are still there. Jewish, Christian, and Muslim communities flourished and declined in Caesarea over the ages. Today, the town has some of Israel's most interesting archeological discoveries, and is growing into a major seaside resort.

Caesarea.

CAIN. *See* **Abel**.

CAHAN, ABRAHAM (1860-1952). Socialist leader and founder and editor of the influential Yiddish newspaper in **New York**, *The Forward*. He was educated for the rabbinate in his native **Russia**, but soon turned toward radical and socialist views. Upon his arrival in America in 1882, he found a fertile field for his ideas among immigrant Jewry. Cahan worked actively as labor organizer, lecturer, and editor of various Yiddish periodicals. In 1902, he became the editor of *The Forward*, a post he held until his death. A talented writer, he published successful short stories and novels in English, notably *The Rise of David Levinsky*. In this work Cahan described his generation's problems in a way that has been recognized as a classic of immigrant literature in the U.S.

Abraham Cahan. Courtesy Jewish Daily Forward.

CALENDAR. Unlike the general, solar-based calendar, the Jewish calendar is lunar, consisting of twelve 29- and 30-day-long months, based on the new moon. Thus, the year has 354, rather than 365 days. To make up for this difference, the Jewish leap year has an additional month after **Adar**, called Second Adar, which occurs every third, 6th, 8th, 11th, 14th, 17th, and 19th year. In ancient times, before astronomical calculations became mathematically exact, the people of Judea watched the skies for the appearance of the new moon. As soon as the new moon was spotted by witnesses, bonfires were lit on the hilltops to spread the news. Burning torches signaled from mountain to mountain, beginning with **Jerusalem**'s Mount of Olives and on as far as the Babylonian frontier. In the Holy Land the **Sanhedrin**, the highest legislative and judicial council, set the dates of the holidays and the festivals, and fast messengers relayed the information as far as **Babylonia**. By the middle of the 4th century, persecution had made conditions in Palestine difficult and uncertain. The head of the scattered Sanhedrin, Hillel II, introduced then a final and fixed calendar. He published the mathematical and astronomical information for it and made it possible for all Jewish communities in the Dispersion to use this knowledge. This uniformity removed uncertainty from the date of the Rosh Hodesh, the New Moon, and the first day of the year from which the dates of all holidays are set.

HEBREW MONTHS

Month	Occurs during
Tishre	*September - October*
Heshvan	*October - November*
Kislev	*November - December*
Tevet	*December - January*
Shvat	*January - February*
Adar	*February - March*
Nisan	*March - April*
Iyar	*April - May*
Sivan	*May - June*
Tammuz	*June - July*
Av	*July - August*
Elul	*August - September*

CALDER, ALEXANDER. *See* **Art**.

CALIFORNIA. Around the time of the Gold Rush in 1849, Jews discovered California. The first community was established in San Francisco, where the first West Coast Jewish paper, *The Gleaner*, was started in 1855. Soon communities were established in San Diego, Sacramento, San Jose, and **Los Angeles**. Today, there are close to one million Jews living in California, with 490,000 in Los Angeles, 210,000 in the San Francisco area (including San Jose), 75,000 in Orange County, and 70,000 in San Diego. Among the Jewish institutions of higher learning are the University of Judaism (Conservative) and the West Coast branch of the **Hebrew Union College** (Reform), both in Los Angeles.

Sacramento
San Francisco
Santa Barbara
Los Angeles
San Diego

Jews have played a prominent role in the motion picture industry in Los

Beth Tzedec Congregation, Toronto, Canada.

Angeles, accounting for many of the producers who established the big studios, such as MGM, as well as for many of the actors (*see* **Stage and Screen**).

California is second only to New York as a center of Jewish life in the U.S., with many Reform and Conservative congregations, as well as Jewish cultural institutions, such as the Judah Magnes Art Museum in Berkeley and the Simon Wiesenthal Center in Los Angeles. In the U.S. Senate, California has been represented by two Jewish women, Barbara **Boxer** and Diane **Feinstein**.

CALLIGRAPHY. *See* **Ketubah, Scribe.**

CAMPS. Jewish youth camps in the United States are a major source of social and sports activities, as well as Jewish living and learning. Every summer, many thousands of Jewish youth under the age of 18 participate in camp programs throughout the country. These programs are run by local Jewish federations and national Jewish organizations.

Camp Massad, Pennsylvania.

Founded in 1919, Camp Cejwin in Port Jervis, N.Y., was the pioneer of Jewish educational camps.

Ramah camps, run by the Conservative movement, are located in **Wisconsin**, **Pennsylvania**, **Connecticut**, **California**, **New York**, Ontario (Canada), and **Israel**. Ramah also conducts an annual teen study program in Israel and a training institute for future counselors. Organized by the **Jewish Theological Seminary of America** in 1947, Ramah offers a Jewish educational program conducted in Hebrew, with formal instruction in classical Hebrew texts.

The Reform movement has camps in **Massachusetts**, New York, Pennsylvania, **Georgia**, California, Wisconsin, **Illinois**, **Indiana**, **Mississippi**, and **Texas**. The program emphasizes innovative approaches to Jewish learning and worship, social justice, Israel, and Jewish culture.

B'nai B'rith Youth Organization (BBYO) has camps in Pennsylvania and Wisconsin, which focus on leadership training and general Jewish experience. All of these organizations have summer youth programs in Israel.

The Federation of Jewish Philanthropies runs 16 camp sites in New York, **New Jersey**, and Pennsylvania. Some 6,500 youngsters attend Federation camps. The best-known is Surprise Lake Camp in New York.

In recent years Orthodox groups—religious Zionist organizations, the Agudath Israel World Organization, yeshivot (Lubavitch Movement, Torah Vada'ath, and Yeshiva University), and Beth Jacob Schools—have set up camps of their own, where a full program of religious training is offered alongside regular camping activities. The largest of these camps, established in 1964, is Morasha in Pennsylvania.

CANAAN. Son of Ham and grandson of **Noah**, ancestor of seven Canaanite tribes, sometimes identified with the Phoenicians. In the biblical account, Canaan, the coastal plain west of the Jordan, is the land God promised to **Abraham**, "Unto thy seed will I give this land" (Gen. 12:17).

CANADA. Larger in area than the U.S., the British Dominion of Canada has only one-tenth of the U.S. population. In 1998, the

Canadian population numbered more than 29 million. Of these, about 360,000 are Jews, with 100,000 in Montreal and 175,000 in Toronto.

Until 1760, Canada formed a part of a vast French colony in which few Jews had been allowed to settle. In 1763, however, the British defeated the French and established British rule over the country. Several Jews had served as officers in the British army. One of them, Aaron Hart, settled in Trois Rivieres, a small town in the province of Quebec. Later, his son, Ezekiel Hart, was elected to the legislature of Lower Canada. His political opponents objected to his position in the legislature because, as a Jew, he refused to take the prescribed oath, "on my faith as a Christian." For a while, the law was on their side, but in 1829, it was amended to extend equal political rights to Jews. In 1832, the Jews were granted full political equality—25 years earlier than in England.

Growth of the Jewish community in Canada was slow until the middle of the 19th century; until then it had consisted almost entirely of **Sephardic** Jews who arrived from England, Holland, and various countries in the Americas. These early Sephardic settlers played a leading role in developing the new country, pioneering in such enterprises as transatlantic shipping, transatlantic cables, fishing, streetrailways, and mining. By 1768, there were enough Sephardic Jews to enable them to found a congregation. They named it *Shearith Israel*, or Remnant of Israel, also the name of the oldest Jewish congregation in the U.S.

In the middle of the 19th century, a large number of German Jews came to Canada. Being Ashkenazic Jews, they did not feel at home in the Sephardic synagogue. In 1858, when their numbers were sufficient, German and Polish newcomers in Montreal founded the first Ashkenazic congregation in Canada.

During the great Jewish emigration from eastern Europe that began in the 1880's in the wake of persecution and **anti-Semitism**, many arrived in Canada. Since pioneers were needed to develop Canada's vast unsettled areas, the government offered the newcomers such inducements as free land, equipment, and financial help. Moreover, many of the immigrants were under the influence of the "back to the soil" movement among the Jews of Europe. The arriving immigrants were therefore encouraged to choose agriculture as their new way of life. The first Canadian Jewish farm settlement was founded in 1882. Baron Maurice de **Hirsch** of Paris and the **Jewish Colonization Association** (ICA) which he founded helped to settle Jews on Canadian soil. Other immigrant Jews became artisans, instrumental in developing industry in Canada. The modern clothing industry built up by American Jews, for instance, was gradually introduced into neighboring Canada as well. Montreal and later Toronto became Canada's garment centers.

Right, Samuel Bronfman House, National Headquarters of the Canadian Jewish Congress in Montreal. Above, Canadian postage stamp commemorating the victims of the Shoah.

The Montreal Jewish community is the oldest and largest in Canada. While the majority of Montreal's inhabitants speak French, Jews belong to its English-speaking minority. The majority of Jewish children attend the "Protestant," that is, English-speaking schools, and the Jewish taxpayers pay their school taxes into the "Protestant" panel. An attempt in 1923 and 1924 to create a separate Jewish tax-supported school system failed because the higher courts found it to be unconstitutional. Education in Canada, as in the U.S., is under the authority of each province and not of the federal government. The law provides that those who do not wish either of the two prevailing types of education, the Catholic or the Protestant, may conduct schools of their own choice. Many Jewish parents prefer to send their children to all-day private schools. In Montreal, 60% of Jewish boys and 40% of Jewish girls attended some type of Jewish school. The largest number of children, almost 50%, attend Jewish all-day schools.

CANETTI, ELIAS (1905-1994). Bulgarian-born Sephardic Jewish writer who lived in Vienna and wrote plays and novels in German. He was awarded the Nobel Prize for Literature in 1981.

CANTONISTS. Jewish children in **Russia** drafted for military service. In 1827, Czar Nicholas I extended military service to include Jews. The Russian conscripts served in the army for 25 years, beginning at age 18. Jewish children, however, were taken at the age of 12 and placed in "canton," or district, schools of six years of preliminary training. They were sent as far away from any Jewish settlement as possible, and every effort was made to convert them to Christianity. Many cantonists did not survive the cruel treatment in these schools; many saved themselves by conversion. For this reason, Jews did everything in their power to keep their children from being taken into the Russian army. The government simply compelled the heads of each Jewish community to produce the community's quota of children. The rich often tried to buy substitutes for their children, while informers and professional kidnappers added to the terror within the Jewish communities. This state of affairs lasted for 30 years until Alexander II abolished the system in 1857.

CANTILLATION. *See* **Hazan.**

CANTOR. *See* **Hazan.**

CANTOR, EDDIE. *See* **Stage and Screen.**

CANTOR, GEORGE (1845-1918). German mathematician. Born to a converted family of Jewish extraction, he founded the theory of sets, which revolutionized modern mathematics.

CARDOZO, BENJAMIN NATHAN (1870-1938). U.S. Supreme Court justice. Born in **New York City** into a family of **Sephardic** Jews, Cardozo was graduated with high honors from Columbia College, and in 1891, received his degree in law from the Columbia University Law School. He practiced law in New York, and was elected justice of the Supreme Court of the State of New York in 1913. President Herbert Hoover appointed Cardozo to succeed Oliver Wendell Holmes as Associate Justice of the U.S. Supreme Court in 1932.

Cardozo was a trustee of Columbia University; a member of the Board of Governors of the American Friends of the **Hebrew University**; and a member of the executive committees of the National Jewish Welfare Board and of the **American Jewish Committee**. He also distinguished himself in legal literature. His books include *The Nature of the Judicial Process*, *Paradoxes of the Legal Sciences*, and *Law and Literature*. In his writings, he always endeavored to reconcile the law with the spirit and needs of the times.

Benjamin N. Cardozo. Courtesy Fallon Publications.

CARLEBACH, SHLOMO (1925-1995). Rabbi, teacher, neo-Hasidic composer. He became known in the 60's to American and world Jewry as a revitalizer of Jewish faith, peoplehood, and music. His widely popular neo-Hasidic melodies, his participation in causes like the struggle for Soviet Jewry, his work with Jewish students on campus in the U.S. and Israel, and his unique style of storytelling contributed to this rebirth. Jews across the spectrum of the Jewish world have been influenced by his work, and some of his melodies remain popular to this day.

CARO, JOSEPH (1488-1575). Born in **Spain**, Caro settled in Palestine, where he wrote the **Shulhan Arukh**—literally, the set table—which presented Jewish law in a popular vein, and eventually became the standard source for Jewish observance.

CENTRAL CONFERENCE OF AMERICAN RABBIS. Oldest of American rabbinic associations (about 1,100 members), founded for Reform rabbis by Isaac Mayer **Wise** in 1889. A leading spokesman for Reform Judaism, the CCAR publishes prayer books, hymnals, a home prayerbook, proceedings of its annual conventions, reports of its commissions, and other volumes. Since 1954, the conference has had a permanent office in **New York City**. Membership includes Reform rabbis around the world.

CHAGALL, MARC (1899-1985). Artist; born in a small town near Vitebsk, White **Russia**. As a young man Chagall settled in **France**. He is the most eminent member of the *École Juive*, or Jewish School, of Paris which through modern pictorial means transferred recollections of the Jewish past to canvas. Judaism, as he experienced it in his hometown, was always a strong source of inspiration to Chagall. He drew and painted Jewish figures with a bold imagination and little concern for realistic detail. Some of his pictures are like strange dreams in which all objects appear topsy-turvy, without concern for logic or perspective. In one of the early surrealistic painters, Chagall used floating figures in his painting as his personal symbol for the liberation of the spirit through love or art. Among his best known paintings are the vibrantly colored *I and My Village, Over Vitebsk, The Betrothed, Rabbi of Vitebsk, Rabbi with Torah,* and *The Green Violinist*.

Chagall has also painted murals, ballet and theater settings, and costumes. A group of stained-glass windows symbolizing the tribes of Israel was commissioned by **Hadassah** and installed in the synagogue of the **Hebrew University** Medical Center on the outskirts of Jerusalem. In 1966, he executed a mosaic wall for the lobby of the new Knesset building and two murals for the new Metropolitan Opera building in New York.

CHAIN, ERNEST BORIS (1906-1979). Biochemist, discoverer of the curative properties of penicillin and its adapter for use on the human body. Chain was born in Berlin to Russian-Jewish parents, and came to England in 1933. He worked at Cambridge and Oxford universities and was subsequently Director of the Instituto Superiore di Sanita in Rome. He returned to England to become a professor of biochemistry at the Imperial College of Science and Technology in London.

CHARITY. In Hebrew, *tsedakah*, meaning righteousness or justice, since helping the needy is considered a duty. In biblical times, when the Jews were agriculturists, they gave charity by letting the poor glean, that is, gather the grain dropped in harvesting (see Ruth 2: 2-16). According to biblical law the corners of the field were to be left unreaped for the poor, who also had the right to all sheaves found uncollected. A tithe, or tenth, of all farm produce was offered to charity; untithed food could not be eaten. Biblical law required that the tithe be distributed to the needy, particularly "to the stranger, the fatherless, and the widow."

The Green Violinist, by Marc Chagall, Guggeheim Museum, New York.

By Talmudic times each community had a *kuppah*, or charity fund. The community had absolute power to levy taxes for this purpose. From the *kuppah* the community's poor were given money for fourteen meals per week. Distinguished members of the community were collectors for the *kuppah*, and a board of three men was responsible for allocating the funds. Some rabbis divided charity into seven categories: feeding the hungry; clothing the naked; visiting the sick; burying the dead and comforting mourners; ransoming captives; educating orphans and housing the homeless; and providing dowries for poor brides.

The lending of money without interest, helping the non-Jewish poor in the community, and giving preference to women and students were all part of the system of Jewish charity. **Maimonides** listed eight degrees of charity: the lowest was to give grudgingly; the highest to help a person to become self-supporting.

Charity was also an important act leading to the pardoning of personal transgressions or sins. The **Yom Kippur** service states that "repentance and prayer and charity avert the harshness of God's decree." The Jew believes that to ask God to have pity upon one's own misfortune, one must have pity for others' misfortune. Charity is therefore distributed on the eve of Yom Kippur in atonement for one's sins. Because charity is considered effective in redeeming the souls of the dead as well as of the living, alms are also generously distributed at funerals.

Gifts to the poor are not merely associated with mournful occasions and fear of punishment. Rather, they are a basic principle of Judaism and are offered on joyous occasions as well. Thus, the merry **Purim** festivities include the custom of *mishloah manot*, or the delivery of gifts to the poor, and it is customary to raise *maot hittim*, or wheat money, before **Passover**. This money is used to provide matzo, wine, and the other ritual needs of the holiday for those who cannot afford them. Similarly, the Passover Seder ceremony includes an invitation to "all the poor to come and eat." In Eastern Europe it was common for the poor to be invited to all ritual celebrations.

In the U.S. today and throughout the Jewish world, charity continues to be one of the main aspects of organized Jewish life.

CHICAGO. With more than 250,000 Jews, Chicago has the third largest Jewish population in the U.S. Organized Jewish life dates to the 1830's when the first Jews arrived from central Europe. Reform temples were founded in the 1840's and 1850's, and today Chicago has more than 100 congregations of all three major movements.

Chicago's institutions of higher learning include the Hebrew Theological College, the Jewish People's Institute, and the College of Jewish Studies.

One of the most ethnic cities in the U.S., Chicago has absorbed Jewish immigration from many countries. The Skokie suburb is known for its active community of **Holocaust** survivors.

Chicago's Jewry has supported many civic and Jewish causes and produced many outstanding personalities who have enriched Jewish and general culture. One example is Julius **Rosenwald**, who developed the Sears company and contributed millions to general and Jewish causes. Another is Saul **Bellow**, considered America's most distinguished writer of the post-World War II era.

CHILE. Republic on the west coast of South America. In 1998, the total population was 14.4 million; the Jewish population was 21,000. Like other Spanish colonies in South America, Chile had a flourishing **Marrano** community in the 16th and 17th centuries. But while the **Inquisition** succeeded in suppressing such communities elsewhere, Chile is still home to a group of colonial Jews. The Sabatarios, descendants of Marranos who fled to the interior to escape the Inquisition, survive in the mountain province of Cautin. Nothing was known of them until 1919, when a letter requesting admission to the South American Zionist Organization revealed their presence in the country. An investigation disclosed that, despite intermarriage with Spaniards and Indians and a total lack of contact with other Jewish communities, they had preserved a number of Jewish customs and beliefs.

Aside from the Sabatarios, however, the entire colonial community was lost. Jewish life in Chile was renewed only after 1810 when the country gained independence and offered guarantees of religious freedom. The first communities were small. At the time of World War I, there were about 3,000 Jews in Chile, mostly Sephardic Jews from Macedonia and the Balkans. The waves of immigration from Eastern and Central Europe in the following decades, increased the number of Jews to 30,000, and made Chile's Jewish community the fourth largest in Latin America. It is also most highly organized. The Central Committee of the Jewish Community of Chile coordinates the activities of all local organizations, represents Chile's Jews in the **World Jewish Congress**, and is recognized by the government as the spokesman for the community.

Jews in Chile are mainly engaged in trade, crafts, and small industry. They are more active in national politics than Jews in other South American republics. The degree of their cultural integration is shown by the fact that *Nosotros*, the leading Jewish periodical of the country, is published in Spanish, rather than Yiddish or Hebrew. Yet the Chilean Jews have shown concern for Israel, and the Zionist Federation, a central organization of all Zionist parties, is active in the Central Committee of the community.

CHINA, PEOPLE'S REPUBLIC OF. Chinese Jewry consisted of two communities. The older group believed that its forbears reached China after the destruction of the First **Temple** (586 B.C.E.). Early Chinese documents indeed mention Jewish traders several centuries before the Common Era. Much later, in the 14th century, Marco Polo wrote of influential Jews at the court of Kublai Khan. After 1650, this community, which had preserved its religious traditions for more than 2,000 years, declined rapidly. By the middle of the 19th century its last synagogues—beautiful pagoda-like structure at Kai-fung-foo—had disappeared. Today, only a handful of "native" Jews remain. Owing to intermarriage and possibly to conversions in the past, they are indistinguishable in appearance from their Chinese neighbors. The Western community in China was founded in the 1840's, when China was opened to western trade. Its ranks were swelled by refugees from Europe during the Nazi Era. Several European yeshivot, or Talmudical academies, had relocated in China during World War II. After 1948, most of the refugee community settled in Israel. In 1992, Israel and China established diplomatic, trade, and cultural relations.

CHMIELNICKI. *See* **Ukraine**.

CHOMSKY, NOAM (1928-). Leading authority on linguistics, the study of languages. The son of Jewish educator William Chomsky, he has been a professor of linguistics at the

Massachusetts Institute of Technology (MIT) since 1957 and has espoused many radical causes, especially in the 1960's and 1970's.

CHOSEN PEOPLE. According to the **Bible**, God entered into a **convenant** with **Abraham** and his descendants, to be God's servants and witnesses in the world. This concept has been distorted through the ages to mean that Jews regard themselves as God's chosen, thus superior to other people. In actual fact, this "chosenness" puts a heavy burden on the Jewish people, rather than endowing them with special privileges. The Hebrew prophets make it clear that being chosen does not mean being better than others, but rather having a special mission which requires a high moral code and an unshaken faith.

CHRISTIANITY. The most dominant religion of the Western world. Christianity originated in the Land of Israel with a Jew from the **Galilee** named **Jesus**, all of whose disciples were Jews, and was spread throughout the ancient world by another Jew named Saul, whose name was later changed to **Paul**. Today's Catholic Church is more aware than ever of the common heritage of Jews and Christians, and recent Popes have referred to Jews as our "elder brothers."

This, however, was not always the case with the relationship between the two religions. When Christianity first began to spread in the Roman Empire, the rabbis of the time regarded this new offshoot of Judaism as a heresy, and opposed it. As Jews lost their national independence and were scattered in the new Christian world, the Church doctrine developed strong anti-Jewish views, including the view that the Jews, rather than the Romans, were responsible for the death of Jesus, and therefore were cursed by God to roam the earth and find no rest or fulfilment. During the Middle Ages the Church was instrumental in introducing many restrictions against the Jews, and, in effect, forced them to become second-class residents of the host countries in Europe. Perhaps the most radical example of persecution against Jews by the Church was the Spanish Inquisition in the 15th and 16th centuries, which specialized in torture, often against innocents. It was not until the 19th century that Jews started to obtain citizenship rights, and even then the Church did not accept Jews as the equals of their Christian compatriots.

The church, however, never condemned the Jewish people to die, as did the Nazi regime in Germany in the 1930's and 40's. Some argue that centuries of anti-Semitic preaching by the Church culminated in the **Holocaust**, but this may be only partially true. Today, a new era in Christian-Jewish relations has begun, due to the birth of Israel and the Church's awareness of the Holocaust. The Vatican has officially condemned anti-Semitism and recognized the State of Israel, and many Christian groups, both Catholic and Protestant, support the Jewish state.

CHRONICLES. The first and second Books of Chronicles form the last book of the **Bible**. Chronicles retells the history of the Jewish people from Creation to the close of the Babylonian exile. It omits the history of the northern Kingdom of Israel to concentrate on the history of the Kingdom of Judah and stress priestly duties and **Temple** ritual.

CIRCUMCISION. Performed upon the Jewish male child on the eighth day of life. In Genesis 17:10-14, God commands **Abraham** to circumcise the foreskin of all males of the house as the sign of the covenant between God and the children of Abraham. It has become a basic law among Jews. In times of persecution, Jews risked their lives to fulfill the commandment. Traditionally, the ceremony is performed by a trained *mohel*, or circumciser, the child being held by an honored guest, the *sandek*, or godfather, who occupies a seat designated as Elijah's chair in honor of the prophet **Elijah**. This custom stems from the belief that the prophet is witness to the ritual. The circumcision ceremony is an occasion for rejoicing and feasting, accompanied by special blessings and prayers.

CLEVELAND. *See* **Ohio**.

COCHIN, JEWS OF. *See* **India**.

COHEN. *See* **Kohen**.

COHEN, ELI (1924-1965). Israeli spy who penetrated the highest levels of government in **Syria**. He was caught and hanged in Damascus. He is considered a hero of modern Israel.

COHEN, HERMANN (1848-1918). German philosopher. The son of a cantor in a small Jewish community, he attended the Rabbinical Seminary at Breslau for a few years. However, he left the Seminary and instead devoted himself to the study of philosophy. In 1876, he was appointed professor of philosophy at the University of Marburg. At this time, Cohen entertained little interest in Judaism and devoted himself entirely to the development of his philosophic system, a modification of the system of Immanuel Kant. The anti-Semitic outburst of the historian Treitschke, in 1880, stirred Cohen's Jewish consciousness, and he attempted to defend his people. An essay *Love of Fellowman in the Talmud*, written as a reply to a query of a court, about the Jewish attitude toward morality drew him still closer to Jewish matters. From that time on, Cohen wrote many essays on Jewish subjects which were later collected in three volumes. He also wrote a work on the Jewish religion called *Die Religion der Vernunft* (The Religion of Reason). In these works, he formulated his philosophical and ethical principles of Judaism. He dwelt especially on the high value of the Messianic idea—the hope for the triumph of good at the "end of days."

COHEN, MORRIS RAPHAEL (1880-1947). American philosopher. Of his numerous works, the leading ones are *A Preface to Logic and Scientific Method* and *Reason and Nature*. In addition, Cohen wrote many essays on the philosophy of law and was editor of the *Modern Legal Philosophical Series*.

COLOMBIA. Republic in northwestern South America. Marranos—converted Jews who practiced the faith of their fathers in secret—lived in Colombia during the 16th and 17th centuries. Their community was suppressed by the **Inquisition** established in 1910. During the 1850's Sephardic Jews from Curacao settled in Colombia. They were joined by immigrants from Greece, Romania, and Turkey after World War I, and by refugees from Germany and East Europe during the 1930's. Colombia, whose total population in 1998 was 35.6 million, is the home of 5,000 Jews, most of whom live in the cities of Bogota, Baranquilla, Cali, Cartagena, and Medellin. Each of these has its own synagogues, religious schools, and charitable organizations.

COLORADO. Jews first settled in Colorado during the gold rush in the 1860's, and some, like Simon **Guggenheim**, became active in developing silver and lead resources. Today, most of Colorado's 48,000 Jews live in Denver (with smaller communities in Colorado Springs and Pueblo), where the *Intermountain Jewish News* is published. Major Jewish health institutions located in Denver include the National Jewish Hospital and the Jewish Consumptives' Relief Society.

COLUMBUS, CHRISTOPHER (1451-1506). Discoverer of America. He was believed to be of Jewish origin. He had Jews in his crew, and was befriended by powerful Marranos in Spain, to whom he wrote letters bewailing his treatment. Columbus claimed descent from the dynasty of King **David**. His son Ferdinand stated that his father's "progenitors were of the blood royal of Jerusalem, and it pleased him that his parents shall not be much known."

COMMANDMENTS. *See* **Mitzvah**.

COMMUNITY. *See* **Kahal**.

CONCENTRATION CAMPS. *See* **Holocaust**.

CONFERENCE OF PRESIDENTS OF MAJOR JEWISH ORGANIZATIONS. Umbrella organization of close to thirty American Jewish organizations. First organized in 1954, the Conference represents American Jewry to the U.S. Government, and gets particularly involved in U.S.-Israel relations.

CONFIRMATION. Synagogue ceremony in which boys and girls graduating from elementary religious school publicly recognize their dedication to Judaism. Originating in **Germany**, confirmation was introduced in the U.S. in 1847 and now takes place in all Reform, most Conservative, and some Orthodox synagogues. It is celebrated on the holiday of **Shavuot** to signify that the graduates confirm their loyalty to the Torah which, according to tradition, was given on Shavuot.

CONNECTICUT. There are sporadic records of Jews living in the state in the 17th and 18th century. Not until the mid-19th century, however, were Jews permitted to establish synagogues. The first were organized in Hartford and New Haven. Today, there are some 100,000 Jews living in the state, mainly in the Hartford, New Haven, Bridgeport, Stamford, and Norwalk areas. Jews have been active in the state's economic, social, political, and cultural life. One of the best known was Senator Abraham **Ribicoff**. More recently, Joseph **Lieberman** has been serving as U.S. Senator from that state. There are many synagogues and a high level of philanthropic activities. The *Connecticut Jewish Ledger* is published in West Hartford, *The Jewish Leader* in New London.

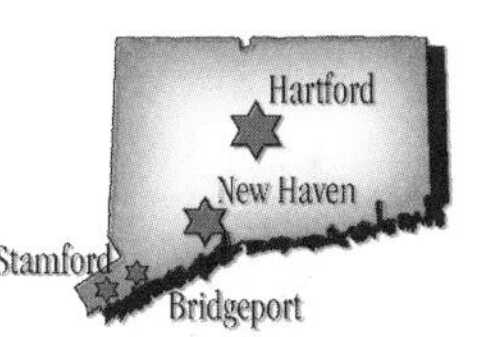

CONSERVATIVE JUDAISM. *See* **Judaism**.

COPLAND, AARON (1900-1990). Composer, pianist, conductor, and author. One of America's leading musicians, Copland distinguished himself both as creative artist and as interpreter of modern music. His work as a composer developed from a dry, ironic modern idiom to more simplified melodic treatment. In both phases he made striking use of American jazz and folk motifs. *Vitebsk, Study on a Jewish Melody* and *In the Beginning*, a choral setting on the theme of Creation, are works on Jewish motifs.

CORDOVERO, MOSES. *See* **Kabbalah**.

COSSACK UPRISING. *See* **Lithuania** *and* **Germany**.

COSTA RICA. Republic in southern Central America. Costa Rica's Jewish community was founded by settlers from Curaçao in the 1890's. Immigrants from Europe have since swelled its number to 2,500 in total population of 3.5 million. The **Ashkenazic**, or East European, majority and **Sephardic** minority have separate organizations. The Central Zionist Organization is the representative Jewish body of that community.

COUNCIL OF FOUR LANDS. *See* **Kahal**.

COVENANT. In biblical times a contract or agreement of friendship between persons or nations was completed in a ceremony in which the two parties walked between the two halves of an animal sacrifice (Gen. 15:9-11). In the biblical covenants between God and Israel, a sign accompanied each renewal of the contract. When God made a covenant with **Noah** after the flood, He set the rainbow as a sign that "the waters shall no more become a flood to destroy all flesh" (Gen. 9:13-15). In the covenant God made with **Abraham**, giving to him and to his children the land of **Canaan** for "an everlasting possession," **circumcision** was the sign (Gen. 17:10). When the Lord renewed the covenant with the Children of Israel at Sinai, His sign was the **Sabbath** (Exod. 31:13). In the Bible, the **Torah** itself is called "the Book of the Covenant," the stone tablets with the Ten Commandments "the tablets of the covenant," a reminder that Israel's part of the contract was faithfulness to God and righteous behavior toward men.

CRÉMIEUX, ISAAC ADOLPHE (1796-1880). Statesman who devoted his life to furthering French democracy and equal rights for the Jews of **France**. He was instrumental in the abolition of a degrading oath which all French Jews were forced to take when appearing in court. Admitted to the bar in 1817, he became an outstanding orator, lawyer, statesman, and defender of human rights. Deeply aroused by the **blood accusation** against his fellow Jews in the **Damascus affair**, Crémieux actively intervened on behalf of the unfortunate victims. This close contact with the misery of Asian Jewry led him to form the **Alliance Israélite Universelle** to promote their welfare. He became president of this important organization and retained the post for life. In the turbulent political scene of 19th-century France, he held various government posts, including that of minister of justice, and in 1873, was made senator for life.

CRESCAS, HASDAI (ca. 1340-1412). Spanish rabbi, statesman, and religious philosopher. The Talmudic scholarship of Hasdai Crescas was so highly valued that his contemporaries simply called him "the Rov [teacher] of Saragossa." Crescas' statesmanship was recognized when he served the Royal Court of Aragon, yet this did not save him from tragedy. His son was killed during the black year of 1391, when Spanish mobs, incited by the eloquence of a monk, raged in many cities and gave Jews a choice between death and giving up their faith. Crescas is best remembered for his philosophical work *Or Adonai*, "Light of the Lord." This book described the major beliefs of Judaism as faith in God's guidance and in Jewish destiny. Crescas opposed the philosophy of Aristotle and stressed his belief in free will. He is considered the last original Jewish thinker of the medieval period, and his work influenced deeply the 17th-century philosopher Baruch (Benedict) **Spinoza**.

CRIMEA. Peninsula in the former Soviet Union, on the shore of the Black Sea. Jews first settled there during the time of the Second **Temple**, more than two thousand years ago, possibly even earlier. Their numbers grew under Roman rule. Old Jewish inscriptions discovered in Crimea indicate that a substantial and prosperous Jewish population existed there at the beginning of the common era. In the 8th and 9th centuries, the **Khazar** Kingdom flourished in the Crimea. First a pagan nation, the Khazars embraced Judaism at an early period in their history. This period of an independent Khazar state ended in 1016, when the Russians and Byzantines united to defeat the Khazars. Jewish communities survived the Tatar invasions in the 13th century. In later periods, prosperous Jewish tradesmen from the Crimea opened routes of commerce to Turkey, Russia, and **Poland**. When Czarist Russia annexed the region in 1784, most of the Jews were artisans and small traders. In addition to the Jewish population, Crimea had substantial **Karaite** communities. This sect, founded by **Anan ben David** during the 8th century, rejected Talmudic tradition, adhering only to biblical law.

In 1924, the Soviet government set aside some of the land of this area for Jewish colonization. Jewish families who had lost their means of livelihood because of the government ban on private enterprise emigrated to the Crimea. A special organization, *Komzet*, the Commission for the Rural Placement of Jewish Toilers, supervised the colonization. The American **Joint Distribution Committee** (JDC) extended financial and technical help to the settlers through the AgroJoint. Before World War II, there were about 80,600 Jews in the Crimea, out of a total population of more than a million. Twenty-five thousand Jews engaged in agriculture. During Nazi occupation, all the Jewish colonies were destroyed, and most Jews perished. Only a small number returned to their homes after the war.

CRUSADES (1096-1291). The Crusades were a series of Christian wars designed to free the Holy Land from Moslem rule. They were uniformly tragic in their effects upon the Jews. Crusaders were exempted from the payment of their debts to Jews. Inflamed to hatred against the "unbelievers" by both church and state, the armies of Crusaders, often no more than armed mobs, began their "holy war" by massacring Jewish communities in **France**, **Germany**, and **England**. Some Jews were forcibly baptized, others were killed for refusing baptism, still others were slain without the opportunity of choice. Emperor Henry IV permitted the forced converts to live as Jews again. A few bishops and archbishops tried to protect the Jews of their districts, but their efforts generally failed. In the Holy Land itself, the few surviving Jewish communities were almost entirely destroyed by the Crusaders. What the pagan Romans had left undone, the Christians completed. The afflicted European communities met the attacks in different ways. Jews of Treves submitted to forced baptism, and later renounced it; those of Cologne tried in vain to hide; those of Worms, Speyer, Mayence, and York took their own lives; those of the French city of Carentan died fighting. Rashi, who was in Troyes, France, during the First Crusade, escaped injury. His grandson, Rabbenu Jacob Tam, was badly wounded, almost killed, in the Second Crusade. Many of the *kinnot*, or poems of lamentation, composed in memory of the victims are still recited on the Fast of the Ninth of Av. As a result of the Crusades, tens of thousands of Jews were massacred, some communities were completely wiped out, and others never recovered their strength. Jewish trade with the Orient was broken, and Jews were gradually forced to earn their living by usury. Above all, suspicion of, prejudice against, and hatred toward them became deep-rooted and lingered on for centuries in the popular mind.

CRYSTAL, BILLY. *See* **Stage and Screen.**

CUBA. Until the 1959 revolution which ended in Fidel Castro's transformation of Cuba into a socialist state, Jews numbered 10,000. In 1998, about 700 Jews remained in a population of 11 million. Cuba won freedom from Spain in 1898 as a result of the Spanish-American War. In the 16th century, **Marranos**, forced converts who practiced Judaism in secret, came to Cuba to escape persecution in other parts of Latin America. For a short time they prospered, playing an important part in developing Cuba's sugar industry. Finally, the **Inquisition**, which sought to wipe out all non-Catholic faiths, reached the island, and the Marrano community disappeared. Although religious persecution ceased in 1783, it was not until Cuba gained its independence that Jews began to immigrate in large numbers. The first to come were American Jews, who formed an independent community. At about the same time, many Sephardic Jews from **Turkey** and **Morocco** arrived. The influx of East European Jews began only after 1924, when the U.S. shut its doors to immigrants. Strict immigration laws passed in the 1930's prevented further growth of the community. Today, about half of Cuba's Jews are descendants of the Sephardic immigrants; the rest are divided between a "North American" and an East European community.

Jewish Community Center in Cuba.

CUKERMAN, YITZHAK. *See* **Warsaw**.

CUP OF ELIJAH. *See* **Passover**.

CURAÇAO. Island in the Dutch West Indies where Jews who originally fled Spain and Portugal settled in the mid-17th century. Their synagogue is the oldest in the Western Hemisphere. Jews occupy positions of social, economic, and political importance on the island. (*See also* **Netherlands Antilles**.)

CUSTOMS. In Hebrew, *minhag*. A practice which, though not based on biblical or Talmudic law, has become, through long observance, as sacred and binding as a religious law. Customs have played an important part in the development of *Halakhah*, or Jewish religious law. The rabbis, seeking to achieve unanimity of practice and usage, established many customs of different times and places as laws. Many biblical laws, such as **circumcision**, began as customs before they became law. "The custom of Israel is law," from *Tosafot*, is a familiar comment. Customs may vary from place to place, and the rabbis maintain that one must follow the local custom, and that sometimes a custom may even override a law. **Sephardic** and **Ashkenazic** Jews vary in many customs, such as Hebrew pronunciation, the text of some prayers, and holiday observances. Reform Jews have instituted new customs, such as the **confirmation** ceremony on **Shavuot**.

CYPRUS. Island at the eastern end of the Mediterranean Sea. It comprises an area of 6,188 m^2, and has a population of close to half a million, consisting chiefly of Greeks and Turks. In the Bible Cyprus is mentioned as Kittim. During the Maccabean period Jews lived on Cyprus. Alexander **Jannaeus** fought the king of Cyprus and conquered him. In the time of Trajan, Jews took an active part in the revolt against **Rome**. As a consequence, Jewish Cypriots were exterminated, and for many years Jews were forbidden to live on the island. At the advice of Don Joseph **Nasi**, the Turks captured the island in 1571 from the city-state of Venice. In 1878, during the time of Lord Beaconsfield (Benjamin **Disraeli**), the island was occupied by the British. In 1960, Cyprus gained independence. Several attempts made by the Jews of Cyprus to start farm settlements failed. In the 1930's a number of families moved from Palestine to Cyprus, and engaged in its citrus fruit trade. After the World War II the British established detention camps on Cyprus for Jewish refugees who tried to enter Palestine illegally. In 1998, about 20 Jews lived on Cyprus, out of a total population of more than 7 million.

CYRUS (6th century B.C.E.). One of the great conqueror-kings of the ancient world and founder of the Persian Empire. When this Median prince took Babylon in 539 B.C.E. he found there Jews who had been led into captivity by Nebuchadnezzar 50 years earlier. Cyrus permitted them to return to Palestine and named Zerubbabel, grandson of Judea's last king, governor of Jerusalem. He assigned a military guard to escort Zerubbabel to his capital. The returning exiles carried with them the plundered vessels of the Temple and funds for its reconstruction. Both were gifts of the emperor.

CZECH REPUBLIC. In 1993, by democratic vote, the former republic of Czechoslovakia, bordering **Poland** on the north, **Germany** on the west, and **Hungary** on the east, was split into two countries, Czech and Slovakia. The Czech Republic's Jewish community in the regions of Moravia and Bohemia dates to the 10th century.

Silver Guilded Kiddush Cup, 1610, Czechoslovakia.

Jews first settled in a suburb of the capital city, **Prague**, and from there spread to other cities. Their numbers increased when they were joined by Jews fleeing the cruel attacks of the Crusaders in the countries of western and southern Europe. Jews prospered in the region, engaging in agriculture and various trades, until the mid-14th century when they suffered persecution and exile. They were accused of poisoning wells and desecrating the bread of the Holy Communion.

The religious war which broke out at this time between the students of Jan Hus and the Catholics brought further suffering to the Jews. In 1542, disaster was narrowly averted when pope Pius IV persuaded King Ferdinand I to cancel the edict ordering Jews out of Prague. After each tragic disturbance, the Jewish community rebuilt its life, and the community became famous for its outstanding scholars. Among these were Rabbi Judah **Loew**, scholar and saint also known as the Maharal, and Rabbi Yom Tov Lipman Heller, author of a commentary on the Mishnah.

The country was for many years the cause of controversy between certain Slavic and German tribes. After continuous battles between the Slavic and the German rulers in the mid-17th century, it fell to the Hapsburg crown and became a part of the Austro-Hungary empire. In 1918, Czechoslovakia again won political independence.

The new republic, established after World War I by Thomas Masaryk, granted its Jewish citizens equal rights in practice as well as in theory. In 1938, there were about 400,000 Jews living in the new Czechoslovakia, in a general population of about 15 million. Jews were represented in the government, civil service, the armed forces, Parliament, trade and commerce, and the professions. A national-cultural Jewish life developed there, and numerous yeshivot and Hebrew schools flourished. Carpatho-Russia was, between the World Wars, an important center of **Hasidism**. Many Jews there engaged in farming. Some of the most famous Czechoslovak communities were Prague, Brno, Bratislava, Moravska Ostrava, and Mukacevo. In the 1930's Czechoslovakia absorbed many Jewish refugees from Germany.

The Munich Pact of 1938, under which large areas were surrendered to Nazi Germany, brought tragedy to Jews in

Czech stamp of Rabbi Loew's grave.

Czechoslovakia. In the area which was ceded to Germany, Czech Jews were persecuted as were other Jews throughout the German Reich. In 1939, the Germans occupied Czechoslovakia, nullified its independence, and turned it into a puppet state. Some Czechoslovak Jews managed to emigrate to other countries, including Palestine, but large numbers suffered the fate of millions of other Jews, and were exterminated in the infamous death camps.

After World War II, the republic of Czechoslovakia was re-established and its Jewish citizens were granted equal rights. But nearly all of the communities were without Jewish residents. In 1946, the Communist regime came into power, and most of the remaining Jews emigrated. In 1998, the Jewish population in the Czech Republic was estimated at about 2,200; most live in Prague and other large centers.

In 1989, the Communist regime came to an end. The new president, Vaclav Havel, visited Israel in 1990 and has shown interest in furthering cultural ties between the two nations.

Czech stamp of the Altneuschul synagogue.

CZERNIAKOW, ADAM (1880-1942). President of the **Judenrat**, or Jewish Council, in the **Warsaw Ghetto** during the Nazi occupation. Despite his many efforts to ward off the Nazi onslaught against half a million Jews in Warsaw, the systematic extermination of this major Jewish population center continued unhindered, and eventually Czerniakov committed suicide.

Below, university seals with Hebrew inscriptions. Clockwise, Yale University, Columbia University, and Dartmouth College. Courtesy Yale University, Dartmouth College, and Columbia University.

DACHAU. Village in Bavaria, **Germany**; site of the first Nazi concentration camp in 1933. Here the Nazis brought from Germany and elsewhere a variety of people, including Jews, who were brutalized and either killed or left to die, and conducted, among other things, medical experiments on humans. It was liberated by the U.S. Army in 1945.

DALET. Fourth letter of the Hebrew alphabet; numerically, four.

DAMASCUS. Syrian city, "half as old as time." When **Abraham** fought King Chedorlaomer for the liberation of Lot, he pursued Chedorlaomer to Hobah, north of Damascus (Gen. 14:15). For intermittent periods beginning with **David**, Jewish kings ruled this capital of Aram. Finally, it fell to the Assyrian empire of Tiglat-Pileser in 732 B.C.E. Ruled at different times by almost every aggressive power of the Mid-East, Damascus fell to the Arabs and became their imperial city in 635 C.E. In 1516 C.E., Ottoman Turks held Damascus as one of their important ruling centers until World War I. To this day, the Jewish settlement of Damascus has been almost unbroken since the time of **King Herod** (40-4 B.C.E.). After World War I, Arab nationalism made life difficult for the Jews, and they began to move away, mostly to Israel. Once the Syrian government allowed Jews to emigrate in 1996, only 200 old and poor Jews remained.

DAMASCUS AFFAIR. In 1840, while **Syria** was under Egyptian rule, the Jewish community in **Damascus** was accused of killing a Franciscan friar, Father Tomaso, in order to use his blood for ritual purposes. Influenced by the French consul Ratti Menton, an inquiry was undertaken by the local governor. Jewish leaders of the community were arrested and tortured. One died in prison, and eight others were condemned to death. Isaac Adolphe **Crémieux** of France and Sir Moses **Montefiore** of **England** came to **Alexandria** to plead with the ruler Mehemet Ali. They succeeded in obtaining the release of the prisoners as well as an expression of Mehemet Ali's disbelief in the charge against them. Meanwhile, Turkey had recovered control of Syria, and Crémieux and Montefiore proceeded to Constantinople, obtaining from the Sultan Abd al Majid a document denouncing the **blood accusation** as a base falsehood. The same document, the *Hatti Humayun*, removed some of the disabilities governing Turkish Jews.

DAN. **Jacob**'s fifth son; founder of the tribe known for its fighting men. The tribe of Dan settled in the area around Ekron in the south of Canaan and along the coast north of **Jaffa**. Dan is also the name of a settlement established later by Danites in the north near the headwaters of the **Jordan**. The modern **Kibbutz** Dan was established in 1939 near the site of its ancient namesake.

Emblem of the tribe of Dan.

DANCE. As in all other ancient cultures, dance in Judaism reaches back to earliest recorded times. It is associated with personal, communal, and historical occasions, often of a religious nature. Invariably it was accompanied by instrumental music. **Miriam** and other women performed a victory dance after crossing of the Red Sea, and other women celebrated this way. Jewish dances are mainly folk dances, performed in a group, often in a circle rather than a solo performance, and most often by women.

With the birth of **Hasidism** (18th century), a new cultural phenomenon emerges: men dancing together, without women, mostly in a circle but also in pair or line formations. In fact, the Hasidim consider dance a form of expressing love and devotion to God.

Hasidim Dancing, by Saul Raskin. Courtesy A. Kamberg Collection.

Zionism seems to have borrowed the Hasidic dancing fervor in creating its own circle dance, the *horah*, and in borrowing folk dances from other cultures such as Russian, Polish, Romanian, and Middle Eastern (notably Yemenite). Dancing helped the early pioneers in Palestine overcome hardship and forged a group spirit.

Dance today has become an important aspect of Israeli culture, and there are Israeli folk dance groups there and around the world. Jews in general have incorporated dancing into all special life occasions, notably Bar Mitzvahs and weddings, and dancing has become a communal experience in all Jewish groups and communities.

DANIEL, BOOK OF. The Book of Daniel is in the section of the **Bible** known as Writings. The book tells the story of the prophet Daniel who was taken captive to Babylon and trained for the king's service. He became a favorite of King Belshazzar by interpreting his dreams. When the mysterious writing *Mene, mene, tekel upharsin* appeared on a wall in the King's palace during a feast, Daniel explained that it foretold the downfall of the King. As a punishment, he was cast into a lion's den but was miraculously saved from death. This story, written in **Aramaic**, occupies the first six chapters of the book. The last six chapters, written in Hebrew, are mystic revelations about the end of days, the day of judgment in which the wicked world powers would be destroyed and the Jewish people would be restored to their home.

DANIEL DERONDA. Novel by George Eliot, published in 1877. It tells the story of Daniel Deronda, English-born and completely unaware of his Jewish ancestry, who finds his way back to Judaism and tries to recreate a Jewish state in Palestine. Written 20 years before **Herzl**'s *The Jewish State*, Daniel Deronda makes a passionate plea for the "revival of the organic center" for the Jewish people.

DAVID (r.1010-970 B.C.E.). Second king of Israel. A shepherd lad, David, youngest son of Jesse, was taken from grazing his father's sheep near **Bethlehem** in **Judah** and brought to court to soothe King **Saul**. David played his harp to calm the king when he was depressed by an "evil spirit," and Saul took a liking to him. A deep friendship also developed between David and Saul's son, Jonathan. When the **Philistine** giant Goliath taunted and challenged Saul's army, David killed the giant with a stone from his slingshot. He distinguished himself in battle and married Saul's daughter Michal. The king grew jealous of David's popularity and repeatedly tried to kill him. David became a refugee, hiding from Saul in the mountains and later among the Philistines. Yet he managed not to fight for the Philistines when they faced Saul in battle on Mt. Gilboa and defeated him. David mourned the death of Saul and his beloved friend Jonathan in a beautiful elegy (II Sam. 1:17-27).

Saul Attacks David, by Gustav Doré.

Long before Saul's death, the prophet Samuel anointed David secretly, and now his own tribe, Judah, chose him king. The other tribes had crowned Saul's son Ishbaal, and the civil war that resulted lasted two years. On the death of Ishbaal, David was acclaimed king over all Israel and ruled for 40 years.

Under David's reign, the tribes of Israel were united and became a nation. He defeated the Philistines so soundly that they were not heard from again for centuries. He subdued the surrounding Canaanite peoples, including Aram and its capital **Damascus** in the north. By defeating the Edomites in the south, David gave the Israelites an outlet to the Red Sea at Ezion-Geber. David's crowning achievement was the capture of **Jerusalem** from the Jebusites; he made this ancient city, sitting up on the rocky heights of Zion, the capital of Israel. There he built a splendid new tabernacle to which he brought up the **Ark of the Covenant**. Thus, David made Zion the center of worship and the holy city of religious pilgrimage. Jerusalem came to be called the City of David, the heart of his kingdom. David extended the boundaries of Israel to an area never again attained, except for a short period under the Hasmoneans.

King David suffered much grief. His greatest sorrow was the rebellion and death of his beloved son **Absalom**. David died at the age of 71, the beloved hero of his people leaving the throne of Israel to his son **Solomon**. He is remembered as a great warrior, as a loyal friend, and as the erring king who bowed with meekness to the prophet's reprimand.

David is remembered as the "sweet singer of Israel"; author of the **Psalms**, or *Tehillim*; and the son of Jesse from whose stem the Messiah would spring to lead a scattered Israel back to Zion.

DAVID, TOMB OF. The **Bible** relates that David was buried in **Jerusalem** (I Kings 2:10). Though the site of the tomb is not certain, it is placed at the south of old Jerusalem, on what is erroneously called Mount Zion. Between 1948 and 1967, when the Western Wall was not accessible to Jews, pilgrimages were made to the tomb on Mount Zion.

DAYAN, MOSHE (1915-1981). Israeli soldier and statesman. Born in Kibbutz Degania "A," he received his early education at Nahalal, a settlement which his parents helped found. He joined the Haganah when still a boy. After the Arab disturbances in 1936, Dayan first served as an instructor in the Supernumerary Police Force and later with General Orde Charles **Wingate**'s Special Night Squads. In 1939, he was arrested by the British authorities and served two years of a five-year sentence. He resumed his service in the Haganah and fought in the Syrian border area. In the invasion of Syria, then held by Vichy France, by the Allied forces, Dayan was seriously wounded, losing an eye.

In the War of Independence, Dayan commanded a battalion on the Syrian front. During the siege of Jerusalem he served as military commander. He participated in the Rhodes Armistice talks with the Kingdom of Jordan and served with the Mixed Armistice

Moshe Dayan.

Commission. In 1953, after attending a course of military studies in England, he became Chief of Staff of the Israeli army with the rank of Major General, a position he held during the Sinai Campaign of 1956. He was released from active service in the Israeli Defense Forces in 1958. He was elected to the **Knesset** and served as minister of agriculture from 1959 to 1964. In 1967, he was appointed minister of defense. He played an important role in planning the strategy that brought **Israel** victory in the **Six-Day War**. He left his post when Golda Meir's government resigned in 1974. In 1977, he quit the Labor party to become Israel's foreign minister under Menachem **Begin**. In this position he played a key role in the negotiations between Israel and **Egypt** initiated by the visit of Egypt's President Anwar el-Sadat to Jerusalem in November 1977. In 1965, he wrote the *Diary of the Sinai Campaign*.

DEAD SEA. Inland sea located at the lowest point on earth. It is 47 miles long by 9.5 miles wide, in the deepest pit of the **Jordan** depression, fed by the Jordan and Arnon rivers. Compressed between the mountains of Moab in the east and the Judean hills in the west, the Dead Sea was the stage for the tragic biblical drama of Sodom and Gomorrah's destruction for their sins. Its historic character is reflected in its numerous names: in Hebrew, the Salt Sea, in Arabic, the Sea of Lot; and to Josephus Flavius, the Asphalt Sea. The Greeks, who called it the Dead Sea, believed that nothing could live in it, though microscopic life has recently been discovered in its silt. Its waters are so heavy that they hold the human body buoyant. The first attempt to tap the treasures of this "fluid mine" was made before World War II, when two plants were set up at northern and southern ends. The northern plant was destroyed by the Arabs in 1948, but the second at Sodom has been restored by Israel for the exploitation of its millions of tons of salt, potash, bromides, and other minerals. A winter health resort and hotels are located on the coast.

DEAD SEA SCROLLS. Ancient biblical manuscripts discovered in the spring of 1947 by Arab Bedouins in the Qumran caves at Ain Fashka on the northwest shore of the **Dead Sea**. As part of a hidden library of hundreds of fragments and scrolls, seven leather manuscripts were salvaged, still wrapped in linen and enclosed in earthen jars. Briefly, they contain:

First, the Book of Isaiah in its entirety, written in 54 columns. This copy differs in some details from the Masoretic text in the Hebrew Bible.

Second, a second Isaiah Scroll, containing most of Chapters 38-66, is closer to the Bible text. This second copy was acquired by the **Hebrew University of Jerusalem** through the efforts of eminent archeologist Eliezer L. Sukenik. He also published the first accounts of his findings in two volumes. After much difficulty all seven scrolls came into the possession of the State of **Israel**.

Third, a **Midrash** on the Book of **Habakkuk**, consisting of a commentary on "the end of the days" and of the imminent visitation of God pronounced by the "Teacher of Righteousness," prefaced by verses from the biblical book of Habakkuk.

Fourth, *The Manual of Discipline*, in two fragments, is a "constitution" of a religious sect, probably the Essenes, setting forth the righteous way of life and admonishing the members of the sect to battle for truth and virtue.

Fifth, *The War of the Sons of Light and the Sons of Darkness*, presumably a manual on the conduct of war on the religious and the military level. The "Sons of Light" are defined as "the sons of Levi, the sons of Judah and the sons of Benjamin," while the "Sons of Darkness" include "the bands of Edomites, Moabites...**Philistines**, the bands of Kittim of Ashur" and the "Kittim of Egypt." The latter, in the opinion of Professor Sukenik, refer to the Seleucids in **Syria** and Ptolemies in **Egypt**. These were the adversaries confronting Jews and Judea. The armed combatants mentioned in this scroll are archers, slingers, horsemen, and charioteers.

Sixth, *Thanksgiving Psalms*, four leaves of leather, includes about 20 psalms similar to those of the Bible. Five of these psalms were published by Professor Sukenik. They are composed in a verse with a rather loose rhythm, with inspiring contents and profound religious feeling.

Last, *The Aramaic Scroll*, previously thought to be the lost Apocalypse of Lamech, now called the Genesis Apocryphon, is written in Aramaic and contains some chapters from the Book of **Genesis**, plus folklore material.

An eighth scroll, probably found in the late 1950's, is the largest and most complete to date. It was acquired by the Israeli government in 1967 during the **Six-Day War**. **Yadin**, who published a translation of the 27-foot-long scroll in 1977, dated it between the 2nd century B.C.E. and 70 C.E.

Dating of the Dead Sea Scrolls has aroused a stormy debate among scholars. The scrolls are generally accepted, on the basis of archaeological evidence and the Hebrew script, as dating from the 1st century B.C.E. Further exploration of caves in the vicinity where the Dead Sea Scrolls were discovered has produced other fragments of biblical scrolls. Of particular interest to archeologists are the "copper scrolls," known to contain a mysterious account of a unique inventory of buried treasures totaling tons of gold, silver, and precious vessels.

The Manual of Discipline scroll (Dead Sea Scrolls).

In September 1991, the **Hebrew Union College** in Cincinnati announced that the school had created a computer program for reconstructing unpublished texts from a previously published concordance to the scrolls. Later that month, the Huntington Library in San Marino, California, announced it would allow researchers unrestricted access to the library's complete set of photographs of the scrolls. This prompted the Israeli Antiquities Authority to lift its long-standing restrictions on the use of the scrolls.

The search for more scrolls and artifacts in the Dead Sea area continues to result in new discoveries.

DEBORAH. Prophet and judge of Israel who held court "under the palm tree of Deborah, between Ramah and Bethel on the mountain of Ephraim." When Yabin, King of Chazor, oppressed the Children of Israel, Deborah summoned Barak to lead the tribes in the battle of Megiddo against the Canaanites. Deborah planned the strategy which brought Barak victory, though the Canaanite general, Sisera, had "900 chariots of iron." She celebrated this victory with a stirring ode of thanksgiving (Judges 4 and 5).

Deborah.

DECALOGUE. *See* **Ten Commandments.**

DELAWARE. Few Jews lived in Delaware prior to the 1880's when the first congregation was organized in Wilmington. Today, most of Delaware's well-organized community of 10,000 Jews lives in that city. The *Jewish Voice* covers Jewish affairs in the state. The Dupont corporation, the most dominant company in Delaware, was the first major industrial corporation in the U.S. to engage a Jewish CEO.

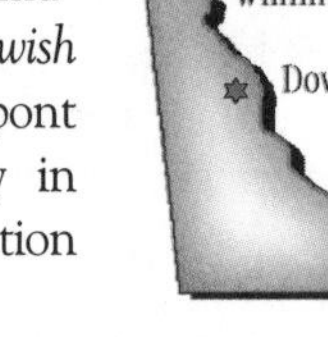

DELVALLE, ARTURO (1937-). The only Jew ever elected head of state in the Western Hemisphere. Member of the old Spanish-Portuguese Jewish community of **Panama** (*see* **Curaçao**), he became president of Panama in 1985. In 1988, he tried to dismiss dictator Raul Noriega and had to flee the country until 1989 when the U.S. ousted Noriega.

DENMARK. Jews have lived in Denmark since 1622, when King Christian IV invited them to migrate from the Netherlands to his country. Enjoying civic rights and the friendship of the rulers, they concentrated chiefly in the capital city, Copenhagen. Danish Jews engaged widely in commerce, and a number of them attained wealth and influence. By the 18th century, leading Danish Jewish families had established close ties with the world of secular Danish culture.

The Jewish community of Denmark was the largest in the Scandinavian countries but small in proportion to the general population. Nevertheless, Jews of Denmark have played a significant role in that country's culture, especially in literature, art, science, music, and the world of finance.

During World War I, Copenhagen served as a haven for many refugees from Eastern Europe. But on April 9, 1940, the Germans occupied Denmark and attempted to persecute the Jews there. Both the government and the people of Denmark protested and succeeded in preventing the maltreatment of their Jewish neighbors. In 1943, when the Danish people learned of Gestapo plans for the deportation and extermination of Danish Jewry, they organized a rescue plan: all Danish Jews were secretly gathered at the ports and smuggled in ships and boats to **Sweden.** Both the Swedish and Danish governments supported this humanitarian operation. As a result, the Germans seized no more than 467 people who were deported to Theresienstadt. What became known as "Little Dunkirk" was the only organized non-Jewish rescue operation during the Nazi period.

After the war, virtually all Danish Jews who escaped to Sweden were repatriated. In 1998, there were 6,500 Jews living in Denmark, more than 90% of whom lived in Copenhagen, the seat of the country's only Jewish congregation. Danish Jews were active in the textile industry, publishing, and book selling. A Jewish elementary school in Copenhagen has existed since 1850, offering general as well as religious education. The Danish Jewish community was pro-Zionist and actively interested in Israel affairs.

DETROIT. *See* **Michigan.**

DEUTERONOMY. In Hebrew *Devarim,* or Words. Latinized version of the Greek, meaning repetition of the law. Fifth book of the **Bible.** Named in Hebrew after the second word of the opening verse of the book: "These are the words which **Moses** spoke unto all Israel on this side of the Jordan, in the wilderness." The book is thought to be identified, in part, with the book of the Torah found in the Temple during the reign of King Josiah (640-609 B.C.E.). It retells the story of Israel from the time of the exodus from **Egypt.** This Book is also termed in Jewish tradition as Mishneh Torah, a "repetition of the laws" given in the books of **Exodus** and **Leviticus.** Many of the ethical ideas found in the earlier books of the **Pentateuch** reach their loftiest form in Deuteronomy. The book closes in noble verse as Moses bids farewell to the people and gives his blessings to the tribes one by one.

DEUTSCH, BABETTE (1895-1982). 20th century American poet. With her husband, Avrahm Yarmolinsky, she is also known for her translations of poets like Rilke, Pushkin, and Blok from German and Russian.

DIASPORA MUSEUM. Leading Israeli museum since 1978, located on the **Tel Aviv University** campus. It has permanent and interactive displays of Jewish life, culture, and history, as well as temporary exhibits. It also maintains a research center with visual archives, a genealogical database documenting the Jewish communities of Europe and the world, and a Jewish music center.

DIBBUK. Literally, attachment. Name given to the soul of the deceased, usually evil, which has entered a living person in order to find its salvation. Belief in the transmigration of the soul is ancient; it is mentioned in the Talmud. The books of the **Kabbalah** gave this belief widespread circulation. Special rites, or exorcism, were prescribed to drive out the evil spirit. By the use of holy names and assurances of salvation, certain "miracle workers" were believed to be capable of inducing the dybbuk to leave. S. Anski made use of the legend in his famous play *The Dybbuk.*

DIETARY LAWS. Code of law restricting the foods Jews may eat and controlling the preparation of permitted foods. According to the story of Creation (Gen. 1:29), all fruits and vegetables may be eaten. The Bible separates animals into clean—*tahor*—and unclean—*tameh* (Lev. 1:1). Israel, as a holy people, is allowed to eat only the flesh of "clean" animals, mammals which chew the cud and have cloven hooves. Rabbis have restricted the birds considered fit for food, since it has been difficult to identify all those mentioned in Leviticus. Permitted animals, before they may be eaten, must be ritually slaughtered. Since the eating of blood is forbidden, the meat must be soaked and salted to withdraw as much blood as possible. It is not permissible to use the hindquarter of cattle unless certain veins are removed. If the animal is sick, or if after slaughtering the vital organs show signs of fatal disease, the animal becomes "unclean." Fish with both scales and fins may be eaten, but shellfish, reptiles, and insects are forbidden.

The products of unclean animals, such as their milk or eggs, are also unclean. In several places the Bible commands, "Thou shalt not seethe a kid in the milk of its mother" (Exod. 34:26; Deut. 14:21). From this comes the command to separate meat and dairy foods to the extent of using separate utensils for their preparation and serving. Explanations for the dietary laws are manifold. Some are hygienic in origin. Historically, they were important in helping Jews maintain their identity and added a measure of sanctity to their daily lives.

DISRAELI, BENJAMIN, FIRST EARL OF BEACONSFIELD (1804-1881). British statesman and author. He was born in **London** to a long line of Jewish ancestors who had come to **England** after having been driven out of **Spain** by the **Inquisition**. Benjamin was twelve when his father, Isaac, a well-known writer, withdrew from his Sephardic congregation. Isaac had his son baptized because of the political and social discrimination practiced against Jews in England at that time. Yet Benjamin Disraeli never lost his pride in his Jewish ancestry. After completing his education, he spent three years traveling in southern Europe and the Near East. Impressions of his travels, particularly of the Holy Land, never left him. In Disraeli's books all the heroes go to Palestine for inspiration. One of his novels, *David Alroy*, is the romantic story of the 12th century Jewish revolt against Persia led by Alroy, who planned to reconquer **Jerusalem** for the Jews.

Disraeli had a trigger-quick wit, and some of his novels, beginning with *Vivian Grey* in 1826, were amusing satires that made him the idol of London society. Disraeli's career in British politics was remarkable. His political novels, pamphlets, and speeches helped reshape the Conservative Party, and his influence continued long after his death. He served for a time as leader of the House of Commons, and twice as chancellor of the exchequer. In 1868, and again from 1874 to 1880, he was Prime Minister. During these years, his domestic policies reflected Disraeli's sympathy for the working class and resulted in a number of progressive health, housing, and factory laws. He consistently supported the struggle for obtaining the vote for Jews, despite opposition from his own party. His foreign policy was outstanding. Disraeli obtained for Britain a controlling interest in the Suez Canal in **Egypt**. He arranged to have Queen Victoria proclaimed Empress of **India** and brought about the cession of **Cyprus** to Great Britain. He enlarged and strengthened the power of the British Empire. His policies and courtliness brought him Queen Victoria's deep affection, while his swift repartee and political and diplomatic victories made Benjamin Disraeli one of the most fascinating figures of the 19th century. For Jews, Disraeli had a rare tenderness and respect. Of them he wrote, "That is the aristocracy of nature, the purest race, the chosen people."

Benjamin Disraeli.

DIZENGOFF, MEIR (1861-1936). Zionist leader and mayor of **Tel Aviv**. Joining the Zionist movement in the 1880's, Dizengoff visited Palestine several times before settling there in 1905. In 1909, he laid the cornerstone of Tel Aviv, the first all-Jewish city, and was elected its mayor in 1921. His devoted efforts were important in making Tel Aviv a flourishing city of 100,000 before he died in 1936.

Meir Dizengoff.

DOCTOROW, E.L. (1931-) American novelist who mixes fiction with historical figures and events, he wrote *Ragtime* about America in the early 20th century.

DOMINICAN REPUBLIC. Republic occupying the major eastern section of the Caribbean island of Hispaniola. Before 1940, few Jews settled in the Dominican Republic, and those who did assimilated rapidly. For a brief period, it became one of the bright spots on the darkening horizons of European Jewry. At a time when most nations were severely restricting immigration, Generalissimo Rafael Trujillo announced that the Dominican Republic would welcome Jewish refugees. Speaking at an intergovernmental conference on refugees at Evian, **France**, in 1938, Trujillo offered full economic assistance and "equality of opportunities and of civil, legal, and economic rights" to all colonists. A farm colony was immediately established at Sosua in the Dominican Republic, and plans were made for transferring refugees from Europe. The outbreak of World War II, however, interfered with the project. Communications were difficult, and Jews could not escape from the countries under Nazi domination. Only 1,200 managed to reach the Dominican Republic. Of these, some 300 stayed on after the end of World War II. The total Jewish population in 1998 was 100, living in Sosua and Ciudad Trujillo. There is one synagogue in each of these cities. The Jewish Congregation of the Dominican Republic is the central Jewish organization recognized by the government.

DORATI, ANATOL. *See* **Music.**

DOUGLAS, KIRK. *See* **Stage and Screen.**

DOV BER OF MEZHIRICH. *See* **Hasidism.**

DOWRY. Money or valuables provided by the bride's family. It was practiced throughout Jewish history, and it is still mentioned in the **Ketubah**, or marriage contract, although for most Jews it has become merely a symbolic gesture.

DRAMA. *See* **Stage and Screen.**

DREIDEL. *See* **Hannukah.**

DREYFUS, ALFRED (1859-1935). The only Jewish officer on the French General Staff, he became the center of one of the most famous cases in legal history and a crucial point in the battle against **anti-Semitism** in the modern world. In 1894, a French court-martial convicted Dreyfus of treason on the basis of documents alleged to have been written in his hand. Two years later, fearing that the army would be discredited, the government suppressed evidence that Dreyfus was not guilty and that the real spy was Major Ferdinand Esterhazy, another member of the general staff. In 1897, however, the issue was brought into the open, and the case became the center of a conflict that embroiled French politics for a decade. Those who insisted on Dreyfus's guilt were both politically reactionary and openly anti-Semitic; winning the majority of voters to their side, they vanquished the liberal forces in the elections of 1898. The following year, however, a new prime minister permitted a second trial. Because Dreyfus's innocence was common knowledge, it was expected that he would be acquitted. Nevertheless, the court found him "guilty with extenuating circumstances," and sentenced him to ten years' imprisonment. Although he was pardoned by the President of France soon after, the battle for Dreyfus's exoneration continued. Finally, in 1906, the Supreme Court of Appeals cleared the prisoner, and Dreyfus was reinstated as a major in the army. In 1998, the French government paid special tribute to Dreyfus and to his main defender, the celebrated writer Emile **Zola.**

Cinq Centimes

L'AURORE

Littéraire, Artistique, Sociale

J'Accuse...!

LETTRE AU PRÉSIDENT DE LA RÉPUBLIQUE

Par ÉMILE ZOLA

Emil Zola's letter to the President of France, insisting on Dreyfus's innocence.

DREYFUSS, RICHARD. *See* **Stage and Screen.**

DROPSIE COLLEGE. *See* **Annenberg Research Institute.**

DRUZES. Followers of a religious sect which split from **Islam** in the 11th century. Most of them lived in **Syria, Iraq, Iran,** and **Lebanon** before coming to Palestine. The Druzes in Israel are loyal citizens of the Jewish state.

DUBINSKY, DAVID (1892-1982). One of America's great labor leaders, Dubinsky was leader of the International Ladies' Garment Workers' Union from 1932 to 1966, and an organizer of the Liberal Party in 1944.

DUBNO, MAGGID OF. *See* **Maggid of Dubno.**

DUBNOW, SIMON MARKOVICH (1860-1941). Russian Jewish historian. Dubnow developed his own interpretation of Jewish history, claiming that the spiritual powers of the Jewish people and their unity were preserved by the organized Jewish community during the 2,000 years of the Dispersion. Dubnow believed that the unity of the Jewish people did not depend upon a national territory, nor upon an independent state. This unity was kept alive by communal organizations within whose framework Jewish culture and religion had continued to grow for 2,000 years after the Dispersion. He therefore believed in cultural autonomy and self-government for the Jewish communities. Dubnow's theories of Jewish nationalism resulted in the formation of the Jewish Peoples Party in **Russia** in 1906. At the **Versailles Peace Conference** after World War I, Dubnow's theory of Diaspora Nationalism motivated the demand for minority rights for Jews of Eastern Europe. Dubnow's *History of the Jews of Russia and Poland* was translated into English, and has been of considerable influence on the writing of Jewish history. His general *History of the Jewish People*, in ten volumes, was published in 1901.

Simon M. Dubnow (center, with cane) on his usual Sabbath walk in Kovno, shortly before his capture by the Nazis. Courtesy Anita L. Lebeson.

DUNASH BEN LABRAT (920-990). Hebrew poet in **Spain** who wrote both religious and secular verse. He introduced Arabic meter into Hebrew poetry and played an important role in the development of Hebrew grammar.

DURA-EUROPOS. Ancient city near the Euphrates where the ruins of a synagogue built in 245 were discovered in 1932 with pictures showing biblical scenes.

DYLAN, BOB. *See* **Music.**

EBAN, ABBA (1915-). Israeli statesman, Eban was born in Capetown, **South Africa**, and grew up in a Zionist home in **England**. He studied Hebrew, Arabic, and Persian at Cambridge University. Having distinguished himself in these subjects, he remained to teach them. During World War II he enlisted in the British Army, became an officer, and was assigned to Cairo headquarters. Part of Eban's duties included flights to Palestine in order to stimulate the Jewish war effort there.

Abba Eban and David Ben-Gurion emerging from the United Nations building in New York in 1951. Courtesy United Nations.

Eban settled in **Jerusalem** where his special background was utilized by its Jewish "shadow government" during the closing days of the British Mandate. In 1947, he was appointed liaison officer with the United Nations Special Commission on Palestine. After the proclamation of the State of **Israel** in 1948, Eban pleaded successfully for the admission of Israel to the United Nations. One of the most eloquent spokespersons on the international scene, he served with distinction as head of the Israeli delegation to the United Nations. In 1950, he became Israel's ambassador to the U. S. In 1953, he was deputy chairman of the U.N. assembly. From 1958 until 1966 he was president of the **Weizmann Institute of Science**. In 1960, he was appointed Minister of Education and Culture; in 1963, Deputy Prime Minister; and in 1966, Foreign Minister of the State of Israel, a post he held until the fall of Golda **Meir**'s government in 1974.

ECCLESIASTES. Greek for *Kohelet*. Seventh book of Writings in the **Bible**. The suggested Hebrew meaning of *Kohelet*, its author, is "the Assembler." One of several Wisdom books, the central idea that "all is vanity" is expressed in pithy sayings. Mostly prose, it has passages of great poetic beauty.

ECUADOR. Republic on the northern Pacific coast of South America. There are about 900 Jews in a population near 11 million. In Spanish colonial times Ecuador was the home of **Marranos,** forced Catholic converts who practiced their Jewish faith in secret. Their settlement disappeared, and nothing is known of it. In the 20th century, Jews from Europe founded a new community in Ecuador consisting of two distinct settlements in Quito and Guayaquil. Each is separately affiliated with the **World Jewish Congress**. Each settlement has Zionist groups and a **B'nai B'rith** organization, but educational facilities are poor. In recent years, there has been a tendency for Jews to emigrate to other South American countries.

EDOMITES. Small tribe in southern Palestine, conquered and forcibly converted to Judaism by Johanan **Hyrcanus**. Traditionally, they are descendants of Esau, who lived by hunting.

EDUCATION IN JEWISH HISTORY. In many ways, Jewish history is the story of the education of a people. From the beginning, many great Jewish leaders were also great teachers who spoke to the world through the Jewish people. When the world's mystery and wonder were fresh in the human mind, the patriarch **Abraham** thought about its mystery and wondered about its Creator. He discarded his father's idols and began to teach his tribe to believe in one God. Thus, the founder of the Jewish people was also the first teacher in Jewish history. **Moses**, the Lawgiver who led the people to freedom, was called *rabbenu*, our teacher. He taught the children of Israel during their years of wandering, and he designated times when the people should come together and study. When the

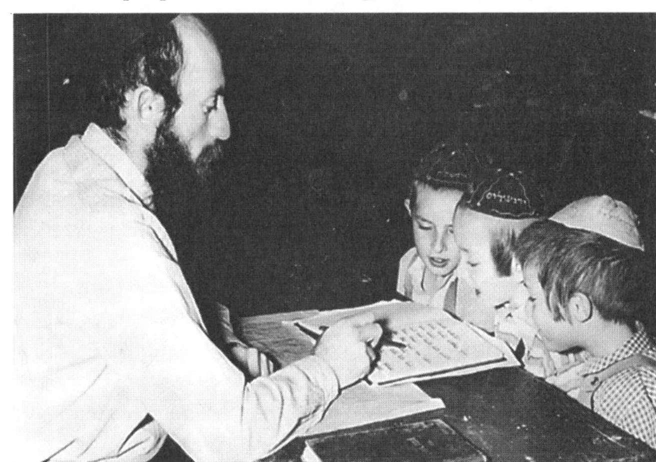
The old heder *was the early "one-room" Jewish school. It is still the format used by some very religious Jews.*

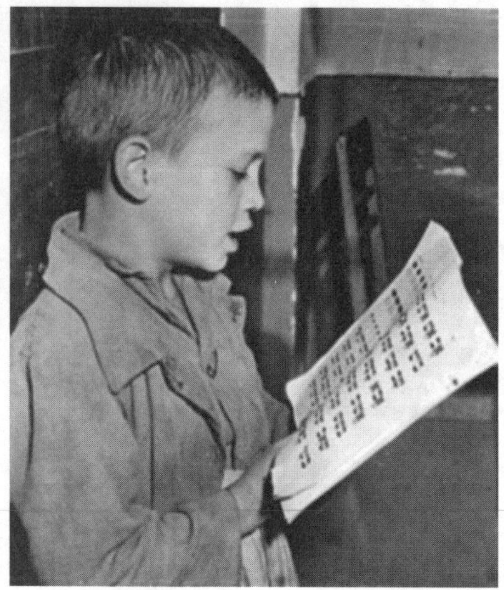

A child of the hara in Tunis learning Hebrew.

Children of Israel settled in the Promised Land and were ruled by judges, there were no schools, so knowledge was handed down by word of mouth from father to son, mother to daughter. The **Judges**, priests, and **Levites** taught the people to reject the idols of their Canaanite neighbors and follow the laws of Moses. Then the greatest teachers of all time, the prophets of Israel, brought to the people a lofty vision of God and taught that to serve Him people must love peace and justice and act rightly toward one another.

A knowledge of reading and writing was common in Israel's earliest days. When he wanted some information during one of his military expeditions, **Gideon**, the fifth of the Judges, found a simple boy who knew enough to "write down for him the princes of Sukkot, and the elders thereof, seventy and seven men." Perhaps the earliest formal schools in ancient Israel were those that trained the priests and Levites in the complicated laws and rituals of bringing sacrifices and conducting **Temple** services. By the 6th century B.C.E., after the return from the Babylonian exile, scribes or soferim had become the teachers of the people, who were required to come regularly to the Temple courts for instruction. **Synagogues**, or houses of prayer, then sprang up all over Judea and served dually as schools. Around 75 B.C.E., **Simeon ben Shetah**, the head of the **Sanhedrin,** a judicial and legislative body, established a system of high schools in all large towns for boys older than 15. Fewer than 100 years later, the high priest, Joshua ben Gamala, set up a system of elementary schools in every town for boys at least age five. The historian **Josephus Flavius** boasted that in **Jerusalem** alone there were more than 300 schools for children.

Education came to be of utmost importance in the life of the people. After the destruction of the Second **Temple** by the Romans, the rabbis taught that study, like prayer, was a form of worship and a substitute for sacrifices. During the Talmudic period in **Babylonia**, the rabbis set up a complete, lifelong system of education that began at the age of five or six. Few details were overlooked, and there was even a place for athletics. In the 6th century, one rabbi stressed that 25 pupils were the ideal number for a class. If there were 40 children, he urged that an assistant teacher be added, and for 50 he advised two teachers. The Bet Ha-Sefer, or House of the Book, was the Bible school for the youngest children. At age 10 they were expected to enter the Bet Talmud or Bet Ha-Knesset, or House of Assembly, for the study of the **Talmud**. These schools taught languages and mathematics; such subjects as astronomy, botany, and zoology were required for certain Talmudic studies.

The highest schools of this system were the great academies of **Babylonia**, where the scholars studied and created the Talmud. One great teacher, Abba Arikha, founded an academy at Sura that lasted, with brief interruptions, for eight centuries. The academy at Sura was never idle or empty. Scholars who had to work all day studied there in the early morning and late evening. In March and September, when there was little work in the fields, the Sura academy held Kallot, or seminars, for farmers and businessmen. There were even scholarships for worthy students who could not afford to take two months off from work and travel to attend the Kallot in Sura.

The education system begun in Palestine and developed in Babylonia moved with the people wherever they went. By the 11th century, persecution and intolerance had driven the Jews out of Babylonia. The great centers dwindled and almost disappeared, and Jews set up new communities in **Spain**, **Italy**, **France**, and **Germany**. New subjects of study were added to the system, others were subtracted, without changing its core. In 12th century Arab Spain, philosophy and Arabic were added to the studies in the higher schools. In Italy the new subjects were Latin, Italian, and logic. To escape the bloody path of the **Crusades**, Jews began to migrate from Germany to Poland in the 12th century. The Kahal, or community organization, in Poland was a strong one. Education was made compulsory for children from six to thirteen years of age, and the system was controlled by a board of study called the Hevra Talmud Torah. This hevra prescribed the studies for the **heder**, or elementary private school, as well as for the **Talmud** Torah, the community free school. The yeshiva, or Talmudic academy, was also supervised by the hevra. The head, or Rosh Yeshiva, was selected by them. During the 16th, 17th, and 18th centuries, when Jewish life became constricted and was limited to the ghetto, education also narrowed, and languages and sciences were no longer studied. These subjects were reintroduced during the **Haskalah**, or enlightenment period. Education for girls was not required at any period. Yet the woman of outstanding abilities usually managed to get an education. Ordinary women shared deeply the general reverence for learning and often made great sacrifices that their sons might become scholars.

During the 20th century, Orthodoxy began providing formal Jewish education for girls and women. One of the outstanding movements working to this end is the Beth Jacob movement, which since its founding by Sara Schenirer in **Cracow** in the early 1920's has spread around the world.

Due to a shortage of books in Yemen, many children studied from one book and learned to read upside down.

Children of Kibbutz Hulata in Galilee studying art. Courtesy Zionist Archives and Library, New York City.

The average male Jew could always read and write, since even the poorest child could get an elementary education. For bright young students who had no means of support, the community provided food and shelter, so that they could devote themselves completely to study at the yeshiva. As a result, ignorance was rare among Jews. During the Middle Ages, when even princes and nobles were illiterate, the Jewish community had many scholars and honored them above other men. Until recent times, Jewish education was considered a lifetime process: the young studied all day, while the adults studied during their leisure hours, evenings, Sabbaths, and holidays. When Jews dreamed of Paradise, study held a place in their vision. (*See also* **Jewish Education in the United States.)**

EFROS, ISRAEL (1890-1981). Hebrew poet, scholar, and educator. He was born in **Poland** and immigrated to the U.S. in 1906. He wrote Hebrew poetry and translated Shakespeare into Hebrew and **Bialik** into English. In 1919 he founded the Baltimore Hebrew College. In 1955, he settled in Israel and became rector of **Tel Aviv University.**

EGYPT. Egypt's recorded history goes back to about 4000 B.C.E. A close neighbor of Israel, Egypt has been linked with Jews and their history from the beginning. The **patriarchs** all stayed in Egypt for various periods of time. Bondage in Egypt and the Exodus mark the beginnings of Jewish history. Historians believe that the first Hebrew migration to Egypt probably took place during the rule of the Semitic Hyksos dynasty of the 18th to 16th centuries B.C.E. The Tel El-Amarna tablets, discovered in 1887, show that the Pharaohs had set up governors in many towns of Canaan, evidence of their domination of the country. One of the Amarna tablets is a letter from the ruler of **Jerusalem**. In it, he complains to Pharaoh that the *Habiru*, or Hebrews, are invading and conquering the land.

Relations between Egypt and the Jewish people continued throughout the period of the Jewish Monarchy. **Solomon** married an Egyptian princess and made a trade treaty with Egypt. After Solomon's death, when the northern tribes broke off and established their own kingdom, the Pharaoh Shishak came to their aid by attacking **Jerusalem**. Two centuries later in 608 B.C.E., Josiah, King of Judah, died in battle at **Megiddo** when he tried to block the march of Pharaoh Necho through his territory. Josiah's son Jehoahaz ruled Judah for only three months. The Egyptians deposed him and set his brother Jehoiakim on the throne.

After the First **Temple** was destroyed in 586 B.C.E., the exiled prophet **Jeremiah** found Jewish colonies in Upper and Lower Egypt. Papyri, discovered in Elephantine, an island on the Nile, describe the life of its Jewish colony and its Jewish temple in the 5th century B.C.E. After **Alexander the Great** conquered Egypt in 332 B.C.E., Jewish immigrants streamed into Egypt where they prospered and established themselves under Hellenist rule. The Alexandrian Jewish community grew until in time it numbered almost one million; in **Alexandria**, a great Hellenistic Jewish civilization developed (*see* **Hellenism**). Jews spoke Greek and tried to work out a viable compromise between Jewish and Greek culture. The philosopher **Philo** is the best known representative of this movement. During the Syrian oppression of Judea, the refugee High Priest Onias founded a Temple in Heliopolis, a city near the Nile. At this time in the 3rd century B.C.E., the **Bible**, translated into Greek at Alexandria, known as the **Septuagint** version, came to exert a great influence, serving both the Jews of the Hellenistic period and the rising Christian Church.

At the same time, the security of Egyptian Jewry was threatened by a great deal of anti-Semitic feeling among the Greek population. Sometimes Greek riots and attacks on the Jewish community had to be stopped by the governing Roman authorities. Developments in Judea also influenced the security of Egyptian Jewry. Refugees from the Judean revolt against Rome stirred up a Jewish rebellion in Egypt in 72 C.E., and again in 115-117 C.E., when Alexandrian Jewry was massacred.

As the Roman Empire became Christian, the situation of Egyptian Jewry deteriorated. In 415 C.E., Alexandrian masses, inflamed by Bishop Cyril, broke out in violent riots and forced hundreds of Jews to undergo baptism. During the following two centuries, the Alexandrian Jewish community dwindled in importance. With the Arab invasion of 639 the situation improved slightly. Under Moslem rule, the community, centered mainly in the new city of Cairo, became Arab in character and culture. Documents found in the Cairo **Genizah**, a storehouse of worn-out books, describe in detail the life of the community. Though the traditional Moslem code treated Jews as inferiors, Jewish cultural life reached a high level. **Saadiah Gaon**, the greatest scholar of his day, was a native of the Fayyum in Egypt. The Jewish community came to be governed by an **exilarch**, and significant academies of learning were established. Except for the period of bitter persecution under Caliph Hakim from 995-1021, conditions were favorable. When **Maimonides** arrived in Egypt in 1165, the great scholar found an appreciative Jewish environment. Maimonides became court physician to the Sultan Saladin, and a number of his great works were written during this period. Maimonides took a leading part in Jewish life in Egypt, and his descendants were dominant there for a long time.

After the Turkish occupation of Egypt in 1517, the Egyptian Jewish community managed to sustain itself, but did not achieve economic or cultural advancement. It was not until the opening of the Suez Canal in 1869 that economic prosperity and Western influence reached the Jewish community, then numbering about 75,000. Many Jews became wealthy businessmen, even pashas and senators. The majority, however, remained poor peddlers and craftsmen, segregated in the Jewish quarters of Alexandria and

Cairo. During World War I, many Jews from Palestine fled to Egypt to escape Turkish persecution. Their influence and the development of Arab nationalism stirred Egyptian Jewry from its lethargy. They began to migrate to Palestine and Europe, and the community declined. Many Egyptian Jews who had European citizenship also suffered because of the general anti-European reaction of the period, and because an anti-Zionist policy had been adopted.

After the establishment of the State of **Israel** in 1948, the position of the Jews in Egypt became increasingly difficult. Jews were arrested and robbed. After the Sinai Campaign of 1956 President Gamal Abdel Nasser passed a law that in effect deprived all Zionists of Egyptian citizenship. Jews were imprisoned and expelled for security reasons. Large numbers of Jews were able to immigrate to Israel by way of Europe.

In 1967 and again in 1973 (*see* **Six-Day War** *and* **Yom Kippur War**), Egypt went to war against Israel with the avowed aim of destroying the Jewish state. In November 1977, Anwar el-Sadat, who had succeeded Nasser as president of Egypt in 1970, surprised the world with the announcement that he would visit Israel and discuss the possibility of peace with the Jewish State. He arrived in Jerusalem late on November 18, 1977, and on the next day addressed the **Knesset**. This marked the beginning of peace negotiations between Egypt and Israel. In September 1978, Sadat met with Israel's prime minister Menachem **Begin** under the auspices of U.S. President Jimmy Carter at Camp David, Md., to draw up a framework for a peace treaty. A formal peace treaty, the Camp David Accords, was signed in 1979 by Menachem Begin, Anwar Sadat, and Jimmy Carter. However, Sadat was assassinated in October 1981 by Arab fundamentalists who opposed his policy of Israeli-Egyptian rapprochement. Despite the treaty, relations between Israel and Egypt have remained strained under the leadership of Sadat's successor, Hosni Mubarak. Now in its second decade, the Peace Treaty between Israel and Egypt has endured.

Egypt's Jewish population at the time of the establishment of the State of Israel was about 90,000. In 1998, there were only about 200.

EHRLICH, PAUL (1845-1915). German scientist. His achievements—discovery of the method of staining the white blood cells, his research in the field of bacteriology, and particularly his discovery of a drug to cure syphilis—made him world-famous. The originator of modern chemotherapy, in 1908 he shared the **Nobel Prize** in medicine and physiology with Elie Mitchnikoff.

Jonathan Eibeschütz. Anonymous engraving.

EIBESCHÜTZ, JONATHAN (1690-1764). Renowned rabbi and Kabbalist. Born in Cracow, **Poland**, he gained fame as a Talmudist early in his life. At age 21, he became head of a yeshiva in Prague. His comments on the **Shulhan Arukh** and his sermons, collected in his *Yaarot Devash* (Forests of Honey), are classics in rabbinic literature.

EICHMANN, ADOLF. *See* **Holocaust**.

EIGHTEEN BENEDICTIONS. *See* **Prayer**.

EINHORN, DAVID. *See* **Baltimore**.

Albert Einstein. Courtesy Yeshiva University.

EINSTEIN, ALBERT (1879-1955). Theoretical physicist. The most outstanding physicist of modern times, Albert Einstein was almost as revered for his honesty, humility, and humanitarianism as for his theories about the nature of the universe. Born in Ulm, **Germany**, he received his scientific education in **Switzerland**, where he was naturalized in 1901. While working at the Patent Office in Berne, he prepared four scientific papers which gained him international acclaim before he was 26. In the years that followed, Einstein lectured and taught in **Prague**, Zurich, Leyden, and Berlin. In 1916, he published his famous general theory of relativity, which has been described as "the greatest intellectual revolution since Newton"; six years later he was awarded the Nobel Prize for his work on photo-electric effects. With the rise of Hitler to power in 1933, he left Berlin, where he had held a distinguished position since 1914, and settled in the U.S. From 1933 until his death in 1955, he served as professor of theoretical physics at Princeton's Institute of Advanced Studies.

In 1939, Einstein called the attention of President Franklin D. Roosevelt to the possibilities of atomic warfare; his own theories played a crucial part in unbinding the energies of the atom. It was, in fact, the great irony of Einstein's life that his work for the advancement of human understanding of the world had also advanced human capacity for deadly warfare. Having experienced **anti-Semitism** early in life and realizing the evils of Prussian militarism, Einstein had early become a crusader for peace and harmony in human relations. He did not hesitate to speak out against injustice. After World War I, he headed the International Committee for Intellectual Cooperation of the League of Nations, withdrawing in protest against the League's failure to take strong measures against Italian Fascism. As the clouds of Nazism gathered over Germany, Einstein spoke out against anti-Semitism and the Nazi threat to intellectual freedom. In the U. S., too, Einstein was an outspoken defender of freedom of thought. To the end, he advocated international cooperation, and even world government, in the hope that the human race might learn to live in peace. He devoted much energy during the last decade of his life to making the world aware of the great dangers threatening it, as the result of his own work in discovering the destructive potential of atomic power.

Einstein was never a practicing Jew. From the 1920's onward, however, he expressed his devotion to his people by dedicating considerable effort to **Zionism** and especially to the development of the **Hebrew University** in Jerusalem. He first visited the U.S. in 1921 on a tour with Chaim **Weizmann** on behalf of the university, and sat on its board of governors until his death. After the death of Weizmann, Einstein was proposed as a candidate for the presidency of the State of **Israel**; Einstein refused on the ground that he was not qualified to fill the position.

ELAT. In Hebrew, *terebinth*. Seaport on the Gulf of Elat, or Aqaba; a finger of the Red Sea, where the borders of **Israel**, **Egypt**, Jordan, and Saudi Arabia meet. About 950 B.C.E. **Solomon** built the twin cities of Elat and Ezion Geber for his navy and copper industry. With the discovery of a sea route around Africa to India, Elat was abandoned. Developed by Israel as a seaport window to East African and Asian markets, Elat now boasts a growing population of 31,300. The nearby Timna copper mines are expanding production, and the port is growing. Elat is also a winter resort, noted for its coral reefs and exotic tropical fish.

ELDERS OF ZION. *See* **Anti-Semitism**.

ELEAZAR BEN AZARYAH. *See* **Tannaim**.

ELIEZER BEN HYRCANUS. *See* **Tannaim**.

ELIJAH. The prophet Elijah the Tishbite lived at the time of **Ahab** from 874-853 B.C.E., the king who "did what is evil in the eyes of the Lord." Ahab married the Phoenician princess **Jezebel** and permitted her to build an altar and sanctuary to **Baal** in **Samaria**.

The biblical story of Elijah, from his first startling appearance before the king, prophesying drought in the land, to his end when he is whirled to heaven in a chariot of fire, established the image of the prophet for ages to come. A gaunt figure clothed in goatskin, Elijah prophesied drought and disappeared into the desert to be fed by ravens. When the punishing drought came, the people cried out for rain. Yet the king did not forbid the idol worship, and Elijah challenged the Baal priests to prove that theirs was the true god. The dramatic public duel on Mt. Carmel between Elijah and 450 priests of Baal ended in the humiliation of the latter. The Lord answered Elijah's prayers. The king and people saw a fire descend

Elijah Carried Off in a Chariot of Fire, by Gustav Doré.

from heaven to consume the offering on Elijah's altar. Then a heavy rain fell and the drought ended (I Kings 18).

Still, the struggle went on. Elijah had to flee from the anger of Queen Jezebel who threatened his life. Ahab desired the fine vineyard of Naboth who refused to sell it. Jezebel had Naboth executed on false charges. When Ahab came to take possession of the dead man's vineyard, Elijah appeared before him and cried out: "Hast thou murdered and also taken possession?...In the place where the dogs licked the blood of Naboth shall the dogs lick thy blood, yes thine also." (I Kings 21:19.) Elijah predicted a grim end for Jezebel and the punishment of the Kingdom of **Israel**. Hazael, the king of Aram, made war upon Israel, and only the "7,000" who "did not bow down to Baal" survived.

But in the closing verses in the Book of **Malachi**, the stern figure of Elijah began to grow milder. Here, Elijah was portrayed as the prophet who descended from heaven before the great Day of the Lord to bring peace to the earth. Elijah's appearance to usher in the Messianic age was discussed in the **Talmud**. When the Talmudic masters had a difference of opinion and could not arrive at a decision, they tabled the discussion by deferring it "till the appearance of Elijah the prophet." Since the time of the Talmud, Jewish literature and legend have presented Elijah as comforter of the poor and the suffering. He appears miraculously when the need is greatest; he reveals himself to mystics, or students of the **Kabbalah**, and to Hasidic wonder rabbis to teach them to reveal the secrets of the future. To this day, at the Seder table on **Passover**, a special cup is filled with wine in honor of the prophet.

ELIJAH, GAON OF VILNA (1720-1797). Great Talmudist and revered spiritual leader of Lithuanian Jewry. Tradition has it that at

Elijah, Gaon of Vilna.

the age of 10 he was already well versed in the **Talmud** and had outgrown the need for instructors. The title "Gaon" was given him because of his extraordinary genius. The Gaon brought a new approach to Talmud study by stressing the factual and logical interpretation of the Bible text and Jewish law. In brief and concise marginal notes to Talmudic and Midrashic literature he shed light on the most difficult passages. His power of concentration and perseverance was extraordinary. It is related that for 50 years he slept no more than two hours a night. Although he gave his entire life to sacred studies, he recognized the necessity for secular learning. This recognition represented a revolutionary idea for the rabbis of his time, who generally considered worldly study as damaging to the traditional Jewish way of life. He wrote a work on mathematics and a Hebrew grammar.

Elijah's fame spread quickly, but he remained a most unassuming and modest man. Sternly pious, he led a life of self-denial, shunning all fame and offers of rabbinical posts. He lived in seclusion on a tiny allowance granted to him and his family by the town's Jewish community. The spread of **Hasidism** drew him out of his retirement. He feared that this new movement would lead its followers astray, and therefore he advocated the harshest measures against them. His favorite pupil, Rabbi Hayim of Volozhin, established a rabbinical college at Volozhin where the Gaon of Vilna's methods of study were put into practice.

ELISHA (Late 9th century B.C.E.). Biblical prophet on whose shoulders **Elijah** placed his mantle as his successor (I Kings 19:19). Elisha was the son of a wealthy landowner who lived east of the Jordan. Like Elijah, he wanted to rid Israel of **Baal** worship. He therefore secretly anointed Jehu, a general in the army, as king of Israel. Jehu led a revolt against Jehoram, son of **Ahab**, destroying him as well as his mother Jezebel, the idolatrous queen. Then Jehu exterminated the priests of Baal.

Elisha mingled with the people, helping them and winning their love. No other prophet in Israel is reputed to have performed as many miracles as Elisha. He is said to have divided the waters of the Jordan, resurrected a child, and healed the Syrian captain Naaman of leprosy. The many stories of Elisha's miracle-working reflect the people's love for the prophet who healed the sick and helped the poor. (II Kings 1-9:4, 13:14-21.)

ELISHA BEN ABUYAH (ca. 80-150 C.E.). Scholar and teacher of the Law. Though he was one of the most learned men of his time, Jewish tradition regards him as a traitor and apostate. He was the son of a wealthy Jerusalem family, and excelled early in both secular and rabbinic learning. He lectured at the academies of **Jerusalem** and was a close friend of Rabbi **Akiba**, as well as teacher and friend of Rabbi **Meir**. He is said to have turned to Greek mysticism and to have informed on his fellow-Jews to the Romans. Because of this reprehensible act his name is scarcely ever mentioned in the **Talmud**, all his sayings being attributed to Aher, "the other." Modern scholars believe that he was a **Sadducee** rather than a convert to a gentile religion. This, they feel, would have been sufficient ground for his excommunication by the dominant **Pharisee** faction, which demanded complete conformity during a period when the Jewish people were struggling for spiritual survival.

EL SALVADOR. Smallest of the Central American republics. Only 350 Jews of a total population of more than 4 million live in the capital, San Salvador. There are Zionist groups and a central, legally recognized organization, the *Comunidad Israelita*, or Jewish Community.

ELUL. Last month of the Jewish civil calendar. Preceding the High Holy Days, it is a month of spiritual preparation and penitence.

EMANCIPATION. The removal of restrictions against the Jews in the western world during the late 18th to early 20th centuries, especially during the 19th century. A major factor in this process was the French Revolution in 1789, which brought emancipation to the general population of **France** and Europe. Until that time, Jews had lived for more than a thousand years under the restrictive rule of Christian Europe, which had prevented Jews from fully participating in the social and economic order, forced them to live in secluded areas called ghettos, and in effect accorded them the status of outsiders. In the New World, particularly in North America, the Jews enjoyed much better status than in Europe. But gradually after 1789, the civil, social, and economic status of Jews throughout Europe, beginning in western Europe, began to improve, while in **Russia** this did not occur until after the Communist Revolution in 1917. This is not to say that Jews in Europe in the 19th and early 20th centuries achieved equality. While European societies changed during that time, attitudes toward Jews and Judaism remained ambiguous at best and outright hostile at worst. Emancipation in Europe did not realize the idealistic goals of the French or Russian revolutions. Rather, it ended in the death fields and death camps of World War II.

EMEK JEZREEL. *See* **Israel**.

EMUNAH WOMEN OF AMERICA. Part of the World Religious Zionist Women's Organization. Organized in 1948 as Hapoel Hamizrachi Women's Organization, the name of Emunah was adopted in 1978 to affect a unity with its sister countries throughout the world.

It is a national movement of 25,000 religious Zionists, encompassing 80 chapters throughout the U.S. Emunah Women of America supports an extensive network of 187 institutions in Israel which includes daycare centers, vocational training schools, teacher schools, and children's villages. Additionally, Emunah provides social welfare services through its "Self-Help" programs for indigent and immigrant mothers, parental guidance programs, absorption and integration services for new immigrants, psychological counseling, community centers, and aid to the elderly.

ENGLAND (UNITED KINGDOM). Island Kingdom off the northwestern coast of Europe. In 1998, it was the home of 300,000 Jews, less than one percent of the total population of more than 57 million. The first Jews in England were financiers who followed William the Conqueror from **France** at the time of the Norman Conquest in 1066. By the middle of the following century, their number had grown to 5,000, with thriving communities in **London**, Oxford, Cambridge, Norwich, Winchester, Lincoln, and other towns. Within another century, there were 70 "Jew Streets" in England. With the expulsion from England in 1290, 16,000 Jews had to seek homes elsewhere.

During this period, England lived under the feudal system. As in all feudal societies, Jews had no official rights. Officially, they were the property, or "chattel," of the king. Because they paid heavy taxes to his treasury, it was in his interest to protect them. But the king was not a kind protector. When he needed money, he had no scruples about confiscating the property of "his Jews," or taxing them to the point of bankruptcy. Despite these handicaps, English Jewry prospered for about 80 years after the conquest and suffered no serious persecution. The majority were not rich, but some of them were great bankers and merchants who founded Talmudic academies and wielded much influence with the king. Before 100 years had passed, however, anti-Jewish feeling began to emerge. In 1144, a charge of ritual murder—the claim that Jews had killed a Christian to use his blood in **Passover** ceremonies—at Norwich set the pattern for oppression throughout the 12th century. An especially violent outburst during the Third Crusade from 1189 to 1190 finally forced Richard I, also called Richard the Lion-Hearted, to take up arms against the rioters. Richard also declared that anyone harming the Jews was sinning against the Crown. Later, to assure a steady flow of gold into his treasury, he set up a special office, the Exchequer of the Jews, which registered all loans and supervised the collection of debts. Under other circumstances, this office might have been a blessing. England, however, was torn by conflict between king and barons, so that the King's Jews were naturally the target of baronial hatred. As a result, the reigns of John from 1199 to 1216 and Henry III from 1216 to 1277 were marked by incessant persecution and exploitation.

By the time Edward I took the throne in 1277, English Jews were in dire straits. Italian bankers had largely replaced them as moneylenders, and they had lost the right to lease land. Church leaders, anxious to expel them, succeeded in convincing the King to take this drastic step by joining with the nobility and promising him one-tenth of all Jewish property. In 1290, on November 1, the Feast of All Saints, the entire Jewish community of 16,000, penniless and with little hope of welcome anywhere, was forced to take the weary path of exile, seeking homes across the sea.

For the following 350 years, England had no Jewish community. The resettlement of Jews in England took place in 1656 when England was in the throes of the Puritan Revolution. Oliver Cromwell, the Lord Protector, believed that Jewish merchants would stimulate English trade. But the merchants of London, fearing competition from Jewish merchants, refused to accept the plan. Nonetheless, an unusual circumstance led to the founding of a Jewish community: England happened to be at war with Spain and had ordered all Spanish property confiscated. Among the goods seized were those of a **Marrano** residing in London. In order to regain his possessions, this man declared that he was not a Spaniard, rather a Portuguese Jew. Together with seven other Marranos he petitioned Cromwell. The Lord Protector, eager to open the country to Jews, accepted their petition. Once it was known that Jews were living openly in the city, other **Sephardic** merchants settled there. Although Parliament had not approved the change, the township of London immediately permitted them to build a synagogue and sold them land for a cemetery. By 1662, there were more than 100 congregants in the synagogue, and two years later, the first Jewish school was founded.

The first Sephardic settlers were followed by Jews from **Germany** and Central Europe. By 1690, there were enough **Ashkenazic** Jews to found a separate synagogue, and by 1700, there were 500 Jews in the capital. In 1760, the community, which had no political rights, founded a **Board of Deputies of British Jews** to handle relations with the government. By 1753, a "Jew Bill," proposing equal rights for the Jews, had been introduced in Parliament. The bill was defeated, but the struggle for political rights had begun. At the beginning of the 19th century, the total number of Jews was 25,000, among them a number of families noted for their wealth and

The Great Synagogue in London. Cantor Kusevitsky intones the prayer for the Royal Family. Courtesy British Information Service.

> *"Who is wise? He who learns from everyone. Who is strong? He who controls his temper."*
>
> — ETHICS OF THE FATHERS

accomplishments. With the general liberalization of political and social life in England, it was inevitable that Jews would succeed in the quest for equality. The 1832 Reform Bill granted Jews and Catholics the right to vote in parliamentary elections. Four years later, the Board of Deputies of British Jews was recognized by the government. By 1858, Baron Lionel de Rothschild was admitted to the House of Commons. In 1872, the last handicap was removed with admission of Jews to England's great universities.

Political and social rights were gained on the eve of another revolution in the life of English Jewry. While the battle for equality was being waged in England, Jews of Eastern Europe were experiencing political persecution and increasing economic hardship. By the early 1880's, the situation had become so unbearable that masses of East European Jews were forced to flee to the West. Many settled in England. Between 1881 and 1905, when the English government imposed restrictions on immigration, between 100,000 and 150,000 Polish and Russian Jews were added to a community that in 1881 had totaled only 60,000.

Most of the immigrants settled in Whitechapel in the East End of London. Others found their way to Manchester, Leeds, Glasgow, Liverpool, and other cities where Jewish communities had not existed before. The immigrants earned their living as tailors, small manufacturers, and peddlers or petty traders. They were active in establishing a ready-made garment industry. Isolated in their own districts and speaking little or no English, they tended to form communities of their own, with Yiddish newspapers, theaters, clubs, and synagogues like the ones they had known "at home." They therefore had little basis for communication with the older, well-established community. The old community, for its part, though suspicious of the newcomers, did its best to help the newcomers adjust through the Board of Deputies and the Jewish Board of Guardians.

The adjustment of the newcomers was successful. Their children attended English schools and within a generation had entered into the current of English life. The solidarity of the two communities was speeded by the fact that all of England was undergoing a social revolution. The gap between rich and poor was narrowing, and class distinctions were becoming less rigid.

Zionism also provided a common cause for the two sectors of the community. At first the old-timers were more conservative and less willing to exert their influence with the government on their behalf. This situation came to an end only when a group of Zionists, comprised of immigrants and led by Chaim **Weizmann**, a Russian Jew naturalized in 1910, succeeded in influencing the government to grant the **Balfour Declaration** in 1917 and in promising the establishment of a Jewish National Home in Palestine. From then on the influence of the "newcomers" was recognized, and Zionism began to play an important part in the official life of English Jewry. From 1919 to 1948, when England occupied Palestine under a Mandate from the League of Nations, the Jewish community actively attempted to influence the English government in favor of the Jewish cause in Palestine.

Today, about 70% of English Jewry is self-employed, chiefly in the professions and small business. Except for a brief flare-up of Nazi propaganda in the 1930's and a short period of resentment against Jews during the struggle between the Palestine Jewish community and the British army in the 1940's, **anti-Semitism** has not troubled the community in recent decades. England was, in fact, the only major West European country which did not suffer seriously from anti-Semitism during the Nazi era.

The center of Anglo-Jewish life is **London**, home of 210,000 Jews. Jewish life in the capital centers around the United Synagogue, an organization of Orthodox synagogues headed by a chief rabbi. More than half of all English Jews throughout the country belong to synagogues, most of them Orthodox, with smaller non-Orthodox movements.

ENGLISH LITERATURE. The treatment of Jewish characters that appear throughout English literature runs the gamut from blatant **anti-Semitism** to great respect and admiration. Shylock in Shakespeare's *The Merchant of Venice*, perhaps the most famous Jewish character in English literature, is commonly seen as an evil person, yet a closer examination reveals that there is more than meets the eye. In Dickens's *Oliver Twist*, Fagin the Jew is a corrupter of youth, yet other Dickens Jewish characters are virtuous. Some English writers, like Hilaire Belloc are outright anti-Semitic, while T.S. Eliot may be considered a latent one. On the other hand, great English poets of the 19th century such as Wordsworth, Byron, and Browning admired and idealized Jews and their culture, and Sir Walter Scott presented the romantic figure of Rebecca in *Ivanhoe*. For the most part, Jews in English literature have been presented as extremes of either virtue or vice, rather than realistic flesh and blood people with a mixture of both.

ENLIGHTENMENT. *See* **Haskalah**.

ENTEBBE RAID. On July 4, 1976, during the height of Arab terrorism against **Israel**, an Air France plane was hijacked by Palestinian and German terrorists in Greece and taken to Entebbe in eastern Africa. After releasing the non-Jewish passengers, some 102 passengers, mostly Israelis, were held hostage. Israel sent an air rescue force which flew 2,500 miles at night over Arab and African countries, landed at the Entebbe airport, and rescued the hostages. The commander of the force, Lt. Colonel Yonatan Netanyahu, was the only Israeli casualty.

EPHOD. *See* **Kohen**.

EPHRAIM. Younger of **Joseph**'s sons; founder of the warlike "half tribe of Ephraim" that settled almost in the middle of the Promised Land on a narrow stretch between the Jordan and the Mediterranean. **Joshua**, the leader who succeeded **Moses**, came from the tribe of Ephraim. The first king of Israel after the division of the kingdom into two rival states, Jeroboam ben Nebat, was also an Ephraimite. So important was the part played by this tribe in the affairs of Israel that Ephraim came to be another name for the northern kingdom.

Emblem of the tribe of Ephraim.

Sir Jacob Epstein. Courtesy British Information Service.

EPSTEIN, SIR JACOB (1880-1959). Sculptor. Born of immigrant parents in **New York**, he moved to **England** where his early work in stone was at first controversial. However, in 1954, he was knighted. Epstein chose biblical subjects such as **Adam**, **Jacob** and the Angel, and Lucifer, for his monumental sculptures. He is also widely known for his busts which, dispensing with superficialities and nonessentials, analyze the sitter's personality. Those who have sat for him include George Bernard Shaw, Winston Churchill, Jawaharlal Nehru, Albert **Einstein**, and Chaim **Weizmann**.

ERETZ ISRAEL. *See* **Israel, State of.**

ESAU. *See* **Jacob.**

ESHKOL (SHKOLNIK), LEVI (1895-1969). Israeli labor leader and statesman. Born in the **Ukraine**, he settled in Palestine in 1914, where he worked in various kibbutzim and became active in HaPoel HaTzair (*see* **Labor Zionism**). Mapai member of the **Knesset** since 1949, he was Minister of Agriculture from 1951 to 1952 and Minister of Finance from 1952 to 1963 before becoming Prime Minister and Minister of Defense in 1963. During his term of office the **Six-Day War** broke out, and he turned over the defense portfolio to Moshe **Dayan**. He remained prime minister until his death.

ESSENES. Sect of pious, ascetic Jews during the time of the Second **Temple**. Evidence of the existence of the sect dates from the **Hasmonean** period. The members of the group dedicated themselves to a life of simplicity and purity. They lived close to nature and shared in common their worldly possessions. The Essenes settled in isolated areas in the Judean desert and in the vicinity of the **Dead Sea.** They eked out a modest living by cultivating the land and through their craftsmanship. Trade was prohibited for they considered it dishonest. Similarly, they refused to produce instruments of death and destruction.

The Essenes were known for their strict observance of the ritual of daily immersion in cold water. Purity of the soul was made conditional upon purity of body. The whole community ate together. Their meals, consisting of bread and vegetables, represented a solemn ritual. Keeping absolute silence throughout their meals, they resembled priests performing their rites during the sacred services in the Temple. New members who wished to join the sect had to go through rigorous tests and initiation rites in order to prove their worthiness. Patience, perseverance, modesty, righteousness, purity of character, and above all, love of truth and readiness to aid the poor and downtrodden were the qualities required of every candidate.

The Essenes' closeness to nature led them to recognize medicinal herbs, and they acquired a reputation as healers and soothsayers. The Essenes refused to divulge their secrets, rules, or knowledge even under threat of death. Although opposed to war, they hated oppression and many joined the fight against the Romans. In recent years, scrolls found in caves near the Dead Sea revealed a rich and valuable literature of sects similar to the Essenes.

ESTHER, BOOK OF. The *megillah*, or scroll of Esther, tells the story of the beautiful Esther, whose Hebrew name was Hadassah, or Myrtle. She was an orphan who lived with her wise cousin **Mordecai** in the capital city Shushan. When King Ahasuerus (thought to be Xerxes, 485-464 B.C.E.) deposed Queen Vashti, he chose Esther to take her place. Neither the King nor his wicked minister Haman the Agagite, knew that Esther was Jewish. Haman plotted to destroy all the Jews of Persia. Queen Esther, after fasting and praying for guidance, pleaded with the King and saved her people from destruction. Purim is the festival celebrated to commemorate this deliverance. The Fast of Esther is observed on the 13th of Adar in memory of the three days the Jews of Persia fasted at Esther's request. The Scroll of Esther is read in the synagogue on the evening and the morning of Purim.

Scroll of Esther. Courtesy The Jewish Museum, New York City.

ETHICS, BOOK OF. *See* **Hebrew Literature**.

ETHICS (OR SAVINGS) OF THE FATHERS. In Hebrew, *Pirke Avot*. Section of the Mishnah. This book is a collection of moral and religious teachings by the rabbis who contributed to the Mishnah. One of the six chapters from the Ethics of the Fathers is read on the afternoon of every Sabbath between **Passover** and **Rosh Hashanah**. The original purpose for the compilation of the Ethics was to teach right conduct and to show the divine source of the traditional law. An enlarged version is called the *Avot de Rabbi Natan*.

ETHICAL WILLS. Rather than a legal document, an ethical will in Judaism refers to instructions written down during one's lifetime for one's children on how to preserve certain aspects of the Jewish heritage or how to live according to certain precepts. Such instructions, albeit verbal, are common in the Bible. During and after the Middle Ages ethical wills appeared in written form, some of which became important historical documents (such as **Ibn Tibbon**'s). Recently in the U.S. the tradition of writing an ethical will was revived.

ETHIOPIAN JEWS. *See* **Falashas**.

ETROG. *See* **Sukkot**.

EVE. The first woman according to the Bible, created from one of **Adam**'s ribs. Eve is tempted by the snake to taste of the forbidden fruit, whereby the first human couple is banished from the Garden of Eden.

EVIL EYE. Superstition dating back to the **Talmud** and common among non-Jews as well, according to which someone may be cursed by someone else's evil glance. Amulets were used to ward off the evil eye.

EXILARCH. *Resh Galuta*, or Prince of the Captivity. Title held by the head of the Babylonian Jewish community until the 11th century C.E. Jews of **Babylonia** had the right to govern themselves according to Jewish law, and the exilarch therefore appointed judges and was the court of final appeal. The exilarch collected and allocated taxes and represented the Jewish community at the Babylonian court. Since, in addition, the exilarch claimed direct descent from the House of David and for a thousand years the office was transmitted from father to son, they were personages of great authority. (*See* **Babylonia**.)

EXILE. *See* **Galut**.

EXODUS. From Greek, meaning "going out." In Hebrew the second book of the **Bible** is called *Shemot*, or Names, because it begins with the words, "Now these are the names of the sons of Israel, who came into **Egypt** with **Jacob**." Exodus tells the story of the Egyptian oppression of the Israelites, the appearance of Moses, the ten plagues, and the exodus from Egypt. It describes how God revealed Himself in thunder and lightning to the Children of Israel standing at the foot of Mt. Sinai and gave them first the **Ten Commandments**, the laws they were to live by, and finally the covenant, or promise of the Land of Canaan. The story of the **Golden Calf** and the making of the **Tabernacle** are in the closing chapters of the book.

EZEKIEL. Literally, whom God makes strong. Third of the major prophets, Ezekiel, son of Buzi, was a younger contemporary of **Jeremiah**. He too witnessed the destruction of **Jerusalem** and Judea, and went into exile to **Babylonia**. Like Jeremiah, he also believed deeply in each person's individual responsibility to God. His prophecies have great poetic beauty and mystic power; the mystical concept of the Divine Chariot in the **Kabbalah** drew its imagery from Ezekiel's first vision. His most famous chapter, 37, is the symbolic vision of a valley of dry bones that are resurrected and rise again as "a mighty army," a prophecy of the rebirth of **Israel**.

EZRA, BOOK OF. This biblical book tells of **Ezra the Scribe** who led the Jews who had returned from Babylonian exile to Judea in the 5th century B.C.E.

EZRA THE SCRIBE. One of two leaders of the return from the Babylonian captivity in the 5th century B.C.E. He was a teacher of the Law and, presumably, author of the Book of **Ezra** in the **Bible**. About 458 B.C.E., 60 years after the Return and the rebuilding of the **Temple**, social and religious conditions in Judea deteriorated, causing great concern among Babylonian Jewry. Ezra, a priest and learned scribe, or *sofer*, led a mission of Babylonian Jewish notables to Judea to correct this condition. He carried an authorization from King Artaxerxes to appoint officials and act as an administrator. Ezra acted vigorously; he instituted religious reforms that preserved the identity and continuity of the Jewish people. By his act, the scribes took over the responsibility of teaching the people. Ezra called an assembly of the people in the Temple courts where portions of the Torah were read out loud to them. The **Levites** circulated among the people explaining the text, and the people pledged obedience. This was the First Great Assembly, an institution that continued for about two centuries. Not the least of Ezra's achievements was the custom he began of reading Portions from the Torah on Sabbaths, Mondays, and Thursdays. This was a form of worship and teaching which spread from the Temple to synagogues all over the Land. It is no wonder that, in the Talmud, Ezra has been compared to **Moses**.

FABLES. *See* **Hebrew Literature.**

FALASHAS. Ethiopian Jews living in separate small villages west of Lake Taana. Although Christian missionaries succeeded in converting tens of thousands, almost 20,000 remained true to their faith. By 1993, most had been brought to **Israel** through a special rescue operation. Their absorption into Israeli society was hindered by their differing Jewish customs. Falashas, meaning foreigners or invaders, is considered a derogatory term.

An art instructor working with a newly-arrived Ethiopian first grader. Courtesy AMIT Women.

FAMILY. The family unit is central to the Jewish religion and life. In biblical times, extended families lived together within a tribal structure, and polygamy was practiced. In post-biblical times, polygamy disappeared for the most part and was forbidden in Europe around the year 1000 (*see* **Gerhsom, Rabbenu**). Among both European and Sephardic Jews in **Israel** and elsewhere the tradition of extended families living in the same community and maintaining strong ties has continued to this day. In the U.S., however, because of the general trend of young adults relocating due to career opportunities, the extended family structure has broken down, negatively impacting Jewish continuity. The synagogue, especially through the **havurah** movement since the 1970's, has had a certain measure of success in addressing this problem.

FARMERS. *See* **Agriculture.**

FAST DAYS. Fasting has always been a part of the profound process of soul purification for Jews. Purity of thought and action were considered the key to happiness in both this world and the next. According to Jewish belief, God keeps a strict accounting of each person's deeds, and in accordance with this record, He metes out justice. If one wishes to ward off divine punishment, he must repent of his sins and cleanse himself of them. When he repents, he first recognizes his transgressions and confesses them to God. This may be done at all times, but is especially auspicious during the Ten Days of Awe and Repentance following the New Year. Therefore the prayers of these days include long confessions of sin and pleading for forgiveness, chanted by the congregation in unison.

In addition to confession and repentance, man must actively atone, or make up, for his misdeeds. The chief way of atoning is the fast, in which man "torments his flesh" and begs forgiveness. **Yom Kippur**, the Day of Atonement, is the chief fast day when observant Jews abstain from food and drink for 24 hours. Pious Jews, however, observe additional fast days. Mondays and Thursdays are favored for this purpose, since they are the days when the **Torah** is read in the synagogue. Any other day may be chosen for fasting, with the exception of **Sabbath** and holidays, when fasting is forbidden. When a fast day falls on a Sabbath its observance is

Painting of a Jewish family by Max Oppenheimer. Courtesy The Jewish Museum, New York.

postponed until the next day, except in the case of Yom Kippur, which takes precedence over the Sabbath.

In addition to the fasts of purification and atonement, there are a series of fast days that are associated with mournful events in Jewish history, especially with the fall of Jerusalem and the destruction of the Temple. Since it is believed that these catastrophes were punishments for the sins of Israel, such fast days are occasions for repentance as well as mourning. They are marked by fasting and the recitation of special prayers and lamentations. Their sadness, however, is tempered by faith that the Messiah was born on the day the Temple was destroyed, and will one day come to redeem the people of Israel from the misery of the exile that began with the Destruction.

The most mournful of these fast days, and the "blackest day in the Jewish calendar," is *Tisha b'Av*, or the Ninth of Av. Tisha b'Av is the anniversary of the destruction of both Temples: the First by Nebuchadnezzar in 586 B.C.E., the Second by Titus in 70 C.E. The fast lasts from sundown of the eighth of Av to sunset the next day. During the morning hours until noon, both work and study are forbidden. The Book of Lamentations, the Prophet **Jeremiah**'s outpouring of grief at the destruction of the First Temple, is chanted. Many *kinnot*, or lamentations, of later origin are also read. Some of these recall other calamities which befell Jews on this day, such as the massacres of whole Jewish communities during the **Crusades**.

Three other fasts are observed in commemoration of events connected with the destruction of the Temple. The 17th of Tammuz marks the day on which the enemy broke through the walls of Jerusalem and entered the city. The three-week interval between the 17th of Tammuz and Tisha b'Av are observed as weeks of mourning. The Fast of Gedaliah, on the third day of Tishri, commemorates the assassination of Gedaliah, the governor of Judea in the days that followed the destruction of the First Temple. After Gedaliah's murder, the last vestiges of self-government were taken from the Jews. The 10th of Tevet was the day on which Nebuchadnezzar began the siege of Jerusalem. These three fast days are observed from sunrise to sunset, rather than from sundown of the preceding day to sunset of that day itself.

FAST, HOWARD (1914-). American author. His many novels are based mostly on historical subjects dealing with the struggle for freedom, including *My Glorious Brothers* (about the **Maccabees**) and a biography of Haym **Salomon.** Fast was a strong advocate of communism until 1956 when he publicly broke with the Communist party.

FEDERATION OF JEWISH MEN'S CLUBS. *See* **Judaism, Conservative.**

FEIERBERG, MORDECAI ZEEV (1874-1899). Hebrew writer in **Russia**, whose novel *Le'an* (Whither) dramatized the hopelessness of Jewish life in eastern Europe at the time, thus presaging Zionism.

FEINSTEIN, MOSHE (1895-1986). The leading Orthodox rabbinical authority of his time, whose rulings on Jewish law were accepted worldwide. He headed the Tiferes Yerushalayim yeshiva in **New York** for many years. His decisions were published in a multi-volume collection titled *Igros Moshe* (Moshe's Letters).

FEINSTEIN, DIANE (1933-). U.S. Democratic Senator from **California** since 1992. She served as mayor of San Francisco and became known as a moderate liberal who, while supporting pro-choice and environmental protection, was nevertheless a hard-liner on crime and supported curbs on illegal immigration.

FELSENTHAL, BERNARD (1822-1908). American rabbi and founder of the **Jewish Publication Society** and the American Jewish Historical Society.

FERBER, EDNA (1887-1968). American writer whose book *Showboat* became a classic American musical and film. She wrote about the diversity of American life in books like *Giant* and *Ice Palace*.

FEUCHTWANGER, LION (1884-1958). German-born novelist and dramatist, famous for his book *The Jew Süss* and the trilogy about **Josephus**.

FIELDS, JACKIE. *See* **Sports**.

FINAL SOLUTION. Term used by the Nazis to describe their secret plan to murder Jews in Europe.

FINKELSTEIN, LOUIS (1895-1991). American scholar and rabbi who served as chancellor of the Conservative **Jewish Theological Seminary**. He was an expert on the post-biblical Mishnaic period.

FINLAND. European republic between **Sweden** and the former Soviet Union. In a population of 5 million, there are about 1,200 Jews, living mostly in Helsinki. Jews settled there under Swedish rule in the 18th century. After Finland became Russian territory in 1809, the only Jews permitted to settle were ex-servicemen and their families. There was never severe persecution as in Russia proper, but Jews suffered many restrictions. After the Finns gained independence in 1917, they granted the Jews full equality. All the Jews of Viipuri, which was annexed by Russia in the war of 1939-40, moved to Finnish territory. Finland was the only part of Europe under Nazi domination from 1941 to 1944 where Jews did not suffer from persecution. Most Finnish Jews are engaged in commerce and trade. Their small numbers and distance from other Jewish communities made a full Jewish life difficult.

FIRST FRUITS. *See* **Shavuot**.

FIRSTBORN, REDEEMING OF. *See* **Pidyon Ha-ben.**

FISCHER, BOBBY (1943-). In 1972, he became the first American to win the chess world championship. A grandmaster at age 15, he is considered one of the greatest chess players of all time.

FLAG, JEWISH. The word "flag" is mentioned many times in the **Bible**. Each tribe had its own standard, though there is no description of the design or color. No information is available about Jewish flags during the First or Second Commonwealth. Not until the 16th century did a specific Jewish flag appear. In 1524, Pope Clement VI received a mysterious visitor

אלת־הנצחון ניקי
GODDESS OF VICTORY
UPON THE GLOBE
SUPPORTED BY ATLAS.
FRAGMENT OF A SIMILAR STATUE

in Rome. He was David **Reubeni**, who claimed to be a forerunner of the Messiah. He brought with him a white flag, embroidered with silver and golden letters.

In modern times, Theodor **Herzl**, founder of political Zionism, suggested in the book *The Jewish State* (1895) that the Zionist organization adopt a flag showing seven gold stars against a white background. The white was to signify new and pure life, the seven stars the seven-hour workday. Instead, the Zionist movement chose a white flag with two horizontal stripes of blue and a blue Star of **David** in the center, inspired by the traditional prayer shawl. By a special act of the government, on November 12, 1948, this flag became the official standard of the new state.

FLORIDA. With close to 700,000 Jews, Florida has become the state with the third largest Jewish population in the U.S., after **New York** and **California**. The first Jew associated with Florida was Moses Levy who in 1819 sought to settle Jews there. His son David Yulee was the first Jew elected to the U.S. Congress. The first Jewish community was organized in Jacksonville in 1850, and the first synagogue was founded in Pensacola in 1875. Before the Civil War there were few Jews in Florida, but as Miami began to develop as a winter resort, a steady increase of Jewish population began. Today, there are major Jewish communities in Miami (145,000), Fort Lauderdale (174,000) Boca Raton-Delray (84,000), Hollywood (63,000), and Palm Beach (63,000). These communities support a large number of temples and synagogues, mostly Reform and Conservative, Jewish community centers, and charitable Jewish organizations.

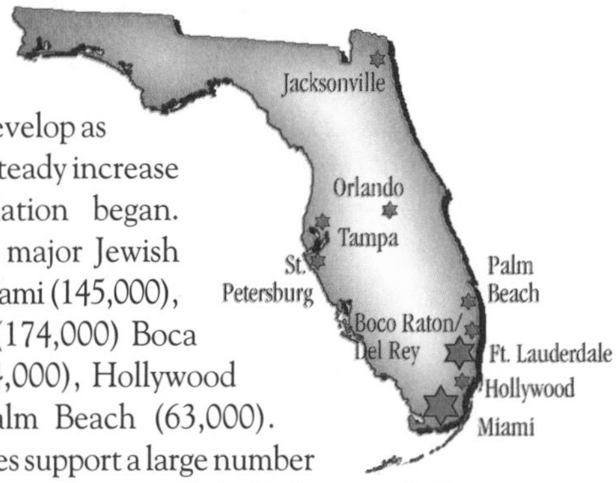

FOLKLORE. Traditions handed down for generations, including customs, legends, superstitions, beliefs, and folk songs current among the folk or common people.

Jewish folklore is varied and rich in content, partly because it has absorbed the folkways of many other peoples. In addition, the Jewish people's close tie to the **Bible** and the long periods of persecution and isolation gave rise to a distinctively Jewish folklore. The **Talmud** and **Midrash**, as well as theological, ethical, and moral works of later centuries, contain a wealth of customs and beliefs. The legend of the **Golem** and of the 36 anonymous righteous men (**Lamed Vav**) for whose sake the world survives, tales about the **Dybbuk**, and superstitions about the **Evil Eye**, or *Ayin-Hara*, are a few examples.

In the modern period beginning in the mid-18th century, Jewish **emancipation** and **assimilation** have led to the disappearance of many of these traditions. The Nazis' destruction of the Jewish culture centers in Eastern Europe during World War II aided the process. A number of individuals and institutions have collected and published volumes on Jewish folkways. The **YIVO** Institute of Jewish Research in New York and the new **Yad Vashem** Institute in Israel are currently making important contributions to the collection and study of Jewish folklore.

FOUR SPECIES. *See* **Sukkot**.

FRANCE. The first Jews to reach France probably traveled in the wake of conquering Roman legions. Historical records show that, in the 7th century, Jewish farmers, artisans, and merchants had settled in most French provinces. During the reign of Charlemagne from 768-814, Jews controlled the country's import-export trade and enjoyed considerable civil and religious freedom. A century later, when Charlemagne's empire began to break up, harsh restrictions were imposed. Then the **Crusades**, beginning in 1096, brought persecution and often death. Entire communities were martyred for their faith. The Church brought every possible charge against them. Beginning in 1171, when all the Jews of Blois were burnt at the stake, the community was beset with **blood accusations** and repeated charges that Jews desecrated Catholic forms of worship. Four years later, the French king ordered 24 wagon loads of the Talmud burnt publicly in Paris after a "disputation" on the merits of the Jewish faith. Nonetheless, two great centers of learning flourished in medieval France: one in the northeast, mainly in Champagne, the other in the south, in Provence and Languedoc. **Rashi**, the "Prince of Bible commentators," was perhaps the greatest French Jewish scholar.

Persecution by both church and state culminated in the decree of 1394, expelling the entire community from France. Nevertheless, scattered settlements remained, especially in the south. These grew during the following centuries, as ever greater numbers of Spanish and Portuguese refugees from the Inquisition sought haven in France. A further addition came in 1648, when Alsace, with its ancient Jewish community, was annexed by France. By the time of the Revolution of 1789, France was home to 40,000 Jews, most of whom were forced to live in ghettos where they were deprived of all legal rights.

The revolution wrought a radical change in this respect. A decree promulgated in 1791 declared Jews to be full citizens of France. Napoleon, however, soon curbed this freedom. Calling a *Sanhedrin* of Jewish notables, he gained approval for a program that placed Jews directly under his control. He then proceeded to restrict their economic and political activities.

These restrictions remained in force after the emperor's downfall; it was not, in fact, until 1846 that the last of the disabilities was removed. Yet even then the battle against **anti-Semitism** had not ended: as Jews began to take a prominent place in the social, cultural, and political life of France, reactionary elements in the Church and army began a campaign to undermine the Jewish position. The strength of these elements was shown in the 1890's, when the conviction on falsified charges of treason of a Jewish army officer named **Dreyfus** set off a conflict between the liberal and reactionary forces in the country. It took almost a decade, and the efforts of such men as Emile **Zola**, to free Dreyfus, despite clear evidence of innocence. His exoneration, however, marked the defeat of Church and army, and the beginning of a new era in the history of France, as well as French Jewry.

The subjugation of France by **Germany** in 1940 brought about a revival of anti-Semitism on a scale never before known to the country: the entire Nazi program of racism became law. Yet with the help of the French population, more Jews survived the war in France than in any other West European country. Since the war, the life of the Jewish community has returned to pre-war normalcy. Again, Jews such as Pierre **Mendes France**, who served as premier in 1955, have risen to eminence. In 1998, there were about 525,000 Jews in France, many of them refugees of World War II. This figure includes those who came to France since 1961 from North Africa: 100,000 from **Algeria**, 30,000 from **Tunisia** and **Morocco**. Jewish life is organized in *consistories*, boards of one rabbi and four laymen, concerned with Jewish affairs in each of the seven districts into which the community is divided. A central consistory, made up of the chief rabbi and a representative of each consistory, coordinates activities on a national level, and serves as a link between the Jewish community and the ministry of public worship. Since 1860, the **Alliance Israélite Universelle** has been an important factor in the life of French Jewry, serving as a link between it and world Jewry. French Jews are active in the textile, garment, fur, leather, and jewelry industries, and have distinguished themselves in law, medicine, journalism, and banking.

FRANK, ANNE (1929-1945). Jewish Dutch girl. Hiding from the Nazis during the occupation she wrote a diary of the events and her thoughts, showing extraordinarily mature understanding. The diary was published and staged as drama in many countries. Her diary is the best known Jewish book to come out of the **Holocaust**.

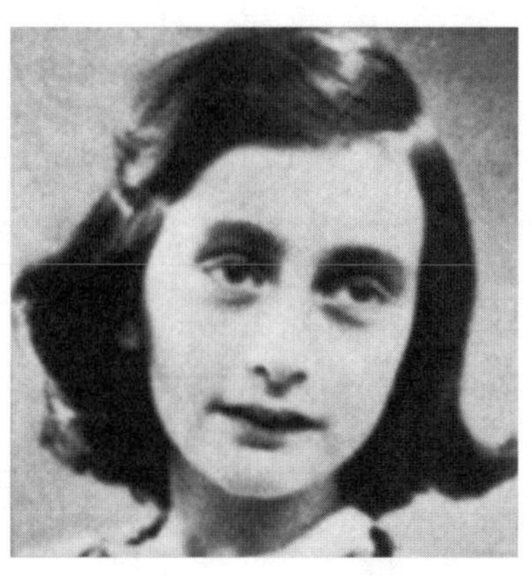

Anne Frank.

FRANK, JACOB (1726-1791). False messiah and leader of a sect that brought pain and strife during half a century of Jewish life. Jacob Frank spent the formative years of his life in **Romania** and **Turkey**. Having little education, his contact through his father with secret followers of **Sabbatai Zevi**, the 17th-century false messiah, proved to be a decisive influence on his unstable personality. He assumed the role of a messiah and went to **Poland** where he proclaimed himself a reincarnation of **Sabbatai Zevi**. Polish Jewry was reeling from the cruel blows of Cossack pogroms and were vunerable to the idea of a messiah who would save them. He began to teach the **Kabbalah** and represented himself as the reincarnation of all the prophets and messiahs who had come before him. He and his disciples outraged the Jewish community with their immoral and unorthodox behavior; finally, the local authorities banished Frank from Poland. Wherever Frank went, he brought trouble and calumny upon the Jewish people, causing a revival of the old accusation that Jews used human blood for ritual purposes. To discipline Frank and his followers, a conference of rabbis met in 1756. They banned the Frankist sect from the Jewish community and forbade the study of the Kabbalah by anyone under 30 years of age. The Frankists appealed to the Catholic bishop Dembowsky, claiming that they were Kabbalists at war with the **Talmud** which was full of error and blasphemy. They hinted that their beliefs resembled Christian tenets. The bishop summoned the rabbis to answer the charges against the Talmud in a public debate. As a result, thousands of copies of the Talmud were seized and publicly burned. Eventually, Frank and a thousand of his followers were baptized. Great pomp attended these baptisms, to which Frank came dressed in magnificent Turkish robes. But the Church, never trusting these converts, watched them closely and later imprisoned Frank for conversion under false pretenses. The Frankist sect survived him for a time but no longer had any importance.

FRANKEL, ZACHARIAS (1801-1875). German rabbi who sought to liberalize Judaism. He took a moderate position between **Geiger**'s Reform and Samson Raphael **Hirsch**'s modern Orthdoxy, since he was unwilling to go to the Reform extreme of giving up such things as Hebrew as the language of prayer.

FRANKFURTER, FELIX (1882-1965). U.S. Supreme Court Justice. He came to the U.S. from Vienna at the age of 12, and earned his law degree at Harvard University in 1906. While at Harvard he was deeply influenced by the new liberal doctrines of a group of rising lawyers that included Oliver Wendell Holmes and Louis **Brandeis**. These doctrines formed the basis of his later teachings. While holding the professorship at Harvard, Frankfurter served intermittently in various government departments. His brilliant plea in defense of the convicted anarchists Sacco and Vanzetti in 1927 earned him a national reputation and brought him to the forefront of American liberalism. During the Roosevelt administration (1933-1945), Frankfurter and many of the young lawyers he had trained played influential roles in drafting much of the liberal legislation of the "New Deal." Appointed to the Supreme Court in 1939, he advocated "judicial restraint" and deference to the will of the people. He resigned in 1962 due to ill health. Throughout his career he took an active interest in Jewish and Zionist affairs; in 1919, he was legal advisor to the Zionist delegation at the **Versailles Peace Conference**.

FRANKL, VIKTOR(1905-1997).Psychotherapist.His *logotherapy*, or therapy through finding meaning in one's life, evolved from his experience in **Auschwitz** where he survived because he was determined to be reunited with his wife. He describes this experience in his widely read book *Man's Search for Meaning*.

FRANKLIN, SIDNEY (1903-1976). Bullfighter, born in Brooklyn. He went to **Mexico** at age 18 and learned the art of bullfighting. In 1929, he went to Spain where, according to Ernest Hemingway, he became one of the best matadors of his day.

FREIER, RECHA (1892-1984). Initiator of **Youth Aliyah**. A teacher and the wife of a Berlin rabbi, she began in 1932 to help Jewish youth in **Germany** prepare for agricultural life in Palestine. After 1933, she organized similar training in other countries. She settled in Palestine in 1941.

FREUD, ANNA (1895-1982). Child psychologist. Daughter of Sigmund **Freud**, she left **Austria** in 1938 after the Nazi occupation and took her father to **England**, where she developed her child psychoanalysis, and became a renowned authority on child and adolescent psychology.

FREUD, SIGMUND (1856-1939). Founder of psychoanalysis. Freud was born in **Austria** to a scholarly, aloof father and a vivacious mother who was usually the center of attention in the household. He graduated from the University of Vienna Medical School, and one of his earliest original research projects in 1884 resulted in his discovery of the anesthetic properties of cocaine. Even as a general practitioner, Freud was interested in nervous disturbances. In collaboration with Joseph Breuer, he published *Selected Papers on Hysteria* in 1895. Before these studies of hypnosis as a means of studying the origins of hysteria were published, Freud replaced the use of hypnosis with his method of "free association" which became a basic technique of psychoanalysis. In 1900, with the publication of his book *The Interpretation of Dreams*, Freud ended his career as a general practitioner and devoted himself completely to the development and practice of psychoanalysis. His investigations into the unconscious strata of the mind helped to raise the curtain on the mysteries of the human personality and have laid the foundations for later investigations.

Sigmund Freud.

Freud was the first to demonstrate the importance of earliest childhood experiences and the crucial importance of the sexual life of the individual in the development of personality. The ideas presented in his books were hotly rejected and disputed. Freud's work remained unrecognized in his native Austria until late in his life, the first acclaim coming to him from **Germany** and English-speaking countries. After the Nazi invasion of Austria in 1938 he settled in **England**.

Freud was constantly aware of being a Jew, though his attitude toward Jewishness was highly complicated, both negative and positive. He was a member of **B'nai B'rith** in Vienna. At a time when **anti-Semitism** was widespread in Vienna, a friend asked Freud whether he ought to baptize his newborn son. Freud advised against this action. "If you do not let your son grow up as a Jew," he said, "you will deprive him of those sources of energy which cannot be replaced by anything else. He will have to struggle as a Jew, and you ought to develop in him all the energy he will need for that struggle. Do not deprive him of that advantage."

FRIEDAN, BETTY (1921-). Born Naomi Goldstein, she is often called the founder of the women's movement. Her book *The Feminine Mystique*, which revealed the unsatisfying lives of American middle-class housewives, made her one of the main figures of feminism in the U.S. In 1966, she co-founded the National Organization for Women (NOW).

FRIEDMAN, BERNY. *See* **Sports**.

FRIEDMAN, MILTON (1912-). American conservative economist. He became one of the leading economists of the post-war era. He advocated minimal government control and saw money supply rather than fiscal policy as controlling the business cycle. He was awarded the **Nobel Prize** for Economics in 1976, and was invited by Prime Minister **Begin** to help transform Israel's economy into a free market economy.

FROMM, ERICH (1900-1980). German-born American psychoanalyst and social philosopher. He wrote about the major social issues of the 20th century, such as the causes of Naziism in *Escape from Freedom*, the meaning of religion in our time in *Psychoanalysis and Religion*, and the meaning of love in *The Art of Loving*.

Overleaf: Sukkot at the Western Wall, following the reunification of Jerusalem in 1967. Courtesy Israel Office of Information.

GABBAI. Synagogue official. Now mainly the person who calls people for **aliyah** during the Torah service.

GABRIEL. *See* **Angel**.

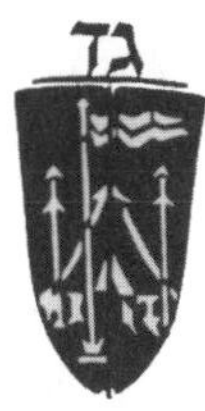

Emblem of the tribe of Gad.

GAD. Seventh son of **Jacob**; head of the tribe of Gad, whose territory lay in the mountains of Gilead, east of the Jordan. The tribe of Gad supplied **David** with some of his best warriors.

GADNA. Hebrew acronym for Youth Battalions. Israeli pre-military training during high school years. (*See also* **Israel Defense Forces**.)

GALILEE. Literally, district. The northern hill country of **Israel** is divided into Upper and Lower Galilee; it extends lengthwise from the Emek Jezreel to the foothills of **Lebanon**, from the Mediterranean on the west to the Jordan rift on the east.

GALILEE, SEA OF. *See* **Kinneret, Lake**.

Galilee.

GALUT. Or *Golah*; from Hebrew, meaning exile. The lands where Jews lived outside of the Land of Israel were called Galut. In early times, Galut also referred to the people-in-exile or captivity. Jewish sages called Israel's stay in **Egypt** *Galut Mitzrayim*, or Egyptian captivity. The second Galut, of **Babylonia**, lasted 70 years, from 586 to 516 B.C.E., the year of the rebuilding of the Second **Temple**. The third Exile, from the destruction of the Second Temple in 70 B.C. to the present day, is called *Galut Edom* or *Galut Ishmael*. The former refers to the Jews under Christian rule, the latter to those under Moslem dominion. A distinction is usually made between Galut, which is forced exile, and Diaspora, which is voluntary. (*See also* **Ingathering of The Exiles**.)

GANS, DAVID BEN SOLOMON. *See* **Prague**.

GAON. Title given to the heads of the Talmudic academies of Sura and Pumbeditha in **Babylonia** between 589 and 1040. The name "Gaon" is derived from the phrase *Geon Yaakov*, or Pride of Jacob, in Psalms 47:5. After the period of the Geonim, the title fell out of use for more than 500 years; it was used again among rabbis and scholars to describe someone of great Jewish learning. The first Gaon was Hanan of the academy of Pumbeditha in 589 and the last was Rav **Hai Gaon** in 1038. There were 48 Geonim in the academy of Pumbeditha and 36 in that of Sura. The Geonim, who were known for their scholarship and wisdom, were the deciding judges in all religious matters. The Geonim also supervised the academies in their districts. Semiannually all the academy teachers would assemble to hear the Geonim render scholarly interpretations of moot questions on the **Torah** and the **Talmud**. In addition, the Geonim replied to written questions sent to them from all parts of Babylonia, and from other countries as well. Responses recorded by various Geonim are still in existence. Among the most famous Geonim were: Judah Gaon, **Saadiah Gaon**, **Sherira Gaon**, and his son, **Hai Gaon**.

GAON OF VILNA. *See* **Elijah, Gaon of Vilna.**

GARDEN OF EDEN. *See* **Heaven and Hell.**

GARFUNKEL, ART. *See* **Music.**

GARY, ROMAIN (1914-1980). French novelist. Born in **Lithuania**, he was a French war hero who wrote about the horrors of war and about human cruelty and greed. His Jewish heroes appear in *The Dance of Genghis Cohn* and *Madame Rosa*.

GAZA. *See* **Israel** *and* **Negev**.

GEDALIAH. *See* **Fast Days**.

GEHINOM. *See* **Heaven and Hell.**

GEIGER, ABRAHAM (1810-1874). Scholar and orator. One of the founders of the Reform movement in **Germany**. At the age of 21 he became the rabbi of the Jewish community of Wiesbaden,

Germany, and immediately started to introduce reforms in the synagogue services. In 1837, he called the first conference of liberal, or Reform, rabbis in Wiesbaden; the next year, he was chosen assistant rabbi and later rabbi of the important community of Breslau. The Orthodox members separated and founded a community of their own. In his works, Geiger strove to show that Judaism has evolved throughout the generations. He considered Jews a religious group whose mission is to spread ethical ideas. He removed all references to Zion from the religious services and eliminated prayers which he considered inconsistent with modern thought.

GEMARAH. *See* **Talmud.**

GEMATRIA. *See* **Kabbalah.**

GENEALOGY. Starting out as a patriarchal and tribal society, ancient Israel was deeply interested in genealogy. This is reflected in the first chapters of **Genesis**, where long genealogical tables are provided, tracing the origin of humanity to **Adam** and **Eve**, and the origin of the Jewish people to **Abraham** and **Sarah**. In later books of the **Bible** we find additional genealogies, including those of kings (for example, the House of **David**), priests, **Levites**, and others. In Jewish tradition, every Jew belongs to one of the Twelve Tribes of Israel, and at one time every Jew could trace his or her ancestry back to a particular tribe. After the destruction of the Northern Kingdom of Israel in the 8th century B.C.E., ten tribes were lost, and after biblical times most genealogical records were lost, and most people were no longer able to trace their ancestry back to a given tribe. One of the few remnants of ancient Jewish genealogy is the preservation of family names related to either **Kohen** or Levi, which has religious significance rather than a specific genealogical connection.

For the past 2,000 years, Jews were subjected to frequent assaults and persecution and forced to migrate across the globe, losing many family records in the process. In modern times it became virtually impossible for any family to trace its origins any earlier than the late Middle Ages. Additionally, family names date back only to around 1800 (*see* **Names**), so that tracing one's family name for most Jews means only going back seven or eight generations at the most.

In recent years, however, there has been a growing interest among Jews in the U.S., in **Israel**, and around the world, in finding their family roots. The **Holocaust** in Europe, which wiped out entire communities, has prompted surviving relatives to study their families' past history. And third and fourth generation American Jews, not unlike other Americans of foreign origin, have begun to show interest in their family's origins. Consequently, the **Holocaust Museum** in Washington and Steven Spielberg's foundation in **Los Angeles** have launched projects to preserve individual and family records from the Holocaust, while the **Diaspora Museum** in **Tel Aviv**, Israel established the Douglas E. Goldman Genealogy Center in 1985. In 1998, the Center reported having records of some 750,000 Jews and more than 1,500 family trees listed in its databases.

The search for family trees has intensified as a result of the Internet. Web-sites such as FTJP, or Family Tree of the Jewish People, enable interested Jews to create a family tree of both deceased and living relatives going back several generations in different parts of the world.

GENERAL ZIONISM. Zionist political party dating back to the 6th Zionist **Congress** in Basle in 1903. At this Congress the Socialist Zionist party, **Poale Zion**, and the religious Zionist party, **Mizrachi**, took up positions to the left and right of the General Zionists, or G.Z., who stressed free enterprise, a unified educational system, and respect for Jewish tradition. After Theodor **Herzl**'s death, the leadership of the Zionist movement as a whole remained with such General Zionists as David Wolffsohn and Otto Warburg. During the years 1914 to 1921, General Zionist leaders Chaim **Weizmann**, Nahum **Sokolow**, and Louis D. **Brandeis** led the Zionist movement. In 1920, the **Revisionists** broke off from the G.Z. and formed their own party. After the birth of Israel, the G.Z. participated in the **Knesset** and in government coalitions, and in 1965, it joined the right-wing Herut and formed the present-day Likud party. (*See also* **Israel, Government and Political Parties; Zionism.**)

GENESIS. From Greek, meaning origin. In Hebrew, Bereshit, or In the Beginning. The first of the Five Books of **Moses**, Genesis tells the story of Creation, the flood, and the stories of the **patriarchs**. It closes with **Jacob**'s descent to **Egypt** to join his son, **Joseph.**

GENIZAH. A literary "cemetery" for worn-out sacred books and manuscripts. One famous Genizah, a treasure trove of ancient manuscripts, was discovered in Cairo by Solomon **Schechter** in 1896.

GEORGIA. Jews were among the first white settlers of Georgia in 1733. **Sephardic** Jewish families lived in Savannah, but many left by 1740 because of hardship. Georgian Jews took an active part in the Revolutionary War, and in mid-19th century German Jews settled in Atlanta and other towns. Today, there are 70,000 Jews in Atlanta, and small communities in Augusta, Columbus, Macon, and Savannah. The main Jewish newspaper is the *Atlanta Jewish Times.*

GERMANY. The existence of Jewish settlements in Germany early in the 4th century has been established by historical evidence. Reference to Jews in Cologne is found in decrees issued by Emperor Constantine. Earlier, Jewish traders had followed in the footsteps of the Roman legions who established military outposts along the northern ports of the Rhine. Little is known about the fate of the Jews in Germany at the time of the fall of the Roman empire and during the succeeding invasions from the East and West. During the reign of Charlemagne (771-814), the Jews engaged in commerce and trade. This wise ruler found Jews useful to the welfare of the state and protected them against undue discrimination. His son Louis the Pious (814-840) extended commercial privileges to Jews. Their importance in the economic field is illustrated by the fact that on many occasions market-day was postponed from a Sabbath to a weekday in order to enable Jews to participate in it. Often, Jews were invited to settle in particular towns in order to increase their prosperity. In the 9th and 10th centuries Jewish communities sprang up in the cities of Augsburg, Mayence, Regensburg, Speyer, and Worms.

The development of Jewish economic life paralleled intensive scholarly activity. The famous family of Kalonymus, a family of scholars and poets, moved from **Italy** to Germany. One of the greatest

authorities on Jewish law, Rabbenu **Gershom**, called "the Light of the Exile," headed a Talmudic academy, or yeshiva, in the city of Mayence, attracting students from distant countries.

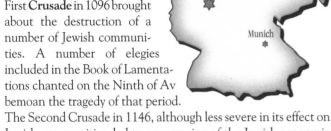

In the Middle Ages. The First **Crusade** in 1096 brought about the destruction of a number of Jewish communities. A number of elegies included in the Book of Lamentations chanted on the Ninth of Av bemoan the tragedy of that period. The Second Crusade in 1146, although less severe in its effect on Jewish communities, led to a worsening of the Jewish economic position. Jews became chattels of the kings, who extended them protection against the attacks of fanatic mobs at the price of their freedom and only in exchange for a heavy tribute.

This humiliating status did not save the Jews from cruel discriminations. In the 13th century, Jews were forced to wear a degrading yellow badge. They were forbidden to hold public office. Ritual murder accusations were leveled against them, even though these were denounced by Pope Innocent IV.

Persecutions of Jews increased at the time of the plague known as the Black Death from 1348-49. The Jews were accused of having caused the plague by poisoning the wells. The resulting widespread pogroms in many German towns caused Jews to seek shelter in Slavic countries. In 1421, Jews were expelled from Cologne. During the next two centuries, the Jewish population continued to be victimized with **blood accusations**, confiscations of property, forced baptism, burning of Jewish books, and physical attacks. The banishment of the Jews from important centers of trade and commerce—Worms, Frankfort, Hamburg, and Vienna—continued well into the 17th century.

The Reformation in the 16th century did not radically change the position of German Jews. However, the interest of German humanists in Jewish scholarship and the emphasis of the Reformation on the **Bible** resulted in some instances in better treatment of the Jewish population. The foremost defender of the Jews, Johann **Reuchlin** (1455-1522), was a Hebrew scholar. He courageously fought the confiscation and the burning of Jewish books. Other humanists joined the right against persecution. The country was divided into approximately 200 small independent states ruled by princes who had only weak ties to the Emperor. The Jewish position varied from one region to the next, depending upon the whim of the local ruler.

The Cossack uprising in the Ukraine in 1648-49 and the messianic **Sabbatai Zevi** movement which brought an influx of Eastern European victims of the massacres to Germany and left a mark on German Jews as well. As late as the second half of the 18th century, traces of the Sabbataian movement were still evident.

The 18th century found the German Jews still sealed off in ghettos. They were divided into two classes, "protected" and "tolerated." Only a few privileged individuals fell into the "protected" category. The struggle to break out of their narrow confines and become a part of German culture and society culminated in the **Haskalah**, or Enlightenment. Under the influence of this movement, great changes took place in Jewish life. At the same time, emancipation efforts gained support among liberal gentile scholars and authors, such as G.E. Lessing. This movement aimed to remove civil and political discrimination and attain equal rights for Jews as citizens of the country. The French Revolution and Napoleon's conquests brought a measure of freedom to Jews of Germany. In the first half of the 19th century, the foremost champion of emancipation was Gabriel Riesser. His fight for equal rights for Jews resulted in a measure of success after the Revolution of 1848.

Emancipation and Reform. The struggle for equality was accompanied by great intellectual activity and sweeping changes in the Jewish way of life. Jewish scholarship was advanced by the great historians and scholars Jost, **Graetz**, **Zunz**, Steinschneider, and **Geiger**. The quest for change in the old traditions and the adoption of new religious forms in harmony with modern thought and practices were expressed in the Reform movement. A considerable number of Jews left the Jewish fold altogether.

While the champions of religious reform were gaining ground in Germany, a new orthodoxy was strengthened by the writings and activities of Samson Raphael Hirsch and Israel Hildesheimer, head of a rabbinical seminary in Berlin. A moderating influence on Jewish life in Germany was exerted by Zacharias **Frankel**, president of the Breslau Seminary. From the middle of the 19th century on, German Jews made outstanding contributions to literature, science, and economics. Jewish religion and philosophy were enriched by the works of Hermann **Cohen**, Martin **Buber**, and Franz **Rosenzweig.**

Despite their integration into the life of the country and their patriotic devotion to Germany, Jews could not escape vicious anti-Semitism. During World War I, 96,000 out of 550,000 Jews served in the German army, and 12,000 died on the battlefield. Yet immediately after the war, the Nazis spread the lie that the Jews had stabbed Germany in the back, causing its defeat. In the 1920's there were only isolated attacks against Jews. But after the rise of Adolf Hitler, anti-Semitism aiming at the total destruction of the Jewish people became the avowed policy of the Nazi regime. During the first years of World War II, the Nazis seized the opportunity to exterminate the Jewish population of Germany and its occupied territories. Six million Jews perished in the greatest slaughter in Jewish history.

Nazi Extermination and Postwar Period. During the early stages of Hitler's rise to power, about 60,000 German Jews managed to emigrate to Israel. Between 1933 and 1941, a total of 310,000 Jews escaped from Germany to other countries, but 130,000 were deported to the gas chambers and

Seder cup from 17th century Germany. The engraving says, "The Son Who Does Not Know How to Ask a Question." Courtesy Israel Museum, Jerusalem.

concentration camps of Eastern Europe. Leo **Baeck**, head of Germany's prewar Jewish community, survived World War II in Theresienstadt.

In 1977, there were approximately 35,000 Jews in West and East Germany. The prewar Jewish population numbered about 600,000.

In 1998, unified Germany had a general population of 82 million; of these 62,000 were Jewish. The largest Jewish communities are in Berlin with 10,000, Frankfurt Am Main with 6,000, and Munich with 5,000.

On September 10, 1952, the Federal Republic of Germany agreed to pay collective reparations to **Israel** and world Jewry for the crimes committed by Nazi Germany against the Jewish people.

Under the terms of the pact, reached after lengthy negotiations among the representatives of the State of Israel, Germany, and the representatives of the Conference on Jewish Material Claims on Germany, Germany was to pay Israel a total of $715 million in "commodities and services" over a period extending until 1962; an additional $107 million was earmarked for the relief and rehabilitation of Jews outside Israel.

This agreement stirred opposition among some segments of the Jewish people, who viewed the acceptance of compensation from Germany as morally indefensible. On the other hand, the Israeli government specifically separated this settlement from the moral issues involved in the case. It pointed out that Israel had assumed the heavy burden of resettling a large number of uprooted and destitute Jewish refugees from Germany and territories formerly under German rule; Israel's claim against Germany for global recompense was intended to defray the cost on the integration of these refugees.

In 1990, East and West Germany became unified. East Germany acknowledged its responsibility toward victims of Nazism and promised to pay reparations to Jewish survivors. During the 1991 Gulf War, Germany, having previously supplied Iraq with materials for chemical warfare, offered Israel protection against chemical weapons, and has sought to play an active part in bringing about peace between Israel, Syria, and other Middle Eastern countries.

GERSHOM, RABBENU. Also known as Gershom ben Judah of Mayence. An outstanding scholar of the late 10th and early 11th centuries, commentator on the **Talmud**, head of several academies in **France** and **Germany**. His learning earned him the title *Me'or Hagolah*, or "Light of the Exile." He was recognized as the leading Jewish religious authority in Europe and his decisions on Jewish law were accepted as legally binding on all European Jews. Around the year 1000 he handed down numerous rabbinic rulings, forbidding the practice of polygamy, insisting on the consent of both parties to a divorce, prohibiting the opening of letters addressed to others, and modifying the laws relating to converts who had been forcibly baptized.

GERSHWIN, GEORGE (1898-1937). Composer and pianist. Born to immigrant Jewish parents in Brooklyn, N.Y., Gershwin had one of the meteoric careers in the history of American music. Beginning as a "Tin Pan Alley" tunester, he burst into serious music with a performance of his *Rhapsody in Blue* in 1924. After this critical success, Gershwin continued to compose for the popular stage. To the end of his life, however, he experimented with classic musical forms. His last work, *Porgy and Bess*, a "folk opera" whose score draws heavily on Negro spirituals, blues, and jazz motifs, has been acclaimed as a masterpiece throughout the world.

George Gershwin.

GERSONIDES. *See* **Levi ben Gershon.**

GET. Bill of divorcement, which by law must be drawn up at the request of the husband and presented to the wife in the presence of two witnesses. It must state that she is free to marry another. To protect the wife, rabbis ruled that her consent is necessary for the divorce to be valid. The earliest extant form of a get, uncovered at the **Genizah** in Cairo, dates from the year 1020.

GHETTO. Area in any city or town inhabited only by Jews. The term "ghetto" has many explanations: the Republic of Venice passed a law in 1516 ordering all Venetian Jews to be limited to one particular section of Venice, known as Ghetto; the word is derived from a Venetian workshop known as *Geto*, where weapons were made; it is an abbreviation of the Italian *borghetto*, meaning suburb.

From the first days of Exile, wherever Jews have lived they have kept to separate neighborhoods by their own choice as well as by decree. Jews often made their living from trade and preferred to live near the marketplace or other such sources of livelihood. Their religious and social needs also caused them to settle in groups. The idea of separating Jewish inhabitants from the rest of the population was conceived by the Catholic Church. But it was not until 1179 that the Third Lateran Council issued an edict forbidding Jews and Christians to live side by side. For a long time this decree was not carried out, but in the 13th century some countries began to limit the Jews to special districts. In 1239, King James I of Aragon relocated the Jews of Valencia in a specific district known as Juderia. In 1276, London Jews were assigned a special area called Jewry. In **Germany**, in the 13th century, Jews were limited to living in streets named Judengasse. In some towns in the south of **France** under the rule of the pope, the Lateran decree went into effect in the 14th century and the ghetto in these places was called Juiverie. In 1555, Pope Paul restricted the Jews of **Rome** to a dilapidated quarter beside the Tiber river known as Giudecca. Later, ghettos were instituted in other Italian towns as well, such as Toscana, Padua, and Mantua.

In the 15th century there were ghettos in various cities in **Poland**—Posen, Cracow, Lublin, and others. Some notable ghettos existed in **Amsterdam**, Frankfort-on-the-Main, and **Prague**.

Generally, the ghetto was enclosed by a wall. Entrance to it was gained through an iron gate that was guarded by special guards inside and out, locked at a stipulated time at night, and reopened in the morning. On Sabbaths and holidays the ghetto gates remained locked.

Because the area was so confined, Jews living in the ghetto were crowded together. Nevertheless, their life was well organized to suit the needs of the community, and the inhabitants

Jewish children in a narrow street of the ghetto in Ghardaia, Algeria. Courtesy Joint Distribution Committee.

benefited from the freedom to conduct their own religious, civic, and social life. (*See* **Kahal**.)

After the French Revolution of 1789, ghettos were dissolved one after another throughout western Europe, although the Roman ghetto continued as late as 1870.

The Nazis created a ghetto in every city they conquered where there were Jews, but they intended the ghetto to serve only as a way station in their highly organized plan of destruction of the Jews. The largest concentrations of Jews in the Nazi-created ghettos were in **Warsaw**, Lublin, Lodz, Bialystok, and Vilna.

The revolt of the Warsaw Ghetto, which broke out on April 19, 1943, and continued for five weeks, will remain a memorable event in Jewish history.

GIDEON. A judge of Israel. He fought the Midianites who were oppressing the Children of Israel and defeated them decisively. In gratitude, the people offered to make Gideon king. Gideon, however, refused immediately, saying: "I will not rule over you, neither shall my son rule over you. The Lord shall rule over you" (Judges 8:23).

GILGUL. *See* **Kabbalah.**

GIMEL. Third letter of the Hebrew alphabet; numerically, three.

GINSBERG, ALLEN (1926-1997). One of the leading American poets of the second half of the 20th century. A founder of the Beat movement in the 1950's and hero of the protest generation of the 1960's, he chastised American materialism and militarism in poems like *Howl*, and memorialized his mother in his major poem *Kaddish*. His poetry is reminiscent of Walt Whitman's *Leaves of Grass.*

GINZBERG, LOUIS (1873-1953). An outstanding Talmudic scholar, born in **Lithuania**, he served as Professor of **Talmud** at the **Jewish Theological Seminary** in **New York** from 1902 until his death. His important works are *Gaonica*, *The Legends of the Jews*, and *Students, Scholars, and Saints*. Ginzberg was also one of the editors of the *Jewish Encyclopedia* published in 1901-06. His studies of the history of the Palestinian **Talmud** are valuable aids in understanding the course of the development of Jewish law and life during the Second **Temple**.

GINSBURG, RUTH BADER (1933-). U.S. Supreme Court justice. She was appointed by President Clinton to the Supreme Court in 1993. With moderate to liberal views, she is known as a pioneer in the movement for legal equality for women.

GLICKSTEIN, SHLOMO. *See* **Sports**.

GLUECK, NELSON. *See* **Archeology**.

GLÜCKEL VON HAMELN (1646-1724). Author of the book Memoirs which preserved a portrait of Glückel's personality, as well as a rich description of the conditions under which Jews lived in her day. Born in 17th-century Hamburg, Glückel was the wife and daughter of merchants. A capable businesswoman, she also managed to raise a dozen children. It was for them that she wrote her fascinating memoirs in Judeo-German. Her memoirs have been translated into German, English, and other languages.

GOD. Many cultures believe in a supreme being or beings who rule the world. Yet the God of the Hebrew Bible creates the world not on a whim, as happens in other cultures, but for a moral purpose (see **Genesis**, chap. 1). He then becomes known to certain people, beginning with **Abraham**. He makes a **covenant** with him and promises to redeem his offspring. Known also as the God of Israel (*see* **God, Names of**), this God becomes the center of both **Christianity** and **Islam**, faiths which, together with Judaism, are considered the three major monotheistic religions of the world. They all accept the one single transcendental God who does not have any human or physical qualities and is beyond human understanding. When **Moses** tries to identify God, he is told, "I am what I am." In other words, God is nameless and remains outside human experience, while in effect, as attested by the Book of **Psalms**, nature, history, and human experience reveal God's existence and power.

GOD, NAMES OF. While **God** is unknowable and nameless, the **Talmud** states that there are 100 names for God in the **Bible**. As **Maimonides** explains it, these names do not reveal the identity or essence of God, but are only ways for human beings to relate to God and achieve a limited understanding of the Almighty. Some names, such as *El* and *Elohim*, simply mean the supreme being. *Adonai*, meaning Lord, is the way of pronouncing YHWH, the way

Gideon.

God's name appears most often in the Bible, yet, consisting of four consonants, cannot be pronounced. In biblical times, the only one who could pronounce it was the High Priest (*see* **Kohen**). Other names of God refer to God's attributes, such as the Creator, Redeemer, and The Holy One. Others refer to God's relationship with the people Israel: Redeemer of Israel, Lover of Israel. Additional names of God appear in the **Kabbalah.**

GOLDBERG, ARTHUR J. (1908-1990). American jurist and statesman. Goldberg became Secretary of Labor in 1961 and was appointed to the Supreme Court the following year, succeeding Felix **Frankfurter**. Appointed U.S. Ambassador to the United Nations in 1965, a position he held until 1968, he was a staunch supporter of Israel.

GOLDEN CALF. When **Moses** went up to Mount Sinai to receive the Law, the Israelites asked **Aaron** to build a golden calf as a visible form of God which they could worship. This act of rebellion against God is considered the major sin of the Jewish people, for which Moses had to obtain special forgiveness from God.

GOLDFADEN, ABRAHAM (1840-1908). One of the founders of Yiddish theater, a playwright, and artist. He organized theatrical troupes which entertained Jewish masses in the Old and the New World for more than a generation. Goldfaden also published a book of Hebrew poetry. In 1887, he paid his first visit to America, where he settled in 1903. Goldfaden's plays became classics of the Yiddish stage.

GOLDMANN, NAHUM (1894-1982). World Zionist leader. In 1936, he helped found the **World Zionist Congress**, which he headed from 1953 to 1977. As chairman of the Conference on Jewish Material Claims against Germany, he was largely instrumental in reaching the reparation agreement with West Germany in 1952. He was the author of two autobiographical volumes and many essays and articles in German, Yiddish, Hebrew, and English.

GOLEM. Statue or image into which life is breathed by supernatural means. The most famous Golem in Jewish history is the one believed to have been created by Rabbi Judah **Loew** of **Prague** (ca. 1525-1609). This Golem served the rabbi and the Jewish community as a spy and intelligence agent. He succeeded in arresting a group of people who were spreading false tales about Jews. It was said that Rabbi Loew used to remove the spirit of life from his Golem every Friday so that the creature would not desecrate the **Sabbath**. The Golem is reputed to have crumbled to pieces; its remains, according to legend, still exist in the "Golem's room" in an ancient synagogue in Prague.

GOLIATH. Philistine Giant in the **Bible** slain by the boy **David**.

GOMPERS, SAMUEL (1850-1924). American labor leader. Founder and first president of the American Federation of Labor in 1886. He served as its president until his death. Gompers refused to participate in any socialistic and political projects, insisting that better wages, shorter hours, and other benefits were the proper aim of trade unions. He came to be recognized as a great public figure, and during World War I served as the head of the War Committee on Labor. Gompers persuaded the A.F.L. to support **Zionism**.

GOODMAN, BENNY. *See* **Music**.

GORDIMER, NADINE (1923-). South African novelist who won the Nobel Prize for literature in 1991. She wrote about Apartheid and advocated black rule in **South Africa.**

GORDON, AHARON DAVID (1856-1922). Labor Zionist thinker and writer. Gordon believed in self-fulfillment through work in the Jewish homeland. With many followers and admirers, he was a source of inspiration and courage to his young comrades and worked at their side despite his age. His influence also extended to the next generation. Gordon expressed his ideals in many articles, purporting that close association with nature was the basis for a healthy and just society.

A.D. Gordon.

GORDON, JUDAH LEIB (1831-1892). Hebrew poet. No other literary personality of the 19th century exerted greater influence on Hebrew readers than did J.L. Gordon. He began as a romantic poet, using biblical themes, and later treated tragic moments in Jewish history. His historical poems are noted for their vigor and dramatic quality. A proponent of the **Haskalah**, he called upon his fellow Jews to leave their self-imposed ghetto life and avail themselves of the educational and cultural opportunities which the gentile world offered them.

GORDON, SIDNEY. *See* **Sports.**

GOTTLEIB, MAURYCY. *See* **Art.**

GRACE AFTER MEALS. *See* **Prayer**.

GRAETZ, HEINRICH (1817-1891). German-Jewish historian. Graetz lived at a time of great change in Jewish history. The **ghetto** walls were coming down, and Jews were mingling in the general life of Europe. His *History of the Jews*, completed in 1876 as a rare combination of scholarship and readability, remains to this day a basic source for understanding the history of the Jews.

GRATZ COLLEGE. Founded in **Philadelphia** in 1897 through a grant by H. Gratz, it is the oldest existing training institution for Hebrew teachers in the U.S., providing a four-year college course leading to a Bachelor of Science degree in Hebrew literature and a teacher's diploma.

GRATZ, REBECCA (1781-1869). Educator noted for her beauty, charm, and good works. Portraits of her were painted by famous artists, and her published *Letters* are rich in descriptions of her home city, **Philadelphia**, and times. In 1838, she established the Hebrew Sunday School Society, the first school of its kind. It is said that she was the inspiration for the Jewess Rebecca in Sir Walter Scott's *Ivanhoe*.

Rebecca Gratz.

GREAT ASSEMBLY. *See* **Talmud**.

GREAT BRITAIN. *See* **England**.

GREECE. Jewish settlement in Greece dating back to the 2nd century B.C.E. Documents of the 12th and 13th centuries indicate Jews were noted for their silk and dyeing industries. Greek Jewry flourished in the 14th and 15th centuries, producing many renowned rabbis and Talmudic scholars. Salonika, which became part of Greece in 1912, was a center of **Sephardic** Jewry. In the late 19th century, 80,000 of its 120,000 **Ladino**-speaking inhabitants were Jewish. The massacres and deportations during the Nazi occupation of Greece in World War II virtually annihilated the Jewish community, which dwindled from 75,000 in 1939 to fewer than 4,500 in 1998.

GREENBERG, HANK. *See* **Sports**.

GREENBERG, HAYIM (1889-1953). Labor Zionist leader, intellectual, and writer. He was the acknowledged intellectual leader of **Labor Zionism** in America, serving as editor of its weekly, *Der Yiddisher Kempfer,* and the English monthly, the *Jewish Frontier*. During World War II, he was chairman of the Executive Council, and during the UN deliberations in 1947 on the establishment of Israel he helped win over many of the Latin American delegates to the Jewish cause. At his death, he was mourned as a leader of great spiritual force.

Uri Zvi Greenberg.

GREENBERG, URI ZVI (1895-1981). One of the greatest Hebrew poets of our time who wrote passionately and eloquently about the rebuilding of **Israel** and the tragedy of the **Holocaust**. Born in Galicia in a Hasidic family, Greenberg at first wrote lyric poetry. In 1924, he came to Palestine, where he identified with the pioneer builders of the land. His later poems are inspired with the vision of Jewish sovereignty over all of historical Palestine. During World War II he wrote powerful and dramatic poems on the Nazi slaughter of the Jewish people, published in the volume *Streets of the River*. He was a member of the Herut Party. (*See also* **Hebrew Literature** *and* **Revisionist Zionism**.)

GREENSPAN, ALAN (1926-). American economist; since 1987, chairman of the Federal Reserve, the agency which controls the nation's money supply. Greenspan believes in limiting the growth of money supply, and has presided over a prosperous U.S. economy in the late 1990's.

GROSSMAN, DAVID (1954-). Leading Israeli novelist and writer of children books. Grossman's major novel, *See Under Love*, deals with the Holocaust, while *The Yellow Wind* covers the Israeli-Palestinian conflict. He is an outspoken critic of many Israeli policies toward Palestinians.

GUATEMALA. Republic in the northernmost portion of Central America. In 1998, there were fewer than 1,000 Jews in a total population of about 11 million. A community of **Marranos**, forced Catholic converts who practiced their Jewish faith in secret, conducted a thriving export trade from Guatemala in the 16th century, when Guatemala was a Spanish colony. The **Inquisition**, established in **Mexico** in 1570, eventually led to the disappearance of this early Marrano community. During the 1860's a small group of German Jews from Mexico and **Cuba**, as well as **Sephardim** from **Turkey** and **France**, settled here. They have been joined by immigrants from East Europe after World War II. All organizations are represented within the *Comunidad Israelita*, or Jewish Community.

GUGGENHEIM FAMILY. Family of American Jewish industrialists, public servants, and philanthropists. Mayer Guggenheim (1828-1905) came to the U.S. from **Switzerland** in 1847. By 1900, he and his seven sons controlled one of the country's great mining empires in **Colorado**. Simon Guggenheim (1867-1941), the sixth son, was U.S. Senator from Colorado from 1907 to 1913. He established the John Simon Guggenheim Foundation, with endowments of more than $10 million to aid scholars and artists. Solomon Guggenheim (1861-1930), a collector of non-objective paintings, set up a fund "for the promotion of art and education in art." Daniel (1856-1930), Mayer's second son, contributed to the development of aviation. Together with his son, Harry Frank, who was U.S. Ambassador to **Cuba** from 1929 to 1933, Daniel established a foundation for aeronautical research. Other beneficiaries of Guggenheim aid include the New York Botanical Gardens, the New York Guggenheim Concerts, the **Jewish Theological Seminary**, and the **Hebrew Union College**.

GÜNZBURG, BARON DAVID (1857-1910). Scion of a distinguished Jewish family in **Russia**, he was intensely interested in Jewish learning. Baron Guenzburg became a patron of Jewish scholarship and amassed one of the largest collections of Jewish books and rare manuscripts. To serve Jewish learning, he founded an academy for Jewish studies in St. Petersburg.

GUSH EMUNIM. Literally "bloc of the faithful," this movement started after the **Six-Day War** in 1967 among religious settlers of the West Bank who were dedicated to the "Greater Land of Israel" concept, which opposes any territorial concessions to the Palestinians.

GUTHRIE, ARLO. *See* **Music**.

Below, Bukharan Jewish family celebrating Hanukkah.

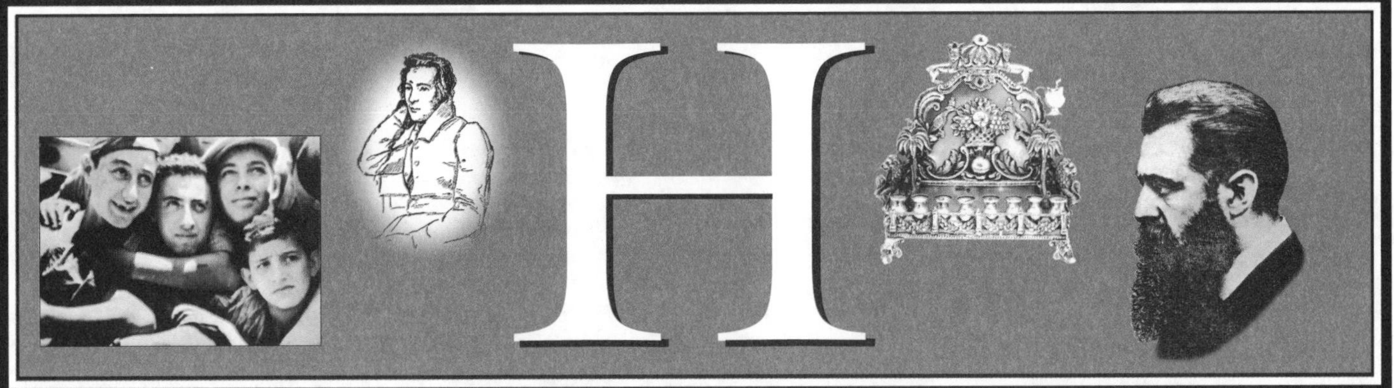

HABAD. *See* **Lubavitch.**

HABAKKUK (c. 630 B.C.E.). Eighth of the twelve minor prophets. In the first chapter of his book, Habakkuk foresees the Chaldean invasion of Judea. In the second, he cries out against injustice; the third and final chapter is a striking poetic prayer.

HABIMAH. Literally, stage. Renowned Hebrew theater in Israel, founded by a group of enthusiastic young artists in Moscow in 1918. In 1928, the Habimah made its permanent home in Palestine. Its repertoire has since grown to more than 100 plays. Its artistry has been acclaimed repeatedly during its several tours of Europe and in its visits to the U.S. It is now Israel's national theater.

Habimah Theater, Tel Aviv. Courtesy Israel Office of Information.

HABIRU. Middle Eastern desert tribes mentioned in 15th century B.C.E. documents found in Egypt. Some scholars believe they might be the ancient Hebrews.

HABONIM. World organization of Zionist youth. In the U.S. it resulted from a reorganization of Poale Zion (*see* **Labor Zionism**) in 1935.

HADASSAH, THE WOMEN'S ZIONIST ORGANIZATION OF AMERICA. The largest Zionist organization in the world, with more than 385,000 members in 1,500 chapters and groups in the U.S. and **Puerto Rico.** It supports health and educational projects in Israel, including Hadassah Hebrew University Medical Center in **Jerusalem,** youth resettlement programs, the Hadassah College of Technology, and the Hadassah Career Counseling Institute. Through its Young Judea movement with its network of clubs, summer camps, and Israel programs, Hadassah seeks to ensure a strong Zionist and Jewish commitment among American youth. It also mobilizes support for its medical work through Hadassah International, an organization of friends of the Medical Center in more than 30 countries around the world.

When Hadassah's two American-trained nurses arrived in Palestine in 1913, the country was suffering from a high infant mortality rate, trachoma (a dreaded eye disease), malaria, and other diseases. The first project set up by the two nurses was a small welfare station in Jerusalem for maternity care and treatment of trachoma. In 1916, during World War I, Hadassah was chosen to provide a medical unit for Palestine. In 1918, the unit established a permanent hospital in **Tiberias,** took over the old Rothschild Hospital in Jerusalem and opened the first nurses training school in the country. The first infant welfare station was opened in 1921.

From these modest beginnings, Hadassah expanded its work, covering Palestine, now Israel, with a network of medical services and a variety of agricultural and vocational education programs. Through the **Jewish National Fund,** Hadassah has participated in the reclamation of thousands of acres of wastelands and in afforestation. Henrietta Szold, the founder of Hadasssah, was the guiding spirit of Youth Aliyah from its inception in 1934 until her death in 1945. Hadassah is the largest organizational contributor to Youth Aliyah and has helped resettle more than 275,000 youngsters from some 80 nations.

Hadassah's Medical Work. The Hadassah Medical Organization practices the principle of equality of treatment of patients regardless of race, faith, or ability to pay. Hadassah's medical and health services are now consolidated into three facilities in Jerusalem: the 700-bed Medical Center at Ein Karem, the 300-bed community hospital on Mount Scopus, and a community health center at Kiryat HaYovel. Half a million patients are cared for annually in these institutions, and a full range of health disciplines is covered in Hadassah's 105 medical, surgical, and health departments.

Also on the Ein Karem campus are the Hebrew University-Hadassah Medical School; the Hebrew University-Hadassah School of Dental Medicine, co-founded with Alpha Omega; the Hebrew UniversityHadassah School of Occupational Therapy, the Hebrew University-Hadassah Braun School of Public Health and Community Medicine; and the Henrietta Szold Hadassah-Hebrew University School of Nursing. The Moshe Sharett Institute of Oncology provides advanced treatment for people with cancer. Inside the hospital's Abbell Synagogue are magnificent stained-glass windows created for Hadassah by the artist Marc **Chagall.**

Hadassah-Hebrew University Medical Center, founded and funded by Hadassah, Jerusalem.

The Hadassah Medical Organization is renowned for its pacesetting work in teaching, healing, and research, setting standards in Israel for health care and medical education. The Medical Center houses the country's first trauma unit and is the designated center for bone marrow transplantation. Twelve percent of the Medical Center's work force is newly arrived Russian immigrants, most of whom have been retrained under Hadassah auspices.

For many years Hadassah has outreached to developing countries in Africa. Hadassah ophthalmologists have carried out thousands of eye operations in 11 different African countries. Together with the U.S. Agency for International Development, Hadassah established a hospital in Zaire. Hadassah physicians have assisted in establishing bone marrow facilities in the Far East and South America.

Hadassah's Education and Child Rescue Programs. Hadassah early on recognized the need to provide quality vocational education and job training for the young people of Palestine. In 1942, it established the Seligsberg Vocational High School for Girls in Jerusalem. Two years later, the Brandeis Vocational Center for Boys opened. The high academic standards and creative approaches in these schools became the model for vocational programs in Israel. In 1969, the schools were merged into a coed high school integrating technical studies with academics. Recently, Hadassah transferred the school to the city of Jerusalem.

In 1970, Hadassah founded the first two-year college in Israel with the goal of providing professional and technological training in an academic setting that would allow students to compete in careers that promised jobs and a stable future. Today, the college offers courses in such highly technical fields as computer science, x-ray and imaging technology, printing, laboratory medicine, industrial design, and television professions.

Each year, more than 35,000 clients use Hadassah's Career Counseling Institute, established in 1944, for its testing, counseling, and evaluation services.

Hadassah is co-owner with Youth Aliyah of Hadassah-Neurim, a residential village for Israeli teenagers, and sponsors day centers where troubled youngsters can receive technical training that will enable them to become useful and productive citizens. Special funds made available by have helped Youth Aliyah educate and absorb Ethiopian youth.

Hadassah in the United States. From Hadassah's inception, its Jewish education program has been basic to its work. Though study groups, classes, and quality educational materials produced by Hadassah, members examine such topics as Zionism, Judaism, Jewish history and culture, Hebrew language and literature, and women's issues. The monthly *Hadassah Magazine* features prize-winning articles on Hadassah's work and on Jewish life in Israel and the rest of the world. Through its Zionist Affairs program, Hadassah serves as a resource center, educating members on issues that directly concern Israel and its relations with the U.S. Hadassah also works actively on the American scene as an advocate for democratic principles and as a force for freedom and equal rights.

Through its peer-led Zionist youth movement, Hadassah has helped thousands of young Americans become committed Jews

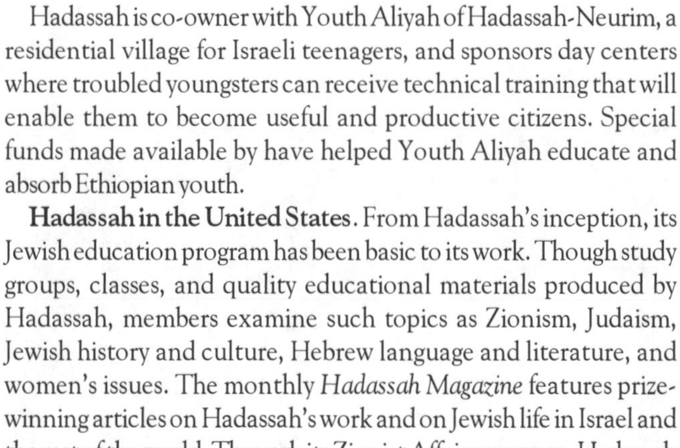

Machinery toolshop in Acre, sponsored by Hadassah-WIZO Organization of Canada.

and ardent Zionists. Cultural programs, sports and recreational activities, traditional religious observances, and summer and year-long Israel experiences instill in Young Judeans a lasting identification with Judaism and Zionism.

HADASSAH-WIZO ORGANIZATION OF CANADA. The largest women's Zionist organization in **Canada**, was formed in 1919 by women and subsequently became a Federation of World **Wizo.** Its 320 chapters in 65 centers across Canada with a membership of 17,000, carrying on fund-raising and educational activities. In Israel it supports 14 nurseries, two kindergartens, two youth clubs and the **Haifa** Community College, four women's clubs, and two large schools: the Children's and Youth Village at Hadassim and the Agricultural Secondary School and Village at Nahalal, which have graduated thousands of students to become productive citizens of Israel. As sole agency for **Youth Aliyah** in Canada, it supports and maintains the Acco Educational and Vocational Youth Village, the Magdiel Comprehensive Secondary School and Youth Village, the Nathanya Day Center, the Child Guidance and Hadassah-WIZO Canada Research Institute in Jerusalem, and the Abe and Sophie Bronfman School in Nehalim.

Canadian Hadassah-WIZO has given study centers and other facilities to the **Hebrew University of Jerusalem**, and has assisted the Asaf Harofe Hospital in many phases of its development.

Hadassah-WIZO of Canada also has planted three forests in Israel through the **Jewish National Fund**.

HAFTARAH. From Hebrew, meaning conclusion. The section from the Prophets recited at the conclusion of the reading from the **Torah**, or Five Books of Moses, on the **Sabbath**, holidays, and during afternoon services on fast days. Each portion of the Torah has a specific Haftorah of its own; there is some connection, however remote, between the Torah reading and the Haftarah. Some Sabbath days are named after the Haftarah reading, such as *Shabbat Hazon* (*Sabbath of Vision*), when the first chapter of Isaiah, which begins with the words "The vision," is read.

The Talmud says that the practice of Haftarah readings on the Sabbath goes back to the 1st century C.E. The early **Tannaim** gradually arranged for the addition of a specific Haftarah for each portion of the Torah.

HAGANAH. Defense force of Jews in Palestine before the establishment of the State of **Israel**. In 1920, in the early days of the British mandatory regime in Palestine, the Arabs attacked the small Jewish settlement of Tel-Hai, near the Syrian border. A few defenders, headed by Joseph **Trumpeldor**, held Tel-Hai but fell in its defense. The Arabs intensified their attacks. The bloody outbreaks in Jerusalem on Passover 1920 and those in Tel Aviv in May 1921, convinced Jews that they could not depend on the British Army for protection, but that they must organize for self-defense. Thus, despite a British ban on Jewish arms, the secret Haganah (Army of Defense) was formed during the 1920's.

In 1929, an attempt was made, under the leadership of the Mufti of **Jerusalem** Haij Amin el Husseini, to undermine the *Yishuv*, the Jewish community of Palestine. The Arabs massacred more than 50 yeshiva students in the Arab town of Hebron, and killed a number of Jews in old Jerusalem and Safed, all of them unarmed and defenseless. Their attacks on new settlements, however, were repelled by the Haganah.

The Arabs repeated their efforts to destroy the Yishuv in 1936. For 32 months, Arab bands harassed Jewish settlements. They caused considerable damage to property and took 500 lives. These repeated widespread Arab attacks hastened the formation of a large and powerful Jewish fighting force. First, units of Jewish special police were organized, and later Special Night Squads (SNS) were trained and led by the colorful British officer Orde **Wingate**. A master tactician, a Bible scholar, and an ally of the Jews, he developed commando methods to defeat the Arab bands. These SNS groups served as a training unit for the famous **Palmach**, the Jewish striking force.

Haganah recruits in pre-state days with light mortar.

On the eve of World War II, the Haganah forces numbered close to 15,000 men. The Yishuv was ready to make its contribution to the victory over the Nazis. Out of a total population of 500,000, 36,000 men and women registered for military and auxiliary services. Palestinian Jews joined all branches of military service and gained valuable experience as sailors, pilots, gunners, and draughtsmen. A Jewish Death Battalion of Commandos took part in the Abyssinian campaigns against the Italian invaders. Some units rendered outstanding service to the British Eighth Army which drove the Nazis out of North Africa.

All in all, close to 30,000 Palestinian Jews served in the Allied armed forces. On September 18, 1944, a **Jewish Brigade** was formed. Units of the Brigade participated in the campaigns in Italy. When the war ended, and before the Brigade was demobilized, it came to the aid of survivors of the **Holocaust**, strengthening their determination to reach the shores of the Jewish homeland.

The doors of Palestine were closed to Jewish immigrants by the British, who sought to appease the Arabs. The task of organizing the illegal entry of Jews into Palestine fell to the Haganah. After the war, it established an "illegal" underground immigration system through which Jews from all over Europe streamed to Palestine. A number of ships carrying Jewish immigrants to Palestine were intercepted and bitter fights ensued.

The issue of free immigration became the central point of the struggle between the British Administration and Palestinian Jews. The British concentrated a force of 100,000 in the area to "pacify" the Jews. Searches for hidden arms were carried on day and night. Haganah leaders were arrested and sent to detention camps, but the Jewish resistance movement continued to grow.

After the partition of Palestine by the UN decision of November 29, 1947, the Arabs embarked on an all-out campaign to destroy the

Yishuv. The armies of seven Arab states invaded Palestine. Overnight, the Haganah was transformed into the **Israel Defense Forces** and held the invading Arab armies at bay. Despite meager equipment and arms, the Israeli artillery, air force, and navy gave an excellent account of themselves and secured the present borders of the Jewish state.

HAGAR. When **Sarah** appeared to be barren, she gave **Abraham** her maid Hagar, who bore him **Ishmael.** Hagar was sent away by divine decree. Her son became the progenitor of the Arab people.

HAGGADAH. From Hebrew, meaning narration. The book containing the **Passover** Seder service. Written in Hebrew with some passages in **Aramaic**, the Haggadah tells the story of the **exodus** from **Egypt**. The original Seder probably consisted of the eating of the Paschal lamb, followed by an informal narration of the Passover story by the head of the house. During the period of the Second **Temple**, when daily and **Sabbath** prayers were assuming a standard form, there was a need for a uniform way of fulfilling the commandment of "telling" the Passover story. The first suggestions for the planning of the Seder service appear in the **Talmud**, where such parts of the present-day Haggadah as the Four Cups of wine and the Four Sons are mentioned. By 200 C.E., the Haggadah had a fairly fixed form; as time went on, additional material such as psalms were added. The Passover service became so long that sometime during the Middle Ages it was divided into two parts. The first part, including the Four Questions, narration of the exodus, and explanations of symbols, was recited before the meal. The second part consisted of the Grace, psalms, and songs after the meal. To make sure everyone understood the Haggadah, it was translated into many languages and often illustrated with biblical scenes and pictures of the Seder service. Many editions of the Haggadah have been written and printed throughout the world. The earliest manuscript available is from the 13th century; the earliest extant printed Haggadah carries the date 1505.

סדר
הגדה של פסח
ונוסף
נדפס
באמשטרדם

First page of the Haggadah, printed in Amsterdam in 1695.

Opposite page: Top, Haifa after dark as seen from Mt. Carmel. Bottom, Haifa Harbor. Courtesy State of Israel Bonds.

HAGGAI. One of the minor prophets in the **Bible.** He encouraged **Zerubbabel,** governor of Judea after the return of the Jews from the Babylonian exile, and urged the rebuilding of the **Temple.** Haggai's prophecy that the Second Temple would be more beautiful than the first was fulfilled.

HAGIOGRAPHA. *See* **Bible.**

HAIFA. Israel's principal port, situated where the mountains meet the sea, had in 1998 a population of 300,000. The city extends over the foot, slopes, and crest of Mount Carmel. Greater Haifa also includes Haifa Bay between the Kishon and Naaman rivers, with its oil refineries and heavy industries, as well as a chain of suburbs and villages. The lower city, fringing the harbor, is the mercantile center. Hadar Hacarmel is the residential and shopping section, interspersed with parks and gardens. Mount Carmel with its splendid forests, terraces of Persian gardens, and white villas commands a matchless view of the city, the sea, and the broad sweep of the bay, with snow-capped Mount Hermon in the hazy distance.

Haifa is not mentioned in the **Bible**, and is referred to only casually in the **Talmud** as a fishing village. **Herzl** called it the "city of the future" when it was still a small town of twisted streets. Until recent times it was cast in the shade by its rival **Acre.**

Its first Jewish community consisted of Moroccan and Algerian Jews who settled there in 1833. Once, it was linked with Damascus by the Hedjaz railway, and later to Cairo. Haifa's growth has been phenomenal, spurred by the construction of the deep sea harbor by the British mandatory government. When the British departed in 1948, the Jewish population took over the city, which has become the metropolis of northern Israel.

The city of Haifa has two institutions of higher learning, the **Technion** and the University of Haifa.

HAI GAON (939-1038). Head of the academy of Pumbeditha, **Babylonia,** Hai Gaon was the foremost authority of Talmudic law in his time. He was the last of the Geonim in Babylonia. In addition to his vast knowledge of Jewish law, he was familiar with Greek philosophy and Arabic literature and wrote poems and commentaries on the **Bible.**

HAITI. Several Spanish Jewish families settled in Haiti in the 16th century. They were driven out when the French, who did not favor Jewish colonists, took the island from the Spanish in 1683. Because the predominantly Black republic of Haiti does not favor white immigration, few Jews have settled here, however, a number arrived during World War II. In 1998, there were fewer

16

than 100 Jews out of a population of about 6 million. All were engaged in commerce. There is no organized Jewish community in this island republic.

HAKAFOT. Literally, encircling. During the **Sukkot** festival, culminating with Simchat Torah, people march around with the scroll of **Torah** carrying a **lulav** and an **etrog**, reminiscent of the procession around the altar in the time of the **Temple**.

HALLAH. Braided egg bread for the Friday night Sabbath meal, symbolic of the bread offering in the **Temple**.

HALACHA. Term applied to Jewish law as interpreted by the masters of the **Talmud** and later authorities. The legal framework of Jewish tradition, especially the Mishnah and rabbinic laws, is known as Halacha, as distinguished from the legendary and narrative portions of the Talmud, called **Aggadah**.

HA-LEVI, JUDAH (1085-1142). Hebrew poet of the Middle Ages. Born in **Spain** when it was under Christian rule, he went to study at the academy of Isaac Al-Fasi in Lucena, near Cordova, in Moslem Spain. Having acquired an extensive knowledge of the **Talmud**, philosophy, Arabic literature, and medicine, he returned to his native town to be a practicing physician. In his youth, Judah's joy of life was expressed in the poems he composed on love and the beauty of nature. Few Hebrew poems can rival the gracefulness, style, brilliance of expression, and tenderness found in the best of his poetry. His religious poems, on the other hand, are radiant with nobility of spirit and longing for the living God.

But he reserved his deepest passion and burning love for Zion; only in the land of Israel's glorious past could the poet find peace and fulfillment. Judah realized his dream. He set out first by boat to **Egypt**, then to **Palestine**. This trip enriched Hebrew literature with ardent and powerful songs of the sea. Legend has it that when Judah reached the ruins of the **Temple** and he knelt at the **Wailing Wall**, an Arab horseman trampled him to death.

Many of Judah's poems became part of the Jewish prayer book. His philosophic work *The Kuzari* greatly influenced Jewish thinking, attempting to prove the Jewish religion superior to the contemporary philosophic systems. Unlike Jewish philosophers before him, Judah Ha-Levi did not find it necessary to reconcile the Jewish religion with philosophic thought. For him, Jewish tradition needs no confirmation by reason; ethical perfection is best attained by religious observance. *The Kuzari* was written in the form of a discussion at the court of the king of the **Khazars** among representatives of the three major religions: Judaism, Christianity, and Islam. The king is finally convinced of the superiority of the Jewish religion. *The Kuzari* also stresses the intimate bond between the Jewish people and the Land of Israel, expressing the thought that "**Jerusalem** will be built when the children of Israel strongly desire it."

Oh Lord, where shall I find You?
All-hidden and exalted is Your place;

And where shall I not find You?
Full of Your glory is the infinite space.

— JUDAH HA-LEVI

HALLEL. Literally, hymns of praise. Consists of Psalms 113-118, which were sung by the **Levites** in the **Temple** in **Jerusalem** on **Sukkot**, **Passover**, **Shavuot**, and later **Hanukkah**. Hallel became part of the synagogue morning service for those days and New Moons. During the chanting of Hallel on Sukkot the *lulav*, or palm branch, is waved. Some congregations recite Hallel on Passover after the evening service, and it is also part of the Seder, or Passover service. (*See also* **Prayer**.)

HALPERN, ROSE (1895-1978). American Zionist leader. She headed **Hadassah** (1932-34, 1947-52) and became head of the American division of the **World Jewish Congress** in 1969.

HALUKAH. Literally, distribution. A system for the support of Jews in **Palestine** with funds raised abroad. The tradition of subsidizing Palestinian Jews goes back to Talmudic times when higher institutions of Jewish learning received such support. Systematic halukah began in 1600, when fairly large numbers of Jews settled in the Holy Cities of **Jerusalem**, **Safed**, **Hebron**, and **Tiberias** to pray for the coming of the Messiah. Lacking means of support, they sent messengers, or *meshulahim*, to raise money in the Diaspora. During the 19th century halukah contributions came from the entire Jewish world. When the Zionist movement replaced Messianic longings with the ideal of self-help, halukah fell into disrepute. It still exists, but its scope has been reduced to a minimum.

HALUTZIM. Literally, pioneers. The term came into widespread use after World War I, when Joseph **Trumpeldor** helped found the Hechalutz movement in **Russia**. Inspired by the ideal of rebuilding Palestine as a Jewish homeland, Halutzim came from countries ravaged by war and revolutions. To reach their goal, Russian Halutzim traveled dangerous roads over the Balkan lands and Caucasian mountains. Halutzim made up the bulk of the Third Aliyah, or immigration, to Palestine from 1918 to 1924. They undertook the most difficult tasks, building roads, draining swamps, and establishing colonies.

The first World Conference of the Hechalutz movement took place in Carlsbad, Czechoslovakia, in 1921. The movement established *hakhsharot*, or training farms, in many countries, particularly in Poland and other East European nations. The farms prepared the young Halutzim for agricultural life in Palestine, learning Hebrew and receiving a deeper knowledge of their people's history. Before World War II, Hechalutz members numbered in the tens of thousands. At the present time, Hechalutz organizations exist in North and Latin America, North and South Africa, and several European countries.

HAM. Literally, warm or hot. Second son of Noah, whose descendants are described in Gen. 10:6-20 as inhabiting the southernmost regions of the earth.

HAMAN. *See* **Purim**.

HAMETZ. *See* **Passover**.

HAMMER, ARMAND (1898-1990). American industrialist and art collector. He had business deals with Soviet Russia and became the owner of Occidental Petroleum Company, the world's largest privately-owned oil company. An art museum in **Los Angeles** in named after him.

HAMMERSTEIN, OSCAR Jr. *See* **Music**.

HA-MOTZI. Literally, he who brings out. Referring to God's bringing bread from the earth, this blessing is said before every meal.

HANNAH. Mother of the prophet **Samuel**, Hannah is famous for her story of barrenness and miraculous birth, which is recited on **Rosh Hashanah.**

HA-NOAR HA-OVED. Literally, working youth. A youth organization affiliated with the **Histadrut**, founded in 1924. Its members study handicrafts or prepare for agricultural settlement. It has branches through Israel, including the Arab and **Druze** sectors.

HA-NOAR HA-TZIONI. Literally, Zionist Youth. It started as a pioneering youth organization in Eastern Europe. Most of its members perished during the **Holocaust**. After the war it flourished in **Latin America** and western Europe. It has seven kibbutzim and five youth villages in Israel.

HANUKKAH. The Feast of Dedication and Lights, which falls on the 25th of **Kislev** and lasts for eight days. It marks the rededication of the **Temple** by Judah **Maccabee** in 165 B.C.E. after his victory over the Syrians who had defiled the sanctuary. Tradition relates that Judah could find only a single cruse of oil which had not been contaminated by the enemy. Although it contained only enough oil to light the **menorah** for one day, a miracle took place, and it burned for eight. Therefore, candles are lit throughout the holiday, one on the eve of the first day, two on the eve of the second, and so forth, until eight are kindled on the last evening.

A feast of liberation symbolizing the victory of the few over the many and of the weak over the strong, Hanukkah is one of the

Hanukkah menorah, 18th-century Poland. Courtesy the collection of Miriam Lipstadt Roth.

> *My heart is in the East,*
> *But I am in the uttermost West,*
>
> *How then can I taste what I eat,*
> *And how can food to me be sweet?*
>
> — JUDAH HA-LEVI

most joyful Jewish holidays. Gifts are given to children at candle-lighting time, and it is customary to play with a small top, or the dreidel, inscribed with the Hebrew letters N, G, H, and S. These stand for the words, *Nes Gadol Hayah Sham*, meaning, "A great miracle happened there."

In the synagogue, the **Torah** is read every day of Hanukkah, and **Hallel**, or Hymns of Praise, consisting of Psalms 113-118, is chanted. One of the hymns sung after the candles are lit is *Maoz Zur* (Rock of Ages). The prayer of *Al Ha-Nissim* (For the Miracles), which recounts the story of Hanukkah, is added to the Eighteen Benedictions and the usual order of Grace after meals.

The story of Hanukkah, which tells of the evil decrees of Antiochus Epiphanes against the Jews and the triumph of the **Maccabees** over their enemies, is related in the Book of the Maccabees of the **Apocrypha**. The second book contains the story of Hannah and her seven children who refused to bow before an idol and suffered a martyr's death at the hands of Antiochus' henchmen.

HARBY, ISAAC (1788-1828). Critic, playwright, precursor of Reform Judaism. Born in Charleston, S.C., Harby received a thorough classical education, studied law, and became a journalist. His critical essays and dramatic plays brought him considerable reputation. In 1824, he organized the Reform Society of Israelites, which sought to make changes in the traditional synagogue service. This organization lasted less than a decade; but it pointed the way to the later Reform movement in American Judaism.

HART, MOSS. *See* **Stage and Screen**.

HASDAI IBN SHAPRUT. *See* **Spain**.

HASHOMER. Literally, the watchman. From the beginning of modern Jewish settlement in Palestine in 1882, the settlers were exposed to attacks by their Arab neighbors. They resisted vigorously, and the Arabs soon realized that they faced a new type of Jew. Unlike their predecessors who had come to Palestine only to pray and die, the new settlers refused to be intimidated by physical threats. Some of these early heroic defenders became legends. They often fought the Arab marauders single-handed. At the same time they learned Arabic, studied Arab ways of thinking and living, and succeeded in establishing friendly relations with their Arab neighbors.

The first organized self-defense group was established in Palestine in 1907. The valor of this group of watchmen, which called itself Hashomer, soon became famous throughout Palestine. Galloping on their thoroughbred horses along the narrow paths of the Galilee mountains and valleys, the Shomrim were romantic figures. They paid a heavy price for their daring. Many of them fell fighting off armed marauders. They were also among the first to establish frontier settlements in Palestine; K'far Giladi in the north was an outstanding example.

HA-SHOMER HA-TZAIR. Literally, the young guard. Left-wing Zionist youth organization, first started in **Poland** in 1913. It became a major founder of kibbutzim in Israel and became prominent in Europe before the war. For a time it came under the influence of Marxism, which it eventually disavowed. It advocated close cooperation between Jews and Arabs. It was a major force in the founding of **Israel**, the **Palmach,** and the **Haganah**.

HASIDISM. Religious movement which began in the 18th century. At that time, life for the masses of Jews in the **Ukraine** and southern Europe was bitter and difficult. Jewish communities were destroyed or annihilated by the Cossack and peasant uprisings, and most Jews lived in stark poverty. Economically helpless, they were unable to acquire much learning. The scholarly rabbis and community leaders looked down upon the illiterate and semi-literate masses who spent their lives in poverty and ignorance.

To the common people who craved spiritual uplift, the personality and teachings of **Israel Baal Shem Tov** offered hope and dignity. The "Baal Shem" (ca. 1700-1760), founder of the Hasidic movement, placed prayer and faith on an equal level with scholarship and knowledge of the Law. Hasidism, therefore, appealed greatly to these "forgotten" Jews, for they no longer had to feel inferior to the scholar. Even the ignorant person, the Baal Shem taught, could find grace in the eyes of God if he prayed with purity of heart, devotion, and enthusiasm. Hasidism also introduced the idea of serving God with joy and happiness. It was opposed to excessive mourning and fasting as weakening to both the body and the soul.

The Hasidic movement encouraged a close bond among its followers. Mutual trust and companionship fostered a spirit of brotherhood. In the center of the closely knit group stood the *tzaddik*, or righteous man, the spiritual leader of the community who had reached a close union with God. He served as an intermediary between the Heavenly Power and man. His disciples' admiration for the *tzaddik* and the faith in his powers were boundless. The Hasidism believed that through prayers the *tzaddik* could alter the decrees of God and even perform miracles. The position and ability of the *tzaddik* were believed to be hereditary. This trust and loyalty in the leader was at times carried to excess, and obscured the true meaning of Hasidism.

The Hasidic Rabbi of Ger and his followers.

The Hasidic movement spread rapidly through the Ukraine, **Poland**, Galicia, and penetrated even the fortress of Jewish scholarship, **Lithuania**. The stress on prayer by the new popular movement; its lesser emphasis on Talmudic study; the creation of separate houses of prayer with some changes in liturgy; the extreme reliance on the *tzaddik*; and the inspired singing and dancing which was new to traditional services of the time: all of these deviations aroused bitter opposition from the Mitnagdim, the opponents of Hasidism. The opposition to the movement spread to many communities. Rabbis and leaders were alarmed at the rapid growth of Hasidism. The memory of the tragic **Sabbatai Zevi** affair contributed to the rabbis' fear that Hasidism might cause a rift in Judaism. The greatest rabbinical authority of the 18th century, the Gaon **Elijah** of **Vilna**, shared this distrust of Hasidism. In a letter to all Jewish communities in Lithuania, he urged an all-out campaign against the Hasidic movement. This internal conflict at times took on ugly forms; false accusations were made to the governmental authorities, opponents were excommunicated, and physical violence was not uncommon.

Yet all these persecutions did not stop the advance of Hasidism. Opposing rabbis and leaders finally realized that the new movement did not represent a threat to Jewish unity. Hasidism, on the other hand, recognized the value of the study of the law, while retaining its own character and appeal to the Jewish masses. In fact, Hasidism today is associated with extreme Orthodoxy, and its followers often wear distinct garb and oppose secular studies.

After the death of the Baal Shem Tov, the movement was led by his disciple, Rabbi Dov Ber of Mezhirich (1710-1772), also known as the great **Maggid**, or preacher. His "court" at the small town of Mezhirich became the center for the movement. Thousands of Jews flocked there to benefit from his wisdom and learning. His position as a scholar, preacher, and mystic contributed greatly toward the popular spread of Hasidism: eventually, it came to influence scholars as well.

Numerous disciples of Ber of Mezhirich established themselves as tzaddikim in their own right. They settled in various towns where they gained followers and influenced large numbers. Each one of them left an individual mark on Hasidism. Prominent among the famous Hasidic rabbis was Levi Yitzhak of Berditchev (1740-1809). His love for the individual was the predominant facet in his personality. In moving prayers, he appealed to God to put an end to the suffering of the Jewish people. His devotion to simple people and his kindness and understanding for the weaknesses of human nature became the subjects of numerous legends.

Another great disciple of Dov Ber of Mezhirich was Shneour Zalman (1748-1812), known as the Rabbi of Ladi. He introduced to Hasidism a more rational concept of Judaism, based on a profound knowledge of the **Talmud** and the **Kabbalah,** or teachings of Jewish mysticism. In the *Tanya,* Shneour Zalman formulated the three bases of his form of Hasidism: Wisdom, Understanding, and Knowledge (*habad*). Shneour Zalman emphasized scholarship as one of the pillars of Hasidism. He was among those falsely denounced for plotting against the Russian government. He was imprisoned and not released until his innocence had been clearly

Member of the Habad (Lubavitch) Hasidic movement helping visitors to the Western Wall in Jerusalem put on tefflin.

established. The branch of Hasidism begun by Shneour Zalman eventually became known as the Habad or Lubavitch movement. (*See* **Shneerson.**)

One of the most original and creative Hasidic teachers was **Nachman of Bratzlav**, the grandson of the Baal Shem. Close to nature and poetic, he preached the doctrine of simple and direct faith. For a short time he lived in Palestine and for the remainder of his life cherished a burning love for Zion. Nachman was a master of parable and fairytales in which he displayed a rich imagination and a deep morality.

Hasidism branched out in different directions and assumed various forms. The movement produced great teachers who enriched Jewish values and exerted great influence on the spiritual life of Jews for 200 years. Pinkhas of Koretz, Elimelekh of Lizhensk, Jacob Yitzhak of Lublin ("The Seer"), Mendel of Kotzk, and many others were leaders who extended the influence and scope of Hasidism. To this day, Hasidism remains a vital force among Jews around the world. Many Hasidic rebbes who survived the Holocaust resettled in the U.S. and **Israel** and established new communities. In modern times, Hasidism has served as a source of inspiration for such non-Hasidic literary masters as **Peretz, Berditchevsky, Asch,** and **Agnon.** Jewish culture as a whole owes a great debt to the movement. Almost every form of artistic expression—the stage, music, dance—have used Hasidic themes and motifs.

HASKALAH. Literally, enlightenment. Great social and cultural changes began to take place in Western Europe in the 18th century. Philosophers such as Montesquieu, Voltaire, and Locke in **France** and **England** began to question the existing authority of Church and State and the prevailing social order. They introduced new concepts of freedom, religious tolerance, equality, and reliance on reason rather than tradition. These ideas ushered in a new era of rationalism and enlightenment.

During the early Enlightenment period, Jewish life in most European countries was still enclosed in the **ghetto.** As a result of generations of persecution and isolation, Jews differed from their neighbors not only in religion and education but also in language, dress, and habits. The hostile attitude of the gentile world forced Jews to seek security and peace within their own community. As the Enlightenment movement began to take hold educated Jews in Prussia and those who held high economic and financial positions clamored for equal rights. They sought to abolish the degrading and discriminating laws directed against them. Believing that emancipation was at hand, they sought to break down the ghetto walls; many broke with Jewish religious traditions as well.

More Jews began to participate in the cultural and literary life of **Germany.** Berlin became the center of the Jewish Enlightenment movement. The leading spirit of this group was Moses **Mendelssohn** who began as a poor rabbinical student and gained fame as a German author and philosopher. Mendelssohn sought to bring Jews closer to European culture and lifestyle without giving up their own cultural and religious values. Under his guidance and inspiration there was a short-lived revival of **Hebrew language** and **literature.**

By the beginning of the 19th century, a large part of German Jewry was well on the road to **assimilation.** From Germany, the Enlightenment moved first to Galicia and later to **Russia.** In both countries, the Jewish masses followed their traditional way of life, and outside influences had little effect. Hence, they turned inward to the development of Jewish literature, enriching it with new forms and ideas. Rabbi Nachman **Krochmal** in Galicia, Yitzhak Ber Levinson, Abraham **Mapu**, Judah L. **Gordon**, and Peretz **Smolenskin** in Russia were the outstanding leaders of the Haskalah movement.

In Eastern Europe, the Haskalah movement developed a national purpose and a practical approach to the Jewish problem. It proposed that Jews improve their economic condition by engaging in agriculture and other useful trades. It also called for the inclusion of secular subjects in Jewish schooling and the relaxing of rabbinical restrictions. On the whole, the movement aimed at striking a happy medium between faith and enlightenment. Orthodox Jews, however, were frightened by the assimilation and conversion that had resulted from the Haskalah movement in Germany. They opposed every effort to institute innovations and bring about changes in traditional Jewish life.

The writers of the Haskalah were the forerunners of the Jewish national revival which took place after the Russian pogroms in 1881. This revival later gave rise to the Zionist movement, which finally culminated in the establishment of the State of **Israel.**

HASMONEANS. *See* **Maccabees.**

HA-TIKVAH. Literally, *The Hope.* The national anthem of **Israel.** Written in 1878 by the poet Naphtali Herz **Imber** and set to music by Samuel Cohen, it was adopted as the Zionist national anthem early in the 20th century. Since then, it has been accepted by Jews throughout the world. *Ha-Tikvah* expresses the eternal hope of Israel to live as a free nation in the land of Zion. When the State of Israel was established in 1948, *Ha-Tikvah,* with a slight change of the wording in its last two lines, became the national anthem.

HAVDALAH. *See* **Sabbath.**

HAVURAH. Literally, fellowship. Small groups of Jews who meet for study and fellowship, begun after the destruction of the Second **Temple** in the 1st century C.E. In the U.S. in the late 1960's, because of their discontent with organized Jewish life and the alienation of individuals and families in society, Jews inside and outside the organized community formed such groups to revitalize the Jewish experience. Some of those Havurot have endured as a new expression of the grassroots American Jewish experience.

HAWAII. Fiftieth state of the U.S., admitted on August 21, 1959. In 1998, there were about 7,000 Jews in Hawaii, most of them in Honolulu, comprising less than one percent of the general population. The majority came to the Islands during the past 20 years. Community life centers around Temple Emanu-El which conducts a religious school and adult education courses.

HAZAN. Originally, at the time of the **Talmud**, the hazan was a caretaker of the synagogue and a functionary at the religious ceremonials. Today, the term *hazan*, or cantor, is applied to one who chants the religious services at temple and synagogue.

Modern cantonal music had its origin in the work of the Jewish Italian rabbi and composer, Salomon Rossi. Salomon Sulzer, Louis Lewandowsky, and many other hazanim in the 19th century helped develop the cantonal music used extensively in the synagogue to this day. Among the great cantors of our time, Rosenblatt, Kusevitsky, and Oysher stand out.

HAZAZ, CHAIM (1898-1973). One of the great masters of Hebrew prose. He won early recognition with his portrayal of life in a Jewish small town during the Russian revolution and civil war of 1917. His range of writing embraces Jewish life in many countries and generations. One of his penetrating satirical novels on the life of Yemenite Jewry has been translated into English and published as *Mori Said*. Born in **Ukraine**, he settled in Palestine in 1931.

Ha-Tikvah. The National Anthem of Israel.

HEH. Fifth letter of the Hebrew alphabet; numerically, five.

HAZOR. Fortress on a hill in northeastern **Galilee**; site of one of the major **archeological** discoveries of our time (*see* **Yadin**). It revealed several ancient civilizations, inspiring James Michener's *The Source*, a historical novel about Jews and **Israel**.

HEAVEN AND HELL. In the Hebrew **Bible** there is little mention of life after death. Basically, life in ancient Israel was here and now, and posterity simply meant the perpetuation of life through one's descendants. In the story of creation, life begins in the Garden of Eden, or paradise, which lasts for only one generation (*see* **Adam** *and* **Eve**). Later, we find allusions to a netherworld called Sheol, where one goes after death, but it is never explained in any detail.

It is not until the post-biblical period that new beliefs in life after death and in reward and punishment in the next life begin to emerge. These new beliefs coincided with similar ideas in **Christianity**, the new religion of that time to which those beliefs were central. But even in Talmudic literature the ideas about heaven and hell remain vague, more allegorical than dogmatic. In Hebrew "heaven" is referred to as *Gan Eden*, or Garden of Eden, and "hell" is *gehinom*, the name of a valley outside Jerusalem where the scapegoat was sacrificed on **Yom Kippur**. In one Talmudic story, heaven is described as the place where the righteous people sit in a circle with crowns on their heads and learn divine wisdom directly from God.

In the Middle Ages, a time of supernatural belief and superstition, the idea of heaven and hell became well established and quite vivid, and many Jews lived in fear of hell and deep hope for heaven. In modern times, however, Reform Jews choose to believe in the immortality of the soul, while the Orthodox continue to believe in heaven and hell. Conservative Judaism leaves this belief to the individual.

A belief related to heaven and hell is the resurrection of the dead, one of Maimonides' **Thirteen Principles** of the Jewish faith. Yet even Maimonides vacillates when he discusses this belief. Another related idea is the transmigration of souls, which appears in the **Kabbalah** as *gilgul neshamot*.

Regardless, however, of individuals' belief in heaven and hell, the focus of Judaism has always been on life here and now, the time during which one must live a worthy life.

HEBREW LANGUAGE. Hebrew belongs to the northern group of Semitic languages, which also includes **Aramaic**, Assyrian, Arabic, and Syriac. Most of the ancient peoples in the lands adjoining Palestine—the Moabites, Amorites, and Edomites—seem to have spoken a common language.

The ancient Ugaritic tablets dating back to the 14th century B.C.E. and found in the city of Ugarit in Northern Syria, and the Moabite Stone of King Mesha from 9th century B.C.E. are both written in Hebrew or in a closely related dialect. Although Hebrew underwent many modifications in the course of generations, it has retained its ancient structure and character. It is basically the same language today as 3,500 years ago in the days of the **Patriarchs**. The rich literature of the **Bible** has preserved for us some of the ancient forms of the language as well as its basic characteristics.

The **Hebrew alphabet** consists of 22 letters, all consonants. Vowel signs were invented much later for easier reading and are

Book of Roots, by Hebrew grammarian David Kimhi (1160-1235).

placed under and above the consonants. However, even in ancient times, some letters, such as *Aleph*, *He*, *Vav*, and *Yod*, served the purpose of vowels. All the parts of speech and word forms are based on a root, generally consisting of three letters. This root is expanded by means of prefixes and suffixes, as well as by changes in sound or vocalization. A verb may be used in several and sometimes all of the seven conjugations, giving the language flexibility.

Biblical Hebrew is distinguished by its simplicity and directness. It is vivid and expressive, lending itself beautifully to the poetic form. At the same time, it has few abstract forms, adjectives, and adverbs.

During the Babylonian Exile (586 B.C.E.) the development of Hebrew was marked by the ever-increasing influence of the Aramaic language on Hebrew grammar and vocabulary. During the period of the Second **Temple**, Mishnaic Hebrew came into being. The language of the Mishnah essentially follows the rules of biblical Hebrew, but it is enriched with new words and grammatical forms. Greek and Latin terms were assimilated and given Hebraic form. The language became more descriptive and now better equipped to express ideas, both practical and abstract.

Although Hebrew was rarely used again as an everyday language until the growth of modern Zionism in the 19th century, it continued as the language of prayer and literature. Jews at all times displayed love and affection for Hebrew as their holy tongue, in which the Bible was written and the Law proclaimed. It was a reminder of the days of their independence and glory. Throughout the ages, poets, scholars, philosophers, grammarians, and translators all contributed to the development of Hebrew. In the Middle Ages, Hebrew was influenced by Arabic. The scientific works translated into Hebrew from the Arabic enriched the Hebrew vocabulary and increased its power to express new ideas.

A revival of the Hebrew literature and language took place in the 19th century. This revival was marked in the beginning by a return to biblical Hebrew. But in the course of time, it was recognized that classical Hebrew required expansion and modification if it was to be used as a modern tongue. It became necessary to coin new words and expressions and to adapt old ones for modern needs.

In the 1880's, Eliezer **Ben Yehudah** pioneered in the revival of Hebrew as a spoken language. His example was taken up enthusiastically by many followers. Hebrew-speaking groups were formed throughout the world. A mass of technical and scientific terms in all fields of human endeavor were created. The ancient tongue has displayed remarkable adaptability to modern needs. Today, Hebrew keeps pace with the steady progress of science and technology. It is the living language of the State of **Israel**. (*See figure on page 122.*)

HEBREW LITERATURE. Hebrew literature from the biblical days to the present embraces a period of approximately 3,500 years. The **Bible**, the cornerstone of the Jewish religion, law, and ethics, has been the source of inspiration for Hebrew literary activity throughout Jewish history. The monumental works of the **Talmud** and **Midrashic** literature are essentially interpretations of and commentaries on the Bible, or writings stimulated by it.

The books of the Bible were not the only spiritual and literary treasures of this early period in Jewish history. The Bible itself mentions the Book of Wars of the Lord, The Book of the Righteous, and the Chronicles of the Kings of Judah and Israel, all of which have been lost in antiquity. It is likely that many more such epic works have similarly disappeared.

The period following the return of the Jews from **Babylonia** (538 B.C.E.) and the reestablishment of the Jewish commonwealth witnessed the revival of Hebrew literary activity. Many works followed the pattern and character of the Bible. Because they were of a later period, these works were not deemed worthy to be included among the sacred books of the Bible. Most of the **Apocrypha**, as these books are called, were written in Hebrew and represent a link between the Bible and the subsequent Midrashic literature. Parts of the original Hebrew text of one of the Apocryphal Wisdom books, **Ben Sira**, have recently been recovered. Other Apocrypha have come down to us in their Greek, Latin and Syriac translations. Of great historical and literary value are the recently found **Dead Sea Scrolls**—the oldest Hebrew manuscripts in existence.

The Talmud is mainly a compilation of Jewish law, remarkable in its encyclopedic scope and character. It reflects Jewish creativity for nearly a thousand years. The **Aggadic** parts of the Talmud are rich in stories, legends, moral and ethical instruction, parables, songs, prayers, dramatic dialogues, and fanciful, symbolic visions of the world-to-come, or of the Messianic times.

Geonic Period. After the close of the Talmud (about 500 C.E.), its laws, enactments, and discussions were further interpreted and extended during the Geonic period in Babylonia (from the seventh to the end of the 11th century C.E.). One of the outstanding works of the period is *Halakhot Gedolot*, a compilation of laws attributed to Judah Gaon in the 8th century. Some of the Geonim produced historical accounts (such as the Letter of **Sherira** Gaon) as well as works on grammar, and liturgical poetry. **Hai** Gaon and **Saadiah** Gaon employed the poetical

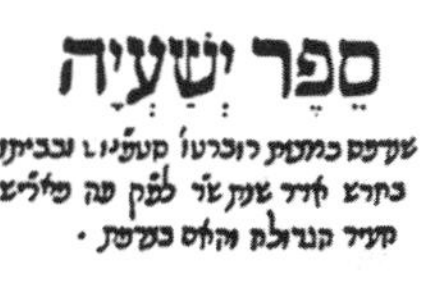

Prophetia Isaiæ.

A Bible published in Paris in 1544. Left, Book of Isaiah. Right, Book of Exodus.

form even in explaining the Law. They also composed meditations or prayers in which lofty thoughts and delicate emotions mingled with deep religious fervor. The Masorites, who arranged the Masoretic text of the Bible (*see* **Masorah**), were active primarily during the Geonic period in Palestine. The punctuation and vocalization of the biblical text took place around the 8th century. The chief authority in this field was Aaron Ben Asher.

Liturgy. Liturgical poetry flourished in Palestine from the 6th to the 8th century. However, a number of moving prayers and poetical passages have come down to us from earlier times. An example of these is the **Sabbath** prayer, *El Adon* (God the Master). The early liturgy was still under the influence of the poetic majesty and simplicity of the Bible. Representative religious poets of that period were Jose ben Jose, Yannai, and Eliezer **Kallir**. The latter was particularly prolific. His style is most flowery, introducing new forms and coining new Hebrew words. The liturgical poets drew on the legends and teachings of the Talmud and Midrashim, as well as the Bible, for themes. Jose ben Jose is remembered for his imposing portrayal of the **Yom Kippur** service in the **Temple** before its destruction. A further development of liturgical poetry took place in Italy during the 10th and 11th centuries. This poetry, generally striking a plaintive note, bewailed the bitter lot of the persecuted Jew and pleaded with God to save his people. A number of these poems, hymns and lamentations are recited on **fast days** and days of mourning.

The Zohar, Mantua, Italy, 1560.

Italian Scholarship. The Hebrew scholars in Italy also produced historical works. One of these, called Yosippon, was based on the historical masterpieces of Josephus **Flavius**. The *Sefer Ha-Kabbalah*, by Abraham Ibn Daud (1110-1180), another important historical source, traced the development of rabbinic tradition and scholarship. In the 11th century, Nathan ben Yehiel Ha-Romi completed a comprehensive dictionary of the Talmud and Midrashim. In the 10th century, works on medicine were contributed by Sabbatai Donnola, who drew extensively on the knowledge of the Greeks.

Golden Age in Spain. In the beginning of the 10th century a great revival of Hebrew literature took place in **Spain**. The patronage of Hasdai **Ibn Shaprut**, a physician and chief counselor to the Caliph, stimulated the spread of Jewish learning and creativity. This was the opening of a new era, called the "Golden Age of Spain." Stimulated by Arab scholarship, Jewish scholars contributed to all fields of Jewish literature and the sciences, including poetry, grammar, philosophy, astronomy, mysticism, medicine, and biblical and Talmudic commentary.

The foremost grammarians—among them Menachem, Jonah Ibn Jannah, and Judah Hayyuj—formulated the rules of the Hebrew language, its structure and character. Outstanding poets, such as Samuel **Ha-Nagid**, Solomon **Ibn Gabirol**, Judah **Ha-Levi**, and Abraham and Moses **Ibn Ezra**, introduced new and secular themes to Hebrew poetry. They sang of battles, love, wine, friendship, and travels, often with satirical and humorous overtones. In the Dark Ages, when Jews were subjected to constant persecution and suffering, the Hebrew poets of Spain opened new horizons of beauty and thought. However, the greater part of their poetry was dedicated to religious themes and to the passionate plea for the restoration of the Jewish people to Zion. Judah **Alharizi**, 13th century author of *Tahkemoni* (Academy), a collection of stories in rhyming prose, was one of the last representatives of the Golden Age in Spain.

Philosophical Writings. Jewish philosophic works were as a rule written in Arabic. Many were translated into Hebrew by members of the **Ibn Tibbon** family. The most influential of the philosophic works include *Emunot Ve-Deot* (Beliefs and Opinions) by Saadiah Gaon; *Moreh Nebukhim* (Guide for the Perplexed) by **Maimonides**; and the *Kuzari* by Judah Ha-Levi. Each one of these books had overwhelming influence on Jewish religious thought. Other works of note in philosophy and ethics are *Mekor Hayyim* (Fountain of Life) by Solomon Ibn Gabirol, and *Hovot Ha-Levavot* (The Duties of the Heart) by Bahya **Ibn Pakuda**. Levi ben Gerson, also known as **Gersonides** (1288-1344), an adherent of Aristotelian thought, defended the philosophic principles of Maimonides in his *Milhamot Adonai* (Battles of the Lord). *Or Adonai* (Light of the Lord) by Hasdai **Crescas** (c. 1340-1412) and *Sefer Ha-ikkarim* (Book of Principles) by Joseph **Albo** (1380-1440) explained the fundamental principles of the Jewish faith, defending it against Christian and rationalistic criticism. The latter three philosophic works were written in Hebrew.

Studies in Bible, Talmud, Mysticism, and Ethics. Throughout the ages, commentaries on the Bible and the Talmud were rich and fruitful fields of Hebrew literature. Some commentaries of the Bible stem from the days of the **Tannaim**. The greatest contribution toward the understanding of the Bible and Talmud, especially the latter, was made by Shelomo Yitzhaki (**Rashi**). The literal, or factual interpretation of the biblical text preoccupied many of the commentators. The most distinguished of these were Samuel ben Meir, Rashi's grandson, Abraham **Ibn Ezra**, and David **Kimhi**. Other scholars wrote ethical, philosophical and even mystic interpretations of the Scriptures-e.g., **Nahmanides**, Gersonides, and Don Isaac **Abravanel**.

Numerous works dealing with all phases of Talmudic study have been produced since the final editing of the Talmud. These include codes of Jewish law and Responsa, or rabbinical discussion of particular religious and legal problems. The Tosafists, who came after Rashi and were active in the 12th and 13th centuries, continued the process of expanding and advancing the knowledge of Talmudic law. Keen reasoning power, thorough knowledge of the vast Talmudic literature, and exhaustive discussion of the principles of Jewish law characterize the commentaries of the great Polish scholars in the 16th century. Outstanding were Solomon Luria (Maharshal), Rabbi Meir of Lublin (Maharam), and Samuel Edels (Maharsha). Their works together with those of their predecessors (**Alfasi**, Rabbi Hananel of Kairwan, Rashi, Nissim ben Reuben of Gerona, known as Ran, and the Tosafists) are published with every edition of the Talmud.

Since the 13th century, study of **Kabbalah**, the mystic trend in Judaism, has produced a variety of literary works. The **Zohar**, the Principal book of Kabbalah, stimulated the creation of a rich literature of mysticism in the 16th century. Even the literal interpreter of Jewish law, the great codifier, Rabbi Joseph Karo, came under the spell of the Kabbalah; together with other mystics, he sought to hasten the coming of the Messiah.

With the expulsion of the Jews from Spain in 1492 and the formation of new centers of learning in **Poland**, Jewish creativity centered on Talmudic studies. In the yeshivot of Poland a system of study known as **pilpul** evolved. A rich rabbinic literature of Responsa accumulated. Ethical works, expressing the pietistic spirit of the times, became extremely popular. The new books of morality included *Menorat Ha-Maor* (Candelabrum of Light) by Isaac Aboab, *Reshit Hokhma* (The Beginning of Wisdom) by Elijah de Vidos, and *Shevet Musar* (The Rod of Instruction) by Elijah Ha-Kohen.

Italy, however, saw the development of a more secular literary tradition. Dante's *Divine Comedy* was the model for such Hebrew works as the sonnets and *Ha-Tofet Ve-Ha-Eden* (Hell and Eden) by Immanuel of Rome, which found many imitators. Immanuel's influence extended well into the 17th century, when Moses Zacuto (1625-1697) composed the first Hebrew drama.

Enlightenment Period (*see* **Haskalah**). New "enlightened" social and political ideas emerged in the 18th century. Under the influence of the Enlightenment movement, Jews began to call for a reappraisal of traditional Jewish values. There was the feeling that the strictness of Jewish religious organization isolated the Jew from his environment. In **Germany**, a group of Maskilim, or "enlightened" Jews, undertook to revive the Hebrew language and literature, under the leadership of Moses **Mendelssohn**. In 1784 they began to publish a Hebrew monthly called *Ha-Meassef* (The Gatherer). In the course of time *Ha-Meassef* became a quarterly and then an annual journal. Finally, as the German Jews forsook Hebrew for the language and culture of their native land, it ceased publication altogether.

Earlier, the Italian Moses Hayim **Luzzato** (1707-1747) had ushered in a new phase of Hebrew literature. Though he was deeply religious, his plays were worldly in their approach to man and nature. He was followed by the poets David Franco-Mendes; Naphtali Herz Wessely (or Weisl), author of *Shire Tiferet* (Poems of Glory); Shalom Hacohen and Shlomo Levinson (or Lewisohn), a poet and scholar of note who set forth his appreciation of beauty in a masterful poem, *Ha-Melizah Medaberet* (Poetry Speaks). Perhaps the most noteworthy contribution of the early Maskilim to Hebrew scholarship was Mendelssohn's *Biur*, (translation), a new, more scientific and rational interpretation of the Bible.

During the second period the Enlightenment centered in Galicia, a province of Austro-Hungary, where the Jews clung to their traditional way of life. Here the new ideas of the maskilim were bitterly opposed by the pious, especially the Hasidim. Outstanding among the Hebrew authors, some of whom developed the satiric novel to combat their opponents, were Joseph Perl and Yitzhak Erter.

This period was also noteworthy for its important scholarly contributions. Solomon Judah Rapoport produced some important scholarly works based on historical research. *Moreh Nebukhe Ha-Zman* (Guide for the Perplexed of Our Time) by Nachman **Krochmal** represented an historical approach to the development of the Jewish spirit and religion that greatly influenced subsequent Jewish philosophy and scholarship. At about the same time, Samuel David **Luzzato** produced scholarly essays on the Bible, the Hebrew language, and philosophy. In contrast to most of the other Enlighteners, Luzzato advocated strict adherence to Jewish traditions and considered the ethical teachings of Judaism superior to any philosophical system of thought. Jewish scholarship was greatly enhanced by the five-volume work by Isaac Hirsch Weiss on the history of Talmudic literature-the most comprehensive work of its kind, tracing the origin of Jewish law from the Bible to the end of the 15th century.

Russia. By the middle of the 19th century, modern Hebrew literature had begun to develop in **Russia**. One of the first of the modern Hebrew authors, Isaac Baer Levinsohn, advocated the introduction of secular studies and the teaching of trades in the Jewish school system. Brief texts on general and Jewish history, geography, and biography, in a modernized biblical Hebrew, were written by Mordecai Aaron Ginzburg (1796-1846) and Kalman Shulman (1819-1899). The first significant Hebrew poet in Russia, Abraham Dov Levinsohn (Adam Ha-Kohen, 1794-1878) composed reflective poetry. The lyric genius of his son, Micah Joseph Levinsohn (1828-1852), was expressed in tender, lyrical poems bearing the tragic foreboding of his early death. His greatest contribution to Hebrew verse consists of six biblical narrative poems expressing the conflicts of universal human emotions. His poems on biblical themes were matched only by Abraham **Mapu**'s popular novels describing the glories of Israel in biblical times.

The leading spirit of the Enlightenment in Russia was J. L. **Gordon**. Toward the end of his life Gordon, who had been in the forefront of the battle against the old stultifying ghetto traditions, admitted his disappointment with the results of the Enlightenment. The greatest poet of his day, Gordon enriched all forms of Hebrew verse: historical, narrative, and satirical. During the same period, Hebrew novelists often subjected the contemporary Jewish scene to scathing criticism. The greatest of these novelists, Peretz **Smolenskin** and Reuben Asher Brodes, ridiculed the ignorance, narrow-mindedness, and backwardness of Jewish life. The Hebrew press which emerged at the end of the 1850's joined in the struggle for the spiritual and social emancipation of the Jewish people. The Hebrew periodicals, *Ha-Melitz* (The Advocate), *Ha-Carmel* and *Ha-Tzefirah* (Daybreak), spread the ideas of the Enlightenment throughout Eastern Europe.

The pogroms of 1881 in Russia hastened the disillusionment of the "Enlighteners." M.L. **Lilienblum**, formerly a leader in the fight for change in Jewish religious life, the novelist R. A. Brodes, and some of the Hebrew writers who had been attracted to Socialism now turned to Jewish nationalism.

The 1880's was a transitional period in Hebrew literature. The theme in the Hebrew poetry of the period was the yearning for Zion. N. H. **Imber**, K. A. Shapiro, a true and pure lyricist, M. M. Dolitzky, and M. Z. Maneh, all sang romantically of Zion. But the period was also a turning point in the revival of the Hebrew language. Eliezer **Ben Yehudah** became the advocate of spoken Hebrew. Very few believed that the language of the Bible could again come alive. Soon, however, Hebrew-speaking groups sprang up all over the Diaspora. The Hebrew press grew. The first Hebrew daily, *Ha-Yom* (The Day), made its appearance in 1886. Writers and literary critics of note, such as Nahum **Sokolow**, David Frischmann, and Reuben Brainin, contributed greatly to the modernization of Hebrew literature.

Renaissance of Hebrew Literature. Mendele Mocher Sefarim (Shalom Jacob Abramowitz) opened new horizons for the realistic novel. Mendele, who had begun his literary career in the Enlightenment period, ushered in a new era in the Hebrew language and literature at the end of the 1880's. He realized that biblical Hebrew was inadequate for portraying present-day life in its great variety. Mendele therefore drew upon the rich stores of the language in the Mishnah, Midrash, and the literary sources of the Middle Ages, to create a vigorous new Hebrew.

Mendele was followed by two important figures: **Ahad Ha-Am**, the brilliant essayist and pleader for a spiritual center in Palestine, and Chaim Nachman **Bialik**, the poet who best expressed the essence of East European Judaism. Saul **Tschernichowsky**, Jacob Cohen, and Zalman **Shneur**, three of Bialik's contemporaries, each left an individual and distinctive mark on Hebrew poetry: Tschernichowsky through mastery of form, Cohen in lyrical verse, and Shneur in his striking nature poems.

The poetry of David Shimoni (1886-1956), Jacob Fichman, Yehudah Karni (1884-1948), and Jacob Steinberg (1886-1948), was considerably influenced by Bialik. Yet each of these poets succeeded in striking an individual note and in making his own, unique contribution as a critic of great persuasion and charm. Shimoni sang of the *halutz* and portrayed the new life in pioneer Palestine in his romantic and appealing idylls, while Karni is one of the most colorful poets of **Jerusalem**.

The 1890's and the beginning of the 20th century saw the rise of the realistic modern Hebrew novel. Joseph Chaim **Brenner**, S. Ben-Zion, Isaiah Bershadsky, described the bitter poverty and despair prevalent in the Jewish towns of Eastern Europe. The short novel achieved artistic perfection in the masterly works of Uri Zvi Gnessin, Gershon Schoffman, and Itzhak Dov Berkowitz. Berkowitz skillfully translated most of the works of Sholom **Aleichem**, the great Yiddish humorist, into Hebrew. The Hasidic tale, as well as the life of the simple folk, were reproduced in classic style by J.L. **Peretz**, Micah Joseph **Berditchevsky**, and Judah Steinberg. Hasidic lore was also the subject of philosophic and historic essays and works by Hillel Zeitlin and S.A. Horodetzky. The philosophic Hebrew essay reached its height in the writings of Jacob Klatzkin (1882-1948).

In the years immediately preceding World War I, the Hebrew writers who emigrated to Palestine continued to write of the Old Country. These writers included Dvorah Baron, Samuel Joseph **Agnon**, Asher Barash, and Abraham Aaron Kabak. Kabak is the author of a number of historical novels, the most famous of which deal with the life of the mystic Solomon **Molkho**, and with Jewish life in the 19th century.

Hebrew Literature in Israel. After World War II, the State of **Israel** became the center of Hebrew literature. The new life in Israel produced a number of romantic and realistic novels from the pens of Moshe Smilansky, A. Reubeni, Dov Kimhi, and Avigdor Hameiri. The latter, a poet and novelist, was born in Hungary and served as officer in the Austrian army during World War I. His short stories and novels dealing with his war experiences are gripping accounts of human cruelty, degradation, and suffering. Later arrivals to the Holy Und were Chaim **Hazaz**, a novelist of deep insight and brilliant style, Yehudi Yaari, Yitzhak Shenhar and Israel Zarhi. Yaari describes the new immigrant and his impressions of the new land. Shenhar combines sober realism with lyric undertones, and his stories have a clever satirical twist. Zartli, who died young, reflected the life of the first settlers in his novels.

One of the most prolific and highly talented writers, Eliezer Steinman, produced numerous novels, essays and anthologies of Hasidic and Talmudic lore.

Born in Israel, Yehuda Burla describes in his novels the life of Oriental Jews, often with much warmth and local color. One of his best novels, *The Adventures of Akavyah,* is the life story of the son of a Turkish-Jewish family, who grows up in the mountains of Anatolia and meets with strange adventures before reaching Jerusalem. Fate, passion, and romance are the interesting ingredients which makes up most of Burla's fascinating stories. His historical novels center around the life and experiences of Yehuda Ha-Levi and of Rabbi Yehuda ben Solomon **Hai Alkalai**.

Hebrew poetry was enriched between the two World Wars by the works of Yitzhak Lamdan (1889-1954) and Abraham **Shlonsky** (1900-1973). Lamdan is best known for his dramatic poem *Massadah*. This poem became a symbol for a generation of pioneers who dedicated their lived to the upbuilding of the land. For the last twenty years of his life, Lamdan was also editor of the excellent monthly, *Gilyonot*. Shlonsky was a versatile modern poet and a masterful translator. Noteworthy also were Rachel Bluvstein's (*see* **Rachel**) tender, lyrical songs; Sh. Shalom's mystical and nationalistic verses, the modem poetry of Nathan Alterman and Leah Goldberg, and the quiet Hasidic poems of Shimshon Meltzer. Other poets of note were Yockeved Bat-Miriam and Anda Amir-Pinkerfeld.

Uri Zvi **Greenberg** (1895-1981) stands out as one of the giants of Hebrew poetry in the 20th century. His bold use of classic as well as modern Hebrew, his powerful narrative poetry covering both the rebirth of the Jewish nation and the horrors of the Holocaust, his moral indignation reminiscent of the biblical prophets, put him on par with Bialik.

A number of Hebrew writers were active between the World Wars outside Palestine. Matthias Shoham, brilliant poet and dramatist, probed into the roots of Jewish faith and destiny. Hayim Lensky struggled to break out of his isolation in Soviet Russia to sing of a new life in poetry which is a mixture of traditionalism and modernism.

New talents in the field of poetry and the novel have appeared in the last four decades. These were native Israelis who grew up during the turbulent years of building the land and developing a new culture, and who fought in the War of Independence. The varied experiences of the then young generation of Israelis are reflected in the deeply lyrical novels of S. Yitzhar, in the works of Moshe Shamir, who has written a notable historical novel on King Alexander **Jannaeus**, and in the writings of Igal Mossensohn, Aaron Meged, Nathan Shaham, Nissim Gloni and others.

In the 1960's and 1970's there emerged a new generation of poets and novelists of note. Some of them have already left their mark on Hebrew letters. Their works in translation have gained recognition for their craftsmanship and imagination in many lands.

Among these talented poets, Yehuda Amichai ranks as an innovator. His use of everyday language in his poetry, his ironic imagery, and existentialist intellectual and emotional posture have created a new trend in Hebrew poetry. Other poets, who are highly individualistic, and yet express national and social experiences were Reuven Ben-Yosef, T. Carmi, Chaim Guri, Amir Gilboa, Dan Pagis, and Abba Kovner.

Among the novelists Hanoch Bartov, Binyamin Tammuz, Yehudit Handel, Amalia Kahana-Carmon, Yitzhak Oren, David

Amos Oz.

Yehuda Amichai.

Aharon Appelfeld.

David Grossman.

Dahlia Rabikovitch.

A.B. Yehoshua.

Shachar, M. Tabib and others are exponents of the generation that saw the establishment of the State of Israel and depicted changes in Israeli society, attitudes and aspirations affected by new conditions and problems faced by individuals or the country as a whole.

More perplexed and complex are the characters and themes in the works of talented writers such as Yoram Kaniuk, Yitzhak Orpaz, Meir Shalev, Yitzhak Ben-Ner, Sammy Michael, Amos **Oz**, Pinchas Sadeh, A. B. **Yehoshua**, Yehoshua Kenaz, and David **Grossman**. Oz and Yehoshua gained universal recognition for their works depicting the many-faceted Israeli scene, complex situations and experiences, both individual and collective. Oz was awarded the highest Israeli cultural recognition, the Israel Award, in 1998, and is considered the leading Israeli novelist of his generation. Another major Israeli novelist is Aharon **Appelfeld**, the leading writer on Holocaust themes in Israel.

Israeli Hebrew verse has likewise been enriched by new forms and poetic innovations. Books on poetry appear every year in the hundreds. The more established names are: David Avidan, Dalia Rabikowitch, T. Ribner, Ein Tur-Malcha, Natan Yonatan and Natan Zach. Rabikowitch won the Israel Award along with Oz in 1998.

The late Yonatan Ratosh and the late Zelda expressed each in his or her unique medium their beliefs and attitudes, one his attachment to ancient symbols and rituals, and the other her religious sensibilities.

Modern Hebrew Literature in America. Modern Hebrew literature assumed significance in America on the eve of World War I, with the arrival of a number of young poets. The best known of these were B.M. Silkiner, Ephraim A. Lisitzky, A.S. Schwartz; later came Hillel Bavli, Israel Efros, and Simon Ginzburg. These poets were under the influence of their great contemporaries in Eastern Europe: Bialik, Tschernichowsky, Shneur and others. This influence was especially pronounced in their earlier works, which, in theme as well as in form, were rooted in the classic Hebrew tradition. Nevertheless, the influence of the New World was not absent from their work. B.N. Silkiner was inspired by American Indian lore, to write his poem *Mul Ohel Timura* (Opposite the Tent of Timura). This was a unique experiment in Hebrew poetry. The lot of the Indians also found sympathetic expression in the poetic work of Israel Efros. The influence of American motifs is evident in the poetry of Simon Halkin, Abraham Regelson, and Gabriel Preil. Reflecting both Hebrew and American culture, their poetry has had a refreshing and invigorating effect on Hebrew verse in America. Prior to World War II, Hebrew novels, essays, and articles appeared regularly in the U.S. Thereafter, this activity has declined, with the center of Hebrew literature shifting to Israel.

Hebrew Pen Club, New York, 1940.

HEBREW UNION COLLEGE-JEWISH INSTITUTE OF RELIGION. Reform rabbinical seminary founded in Cincinnati in 1875 by Isaac Mayer **Wise**. After two earlier failures, Wise succeeded in starting the school under the auspices of the **Union of American Hebrew Congregations** which he helped establish in 1873. Meeting first in the basement of Rabbi Wise's Temple Bnei Jeshurun, the school graduated four rabbis in its first class in 1883. Since its founding the school has ordained more than 1,879 Reform rabbis, of which 72 are women.

Merged in 1950 with the Jewish Institute of Religion in New York, the school, now known as HUC-JIR, has four campuses: one in Cincinnati which includes the American Jewish Archives; another in **New York** which includes the Jewish Institute of Religion building; a third in **Los Angeles**, and a fourth in Jerusalem. The New York and Los Angeles campuses include schools for the training of cantors and religious teachers; in addition, the Los Angeles campus has a training school for professional workers in American Jewish community agencies. In 1996, Rabbi Sheldon Zimmerman became president of HUC, replacing Dr. Alfred Gottschalk.

HEBREW UNIVERSITY OF JERUSALEM. Its six Faculties—Humanities, Science, Social Science, Medicine, Law and Agriculture—and the Schools of Education, Economics, Dentistry, Pharmacy, Social Service Work, Graduate Library School, Asian Studies, the Institute of Jewish Studies, and School of Public Administration serve the practical needs of Israel and act as a cultural center for all Jewry. In time, the University will serve the entire Middle East region.

The Hebrew University's average total enrollment of graduate and undergraduate students for the academic year is about 18,000. Its faculty of about 2,500 men and women is drawn, as is the student body, from almost every part of the world. The University's *Magnes Press* has issued many distinguished publications.

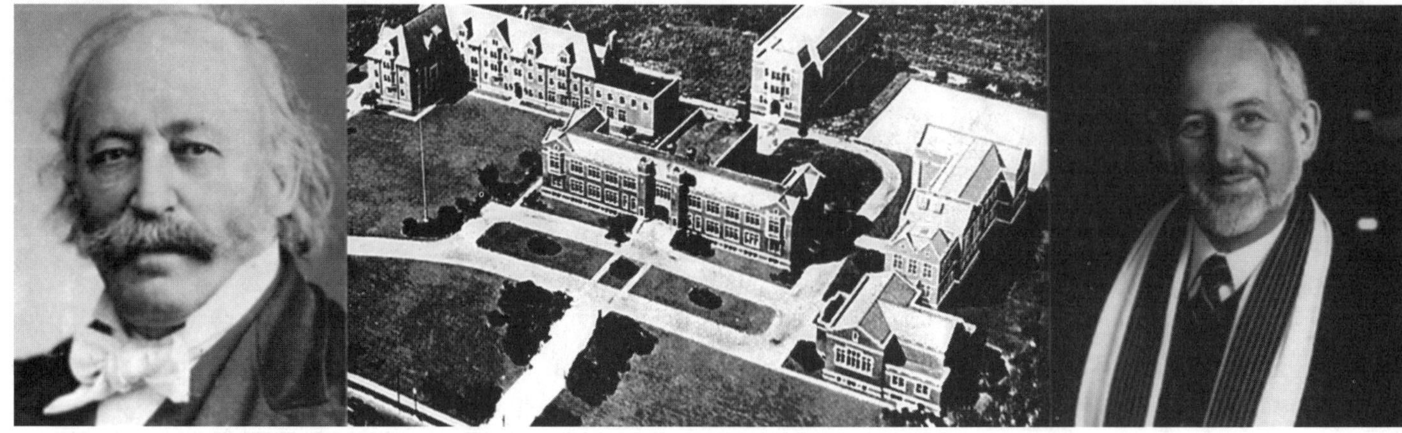

Left, Isaac Mayer Wise. First President of the Hebrew Union College. Center, Cincinnati campus of the Hebrew Union College. Right, Rabbi Sheldon Zimmerman. President of the Hebrew Union College since 1996.

The idea for a Hebrew University was first proposed in 1897 by the mathematician Professor Hermann **Schapira** of Heidelberg. Thus, the University idea, born in the infancy of Zionism, developed simultaneously with the movement. At the 1913 Zionist Congress in Vienna, it was decided to form the University of the Jewish People. Then and there, David Wolffsohn, former president of the **World Zionist Organization**, contributed $25,000 toward its foundation. The first meeting of the University Committee, consisting of Professor Paul **Ehrlich**, Frankfurt; Otto **Warburg**, Berlin; Baron James de **Rothschild**, London; Martin **Buber**; **Ahad Ha-Am**, and Chaim **Weizmann**, was to be held in Paris on August 4, 1914. This meeting never took place for on that day World War I broke out. In the midst of the war, while Palestine was still under Turkish control, a villa and a portion of the University site on Mount Scopus were purchased from its London owner, Lady Gray Hill. Four months before the end of the war, on July 24, 1918, the cornerstone of the University was laid on Mount Scopus by Weizmann in the presence of General **Allenby**, commander of the British Forces in Palestine.

The Hebrew University was opened by Lord **Balfour**, on April 1, 1925, at a memorable ceremony in the natural amphitheater of Mount Scopus. At this inauguration, the first Institutes of Biochemistry, Microbiology, and Jewish Studies were already housed in the rebuilt Gray Hill villa. The Faculty of the Humanities followed in 1928, Biological Sciences in 1931, and Science in 1935.

The Mount Scopus campus of the Hebrew University, Jerusalem.

The Wolffsohn Memorial of the Jewish National and University Library and the Hadassah Hospital, erected in 1939, were among the key University buildings which crowned Mount Scopus until Israel's War of Liberation in 1948, in which many of its students gave their lives. Cut off from the New City of Jerusalem by the fighting, the area of Mount Scopus was demilitarized after the Armistice.

Until its reoccupation by Israeli forces in 1967, the Mount Scopus campus stood untenanted except for Israeli guards. The road leading from Jerusalem to Mount Scopus was controlled by the Jordanians.

After a year of disruption, the University was reorganized in the New City in Terra Sancta College, and in some 50 other scattered quarters. In 1949, the Hebrew University-**Hadassah** Medical School was opened, and out of necessity also scattered in several buildings. The considerable overcrowding and discomfort hampered instructors and students alike, and in 1954, construction began on a new University campus at Givat Ram to the west of Jerusalem. The new campus was not intended to supersede, but rather complement that on Mount Scopus. In 1970, the University used the campuses at Givat Ram and on Mount Scopus, the latter having been rebuilt and expanded. The Faculty of Agriculture is situated in Rehovot.

The first president of the Hebrew University was the educator Dr. Judah L. **Magnes**, who headed the University for almost 25 years. A Board of Governors of distinguished scholars and laypersons of Israel, the U.S., and a number of other countries in the world give active service to the University. The American Friends of the Hebrew University act as foster alumni, supporting it with funds and educational know-how.

HEBRON. Ancient city south of **Jerusalem**. It is the site of the Machpelah cave where **Abraham** buried **Sarah**. **David** reigned there before transferring his court to Jerusalem. In recent centuries, Hebron maintained its Jewish community, as it became an Arab town. In 1929, Arabs massacred many of the town's 700 Jews. After 1948, Hebron came under Jordanian rule, but was captured by Israel in the 1967 **Six-Day War.** Today, Hebron is home to some 100,000 Arabs, with a small Jewish settlement in the center of town. Following the Oslo Agreement (*see* **Israel, State of**), most of Hebron was transferred to Palestinian control.

HEDER. Literally, room. Since the 16th century, possibly even earlier, the term has been applied to one of the most important institutions in Jewish life: the traditional school. The program of the heder included learning the Hebrew alphabet, reading and study of the Bible with **Rashi**'s commentary. The **Talmud** was studied next. The fundamental aim of the heder was preparation for individual study of the Talmud and its commentaries. The heder was generally a private enterprise, usually comprising one room in the house where the rabbi lived. The school year was divided into winter and summer terms. By the end of the 19th century, the heder had fallen into disrepute. More and more parents began to demand modern teaching methods and facilities, as well as the inclusion of secular subjects. The *heder metukan*, or modernized heder, established in Russia at the beginning of the 20th century, aimed to correct some of these shortcomings.

HEIFETZ, JASCHA (1901-1987). Violin virtuoso. A child prodigy, Heifetz entered the Royal Society of Music in Vilna, **Russia**, before he was four. His first concert was held two years later; by the age of nine he was appearing with the great orchestras of Europe. Enthusiastic response to his **New York** debut in 1917 led him to settle in the U.S. Although Heifetz's technique was perfected before he was 18, his career showed continuous musical development. His own experiments in composition are believed to have contributed to this development. Heifetz is considered one of the most brilliant violinists of the concert stage.

HEINE, HEINRICH (1797-1856). One of the greatest German poets. The French Revolution, which started eight years before Heine's birth, shook the **ghettos** of **Germany**, influenced Heine and made him a poet of liberty. Sent to Goettingen to study law, he obtained his degree only after baptism, because the University of Goettingen did not grant degrees to Jews. Bitterness entered Heine's soul and made his pen razor-sharp. He never practiced law, instead traveled and wrote his exquisite *Harzreise* (The Harz Journey) in 1826. Heine's brilliant political satires attacked tyranny in high places. A pamphlet against the German nobility made him a fugitive. He settled in **Paris** where he lived and wrote until his death. He spent the last ten years of his life on his "mattress-grave," suffering from a crippling disease.

Heine's lyrical poems are masterpieces of world literature. Even the Nazis who burned his books could not erase the love of these poems from the people. Since the Germans persisted in singing *Die Lorelei*, it was reprinted without the author's name. Heine's baptism was never more than expedient. He called it "the admission ticket to European civilization." His work is full of references, sometimes tender, sometimes ironic, to his Jewishness and to Judaism. Heine's Jewish sensitivity emerges as tense drama in the unfinished novel *Rabbi of Bacharach*; it flashes with superb irony in the play *Almansor*, whose Moslem character disguises Jewish themes. Heine's *Hebrew Melodies* contain some of the best Jewish poems ever written outside the Hebrew language.

Heinrich Heine.

HELL. *See* **Heaven and Hell.**

HELLENISM. Greek civilization of antiquity. It was **Alexander the Great**'s policy to introduce the Hellenistic culture in the vanquished countries of the Near East. Adopting elements of Near Eastern cultures, Hellenism lost much of its pure Greek spirit. However, it held a great attraction for the conquered people, who were fascinated by the Greek language, arts and science, and the Hellenist cult of body perfection. Of the Near East cultures only Judaism opposed Hellenism. The Greek belief in many gods and Hellenistic sensuality conflicted with Jewish monotheism and strict morality. The struggle between Hebraism and Hellenism came to a head in the Maccabean rebellion. Hebraism was victorious, the Judeans regained their independence, and the spread of Hellenism was checked in Judea.

The large Jewish communities in the Hellenistic kingdoms in Asia, particularly **Alexandria** and Antioch, were deeply influenced by Hellenism. They became largely Greek-speaking, and the **Bible** was translated into Greek and called the **Septuagint** for their use. A Greco-Jewish philosophy developed; the interpretation of the Bible by **Philo** of Alexandria is outstanding. Traces of Greek influence remain in some of the Jewish Wisdom literature of this period, such as *Apocrypha*, and in such words as *synagogue*, *sanhedrin*, and *parnas* which passed into the language spoken by Jews.

HELLER, JOSEPH(1923-1999). American novelist. Best known for his satire *Catch 22*, Heller draws on his Jewish background in other satirical novels as *Good As Gold* and in his memoirs.

HELLER, YOM TOV LIPMAN. *See* **Prague.**

HELLMAN, LILLIAN (1905-1984). American playwright. Known for plays like *The Children's Hour*, she was involved in the dramatization of the *Diary of Anne Frank*.

HEREM. In the **Bible** this term applied to that which is accursed, put under a ban, and therefore not fit for use. Later, it came to mean excommunication or expulsion from the community. The person upon whom the herem was pronounced was alienated from all social and trade relations with other Jews. In extreme cases the offender was denied such basic Jewish rights as marriage into a Jewish family, circumcision for his children, or even a Jewish burial. However, the religious authorities resorted to such extreme measures only when they felt that the future of Judaism was at stake. Such was the case in the 17th century, for example, when the herem was pronounced on the followers of the false messiah, **Sabattai Zevi**.

During and after the Middle Ages the herem was used extensively by religious authorities to ensure obedience to their religious decisions. The most celebrated herem was introduced by Rabbenu **Gershom** and forbade Jews under penalty of excommunication from taking more than one wife in marriage, or divorcing a woman against her will.

In later centuries the powerful weapon of the herem was wielded more capriciously.

HEROD THE GREAT (ca. 73-4 B.C.E.). King of Judea. Son of Antipater and grandson of Antipas, rulers of Edom. Antipater was the friend and advisor of Hyrcanus II. When the Romans conquered Palestine, Antipater was appointed to an important political post. As a result of his influence, his son Herod became governor of Galilee. Herod married Mariamne, granddaughter of Hyrcanus, in order to be related to the Hasmonean family. He was friendly with the Romans and won their favor by his loyalty. In the year 40 B.C.E., the Roman Senate crowned him king of Judea. The Jews hated Herod not only because he was an Edomite and a friend of their Roman enemies but because he did not respect their religion. He waged war against Antigonus, the son of Aristobulus of the house of the Hasmonean dynasty who demanded the throne of Judea for himself. In this battle (37 B.C.E.) Herod captured **Jerusalem**, put Antigonus to death, and destroyed the Hasmonean house. He showed no mercy even for his own wife and children whom he ordered killed some years later.

Herod deprived the **Sanhedrin** of its executive powers, but allowed it to function in religious matters. With the Romans' permission, he extended the borders of Palestine from **Damascus** to **Egypt**, developed foreign trade, and built Samaria and Caesarea. He won fame for rebuilding the Temple (20-19 B.C.E.), which he decorated lavishly. He had beautiful buildings constructed in Jerusalem, too. Nevertheless, the people's hatred of the tyrant was not lessened by these acts. Legend has it that, feeling death at hand, he commanded his men to execute a number of Jewish leaders the day he died, in order to lessen the popular joy at his passing. This final act of cruelty, however, was not carried out.

HERTZ, HEINRICH (1857-1894). German physicist; pupil of the German scholar Helmholtz. He became world-famous through his experiments on the propagation of electrical waves. These experiments proved the electromagnetic theory of light that had been developed in 1865 by the British physicist Maxwell. Hertz's work paved the way for the era of electronics, culminating in the discovery of wireless telegraphy, radio, and television.

HERTZ, JOSEPH HERMAN (1872-1946). Chief Rabbi of the British Empire from 1913 to his death. Hertz was one of the leaders of the **Mizrachi** Organization in England. He assisted in obtaining the **Balfour Declaration** in 1917, which proclaimed Palestine as a Jewish homeland. During World War II he worked untiringly to save Jews from death in Nazi-occupied lands. Of his written works, the best known are *The Book of Jewish Thoughts*, a translation and commentary on the **Torah**, and a translation and commentary on the prayer book.

HERTZBERG, ARTHUR (1921-). American rabbi and leader. Known for his book *The Zionist Idea,* he headed the American Jewish Congress from 1972 to 1978.

HERZL, THEODOR (1860-1904). Founder of modern political **Zionism**. Born in Budapest to an affluent intellectual Jewish family, he was educated at the University of Vienna, admitted to the bar in 1884, and shortly afterward turned to writing. He became a journalist and playwright, particularly famous for his feuilletons, a special type of literary column. In 1891, Herzl became the **Paris** correspondent of the *Neue Freie Presse*, the leading liberal newspaper of that day. All his life, he had faced the **anti-Semitism** of fellow students and professors. At first he advocated **assimilation**. But later in Paris he tried to counteract this hatred by writing a play on anti-Semitism, *The New Ghetto*. But then the **Dreyfus** Case occurred, shocking Herzl and changing the whole course of his life. As a newspaper correspondent, Herzl attended the trial and discovered that it was not Dreyfus the army captain, but Dreyfus the Jew who was on trial. Deeply shaken, Herzl took action. He proposed a solution to the problem of anti-Semitism: the creation of a Jewish State. He started to write down his ideas as he tried to put them into action. While writing *Judenstaat* (The Jewish State), he began to search for financial support and leadership. Herzl first approached the philanthropist Baron Maurice de **Hirsch** who dismissed the idea as "fantastic." Herzl then wrote to Albert **Rothschild** of Vienna and got no reply at all. The paper he reported for, the *Neue Freie Presse*, refused to print any articles about a Jewish state. In 1895, it looked as though Herzl's ideas would never take hold, but then Max **Nordau**, the Paris physician who was famous as a writer and social philosopher, encouraged him to continue with his cause.

Theodor Herzl.

In 1896, Herzl's *Judenstaat* was published. Popular response grew, and in January 1897, Herzl issued a call for a Zionist congress. The first **Zionist Congress** met in Basle, **Switzerland**, on August 27, 1897. The congress was attended by 204 delegates from 17 countries. Herzl, a magnetic figure, stood before them and declared that "Zionism was the Jewish people on the march." He reported his efforts to get European nations' approval and assistance for the formation of a Jewish state in Palestine by obtaining a "charter" from **Turkey**. He won over the Duke of Baden, uncle of Kaiser Wilhelm II. He went to Constantinople and negotiated with important Turkish ministers, and he was received by King Ferdinand of **Bulgaria**. In **London**, he won over the Jewish masses and interested the writer Israel **Zangwill**. Finally, to provide a forum which would serve as the voice of Zionism, he founded with his own funds the journal *Die Welt*. During three days of deliberation, the first Zionist Congress created the **World Zionist Organization** and formulated the Basle Program, stating that "Zionism aims to create for the Jewish people a home in Palestine secured by public law." For this purpose the Congress decided to obtain the necessary backing of various governments as a legal foundation for the Jewish homeland. Herzl was elected president of the World Zionist Organization. The next, and last, seven years of his life were years of feverish work. At the next five Zionist Congresses (1898-1903), over which he presided, the policies and institutions of the movement were hammered out. The Jewish Colonial Trust (the Zionist banking arm) and the Jewish National Fund (its land purchasing agency) were established. Herzl con-

> *"If you will it, it is no legend."*
>
> — THEODOR HERZL

ducted diplomatic negotiations and was received by the German Kaiser Wilhelm II, by Sultan Abdul Hamid of Turkey, and by British statesmen. In the midst of it all, he wrote the novel *Altneuland*, a Utopian vision of the Zionist state. To obtain a promise of diplomatic support in Turkey, Herzl traveled to **Russia** where he was received by two key members of the Government, Minister of the Interior Vyacheslav von Plehve and Finance Minister Sergei Witte. Traveling through Russia, Herzl saw the dreadful suffering of Russian Jews, who were subjected to periodic pogroms. He was so deeply affected that he decided to accept the British offer of Uganda in East Africa as a temporary asylum for Russian Jewry. In August 1903, Herzl presided over a Zionist Congress for the last time. This time 592 delegates attended, and the democratic temper was clearly demonstrated. The Uganda project was rejected after painful sessions. The delegates wanted the Land of Israel or nothing, and the Zionist movement seemed badly split. Herzl continued working for a "charter" for Palestine. In January 1904, he was received by King of Italy Victor Emmanuel III, who responded favorably. Pope Pius X, however, gave Herzl a clear "no." In April 1904, Herzl met with Zionist executives and made every effort to unify the movement. Worn out, his heart failing, he attended some of the sessions with an ice pack under his frock coat. On July 3, 1904, he died, but the work he had begun carried on. Fifty years after the first Zionist Congress, the State of **Israel** was proclaimed on May 14, 1948. Over a year later, Theodor Herzl's remains were flown from Vienna to Israel. The author of the *Jewish State* was laid to rest on Mt. Herzl in **Jerusalem** on August 17, 1949.

HERZOG, CHAIM (1918-1997). Israeli soldier and statesman. Born in Belfast, **Ireland**, the son of Rabbi Isaac Halevi **Herzog**, he immigrated to Palestine in 1935 and obtained a thorough schooling in religious and secular studies. In 1939, he enlisted in the British army and participated in the liberation of the concentration camps in 1945. He returned to Palestine in 1947 and rejoined the Haganah. Upon formation of the Israel Defense Forces in 1948, Herzog served as chief of military intelligence until 1950 and as defense attaché at Israel's embassy in Washington from 1950 to 1954. He was Israel's leading political and military commentator in both Hebrew and English during the 1967 **Six-Day War** and the 1973 **Yom Kippur War**.

Chaim Herzog.

From 1975 to 1978, Herzog was Israel's ambassador to the UN and, in 1975, he publicly tore up the U.N.'s "Zionism is racism" resolution. A noted writer on political, military, and economic affairs, he served as Israel's fifth president from 1983 to 1993.

HERZOG, ISAAC HALEVI (1888-1959). Chief Rabbi of the State of Israel. Born in Lomza, **Poland**, he acquired a thorough schooling in the **Talmud** and secular studies, specializing in law, philosophy, and Asian studies. In 1925, Herzog became Chief Rabbi of **Ireland**, where he gained the respect and love of all classes of Jewry. In 1936, he was elected Chief Rabbi of Palestine, and remained so until his death. A profound scholar, Rabbi Herzog took an active part in the life of his people and land. After the end of World War II, he devoted all his energies to saving the remnants of European Jewry. He made special efforts to save Jewish children who had been hidden in Christian homes and churches and forcibly converted during the war. Herzog published important works in Talmudic and Rabbinical studies, including five volumes on *The Main Institutions of Jewish Law*.

HESCHEL, ABRAHAM JOSHUA (1907-1972). American Jewish religious philosopher. He is considered a neo-hasidist. In eloquent and inspiring language, his writings about the Sabbath, the prophets, and man and God had a deep effect on his generation. During the 1960's he was active in the civil rights movement and later in the struggle for Soviet Jewry.

Moses Hess.

HESS, MOSES (1812-1875). Political leader, writer, and forerunner of modern Zionism. He was born in Bonn, **Germany**, and died in Paris. As a youth he was attracted to the study of philosophy and later participated in the Socialist movement with Karl **Marx** and Friedrich Engels. Then he turned to Ferdinand Lassalle, founder of the German Socialist Democratic Party, and became active in the workers' movement. After the failure of the 1848 Revolution in Germany, Hess settled in **Paris**, where he began to study the problem of the Jewish people and to think about its destiny. In 1962, he published a small book titled *Rome and Jerusalem* in which he wrote that Jewish national consciousness could not be erased, as the German Jewish Reform movement attempted. Humankind is a family of many nations, and small peoples have the right to an equal place in it. Every cultural group has something to contribute to world civilization, he said, and Jewish people, too, have much to contribute. The only solution to the Jewish question is the settlement of Palestine, under the protection of some European power. His ideas in *Rome and Jerusalem* came to be a basic part of Zionist thinking, and for them Moses Hess is remembered.

HET. Eighth letter of the Hebrew alphabet; numerically, eight.

HEVRA KADISHA. A group of Jews that performs the traditional preparations for burial of the dead.

HIAS. *See* **United Hias Service**.

HIGH HOLY DAYS. *See* **Rosh Hashana** *and* **Yom Kippur.**

HIGH PRIEST. *See* **Kohen.**

HILLEL (ca. 1st century B.C.E.). Talmudic authority. Born in **Babylonia**, he came to Palestine to study Law. His fame as a brilliant scholar grew, and he became the leader of the **Pharisees** and head of the liberal school of interpretation of the Jewish law.

> *"In a place where people do not behave like human beings, try to be a human being."*
>
> — HILLEL

Many legends are told about Hillel's devotion to learning, simplicity, and modesty. In his youth, he was a laborer, spending a large portion of his earnings on his tuition. Once, when he lacked the price of admission to the house of study, he climbed onto the roof and through the skylight listened to the discussions of the rabbis. He became so absorbed that he did not mind the snow that covered him almost completely. Half-frozen, he was finally noticed by the scholars inside, taken down, and revived.

In his interpretation of the law, Hillel's first consideration was the welfare of the people. He established regulations which were aimed at reconciling the ancient law with new conditions. One of these, the "prosbul," made it possible for the poor to borrow money at the approach of the seventh, or sabbatical, year when people were reluctant to lend money, since all debts were canceled during that year.

There is a tradition that Hillel was a descendant of the House of David. His saintliness and scholarship earned him the love and respect of his countrymen. King **Herod** appointed him head of the **Sanhedrin**. He remained the spiritual leader of the Jews for a period of 40 years. His utterances reveal his nobility of character. His love of peace was great. He said, "Be of the disciples of **Aaron**, loving peace and pursuing peace, loving thy fellow creatures, and drawing them close to the Torah." His tolerance is illustrated by the story of the heathen who asked Hillel to teach him all of the principles of Judaism while he stood on one foot. Hillel replied, "Do not unto your neighbor what you would not have him do unto you. This is the whole law; the rest is commentary." As contrasted with his great opponent **Shammai**, Hillel stands out as the liberal interpreter of Jewish law.

HILLEL FOUNDATION. *See* **B'nai B'rith.**

HIRSCH, BARON MAURICE DE (1831-1896). Financier and philanthropist. From a titled and wealthy family, he became one of the richest men in Europe by investing his inheritance in railroads, banking, and other industries. When his plan to improve the deplorable condition of Russian Jews failed to receive the Czar's approval, he formed the **Jewish Colonization Association** in order to resettle Jews in various parts of the world and to establish colonies in North and South America, particularly **Argentina**. Hirsch believed that the condition of Jews could be greatly improved if they were to become farmers and industrial workers in less densely populated areas of the world. To this end, he established agriculture and industrial schools in both Europe and the New World. Baron de Hirsch gave millions of dollars to charitable causes of all sorts. In 1887, his only son died. "I have lost my son but not my heir," he said. "Humanity is my heir."

HIRSCH, SAMSON RAPHAEL (1808-1888). German rabbi and champion of neo-Orthodoxy. Hirsch was violently opposed to the Reform movement and advocated the separation of his followers from any community where Reform Judaism had gained the upper hand. Due to his initiative, the German Parliament in 1876 legalized the secession of Orthodox Jews from the Jewish community. In 1836, Hirsch published an uncompromising defense of the institutions and laws of Judaism and a statement of his theories on neo-Orthodoxy. In opposition to the German Reform movement, Hirsch maintained that the acceptance of biblical and Talmudic authority was necessary to a true understanding of Judaism. He felt Judaism needed a reinterpretation and spiritualization of the traditional laws and practices to give them deeper meaning and significance in the modern world. Hirsch founded a day school which combined a thorough Jewish education with modern secular training. He published *Horeb*, a book on the religious duties of the Jewish people in exile, and voluminous commentaries on the **Pentateuch** and the Book of **Psalms**. A commentary on the Jewish prayer book, based on his writings, was published after his death.

HISTADRUT. General Federation of Jewish Labor in Israel. Founded in 1920 by representatives of 4,500 Jewish workers in Palestine, the Histadrut has become the most powerful non-governmental organization in Israel, an institution unique in the history of labor movements. David **Ben-Gurion**, Yitzhak **Ben-Zvi**, and Joseph Sprinzak were among the early founders and leaders of the organization. By 1993, the Histadrut membership was about 1.8 million. Each member pays dues to the federation and receives in return full medical coverage through *Kupat Holim*, or the Workers' Sick Fund, old age and disability benefits, and the right to participate in all its cultural and social activities and elections. On joining the Histadrut, the worker automatically becomes a member of the General Cooperative Association of Israel, founded by the Histadrut to facilitate the growth of new industries. Most of Israel's consumers' and producers' cooperatives belong to it. About 25% of Israel's GNP is attributed to Histadrut owned and centrally-managed enterprises. Most workers also belong to one of 35 trade and industrial unions affiliated with the Histadrut. These unions include both skilled and unskilled laborers, as well as professional, academic, and clerical workers. Through coordination of bargaining policy, the Histadrut has striven to maintain uniform standards throughout Israel. Nationally, the Histadrut has been active in preparing labor legislation for consideration by the Knesset, Israel's Parliament. The Histadrut also maintains local labor councils in towns and villages; a Working Women's Council; a Working Youth Organization; an Agricultural Workers' Center; and *Shikun Ovdim*, which builds low-cost homes for workers and their families. Its cultural activities has included publication of two daily newspapers, *Daver* and *Omer*, the latter a publication for newcomers; Ohel, a full-scale repertory theater; Hapoel, a national sports organization; a publishing house; vocational and general schools for both children and adults; libraries; and a

Bellinson Hospital of Kupal Holim.

Executive Headquarters of Histadrut, Tel Aviv. Courtesy Histadrut.

department for the organization of lectures, concerts, and discussion groups. Since the establishment of the State of Israel in 1948, the Histadrut has accepted Israel's Arabs for membership in its unions; the Israel Labor League, an all-Arab union, is a Histadrut affiliate. To facilitate the integration of Arabs into the economic and cultural life of Israel, the Histadrut maintains a special Arab Department.

HISTADRUTH IVRITH OF AMERICA. American organization of Hebraists, founded in **New York** in 1916 to promote the Hebrew language. It publishes *Hadoar*, the only Hebrew-language weekly outside Israel.

HOFETZ HAIM (ca. 1837-1933). Scholar, author, and one of the prominent leaders of Polish Orthodox Jewry. Born Israel Meir Kahan in Zhitil, **Poland**, he derived his surname from his book *Hofetz Haim* (He Who Desires Life), a treatise against slander. Rabbi Kahan founded a yeshiva in Radin and, refusing important rabbinical positions, devoted his time to writing and teaching. When World War I erupted, he was active in raising funds for the support of Polish and Russian Jewry. Often he interceded in their behalf before the Russian government. In 1930, he personally protested to the Polish government against government interference with Jewish religious and economic rights. A learned man, he was the author of thirty books on Jewish ethics and law. *Mishnah Berurah*, a six-volume treatise on Joseph **Karo**'s *Orah Haim*, is a highly valuable manual for rabbis today.

HOFFMAN, DUSTIN. *See* **Stage and Screen**.

HOL HAMOED. Days between the beginning and the end of the festival, which are only semi-holidays.

HOLLAND. *See* **Netherlands**.

HOLOCAUST. In the Jewish people's long history of martyrdom, the catastrophe that eventuated from the six years of Nazi conquest in Europe between 1939 and 1945 was unprecedented in suffering and death. The Jewish people lost more than 6 million people, or two-thirds of its European community, and one-third of the entire Jewish people.

On February 24, 1920, an ex-corporal in the German army named Adolf Hitler and a group of professional anti-Semitic agitators, including Julius Streicher, Alfred Rosenberg, and Gottfried Feder, met in a Munich beer hall and founded the National Socialist Party. (Streicher and Rosenberg were later sentenced to death by hanging by the International War Crimes Tribunal at Nuremberg in October 1946. Hitler escaped the world's verdict by committing suicide in his private bunker in Berlin at the end of April 1945.)

Nazi Program. The core of the National Socialist Party (Nazi) program was the racist doctrine that "only he in whose veins German blood flows" might be considered a citizen of **Germany**, and therefore "no Jew can belong to the German nation." **Anti-Semitism** was the emotional foundation of the Nazi movement; every member of the Nazi party was an anti-Semite.

Hitler, the *Fuehrer*, or dictatorial leader, of the Nazi Party, announced his anti-Semitism as well as his inhumanity proudly: "Yes, we are barbarians! We want to be barbarians! It is an honorable title. We shall rejuvenate the world! This world is near its end...We are now at the end of the Age of Reason...The **Ten Commandments** have lost their validity. Conscience is a Jewish invention. It is a blemish, like circumcision...There is no such thing as truth, either in the moral or in the scientific sense...We must distrust the intelligence and the conscience, and must place our trust in our instincts...And was not the whole doctrine of **Christianity**, with its faith in redemption, its moral code, its conscience, its conception of original sin, the outcome of Judaism? The struggle for world domination will be fought entirely between us, between Germans and Jews."

This, then, was the double aim of the Nazi revolution: to destroy

Prelude to mass murder: Top, forced labor in the ghetto; middle, mass deportation; bottom, labor camp.

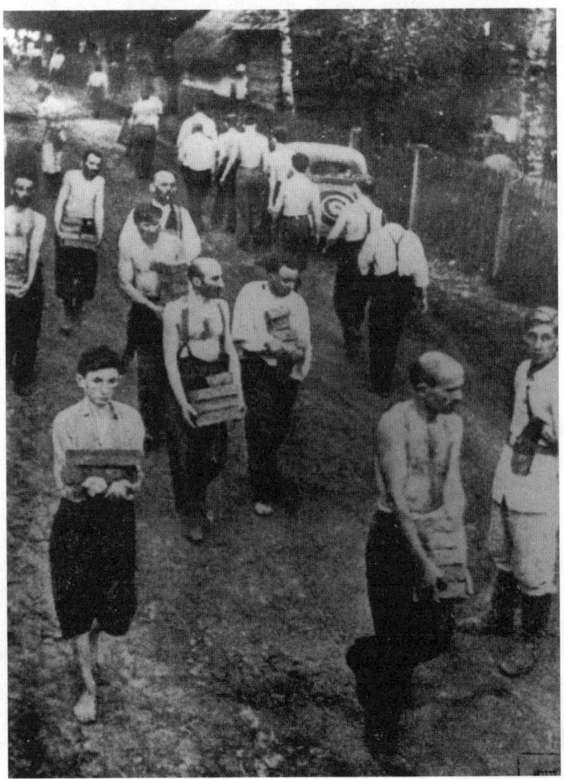

both the Jew and the spirit of Judaism and, simultaneously, the spirit of Christianity. The Nazi regime came into power in Germany in 1933. It trained its weapons, during the first, prewar phase (1933-1939), on the Jewish spirit. Christianity suffered persecution and harassment at the same time. The climax of Nazi barbarism against Jewish culture occurred when hundreds of books by Jewish and anti-Nazi authors were burned in a gigantic bonfire in the square before the famed Berlin Opera House on May 10, 1933.

In its second phase (1938-1944), Nazism broke through the boundaries of Germany and embarked on a war of conquest against Europe. During these years, as country after country fell to the Nazis, the character of the war changed from one of hate propaganda to one of organized mass murder. Men, women, and children were sent into the death camps' gas chambers and crematoria.

The Nazi blueprint for the extermination of European Jews from 1939 on was conceived and carried out in two systematic stages. The first stage began in 1939 with the Nazi occupation of **Poland** and lasted until June 1941 when Germany attacked Soviet Russia. Jews were physically isolated in ghettos, concentration camps, and special forced-labor camps, sealed off from the outside world. The second stage entailed the systematic mass murder of the entire Jewish populations of all Nazi-occupied areas by means of mass executions before open graves, convoys of sealed boxcars, and specially constructed death-factories like Auschwitz, Treblinka, and Maidanek, in which millions were methodically gassed and then cremated. This stage lasted from the summer of 1941 until the Nazi collapse in the spring of 1945.

Typical of what was happening in Germany during the pre-war stage of the anti-Semitic program was the Nazi crusade against German-Jewish scientists and intellectuals. Within the ranks of German Nobel Prize winners Jews numbered 25 percent, although only one percent of the German population was Jewish. Despite records like this one of brilliant achievement and high international standing, Jewish professors were excised from the universities, Jewish doctors from the hospitals, and Jewish scientists from the laboratories. Internationally known refugees who sought haven at this time in the U.S. and other free nations were received with open arms and urged to carry on their work. Later, many of these scientists lent vital assistance to the free world in the decisive battle for strategic and military superiority over Nazi Germany.

Although the war against Jewry continued unabated, the Nazis attempted at all times to mask their real intentions. In Nuremberg in 1935, for example, when the first of a series of anti-Semitic laws was passed depriving Jews of equal citizenship rights and forbidding intermarriage between Jews and non-Jews, Nazi leaders declared that they asked the Jews of nothing more than peaceful withdrawal "to their own areas" and cessation of intermingling "with alien peoples." These same protestations later accompanied the creation of the ghettos.

The Ghettos. After the Nazis occupied Poland, their first move was to isolate Jews from the rest of the Polish population. In February 1940, the **Ghetto** of Lodz, renamed *Litzmanstadt* by the Nazis, was formed, to be followed in October by the **Warsaw** Ghetto. Determined to preserve to the end the pretext of "legality," the Germans set up "Jewish Councils," or governing bodies and a system of Jewish police within the ghetto walls. These devices were intended to prove that the ghettos enjoyed a measure of "Jewish autonomy," to cloak their real function as death traps for Polish Jews, for which they had been designed from the beginning. To

Behind the barbed wire of a Nazi concentration camp.

allay suspicion, Nazi leaders pointed out that they were doing nothing worse than reviving an old medieval institution: providing separate living areas for the Jewish population. But the electrified barbed wire surrounding the ghetto walls told a different story, as did the heavily armed Nazi patrols on constant watch at the ghetto gates. And whereas Jews of the Middle Ages had unrestricted freedom of movement outside of the ghetto walls by day, the penalty for leaving a Polish ghetto without official permission at any time was instant death.

Within the ghetto walls, hunger and privation held sway. Because of unspeakably cramped living conditions, epidemics were rampant. The ghetto population was constant prey to attacks of indescribable cruelty at the whim of its Nazi overseers. Yet despite these hardships, the ghettos displayed a remarkable vitality and almost unbelievable capacity for survival. Cultural and religious activities animated the underground life of the ghetto. Moving dramas of devoted selflessness were played out within its walls. And in perhaps the most sublime triumph of the human spirit to be written in the annals, Jews of the Polish ghetto, tortured, doomed, and alone, summoned up the magnificent courage to rise in revolt against their Nazi jailers.

Camouflage and deception were also characteristic of the mass murder of European Jewry, which the Nazis disguised as "the final solution to the Jewish question." The infamous death camp at Auschwitz was disguised as a labor camp with

Scene in the Warsaw ghetto: Nazi soldiers search for surviving Jews.

numerous factories and workshops. Over the entrance, a gate was emblazoned with the slogan: FREEDOM THROUGH WORK. The transports which daily drove into the center of the camps, bearing victims from all corners of Nazi-occupied Europe, were falsely identified as part of the "Resettlement Project for Colonization in the East." The gas chambers with crematoria-ovens were disguised as public baths for the purpose of disinfection.

The Balance Sheet of Annihilation. Statistics on the Jewish catastrophe are indicated in the table on the next page, published by the **World Jewish Congress**. It should be noted that the only unclear part of the record refers to the fate of Jews in the Soviet Union.

The table representing the percentage of Jewish losses in individual countries warrants closer scrutiny. Significant differences are apparent, for example, the disparity between the 14% loss suffered in **Bulgaria** and the 90% toll in **Latvia** and **Lithuania**. The Polish figures particularily demand clarification.

A display at the museum of Kibbutz Lochamei Hagetaot. Musical instruments made by Nazis out of captured Torah scrolls, and the yellow stars worn by Jews in Europe during the Nazi occupation. Courtesy Zionist Archives and Library, New York City.

Deducting from the total number of Polish survivors the more than 200,000 who were temporarily evacuated by the Russians to a point deep within the heart of Soviet territory out of reach of the Nazis, the proportion of the victims who remained in Poland becomes more than 90 percent, the highest toll of all European Jewry. Individual political, social, and technical factors also affected the fate of Jews in different countries. In **Hungary**, for example, the Nazis were thwarted in their attempt at the extermination of Jews by heavy losses at the war front. In other countries, such as **Italy**, **France**, and **Belgium**, the non-Jewish population helped rescue its Jewish neighbors. These acts of generosity were most frequent in rescuing children. Unusual instances of individual heroism occurred in nearly all the occupied countries. Unfortunately, only **Denmark** organized mass resistance to the extermination of its Jewish citizens.

At the end of 1942, when the Nazi conquerors invaded Denmark and proceeded to set in motion their war of Jewish extermination, King Christian X registered instant protest. He threatened to abdicate; when the Nazis made it known that henceforth every Jew was to be identified by a yellow arm band bearing a Star of David, King Christian announced that he would be the first to don the badge of Judaism. Finally, just as the Gestapo, the dreaded German secret police, had completed their plans for dealing with Jews without Danish assistance, there occurred a noble example of human solidarity. Of the 6,500 Danish Jews officially marked for death by the Nazis, approximately 6,200, or 95%, were secretly smuggled out of Denmark into Sweden with the help of a special rescue fleet of small Danish fishing ships. Between September 26 and October 12, 1942, the Danes rescued all but a few hundred Danish Jews from the gas chambers.

PERCENTAGE OF JEWS EXTERMINATED IN EUROPE

Austria	66.6
Belgium	44.4
Bulgaria	14.0
Czechoslovakia	82.5
France	30.0
Germany	81.0
Greece	80.0
Holland	60.0
Hungary	49.5
Italy	26.3
Latvia	89.5
Lithuania	90.0
Poland	85.0
Romania	50.0
Soviet Union	71.4
Yugoslavia	73.3

Survivors. Each Jewish survivor of the catastrophe owed his or her life either to a freak accident or a chain of fortunate coincidences. The Nazi murder-decree against the Jews lasted until the final moment of the war. Soviet troops entering Poland in 1944 seized the death camp Maidanek, near Lublin, while it was still operating its ultra-modern machinery for murder for the world to see. In April 1945, when the victorious Allied armies under General Eisenhower marched into Germany, they succeeded in taking the still functioning camps at **Dachau, Buchenwald,** and **Bergen Belsen** by surprise.

The full extent of the Jewish tragedy came to light only with the final collapse of Nazism and the Allied liberation of Europe. Gradually the survivors began to emerge from their hiding places to make their stories known. There were Jews who had been living in concealed underground bunkers, women who had lived as "Aryans" on forged documents, children, mainly orphans, who had been sheltered in monasteries or among kindhearted Christian neighbors, and brave men and women who fought the Nazis as partisans in the forests of Poland.

In May 1960, Adolf Eichmann, one of the cruelest masters of the Nazi extermination system, was captured in **Argentina** by Jews and brought to **Israel** for trial. After lengthy hearings in 1961, he was convicted and executed in May 1962.

Jewish orphans found among the survivors of the notorious Buchenwald murder camp and brought to Israel. Courtesy Joint Ditribution Committee.

Fifty years later. Unlike most historical events, the Holocaust refuses to recede into the past. It continues to prey on the collective consciousness of the Jewish people and the human race. In Israel, such organizations and museums as **Yad Vashem** and the **Diaspora Museum** document and study the Holocaust. The U.S. Government has established a major **Holocaust Museum** in the Nation's Capital, which is attended yearly by millions. Holocaust museums and memorials have proliferated throughout the world. Books, articles, documentary films and plays about the Holocaust appear nearly every day. Many thinkers, both Jews and non-Jews, regard the Holocaust as the turning point in the moral history of the world. On the other hand, there are writers, professors, or hate-mongers around the world, including in the U.S., who spread theories denying or minimizing the Holocaust. It is still too early to determine what the lasting impact of the Holocaust on the Jews in particular and the world in general will be. But there is little doubt that it will be profound.

HOLY LAND. *See* **Israel.**

HONDURAS. The first Jews to reach Honduras were East Europeans who came from other Latin American countries in the 1920's. In 1998, there were fewer than 50 Jews in Honduras, in a general population of 5.5 million. Almost all live in Tegucigalpa, the capital, and engage in trade.

HOROWITZ, VLADIMIR (1904-1989). Concert pianist. Born in Kiev, **Russia**, Horowitz studied music at the conservatory in his native city. He performed his first solo concert in 1921 and made his American debut seven years later. He settled in **New York**, and in 1933 married Wanda Toscanini, daughter of the famous conductor. A great interpreter of classical music, Horowitz has appeared with outstanding orchestras everywhere. His numerous recordings have made him a household name.

HOSEA (c. 784-725 B.C.E.). First of the minor prophets. He lived in the turbulent idolatrous northern Kingdom of **Israel** when it was at the height of its power under the rule of Jeroboam II. Hosea's prophecies thunder against moral, religious, and political evils as offenses against God. He predicted the doom of Israel as punishment for its idol worship and social injustice. Yet he loved his people and saw visions of its restoration after the punishment. Then a reconciliation between Israel and God would come about, arising out of God's love of Israel and all humanity. Hosea's all-consuming ideal is love; in striking phrases he compares God to a loving father and faithful husband.

Hosea's words (2:21-22) are recited by the observant Jew when he puts on his **tefillin**, or phylacteries, each morning. As he winds the thong of the hand phylactery three times around his middle finger, he pledges himself anew to the three-fold ideal first pronounced by Hosea.

HOSHANA RABA. *See* **Sukkot.**

HOUDINI, HARRY (1874-1926). World's most famous magician. Born Ehrich Weiss, he was known mainly as an escape artist, who could be chained inside a water-filled tank and still be able to escape. His exploits have never been surpassed.

Vladimir Horowitz. Courtesy RCA Victor Red Seal.

HOVEVE ZION. Literally, Lovers of Zion. A 19th-century East European organization for the settlement of Jews in Palestine. A direct reaction to the widespread pogroms in Tsarist **Russia**, it grew out of the thinking and writing of a few men and from scattered colonization societies that began to spring up in the 1860's. The Hoveve Zion federation was organized formally at a conference in Kattowitz, Silesia, in November 1884. (*See also* **Zionism**.)

HUBERMAN, BRONISLAW (1882-1947). Violinist. Huberman began to study the violin in his native **Warsaw** at the age of six and made his first public appearance a year later. He pursued a successful career in **Germany** until Hitler's rise to power in 1933. In 1936, he visited Palestine, where he conceived the idea of founding a Palestine Symphony Orchestra. Owing to his unstinting efforts, the orchestra was founded, and Arturo Toscanini conducted its first concert in December 1936. This was the forerunner of the Israel Philharmonic Orchestra.

HUNGARY. Jews lived in Hungary as far back as Roman times, when the area was part of the Roman province of Dacia. Conquest of the land by invading Magyars in 897 meant for Jews continuous plunder and persecution at the hands of Catholic kings. Under Turkish rule from 1526 to 1686, the situation of the Jewish populace greatly improved. Austrian domination, however, again changed their circumstances for the worse. France Joseph II (1741-1790) emancipated the Jews, but his decree was carried out only partially. A number of Jews fought on the side of Hungary against Austria in the revolution of 1848.

At that time there was a severe struggle between the Orthodox and Reform elements of Hungarian Jewry, which led to a split in 1871. Three congregational groupings emerged: Orthodox, Reform, and "status quo." Modern Hungarian Jewry has been characterized by sharp contrasts: on the one hand, extreme piety; on the other, extreme **assimilation**, even to the point of conversion to Christianity.

By the beginning of the 20th century, Hungarian Jews were occupying important positions in the economic and cultural life of the country, in the arts, the press, and the sciences. However, the interval between the two World Wars was marked by the growth of **anti-Semitism**.

Before World War II ended, the Germans had occupied Hungary. In the summer of 1944 they transported 400,000 local Jews to **Auschwitz**.

The end of the war found some 120,000 Jewish survivors in Hungary, of whom about 80,000 lived in Budapest. The Jewish community, like the rest of the population, was in dire economic straits. In addition, anti-Semitism was no less virulent than at the height of the Nazi terror. When Hungary came under Soviet domination in 1948, Jews suffered especially from directives aimed at eliminating middle-class elements from the nation's economy. Although official Communist doctrine forbade anti-Semitism, an unusually high percentage of Jews were included in the mass deportations of "undesirables" from the larger cities begun in 1951 and continued into 1952. The Hungarian Zionist movement was outlawed. All contact with Western Jewry and Israel was severed. Emigration was barred. The **American Jewish Joint Distribution Committee**, responsible until 1953 for most welfare and economic aid to the Jewish community, was forced to leave. The Hungarian uprising of October-November 1956 was accompanied by some anti-Jewish acts, and 18,000 to 20,000 Jews fled the country, streaming mainly into Austria. The Jewish population in 1998 was close to 100,000. Eighty percent of the Hungarian Jews live in the capital, Budapest. There are also small communities in Debrecen, Miklosc, and Szeged. The community has a high proportion of Holocaust survivors.

HUPPAH. *See* **Marriage Customs**.

HYRCANUS, JOHANAN. Of all the Hasmonean rulers who re-established and strengthened the independence of Judea, Johanan Hyrcanus was the most successful. Son of Simon the **Maccabee**, Hyrcanus ruled from 135 to 104 B.C.E. His defeat of the allied Samaritans and Syrians and conquest of their cities ended forever the threat of Syrian rule and extended the borders of Judea to the west and north. Hyrcanus turned next to the south and conquered the Edomites, forcing them to accept Judaism. During his thirty-year rule, the Second Jewish Commonwealth attained its greatest independence and power. At the end of his rule, he came into conflict with the **Pharisees**, one of the two political parties that had developed in Judea. The Pharisees wanted to deprive him of his position as high priest, but this group paid heavily for their opposition to Hyrcanus, who drew closer to their opponents, the **Sadducees**.

> *"And I will betroth you unto Me forever;*
> *I will betroth you unto Me in righteousness,*
> *and in loving kindness, and in mercy.*
> *And I will betroth you unto Me in faithfulness,*
> *and you shall know the Lord."*
>
> — HOSEA 2:21-22

HEBREW WORDS COMMONLY USED IN AMERICAN ENGLISH

Adam *Man, person (first man)*
Adon Olam *Master of the Universe (religious hymn)*
Adonai *Lord (of the universe)*
Aliyah *Going up (to the Torah; to Israel)*
Amen *Yes; it is so*
Amidah *Standing (prayer)*
Aviv *Springtime (Tel Aviv)*

Baruch *Blessed*
Bar Mitzvah *Son of the Commandments*
Bet(h) El *House of God*
B'nai B'rith *Children of the Convenant (organization)*
Brit (Bris) *Covenant (also circumcision)*

Chaver *Friend*
Cherub *Angel*
Chutzpah *Impudence*
Cohen *Priest*

David *Friend; beloved*
Dayeynu *Enough (Passover song)*

El *God*
El Al *Toward the heights (Israeli airline)*
Elohim *God*
Erev *Eve*

Gadol *Big; large*
Goy *Nation; people*

Hadassah *Myrtle (name of Queen Esther and of organization)*
Haftarah *Conclusion (reading of concluding prophetic portion in the synagogue)*
Haganah *Defense*
Hallah *Bread (for the Sabbath)*
Halleluyah *Praise the Lord*
Halutz *Pioneer*
Hametz (Hometz) *Leaven; leavened bread (Passover)*
Hamotzi *Who brings forth (blessing before eating)*
Hannukah *Dedication*
Ha'tikvah *The hope (Israel's national anthem)*
Hava naguilla *Let's rejoice*
Havdalah *Separation (Sabbath)*

Kasher (Kosher) *Proper; fit (Jewish dietary laws)*
Kiddush *Sanctification (prayer over wine)*
Kippah *Cap; headcover; dome*

Knesset *Assembly (Israel's parliament)*
Kol Nidre *All the vows (Yom Kippur Eve service)*

L'chaim *To life (Jewish toast)*
Leviathan *Whale*

Maror *Bitter herbs (Passover)*
Matzah *Unleavened bread (Passover)*
Mazal (Mazel) tov *Good luck*
Meguillah *Scroll (Purim)*
Menorah *Candelabrum*
Mezuzah *Doorpost (scroll box attached to doorpost)*
Mitzvah *Divine commandment (also "good deed")*

Nes *Miracle*

Oneg *Joy; enjoyment*

Pesach *Passing-over (Passover)*
Purim *Cast lots*

Rav *Teacher, rabbi*
Rosh Hashanah *Head of the Year*

Satan *Satan; the devil*
Seder *Order (Passover)*
Shabbat (Sabbath) *Ceasing from work*
Shalom *Hello, goodbye, peace*
Shavuot *Weeks (Feast of)*
Seraph *Fiery angel*
Shekel *Weight (coin)*
Shma *Hear (watchword of the Jewish faith)*
Shofar *Horn*
Siddur *Order (prayerbook)*
Simchat Torah *Rejoicing of the Torah*
Sukkah *Booth*

Talit (talis) *Shawl (for prayer)*
Tel *Mound (archeology)*
Torah *Teaching (the Five Books of Moses)*
Tzdakah *Charity*
Tzaddik *Righteous person*

Yom Kippur *Day of Atonement*
Yom Tov (Gut Yontiff) *Good Day; holiday*

Zohar *Splendor (Kabbalah)*

For a representative list of Yiddish words commonly used in English, see **Yiddish**.

IBN EZRA, ABRAHAM (1092-1167). Hebrew poet, philosopher, and Bible commentator. Born in Toledo, **Spain**, he traveled widely, visiting **Italy**, **France**, **England**, North Africa, and the Middle East. Ibn Ezra contributed greatly to the spread of Arab-Jewish culture among Western European Jews. He suffered poverty and often complained bitterly about his situation in biting satirical poems. His **Bible** commentaries are distinguished by their logical and penetrating interpretation of biblical language and content. Also of considerable importance are his books on mathematics, philosophy, astronomy, and Hebrew grammar. Ibn Ezra's grammatical works were translated into Latin. In contrast to most of the Jewish scholars in Spain, he wrote in Hebrew, not Arabic. As a poet, Abraham Ibn Ezra did not measure up to the stature of the great Hebrew masters during the "Golden Age" in Spain. Yet some of his liturgical poems possess depth of feeling. He composed remarkable hymns on creation and on the qualities of angels. His poetic darts of ridicule and wit strike at the root of human weaknesses. Ibn Ezra's contrasting qualities are revealed in his truly moving religious poetry on the one hand, and the rhymed riddles and puzzles—the product of a keen and quick-witted mind—on the other. A number of his liturgical poems are included in the traditional prayer book.

IBN EZRA, MOSES (ca. 1070-1150). Hebrew poet and contemporary of Judah **Ha-Levi**. He came from a famous Jewish family in Granada, **Spain**. At first he was fascinated by the beauty of nature and the pleasures of life. After experiencing rejection and disappointment in love, he took to wandering. He wrote so many religious poems pleading for forgiveness that he became known as *Hasallach*, or the penitential poet. A master of form and literary technique, Ibn Ezra made excellent use of the riches of the Hebrew language in his secular and religious poetry. His book *Shirat Yisrael* (The Poetry of Israel) is of great value for the study of Hebrew poetry and its Arabic influences.

IBN GABIROL, SOLOMON (1021-1058) Medieval Hebrew poet and philosopher. Born in Malaga, **Spain**, he was orphaned as a child. At 16, his genius had already become evident. The tragic experiences of his short life—poverty, illness, and loneliness—are reflected in his subtle and pessimistic poems. His outstanding creative intelligence is revealed in his philosophical works as well. Many of Ibn Gabirol's poems, or *piyyutim*, became part of Jewish religious liturgy. His *Keter Malkhut*, a paean to the greatness of God, is recited on **Yom Kippur** Eve.

As a penetrating philosopher, Ibn Gabirol influenced both Christian theology and Jewish mystic thought. His philosophic work *Fons Vitae* (Source of Life), originally written in Arabic and later translated into Latin, was for centuries credited to "Avicebron"; it was not until the middle of the 19th century that Jewish scholar Solomon Munk discovered a fragmentary Hebrew translation by means of which he was able to prove that Avicebron was actually Ibn Gabirol. Ibn Gabirol's end is surrounded by mystery. An envious Arabic poet was said to have murdered him and buried his remains under a fig tree. To the astonishment of all, the tree bore unusually beautiful fruit. The king questioned the owner about his marvelous tree until he broke down and confessed his crime.

IBN JANNAH, JONAH (990-1050). Scholar and Hebrew grammarian. A physician by profession, he practiced medicine first in Cordova, **Spain**. When the Berbers destroyed Cordova, he settled in Saragossa.

Ibn Jannah's primary interest, however, was the study of Hebrew grammar. He wrote two important books, classics of their kind, one on grammatical construction and the other on sources of the Hebrew language. These books were translated from the Arabic into Hebrew by Judah **Ibn Tibbon**.

IBN PAKUDA, BAHYA BEN JOSEPH (Mid- 11th century). Philosopher and dayan (rabbinical judge) of Saragossa, **Spain**, Ibn Pakuda is best known for his classic book on Jewish ethics, *Hovot ha-Levavot* (*Duties of the Heart*). Little is known about his life, except that he was deeply learned and well acquainted with both Arabic and Jewish philosophical and scientific writing. In his work he urges humans to love and accept God with their hearts. Yet one must also exercise his reason in order to understand his obligations in this world. Ibn Pakuda believes that gratitude to God for His marvelous universe requires us to live ethically. Ibn Pakuda also wrote several beautiful hymns and poems; especially noteworthy is the *Admonition* to his soul that begins with the verse from the Psalms, "Bless the Lord, O my soul."

IBN SHAPRUT, HISDAI (915-970). Jewish statesman in **Spain**, whose support of Jewish scholarship helped promote important Jewish scholars and writers in Spain during the "Golden Age."

IBN TIBBON FAMILY. Famous family from **Spain** that lived mostly in Southern **France** during the 12th and 13th centuries. They are best known as translators of Arabic works into Hebrew. In doing so, they enriched the Hebrew language by creating new words and expressions for philosophic and scientific terms previously unknown in Hebrew. They also made available the works of outstanding Jewish philosophers and scholars to a wider public which could not read Arabic. Some noteworthy family members are:

Judah Ben Saul (1120-1190), who practiced medicine at Lunel in Southern France. Among the works he translated are *Emunot Vedeot* (Beliefs and Opinions) by **Saadiah Gaon**; *Hovot haLevavot* (Duties of the Heart) by Bahya **Ibn Pakuda**, and the *Kuzari* by Judah **Ha-Levi**.

Judah ben Samuel (1150-1230), who was the most important of all translators. He rendered into Hebrew **Maimonides**' *Moreh Nebuchim* (Guide to the Perplexed) and other works. Judah corresponded with this great scholar and philosopher, discussing various problems that arose with the translations.

Moses ben Samuel (1240-1283), who was a practicing physician in Provence. He translated Maimonides' commentary on the Mishnah (*Peirush Hamishnayot*), his *Sefer Hamitzvot*, and *Milot Hahigayon* (Terms of Logic), as well as scientific and philosophic works from the Arabic.

IDAHO. Jewish life in Idaho started around 1860. From 1915 to 1919, Moses Alexander served as the first and, so far, only Jewish governor of the state. Today, Idaho has about 400 Jews, half of whom live in Boise, with only one active Jewish congregation and school.

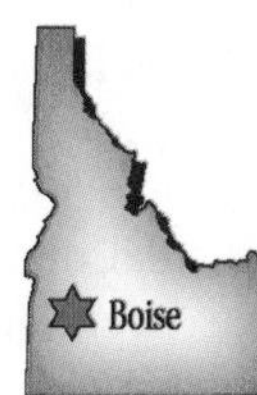

IDOLS, IDOLATRY. Throughout antiquity, Jews lived in a world that worshiped visible objects, such as statues of stone and wood representing the powers ruling the world. While each idol-worshiping group or nation accepted the validity of other groups' idols, Jews rejected all idols as false gods and considered their one invisible god as the only true ruler of the universe. Throughout the **Bible** there is conflict between idolatry and Jewish monotheism. With the birth of **Christianity** and later **Islam**, two religions also based on the belief in one divine power ruling the universe, idolatry became less accepted.

ILLINOIS. With a Jewish population of some 270,000, more than 260,000 live in **Chicago** alone, while the rest are spread in small communities of a few hundred each. Though the first Jews reached Illinois in the 18th century, Jews did not start settling throughout the state until the second half of the 19th. More than 100,000 arrived at the turn of the century, and most settled in Chicago. Henry Horner served as governor from 1932 to 1940.

IMBER, NAPHTALI HERZ (1856-1909). Author of ***Ha-Tikvah***, Imber was a poet and an incurable wanderer. He left his home in Galicia when quite young and roamed Europe. In 1878, he wrote *Ha-Tikvah* (The Hope), a poem of nine stanzas expressing the Jewish longing to return to the Land of Israel. *Ha-Tikvah* is now the national anthem of the State of **Israel**. Imber lived in Palestine from 1882 until 1887, when he went to Europe and England. Later, he came to the U.S. and traveled all over the country, writing Hebrew poems and articles for many Jewish magazines. He died in **New York**.

IMMANUEL BEN SOLOMON OF ROME (1270-1330). Hebrew scholar and satirical poet. Immanuel, named Ha-Romi because he was born in **Rome**, came from a rich and distinguished Jewish family. In his youth, he studied the **Talmud** as well as mathematics, astronomy, medicine and languages. He served as secretary to the Jewish community of Rome, and excelled as an orator. However, Immanuel's biting tongue made him many enemies, and he was forced to resign his position. Shortly afterward, he lost all his possessions and took to wandering. Immanuel's best known work, *Mahberot Immanuel*, is a collection of poems written in narrative sequence. The section titled "Tofet and Eden" is modeled after Dante's *Divine Comedy*. He also wrote in Italian, one of the first to introduce the sonnet into Hebrew poetry. Some Talmudic scholars were critical of his writings, because of the frivolous and irreverent nature of some of the passages in his *Mahberot*.

INCLINATION, GOOD AND EVIL. *See* **Yetzer ha-rah, ha-tov.**

INDIA. Republic in southern Asia. In 1998, India's 4,400 Jews fell into three distinct groups: the *Bene Israel* (Sons of Israel), Jews of Cochin, and a series of loosely organized communities from Persia and the west. The Bene Israel, largest of the groups, speak Maharati, wear Indian dress, and are divided into caste-like groups of "black" and "white" Jews who have separate synagogues and do not intermarry. They believe they settled in the Bombay District in about 175 B.C.E. around the Maccabean uprising in Palestine. When first discovered by the West about 200 years ago, they knew no Hebrew and owned no prayer books. *Shema Yisrael*, one of the few prayers they remembered, was recited at all their religious ceremonies. Several thousand of them have emigrated to Israel.

A rabbi and his family in India. Courtesy Hazel Greenwald.

Indian Jews of Iraqi origin, the second largest group, live predominantly in Bombay and Calcutta and engage mainly in commerce. They are descendants of Jews who followed their leader David Sassoon from Iraq to India in 1832 where he founded the house of **Sassoon**, known for its great wealth and generous contributions to Jewish charitable causes.

Cochin Jews, the third largest group, who live in Cochin and other cities on the Malabar Coast, came from Persia and Arab countries during the early Middle Ages. They spoke Malayalam, the language of the Dravidians, India's original inhabitants. Hebrew, however, was known and used in their strictly Orthodox religious ritual. The first written record of Cochin Jews is a copper inscription dated 1020 C.E., in which the maharajah of the district grants privileges of nobility to the head of the community. The "white," "black," and "brown" Jews of Cochin all believe they stem from exiles who left Palestine in 70 C.E. after the destruction of the Second Temple. It is more probable that the "black" Jews arrived in India after the Moslem conquest of Persia in the 7th century, and that the "whites" came after the expulsion from Spain in 1492.

The smallest group is of European origin, consisting of refugees who emigrated to India to escape Hitler's persecutions in **Germany** in 1933.

Jews of India live in comparative freedom and security. Many of them have risen to high ranks in the armed services; others have prospered in business and the professions.

INDIANA. Jewish traders arrived in the mid-18th century, but settlement did not start for another 100 years. Indiana, mainly a rural state, never achieved large Jewish settlement. Of the 18,000 Jews who live in the state, some 10,000 live in Indianapolis, 2,200 in Fort Wayne, 2,000 in South Bend, and 1,000 in Bloomington. The last is home to Indiana University, which has a well-known Judaic studies program. Indianapolis has well-established congregations and Jewish organizations. Indiana Jews have been active in civil and philanthropic life in the state.

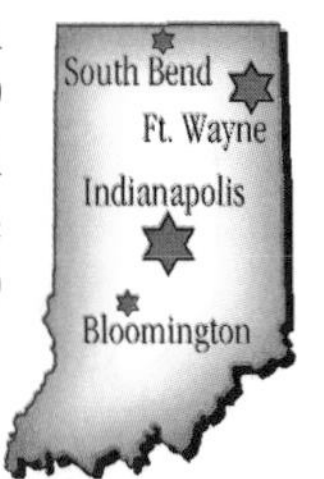

INGATHERING OF THE EXILES. In Hebrew, *Kibbutz Galuyot*. The hope for the reunion of the people of Israel in the land of Israel is fundamental to the prophetic idea of redemption: "The redeemed of the Lord shall return and come with singing into Zion; and joy shall be upon their head" (Isa. 51:11). For centuries Jewish prayers echoed the fervent desire for the ingathering of the exiles: "Sound the great trumpet for our freedom...and gather us from the four corners of the earth." Not until the rise of the Zionist movement did the reunion of Israel became a reality. Unfortunately, only a small portion was able to return to Zion before the Nazis exterminated 6 million European Jews.

After the establishment of the State of **Israel** on May 15, 1948, the ingathering of the exiles assumed undreamed-of proportions. The greatest number of Jews came during the first five years of Israel's existence. From mid-May 1948 to the end of 1992, close to 1.8 million Jews came to Israel from all five continents and from more than 90 countries. In 1990, the flow increased, and in the next several years more than 500,000 Jews from the former Soviet Union arrived in Israel, along with an additional 20,000 Jews from Ethiopia.

Operation "Magic Carpet" in which an entire Yemenite community was transported by planes to Israel in 1949-1950.

INQUISITION. The special courts set up by the Catholic Church to check the spread of heretical opinion among the faithful, first formed in the 13th century. It was most active, however, in **Spain**, where it began in 1480. In time, the dreaded activities of this agency of the Church came to be directed mainly at ferreting out the **Marranos**, Jews who had been forcibly converted to **Christianity** and were found secretly observing the practices of Judaism.

It is estimated that in 350 years of Inquisition activities (roughly from 1480 to 1821), about 400,000 Jews were brought before these ecclesiastical tribunals; 30,000 were put to death. Punishment was carried out in public squares to serve both as a warning and a demonstration of "the glory of the Church." Hence, an inquisitorial execution was known as **auto-da-fe**, an act of faith. Most notorious of the inquisitors was Thomas de Torquemada, who was largely responsible for the edict issued by Ferdinand and Isabella of Spain on the Ninth of Ab 1492, expelling all Jews from Spanish territory.

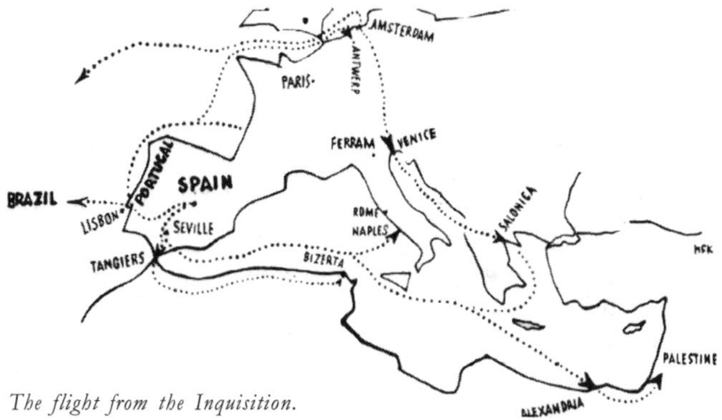

The flight from the Inquisition.

IOWA. One of the smaller Jewish communities in the U.S., there are 2,800 Jews in Des Moines, 1,200 in Iowa City, and 520 in Sioux City. Jews first arrived in Iowa in the 1830's, and in the beginning of the 20th century, some 1,500 Jews were sent by the U.S. Government to live in Iowa.

Des Moines
Iowa City

IRAN. Iran, the ancient Persia, included at its height of power Asia Minor, Mesopotamia, **Babylonia**, and the mountainous lands east and south. Jews first came under Persian rule in 539 B.C.E. when King **Cyrus** conquered Babylonia. The Judean captives, exiled to Babylonia after the destruction of the **Temple** in 586 B.C.E., welcomed the Persian rulers. Forty thousand of them returned to Judea and rebuilt their homeland. For two centuries of Persian rule, the Jewish communities of Persian Babylonia flourished, and close links were maintained with the communities of Judea. In later centuries, when the Persian Empire fell successively under Greek, Parthian, and Arab domination, Jews continued to live in its territories, notably in the Babylonian cities of Sura and Pumbeditha, where great academies flourished and where the immense work of compiling the **Talmud** was completed in 500 C.E.

During the 12th century, there were large Jewish communities in the cities of Isfahan, Shiraz, and Hamadan, part of present-day

Iran. Under the Safavid Dynasty from 1499 to 1736, Jews suffered severe discriminatory measures against them. Many converted to **Islam**, living secretly as Jews. Some fled to **Afghanistan** and Palestine where their descendants are still to be found. The Kadar Dynasty from 1795 to 1925 continued the harsh anti-Jewish policy of the Safavids. They considered the Jews ritually unclean, humiliated them, and taxed them heavily. Under this treatment, the Jewish community declined. In the late 19th century, the situation for Persian Jewry improved somewhat when Western European Jews interceded on their behalf. In 1898, the first school of the **Alliance Israélite Universelle** was organized at Teheran. Today, the Alliance conducts a network of 21 schools throughout Iran which has contributed greatly to raising the cultural and economic standards of Persian Jewry. Since May 15, 1948, there has been a mass emigration of about 60,000 Persian Jews to **Israel**. Emigration is still continuing at a slow pace.

A Jewish child of the Teheran ghetto in Iran.

Under the Shah Reza Pahlevi in 1979, the Jewish community was estimated at 70,000. In 1998, there were about 14,000 Jews, the majority living in Teheran. Other Jewish centers are Shiraz, Isfahan, and Hamadan. Only a handful of Iran's Jews live in comfortable circumstances. Many, particularly in the smaller towns and villages, live in conditions bordering on destitution.

Since the triumph of the Ayatollah Ruholla Khomeini's Islamic Revolution in 1979, the 2,500-year-old Jewish community of Iran has experienced a dramatic decline. **Zionism**, defined on the basis of ties with Israel, is regarded as a crime punishable by death. At present, the outlook for Iranian Jewry is uncertain.

IRAQ. Jews in Iraq constitute the oldest Jewish community in the world aside from **Israel**. Iraq, the **Babylonia** of the **Bible** and the **Talmud**, was the Jews' first land of exile, to which they were driven from Palestine by Nebuchadnezzar after he had destroyed the First **Temple** in 597 B.C.E. The Babylonian **Talmud** was composed there. But due to repeated unrest and disorder in the country caused by a series of wars, Jews steadily emigrated to India and to Persia where they created communities, known as Baghdad Jews, which still exist today. In the 7th century, Arabs conquered the country. Under Harun-al-Rashid's rule from 786 to 809, the scholars and leaders of the Talmudic academies began to make contact with the various Jewish communities in Europe. Their influence extended to Jews in both Europe and North Africa.

In 1534, **Turkey** conquered that area which today comprises the land of Iraq and ruled it until 1917 when Great Britain won it. In 1932, the independent kingdom of Iraq was established. Both under the British mandate and under Iraqi sovereign rule, Jews lived in comparative freedom. A good number enjoyed prosperity and even wealth, especially in the capital city of Baghdad. About 50,000 Jews resided there, representing approximately 20 percent of the population.

Spiritually, the Jewish community in Iraq had deteriorated since its original growth and development. The **Alliance Israélite Universelle** played a significant educational role in Iraq early in the 20th century by founding a broad network of schools.

In 1948, the outbreak of the Arab war against the newly established State of Israel was marked by legal plunder and persecution of Iraqi Jews. The "great exodus" of Jews followed in 1951 and 1952. Of the 130,000 Jewish inhabitants who were in Iraq in 1948, fewer than 350 have remained. The remnants of the Iraqi Jewish community are settled mainly in Baghdad. Anti-Jewish feeling has heightened with the unrest in the Middle East. Jews have lost property rights, and mass trials have been held to uncover "Zionist spy rings."

In February 1991, Iraq launched a missile attack on Israel which caused extensive damage in the **Tel Aviv** area. Miraculously, loss of life was minimal. After the swift victory of the Allied forces against Iraq, the political situation in that country is uncertain. After the defeat of Saddam Hussein, it was hard to determine whether any Jews were left in Iraq, but before the outbreak of the war, there were about 120 Jews left.

IRELAND. The earliest evidence of Jewish settlement in Ireland is a grant made in 1232 to a certain Peter de Rivall, giving him "custody of the King's Jews in Ireland." In 1290, Irish Jews, like their English brethren, were expelled from Ireland and did not return until around 1655, the days of Oliver Cromwell and the Commonwealth. It was then that the first **Sephardic** community was founded in Dublin; Jewish settlement in Ireland has been small but continuous ever since.

In 1998, most of Ireland's 1,300 Jews live in Dublin, the capital city. They are mostly shopkeepers and tradesmen. The clothing and furniture industries were introduced into Ireland by Lithuanian immigrants. Dublin, with its two large and four small synagogues, its charitable organizations, and Talmud Torah, is the center of religious and cultural life of Irish Jewry. More than half of Northern Ireland's Jews live in the capital city of Belfast, whose present Jewish community was founded in 1870. An earlier Jewish community was founded there a century before, but later dissolved.

IRGUN Z'VAI L'UMI. Underground military force organized by the **Revisionists** in April 1937 to combat British repressions in Palestine and the Arabs' growing rule of terror. The Revisionists were impatient with the policy of restraint practiced by Jewish leaders in **Palestine** in the face of constant Arab attacks. The Irgun was guided by two fundamental principles: that a Jewish state had to be established in the immediate future, and that every Jew had a natural right to come to Palestine. The Irgun believed the time was right for military action in order to achieve the legitimate aim of establishing a Jewish state. The Irgun's symbol, a hand gripping a rifle over a map of Palestine that included eastern Palestine, began to appear on all the organization's posters.

In 1938, a member of the Irgun, Shlomo Ben Yosef, was accused of attacking an Arab vehicle in retaliation for numerous killings of Jews. He was sentenced to the gallows. Ben Yosef became a symbol of the determination of Irgun members to fight to the death for the cause of Jewish liberation.

When World War II broke out and the free world was engaged in a deadly struggle with the Nazi armies, the Irgun committed its small force to fight the common enemy on the side of the British. The first Irgun commander, David Raziel, was killed in 1941 in a commando operation in Iraq. Command of Irgun was then taken over by Yaakov Meridor, and later in 1943, by Menachem **Begin**. In February 1944, the Irgun called for the end of the British mandate, the freeing of Palestine from "foreign domination," and the immediate establishment of a provisional government. The British began a ruthless campaign to destroy the Irgun. Several hundred of its members were arrested and exiled to Eritrea, a British colony in Northeast Africa. The arrests swelled to thousands after the Irgun blew up the King David Hotel, the administrative offices of the Palestine (British) government. Each Irgun exploit was countered by an act of British repression. In the spring of 1947, Dov Gruner and four other members of Irgun were hanged at the Acre prison.

Though the **Jewish Agency** and the **Haganah** frequently condemned Irgun for its extremist policies, there was a short period after World War II when Haganah and Irgun cooperated in the struggle against the British. This happened when the British Labor party, on coming to power in 1945, failed to fulfill its pre-election promises to open Palestine without restrictions to survivors of the **Holocaust**. To allegations that Irgun was a terrorist organization, Begin replied that Irgun's aim was not to cause loss of life, but to hasten the British evacuation of Palestine. After the establishment of the State of Israel in May 1948, the Irgun, numbering several thousand, cooperated with Haganah in fighting off Arab invaders.

Open hostility briefly erupted between the Irgun and the Haganah (by then the official army of the State of Israel) in June 1948 when the Irgun brought to Israel the S.S. Altalena, a boat carrying volunteers and munitions for use in the War of Independence. The Haganah claimed that it had not authorized the landing and unloading of the boat; its leaders feared that the Irgun would start a revolt to topple Israel's provisional government. The Irgun insisted that they had kept the Haganah informed about the boat and that the Haganah leaders with whom they had consulted had raised no objections to the arrangement. The Altalena was sunk by the Haganah, but contrary to the fears of some, Irgun did not put up a fight against Haganah. On September 21, 1948, the Israel government ordered the Irgun disbanded. Most of its members were incorporated into the **Israel Defense Forces**.

ISAAC. From the Hebrew *Yitzhak*, meaning laughter; second of the three patriarchs. In his youth, Isaac was willing to serve as a sacrifice. He married his cousin **Rebecca**, who bore him twins, Esau and **Jacob**. He prospered and the Lord renewed His promise to give Canaan to the Hebrews by telling Isaac, "To you and to your seed I give all these lands...And I will cause your seed to multiply as the stars of heaven" (Gen. 26:2-4). Isaac was 40 years old when he married. By the time his sons were grown, he was feeble and blind. Rebecca was therefore able to trick him into giving the blessing of the firstborn to Jacob instead of the unworthy Esau.

ISAAC ELCHANAN. *See* **Spector, Yitzchak Elchanan**.

ISAAC, JULES (1877-1963). French Jewish historian. Having lost his entire family during the Nazi occupation of **France**, he became interested in the roots of **anti-Semitism** and wrote the books *Jesus and Israel* and the *Genesis of Anti-Semitism*, which played a decisive role in the Vatican's decision under Pope John XXIII to change the attitude of the Church toward the Jewish people.

ISAIAH. First of the major prophets in the Bible. Isaish, son of Amoz prophesied during the 8th century B.C.E. in Jerusalem, from the death of King Uzziah until the middle of Hezekiah's reign. He protested strongly against moral laxity and injustice. His great visions include world peace at the end of days (2:1-4) and the vision of the divine presence in the **Temple** (6:1-5). Isaiah maintained that God is more interested in justice to the weak and the poor than the offerings of sacrifices in the Temple.

Three major events are reflected in Isaiah's prophecies: the invasion of the kingdom of **Judah** by the armies of Israel and **Damascus** for the purpose of forcing King Ahaz into an anti-Assyrian alliance in 734 B.C.E.; the destruction of the Kingdom of **Israel** by the Assyrians in 721 B.C.E.; and Sennacherib's invasion of Judah in 701 B.C.E. Throughout this time, the small kingdom of Judah faced a dual danger: the risk of being swallowed up by neighboring empires, and spiritual destruction through the loss of its belief in one God. Isaiah's political wisdom impelled him to advise strict isolation for Judea and avoidance of entangling alliances with foreign nations. In chapters 40 to 66, called by some authorities the Second Isaiah, the prophet comforts the exiled, suffering, and despairing people in the great poem beginning, "Comfort ye, comfort ye, My people, saith your God" (chapters 40-44).

ISHMAEL. Son of **Abraham** and **Sarah**'s maid, **Hagar**. He was **Isaac**'s older half-brother, and is considered the father of the Arab people, who are sometimes referred to as Ishmaelites.

ISLAM. Also known as Mohammedanism; youngest of the three monotheistic religions of our time. Islam was founded by Mohammed, son of Abdallah, a camel driver of Mecca, **Arabia**. He was born in 571 C.E. and died in 632. Islam's bible, the Koran, which is in its entirety the work of the founder, is based to a large extent on the Old and New Testaments, whose contents must have been transmitted to the illiterate Mohammed in oral form colored by the interpretations of the rabbinic commentators and the Church Fathers. Though it incorporates elements of both Judaism and **Christianity**, accepting both **Moses** and **Jesus** as prophets, the faith of Mohammed is closer to **Judaism** than to Christianity. It insists that there is only one God and rejects the idea of a son of God or a Trinity. It allows no sculptured figures or painted pictures to appear in its houses of worship. It forbids its communicants from eating pork or drinking liquor. It subscribes to the doctrines of life after death, a day of judgment, reward and punishment, and paradise and hell. Mohammed is, according to Islam, the last and greatest of all prophets and his Koran, which deviates in a number of places from the data of the Hebrew and the Christian Scriptures, is the correct version of the Word of God.

Today, some 800 million Muslims live in a belt of countries extending in a continuous line from **Morocco** in the west to Indonesia in the east. Their five fundamental duties are to declare that there is no God but Allah and that Mohammed is his prophet; to recite the five daily prayers; to give alms; to fast during the month of Ramadan (during the periods of daylight only); and to make the pilgrimage to Mecca at least once during a lifetime.

Islam is divided into sects, the two most important being the Sunnites, or traditionalists, and the Shi'ites, the more mystically inclined followers of the Caliph Ali. It is theoretically tolerant of Jews and Christians, but in practice Moslem states treat non-Muslims as second-class citizens.

The position of Jews has been more favorable under Islam than under Christian rule. During the Middle Ages, when the Muslim civilization peaked, there was often close cultural collaboration between Jewish and Muslim scientists and thinkers. At the courts of such enlightened Muslim princes as Abdurrahman of **Spain** in the 10th century, Saladin the Great of **Egypt** in the 12th century, and Suleiman and Selim of **Turkey** in the 16th century, gifted Jews were influential and eminent. This situation, however, was neither universal nor permanent, proven by the fact that **Maimonides** was compelled by the fanatical Almohades to leave his native city when he refused to renounce Judaism in favor of Islam.

ISRAEL. Literally, one who strives with God. The name given to **Jacob** after he wrestled with the angel (Gen. 32:28); the collective name of the twelve tribes. Later, it became the name of the northern Kingdom of **Israel** (931 B.C.E.-721 B.C.E.), formed when the ten tribes seceded after the death of King **Solomon**. Eventually, the name came to be applied to the Jewish people as a whole. The land of their origin was known as *Eretz Israel*, the "Land of Israel"; the modern state is named *Medinat Israel*.

Jacob Struggles With the Angel, by Gustav Doré.

Israeli soldier in a parachutist training course.

ISRAEL DEFENSE FORCES. In Hebrew, *Tz'va Haganah L'Yisrael*. The Israel Defense Forces (IDF) grew out of the **Haganah**, the Jewish self-defense organization formed during the period of the British Mandate and the **Jewish Brigade**, a military unit which fought alongside the Allied Forces during World War II. Its purpose was to defend Jewish life and property in **Palestine** against Arab marauders. Since its creation in 1948, Israel's army has been called upon four times to fight for the survival of the country: in 1948, 1956, 1967, and in the **Yom Kippur War** of 1973. In February 1991, the IDF planned to launch an air and ground attack on western Iraq to put an end to the Scud missile attacks against Israel, but the U.S. dissuaded Israel from doing so.

The IDF must be constantly on the alert to defend Israel's borders against attacks from hostile neighbors. The IDF has a nucleus of career soldiers, but it is basically a citizens' army. All men from the age of 18 to 29 and women from 18 to 26 are called for regular service of up to 30 months for men and 20 months for women. Married women, mothers, and pregnant mothers are exempted from the draft. Women from strictly Orthodox homes who have religious objections to serving in the army must perform national services as teachers or nurses. Israeli Arabs are exempt, but Druzes are drafted at their own request, and a number of Muslims and Christians have volunteered. Following their term of national service, men and women without children are in the Reserves until the ages of 55 and 34, respectively, and men must report each year for various periods of training. With this arrangement, able-bodied citizens can be mobilized for combat within hours if a national emergency erupts.

> *"And he said, 'No longer will your name be Jacob, but Israel, for you have struggled with beings divine and human and you have prevailed.'"*
>
> — GENESIS 32:28

Organization. The IDF includes all three branches of modern armed services: army, navy, and air force. Ranks are uniform throughout, under the orders of one General Staff, headed by a chief of staff with the rank of lieutenant-general. The General Staff consists of the chiefs of the General Staff, Manpower, Logistics and Intelligence, the Commanders of the Navy and Air Force, and the officers who command the Northern, Central, and Southern regional commands into which the country is divided.

Women in the Army. The women's force, known as *Hen* (an abbreviation of *Hel Nashim*, or Women's Force); the word *hen* also happens to be the Hebrew word for charm. This force provides non-combatant personnel such as nurses, mechanics, communication workers, and other specialists, thus freeing the men for active combat duty. Some women serve as combat personnel.

Nahal (No'ar Halutzi Lohem). This pioneer youth group combines soldiering with pioneering. After a few months of intensive military training, Nahal groups are assigned to agricultural settlements for about a year to gain practical experience in farming. A Nahal group joins a frontier settlement or sets up one of its own, often in areas too dangerous or difficult for settlement by civilians.

Gadna (G'dude HaNo'ar). The "Youth Battalions" are pre-military organizations for boys and girls between the ages of 14 and 18, supervised jointly by the Ministry of Defense and the Ministry of Education and Culture. Training is along scout lines, and there are also naval and air sections. Emphasis is placed on pioneering and practical training in agriculture. Many developing countries, especially in Africa and South America, have formed youth movements modeled on Nahal and Gadna.

Role of the Army in Education and Citizenship. In addition to fulfilling Israel's defense needs, the Army helps weld the many different elements of the country's population into a unified whole. Soldiers are taught Hebrew, Jewish history, and the geography of the country. In this manner the Army has helped new immigrants become integrated into Israeli life. No soldier leaves the army without getting a basic education. Soldiers are also trained in trades of their choice so that they return to civilian life better prepared for the productive work necessary for the nation's continued growth and welfare.

Israeli soldier in the Negev during morning prayer.

ISRAEL, GOVERNMENT AND POLITICAL PARTIES. The State of **Israel** is a democracy, and its government represents the people and is responsible to them in periodic elections. There are a number of forms of democratic government, such as the American, or presidential system, and the European, or parliamentary system. The government of Israel is parliamentary.

Israeli-made Merkava tank, one of the most advanced tanks in the world.

Legislature. The **Knesset**, or Parliament of Israel, is the unicameral legislative branch of the government. The 120 representatives to the Knesset are elected to serve four-year terms in free, secret elections. If the government fails to hold the confidence of the Knesset (*see* Executive), an election may be held before the four-year term is over. All citizens, men and women, Christians, Muslims, and Jews, 18 years of age or older, have the right to vote. Both the Cabinet and the Knesset members may introduce new bills. A bill becomes a law after it has passed three readings and been published in the official *Reshumot*, similar to the American Congressional Record.

Proportional Representation. Israel has many political parties, and Knesset members are elected according to proportional representation. This means that each party presents to the country its own list of candidates, and the voters cast their ballots not for an individual candidate but for the whole party list. The number of members each party elects to the Knesset is proportional to the percentage of the popular vote it receives. As of 1998, no party in Israel has ever received an absolute majority. As a result, several parties combine to form a working majority in the Knesset. This coalition works out a program for which it assumes collective responsibility. Severe disagreements among the members of the coalition bring about resignations, and the coalition loses its legislative majority. The Knesset must then be dissolved and new elections called.

Memorial at Hulda to those who died defending the road to Jerusalem in 1948.

Executive. The Cabinet is the executive branch of the government, and its task is to carry out and administer the laws enacted by the Knesset. Under the Israeli system, the Cabinet is directly responsible to the Knesset. It has no veto power and can continue in office as long as it retains the confidence of the Knesset. If defeated in a vote of confidence the Cabinet must resign, and a new one must be formed. If the Knesset cannot form a new Cabinet which has its confidence, it must turn to the people and call for new elections.

Prime Minister's Office. The cabinet is headed by the prime minister who is the chief executive. His office coordinates the work of all the ministries and administers the civil service. The smooth and efficient working of the whole machinery of government is the responsibility of the prime minister.

Presidency. The President of Israel, unlike the American President, has little actual power. Serving as a symbol of the people's unity, he is not chosen in the competitive general elections, but is elected in a secret ballot by an absolute majority of the Knesset. The president's term of office is five years, but there is no limit on the number of times he may be re-elected. The duties of the president are largely honorary. These include the task of summoning a member of the Knesset, usually the leader of the majority party, to form a new government. Upon the recommendation of competent bodies, he appoints judges, diplomatic representatives, the governor of the Bank of Israel, and the comptroller. It is also in his power to grant amnesty to prisoners and to commute their sentences. Major documents, such as treaties with foreign states, are signed by the President together with the prime minister or another competent minister.

The Knesset building in Jerusalem.

Judiciary. Israel's judicial system is made up of two branches, civil and religious. There are Jewish, Christian, and Moslem religious courts, so that the followers of each religion come under the jurisdiction of a religious court of their own faith. Matters of marriage and divorce are under the sole jurisdiction of the religious courts.

Judicial authority is independent of the executive and legislative branches of government, as is essential in a democracy. Judges are appointed for life, and the appointments are made by the President on the recommendation of an eight-member committee. The President and two members of the Supreme Court, the minister of justice, and one other Cabinet member, two members of the Knesset selected by that entire body, and two lawyers chosen by the Bar Association serve on that committee.

The highest court of appeal is the ten-member Supreme Court. This court sits also as a high court of justice to which a citizen may bring his complaints against the authorities, and the court acts to protect the rights of the individual citizen. The Supreme Court of Israel, unlike that of the United States, does not have the power to review laws and declare them unconstitutional because Israel has no written constitution. Israel inherited its legal code when the state came into being in 1948.

This code is a mixture of British common law, remnants of Turkish Ottoman law, decrees of the British mandatory administration, and new laws enacted by the Knesset. By a resolution passed by the Knesset on June 13, 1950, a committee on constitution and law was authorized to prepare a draft constitution. As each article of this draft constitution is completed, it must be submitted to the Knesset for approval. When all the articles are approved, they will form the state constitution.

Political Parties. Israeli political parties date back to the beginning of the Zionist movement. From the early days of Zionism in Europe, Zionists ranged along a broad political spectrum, from the extreme left socialists to the extreme right nationalists. In the middle were religious and general Zionist parties. When Israel was founded in 1948, the socialist Mapai (*see* **Labor Zionism** *and* **Ben-Gurion**) got 46 seats, and formed a government coalition with the United Religious Front (16; *see* **Mizrachi** *and* **Agudath Israel**), the Progressive Party (5; *see* **General Zionism**), the Sephardic Party (4), and the Arab Party (2). The opposition consisted of the Mapam (19; *see* **Hashomer Ha-tzair**), Herut (14; *see* **Revisionist Zionism**), General Zionists (7; *see* **General Zionism**), the Israeli Communist Party (4; non-Zionist), and assorted small parties won one or two Knesset seats.

For the next 30 years, Mapai remained in power, while the political map kept changing, with splinter groups forming in nearly every party, and with parties reorganizing and renaming themselves. The General Zionists and the Progressives were absorbed by Herut, now called Likud. The Mizrachi became the NRP (National Religious Party), the Sephardic Party became Shas, Mapam became Meretz, the communists disappeared within the United Arab List, the newly arrived Russian Jews in the 90's formed their own party (Yisrael Be'aliya). The ruling Mapai became the Israel Labor Party. The two main players today are Likud, which first came into power in 1977 (*see* **Begin**), and Labor. In 1996, Likud (32 seats) formed a government coalition with Shas (10), NRP (9), Yisrael Be'aliya (7), and two smaller parties with 4 seats each. The opposition consisted of Labor (34), Meretz (9), United Arab List (4), and a few small parties.

ISRAEL, STATE OF. The third Jewish Commonwealth came into being on May 14, 1948, almost six months after the UN decision to partition Palestine into one Jewish and one Arab state. The proclamation of the State of Israel marked the climax of a half century of political **Zionism** that sought to reunite the scattered Jewish people with its ancient "Promised Land."

Boundaries. In the Bible, the boundaries of the land of Canaan, promised by God to **Abraham** and his seed, extended from the Euphrates River to the Red Sea, from the Mediterranean to the great desert in the east, a geographical and economic unit corresponding roughly to the southern horn of the Fertile Crescent. These ideal boundaries were achieved only by **David**.

Geography. The present area of Israel is only part of the original land and is made up of three longitudinal strips: the coastal plain along the Mediterranean, the range of hills forming the backbone of the Country, and the Jordan depression with its prolongation, the Plain of Araba. These strips are divided by the fertile Valley of Jezreel, which separates the mountains of **Galilee** in the north from the stern hills of Judea in the south, and by the Plain of Beersheba, which forms the northern boundary of the **Negev**. The Jordan depression follows the Jordan River from its freshwater lakes in the north (**Kinneret**) to the **Dead Sea** in the south, and along the barren Araba to the Red Sea port of **Elat**.

Climate. The climate of Israel varies with the altitude and with the proximity of various regions to the Mediterranean or the desert; generally, it is a Mediterranean climate, characterized by a long, hot, dry summer from April through October, and a cool rainy winter that lasts from November to April. The heaviest rainfall is in the north, the lightest precipitation at Elat in the south. The coldest month of the year is January, and the hottest month is May or June when the temperature is capable of rising to 98 degrees in the hill city of **Jerusalem**, and as high as 120 degrees in the depth of the Jordan valley. Like the landscape of the country, the climate of Israel is extraordinarily diverse.

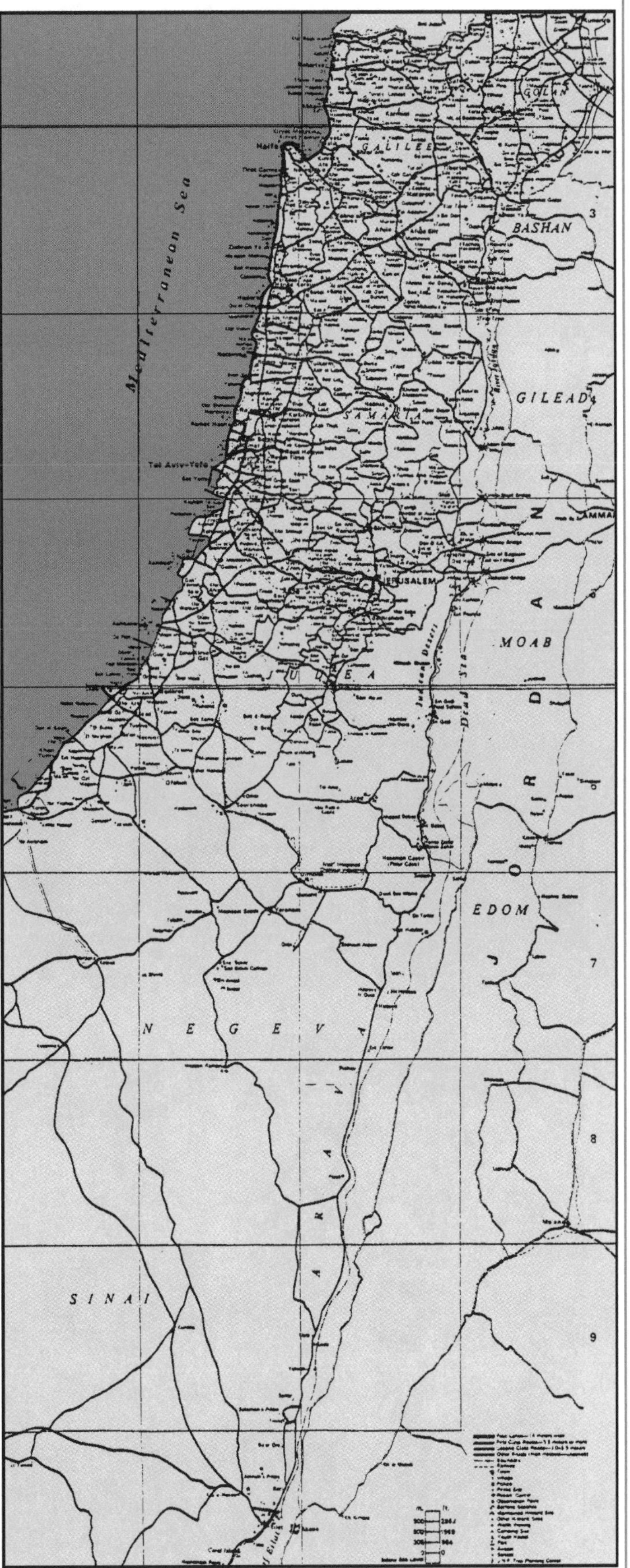

Map of Israel.

Natural Resources. The natural resources of Israel were enriched in 1955 by the discovery of oil in the Negev. This southern area provides the country with a large variety of minerals, ranging from copper and manganese to mica and glass-sand. The **Dead Sea** yields many minerals, particularly large quantities of magnesium, potash, and bromide. The variegated structure of the country affords a rich and diversified agriculture with crops of grain, vegetables, and fruits. Citrus fruits provide a large part of Israel's exports; also a wide range of products are manufactured, processed, or finished in Israel. Not the least of the country's resources is its population, increased by constant immigration. When the State of Israel was established in May 1948, its Jewish population numbered about 650,000. In 1998, the population of Israel was more than 5.8 million, of whom 4.8 million were Jews. The **Ingathering of the Exiles** has brought to Israel Jews from about 90 countries.

History. From the beginning, Israel's history was determined by its strategic situation at the crossroads of empires and established routes of trade. It connected the Plain of the Nile in the south with Mesopotamia, the land of the Tigris and Euphrates rivers, in the northeast. **Canaan**'s harbors looked westward to Crete and **Greece**; Elat faced toward the rich lands of the south and Far East, the ancient sources of civilization. About 2300 B.C.E. Sargon I marched down from Mesopotamia and reached the Mediterranean. Later, Egypt

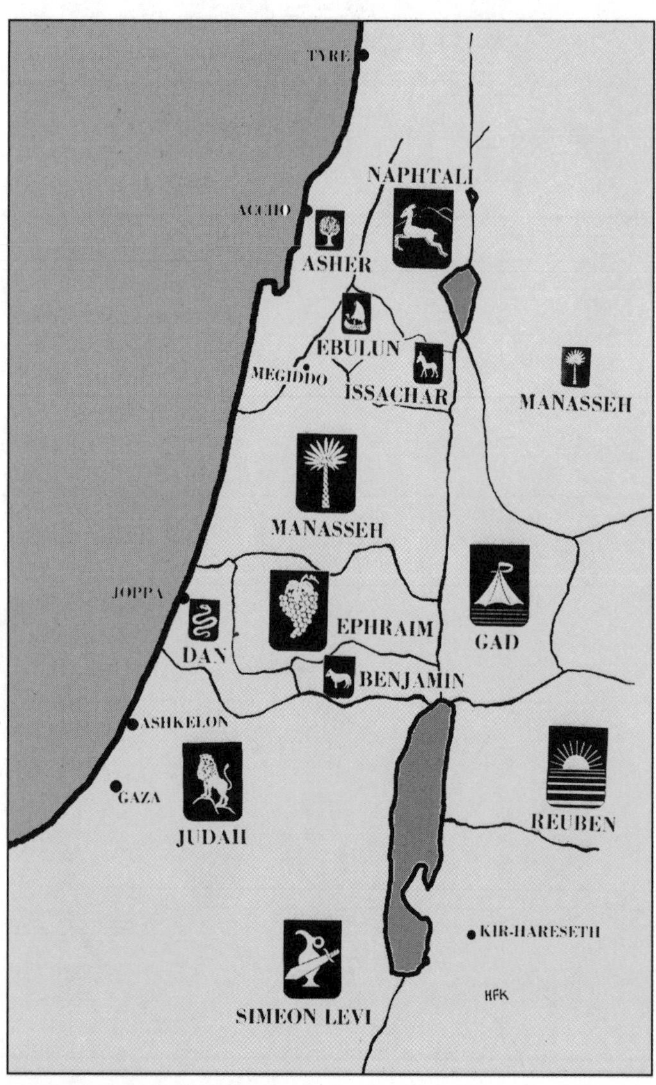

Map of the Twelve Tribes.

Danish volunteer doing farm work in Israel.

subdued Canaan, and its governors exacted tribute from the people. The earliest Hebraic association with the Promised Land occurred in the time of the patriarch **Abraham** around the 20th century B.C.E. In the biblical story of the **Covenant**, God gave the land of Canaan to Abraham and his children as an "everlasting possession." The invasion of the Israelites came in the 13th century B.C.E. In the biblical story of the Exodus, **Moses** began the conquest of Canaan by overcoming the kings of the Amorites in East Jordan, where the tribes of **Reuben**, **Gad**, and half of Manasseh settled. **Joshua** completed the conquest, particularly of the northern hill country, dividing the land among the other tribes of Israel. But the plains and coastal regions remained settled by the Canaanites and the seafaring Philistines. These peoples were thorns in the flesh of the Israelite tribes, whom they harassed constantly so long as they remained loosely organized under the rule of **Judges**.

First Commonwealth. During the 11th century B.C.E. under **Saul**, the unification of the tribes into a nation began. But it was **David** who unified the Jewish state by his decisive victories over the **Philistines**, and by the conquest of the Jebusite stronghold, **Jerusalem**, which he made the nation's capital. David's son, **Solomon**, consolidated his father's gains; his reign marked the climax of the independent history of Israel. Solomon's empire stretched from Mount Hermon in the north to Elat on the Red Sea and from the plain in the east to the Mediterranean. He trained his people, mere farmers and shepherds, in the arts of building, crafts, and trade.

Solomon built a navy and sent his ships as far as **Ophir** and Tarshish to bring back precious cargoes. But although he enriched his kingdom, the extravagance of Solomon's court and his passion for building imposed a heavy tax burden upon the people. Revolt broke out during the reign of Solomon's son Rehoboam, and the country divided into two small kingdoms, Judah and Israel. The vassal states which David had subjugated now began to break free. The giant empires to the north and south awaited their opportunity to pounce. The Kingdom of Israel, though three times greater in territory and with twice the population of Judah, was the first to fall. It surrendered to the **Assyrians** in 722 B.C., and most of its residents were captured. The rest fled to Judah. As a hill country separated from Egypt by the desert and sheltered by Israel on the north, Judah was easier to defend, but it fell at last in 586 B.C. to Nebuchadnezzar, king of Babylonia, who deported a great part of the population.

The conquered people of Judah did not merge with the mighty Babylonian nation, like others who had been held captive, because in exile they learned to value and understand the teachings of their great prophets, such as **Isaiah, Jeremiah**, and **Ezekiel**. The exiles became convinced that just as the prophecies of destruction had been fulfilled, so would be the prophecies of a return to their land. And they accepted the prophetic vision of an age of ultimate peace and justice, not only for themselves but for the entire world. It was in the Babylonian exile that the people absorbed the idea of a Messiah as described in the Book of Isaiah.

The First Return. Thus, when **Cyrus** of Persia liberated the subject people from the Babylonian yoke in 538 B.C., a movement to return to Zion developed under **Zerubbabel, Ezra**, and **Nehemiah**. In the desolated land occupied by hostile strangers, the Judeans, as they were now called, labored with a tool in one hand and a sword in the other to rebuild the Temple in Jerusalem and construct a wall around the city. During the period that followed, high priests instead of kings ruled the people, scribes took the place of prophets as the teachers of the people, and the **synagogue** developed into a permanent institution. The Persian rule ended with the conquest of the Persian empire by **Alexander the Great** (356-323 B.C.E.). After Alexander's death, his empire was divided. Judea then fell first to the Ptolemies of **Egypt**, then to the Seleucids of **Syria**. But Jews, too weak to resist, remained almost indifferent to the changes of rulers. Concentrating upon their inner life, they developed religious institutions and great religious books, and collected and edited the books of the Bible. It was only when Antiochus, King of Syria, tampered with their religion that the docile people were stirred to rebellion. Led by the **Hasmoneans**, they hurled the defilers from the land in 165 B.C.E. Twenty-six years later Simon the Hasmonean declared Judea a free commonwealth.

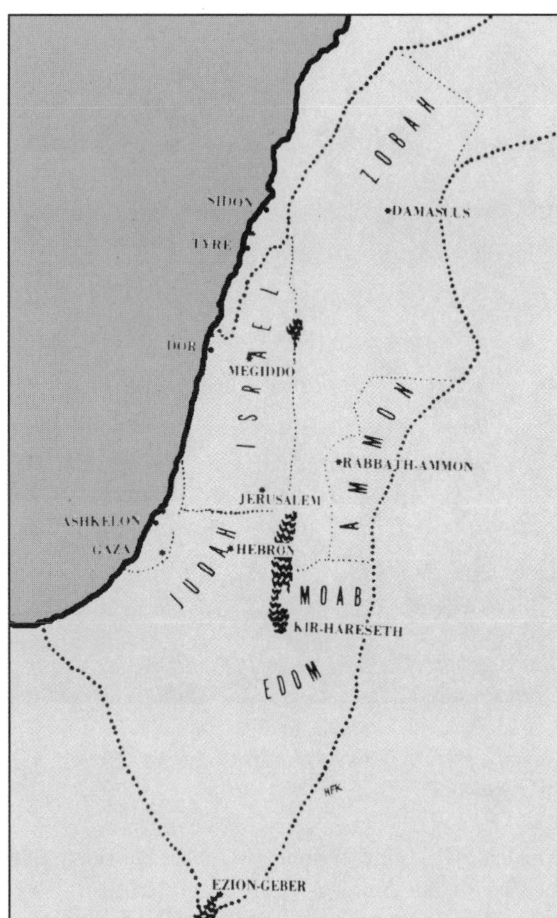

Map of the Kingdom of David and Solomon.

View of the old city of Jerusalem.

The Second Commonwealth. The Hasmonean dynasty not only restored the land of Israel to its ancient boundaries, but also increased the population by converting the mixed population of Galileans and the **Edomites** to Judaism. A powerful kingdom might have developed, but in 63 B.C.E. the Romans invaded Judea. The unequal struggle ended in the complete destruction of Jerusalem and the Second Commonwealth in 70 C.E. The fires of rebellion were rekindled by **Bar Kokhba** in 132-35 C.E. They were quenched once more, this time for nearly 2,000 years.

The Long Night. The Romans now called the land **Palestine** to erase all Jewish associations, while Jerusalem was rebuilt as a soldiers' colony and renamed Aelia Capitolina. Yet the invisible chains that bound the Jews to Israel were never broken. With Jerusalem gone, a new center of Jewish study was built in **Yavneh**, and the **Sanhedrin**, a scholarly governing body, was created. As the Romans persecuted the tiny community, the center was moved north to **Tiberias** where the Mishnah, a systematic code of law, was completed in 200 C.E. The situation worsened when Rome adopted Christianity in 320 C.E., for now the land was holy to Christians. Persecutions continued with unabated cruelty under the Byzantines of the Eastern Empire, until the Arab invasion of 636 opened the era of **Islam**. The Muslims found only a few Jews in Palestine. The first centuries of Muslim rule were marked by prosperity and a measure of tolerance. Lacking experience in civil life, the Muslims at first engaged Jews as administrators. In time, however, a decline set in as Arab power weakened. In the 11th century the land came under the control of the Seljuk Turks, who annoyed the Christians and provoked the **Crusades**. The 100 years

Immigrant from Hadramaut, Southern Arabia, learns vegetable gardening from a Romanian immigrant. Courtesy Zionist Archives and Library, New York.

of Crusaders in Palestine, beginning in 1099, were a long nightmare to the Jewish community; nearly all Palestinian Jews were slaughtered during the period of the Latin Kingdom of Jerusalem. This period ended when Saladin vanquished the Christians in 1187 and called on the Muslims and Jews to resettle in the land. Palestine was never completely without a Jewish population.

In 1211, the Palestine Jewish community was strengthened by the arrival of a group headed by 300 rabbis from **France** and **England**. Their piety was equaled only by their poverty, and their need gave rise to the system of **Halukkah**, funds gathered throughout the world for the support of the Jewish community in Palestine. Still, the land had no peace. In 1260, Mongol hordes poured in from the north, pillaging and murdering as they advanced, until they were halted at Gilboa. Once again the land was laid waste, and in Jerusalem there remained only two Jews. Then Rabbi Moses ben **Nahman** (Nahmanides) of Gerona settled in Jerusalem. He became the father of Jerusalem's modern Jewish community; since Nahmanides' day the Holy City has never been without Jews.

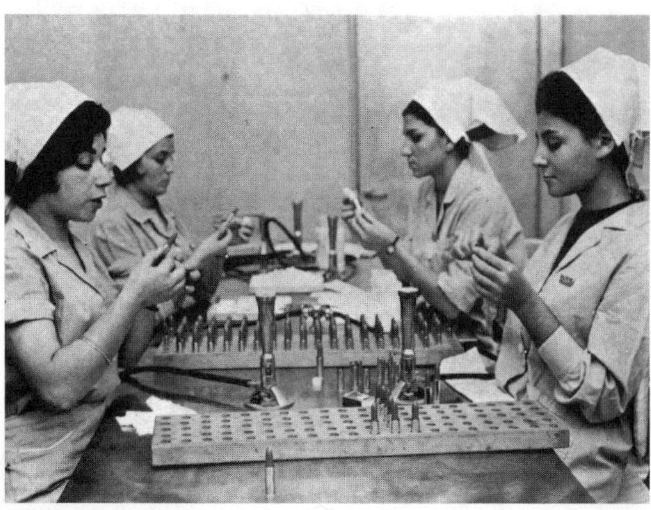

Workers at a cosmetics plant in Ashdod.

In 1516, Palestine was conquered by the Ottoman Turks. Around 1492, many Jews expelled from Spain found refuge in Palestine. Spanish Jews brought with them knowledge and skill, and in 1563, one of them, Don Joseph **Nasi**, attempted to create a colony of Spanish refugees in Tiberias as a starting point for the resettlement of the entire country. Some of the exiles settled in Safed where they created a center of **Kabbalah**. Until that time most of the Jewish population of Israel had been **Sephardic**, or Mediterranean, in origin. But with the development of the Hasidic movement in Eastern Europe, **Ashkenazic** Jews began to trickle into the country. A forerunner of this movement was Rabbi Judah the Pious, from Poland, who came to Jerusalem in 1700 at the head of a group of disciples. Their synagogue was destroyed by the Arabs. Later rebuilt, it became known as the Hurva, or Ruins, Synagogue, a famous landmark until its destruction in the War of Independence in 1948. As the Ottoman Empire decayed, the local pashas oppressed and impoverished Palestinian Jews; but the community was again strengthened when a group of Hasidim from Europe settled in Safed in 1777 and later in Tiberias. These newcomers formed the nucleus of the present Ashkenazic community of Israel. They were followed at the beginning of the 18th century by groups of *Mitnagdim*, opponents of **Hasidism** who flocked to Jerusalem; later, more Hasidim settled in Hebron. Between 1827 and 1875, the philanthropist Sir Moses **Montefiore** tried to help the Jewish community through constructive projects. The French **Alliance Israélite Universelle** set up an agricultural school at **Mikveh Israel** and trade school in the cities in 1870. These efforts were the beginning of the modern resettlements of the country.

The Lovers of Zion and the First Aliyah. The pogroms in **Russia** and growing **anti-Semitism** in Western Europe, in an age when liberalism was being paid lip service, finally brought Jews to the conviction that as a nation, the only road open to them was the road back to Zion. Out of this conviction developed modern Zionism. In 1882, a year after the murderous attacks upon Russian Jews, the movement of **Hoveve Zion**, or Lovers of Zion, developed. The object of this movement was the acquisition of land in Palestine and the promotion of Jewish settlement there. The newcomers founded **Rishon-Le-Zion** in 1882 and later Zikhron Yaacov. Among the first settlers of these colonies were the **Bilu**, a group of young Jewish students from Russia who founded Gedera in 1884. The settlers of the **First Aliyah** endured ordeals resulting from their ignorance of agriculture, as well as from malaria, excessive poverty, and the hostility of their neighbors. They were eventually taken under the wing of Baron Edmond de **Rothschild** of Paris, a philanthropist who did more than any other individual for the practical resettlement of Palestine.

Political Zionism and the Second Aliyah. It was not until 1897 that political Zionism was formulated by Theodor **Herzl**, the father of the idea of the Jewish State. He rekindled Jewish nationalism throughout the world and set in motion a chain of events that culminated fifty years later in the establishment of the State of Israel. Between 1904 and 1914, the Second Aliyah, mainly young people, came streaming into Palestine from **Russia** and **Poland**. Though comparatively few in number, it was the settlers of the First and Second Aliyot who laid the agricultural, economic, and political foundations of modern Israel. Each new village was in fact a cell of the future state. The settlers waged a struggle against primitive conditions, hostile neighbors, and Turkish obstructionism.

The Balfour Declaration and the Rebuilding of the Land. World War I, in which Turkey was allied with **Germany** and **Austria**, seriously set back the movement of Jewish upbuilding and resettlement. Much of the Jewish population was deported, and starvation and epidemics harried the remainder. Then came the issuance of the **Balfour Declaration** in 1917, promising a national home for Jews in Palestine. With new hope, the Third Aliyah established new agricultural cooperatives. The Fourth Aliyah was composed mainly of tradespeople, manufacturers, and business people with some capital for investments. **Tel Aviv** and **Haifa** grew in population, and new industries were established. School systems and hospitals were developed, and the Jewish community of Palestine organized itself for democratic self-government. The Keren Kayemet, or **Jewish National Fund**, provided the land for the **Halutzim**, and the Keren Hayesod, or Palestine Foundation Fund, provided the credit and other forms of assistance for the new immigrants.

A reversal in British policy, due partly to the recurrence of Arab outbreaks, was reflected in the shearing away of Transjordan from the area of the Jewish national home in 1922. The mid-1920's saw economic and political setbacks. Arab hostility to Jewish settlement of Palestine was inflamed by Arab leaders. The British administration either did not see or chose not to see to the threatening danger. In 1929, Arab riots broke out in Jerusalem, **Hebron**, **Safed**, and other parts of the country; Jewish lives and property were destroyed. In this new political situation, the British further whittled down the original meaning of the Balfour Declaration. The major provisions of the Passfield White Paper cut down Jewish immigration drastically, and stopped altogether the purchase of agricultural land by Jews. A storm of protest and indignation from Jews and non-Jews alike broke out. As a result, the worst features of the Passfield White Paper were modified.

The situation in Palestine quieted down, and there were no further serious Arab disturbances until 1936. The country escaped the worldwide economic depression and progressed. Fleeing from the lengthening shadow of the Nazi terror in Germany, thousands of Jews came into Palestine. During the Fifth Aliyah of 1933-1939, 300,000 newcomers were absorbed by the Jewish community.

In addition, 55,000 adolescents of the **Youth Aliyah** came into the country. These immigrants had to adjust quickly to a new climate, the new Hebrew language, new jobs, and a people for whom hard menial work was part of their "Religion of Labor." In the meantime, Arab riots broke out anew. From 1936 to 1939, Arab terrorists attacked Jewish settlements, burned fields and forests, and murdered and intimidated Arabs friendly to Jews. British counteraction against the terror was neither consistent nor effective. The British did not permit the **Haganah**, the Jewish militia, to protect the settlements. A period of self-defense and "illegal" immigration followed; this activity was intensified during World War II, when Jews of Palestine strove to save as many Jews as possible from the Holocaust. At the same time, the Jewish settlement contributed actively to the Allied war effort, serving not only as a source of industrial supplies but also as a fighting force in North Africa and in the European campaigns.

By the end of the war the Jewish population of Palestine had risen to 500,000 while the Palestinian Arabs were one million. The

The diamond exchange buildings on the Ramat-Gan Highway. Courtesy Israel Office of Information.

resurgence of Jewish national aspirations after the war was opposed by the British, whose vacillation further encouraged Arab opposition. Numerous commissions were sent to investigate the Palestine situation and make recommendations. President Harry S. Truman recommended in a personal message to the newly elected British Labor Government that 100,000 Jewish survivors of Nazi concentration camps be admitted without delay into Palestine. The British suggested, in reply, an Anglo-American Committee of Inquiry, to which President Truman agreed. This committee subscribed to the recommendation to admit 100,000 immigrants, but the British again rejected it. Matters came to a head when the U.N. decided in November 1947 to partition Palestine into separate Jewish and Arab states. The Arabs reacted to this announcement by attempting to terrorize the Jewish community through attacks on settlements, ambushes on roads, and sabotage in cities. The British administration began to disintegrate, although it had undertaken to function until May 15, 1948. But despite the prevailing chaos and terror, the Jews of Palestine did not panic. They kept the situation under control through their self-defense organization, the Haganah, a forerunner of the Israeli Defense Forces.

The Third Commonwealth. On May 14, 1948, the State of Israel was proclaimed in Tel Aviv. Ten minutes after the proclamation, President Truman extended *de facto* recognition to

Celebrating the 70th anniversary of the founding of Zichron Yaacov in 1952.

the new State. The five surrounding Arab states immediately attacked Israel from the land, sea, and air. Urged on by their leaders, who told them that they could all return after the Jews had been driven out, most of the Arab population fled the country. Eventually, however, Israel's enemies were driven off, and an armistice was signed in 1949. After that time, an uneasy peace prevailed in the area. Notwithstanding political tensions, a fierce Arab boycott, and sporadic border incidents, the new republic made remarkable progress.

Schools and universities helped to weld together a multilingual mass of immigrants into a Hebrew speaking community. Agricultural settlements increased to more than 700. New industrial crops were introduced. Agricultural development was paralleled by industrial expansion. New sources of water and oil were tapped, the Huleh swamps were drained, and water was piped from the Yarkon River to the thirsty **Negev**. Though still beset by menacing enemies and struggling in a morass of problems and difficulties, Israel is again a nation and a land, the Third Commonwealth of the Jewish people.

This basic unity was first demonstrated effectively in a few autumn days in 1956. Israel's long borders had been subjected for years to sabotage, pillage, and murdering raids, particularly by *fedayeen*, or commandos, from Egyptian bases and from the Gaza strip. Harassed beyond endurance, Israel undertook a four-day campaign on October 29, 1956, which resulted in the conquest of the Sinai Peninsula and the Gaza strip. Enormous quantities of arms and material, as well as documents captured by the Israeli Army, revealed that the area was being prepared as a springboard for an Egyptian assault on Israel. Following a request by the UN, Israel withdrew its army from the Sinai and Gaza.

When these attacks, or Israel's retaliations, were brought before the UN's Security Council, Israel did not receive justice primarily because of the constant hostility of the Soviet Union, which could veto the passage of any decision that would displease the Arab governments.

The situation steadily deteriorated until June 1967 when Israel struck back at the hostile Arab nations surrounding it (*see* **Six-Day War**). This war took less than a week to end in a brilliant victory for Israel. However, the Arabs refused to make peace with Israel or even recognize its existence. On Yom Kippur in 1973, Egypt and Syria launched an attack on the country (*see* **Yom Kippur War**). Following the cease-fire imposed by UN, the U.S. made initiatives toward permanent peace in the Middle East.

On May 29, 1974, Syria, the most implacable of Israel's enemies, agreed to sign a disengagement pact with Israel under terms similar to those agreed upon by Israel and Egypt. On June 5, 1974, the agreement between Israel and Syria was signed in Geneva. None of these agreements, however, even remotely implied a full peace and Arab recognition of Israel's existence.

In May 1977, an important political change took place in Israel. The Labor Alignment which had led Israel's governing coalition without interruption since the establishment of the state suffered an electoral defeat and was replaced by Likud, a nonsocialist parliamentary block led by Herut, successor of the right-wing Revisionist movement in Zionism. Menachem **Begin** became prime minister. Later in November, Begin became the first Israeli prime minister to meet officially with an Arab chief of state when Egypt's President Anwar el-Sadat paid a surprise visit to Jerusalem to discuss the possibility of peace with Israel. In September 1978, at a meeting between Begin and Sadat at Camp David, Md., under the auspices of President Jimmy Carter, a framework for a peace treaty between Israel and Egypt was drawn up, and on March 26, 1979, the two countries signed a peace agreement in Washington, D.C. Under this treaty which promised the establishment of normal relations between Israel and Egypt, Israel returned to Egypt the entire Sinai peninsula which Israel had occupied in the Six-Day War. In mid-1979, none of the other Arab countries showed a willingness to make peace with Israel or even recognize its existence, but it was hoped that if subsequent negotiations between Israel and Egypt, the leader of the Arab world, went well, other countries might follow Egypt's example bringing peace to Israel and the entire Middle East.

In the late 1980's Palestinian unrest in Israel grew, resulting in a long struggle against the Israeli occupation of Gaza and the West Bank. This struggle, known as the *Intifada* (Arabic for "liberation"), continues; the Palestinian problem remains unsolved, while all parties look for a solution.

In 1990, immigration of Soviet Jews to Israel increased dramatically, and the flow continues unabated. The total number of Soviet Jews who settled in Israel since 1970 approached one million during the 1990's. (*See* **Ingathering of the Exiles.**)

In February 1991, Iraqi dictator Saddam Hussein launched a missile attack against Israel. Some 40 Scud missiles were fired, landing mostly in the Tel Aviv area, where more than 2,000 homes were damaged. Miraculously, the loss of life was minimal. At the request of the U.S., Israel did not join the Gulf War against Iraq. After the Iraqi defeat on Purim in 1991, Israelis were able for the first time in weeks to take off their gas masks and resume normal life. In the aftermath of the Gulf War, the U.S. and its allies renewed their efforts to bring about a comprehensive Arab-Israeli peace and settle the Palestinian problem. (*See* **Lebanon.**)

In 1992, another important political change took place. The Labor Alignment took over the government. A new coalition replaced the Likud and made Yitzhak **Rabin** its prime minister. In 1993, Israel and the PLO signed the Oslo Agreement, which led to turning over the Gaza Strip and Jericho to Palestinian rule under

Oranges and other citrus fruits are among Israel's exports.

Russian immigrants arriving in Israel in 1991. Courtesy UJA Archives.

Yasser Arafat. This transfer effected in 1994 a full peace treaty with Jordan, while Israel and Syria continued their peace talks. New economic growth and prosperity resulted from this new political stability.

In late 1995, Prime Minister Rabin was assassinated at a peace rally in Tel Aviv. The new prime minister, Shimon **Peres**, announced early elections when a wave of bus bombings by Hamas terrorists shook the country. In the first-ever direct elections for the post of Prime Minister, the Likud party candidate, Benjamin **Netanyahu**, won, promising the electorate "peace with security."

In 1998, Israel celebrated the 50th anniversary of its founding. During the half-century of its existence, the state changed from a small community of barely over half a million Jews, to a strong nation of close to 5 million. It was also transformed from a basically agricultural economy with some industry, to one of the world's leading high-tech economies with more companies on the New York Stock Exchange than most countries. In 1999, Ehud **Barak** became Prime Minister, pledging to make peace with the Palestinians. Despite far-reaching concessions on Israel's part, the peace talks failed in late 2000, followed by a long Intifada (Arab riots), causing the death of hundreds of Palestinians and Israelis. In early 2001, Ariel **Sharon** of the Likud party was elected Prime Minister in the midst of an unresolved conflict.

ISRAEL OF RIZHIN, RABBI. *See* **Hasidism**.

ISRAELS, JOSEPH (1824-1911). Artist. This Dutch Jew was among the first painters to free his palette from the influence of the dark studio and to execute his sketches in the open air. He was also among the first to capture the spirit of the common people, the humble fishermen in little villages and to paint them at work and at leisure, in happiness and grief. Israels painted many Jewish subjects; notable among them is *A Son of the Old People,* a sad old clothes dealer sitting before his modest shop, and *The Old Scribe*, based on a sketch he made while traveling through Tangier, North Africa.

ISSACHAR. Literally, reward bringer. Fifth son of **Jacob** and **Leah**; ancestor of the tribe that settled on the west bank of the **Jordan** near the Sea of Galilee.

ITALY. Italy's Jewish community is the oldest with a continuous history in Europe. During the 2nd century B.C.E. Jewish farmers and traders lived in **Rome**, Naples, Venice, and other cities. For several hundred years they shared the rights that Rome liberally granted to members of conquered nations. When Christianity became the state religion in the 4th century, these privileges were revoked. Restrictions were relaxed, however, after the fall of Rome. By the 9th century Jews were playing an important part in the commercial life of Italy. In addition to trade, they worked in all the handicrafts and professions; it was only later that Jews were forced into the field of money-lending. During the early Middle Ages, Jewish prosperity and freedom permitted the establishment of great academies at Bari and Otranto, where Italian Jewish grammarians, Talmudists, philosophers, physicians, and poets became famous.

Although many of the decrees which plagued other medieval Jewries had their origin in Rome, Italian Jews were long spared their enforcement. Not until the 13th century did Pope Innocent III succeed in implementing discriminatory measures. Yet even these measures, and the popular outbreaks that became frequent in the following centuries, did not succeed in crippling the economic and cultural life of Jews. Italy was then organized in independent city-states; Rome did not have the power to enforce its decrees in the powerful commercial centers where Jewish merchants contributed to the wealth of the community. In addition, the Renaissance spirit of tolerance had already been born. Papal Rome found room for a thriving center of Jewish culture. Immanuel ben Solomon of Rome (ca. 1270-1330) dedicated Hebrew verses to his friend Dante; scholars such as Pico della Mirandola studied Hebrew with Jewish colleagues in the faculties of medicine, law, and philosophy at the great Italian universities. Between 1230 and 1550, poets, scholars and philosophers writing in Hebrew, Latin, and Italian created a "golden age" of Jewish learning paralleled only in Muslim **Spain**.

By the mid-16th century, this renaissance began to fade. Italy, torn by civil strife, fell prey to French and Spanish invaders. The Spanish Jews who had swelled the Italian community after their exile from Spain in 1492 were overtaken by the **Inquisition**, which accompanied the Spanish invaders to Italy. Rome, threatened by the Reformation in the north, adopted the fanatical tactics of the Spanish Inquisition to stamp out heresy at home. The expulsion of the Jewish community from Genoa was the first sign of the change. Soon after, Pope Julius III (1550-1555) ordered the **Talmud** burned in the streets of Rome and nearly succeeded in expelling the Jews from the Eternal City. His successor confined the Jews of the Papal States to ghettos. As part of a campaign to convert the Jews to Catholicism, the entire community was forced to attend special church sermons.

Many Jews fled from Rome; those who remained suffered from discrimination. The leadership of Italian Jewry then fell to the communities of Venice, Ferrara, and Mantua. A printing press was founded at Mantua, where a new edition of the Talmud appeared in 1590. Also published were popular and scholarly works by writers such as Azariah dei **Rossi** of Ferrara. Within several decades, however, Spanish and Austrian invaders decimated the communities of Ferrara and Mantua as well, leaving Jews of Venice to bear the burden of Jewish culture. For a century and a half Venetian Jewry produced a line of distinguished scholars and poets. The last and greatest of these was Moses Haim **Luzzato**, Kabbalist, linguist, scholar and poet. Leghorn (*Livorno*), where the Jews had some autonomy until the 19th century, remained a center of Kabbalistic learning.

Napoleon's conquest of Italy in 1797 was the start of the emancipation of Italian Jewry. As in **France**, he convened a

Synagogue in Turin, Italy, one of Europe's most beautiful temples, destroyed by the Nazis.

"Sanhedrin" to organize the affairs of the Jewish community and granted full civil rights to Jews. Napoleon's defeat and the strong reaction that followed led to a revival of the Inquisition. The national movement, which sought the liberation of Italy from foreign rule and the unification of its many states, soon provided a rallying point for Jewish hopes. Espousing the cause of civil rights for all, it drew many young Jews to its ranks. With the final unification of all Italy under King Victor Emmanuel II in 1870, Jews were again granted full citizenship.

The Jews of Italy were grateful for their freedom. Having fought valiantly for independence, they remained ardent patriots and threw themselves vigorously into public life. Within a short time they were finding important positions in government, politics, and society. The urge to take full advantage of their newly acquired rights was so strong that large sections of Italian Jewry began to lose touch with the Jewish community. Intermarriage became common, especially among the upper classes, and the number of conversions was great. Though closely organized communities remained, and scholars maintained the "enlightened" tradition of Jewish scholarship established by Samuel David **Luzzato** earlier in the century, the threat of assimilation was serious.

But the period of unrestricted freedom was short-lived. The Italian Fascist movement was founded in 1919, and in 1923, Benito Mussolini came to power. At first Mussolini fought the anti-Semitic elements in his party, which was supported by many influential Jews.

In the hope that the ties of Italian Jews with other Mediterranean and Balkan Jewish communities would be aid his plan for imperialist expansion, he encouraged **Zionism** and helped German-Jewish refugees settle in Italy. When Hitler came to power in 1933, Mussolini took a stand against Nazi anti-Semitism. By 1936, however, Mussolini found himself in need of German aid for his Abyssinian war and began to adopt the racist Nazi doctrines. By the outbreak of World War II, Jews had been banned from the army, government service, professions, and many branches of trade. Jewish schools, which Mussolini had encouraged and subsidized, were closed. All large-scale Jewish businesses were confiscated, and Jews were forbidden to hold land of any value. Toward the end of the war, when the Italian defense system had broken down and German troops moved into the country, Hitler proposed the deportation and destruction of Italy's Jewry. Official **anti-Semitism** had never struck deep roots among the people, however, and the Italian Jews found protection among their neighbors. The Allied forces invaded and the war was over before Hitler's plan could be executed.

With the overthrow of Mussolini, Jewish rights were restored. After the war, Italy was the temporary home of more than 35,000 refugees, all but 1,500 of whom left for Israel and other countries. Because of its location, Italy was for a while the chief sailing point for "illegal" immigrants on their way to Israel.

Today, there are approximately 30,000 Jews permanently settled in Italy, a little below the prewar total. They live under the law of 1930 which requires that all Jews affiliate with the official Jewish community to which they pay taxes. Rome has the largest concentration with 13,000; Milan follows with 8,000. The rest of the Jewish population is scattered in 21 other cities, only six of which have communities of more than 1,000. This dispersion again raises the problem of **assimilation**, a problem which community leaders tried to solve by means of an intensive educational program. The educational system now includes Jewish day schools in eight cities, a rabbinical seminary in Rome, and special courses for Hebrew teachers. In Rome, a vocational training school is maintained by **ORT**. A monthly magazine is published by the community. There is an active Zionist organization, and close ties are maintained with **Israel**.

In recent years, Italy has been almost completely free of anti-Semitic activities, and Jews have again achieved prominence in national life. Alberto Moravia, Paolo Milano, Carlo Levi, and Primo **Levi** are leading literary figures. Jews are prominent in the professions and several branches of the economy.

Italy has served as an important transition place for the massive immigration from the former Soviet Union to Israel during the last two decades.

IYAR. Eighth month of the Jewish civil calendar, falling during the **Omer**. Israel's Independence Day is celebrated on the fifth of Iyar.

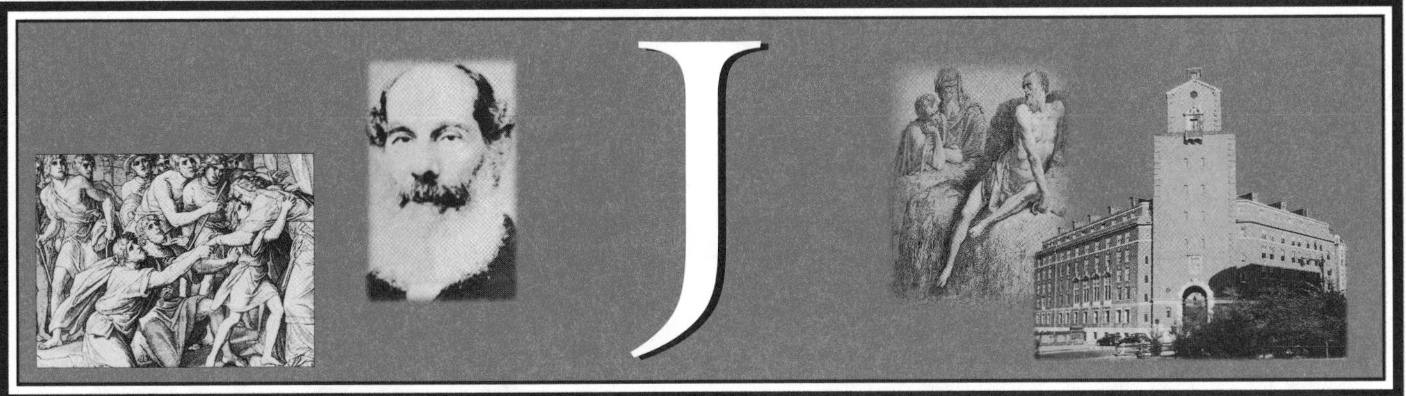

JABOTINSKY, VLADIMIR (ZEEV) (1880-1940). Writer and founder of **Revisionist Zionism**. He came from an assimilated Jewish family in Odessa, **Russia**. He studied law and Russian literature. As a student he won recognition as a Russian writer and orator. At the age of 25, he was already a leading figure among Russian Zionists. During the early part of World War I, he served as war correspondent in France for an important Moscow newspaper. When **Turkey** entered the war in 1915 and drove many Palestinian Jews into exile, Jabotinsky conceived the idea of a **Jewish Legion** that would fight on the side of the Allies and help capture **Palestine** from the Turks. In his efforts to establish such a legion he approached the British, Italian, and French authorities. Success came finally in June 1917 when the British officially announced the formation of Jewish battalions to serve with the British Royal Fusiliers in the Palestine campaign. Jabotinsky, who enlisted as a private, was the only foreigner to be made an honorary lieutenant by the British during World War I.

Vladimir Jabotinsky, by Elias Grossman. Courtesy Zionist Revisionists, New York.

After the end of the war, Jabotinsky remained in Palestine, and in 1919, when the country was threatened with Arab riots, he joined Pinhas Rutenberg in organizing a Jewish self-defense corps. On April 4, 1920, Arab rioters attacked the Jewish quarter in old **Jerusalem**, and the self-defense corps tried to defend the area. The British arrested them and later tried them before a military court. Jabotinsky and twenty comrades were sentenced to twenty years' imprisonment. There was great public protest, and after three and a half months in the **Acre** prison, Jabotinsky was freed. He returned to **England** and joined the Executive of the **World Zionist Organization**. On this body he differed sharply with its leader, Chaim **Weizmann**, whom he considered too conciliatory toward Britain, and he resigned in 1921. In 1925, he organized the Revisionist Zionist party. His program pressed for the speedy creation of a Jewish state on both sides of the Jordan. The last years of Jabotinsky's life were shadowed by Hitler's rise to power in **Germany** and the beginning of World War II. He who had fought the British for so long because they obstructed the realization of the Jewish homeland in Palestine now pleaded for a Jewish army to fight on the side of England against Hitler. He died in 1940 before the formation of the Jewish Brigade.

Jabotinsky was a brilliant, versatile writer in six languages. He wrote the novel *Samson the Nazirite* and translated voluminously from Hebrew into Russian and from English, French, and Italian into Hebrew. Jabotinsky was a master of prose in English, French, and Yiddish. As an orator he was dramatic and incisive with a magnetic personality.

JACOB. Literally, one who supplants another. The younger of **Isaac** and **Rebecca**'s twin sons; third of the biblical **patriarchs**. Jacob bought the family birthright from his elder brother, Esau, "for a mess of pottage," and with his mother's help received the blessing of the firstborn from his father, whose eyes were dimmed by age. Jacob then fled from Esau's anger to his mother's father, Bethuel, in

Jacob's dream. From an old engraving.

Padan Aram. On his way he slept in a field with a stone for his pillow and had a strange dream: he saw a ladder reaching up to heaven with angels ascending and descending it. God promised Jacob that he would inherit the land upon which he had slept. When Jacob arose in the morning, he called the place Bethel, meaning "House of God."

In Haran, Jacob served his uncle **Laban** for twenty years, marrying Laban's two daughters, **Leah** and **Rachel**. Then he started back to the land of his fathers, taking with him his wives and children, his flocks and rich possessions. On the banks of the river Jabbok he wrestled all night with an angel and received the name of **Israel**. His brother Esau came to meet him, and Jacob made peace with him. Later, on the way to Bethel, God appeared to Jacob and confirmed his promise to give him the Land of Canaan as an inheritance. There, his beloved wife Rachel died giving birth to his twelfth and youngest son, **Benjamin**. Jacob lived in Canaan with his twelve sons and prospered, until grief came to him in his old age: his favorite son, **Joseph**, disappeared, having been sold by his envious brothers as a slave to Ishmaelite traders who took him to **Egypt**. Eventually Jacob and his sons settled in Egypt, where Joseph had become the Pharaoh's second-in-command. Jacob died in Egypt in his 147th year. His body was borne to Canaan where he was buried in the patriarchal burial place, the cave of **Machpelah**.

JACOBI, KARL GUSTAV JACOB (1804-1851). German mathematician, born of Jewish parents. Along with the Norwegian Abel, Jacobi established the theory of elliptic functions. Jacobi was one of the greatest mathematicians of all time.

JAFFA. Biblical Joppa. Situated on a steep rocky promontory 116 feet above the sea, it was **Israel**'s oldest seaport and the natural outlet for **Jerusalem**, with whose fate it was linked. King Hiram of Tyre floated the cedars of **Lebanon** down to Jaffa for the building of Solomon's **Temple**. From Jaffa the prophet **Jonah** set out for Tarshish. Although allotted to **Dan** during the conquest of Canaan, Jaffa did not become a Jewish city until after the **Maccabean** victory. Ships from Jaffa played a part in the **Bar Kokhba** insurrection against Rome. Jaffa figures in the history of the **Crusades** and in Napoleon's invasion. Its modern Jewish community dates to the early 19th century. Jaffa remained, however, an Arab town with a Jewish minority until it was captured by Israel in 1948 and incorporated into **Tel Aviv**. Most of the Arabs fled, leaving only 4,000 behind. The city has become a center for the new Jewish immigrants. The "Jaffa orange" developed in the coastal area of Israel is internationally famous.

JAPAN. Island country in the Far East consisting of four main islands and many smaller ones, lying off the northeast coast of Asia. By the 9th century C.E., Jewish merchants from the West were trading in Japan, but no permanent colony had been established. Legends that some Japanese clans are of Jewish origin may refer to the descendants of these early visitors. After Japan was opened to the West by Commodore Perry in 1854, Jews came from Europe, **Turkey**, **Iraq**, and **India**. The first synagogue was built in Nagasaki in the 1890's. It belonged to Russian Jews. A **Sephardic** colony was soon settled in Kobe and is still there. Yokohama was settled next, then Tokyo. Jewish refugees from Germany arrived during the 1930's. At first there was no **anti-Semitism**, but Japan's signing of the Axis Pact with the Nazis brought familiar trouble. Many Polish and Lithuanian Jews, including the entire *Mir yeshiva* en route to the Americas were caught in Japan by World War II. They were sent to the Hongkow ghetto in Shanghai. Although some Jews left Japan at the end of the war, others entered when the Communist conquest of **China** imperiled Jewish life there. The arrival of American Jewish chaplains to serve the occupation forces stimulated Japanese interest in Judaism. Several Japan-Israel Friendship Societies were formed. In 1998, there were about 1,200 Jews in Japan.

Courtesy Musaf Lakore Hatzair (Hadoar Weekly).

JAVITS, JACOB K. (1904-1986). U.S. Senator and attorney. Javits grew up on **New York**'s Lower East Side with his immigrant parents. After receiving a law degree from New York University in 1926, he was admitted to the New York State Bar in 1927 and practiced law in New York until his appointment as special assistant to the chief of the Chemical Warfare Service. He began his political career in 1946 when he was elected to the U.S. House of Representatives from New York City's 21st Congressional District. In 1954, Javits was elected New York State Attorney General and, in 1956, U.S. Senator from New York. Throughout his career, Javits favored increased foreign aid, national housing, and rent control legislation. He drafted a

Senator Jacob K. Javits with Rabbi C.H. Lipschitz, U.S. Ambassador to Israel Kenneth Keating, and President Lyndon Johnson.

Selective Immigration Act establishing an immigration quota based on skills of prospective immigrants rather than their national origins. Javits took a consistently pro-Israel stand. He was a member of the Board of Overseers of the **Jewish Theological Seminary of America**.

JEREMIAH (ca. 626-585 B.C.E.). Second of the major prophets. His book is a masterpiece of biblical literature. Jeremiah, son of Hilkiah, a priest of Anathoth, witnessed the tragic events in the history of **Judea** that ended in the destruction of **Jerusalem** and in the exile to **Babylonia**. He is deeply affected by his people's betrayal of their God. His prophecies foretell the doom of his people as punishment for their sins. Jeremiah envisions a universal God governing all humankind, forgiving even those sins that had been "written with a pen of iron and a point of diamond." The people will survive only if they uphold justice, and each person is responsible for his own acts. At the end of days the Lord will bring the people of Israel back from their captivity, and a righteous Israel will dwell in safety in its own land (Jer. 33:14-16). Jeremiah's love for his people is unsurpassed in the Bible. With the birth of the state of **Israel**, Jeremiah's prophecy regarding Israel's return to its land was fulfilled a second time.

Jeremiah proclaims the law. 16th century French engraving by C.P. Marillier.

Fall of the walls of Jericho. 18th century engraving.

JERICHO. Literally, the Moon City or Fragrance. Also known in the Bible as the City of Palms. Situated five miles north of the **Dead Sea**, Jericho is a rich tropical oasis in the salt encrusted plain, nourished by the springs of Elisha and other rivulets. It is 820 feet below sea level. The strategic key to Jerusalem and all **Canaan** from the east, it was stormed by **Joshua** and all the succeeding conquerors attacking the land from that direction. Destroyed and rebuilt many times, modern Jericho stands on the foundation of the Crusaders' city. It is now a small town where a thousand farmers live in mud huts. Orange groves and banana trees replace the balsams, sycamores, and palms of antiquity.

JERUSALEM. Capital of Israel, ever since **David** established his throne there about 1000 B.C.E.; the Holy City of Judaism, from the time David had the Ark of the **Covenant** borne in triumph into Jerusalem and **Solomon** built the **Temple** to house it on Mount Moriah. Jerusalem has also been called Zion, the citadel of peace and faith, since the days of the prophets **Isaiah** and **Jeremiah**.

The city is situated in the heart of the hills of Judea more than 2,000 feet high. It sits at the crossroads where the highway running from north to south intersects the road leading from the sea to the Jordan. A triad of hills—Zion, Moriah, and Mount of Olives—separated from other hills by the deep ravines of Hinnom and Kidron, make Jerusalem a natural stronghold.

Jerusalem's origins are lost in the mists of antiquity. It was already a center of Canaanite civilization in **Abraham**'s time around 1900 B.C.E. It was twice destroyed, once by Nebuchadnezzar of **Babylonia** in 586 B.C.E. and again by Titus of Rome in 70 C.E. It was restored by Jews 70 years after the first destruction. The Hasmoneans made it their capital and rebuilt the Temple, and Herod the Great adorned and fortified it. After the second destruction Jerusalem remained in ruins for over a century, until the Emperor Hadrian in 134 C.E. turned it into a colony for Roman veterans and renamed it Aelia Capitolina. Jews were prohibited from entering the city upon penalty of death. When the Romans adopted Christianity, however, they not only restored Jerusalem's ancient Hebrew name but made it the highest altar in the Empire. The city became the mystical center of Christendom, particularly after the Church of the Holy Sepulcher was erected by the Emperor Constantine in the 4th century.

A view of the new city of Jerusalem.

In 637 C.E., the new religion of **Islam** invaded the city, adding its mosques to the skyline of the city. Jerusalem became the second holiest Muslim city after Mecca and the seat of the famous Dome of the Rock on Mount Moriah over the site of Israel's Temple. More tolerant than their predecessors, the Arabs allowed Jews to settle in the city. In the 10th century, the Jewish community of Jerusalem centered around the *Avele Zion*, or Mourners of Zion, ascetics who bewailed the loss of Zion's ancient glories and prayed for its early restoration.

Jerusalem again fell to the Christians when the Crusaders captured the city in 1099, massacring much of the Jewish and Moslem population. During most of the 12th century it was the capital of the Latin Kingdom of Jerusalem, but in 1187 Jerusalem was retaken by the Muslims. Thereafter, despite the heavy burden of taxation, the Jewish community found existence tolerable, except during the cruel and destructive Mongol invasions. In 1517, Jerusalem was taken by the Turks. The present walled city, with its 24 towers and eight gates, dates from the period of Suleiman the Magnificent, Sultan of the Turkish Empire. Until the 16th century, the Jewish community of Jerusalem consisted mainly of pious pilgrims who had come to die on its holy soil. After the expulsion from Spain in 1492, many refugees settled there under the fairly tolerant rule of the first two Turkish sultans. In the 18th century, 1,000 Polish Hasidim led by Judah the Pious settled in Jerusalem.

Israel Independence Day parade passing by the Old City of Jerusalem.

Under the urging of Sir Moses **Montefiore** around 1860, the Jews of Jerusalem first ventured outside the protecting walls of the Old City. They built the Yemin Moshe quarter and a windmill for the grinding of grain. The colorful Mea Shearim quarter was established in 1875. The early **"Lovers of Zion"** of the 1870's and 1880's settled in Jerusalem and agricultural colonies. At this time the building of the new city with its modern residential quarters, parks, and imposing public buildings began. But along the dark lanes of the old city, the aged and the pious continued to live on the **Halukkah**, funds gathered from around the world for their sustenance.

The **Balfour Declaration** during World War I and the assumption by the British of the mandate for Palestine occasioned changes in Jerusalem. The ancient city became the home of the British administration governing the country, of the Jewish settlers' shadow government, and of the Palestine section of the **World Zionist Organization**. The **Hebrew University** was built on Mount Scopus; structures housing the **Jewish Agency** and other Zionist institutions were erected in the New City. Arab riots shook the old city in 1929, a foretaste of the disturbances of 1936-39 and those following World War II.

The sponsors of the plan that partitioned Palestine into one Jewish and one Arab State originally envisioned Jerusalem as an international city with access to the Holy Places of the various religions open to all. However, during the War of Independence of 1948, the Old City was seized by Jordanian forces and annexed by the Kingdom of Jordan. Jews were not permitted access to the Western Wall or any part of the Old City; synagogues were destroyed and Jewish graves desecrated by the Arabs. The Hebrew University campus and the **Hadassah** Hospital on Mount Scopus were isolated. Jews were confined to the New City which, in 1949, became the seat of Israel's Parliament and government. At the beginning of the **Six-Day War** in 1967, Israel informed King

Hussein that it would not attack Jordan if the Jordanians did not enter the war on the Arab side.

When Jordanian forces began to shell the New City of Jerusalem, the Israeli army struck back and within two days had liberated the Old City. On June 29, 1967 the two sectors of Jerusalem, the Old City and the New, were officially reunified. Since the reunification of Jerusalem, the city has grown rapidly; the ruins of the Old City are being rebuilt, and many Jews have already moved into that section.

Archaeologists have been making extensive excavations in the area, particularly around the **Western Wall**. Currently, the population is about 600,000, of whom 480,000 are Jews.

JESSEL, GEORGE. *See* **Stage and Screen.**

JESUS. Galilean Jew who lived in the beginning of the common era, during the Roman rule of Judea. Contemporary Jewish sources do not provide any information about his life, which is described in the New Testament, written after his death. Some of the teachings of Jesus concerning kindness and tolerance are reminiscent of the Jewish sage **Hillel**, who preceded him. While Jesus himself did not found a religion, but rather lived and died a Jew, the stories about him and the sayings and parables attributed to him were compelling enough to give rise to a worldwide religion called **Christianity** (Christ means messiah or savior). Jesus lived at a time when there was great turmoil and messianic fervor in Judea, and the stories about him can be understood against the background of an entire people yearning for salvation or redemption.

JEW BY CHOICE. Term which has become popular in the U.S. with the recent increase of conversions to Judaism. Refers to those who choose to become Jewish, unlike those who are Jews by birth.

JEW. From the Hebrew *Yehudah*, or **Judah**, meaning "Praise to the Lord." Judah was one of the twelve tribes of Israel, descended from the fourth son of **Jacob**. After the exile to **Babylonia**, the term Jew came to be used synonymously with Hebrew and Israelite.

JEWISH AGENCY. Originally, the **World Zionist Organization** was designated as the Jewish Agency in the mandate for Palestine given by the League of Nations to Britain and ratified in 1922. According to Article IV of the mandate, the **World Zionist Organization** was the appropriate Jewish agency "for the purpose of advising and cooperating with the Administration of Palestine" in matters concerning the establishing of the Jewish national home. In order to speed the work of building, a movement began among Zionists in 1923 to obtain the support of all Jews, including non-Zionists, for the national home in Palestine. To achieve this aim, it was suggested that an extended Jewish Agency be created with 50 percent non-Zionist representation. This idea, actively supported by Chaim **Weizmann**, had many opponents who feared that Zionism would be weakened by the non-Zionists. The discussions lasted until 1929 when at the 16th Congress in Zurich, the enlarged Jewish Agency was launched, and its constituent assembly met immediately. Among those who took part in it as non-Zionists were Louis **Marshall** from the U.S., Sir (later Viscount) Herbert **Samuel** and Lord **Melchett** from England, **Albert Einstein** and Oscar Wasserman from **Germany**, and Leon **Blum** from **France**. After the death of the two outstanding non-Zionists, Louis Marshall and Lord **Melchett**, many of the non-Zionists drifted away and the Jewish Agency Executive became almost identical with the World Zionist Executive. (*See* **Zionism.**)

JEWISH BRIGADE. An infantry brigade in the British army during the close of World War II, formed to enable Jews from Palestine to fight against the Nazis. The Brigade saw action in Italy in 1945, then made contact with **Holocaust** survivors and helped start the process of rescuing them and taking them to Palestine.

Masthead of The Jewish Chronicle, dated November 12, 1841.

JEWISH CHRONICLE. Anglo-Jewish weekly, founded in **London** in 1841. Over the years the journal has acquired an unchallenged position as the central press organ of Anglo-Jewry, and one of the best Jewish newspapers in the world.

JEWISH COLONIZATION ASSOCIATION. Founded in 1891 by Baron Maurice de **Hirsch**, a wealthy French philanthropist, who felt that **anti-Semitism** could be lessened if Jews were dispersed geographically and occupationally, especially to farm areas. This organization, known as ICA, aided immigration and agricultural projects for Jews in many places, including southern Russia, **Argentina, Brazil, Bolivia, Poland,** and the U.S. Since 1932, ICA funds, originally more than $10 million, have also been used to aid refugees and to supplement the work of other groups that help immigrants.

JEWISH COMMUNITY CENTER. First organized under the name Young Men Hebrew Association (YMHA) in the mid-19th century in cities such as **Baltimore** and **New York**, most have become known as JCC's, or Jewish Community Centers, and today there are close to 300 such centers throughout the U.S.

The JCC's have made a great contribution to Jewish communal life in the U.S., unlike the synagogue which is basically a religious center with added social activities.

JEWISH DEFENSE LEAGUE. Militant Jewish group in the U.S. Founded in Brooklyn, N.Y., in 1968, the JDL was originally organized to protect Jews in poor neighborhoods from physical attacks. Later, under the leadership of Meir Kahane, who was assassinated in New York by an Arab in 1990, and using the slogan "Never Again" with reference to the **Holocaust**, the JDL engaged in violent demonstrations and employed physical force to draw public attention to the plight of Jews in Soviet Russia and in Arab lands and to the precarious situation of the State of **Israel.**

JEWISH EDUCATION IN THE UNITED STATES. The vast majority of Jewish children in the U.S. who receive Jewish education, attend Jewish school after public school hours. It is estimated that between 60% and 70% receive some kind of Jewish education during their school years, quite remarkable considering that Jewish education is voluntary in the U.S. No one can force parents to send their children to a Jewish school. But the vast majority of American Jews do so because they believe, as Jews have always believed, that a Jewish education is essential for their children to understand what it means to be a Jew and respect themselves.

While almost all American Jews agree on the need for Jewish education, they differ as to the kind of Jewish education that is best for their children. Thus, different types of Jewish schools function on the American scene.

Congregational Schools. The majority of American Jewish children attend synagogue schools conducted by various Orthodox, Conservative, and Reform congregations. The synagogues conduct two types of schools.

Week-Day Afternoon Schools. Children attend from three to five days a week after public school hours and receive from three to eight hours of instruction weekly. These are conducted largely by the Orthodox and Conservative synagogues. The Hebrew language, prayers, Jewish customs and ceremonies, Jewish history, and the Bible are the major subjects studied. These schools conduct their own children's services on the **Sabbath** and holidays, and many of them also conduct a variety of club activities. The course of study covers four to six years.

The One-Day-A-Week School (Sunday School). Children attend either Saturday or Sunday mornings and receive from one to three hours of instruction. These are conducted chiefly by the Reform synagogues, and more than 35% of the total number of children attending Jewish schools are enrolled in this type of school. Jewish history, **Bible**, and Jewish customs and ceremonies are the major subjects studied. More and more synagogues are adding one or two sessions a week for Hebrew studies. Most of the Orthodox and Conservative synagogues also have one-day-a-week departments attended by young children before they enter the weekday Hebrew school. In the Reform religious schools, the course of study usually leads to confirmation at age sixteen.

The Yeshivot Ketanot, or **All-Day Schools**. This full-time program combines Jewish studies and all subjects covered by the general public school. This type of school offers the most thorough Jewish education. Pupils receive about fifteen hours a week of instruction in Jewish studies (in the Hebrew language or Yiddish, in some instances), prayers, the Bible in its original Hebrew, Mishnah, Talmud, Jewish history, and Jewish laws and customs. This has been the fastest growing type of school in recent years. In 1935, there were 17 such schools in three communities. In 1959, there were over 230 such schools in more than 50 communities. Today, there are more than 500 such schools in the U.S. Most of these day schools are Orthodox institutions, but in recent years the Conservative movement has developed its Solomon Schechter Day School program, the Reform movement has begun to establish its own day schools, and there are non-denominational day schools in many large Jewish communities, some of which rival the best private schools in the U.S. Many consider the day school the best hope for Jewish survival outside Israel.

The Communal Talmud Torah is a non-synagogue weekday Hebrew school that children attend five days a week after public school hours and receive from six to ten hours of instruction weekly. The subjects covered are similar to those in the congregational weekday afternoon school. The communal Talmud Torah, the most flourishing type of school a generation ago, has declined rapidly in recent years and been replaced largely by the congregational school and the all-day school. It is still found in the larger Jewish communities.

Yiddish Schools are sponsored by the Workmen's Circle and the Sholom Aleichem Folk Institute, national organizations which originated among Jewish socialists. In these schools, Yiddish is the language of instruction. Children attend three to five afternoons a week and study Yiddish language and literature, Jewish history, Jewish holidays, and the Bible in Yiddish. In some of these schools, Hebrew is taught in the upper grades. The Jewish National Workers Alliance (Labor Zionists) conducted similar schools, except that in these schools Hebrew as well as Yiddish was taught from the outset. These are generally small schools, and only a small percentage of the total number of Jewish children attend them.

Yeshivot. During the 20th century, especially with the destruction of European Jewry, *yeshivot*, or Talmudical academies or rabbinical colleges, have assumed a place of increasing importance in American Jewish religious life. Some of these institutions were transferred to the U.S. from Europe. Among the most prominent American Yeshivot are the Yeshiva of Mir, the United Lubavitcher Yeshivot, Yeshiva and Mesivtah Chaim Berlin, Yeshiva and Mesivtah Tifereth Jerusalem and Yeshiva and Mesivtah Torah Vodaath (all in the New York area), the Yeshiva of Lakewood, N.J., the Yeshiva of Spring Valley, N.Y., the Ner Israel Rabbinical College in Baltimore, Md., and the Yeshiva of Telz in Cleveland.

History. The various systems of Jewish education now existing in the U.S. did not come into being all at once, but rather developed gradually with the growth of the American Jewish community. Jews came to this country from different countries, each group bringing its own traditions and ways. The schools they set up at the beginning followed the patterns of their homelands, but soon these schools were modified to conform more closely with the type of schools that were growing up on the American scene.

The first Jewish school in the U.S., the Yeshivah Minchat Areb, was founded as an all-day school in 1731, and was associated with the first synagogue established in New York City. At first, only Hebrew subjects were taught, but later general subjects, such as reading, writing, arithmetic, and Spanish, were added. At this time, the Jewish community was responsible for the education of its children just as other religious groups provided education for their children. As time went on, these schools became private schools where the attention was given mostly to general subjects and little to Hebrew subjects. In the early 1800's, synagogues began to provide some instruction in Hebrew subjects after school. For a brief period from 1845 to 1855, a number of all-day schools similar to present-day yeshivot began and flourished, but they went out of existence soon after that. After 1850, the free public school became the generally accepted type of school, attracting the greater proportion of American children. Almost all Jewish children attended public schools for their general education, and the Jewish school became largely supplementary.

In 1838, the first Sunday school was established in Philadelphia and became the most widely accepted type of school by Jews during the last half of the 19th century. The majority of Jews who immigrated to America during this period came from Germany, from where they brought Reform Judaism. They minimized the importance of Hebrew and considered one day a week of instruction sufficient. They patterned their Jewish religious schools after the Protestant Sunday Schools which had grown up in America.

After 1880, when Jewish immigration from Eastern Europe swelled into the millions, the heder entered the American scene. This was a private one-teacher school, conducted by poorly trained teachers. Gradually the heder gave way to the Talmud Torah, also an East European type of school, but on a much higher plane. The Talmud Torah was well organized and provided a rich program of instruction. Its teachers were well trained, its textbooks challenging, and its school buildings new and substantial. Hebrew was taught as a living language. The Zionist goal of establishing Palestine as a Jewish homeland was an important part of its program. Talmud Torah became the heart of intensive Jewish education in America and held that position until recently. Shortly before World War II the congregational and all-day schools supplanted the Talmud Torah to a large extent. During the period after 1880 the Yiddish schools were also organized.

As schools grew and became better organized, the demand for American-trained teachers increased. In 1867, the first teacher training school, Maimonides College, was established in Philadelphia. Thirty years later, Gratz College was established in Philadelphia for the same purpose. There are now fourteen recognized teacher training schools throughout the country.

In 1910, New York City's Jewish community established the Bureau of Jewish Education, the first of more than 40 community bureaus of Jewish education which now exist in the U.S. These central bureaus were established to meet the problems that the individual schools could not handle alone. In many instances, these bureaus of Jewish education give subsidies to schools to enable them to provide more scholarships. They help schools get qualified teachers; they prepare better textbooks and other teaching materials to improve instruction; they offer expert guidance to help teachers improve their methods; and they provide other services through which the community helps its Jewish schools to improve.

In today's Jewish school, teachers use well prepared and colorful textbooks, workbooks, filmstrips, records, movies, and other modern teaching aids. In today's Jewish classroom children learn not only from books, but also through play, art, dance, and other activities.

Jewish education has spread to the summer camps. In various parts of the country there are camps where Hebrew is spoken as a matter of course, and children actually attend classes for part of the morning. Other camps provide a rich program of Jewish educational activities, such as Sabbath services, Jewish music, dance, arts, and drama. Thousands of Jewish children today take their Jewish education with them on vacation and make camp life a richer and more meaningful experience. (*See also* **Education in Jewish History**.)

JEWISH EDUCATION SERVICE OF NORTH AMERICA (JESNA). Comprehensive educational agency in American Jewish life, founded in 1938. JESNA aims to advance instructional and professional standards, engage in research and experimentation, stimulate communal responsibility, certify teachers, provide supervisory and administrative personnel conduct local surveys, supply educational materials, and assist other national agencies. It publishes newsletters, bulletins, curricula programs, and the widely distributed *Pedagogic Reporter* and *Jewish Audio-Visual Review*; and it sponsors the National Council of Jewish Audio-Materials. The Association organizes local and national conferences on Jewish education, and sponsors the National Curriculum Research Institute.

JEWISH LEGION. *See* **Legion, Jewish.**

JEWISH MUSEUM. Located in the former family mansion of Felix M. **Warburg**, presented to the **Jewish Theological Seminary of America** by his widow, in memory of her husband, her father, Jacob H. **Schiff**, and her brother, Mortimer L. Schiff. The present building on **New York**'s Fifth Avenue was first opened to the public in May 1947. The museum's collections, which started in 1904, now comprise more than 9,000 objects. The Jewish Museum is dedicated to the exhibition of Jewish ceremonial art and the promotion of the visual values in Judaism. The first floor is reserved for temporary exhibits of artistic and historical merit. The second and third floors are devoted to the display of part of the museum's collections of Jewish ceremonial art; the fourth contains a display of coins, plaques, and medals, as well as a Junior Gallery of interest to young visitors. In 1963, a modern wing, donated by Mr. and Mrs. Albert A. List, was completed on an adjacent Fifth Avenue plot. It provides more room for the museum collections and serves as a showcase for young modern artists.

JEWISH NATIONAL FUND (*Keren Kayemet LeIsrael*). Agency responsible for afforestation and land reclamation in **Israel**, established in 1901 by the World Zionist Organization at its fifth Zionist Congress in Basel, **Switzerland**. Its initial purpose was to purchase land in Palestine through small donations from Jews around the world. The JNF's principles were greatly influenced by the agricultural laws of the Bible. They provided that land purchased by the JNF must remain the inalienable possession of the Jewish people. It cannot be sold or mortgaged; it may be leased only to individual pioneers or groups of settlers at a normal rental period of 49 years, renewable only by the original contractor. In 1903, the Jewish National Fund made its first land purchases in the lower

JNF leaders with New York Governor George Pataki, third from right, and JNF President Milton Shapiro, third from left.

Galilee and continued to make purchases that would form the foundation of what would become the State of Israel. These purchases determined the future sites of forests, cities, kibbutzim, universities, settlements, and strategic outposts. Many of the first Jewish settlements in Palestine were founded with the aid of the JNF which, in addition to land, provided farm equipment, livestock, and expert advice. Arab riots and the British Mandatory government's legal restriction on land purchase failed to curtail JNF land acquisition. The United Nations' 1947 Partition Plan for

Palestine drew Israel's borders along the lines of the JNF's land holdings. After the founding of the State of Israel in 1948, JNF work shifted from land purchase to reclamation and afforestation. The JNF's major projects have included the reclamation of thousands of acres for agriculture, recreation, housing, industry, tourism, reservoirs, and roads. The JNF's historic achievements include the planting of more than 200 million trees; the reclamation of 875,000 acres of difficult terrain for farming, housing, and industry; the preparation of land for 1,100 rural villages; the building of more than 3,750 miles of rural roads, and the creation of 440 major parks and picnic areas throughout Israel. Thirty percent of Israel's population lives on land which the JNF has prepared.

JEWISH PUBLICATION SOCIETY OF AMERICA. Founded in 1888, the JPS's purpose was the "publication and dissemination of literature, scientific and religious works, and also the giving of instruction in the practices of the Jewish religion, history and literature." Its first publication was an *Outline of Jewish History*; in 1890, its first popular success, Israel **Zangwill**'s *Children of the Ghetto*, appeared in 1892. The next year, plans for a new translation of the Bible began, a task not completed until 1917. Another translation of the books of the **Bible** was released in the 1960's. Beginning in 1899, the JPS published the *American Jewish Yearbook*, now prepared by the **American Jewish Committee** with the JPS collaborating in its distribution. Several important series have been published by the JPS. These include the Schiff Memorial Library of Jewish Classics; a Historical Jewish Communities series; a series of commentaries on the Bible; and a series of children's books. Editors of the JPS have been Henrietta **Szold**, Solomon Graysel, Chaim **Potok**, Maier Deshell, and Ellen Frankel.

JEWISH THEOLOGICAL SEMINARY OF AMERICA. Seminary of Conservative Judaism for the training of rabbis, teachers, and cantors. Founded in 1887 with a class of seven students, its program now includes projects for the advancement of Jewish scholarship and research. Rabbi Sabato **Morais**, first Seminary president, and H. Pereira Mendes, its co-founder, were

The Jewish Theological Seminary of America, New York.

Left, Sabato Morris, the first president of the Jewish Theological Seminary. Right, Ismar Schorsch, Chancellor since 1986.

also its first instructors. In 1902, Solomon **Schechter** was brought from Cambridge University in **England** to become the second president of the Seminary. The establishment of the Seminary Library by Judge Mayer **Sulzberger** came under Schechter's auspices, and he transformed the Rabbinical School into a graduate institution. Upon Schechter's death in 1915, Cyrus **Adler** succeeded to the presidency. The Seminary then moved into its new buildings on Morningside Heights in New York City, where it presently resides. Since 1940, Louis **Finkelstein** became president of the Seminary in 1945, having been chancellor. The Seminary chancellor in 1979 was Gerson D. Cohen, succeeded by Ismar Schorsch in 1986. Among the activities launched by Finkelstein was the Institute for Religious and Social Studies which aims "to develop a keener awareness of the unique contributions which the various religious traditions have made to the advancement of civilization."

Besides the Rabbinical School, the Seminary includes a Teacher's Institute, Cantor's Institute, Seminary College of Jewish Studies, Seminary College of Jewish Music, and the Seminary School of Jewish Studies. The University of Judaism in Los Angeles operates on the West Coast. The Bet Midrash/Seminary of Judaic Studies in Jerusalem is its Israeli affiliate. Other global affiliates include the Seminario Rabbínico Latino Americano in Buenos Aires, Argentina, and the Jewish Theological Seminary of Hungary in Budapest.

In more than a hundred years of existence, it has graduated thousands of rabbis and teachers who now serve synagogues and schools throughout the U.S. and **Canada**.

The Rabbinical Assemble of America is the organization for rabbinical graduates of the Seminary. Two programs with strong ties to the Jewish Theological Seminary are the Women's League for Conservative Judaism and the Federation of Jewish Men's Clubs which strive to instill ideals of Judaism into the lives of its members and promote youth-oriented projects.

JEWISH WAR VETERANS OF THE UNITED STATES. Organization of Jewish men and women who have served in the U.S. armed forces. The JWV is an outgrowth of the Hebrew Union Veterans Organization, founded in 1896 by 78 Jewish veterans of the Civil War. Limited to veterans of the Civil War, its membership became depleted over the years, and the remnants were ultimately absorbed into the Hebrew Veterans of the War with Spain, organized as an independent veterans' group after the Spanish-American War. After World War I this organization changed its name to Hebrew Veterans of the Wars of the Republic to include veterans of all wars. The organization adopted its present name in 1929.

The Jewish War Veterans has its headquarters in Washington, D.C. and a post in every major city and many suburbs throughout the U.S. It is the official representative of Jewish soldiers and sailors confined to the various hospitals for veterans under the care of the U.S. Veterans' Administration. It aids the families of deceased Jewish veterans to obtain their entitled benefits. It officially represents American Jewry at patriotic functions. In its program to promote Americanism, the JWV is vigilant of ideologies which pose a threat to American freedom. Each year it presents an award for Americanism.

JEWS' COLLEGE. Rabbinical seminary in London, **England.** It is the main agency for training Orthodox rabbis, cantors, and teachers in Great Britain. The college, founded in 1855 by Chief Rabbi Nathan Marcus Adler, has been incorporated into the University of London. According to the constitution of the college, the chief rabbi of Great Britain is always its president. The college library, particularly rich in items on Anglo-Jewish history, is larger than that of any other European theological seminary.

JEZEBEL. Biblical queen in 9th century B.C.E.; wife of King **Ahab.** She is considered one of the evil persons in the Bible, who brought **Baal** worship to Israel. In English, her name became synonymous with a scheming and devious woman.

JOB. Third book in the biblical section Writings. The theme of Job is divine justice, asking and discussing the question "Why do the righteous suffer?" Job of Uz, a good man, suddenly has a series of terrible misfortunes: he loses his wealth, his children die, and he becomes ill with a loathsome disease. Three of his friends, Eliphaz, Bildad, and Zophar ,come to console him. They assume that his troubles have come to him as punishment for his sins, and urge Job to confess his guilt and accept his suffering as God's righteous judgment. Job insists that he is innocent and pours out the bitterness of his soul. Finally, a fourth friend, Elihu, son of Barachel, scolds Job for lacking trust in God. The book has a happy ending. Job learns that humans cannot really understand the mystery of the Lord's ways, when God speaks to him "out of a whirlwind" and restores his health and happiness. Job has more sons and daughters and lives to be 140. With its magnificent poetic description of Job's trials and his patient faith, together with the majestic descriptions of Divine power, the Book of Job is the greatest of the Wisdom books in the **Bible.**

JOEL. Second of the minor prophets in the **Bible.** The Book of Joel calls the people of Judea to repent because the Judgment Day is at hand. It ends with the promise that the enemies of Israel will be overturned, **Jerusalem** and Judah will be restored, and God will dwell in the midst of His people once again.

JOEL, BILLY. *See* **Music.**

JOHANAN BEN ZAKKAI (1st century C.E.). Religious leader. A student of **Hillel** and a member of the **Sanhedrin,** Ben Zakkai advocated a policy of peace with the Romans. The **Talmud** relates that during the siege of **Jerusalem** for no reason was anyone allowed to leave the city except to bury the dead. Ben Zakkai instructed his disciples to carry him in a coffin across the city walls.

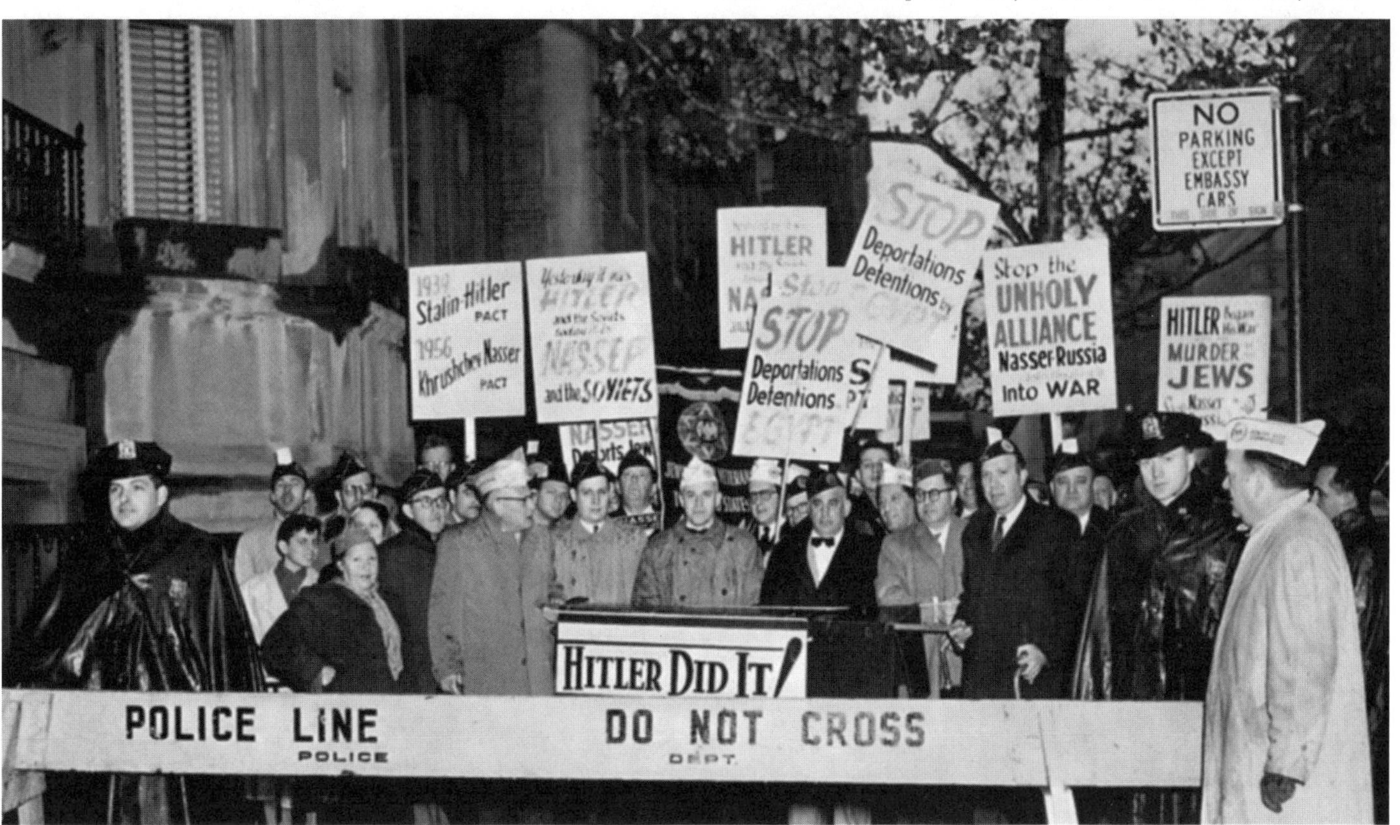

Members of the Jewish War Veterans picket the Egyptian Consulate in New York in 1957.

Job Visited By His Friends, by Gustav Doré. "And he took a potsherd to scrape himself, and sat down among the ashes." — Job 2:8.

There he met the Roman commander Vespasian who granted him permission to open a Talmudical academy at **Yavneh**. There, he continued the work of the Sanhedrin, instituting laws and regulations which exerted a lasting influence on the development of Jewish spiritual values.

JOHANAN OF GUSH HALAV (John of Gischala, 1st century C.E.). One of the leaders of the Judean rebellion against **Rome**, 66-70 C.E., Johanan was a man of frail body and peaceful habits. An attack on his town forced him to take up arms and transformed him into one of the fiercest opponents of Roman tyranny. After Gush Halav fell to the Roman legions, Johanan fled to **Jerusalem** with several thousand followers. There he joined in the ruthless struggle between the peace party and the Zealots, who favored war. Only after Titus had already laid siege to Jerusalem did Johanan join forces with **Bar Giora**, another Zealot leader, for defense of the capital. After five months of heroic fighting, Jerusalem was taken by sheer force of numbers. Johanan was among the last to be captured. He was forced to march in Titus's triumphal entry into Rome and later sentenced to life imprisonment as a rebel.

JOINT DISTRIBUTION COMMITTEE. *See* **American Jewish Joint Distribution Committee.**

JOLSON, AL. *See* **Music.**

JONAH. Literally, dove. Fifth and perhaps most familiar of the minor prophets in the Bible. The first two chapters of the book of Jonah tell how the prophet unwillingly set out on his mission to save the people of Nineveh, how he was swallowed by a great fish and prayed for salvation, and how he was spewed out safely on the shore. The third chapter tells how Jonah obeys the word of the Lord and prophesies the destruction of Nineveh because of its wickedness, and how the people repented. The final chapter describes Jonah's displeasure because God forgave the people of Nineveh and his prophecy of destruction did not come true. It also tells how the Lord taught Jonah the meaning of mercy and forgiveness.

JORDAN. In Hebrew, *Yarden*. Israel's largest river, flowing into the Red Sea. It is the natural border between Israel and Jordan.

JORDAN, HASHEMITE KINGDOM OF. Modern name for kingdom of **Transjordan**, which was formed in 1922. In 1948, Jordan annexed the territory on the **West Bank** originally assigned in 1947 for a new Arab state under the UN partition resolution and also occupied the Old City of **Jerusalem**. In 1967, Israeli forces occupied Jerusalem and the West Bank territory. In 1994, Jordan signed a peace treaty with Israel.

JOSEPH. Literally, He (i.e. God) will add. Son of **Jacob** and **Rachel**. The favorite child, he was given "a coat of many colors" to wear. Both a dreamer and an interpreter of dreams, Joseph aroused the jealousy of his brothers and was sold as a slave to an **Egypt**-bound caravan. In Egypt he gained a position of authority on the estate of his master, Potiphar, but was imprisoned because of a false accusation by Potiphar's wife. His old skill at interpreting dreams brought his release from prison and his rise to the office of the Pharaoh's viceroy and governor of Egypt. The stories of his dramatic reunion with his family which came down to Egypt during the years of famine in Canaan and the comfort he brought to his father who had thought Joseph dead form the final chapter in his story. Joseph was not forgotten by his people. Years later, when they fled Egypt to return to their Promised Land, they took Joseph's embalmed body along on their 40-year journey to Canaan and gave him final burial near Shechem. Rabbinic tales and Jewish folklore have spangled the Joseph story with numerous

Joseph and his brothers. From an 18th century engraving. "And Joseph said to his brothers, 'Is my father still alive?' And they could not answer him." — Genesis 45:3.

legends. Folk plays on the theme of his life came into being as traditional entertainment for **Purim**, to be performed by strolling players or the townspeople themselves. The imagination of humankind has been gripped by the story, and countless dramas and tales have been written about Joseph, culminating in Thomas Mann's great trilogy, *Joseph and His Brothers*.

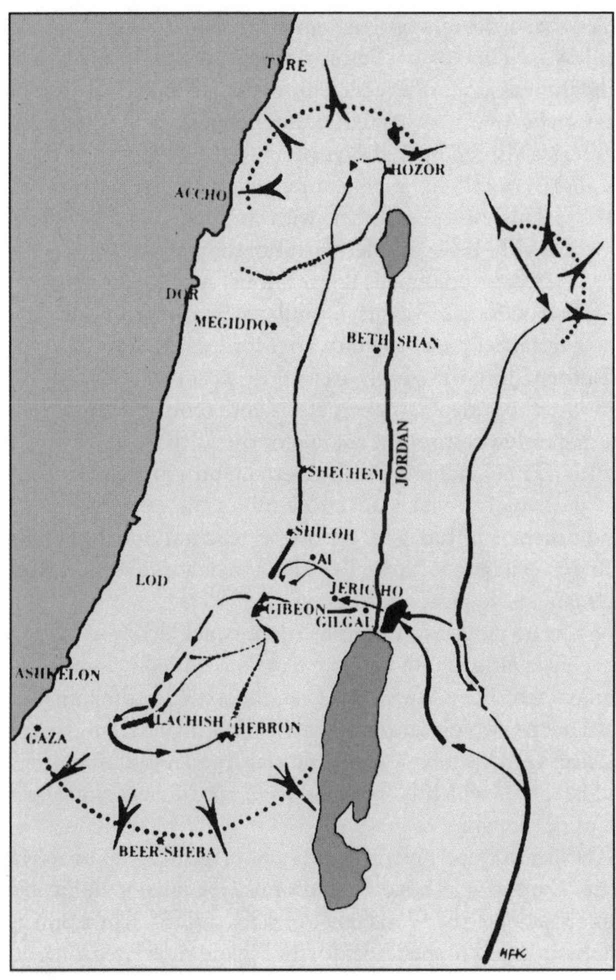

Joshua's battles.

JOSEPHUS FLAVIUS (ca. 37-ca. 105). Soldier and historian. Born in **Jerusalem**, Joseph ben Mattathias came from a priestly family and was educated in the schools of the **Pharisees**. At age 26 he was sent on a mission to **Rome** where he remained for two years at the court of Nero. Returning home in 65 C.E., Josephus found the country in open rebellion against Roman rule. Entrusted with the command of **Galilee**, he fortified its cities against Vespasian and his invading Roman legions. From the beginning, Joseph's loyalty was suspected by **Johanan of Gush Halav**, leader of the extremist Zeolot party, and the feud between them was bitter. Vespasian invaded Galilee in 67 and conquered the fortresses one by one. In Jotapata, Josephus held out for three months. When the garrison was captured, Josephus saved his life by surrendering. He won his way into Vespasian's good graces by predicting that he would become emperor of Rome. The prediction came true, Vespasian returned to Rome to mount the imperial throne, and Titus took over command of the war in Judea. During the siege of Jerusalem, Titus used Josephus to urge the Jews to surrender. After the fall of Jerusalem, Joseph accompanied Titus to Rome, and was rewarded by the favor of the Flavian emperors, Vespasian and Titus. In gratitude, he took their name and called himself Josephus Flavius. Josephus appears to have been torn between his inescapable Jewishness and his need to please the Romans. He turned to writing and wrote first *The Judean Wars* (against Rome). Then he wrote the *Antiquities of the Jews*, a history glorifying the Jewish people. In *Against Apion*, a reply to the Alexandrian schoolmaster and anti-Semite, Josephus passionately defended Jews against slander. *Vita* is the autobiography that Josephus wrote to answer the charges made against him by another Jewish historian, Justus of Galilee. The writings of Justus on the Jewish revolt have been lost. The books of Josephus have survived, and serve as the only source of knowledge for a good part of the Jewish history of that period.

JOSHUA. Literally, the Lord will help. According to the **Bible**, Joshua, the son of Nun, was chosen by **Moses** to be his successor. Joshua led **Israel** across the Jordan in about 1260 B.C.E., conquered the **Jericho** fortress, and defeated the six hostile Canaanite tribes. After six years of battle, he began the division of the conquered territory among the tribes. The Book of Joshua is the sixth in the Bible, following **Deuteronomy**; it tells the story of the conquest and division of **Canaan**, and ends with Joshua's farewell address and death.

JOSHUA BEN HANANYAH. *See* **Tannaim**.

JUDAH. Literally, Praise to the Lord. Fourth son of **Jacob**, born of **Leah**; founder of the tribe of Judah, whose emblem was the lion. Just as Judah came to be the leader of all the sons of Jacob, so the tribe of Judah took the leading role in the life of the people. Much of Chapter 15 in **Joshua** is devoted to a description of Judah's territory, which extended from the end of the Salt Sea in the south to the Great Sea in the west and was crowned with **Jerusalem** on its heights. Judah was also the name of the southern kingdom, which included the tribes of Judah, **Simeon**, and part of **Benjamin**. This kingdom came into being after the northern tribes had seceded at the death of **Solomon**, forming their own northern kingdom of **Israel**.

Emblem of the tribe of Judah.

JUDAH HA-LEVI. *See* **Ha-levi, Judah**.

JUDAH, KINGDOM OF. The southern kingdom which included the territory belonging to the tribes of **Judah**, **Simeon**, and part of **Benjamin**. The kingdom of Judah came into being after the northern tribes had seceded from the House of **David** at the death of **Solomon**, forming their own northern kingdom of Israel.

JUDAH MACCABEE. *See* **Maccabees**.

JUDAH THE PRINCE (*Yehudah Hanasi*; ca.135-222 C.E.) Also called Rabbi and *Rabenu ha-Kadosh*, our Holy Rabbi. His life work consisted of editing, compiling, and classifying the Mishnah, the entire body of Jewish oral law which had been accumulated during the preceding four centuries. He arranged the Mishnah in six sections, each one dealing with a particular set of laws. This work exerted a crucial influence on the development of the religious, cultural, and social life of the Jewish people.

Judah the Prince was born on the day Rabbi **Akiba** died, a coincidence symbolic of the continuity of Jewish scholarship. A descendant of **Hillel**, who established a famous school of interpreters of the Law, he succeeded his father as *Nasi*, or head of the **Sanhedrin**, the highest legislative and judicial council of the time. His preoccupation with Jewish law did not prevent the great rabbi and scholar from acquiring a thorough knowledge of Greek language and culture. But it was his vast knowledge of Jewish law which earned him the recognition of the scholars of his time. His learning as well as his wealth added dignity and splendor to his leadership of the Jewish people as head of the Sanhedrin. Even the Roman authorities respected his station. His house resembled a royal court. Yet Rabbi Judah himself was a modest and self-denying person, highly responsive to the needs of his fellow man. In time of famine, he distributed his wealth freely to the poor. His main interests lay in learning and in his students whom he loved deeply. "I learned much from my teachers," he once said, "much more from my comrades, and most of all from my students."

Judah the Prince lived first in Bet Shearim and then in Zippori, Galilee. He was the last of the **Tannaim**, closing a great period of Jewish scholarship.

JUDAISM. Judaism is based on the **Bible**, each age reinterpreting and redefining biblical laws. The Talmud is the result of such a process of interpretation. Changing conditions and circumstances resulted in further interpretations by rabbinic authorities of every generation. Hence, Judaism never froze into a fixed and rigid philosophy and was always more concerned with the practice of the commandments regulating human's relations with each other and with God.

Orthodox Judaism. The way of life that adheres to the traditional aspects of Judaism came to be called "Orthodox" in the early 19th century when Reform and Conservative Judaisms, which differ somewhat from the original tradition of Judaism, developed. Orthodox Jews continued to follow the laws, customs, and ceremonies prescribed in the **Shulhan Arukh**. This code of Jewish law, however, deals only with obligatory practices. In addition, there are many customs which have evolved over the ages. These customs have been so hallowed by time and tradition that they now have almost the binding force of law for the communities in which they are practiced. Numerous collections of such customs have been made, and many of them have become an organic part of Jewish life.

At the center of the Orthodox way of life lies the idea that God chose His people Israel from among the nations and bestowed His law upon them as a symbol of this love. In receiving the **Torah**, the Jews took upon themselves the task of becoming "a nation of priests and a sacred folk" by dedicating themselves to fulfilling the ideals of justice and holiness embodied in the Law. For the Orthodox Jew, the Law embodies all the rules for the good life. When he or she acts according to the letter and spirit of the Law, the Jew realizes the will of God and reflects upon the goodness of God and the love lavished by Him upon Israel and all humankind. In fact, a large number of customs and ceremonies observed by Orthodox Jews serve directly to remind them of this love.

Conservative Judaism. The history of Conservative Judaism began with the Historical School of Jewish Learning founded by Zechariah Frankel in **Germany** in 1850. Frankel held that Judaism was a living spirit which had undergone many changes in its long history to adjust itself to the changes in its surroundings. The Historical School he initiated aimed to use modern scientific methods to study the Jewish past. As long as every effort was made to preserve and understand the Jewish tradition, Frankel believed that in the future, as in the past, changes in customs or ceremonies would evolve naturally in the spirit of Judaism, as well as in the spirit of the times.

A leader of this school of thought was Sabato Morais, a founder of the **Jewish Theological Seminary of America**. When Solomon **Schechter** assumed the leadership of the Seminary, Conservative Judaism in America was greatly strengthened. Schechter felt that "Universal Israel" had always permitted differences of opinion because of the all-embracing unity of Judaism, past, present, and future. This unity together with tradition and scholarship constituted, he believed, a fertile soil for the growth of a program for Conservative Judaism. The religious movement known as **Reconstructionism** was first formulated by a member of the Jewish Theological Seminary's faculty, Dr. Mordecai M. **Kaplan**.

Reform Judaism. Early Reform Judaism was rooted in the period of political emancipation and cultural adaption of European Jewry from the middle of the 18th through the 19th century. Israel Jacobson in the German province of Westphalia was perhaps the first leader to express the current desire for modifications in Judaism. He introduced a number of changes into his synagogue: a mixed choir, a few prayers recited in German, and a sermon in German.

When he moved to Berlin in 1815, Israel Jacobson instituted these innovations in a new synagogue founded by him and the banker Jacob Beer. It was, however, the scholar Abraham **Geiger** who laid the ideological foundation for Reform Judaism. Geiger saw Judaism as an historical, developing faith and rejected basic beliefs and practices which he believed were contradictory to modern scientific thought.

The first to found Reform institutions in the U.S. was Isaac Mayer **Wise**. The principles he advocated formed the basis for the Pittsburgh Platform adopted by a conference of rabbis in 1885. These principles emphasized the prophetic ideas of the Bible and declared some of the biblical and Talmudic regulations no longer applicable. The Platform separated Jewish religion from Jewish nationalism and rejected a return to Palestine and the belief in a personal Messiah. For the Messianic era of peace and perfection it substituted the hope for a perfect world achieved by cultural and scientific progress. Reform Judaism thought of Jews as a group with a mission to spread godliness in the world. A revision of these principles took place in 1937 at the meeting of the Central Conference of American Rabbis in Columbus, Ohio. The conference defined Judaism as the "historical religious experience of the Jewish people," thereby including not only Jewish belief and ethic, but also traditional culture and peoplehood. Today the Reform movement sponsors ARZA, or American Reform Zionist organization, which is dedicated to the cause of Israel. Since the 1960's, there have been two major ideological trends within Reform. On the one hand, many Reform rabbis have become more traditional and observant, and have even advocated a "Reform Halachah." On the other hand, other Reform rabbis, including the former leader of the movement, Alexander **Schindler**, broke ranks with the other Jewish movements by introducing new concepts such as patrilineal descent (recognizing one as a Jew even if not born to a Jewish mother, only a Jewish father). Moreover, a growing number of Reform rabbis began to officiate at marriages between Jews and non-Jews.

A somewhat similar phenomenon could also be detected in the Conservative movement, where the approval of the ordination of women drove a wedge between traditionalist and liberal Conservative rabbis. In the Orthodox camp, a trend toward the right could be seen among some young rabbis, who refuse to recognize the validity of non-Orthodox movements, while others have been seeking dialogue and reconciliation.

JUDENRAT. From German, meaning Jewish Council. During World War II, the Nazi occupiers of Europe set up a *Judenrat* in every Jewish community, whether as large as the half million Jews of Warsaw or as small as a village of a handful of families. The members of the *Judenrat* were put in the painful position of serving their own people's executioners, and while many of them sought to alleviate their people's situation, there was little they could do.

JUDGES (12th and 11th centuries B.C.E.). The Book of Judges spans the period from the death of **Joshua** to the time when **Saul** was anointed king. The conquest of **Canaan** under Joshua had been incomplete. The tribes of Israel had not reached the coast which remained occupied by the **Phoenicians** and the **Philistines**. In the Great Plain the unconquered fortresses of Taanach, Megiddo, and Beth-Shean were arranged as a formidable barrier separating the tribes of **Dan**, **Asher**, **Zebulun**, **Naphtali**, and **Issachar** in the north, from the tribes of **Manasseh**, **Ephraim**, **Benjamin**, and **Judah** in the south. Aloof across the Jordan, **Reuben** tended its sheep, and **Gad** dallied in Gilead. The physical separation, as well as the nature of tribal society, prevented the Judges from effecting the unification of the people, even though they were popular heroes. During their era, Mesopotamian enemies from the north, the Moabites from across the Jordan in the south, and the nomad Midianites from Sinai subjugated the Israelites for varying periods of time. In such times of crisis, the Judges were called to leadership by the people and their battles eventually extended Israelite mastery of the Land. There were sixteen Judges. Two of them, **Deborah** and **Samuel**, were also prophets. One, Eli, was a priest, while **Samson** was a folk-hero rather than a military or religious leader. Another kind of battle characterized the period of the Judges: the battle of Israel's religion of one God against the fertility and nature gods of Canaan. In both these struggles, the Judges were the leaders of the people.

JUDGES

OTHNIEL, *son of Kenaz, was the first to judge Israel after Joshua's death.*

EHUD, *son of Gera, fought the Moabites.*

SHAMGAR, *son of Anath, led the Israelites against the Philistines.*

DEBORAH, *prophetess, guided Barak to victory over the Canaanites.*

GIDEON, *son of Yoash, defeated a host of Midianites with 300 men.*

ABIMELECH, *son of Gideon, the only judge to gain leadership by treachery.*

TOLA, *son of Puah, judged Israel for 23 years.*

YAIR, *the Gileadite, judged the people for 22 years.*

JEPTHAH, *son of Gilead, defeated the Ammonites.*

IBZAN *of Bethlehem judged the people for 7 years.*

ELON, *from the tribe of Zebulun, judged for 10 years.*

ABDON, *the son of Hillel, ruled for 8 years.*

SAMSON, *son of Manoah, fought the Philistines singlehanded.*

ELI, *the priest, ruled the people from the sanctuary at Shiloh.*

SAMUEL, *the prophet, the last to judge Israel before it became a kingdom under Saul.*

Overleaf: Early engraving of Jerusalem.

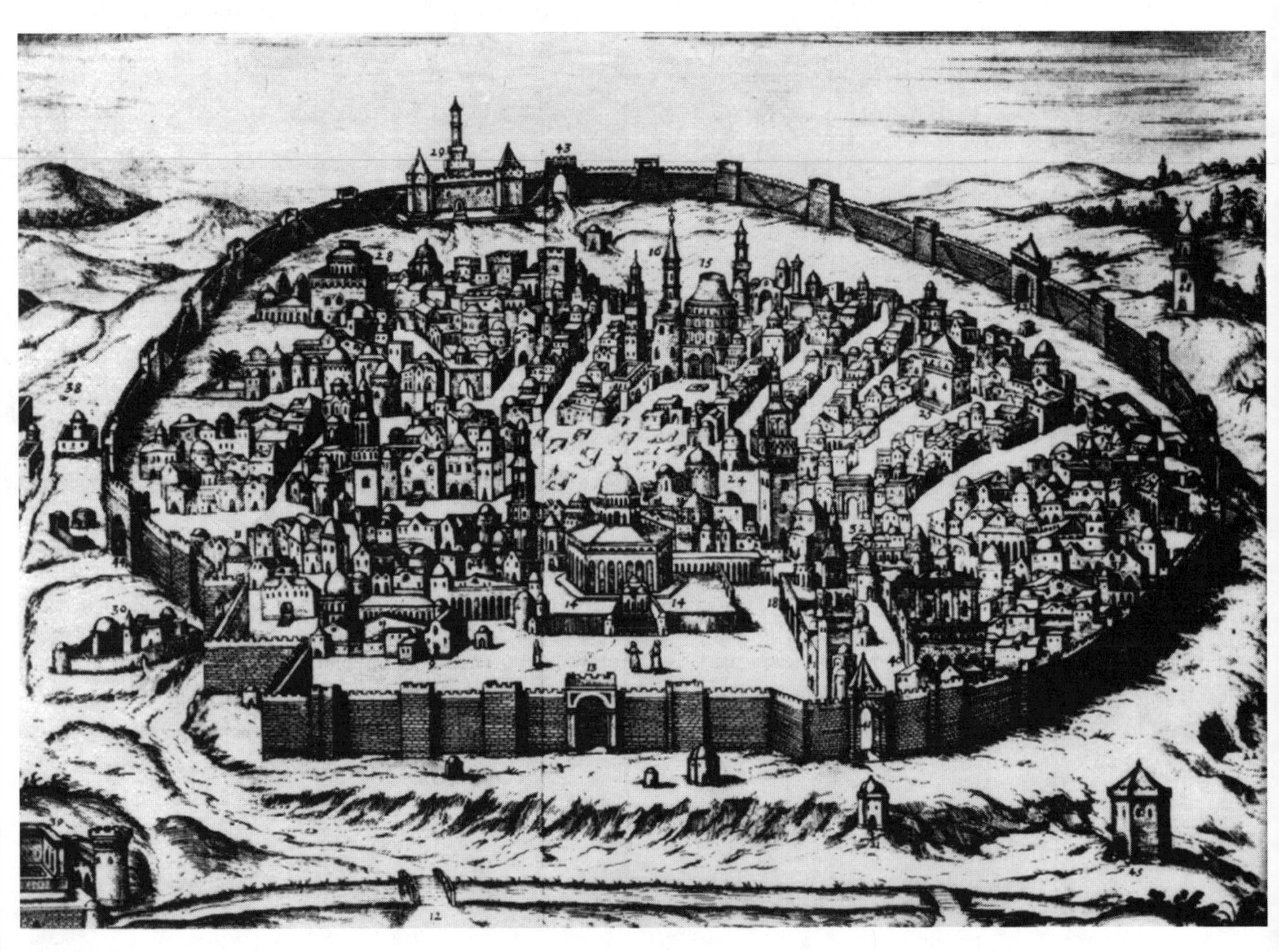

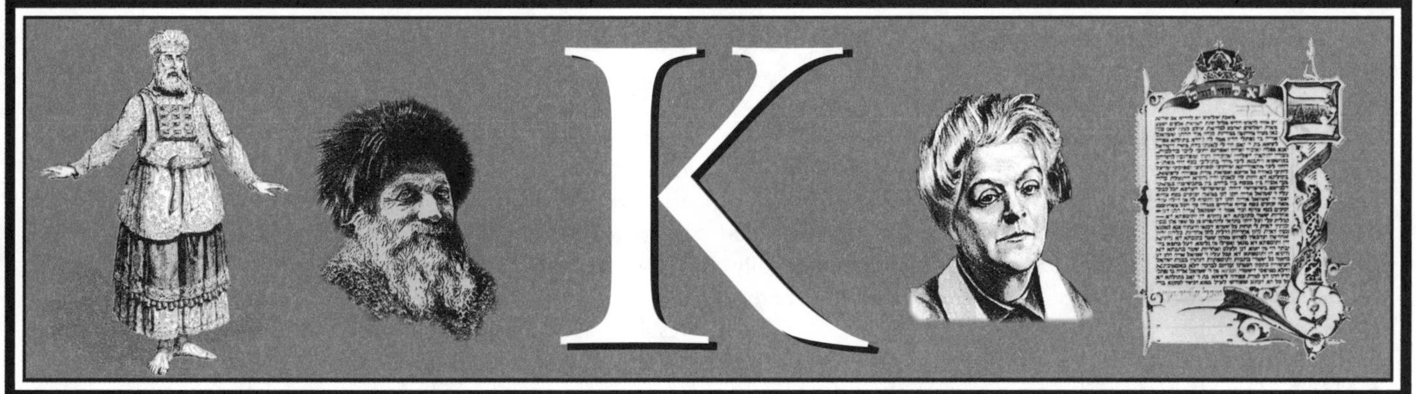

KABAK, A.A. *See* **Hebrew Literature**.

KABBALAH. Literally, received tradition. Refers to Jewish mysticism. In an attempt to fathom the mysteries of God and Creation, the Kabbalists developed a complete philosophic system during the Middle Ages. The **Talmud** contains mystical interpretations of the biblical story of Creation. With the appearance of the **Zohar** in the 13th century, the study of the Kabbalah gained popularity. Among the earliest mystic works are the *Alphabet of Rabbi Akiba* and *Sefer Yetzirah* (The Book of Creation) attributed to **Abraham**. The *Sefer Yetzirah* attaches great mystic power to numbers and enumerates the ten *sefirot*, or diven emanations, which later assumed great importance in the Kabbalistic system. God, the *En Sof*, or Infinite One, makes His divine existence known by means of these ten emanations. The first sefirah is called *Keter* (Crown). The others follow in this order: *Hokhmah* (Wisdom); *Binah* (Intelligence); *Hesed* (Mercy); *Din* (Judgment) or *Gevurah* (Strength); *Tiferet* (Beauty); *Netzah* (Victory); *Hod* (Glory); *Yesod* (Foundation); and *Malkhut* (Kingdom).

Jewish mysticism attracted remarkable personalities, some of whom considered themselves Messiahs. Abraham Abulafia (1240-1291), who regarded himself as a forerunner of the Messiah, even attempted to convert the Pope to Judaism.

Kabbalistic teachings gained in intensity and scope in 16th-century Safed. This town in upper **Galilee** in Palestine became a center of Jewish mysticism; among its foremost teachers of Kabbalah was Isaac Luria (1534-1572). A practical or miracle-working mystic, Luria claimed that the secrets of Creation had been revealed to him by the prophet **Elijah**. Luria believed that human beings could attain identification with the Divine Spirit through intense concentration, or *kavanah*. This theory was described by Luria's disciple Hayim Vital in his book *Etz Hayim* (The Tree of Life). Other Lurianic ideas transmitted by Vital are *tzimtzum*, literally contraction, whereby the infinite God reduces Himself to enter the world; *shevirat ha-kelim*, or breaking the vessels, referring to the destructive impact of God's creation, which gave rise to evil; this evil is countered by *tikkun*, or restoration, which is done by a person releasing the holy sparks of the divine within oneself.

Another famous Kabbalist, Moses Cordovero, formulated Kabbalistic teachings in a philosophic system. His contemporary Isaiah Horowitz (1555-1625) interpreted the teachings of Judaism in the light of Kabbalah. He sought, with the other inspired mystics of his generation, to hasten the coming of the Messiah.

The teachings of the Kabbalah contributed to the rise of Messianic hopes and in time influenced **Hasidism** profoundly. Hasidic religious fervor is based on Kabbalistic teachings. Jewish folklore thrived on the Kabbalah's poetic and magical elements, and many non-religious Jews, as well as non-Jews, have been and still are influenced by it.

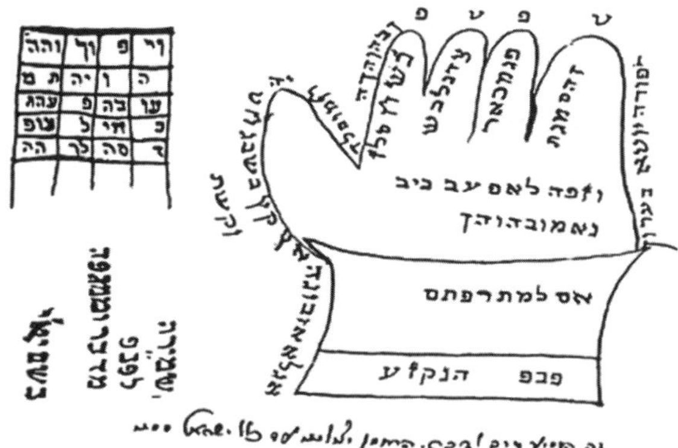

Symbolic representation of the Kabbalistic doctrines.

KADDISH. Literally, santification. One of the most ancient prayers in the Jewish prayer book, generally recited in the **synagogue** during religious services. It became popular as the mourner's prayer. Kaddish is traditionally recited in the presence of a *minyan*, or quorum of ten adult male Jews. The essential part of the prayer is the verse from Psalm 113 in its Aramaic version: "Let His great name be blessed forever and to all eternity." The mourner's Kaddish is recited at synagogue services for eleven months and on every anniversary of the relative's death.

The so-called Rabbinical Kaddish is recited at the close of a lesson or the completion of the study of any portion of the Talmudic law.

The Kaddish glorifies the name of the Lord, reaffirms faith in the establishment of the Kingdom of God, and calls for peace in the house of Israel. Beautiful and stirring melodies accompany the reciting of the Kaddish on the High Holy Days of **Rosh Hashanah** and **Yom Kippur**.

KAF. Eleventh letter of the Hebrew alphabet; numerically, twenty.

KAFKA, FRANZ (1882-1924). Writer. Born in **Prague**, he was a strange genius whose short life was unhappy. From his youth he lived only for his writing. Kafka's family life was difficult; he never succeeded in gaining his father's approval, nor did he agree with his father's views. Kafka never married. His first engagement was broken after several years when he became ill with tuberculosis.

Franz Kafka.

The second woman he fell in love with was forbidden to marry him. This personal unhappiness and Kafka's Jewishness are thought to be reflected in his novels, stories, and sayings. Outstanding among his writings are the short story *Metamorphosis* and the novels *The Trial* and *The Castle*. These works have a strange poetic beauty and an eerie, dream-like quality. Yet they continually startle readers with the recognition of reality and the hero's hopeless, tragic fate.

KAHAL. Also *kehilla*. Literally, community. During the Middle Ages, Jewish localities were organized into communities which had considerable power to govern themselves. The make-up of the Jewish community had developed over the ages in Palestine and in **Babylonia** and continued with some changes in the West. The community derived its power to manage all Jewish affairs and institutions of the Jewish community from several sources. First was the personal obligation and need for Jews to live according to Talmudic religious and civil law. Therefore, every member of the community had definite rights and duties that could not be taken away. Second, the Jewish community was granted power by the non-Jewish world to conduct its own affairs and enforce its rules.

The feudal barons, kings, and princes of the Church who "owned" the Jews living in their various domains held the kahal responsible for a tax placed on the entire Jewish community. Christian governments throughout the Middle Ages followed the same practice. Community officials, consequently, had the authority to decide how much individuals were to be taxed.

The term *kahal* came to be applied to the local governments of the Jewish communities in **Lithuania**, **Poland**, and **Russia** during the 16th century. The head of the kahal was called the *rosh ha-kahal*, or the *parnas*, and had considerable authority and prestige. He was assisted by *gabbaim*, or overseers, usually seven. The kahal had its own courts of law to which Jews reported all disputes. The community had the right to enforce its decision by means of imprisonment, flogging (no more than 39 lashes), or temporary or permanent excommunication, or *herem*, which was the most dreaded punishment because it meant being barred completely from contact with any other Jew, including members of one's immediate family.

Life within the kahal proceeded according to age-old tradition. Public life revolved around the synagogue, since not only religious worship, but also meetings and weddings took place there. The community school, or Talmud Torah, open to the destitute, was housed in some part of the synagogue. Often, the hostel, or *hekdesh*, provided by the community for strangers, was located in a synagogue annex, as was the public bathhouse, or *mikveh*. Public charities in the community were well organized, and no Jew was ever left without help. Learning was highly valued, and illiteracy was rare. Most of the officials, usually chosen for their learning, served without salary. For a time, the rabbi also served without salary, and was the religious authority, the teacher, and the guide of the community. Between 1580 and 1764, the kahal reached a high form of development in the Council of the Four Lands. Delegates of the communities from Great Poland, Little Poland, Podolia, and Galicia met, at first once and later twice a year, to regulate the affairs of the people.

KAHANE, MEIR. *See* **Jewish Defense League**.

KALISHER, Z'VI HIRSCH (1795-1874). Rabbi, scholar, and early proponent of **Zionism**. Born in **Poland**, he was the first outstanding Orthodox rabbi to preach that Judaism permitted Jews to work actively for the Zionist cause and that they were not restricted to waiting and praying for the coming Messiah. In his Hebrew pamphlet, *The Quest for Zion* in 1862, he outlined methods for the settlement of Palestine. His pioneering effort actually resulted in the organization of the first Palestine colonization society. His pamphlet influenced the French **Alliance Israélite Universelle** to establish the **Mikveh Israel** Agricultural School in Palestine. In 1866, he influenced 80 Jews to buy land for an agricultural settlement in Palestine.

KALLIR, ELEAZAR (7th century). Early Hebrew poet in Palestine whose religious verse (*piyutim*) appears in the prayer book. He wrote more than 200 piyutim and introduced rhyme into Hebrew poetry.

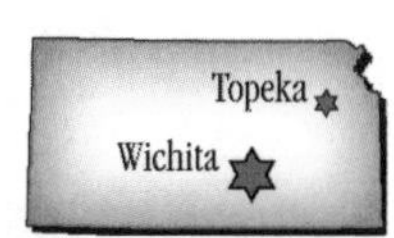

KANSAS. With 1,300 Jews in Wichita and 500 in Topeka, Kansas's Jewish population is one of the smallest in the U.S. Jewish merchants arrived in Kansas in the mid-19th century. In 1882, Jews tried but failed to establish agricultural settlements in several parts of the state. For years, there were small Jewish communities throughout the state, but most have disappeared.

KAPLAN, LOUIS. *See* **Sports**.

KAPLAN, MORDECAI (1881-1983). Born in Lithuania and raised in the U.S., Kaplan developed an originally American brand of Judaism, called **Reconstructionism**. In his book *Judaism as a Civilization* he argues that Judaism is not strictly a religion, but a civilization which encompasses people, land, religion, and culture. His movement has remained small in size, but he has exerted great influence on many Reform and Conservative rabbis. He also originated the Jewish Center (*see* **Jewish Community Center**).

KAPPAROT (or *kapores*). An old Jewish custom of swinging a chicken over the head before **Yom Kippur** to transfer one's sins to the fowl. It is only practiced today by the most strictly Orthodox.

KARAITES. Jewish sect founded in the late 8th century by **Anan ben David**. Karaism rejected the rabbinic tradition of Talmudic law and based its religious life on the literal interpretation of the **Bible**.

Anan ben David, nephew of the deceased **Exilarch** of the Bustanai dynasty, also aspired to this high position. The Geonim, the highest religious authorities in **Babylonia**, doubted Anan's devotion to Talmudic law and appointed instead his younger brother, Hananiah. Angered by the rejection from the Geonim, Anan proclaimed openly his opposition to the **Talmud**. His followers rebelled against the Talmudic tradition. They were influenced by the controversy raging in **Islam** at that time between traditionalists and their opponents. When Anan's supporters increased in numbers, he became head of the new religious sect which later came to be known as Karaism, from the Hebrew *Karaim*, or (strict) readers of the Scripture.

Anan recognized the authority of the Bible only. He urged his pupils to search in the Scriptures for the true or literal interpretation of the law. By their strict adherence to the biblical text the Karaites defeated their own purpose. As time went on, the Karaite teachers engaged in hair-splitting interpretations of the Bible no less than the rabbinical authorities whom they criticized. Much confusion resulted from the varied and often conflicting interpretation of Karaite scholars. In many instances the Karaite restrictions were more severe than those of the Talmud. They prohibited the use of light on the Sabbath day altogether, and were even more rigorous in observance of the laws of ritual cleanliness and fasting.

The debates between the Talmudists and Karaites stimulated Jewish scholarship. The defense of traditional Judaism required a thorough knowledge of the Bible and the Hebrew language. Jewish philosophic thought was also mobilized in defense of tradition.

Between the 9th and 12th centuries Karaite communities were established in **Babylonia**, Persia, **Egypt**, and Palestine. In the 13th century many Karaites settled in the Crimea in **Russia**, and spread from there to **Lithuania** and Galicia. During the last few centuries the Karaites have gradually separated from the Jewish community. For instance, in order to avoid the restrictive measures directed against Jews by the Tsarist regime in Russia, Karaites tried to prove that they were not Jews.

Before World War II, there were about 12,000 Karaites, most of them in the Crimea. The Karaites have at all times professed a love for **Zion**. Since the establishment of **Israel**, many Karaites from Egypt have settled in the Holy Land. They have founded several settlements, and have tended to draw nearer to other Jews.

KARO, JOSEPH BEN EPHRAIM (1488-1575). Famous Talmudic scholar and author of the **Shulhan Arukh**, the core of Jewish law. Orthodox Jewish life for the last 400 years has been regulated by the *Shulhan Arukh*. Born in Toledo, **Spain**, Karo was forced to go into exile with his parents when only four years old. After much wandering, the family finally settled in **Turkey** where he received his education. Karo acquired his greatest fame in **Safed**, Palestine, at that time a center for the study of the **Talmud** and of Jewish mysticism, or **Kabbalah**. In this city, high on the mountains of upper **Galilee**, Karo founded a yeshivah and wrote most of his books. Before compiling the *Shulhan Arukh*, he spent many years in the writing of *Bet Joseph*, a commentary on the *Arbaah Turim*, an earlier code of Jewish law composed by Jacob Ben Asher. Other works by Karo are *Kesef Mishneh*, a commentary on the famed **Maimonides** Code. Joseph Karo, himself steeped in the Kabbalah, greatly influenced his students, many of whom were famous Kabbalists.

KASHRUT. *See* **Dietary Laws**.

KATZ, ELIAS. *See* **Sports**.

KATZIR, EPHRAIM (1916-). Professor, biochemist, biophysicist, and fourth president of Israel. Born in Kiev, **Russia**, he was brought to Palestine by his parents at age nine. A graduate of the **Hebrew University**, in 1949 he was appointed Acting Head of Department of Biophysics in the **Weizmann Institute of Science** at Rehovot, and later its substantive director. From 1966 to 1968, he was Chief Scientist to the Ministry of Defense. He has written extensively on proteins and such natural products as nucleic acids and is a member of a number of national and international societies. In 1966, he was the first Israeli to be elected to the U.S. National Academy of Sciences. He was president of the State of Israel from 1973 to 1978.

Ephraim Katzir.

KATZNELSON, BERL (1887-1944). Writer, editor, and Israel labor leader. Honored for many years as the "conscience" of Israel labor, Katznelson came to Palestine from **Russia** in 1909. In 1920, after working for many years as an agricultural laborer and serving in the **Jewish Legion** during World War I, he was instrumental in founding the **Histadrut**, the Israel Federation of Labor. Five years later he established *Davar*, the Histadrut daily which he edited to the end of his life. A founding member of Mapai, the Israel labor party, he was active in public life as a member of the executive committee of the Histadrut, the **Jewish Agency**, and the **World Zionist Organization**. During the late 1930's Katznelson was a strong partisan of "illegal" immigration. Recognizing the imminent danger to European and world Jewry, he was an active supporter of the underground which smuggled Jews out of Europe and into Palestine.

KATZNELSON, YITZHAK. *See* **Hebrew Literature.**

KAUFMAN, GEORGE S. (1899-1961). American playwright known for such comic plays as *You Can't Take It With You* and *The Man Who Came to Dinner*.

KAUFMANN, YEHEZKEL (1889-1963). Hebrew philosopher and scholar. He was born in **Ukraine** and educated in Talmudical academies and European universities. In his comprehensive sociological study *Golah Ve-Nekhar* (Exile and Dispersion), Kaufman points out that the problem of Jewish nationalism is unique in character and historical development and therefore requires its own solution. His eight-volume history of the Jewish religion, *Toldot Ha-Emunah Ha-Yisraelit* (A History of the Israelite Faith), is an exhaustive and analytical work on the development of Jewish religious thought and practices. Kaufman was professor of biblical research at the **Hebrew University** in **Jerusalem**.

KAYE, DANNY. *See* **Stage and Screen**.

KEDUSHA. *See* **Prayer (Eighteen Benedictions)**.

KELETI, AGNES. *See* **Sports**.

KENTUCKY. The two main Jewish communities are in Louisville (8,700) and Lexington (1,850). German Jews arrived in the state in the mid-18th century, East European Jews after 1880. Communities were established in many towns, but most have now disappeared. Distinguished Jews from the state include Joseph Jonas, a friend of Abraham Lincoln who helped found the Whig Party, and Louis **Brandeis**, one of America's leading jurists.

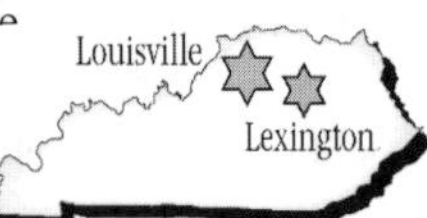

KEREN HAYESOD. *See* **Israel, State of** *and* **Zionism.**

KEREN KAYEMET. *See* **Jewish National Fund.**

KETUBAH. Jewish marriage contract listing the details of the marriage agreement with particular emphasis on the promise of the husband to provide for his wife both during marriage and in case of divorce. The oldest ketubah preserved dates from the 5th century, though the Aramaic form used today probably dates only to the 12th century. The margins of many ketubot were artistically ornamented with designs and biblical verses.

Illuminated Ketubah by Sol Nadel. Commissioned for the marriage of Mr. and Mrs. Maximilian, Toronto, Canada.

KHAZARS. People of Turkish origin who lived in southern **Russia** and adopted Judaism in the 8th century. Originally, the Khazars were only a small nomadic tribe, but by alliance with stronger tribes of Arabs, Russians, and Byzantines and through constant warfare, they succeeded in establishing an empire that stretched from the steppes of Eastern Europe and from the Volga Basin to the Chinese frontier. In 960, Hasdai **Ibn Shaprut**, a Jewish scholar and physician to the Caliph of Cordova, received a letter from King Joseph of the Khazars, telling a remarkable story. Some centuries before, King Bulan of the Khazars had asked the religious leaders of the Jews, Christians, and Mohammedans to explain their religions to him. Most impressed by the description of the Jewish faith, Bulan adopted it for his entire kingdom and invited Jewish scholars to establish schools for the instruction of his people in the **Bible**, **Talmud**, and Jewish ritual. Bulan's successors took Jewish names and encouraged the practice of Judaism within the country. Fascinated by the story, and grasping at the possibility of obtaining a land of refuge for persecuted Jews, Hasdai entered into correspondence with King Joseph and learned about the country of the Khazars. At a time when much of Europe was fanatically bigoted, the Khazars had established a rule of tolerance. The King's palace was located on the Volga River near the site of modern Astrakhan. The Khazar capital conducted a flourishing trade in grains, hides, and fruit. Unfortunately, early in the 11th century, Russian attacks destroyed the Khazar kingdom completely. The people were scattered throughout Crimea, **Hungary**, and even **Spain**; most of them adopted Christianity and disappeared as a separate group. The story of the conversion of the Khazars to Judaism has been interpreted variously. Some scholars call it a fable; others claim that only the ruling class adopted Judaism. Fascinated by the story, the medieval poet Judah **Ha-Levi** described the philosophic discussion between King Bulan and the three religious leaders in his book *Ha-Kuzari*.

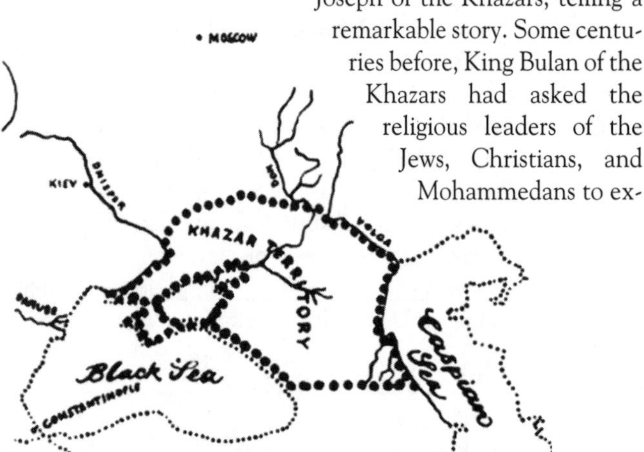

The Khazar Kingdom. Courtesy Zionist Archives and Library, New York.

KIBBUTZ, KVUTZAH. Literally, group or collective. Forms of communal settlement in **Israel**. The early **halutzim**, or pioneers, established the kibbutz on the principle of complete equality. The members of each settlement own the property in common. Every member has one vote in the assembly which manages the settlement. All members must work; hired labor is employed only in times of crisis. Women share fully in the life and work of the community. Children spend the day in daycare. Their parents come for them immediately after work and they spend their free time, evenings, and Sabbaths together.

The kibbutz and the kvutzah differ in several ways. The kvutzah has fewer members and was originally devoted solely to agriculture. Both types trace their origins to *Degania*, or the mother of kvutzot founded in 1909. The large kibbutz appeared many years later when the number of immigrants flowing into the country rose. It was felt that larger units would better serve the needs of the country. Industrial enterprises were introduced to increase employment opportunities, lessen the dependence of the settlements on the cities, and raise the standard of living. At present, virtually all kibbutzim and kvutzot belong to one of three national federations. These federations coordinate the activities of their members in such matters as marketing, education, culture, credit, and relations with the government and other outside groups.

KIBBUTZ GALUYOT. *See* **Ingathering of The Exiles.**

KIDDUSH. *See* **Prayer.**

KIDDUSH HA-SHEM. Literally, sanctification of God's name. This term was applied to the act of martyrdom in Jewish history, especially during the Middle Ages at the time of the **Inquisition** and during the Cossack massacres led by Bogdan Chmielnicki in **Ukraine** in 1648. Kiddush Ha-Shem also defines an act that brings honor to the Jewish people. The opposite of *Kiddush Ha-Shem* is *Hillul Ha-Shem*, desecration of God's Name.

Perhaps it never happened
Perhaps
I never rose at dawn
To till the soil with the sweat of my brow.

— RACHEL, 1927

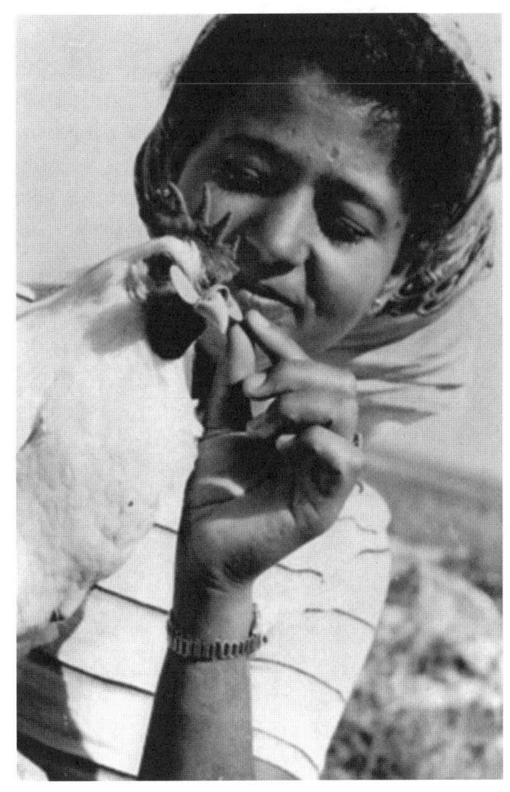

Kibbutz Life. Above, Nahal women farming on the Golan Heights. Top right, farming in a border kibbutz under protection of guards. Right, a member of a kibbutz treating a chicken. Below, kibbutz Lohamei ha-getaot (Ghetto Fighters), north of Haifa.

KIMHI, DAVID (1160-1235). Hebrew grammarian and biblical commentator. He provided biblical students with logical, grammatical explanations of difficult words and passages. His grammatical works, encyclopedia, and *Book of Roots* were translated into Latin and used extensively by Christian scholars. Kimhi ably defended his faith in debates with various Christian scholars.

KINGS, BOOK OF. In the **Bible**, the First and Second Books of Kings cover the history of the kingdoms of Israel and Judah from **Solomon** in 970 B.C.E. to the destruction of Judah by Babylonia in 586 B.C.E. Beginning with the last days of King **David**, one dramatic story follows another. After Solomon's brilliant reign and the building of the **Temple** in **Jerusalem**, war split the country into two separate kingdoms: Israel in the north and Judah in the south.

The story of the Kingdom of Israel spanning the years between 993-721 B.C.E. follows. Throughout his life the prophet **Elijah** battled against Israel's idol worship; the prophet Elisha who followed him continued this struggle. In its nearly three centuries of existence, the northern kingdom never managed to rid itself of idol worship. After describing the fall of the northern kingdom, the Book of Kings continues with the southern Kingdom of Judah whose capital was Jerusalem and whose center of worship was the Temple. Great prophets came to Judah, taught its people, and prepared and strengthened them for the time of their defeat and exile in 586 B.C.E.

KINGS OF ISRAEL AND JUDAH

All years B.C.E.

KINGS OF THE UNITED KINGDOM OF ISRAEL

Saul	*1030-1010*
David	*1010-970*
Solomon	*970-931*

KINGS OF ISRAEL		KINGS OF JUDAH	
Jeroboam	*931-910*	*Rehoboam*	*931-913*
Nadab	*910-909*	*Abijah*	*913-911*
Baasha	*909-886*	*Asa*	*911-870*
Elah	*886-885*	*Jehoshafat*	*870-848*
Zimri	*885*	*Jehoram*	*848-841*
Omri	*885-874*	*Ahazia*	*841*
Ahab	*874-853*	*Athalia*	*841-835*
Ahaziah	*853-852*	*Joash*	*835-796*
Jehoram	*852-841*	*Amaziah*	*796-781*
Jehu	*841-814*	*Uzziah*	*781-740*
Jehoahaz	*814-796*	*Jotham*	*740-736*
Joash	*798-783*	*Ahaz*	*736-716*
Jeroboam II	*783-743*	*Hezekiah*	*716-687*
Zechariah	*743*	*Menasseh*	*687-642*
Shallum	*743*	*Amon*	*642-640*
Menahem	*743-738*	*Josiah*	*640-609*
Pekahiah	*738-737*	*Jehoahaz*	*609*
Pekah	*737-732*	*Jehoiakim*	*609-598*
Hoshea	*732-724*	*Zedekiah*	*598-587*
Fall of Israel:	*721*	*Fall of Judah:*	*587*

KINNERET (Sea of Galilee). A harp-shaped fresh-water lake in Israel. It is thirteen miles long and seven and a half miles wide at its broadest point, surrounded by the hills of **Galilee** and Golan. A rich fishing ground, Kinneret is encircled by towns and villages, including *Tiberias*, Kfar Nahum (Capernaum), Migdal, Ginossar, and Ein Gev. The lake has always had a romantic appeal, and many songs and poems were written about it.

KIRSZENSTEIN-SZEWINSKA, IRENA. *See* **Sports.**

KISLEV. Third month of the Jewish civil calendar. **Hanukkah** falls on the 25th of this month.

KISSINGER, HENRY ALFRED (1923-). American political scientist and statesman. Born in Fuerth, **Germany** to Orthodox Jewish parents, he came to the U.S. as a refugee in 1938. After serving in the U.S. Army during World War II, he completed his studies at Harvard University, where he subsequently served as faculty member, working primarily in the fields of government and international affairs. He was consultant to the U.S. Arms Control and Disarmament Agency from 1961 to 1967 and to the U.S. Department of State from 1965 to 1969. From 1961 to 1962 he was an advisor on national security affairs to President John F. Kennedy. In 1969, he became National Security Advisor to President Richard M. Nixon, and from 1973 to 1977 served as Secretary of State, the first foreign-born person and the first Jew in U.S. history to hold that office. In 1973, he received the Nobel Peace Prize (together with Le Duc Tho of North Vietnam) for his efforts to bring about peace in Vietnam. Following the **Yom Kippur War** of 1973, he initiated a cease-fire between Israel and its Arab neighbors and shuttled back and forth among Israel, **Egypt**, **Syria**, and Jordan to effectuate troop disengagements on Israel's frontiers with Egypt and Syria.

KLAUSNER, JOSEPH (1874-1958). Hebrew scholar, writer, and historian. As a youth of 15 in Odessa, **Russia**, Klausner dedicated himself to the task of modernizing Hebrew. He published books in Hebrew on a variety of subjects: literature, philosophy, philology, history, and Asian studies. He was editor of *Ha-Shiloah*, one of the finest Hebrew publications for more than 20 years, and served as professor of modern Hebrew literature at the **Hebrew University** in **Jerusalem** since its establishment in 1925. Klausner was chief editor of a Hebrew Encyclopedia. His two studies on the rise of Christianity, *Jesus of Nazareth* and *From Jesus to Paul*, are available in English.

KLEZMER. Literally, musical instruments or musicians. Small musical bands in Eastern Europe before World War II, with the fiddle being the main instrument. They entertained at weddings and other festive occasions. In the U.S. today there has been a revival of klezmer music, consisting mostly of traditional Yiddish melodies.

KLUTZNICK, PHILIP (1907-). American communal leader. He held a position in Franklin D. Roosevelt's administration and from 1979 to 1980 served as Secretary of Commerce. One of the leaders of **B'nai B'rith**, he played a major role in that organization for many years.

KNESSET. Parliament of Israel. *See* **Israel, Government of.**

KOESTLER, ARTHUR (1905-1983). Writer. He was born in **Hungary**, lived briefly in Palestine, and settled in **England**. He wrote mainly about the political events of his time. His political novel *Darkness at Noon* was a major expose of communism. *Thieves in the Night* was about kibbutz life.

KOF. Nineteenth letter of the Hebrew alphabet; numerically, 100.

KOHELET. *See* **Ecclesiastes**.

KOHEN. Literally, priest. **Aaron**, the elder brother of **Moses**, was the first high priest and ancestor of all the priests and high priests who performed the sacrificial rites and conducted services in the Sanctuary. According to the Bible, the meeting tent, or **Tabernacle**, was built by the Israelites in the wilderness after their exodus from **Egypt**. It was the first sanctuary in which a kohen, or priest, served the Lord (Exod. 25:8). There, Aaron brought the offerings of the people in the desert. When he performed the services in the Tabernacle, Aaron wore priestly robes called the *hoshen* and *ephod*. On the shoulder-pieces of the ephod were two stones on which the names of the twelve tribes of Israel were engraved. On his chest, Aaron wore a breastplate made of gold, blue, purple, and scarlet yarn set with precious stones (Exod. 28).

The High Priest wearing the breastplate.

When the Children of Israel settled in the Land of **Canaan**, the priests, like the rest of the tribe of **Levi**, received no portion of land, because they were completely dedicated to the service of the Lord. Instead, biblical laws assigned to them a part of levitical taxes paid by the people and some of the voluntary offerings from the crops and produce. Certain portions from the sacrifices and first fruit offerings were also set aside for the priests.

The Tabernacle rested in Shiloh, almost in the center of the land. Eli, the priest, officiated there for 40 years and served as Judge of Israel. In the time of King **David**, the role of the priest assumed new importance in the life of the people. Worship became centralized in **Jerusalem**, the new capital of the nation. When King **Solomon** built the **Temple**, gleaming with gold and bronze, high on Mt. Moriah, Zadok served as high priest and his son Azariah after him. For a thousand years, this position passed from father to son in the family of Zadok. As the centuries passed, triumph and disaster followed in turn, changing the life of the nation. The First Temple was destroyed, then rebuilt by the people returned from exile. The priests were the teachers and leaders of the people at that time, and their power was great. As foreign empires came and went, they interfered with people's lives and worship in the Temple. Corrupt Greek and Roman governors ignored the required religious qualifications for priests and allowed men to buy their way into the position with gold. Then the Second Temple was destroyed, and the people were scattered in the lands of the dispersion, where prayer took the place of sacrifices. The kohanim went into exile with their people, retaining their identity by the surname Kohen. The spelling of the name has varied at different times and in different countries: Cohen, Coen, Cahn, Cahen, Cohan, Cahan, Kagan, Kahn; or Cowen, Kohn, Kann, and Katz (from the initials of *kohen tzedek*, priest of justice). All these variations identify members of a family whose ancestors acted as priests in the Sanctuary. Descendants of the original kohanim still rise up in Orthodox synagogues during the holiday services, cover their faces with prayer shawls, and bless the people with the triple benediction of the ancient priests of Israel.

KOHLER, KAUFMAN (1843-1926). Rabbi, educator, and leader of Reform Judaism. A descendant of a family of rabbis, Kohler was born in Fuerth, Bavaria. He studied in Frankfurt-am-Main under the Orthodox philosopher Samson Raphael **Hirsch**. Later, he came under the influence of the famous Reform leader Abraham **Geiger**, who urged him to go to America. He arrived in the U.S. in 1869 and held Reform pulpits in Detroit, **Chicago**, and **New York**. Kohler convened the conference of 1885, which drew up the "Pittsburgh Platform," a statement of Reform views which retained its influence until the late 1930's. He introduced Sunday services into his temples. Kohler was President of **Hebrew Union College** and of the **Central Conference of American Rabbis**. He also served as editor of the **Jewish Publication Society**'s 1917 translation of the Bible.

KOHUT, ALEXANDER (1842-1894). Rabbi and scholar. Ordained in Hungary, Kohut arrived in New York in 1885 and became one of the founding fathers of Conservative Judaism in the U.S. He is best known for his exhaustive Talmudic dictionary and his work in behalf of the **Jewish Theological Seminary of America** with Sabbato Morais.

KOHUT, REBECCA BETTELHEIM (1864-1951). Educator and communal worker. Brought to America from **Hungary** as a child, Rebecca Bettelheim studied literature and history before her marriage to Alexander Kohut in 1887. After his death in 1894, she embarked on a long career as lecturer, author, educator, and communal worker. She founded the Kohut School for Girls, and served as president of the first World Congress of Jewish Women and of the National Council of Jewish Women. Her writings include *My Portion*, an autobiography.

Rebecca Kohut. Drawing by Isaac Friedlander.

KOL NIDRE. *See* **Yom Kippur**.

KOLLEK, THEODOR (TEDDY) (1911-). Israeli public figure. Born in Vienna, he came to Palestine in 1934. In the 1950's he played a major role in building Israel's tourist industry and founding the Israel Museum in **Jerusalem**. He was mayor of Jerusalem from 1965 to 1993, becoming well known as a developer of the city and a seeker of peace between its Jewish and Arab residents.

KOOK, ABRAHAM ISAAC HACOHEN (1865-1935). Religious thinker and famous Chief Rabbi of Palestine. Born in a small town in **Latvia**, he studied at famous *yeshivot*, or Talmudic academies, and became known as a brilliant Talmudic scholar when young. He served as rabbi in several important Jewish communities. He also gained renown for his knowledge of Jewish mysticism, or **Kabbalah**, **Hasidism**, and religious philosophy. He was among the few religious leaders of his time who saw in the return to Zion the fulfillment of a basic doctrine of Judaism.

Rabbi Abraham Isaac Kook. Courtesy Hadoar Weekly.

In 1904, he became Rabbi of **Jaffa**, thus realizing his wish to settle in the Holy Land. In 1922, he was chosen Chief Rabbi of the Ashkenazic Jews in Palestine. In **Jerusalem**, he founded his Yeshivah Merkaz-Harav. He wrote and published distinguished Talmudic works and philosophic-poetical essays. He identified with the pioneers and exerted great influence on younger generations. His devotion and tolerance endeared him to all the builders of Palestine, the freethinking as well as the Orthodox. Every pioneer was close to his heart. When criticized for his tolerance of the irreligious **Halutzim**, he gave this characteristic reply: "When the Holy **Temple** existed, it was forbidden for a stranger or even an ordinary priest to enter in the Holy of Holies. Only the High Priest was permitted to enter it, and that but once a year during the Day of Atonement...However, when the Temple was being built, any worker engaged in the enterprise would go into its innermost chambers in his ordinary work clothes."

KORCZAK, JANUSZ (1878-1942). Polish writer and educator. He developed a theory of education based on treating children with respect, and was well known for his children books. He ran a home for children in the **Warsaw** ghetto during the Nazi occupation, and chose to go to his death when his charges were sent to a Nazi concentration camp.

Janusz Korczak.

KOSHER. *See* **Dietary Laws.**

KOSTELANETZ, ANDRE. *See* **Music.**

KOVNO. *See* **Lithuania.**

KOTSK, MENACHEM MENDEL. *See* **Hasidism.**

KOUFAX, SANDY. *See* **Sports.**

KOUSSEVITZKY, SERGE. *See* **Music.**

KOVNER, ABBA (1918-1987). Hebrew poet. Born in Crimea, he led a group of young Jews who escaped from **Vilna** during the Nazi occupation, and became known as a partisan commander. After the war he settled in Palestine and became a leading Israeli poet.

KREBS, SIR HANS ADOLF (1900-1981). Whitley Professor of Biochemistry at Oxford University from 1954 until his death. He was born in Hildesheim, **Germany**, and was educated in that country. He had to give up his post as lecturer in medicine at the University of Freiburg, Bavaria, and emigrate to **England** with the advent of the Nazis. He shared the 1953 **Nobel Prize** for Medicine for his discovery of the citric acid cycle which describes the chemical stages of oxidation of foodstuffs in living organisms.

KROCHMAL, NACHMAN (1785-1840). Hebrew philosopher and scholar. Born in Galicia, he shared his profound wisdom with students attracted by his philosophy of Jewish history. After his death his teachings were published in his *Guide for the Perplexed of the Age*. Like **Maimonides**, Krochmal sought to reconcile Jewish religious thought with modern ideas. He believed that the Jewish people had survived because they were endowed with an "absolute Spirit" that was universal and immortal. Krochmal stimulated the Jewish people to think of themselves, once again, as a nation.

KURDISTAN. The "Land of the Kurds" is not a separate country, but is divided among **Turkey**, **Iraq**, and **Iran**. Kurdistan stretches along the south shore of the Caspian Sea. The land is mountainous, with few roads. The Kurds are Moslems ruled by semi-independent tribal chiefs. Many Christian Armenians and Assyrians lived there at one time, but their numbers were greatly reduced by Kurdish massacres. According to an old legend, Kurdish Jews came to Kurdistan from Palestine in the time of **Ezra**, several centuries before the common era. They still speak **Aramaic** a dialect closely related to the language of the Gemara (*see* **Talmud**). Once they were nomads like the local Moslems, but later they settled down like the Kurdish Christians. Kurdistan has always remained uninfluenced by Western civilization. Jewish occupations included farming and fruit growing, shopkeeping, peddling, and handicrafts. Thousands of Kurdish Jews have gone to Israel, where their tall, stalwart figures, beards, and turbans became a familiar sight.

KVUTZAH. *See* **Kibbutz.**

LABAN. **Jacob**'s uncle and later father-in-law. He promised to let his daughter **Rachel** marry Jacob. On the wedding night he substituted **Leah**, Rachel's older sister. After Jacob worked for Laban for seven more years, Laban gave him Rachel as well. In Jewish tradition, Laban became known as a deceiver.

LABOR ZIONISM. Socialist Zionism originated at the close of the 19th century and had to struggle for followers among Jewish socialists who rejected Zionism as a "reactionary movement." Jewish socialists saw the solution of the Jewish problem in a Utopian world that socialism aimed to create for all people. The first Jewish leader to differ with the Marxist idea was Moses **Hess**, who held that Jewish people had the right to a place in humankind's family of nations. As the Socialist Zionist movement grew, it had to make its way against socialist ridicule and opposition. Nachman **Syrkin** and Ber **Borochov** were the leaders in this struggle. Syrkin saw in Socialist Zionism a modern expression of the Hebrew prophets' teachings of justice for all. He founded the first *Poale Zion*, or Workers of Zion, group in **London** in 1903. Borochov felt that the special problem of the Jewish masses could be solved only in a Jewish Socialist commonwealth in **Palestine**. At a conference in 1906, the various Russian Poale Zion groups reconciled their differences and formed the Jewish Social Democratic Party, Poale Zion of **Russia**. This body united with the Poale Zion groups of **Austria** and the United States in 1907 to form the Poale Zion Party as an autonomous body within the **World Zionist Organization**. The Labor Zionists came to Palestine as the famous pioneering Second Aliyah (1904-1914), which established agricultural cooperatives and organized the self-defense that guarded Jewish colonies from Arab attack. Before World War I, the Labor Zionists were divided into two parties: Poale Zion and the *Hapoel Hatzair*, or the Young Worker. The personality and "religion of labor" gospel of Aaron David **Gordon** exerted the greatest influence on both groups. The Poale Zion leaders in Palestine included David **BenGurion**, Yitzhak **Ben-Zvi**, and Berl **Katznelson**. In 1929, Poale Zion and Hapoel Hatzair merged to form *Mifleget Poale Eretz Israel*, the Party of the Workers of Israel. For decades, *Mapai*, the initials by which this party is known, was the largest political party in Israel. (*See also* **Hashomer Ha-tzair**.)

Jacob in the house of Laban.

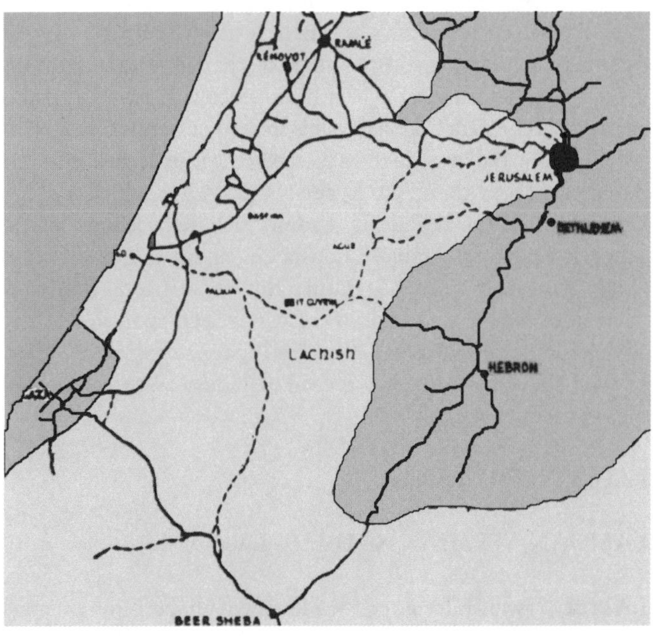

Location plan of Lachish development area.

LACHISH. Canaanite city kingdom conquered by **Joshua** in 1230 B.C.E. and allotted to Judah. It was rice, corn, vine, and olive-growing area lying astride the main trade routes to **Egypt** and Mesopotamia. Lachish was coveted and fought for by Israel's neighbors. Later, it was the scene of **Samson**'s triumphs and **David**'s victory over Goliath. Lachish was a link in the chain of fortresses which King Rehoboam built to guard the southern approaches to Jerusalem. It was attacked by Sennacherib and then by Nebuchadnezzar, as corroborated in the Lachish Letters discovered in 1935. After fourteen centuries of neglect, the 125,000 acres of the Lachish area on Israel's southern border are now being rehabilitated through agricultural settlement. Three training camps have been set up to prepare future settlers, and eight villages have already been established.

LADINO (Judeo-Spanish). When the Jews left **Spain** in 1492, the Spanish language was on the verge of change. The old form is preserved today only in the Jewish dialect called Ladino. It is also called Spaniolish or Castiliano. It is spoken by **Sephardic** Jews in **Turkey**, the Balkans, part of North Africa, in **Israel**, and the Americas. More than 20,000 persons in New York City speak Ladino. From the beginning, Ladino included Hebrew words. Later, it picked up Arabic, Turkish, Greek, French, and Italian words. It is usually printed in **Rashi** script, but in Turkey and Israel a few newspapers print Ladino in Latin letters. Spanish scholars often visit the **Sephardim** to collect old Spanish songs and sayings. In the U.S. there has been a revival of Ladino culture, reflected mainly in songs and folktales.

LAG B'OMER. *See* **Omer**.

LAMDAN, YITZHAK. *See* **Hebrew Literature.**

LAMED. Twelfth letter of the Hebrew alphabet; numerically, thirty.

LAMED VAV TZADDIKIM. Literally, 36 righteous men. The "secret saints" for whose sake the world survives. These secret saints are the center of many stories and mystic legends, all of them based on the saying in the **Talmud** by Abbaye that there are at least 36 righteous men in every generation. They are so pious and modest that they hide their learning and earn their bread by physical labor. According to this legend, before one of the Lamed Vav dies, another is born, and so the sinful world is saved from destruction.

LAMENTATIONS. Third of the five scrolls in the Writings section of the **Bible**. According to tradition, its author is the prophet **Jeremiah**. Lamentations consists of five beautiful elegies or poems of mourning lamenting the fall of **Jerusalem** and the destruction of the first **Temple**. The first four elegies are written in alphabetic acrostics, that is, each verse opens with a letter of the alphabet in consecutive order. Lamentations is chanted in the synagogue on the ninth day of the month of Ab, the day in 586 B.C.E. of the destruction of the Temple.

LANDAU, SAMUEL HAYIM (1892-1928). Religious Zionist leader and philosopher. Born to a Hasidic family in **Poland**, he rose at an early age to a high position of leadership in religious **Zionism**. He worked untiringly for Hapoel Hamizrachi, as well as for Hehalutz and Zionist fund-raising, at first in Poland and later in 1925 in Palestine. Landau was the founder of the movement within religious Zionism that stressed *Torah Ve-Avodah*, or traditional Judaism and labor.

LANDOWSKA, WANDA. *See* **Music**.

LASKER, EMANUEL (1868-1941). German-born world chess champion from 1894 to 1921. He wrote about chess and other subjects.

LASKER-SCHÜLER, ELSE (1876-1945). German-born poet who lived in Palestine from 1936 until her death. She was a leading German poet who turned to Jewish themes inspired by the prophets of Israel.

LATIN AMERICA. All of the Western Hemisphere south of the U.S.-Mexican border and north of Antarctica, including South America, Central America, **Mexico**, and the islands of the Caribbean. This large and variegated portion of the globe is known as Latin America because of the mark left upon it by its Spanish and Portuguese colonizers who spoke Romance languages which were derived from Latin. Spanish or Portuguese is still spoken in most Latin American countries.

Christopher **Columbus** had ventured to cross the Atlantic in search of the "Indies." He believed that by sailing westward he would discover a sea route to India, the home of silk, spices, elephants, gold, and all the "riches of the Orient." Instead, he stumbled on the Americas, which he believed to be the "West Indies." It was soon realized, however, that this was neither India nor the Indies, but a "New World" no less rich and exotic than the fabled Orient. Within 30 years this New World was overrun with Spanish and Portuguese adventurers intent on exploiting the wealth of their newly discovered empire which they came to call "New Spain."

As colonists settled in the Americas, traffic sprang up between New Spain and European countries. Ships bore rich ores to Europe and returned with manufactured goods for the colonies. Soon it was discovered that the riches of the New World lay not in metals alone. Sugar, tobacco, coffee, and other items that could be grown in the fertile valleys and tropical islands of the Americas commanded high prices on the markets of the old world. Trade boomed.

Among the masters of this trade were **Marranos**, Spanish Jews who had converted to Catholicism rather than go into exile or be burned at the stake. The year 1492, when Columbus discovered America, was a monumental year in the annals of Spain—but a dreaded one for Jews. That year, King Ferdinand and Queen Isabella, Columbus's patrons, finally expelled the last Moorish invaders from their land. Declaring Spain a Christian kingdom, they had banished all Jews from their dominions. Only those Jews who accepted Catholicism could remain. Though most chose exile, a good number, however, were baptized, continuing to practice their faith in secret. Such Jews were known as Marranos, or "new Christians," and were singled out for persecution by a branch of the Church known as the **Inquisition**. Seeking to escape the watchful eye of the Inquisition, many Jews had immigrated to the colonies. Experienced in trade and management, they soon prospered. Within a few decades, Marrano communities flourished in

Argentina, **Peru**, **Bolivia**, **Mexico**, and **Brazil**—in fact, wherever Spanish or Portuguese colonists had settled. In Brazil, they were pioneers in the sugar-growing and refining industry; in Bolivia, they monopolized local shipbuilding; elsewhere, they engaged in international commerce.

But their prosperity was short-lived, for the long arm of the Inquisition soon reached out to the New World. Established in Peru in 1569 and Mexico in 1570, it slowly succeeded in destroying virtually all Marrano settlements. In Mexico, even Don Luiz de Carvajal, governor of a province, was burned at the stake. Peru alone had 34 **auto-da-fes**, or acts of faith, between the establishment of the Inquisition and its abolition in 1806. Today, the only known survivors of the old Marrano communities are the Sabbatarios, descendants of Chilean Marranos who escaped to the middle of the continent and intermarried with Indians and Spaniards, and a community of 3,000 in Mexico who claim similar descent.

Not all the Marranos of New Spain and New Portugal were lost. Even at the peak of the Inquisition, there were some places of refuge for Jews in the New World. **England** and **Holland**, the two great mercantile powers of the 17th century, soon demanded a share of trade in the Western hemisphere. By force and by treaty they gained a number of colonies in Latin as well as North America. To such colonies persecuted Marranos could flee. Thus, when **Portugal** in 1654 expelled Brazilian Jews who had confessed their true faith during a brief period of Dutch rule, the exiles made their way to Dutch colonies in the Americas. Twenty-six of them reached the Dutch colony of New Amsterdam, forming the nucleus of the first Jewish congregation in what would become **New York**. Others found their way to Surinam (Dutch Guiana), Curacao, Jamaica, and other colonies held by either the British or Dutch. There they founded communities which survive to present day, the oldest with continuous history in the Western hemisphere.

Over the last 300 years, these settlements made up an historically important but numerically insignificant part of Latin American Jewry, for the bulk of the approximately 400,000 Jews who now live in Latin America are either immigrants or the children of immigrants who arrived fewer than 100 years ago.

Modern immigration began in the 19th century after most Latin American countries had gained their independence. First to arrive were traders and merchants chiefly from the **Sephardic** communities of the Balkans and the Middle East. After 1890, the pace of immigration quickened. Encouraged by the **Jewish Colonization Society** (I.C.A.), an organization which believed that Jewish suffering might be eased by a return to the soil, several thousand newcomers settled on farm colonies in Argentina and Brazil. The greatest influx, however, came between World War I and II. After the U.S. curtailed immigration in 1924, the stream of newcomers from Eastern Europe turned to Latin America. During the 1930's, thousands of German Jews fleeing Nazi persecution settled there. Partly because of the pressure of this immigration and partly because of Nazi propaganda, most Latin American countries closed their gates to refugees in the mid 1930's. Only after World War II were the doors opened to limited numbers of refugees and displaced persons.

Bringing new skills and initiative, these Jews played an important role in the development of Latin American commerce and industry. Most of the immigrants settled in cities where they pursued their old occupations: trade, manufacturing of textiles, furs, furniture, and crafts. New business techniques included installment and direct sales, techniques which opened consumer markets to even the poorest. To the field of banking they introduced "people's banks," cooperative institutions which lend small sums at low interest rates.

The various Latin American communities vary widely in size, organization, and problems. Argentina, the largest settlement, has 250,000 Jews in a highly organized community. All organized settlements participate in the **World Jewish Congress**. Although most communities are clearly subdivided into Sephardic, Ashkenazic (East European), and German Jewish sectors, these subsectors generally unite to participate in national Jewish organizations.

One problem shared by most of the settlements is **anti-Semitism**. During the 1930's and 1940's, Nazi agents actively instigated hatred toward the Jewish population, but their efforts were only partly effective. Since the end of World War II, the problem has become less acute. One sign of change is the favorable attitude of most Latin American governments toward **Israel**, reflected in their voting record in the United Nations. Countries such as Argentina have favored Israel in matters of trade.

Having suffered persecution in their lands of origin and sometimes in their new home as well, Latin American Jews are for the most part ardent Zionists. Almost all communities have Zionist organizations, through which they have made considerable contributions to the development of Israel. Many Latin American Jews, particularly the young, have immigrated to Israel in the past 35 years. In some countries, the Jewish schools are under Zionist control.

LATVIA. Jews have lived in Latvia since the 16th century. There were 2,000 Jews in 1795 when it was annexed by **Russia**. In 1919, when Latvia became independent, Jews were able to develop an active Jewish life, forming schools and organizations. In 1940, the Soviet Union overran Latvia and deported many Jews to Siberia. In 1941, the Nazis occupied Latvia, and some 75,000 Jews fell into their hands. Ghettos were set up in Riga, Dvinsk, Libau, and elsewhere, and by the end of the war most of those Jews perished. After the war some 30,000 Jews returned to Latvia from Russia, but since then a large number has immigrated to **Israel**.

LAUDER, ESTÉE (1910-). American cosmetics magnate. Born in **Hungary**, in 1946 she formed the Estée Lauder company which became a top cosmetics firm known for skin care.

LAUTERBERG, FRANK (1924-). U.S. Democratic Senator from **New Jersey**. He started out as a businessman who developed ADP into a leading computing services company, and became active in Jewish communal life. As senator, he pursued liberal issues such as protection of the environment.

LAW, JEWISH. *See* **Talmud**.

LAWS OF NOAH. Seven biblical laws which according to the rabbis are binding upon the human race. They concern the prohibition of idolatry, blasphemy, murder, adultery, robbery, and eating of flesh cut from a living animal. They encourage the establishment of courts of justice.

LAZARUS, EMMA (1849-1887). American poet. Born in **New York** to an affluent **Sephardic** family, she eventually brought her talent to Hebraic themes. News stories of bloody persecutions of the Jews in **Russia**, followed by contact with refugees in New York, inspired her prose and animated her poetry. "The New Colossus," written on a single sheet of paper and now inscribed on a plaque imbedded in the Statue of Liberty, constitutes an invocation of welcome to the immigrants.

Emma Lazarus.

LEAH. **Jacob**'s first wife and mother of **Reuben**, **Simeon**, **Levi**, **Judah**, **Issachar**, and **Zebulun**.

LEBANON. Literally, white; named after its snow-capped peaks. An independent republic since 1944, Lebanon occupies a mountain range that runs almost parallel with the Mediterranean, north of **Israel**, for about 100 miles, rising at its highest point to 10,000 feet. The country is divided by the Coelesyria, or El Baka Valley into Lebanon on the west and Anti-Lebanon on the east. Lebanon was famous in antiquity for its cedar forests (long since destroyed by reckless cutting), which provided timber for the First and Second **Temples** in **Jerusalem**. In 1998, its population of about 3.4 million included a Christian (that is, Maronite) majority, as well as Moslems and Druzes.

The Jewish community, concentrated mainly in Beirut, has dwindled over the years. A statute passed in 1952 granted the community a large degree of autonomy in internal affairs. Although Lebanon participated in the Arab invasion of Israel in 1948, Lebanese Jewry has enjoyed better treatment than any other Jewish community in the Arab World. There is nonetheless a complete ban on travel and emigration, and Jews are excluded from army and government positions.

During the **Six-Day War**, Lebanon did not participate in the fighting. However, two and a half years later, Palestinian Arab guerillas began to infiltrate into Lebanon and use the southern part of the country as a base for raids into Israeli territory. When it became obvious that the Lebanon government was unable to put an end to these attacks, Israel retaliated in the areas from which the guerillas operated.

In 1982, Israel launched Operation Peace for Galilee, designed to secure its southern border from terrorist infiltration from Lebanon, where the Palestine Liberation Organization (PLO) became, in effect, a state within a state. As a result of the war, the PLO was ousted from Beirut and their military base in Lebanon was destroyed, creating hopes for a unified Lebanon and the possibility of an Israeli-Lebanese peace treaty in 1983. This treaty was abrogated by Lebanon in 1984, owing to internal Moslem and Druze pressure and Syrian opposition. In 1998, both Israeli and Syrian troops were still stationed in Lebanon.

LEESER, ISAAC (1806-1868). American religious leader. A rabbi and founder of Maimonides College in **Philadelphia**, he came to the U.S. while still in his teens. He became a journalist and editor. In 1829, he became Rabbi of Congregation Mikveh Israel in Philadelphia, where he introduced an English sermon into synagogue services. He opposed Reform and carried on a strenuous campaign for the preservation of traditional Judaism. His work and thought were reflected in the pages of *The Occident*, a magazine he edited for 26 years. His 1853 Bible translation served American Jewry as the accepted English version for more than 50 years.

> *Give me your tired, your poor,*
> *Your huddled masses yearning to breathe free.*
> *The wretched refuse of your teeming shore,*
> *Send these, the homeless, tempest-tost to me,*
> *I lift my lamp beside the golden door!*
>
> — EMMA LAZARUS, "THE NEW COLOSSUS"

LEGION, JEWISH. In 1915, during World War I, under the leadership of Joseph **Trumpeldor**, a Zion Mule Corps was founded and served with the British in the Gallipoli Expeditionary Force. This corps' record for bravery helped break down British resistance to establishing of a Jewish Legion. Such a legion, the Royal Fusiliers, was organized in 1917 in London after much effort by Vladimir **Jabotinsky**. In 1918, recruiting for the Jewish Legion began in the United States. David **Ben-Gurion**, later Prime Minister of Israel, Yitzhak **Ben-Zvi**, and Pinhas Rutenberg were the chief architects of the Legion movement in the United States. The Jewish Legion numbered 5,000 and was a part of the British Army that wrested Samaria, the **Galilee**, and Trans-Jordan from the Turks. Another 5,000 men were due to join them, but the Armistice was proclaimed before their arrival.

LEHMAN, HERBERT HENRY (1878-1963). American legislator and statesman. In 1928, he was elected Lieutenant Governor of **New York** and succeeded Roosevelt as Governor in 1932, an office he held for ten years. When the depression started in 1929, Lehman's liberal legislation in such fields as welfare and labor brought economic stability to the state. In 1949, he was elected to the U.S. Senate, where he opposed the McCarran-Walter immigration bill and supported sending arms to Israel. For more than half a century, his numerous philanthropic activities included interest in child welfare institutions, hospitals, and vocational schools. He was active in many Jewish organizations and causes.

Herbert H. Lehman.

LEONARD, BENNY. *See* **Sports.**

LEVENSON, SAM. *See* **Stage and Screen.**

LEVI. Third son of **Jacob** and **Leah.** The tribe of Levi received no allotment of land in **Canaan,** because it was set apart to conduct the worship of God. Instead, the Levites received for their maintenance a portion of the tithes brought by the worshipers to the Temple. (*See also* **Kohen.**)

LEVI BEN GERSHON (GERSONIDES) (1288-1344). Astronomer, mathematician, and philosopher. Born in **France,** he commented on the **Bible,** Aristotelian philosophy, and the **Talmud.** He devised an instrument used in navigation for measuring angular separation between astronomical bodies. His major philosophical work, *Milhamot Adonai*, deals with contemporary Jewish philosophical questions. His views were controversial because, unlike **Maimonides,** he did not always let the Bible be the final word when facing a contradiction between Judaism and Greek philosophy.

LEVI, PRIMO (1919-1987). Italian Jewish writer and chemist. He survived **Auschwitz** and wrote searing memoirs about his experience. His books rank among the most memorable of the **Holocaust.**

LEVI-STRAUSS, CLAUDE (1908-). French philosopher and anthropologist. His studies of culture, linguistics, and mythologies have had a profound influence on 20th century sociology, architecture, literature, and art.

LEVI YITZHAK OF BERDITCHEV. *See* **Hasidism.**

LEVIATHAN. Legendary sea creature described in several places in the Bible, particularly in Job 40. The **Talmud** and Midrash describe the leviathan as a huge fish coiled around the entire globe, reserved for the feast of the righteous in the world-to-come.

LEVI ISAAC OF BERDICTCHEV. *See* **Hasidism.**

LEVIN, MEYER (1905-1981). American novelist. He wrote books on a variety of Jewish subjects, including Hasidic legends and novels about Israel and the Holocaust. His best known work includes *The Old Bunch, Compulsion, Eva*, and *The Fanatic.*

LEVINE, JAMES. *See* **Music.**

LEVINSKY, BATTLING. *See* **Sports.**

LEVINSOHN, ADAM HACOHEN. *See* **Hebrew Literature.**

LEVINSOHN, MICAH JOSEPH. *See* **Hebrew Literature.**

LEVITES. Descendants of **Levi,** the third son of Jacob. From ages 20 to 50, the Levite was consecrated to render service at the Sanctuary where the Israelites worshiped God by bringing sacrifices to the altar. They were gatekeepers and caretakers of the sanctuary and its furnishings; they were judges, teachers of the Law and scribes, temple musicians, and assistants to the priests. Since the tribe of Levi had received no land in Canaan, the Levites were assigned the revenues from 40 cities, as well as certain tithes from all crops and produce. They assisted the prophet **Samuel** at Shiloh in the **Tabernacle** services and in teaching the people. In the First **Temple,** built by **Solomon** in **Jerusalem,** they were the musicians and singers, and performed the menial tasks as well. When the Temple was rebuilt after the Babylonian exile, the Levites led the joyous recession at the dedication festival. When **Ezra** and **Nehemiah** instituted the Great Assemblies and read the Law to the people, the Levites circulated among them explaining and teaching its meaning. To this day, when all traces of the various tribes of Israel have long been erased by the centuries, the tradition of descent from the Levites is still handed down. At synagogue services, a Levite is called up to the reading of the Torah second after a kohen, or priest.

LEVITICUS. Literally, relating to the Levites. Third of the five books of Moses. It contains a manual for Levites, the priestly ritual of sacrifices, the Code of Holiness, rules regarding charity, marriage, and laws governing many other phases of life.

LEVY, ASSER (d. 1681). His full name was Asser Levy van Swellem. He was one of the original band of 23 pilgrims who came to **New York** in 1654. From a penniless immigrant he rose to be a man of property and importance in the community. He initiated several lawsuits which resulted in the clarification of Jewish rights in New Amsterdam. Notable among these was the right to stand guard along with fellow-burghers, rather than pay a tax to be exempt from military duty. A novel by Louis Zara, *Blessed Is the Land*, commemorates Levy's life and accomplishments.

LEVY, URIAH PHILLIPS (1792-1862). U.S. naval officer. He led the crusade to abolish flogging as a form of discipline in the U.S. Navy. Levy's opposition to this and other accepted practices, as well as his Jewishness, made him a target of petty persecution, abuse, imprisonment, and six court-martials. Finally vindicated by an official court of inquiry, he rose in rank from cabin boy to Commodore and flag-officer of the Navy in the Mediterranean under President Abraham Lincoln. In March 1943, the Navy named a destroyer in the memory of Uriah Phillips Levy.

Uriah P. Levy. From the collection of Capt. N. Taylor Phillips.

LEWIS, JERRY. *See* **Stage and Screen.**

LEWISOHN, LUDWIG (1883-1955). American novelist, critic, and outstanding writer on modern Jewish problems. Between 1920 and 1924, a great personal change transformed Lewisohn from an assimilated Jew to one deeply absorbed in his Jewishness. He

Ludwig Lewisohn.

became an active Zionist. With *The Island Within* in 1928, he emerged as primarily a Jewish writer. In this book he analyzed the problems of the assimilated Jew, the difficulties of intermarriage, and the spiritual enrichment that flowed from a rediscovery of Judaism. The last years of Lewisohn's life were spent at **Brandeis University** where as Professor of Comparative Literature, a Jew, a Zionist, and a literary stylist, he influenced young minds.

LIEBERMAN, JOSEPH (1942-). U.S. Democratic Senator from **Connecticut**. He took strong stands on defense, anti-crime legislation, and aid to small business. He was also known as a staunch supporter of Israel.

LIEBERMANN, MAX (1847-1935). Artist. A Berlin native, he followed in the footsteps of Joseph **Israels** and painted Dutch themes. In **Amsterdam** he was attracted by the same colorful ghetto scenes that had fascinated **Rembrandt**. In his old age Liebermann became famous as a painter of portraits of outstanding statesmen, educators, and civic leaders. These portraits are notable for their realistic vigor. He served as president of the Prussian Academy of Arts from 1919 until the Nazis ousted him in 1933.

LIFE, SANCTITY OF. In Judaism, human life is the highest value. Saving a single life is considered equal to saving the entire universe. A Jew is allowed to break a religious law in order to save a life, a practice known as *pikuach nefesh*. Life is seen as the here-and-now, whereas the afterlife is something beyond the purview of this life (*see* **Heaven and Hell**). Judaism does not promote asceticism, removing oneself from the community, or denying oneself the pleasures of this life. A healthy and joyful life is considered the best way to serve **God.** (*See also* **Hasidism**).

LIKUD. *See* **Israel, Government and Parties**.

LILIENBLUM, MOSHE LEIB (1843-1910). Writer, leader in the Enlightenment movement, and early Zionist. Lilienblum's desire for secular education brought him to Odessa. Disillusioned by the lack of spiritual values, he wrote a revealing account of his life called *Hatot Neurim* (Sins of Youth), in which he struck at the evils of ghetto life. After the 1881 pogrom in **Russia**, Lilienblum favored Jewish settlement in Palestine.

LILITH. A female demon and consort of Satan, or Samael. According to one legend in Jewish tradition, she was **Adam**'s first wife.

LINOWITZ, SOL (1913-). American businessman and public figure. He was CEO of the Xerox company which became a major corporation under his leadership. From 1966 to 1969 he was U.S. ambassador to the Organizations of American States, and in 1977 he helped negotiate the Panama Canal Treaty. He was active in Jewish affairs for many years.

LIPPMANN, WALTER (1889-1974). Leading American social and political commentator of the 20th century. His political columns shaped the thinking of many Americans. His books include *A Preface to Politics*, *The Good Society*, and *The Public Philosophy*.

LIPCHITZ, JACQUES (1891-1973). Sculptor. Born in **Lithuania,** he migrated to France, from where he fled during World War II to the U.S. He drew much inspiration from the Bible, and from his experiences as a Jew. Explaining his bronze statue of *Jacob Wrestling with the Angel*, he said: "Man is wrestling with the angel; it is a tremendous struggle, but he wins, and is blessed." Other pieces of Jewish interest include *The Prayer* (an old man performing the **kapparot** ceremony) and *The Miracle*, a tribute to the new state of Israel (a figure, arms raised, facing the Tables of the Law, out of which grows the seven-branched candelabrum). Toward the end of his life he became interested in the Lubavitch Hasidic movement.

LIPSKY, LOUIS (1876-1963). American Zionist leader and writer. As an editor and columnist for various publications, he was introduced into Jewish public life. In 1899, he founded the *Maccabaean*, editing this monthly official Zionist publication. It was transformed into the weekly *New Palestine* in 1918. Lipsky was active in the **American Jewish Congress** from its inception in 1918, and was largely responsible for founding the **World Jewish Congress.** He served as a member of the Jewish delegation to the **Versailles Peace Conference** in 1919, and as a writer, orator, and parliamentarian, he participated in every phase of American Zionist life from the beginning of the 20th century. Lipsky achieved recognition as one of the foremost thinkers in American Zionism and served as President of the **Zionist Organization of America** from 1921 to 1931.

Louis Lipsky. Courtesy American Zionist Council.

LITHUANIA. Jews settled in Lithuania in the 14th century, coming from **Germany** and **Poland,** and were treated well by the local pagan rulers. Most were farmers, artisans, and estate managers. During this period, intermarriage between the ruling families of Lithuania and Poland drew the two countries closer, bringing Lithuania under the influence of Catholicism and reversing the favorable treatment of Jews.

In 1495, the Grand Duke Alexander expelled all Jews from the country. The expulsion edict remained in force for eight years. After returning in 1503, Jews resumed their respected place in the economic life of the country. By the mid-16th century, the influence of the Church and the enmity of the lower nobility intensified, and laws restricting Jewish dress and occupations were passed. The political union of Lithuania and Poland in 1569 brought no marked change to the Jewish position. On the whole, the rulers of the country protected the Jews from excessive restrictions. The Jewish population enjoyed a measure of self-rule within their own communities.

The Miracle, by Jacques Lipchitz.

From 1623 to 1764, Jewish religious, economic, and social life was regulated by the Council of Four Lands (*see* **Kahal**), within which the important Jewish communities of Lithuania were represented. During the years of the Cossack uprisings which began in 1648 and were led by Chmielnicki, thousands of Jews were slaughtered and many communities in Lithuania destroyed. A partial healing of the wounds inflicted by the Cossacks came in the following century. The Jewish community of Lithuania became a center of Jewish learning. Great influence on the spiritual life of Jews was exerted by Rabbi **Elijah Gaon** of Vilna. His pupils, especially Hayim of Volozhin, were the founders of famous Talmudical academies, or yeshivot, in the country. Lithuanian Jewry played an important role in the dispute between **Hasidism** and their opponents, Mitnagdim. The bulk of Lithuanian Jewry remained aloof from the Hasidic movement, and was primarily devoted to the study of the **Talmud**.

During the late 19th century, Lithuania became fertile ground for the growth of the **Haskalah**, or Enlightenment movement. Here, modern Hebrew literature flourished and produced some of the greatest Hebrew writers: Micah Joseph Levinsohn, Abraham **Mapu**, and J.L. **Gordon**. Later in the 19th century, the Zionist movement, as well as the Socialist **Bund**, found numerous followers among Lithuanian Jewry. During the same period, due to economic hardships and Tsarist persecutions, a large number of Lithuanian Jews emigrated to the United States, South Africa, and other countries, where they established flourishing Jewish communities.

After World War I, Lithuania became an independent republic. In 1919, the Lithuanian government appointed a Ministry of Jewish Affairs and granted Jews full cultural autonomy. Jews enjoyed these rights for five years before they were curtailed and economic restrictions instituted. However, Jews retained some of their cultural autonomy and developed a government-supported school system with Hebrew and Yiddish as the languages of instruction. Lithuania also remained a center of Talmudic study. Yeshivot continued to exist in Slobodka, Telz, Panevezsh, and a number of other cities.

At the outbreak of the World War II, nearly 170,000 Jews (about 7% of the general population), lived in Lithuania, 40,000 of them in Kovno, the capital of the country. In 1940, Lithuania was annexed by Soviet Russia, only to fall into the hands of Nazi Germany in the following year. In 1942, mass murders of Jews were carried out with the help of the local populace, until almost all Lithuanian Jews were wiped out, save only those few who had managed to flee to other countries.

After World War II, Lithuania was incorporated into the Soviet Union. In 1993, after Lithuania gained independence from the former Soviet Union, the number of Jews remaining in Vilna and Kovno was about 8,000. Although a few synagogues still function in the cities of Vilna and Kovno, Jewish culture and educational institutions are virtually nonexistent. In 1997, the Lithuanian postal service issued a commemorative stamp of the Gaon of Vilna, now recognized as a Lithuanian historical personality.

LITERATURE, HEBREW. *See* **Hebrew Literature.**

LITERATURE, YIDDISH. *See* **Yiddish Literature.**

LOD. *See* **Lydda**.

LOEW, JUDAH BEN BEZALEL (ca. 1525-1609). Talmudic scholar and astronomer in **Prague**. He was greatly interested in science, an unusual pursuit for a rabbi of his time. Rabbi Judah's advanced views were evident in his many books, in which he criticized the state of Jewish education and expressed ideas which centuries later became known as **Zionism**. Known in Jewish scholarship as the Maharal, he published about 20 books, the most famous of which is a commentary on **Rashi**. He was considered extraordinary, and many legends are woven around his personality. The most famous of these tells about the creation of the **Golem**, an automaton made of clay and brought to life by the Maharal's use of the secret name of God. According to this legend, the Maharal used the Golem during times of stress to save the Jewish community from persecution and evil decrees. As soon as the Golem had fulfilled his mission, the Maharal would return him to his lifeless state. The legend of the Golem has been the theme of many poems, novels, and plays.

Jewish folklore is rich with anecdotes about the wisdom of the Maharal, and the miracles that he performed. His interest in alchemy was probably at the root of his fame as a miracle-maker. Rudolph II of Austria, who took an interest in astronomy and hoped to become wealthy by the use of alchemy, discussed the subject with the Maharal. A statue of the Maharal was erected in front of the city hall of Prague.

LOEWE, FREDERICK. *See* **Music**.

LONDON. Jews have resided in **England**'s capital as early as the Norman Conquest in 1066, if not earlier. For religious and security reasons they lived as a compact community, whose site is remembered by the name of one of the city's oldest streets, Old Jewry.

There was little peace for Jews in those early times. As moneylenders they were not likely to endear themselves to the barons who were in their debt or to peasants who, urged on by fanatical priests, blamed Jews for their woes. However, as the property of the king (and called the "king's chattels"), Jews were under royal protection. But this privilege was withdrawn when, after a series of extortions, Jews were expelled by Edward I in 1290.

A new and happier chapter began with the readmission of Jews in 1656 under Oliver Cromwell. At first, the handful of **Sephardim** from the Mediterranean countries who lived in London met for worship in their small synagogue on Creechurch Lane. However, with the arrival of more Sephardim from Holland, a larger synagogue was erected in 1701 at Bevis Marks. It still stands today, cherished as the mother synagogue of English Jews.

In the wake of the **Sephardim** came the **Ashkenazim** from Central Europe, and they too set up their special house of worship at Duke's Place, where they met for prayer as early as 1690.

London has always been the home of England's Jewish communal institutions: the **Board of Deputies of British Jews**, the elected representative body of British Jewry (1760); the Jewish Board of Guardians (1859); the United Synagogue (1870); **Jews' College** (1855); the Anglo-Jewish Association (1871), and a network of educational, social, and philanthropic institutions. London is also the seat of the Chief Rabbinate of the British Commonwealth, the **Jewish Colonization Association** (ICA), the Maccabi World Union, and the Sephardi World Federation. London's first Jewish Lord Mayor was Sir David Salomons, elected in 1855. The Lord Mayor Sir Bernard Waley-Cohen elected in September 1960 was Jewish. The famous London school, the Jews' Free School, and the old and beloved Ashkenazic Great Synagogue at Duke's Place were demolished by enemy action in World War II.

Today, the Jewish population is roughly 210,000 out of a total London population of about 7.5 million. The mass of Jewish immigrants came from **Russia** and **Poland** beginning in 1882, fleeing Tsarist pogroms. They settled largely in the East End of the metropolis. These immigrants were largely responsible for developing the tailoring, cabinet making, fur trade, and similar industries. In recent years, Jews have moved into the outer suburbs of London. (*See also* **England**.)

LOPEZ, AARON (ca. 1731-1782). Born in **Portugal**, Lopez came to the U.S. with his wife and child and settled in Newport, R.I. He became a successful merchant esteemed by the entire community. Denied naturalization by **Rhode Island**, he was the first Jew to be naturalized in Massachusetts. Lopez owned many ships which, along with his personal fortune, he placed at the disposal of the American Revolution.

LOS ANGELES. With more than half a million Jews, Los Angeles is the second largest Jewish community in the U.S., after **New York**. Jewish life began in the mid-19th century but did not boom until the end of World War I when large numbers of Jews moved there from eastern U.S. In 1911, the Jewish Federation was founded, followed in 1934 by the Jewish Community Council, representing most Jewish organizations.

Los Angeles has more than 50 synagogues, including some of the largest in the country. It has a large Jewish education system, including day schools, and branches of both the **Hebrew Union College** (Reform) and the **Jewish Theological Seminary** (Conservative). It has Jewish museums, including a Holocaust museum, and the Simon Wiesenthal Center. Jewish weekly newspapers include the *B'nai B'rith Messenger*, the *California Jewish Voice*, the *Los Angeles Reporter*, and *Heritage*.

Jews in the 20th century have played a prominent part in the motion picture industry in the city, as producers, actors, script writers, and technical support (*see* **Stage and Screen**).

LOST TRIBES. Ten tribes that composed the Kingdom of **Israel**. When Sargon, King of the Assyrian Empire, completed the conquest of the Kingdom of Israel in 722 B.C.E., he led most of the population into exile. Ever since then, the ultimate fate of these exiles has been the subject of innumerable theories and legends. The **Talmud** presents contradictory opinions. One maintains that the ten tribes were assimilated with the populations among which they lived. Another opinion holds that they survived and joined the exiles from Judea in 6th century B.C.E. who returned to their homeland in the time of **Ezra** and **Nehemiah**.

Medieval Jewish writing is full of references to one or another of the Lost Tribes. Some of the travelers of the Middle Ages, notably Eldad the Danite, claimed to have visited among them. Eldad claimed to have found these tribes in North Africa. Some of them, he said, were called the "sons of Moses" and lived guarded by the **Sambatyon**, a river made impassable six days in the week by its turbulent, stone-throwing waters. To this day, Yemenite Jews and the Bene Israel of **Afghanistan** claim to be descended from the ancient Israelites. Various theories have identified the Tatars, the holy Shindai class of **Japan**, and the American Indians, in turn, as the Lost Tribes. The most popular of these theories, claiming more than a million followers in **England** and the U.S., identifies the people of the British Isles as the Lost Tribes.

LOUISIANA. The Jewish community of Louisiana is one of the oldest in the U.S. Under Roman Catholic rule in the 18th century, the state allowed no religion except Catholicism, yet Jewish life started as early as 1719. In 1828, the first synagogue, Shaaray Chesed, was built in the capital, New Orleans, home to several historical synagogues. During the Civil War, Jews from the state served in the Confederate Army. Three Louisiana ved in the U.S. Senate in the 19th century: Judah Benjamin, Michael Hahn (also governor), and Benjamin Jonas. Today, of Louisiana's 16,000 Jews, 13,000 live in New Orleans, 1,500 in Baton Rouge, and fewer than 1,000 in Shreveport.

Shreveport
Baton Rouge
New Orleans

LUBETKIN, ZIVIA. *See* **Warsaw**.

LUBAVITCH HASIDIM. *See* **Shneerson**.

LUCKMAN, SID. *See* **Sports**.

LUDOMIR, MAID OF (1805-1892). First and perhaps only female Hasidic leader. Hannah Rachel, daughter of Monesh Werbermacher, was known for her piety as a child. After recovering from a long illness, she started to follow Hasidic practice, put on **tefillin** daily, and built her own synagogue. Thousands of Hasidim came to hear her speak. In her old age she traveled to Palestine where she died.

LUDWIG, EMIL (1881-1948). German Jewish biographer, novelist, and playwright. He achieved fame with a series of biographies which include lives of **Jesus**, Bismarck, and Lincoln. In 1932, on the eve of the Nazis' seizure of the German government, Ludwig became a citizen of **Switzerland**. Several years later, the

Nazis burned his books. During World War II Ludwig lived in the U.S. The genre of the critical biography, stressing character and psychology, rather than history, is considered Ludwig's outstanding creative achievement.

LULAV. *See* **Sukkot**.

LURIA, ISAAC. *See* **Kabbalah**.

LUZZATO, MOSES HAIM (1707-1746). Scholar, mystic, poet, and dramatist. Born in Padua, **Italy**, Luzzato acquired great knowledge of the **Talmud**, as well as of classical and modern languages and literature. As a young man, he immersed himself in the study of Jewish mysticism, or **Kabbalah**. This preoccupation led him to believe that the secrets of the **Torah** had been revealed to him by an angel. The rabbis in Italy saw in his fantastic visions the dangerous possibility of a new Messianic movement. Still reeling from the **Sabbatai Zevi** tragedy, they prohibited Luzzato, under threat of excommunication, to study Kabbalah. Consequently, Luzzato moved to **Amsterdam** where he worked as a diamond polisher. In his spare time, he wrote poetry, as well as works of scholarship, mystic philosophy, and ethics. An innovator in Hebrew literature, Luzzato was particularly effective in his allegorical dramas. His classic style, use of symbolism, and ethical thinking exerted considerable influence.

In 1743, Luzzato settled in **Safed**, Palestine, the city of the mystics. A few years later he fell victim to a plague in **Acre**.

LUZZATO, SAMUEL DAVID (1800-1865). Hebrew scholar, thinker, and poet. Born in Trieste, **Italy**, he devoted his entire life to the study of philology, literature, philosophy, and history. Great Jewish scholars, such as **Zunz**, **Geiger**, and **Graetz**, drew on his vast knowledge.

Luzzato was also a religious thinker and a notable poet. Living at a time when assimilation threatened traditional Jewish life, Luzzato stressed the superiority of Judaism. In a number of articles and poems he expressed his hope for the restoration of Zion and his love for the Hebrew language. As a teacher of Bible, history, and religious philosophy at the Rabbinical College at Padua, Italy, he carried on a voluminous correspondence with Jewish scholars around the world. Published after his death, his letters fill nine volumes and served as a great reservoir of knowledge in all fields of Jewish literature from biblical to modern times.

Immigrants arrive at the Lod Airport (now Ben-Gurion Airport) from the Soviet Union after the Yom Kippur War of 1973.

LYDDA (Lod). Ancient town southeast of **Tel Aviv**, on the road to the Judean hills. Lydda had a considerable population after the Jewish return from Babylonian captivity in 537 B.C.E., serving as an important commercial center between **Damascus** and **Egypt**. The Romans called it Diospolis, "the City of God," and burned it down during the **Bar Kokhba** revolt. In the 2nd and 3rd centuries, Lod was known for its Talmudical academy. It was conquered by the Israel Army during the War of Independence in 1948. Israel's largest airport is now located near the town.

Overleaf: Jewish musicians in Eastern Europe. A relief on a copper plate by Haim Goldberg. Courtesy Zionist Archives and Library.

MAABARAH (plural, *Maabarot*). Transition camps in Israel in the early years of the state built to accommodate the vast numbers of immigrants who streamed into the country. *Maabarot* were set up in large towns or in development areas where employment was available. Each family was provided with a hut or tent and some essential equipment, and offered an opportunity to work for a living. By the end of 1952, there were *maabarot* with a population of 230,000, extending from the **Galilee** to the **Negev**. By the late 1950's nearly all the *maabarot* had either been liquidated or turned into permanent settlements.

MAARIV. *See* **Prayer**.

MACCABEE, JUDAH. *See* **Maccabees**.

MACCABEES. Name given to Judah and his brothers of the Hasmonean priestly family from the town of Modin near Jerusalem. The Maccabees led the struggle from 167-160 B.C.E. against Antiochus Epiphanes, King of **Syria**, freeing Judea from Syrian oppression. The family consisted of the father, Mattathias, and his five sons, Johanan, Simon, Judah, Eliezer, and Jonathan. Judah was dubbed Maccabee, or "The Hammer," alluding to the way in which he pounded his enemies.

The Seleucid rulers of Syria sought to establish their empire over the lands that had originally been conquered by **Alexander the Great**. They wrested control of Judea from Egypt, then tried to force the Greek culture and religion on the Jews. In 167 B.C.E., when Antiochus prohibited the practice of Judaism and the Temple was desecrated, the peaceful farmers of Judea transformed into warriors. Led by Mattathias and his sons, they rebelled against the Syrians. Few in number, untrained, and poorly armed, they fought for a year as guerillas in the hills and mountain passes of Judea. When Mattathias died in 166 B.C.E., Judah took over leadership. The little army of farmers repeatedly defeated the trained legions sent against them, captured arms and supplies, and grew in numbers. In several successful battles, the Maccabees achieved great victories against overwhelming odds. In 165 B.C.E., they entered Jerusalem. The Temple was cleared and worship restored, giving rise to the festival of **Hanukkah**.

In the foreground, maabarah. In the background, new housing for immigrants temporarily living in the maabarah. Courtesy Israel Office of Information.

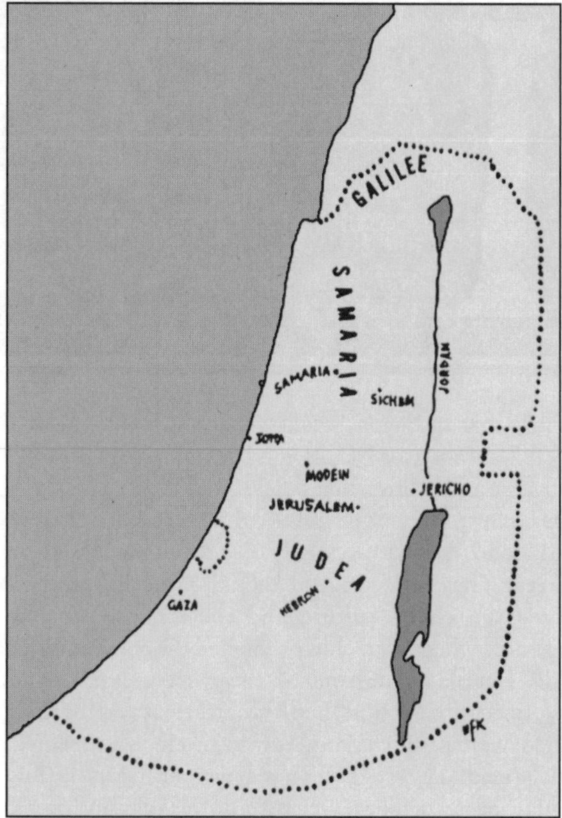

Palestine in the Hasmonean Period.

To secure their victory, the Maccabees undertook expeditions against the hostile neighbors who had aided the Syrians. In one of the ensuing battles, Eliezer was killed, crushed by a war elephant he had stabbed. Another brother, Johanan, fell in a battle with an Arabian tribe. In 160 B.C.E., when the Syrians returned to conquer Judea, Judah Maccabee, leading 800 men, faced a huge Syrian force and died in battle. Jonathan succeeded Judah, carried on the struggle with the Syrians, and strengthened Judea and widened its boundaries. In 143 B.C.E., he was treacherously killed by a Syrian general who had posed as his friend. Simon, the last of the five Maccabee brothers, was elected as ruler and high priest. Beloved by the people, Simon governed them and served as their high priest, leaving the military activities to his sons when he became old.

MACCABIAH. *See* **Sports.**

MACHPELAH. Cave near Hebron. When **Sarah** died, **Abraham** purchased it from Ephron the Hittite (Gen. 23). It became the burial crypt of the **patriarchs** and **matriarchs** and a place of pilgrimage. Long held as a Moslem shrine, admission was denied to non-Moslems until after the **Six-Day War.**

MAGEN DAVID. Literally, shield of David. The six-cornered star made by overlapping two triangles is an ancient and widespread symbol. Many ancient architectural ruins carry the engraving of this Hebrew seal. The 3rd- or 4th-century synagogue dug up in Capernaum, Israel, has not only the six-pointed Magen David upon it, but also the rarer five-pointed Seal of Solomon. In 1345, the Emperor Charles IV permitted Jews of **Prague** to use a flag bearing "the Shield of David and the Seal of Solomon" upon a red field. In modern times, the Shield of David has been the symbol of **Zionism** and the State of **Israel.**

MAGEN DAVID ADOM (MDA). Literally, Red Shield of David. Israel's emergency medical, health, and disaster service was authorized by the Knesset on July 12, 1950. It was entrusted to carry out the functions assigned by the Geneva Convention, equivalent to other Red Cross societies. MDA cooperates with the international Red Cross in disaster areas throughout the world.

American Red Magen David for Israel (ARMD) is the support arm in the U.S. A member organization with chapters throughout the country, it educates and involves members in activities of MDA. It raises funds for MDA's emergency medical services, including collection and distribution of blood and blood products for Israel's military and civilian population. It also supplies ambulances, bloodmobiles, and mobile cardiac rescue units serving all hospitals and communities throughout Israel. Finally, it supports MDA's 73 emergency medical stations and helps provide training equipment for voluntary paramedical corps.

MAGGID. Literally, to tell. The Maggid was a folk preacher who used biblical and **Midrashic** quotations, parables, and stories to preach morality and repentance. Traveling from town to town, the Maggid attracted great masses with his chanting oratory. Although he was not very scholarly, his influence was more widespread than that of scholars and rabbis.

Outstanding among maggidim were Jacob Kranz, the **Maggid of Dubno**, in the 18th century; Moses Isaac ben Noah Darshan, the Kelmer Maggid; and Rabbi Jacob Joseph of New York, originally the Maggid of Vilna, in the 19th century.

MAGGID OF DUBNO (JACOB KRANZ) (1740-1804). Popular preacher and one of the best loved personalities in East European Jewish life. The fables of the Maggid of Dubno always had a moral or ethical message, enjoyed by young and old, scholar and layperson alike. **Elijah, the Gaon of Vilna**, was fond of his sermons.

MAGNES, JUDAH LEON (1877-1948). Rabbi, community leader, and educator. Magnes played an important role in the organization of Jewish community life in the U.S. during the early years of the 20th century. He was secretary of the Federation of American Zionists from 1905 to 1908, and was director of the New

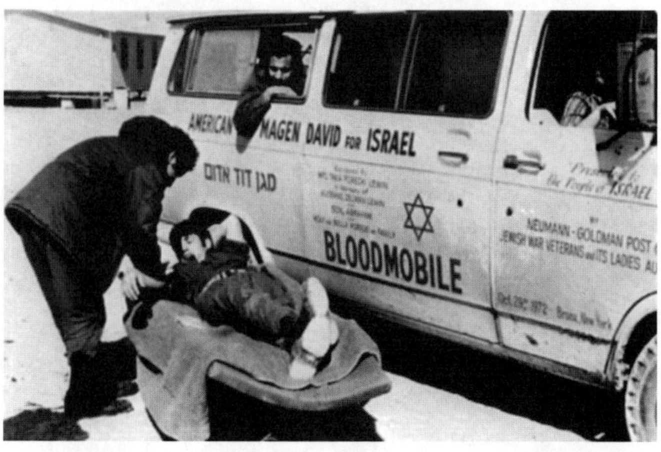

Israeli soldiers giving blood. Courtesy American Red Magen David for Israel.

York *Kehilla*, or community, from 1909 to 1922. After World War I he was called to organize the **Hebrew University** in Jerusalem and served as president of the University from 1925 until his death in 1948. In Palestine, he was one of the leaders of the movement which called for a binational (Arab-Jewish) state in Palestine.

MAHARAL. *See* **Loew, Judah Ben Bezalel**.

MAHLER, GUSTAV (1860-1911). Conductor and composer. He was born in Bohemia and baptized as a child. Mahler served as conductor at the opera in **Prague**, Hamburg, and at the Imperial Opera in Vienna. For a number of years, he conducted German opera at the New York Metropolitan Opera House, and from 1909 to 1911 he was the conductor of the New York Philharmonic. When he died in Vienna, Czechs, Austrians, and Jews all laid claim to him as a great son. Mahler wrote nine symphonies and many songs. He is considered one of the greatest composers of modern times.

MAHZOR. Literally, cycle. A book of prayers, hymns, and liturgic poetry; more generally, the prayer book for the High Holy Days and **Passover**, **Shavuot**, and **Sukkot**. There were several versions of the Mahzor, each following the customs and traditions of a different locality: the Roman Mahzor, based on the 16th-century Mahzor Romania, originated in the Byzantine Empire; the Ashkenazic Nusah of German Jews; and the Mahzor Sephardi, compiled during the early part of the Middle Ages by Spanish Jewry. Today, the two accepted texts are the Ashkenazic and Sephardic versions.

MAIDANEK. Nazi concentration camp near Lublin, **Poland**. Here, a quarter-million Jews and at least 100,000 non-Jews were exterminated, mainly in gas chambers, between 1941 and 1944.

Polish stamp commemorating Maidanek.

MAILER, NORMAN (1923-). American novelist. He first became famous with his World War II novel *The Naked and the Dead*. A keen observer of culture, his later novels fail to measure up to his early potential.

MAIMON, (FISHMAN) JUDAH LEIB (1876-1962). Scholar and leader of religious **Zionism**. Born in Bessarabia, he was inspired at an early age by the idea of a return to Zion. In 1913, Rabbi Maimon and his family settled in Palestine, where he began to take an active part in the rebuilding of the land. He was appointed Minister of Religions in the first Cabinet of the State of **Israel**. Rabbi Maimon was head of the Rabbi Kook publishing house and editor of the scholarly monthly, *Sinai*. He published many important volumes on Jewish holidays, Zionism, law, and monographs on famous personalities. He possessed one of the largest private collections of Judaica books.

MAIMONIDES (1135-1204). Jewish philosopher, religious thinker, and physician. Few have attained the heights of thought and scholarship scaled by Maimonides, also known as Moses ben Maimon, or Rambam. His genius revealed itself in many fields of spiritual and scientific activity: in law, philosophy, medicine, astronomy, and logic. He wrote many extraordinary scholarly works, and was the acknowledged head of the Jewish community in **Egypt** and the revered leader of all Jewry. His authority extended as far as the distant land of Yemen; to this day, Yemenite Jews pay homage to his memory in their prayers.

Maimonides (Rabbi Moses ben Maimon).

Maimonides was born in Cordova, **Spain**, where his father, Rabbi Maimon, was the religious head, or dayan, of the community. He was only thirteen years old when Cordova was conquered by the Almohades, a fanatic Muslim sect. His family was forced to flee; after much wandering, they reached Fez, **Morocco**. Through this troubled period, Maimonides continued his studies. In Fez, he published a letter to Jews who were forced to accept the Islamic faith, urging them to observe secretly the Jewish commandments. When Yemenite Jews were bitterly persecuted, Maimonides wrote to them the famous *Iggeret Teman* in which he advised his distant brethren not to despair, for all persecutions are challenges to prove the truth and purity of the Jewish faith.

Maimonides' outspoken and courageous leadership endangered his position in Morocco, and he and his family were forced to flee again. He remained briefly in Palestine. In 1165, he left for Egypt, where he settled in Fostat near Cairo. He had many obligations as head of the Jewish community and as court physician to the Vizier Al-Kadi al Fadil and later to the Caliph Al Fadal. Yet Maimonides still devoted much time to study.

Even during his lifetime Maimonides was held in the highest regard. His commentary on the Mishnah and his great code *Mishneh Torah* are the work of a genius. The code is divided into fourteen books and embraces the entire field of Jewish law. The *Mishneh Torah* is written in clear, rich, and precise Hebrew. In the first of these volumes Maimonides explained the foundations of the Jewish religion and its principles in the light of reason and logic. To explain further the philosophic principles of Judaism he wrote in Arabic a *Guide for the Perplexed*.

Maimonides influenced spiritual development throughout generations. His *Guide for the Perplexed*, an attempt to bring philosophy into harmony with religion, has been translated into many languages. It has exerted great influence not only on Jewish thinkers, but also on Christian theologians and philosophers. Maimonides was enshrined in folk legend, and the people of Tiberias erected a tomb in his memory. The inscription upon it reads, "Here lies our master Moses ben Maimon, Mankind's Chosen One."

MAINE. With 3,900 Jews in Portland and another 3,000 in the rest of the state, Maine Jewry is one of the smallest in the U.S. Jews began to arrive in the late 19th century with the large immigration waves from eastern Europe, and settled in Auburn, Bangor, Biddeford, Lewiston, and Waterville.

MALACHI. Last of the biblical prophets. He is considered by some traditional authorities to be an anonymous prophet because Malachi means "my messenger." Malachi lived in **Jerusalem** in the middle of the 5th century B.C.E., perhaps 50 years after the rebuilding of the Temple by the returned exiles from Babylonia. Malachi stresses obedience to ritual and Law; his prophecies teach the universality of God and the natural worth of all people.

MALAMUD, BERNARD (1914-1986). American novelist and short story writer. His work, though written in English, is reminiscent of the great Yiddish writers. *The Assistant* is about a poor Jewish grocer in Brooklyn. *The Fixer*, about the Mendel **Beilis** case, won the Pulitzer Prize in 1967.

MANGER, ITZIK. *See* **Yiddish Literature**.

MANILOW, BARRY. *See* **Music**.

MANSDORF, AMOS. *See* **Sports**.

MAOT CHITTIM. Literally, wheat money. The collection of money before **Passover** to provide poor Jewish families with matzot, wine, and other holiday needs. This **charity** was considered an important religious obligation, and societies were often set up for this purpose.

MAOZ ZUR. *See* **Hanukkah**.

MAPAI. *See* **Israel, Government and Parties.**

MAPAM. *See* **Israel, Government and Parties.**

MAPU, ABRAHAM (1808-1867). First Hebrew modern novelist. His biblical novel *Love of Zion*, published in 1853, opened a new era in the history of Hebrew letters. Born in **Lithuania**, he received a religious education and soon acquired a reputation as a prodigy in the study of **Talmud**. In later years he studied Latin and modern languages as well. In his somewhat naive yet charming novels, written in what now sounds like clumsy biblical Hebrew, he laid the foundation for modern **Hebrew literature** by proving that the language was suitable for writing fiction, and by introducing for the first time themes such as love of nature and love between man and woman.

Abraham Mapu.

MARCEAU, MARCEL (1923-). The greatest mime, or silent comedian, of all time. He achieved international fame at age 24, and is known throughout the world as one of the most original artists of the 20th century.

MARCUS, DAVID (1902-1948). American soldier who served with distinction in World War II, and went to Palestine as a military advisor to the **Haganah**. He was killed during the siege of Jerusalem. *Cast a Giant Shadow*, a novel about his life, was made into a movie.

MARCUS, JACOB (1896-1995). American historian and rabbi, he wrote extensively about American Jewish history. He taught at and was associated with the **Hebrew Union College** for 76 years, and became the friend and mentor of generations of Reform rabbis. In 1947, he established the American Jewish Archives, a major repository and research center for American Jewish history. A street in Cincinnati is named after him.

MARRANOS. Spanish and Portugese Jews and their descendants who were forced to accept **Christianity**, but continued to practice Judaism secretly. In a number of cases, they passed their secret beliefs from generation to generation. In its relentless investigations to root out blasphemers, the **Inquisition** tortured many Marranos until they admitted their heresy, and then burned them at the stake. Those Christians, as they were called, who were not exposed as secret Jews were nevertheless despised and remained under constant suspicion. When Jews were expelled from **Spain** in 1492, many escaped to **Portugal** and South America; there, too, many Marranos met martyrdom at the hand of the Inquisition. Other Marranos found refuge in Holland, **France**, **Italy**, and North Africa. There they either reverted to Judaism openly or remained secret Jews, sometimes for several hundred years, until they felt it was no longer dangerous to reveal their faith. Over the centuries, Portuguese descendants of the early Marranos lost or forgot their connections with Judaism, yet still retained a number of Jewish customs. These they practiced in secret, often believing the secrecy itself to be part of the custom. During the 19th century, considerable numbers of such secret Jews were found in northern Portugal and the Balearic Isles. Although they assimilated into the Christian communities, they observed various Jewish customs and holidays. The Marranos of Belmonte, for example, lit Sabbath candles, fasted on **Yom Kippur**, and refrained from eating pork (only on the Sabbath and holidays). An international committee for Portuguese Marranos, formed during the 1920's, helped some Marranos to return openly to Judaism.

MARRIAGE CUSTOMS. Marriage is one of the most sacred and joyous of Jewish ceremonies. Traditionally, the marriage rites begin with the drawing up of a contract between the groom, bride, and their families. This agreement serves as an engagement. On the Sabbath before the wedding itself, the bridegroom is called up to the reading of the **Torah**, as is the father of the bride. Traditionally, the groom and bride fast on the wedding day. The wedding ceremony takes place under a *huppah*, or canopy, which represents the home. It is traditionally held in the open air. Preceded by the reading of the marriage contract, or *ketubah*, the ceremony consists of a series of benedictions thanking God for establishing the family, for creating man in His image, and for the joy of the wedding festivities. After the first benediction, the bridegroom places a ring on the finger of the hand of the bride, and says, "You are sanctified to me with this ring in accordance with the Law of Moses and Israel." After the benedictions, ending with a prayer for the happiness of the

16th century ceremonial wedding ring. Courtesy Sidney L. Quitman.

Jewish Wedding, by Joseph Israels.

bride and groom and for the rebuilding of **Jerusalem**, the bridegroom breaks a glass. This is done to bring to mind the destruction of the **Temple** and Jerusalem, which must not be forgotten even on the most joyous occasions. Among certain Orthodox Jews, the festivities last for a whole week. Special benedictions for the happiness of groom and bride are said each evening, concluding with a feast on the seventh day.

MARSHALL, LOUIS (1856-1929). World Jewish leader. A brilliant constitutional lawyer, he made his mark in civic and national affairs as a member of a slum investigation committee in **New York** and as chairman of the Commission of Immigration of the State of New York. A tireless worker for the underprivileged, he took a forthright stand on Black rights. He championed conservation and preservation of wild life. A founder and president of the **American Jewish Committee** and chairman of the executive board of the **Jewish Theological Seminary of America**, Marshall also spearheaded the work of the **American Jewish Joint Distribution Committee**. In 1919, he was a member of the U.S. Jewish delegation to the **Versailles Peace Conference** which followed World War I, and he drew up the resolution for Jewish minority rights in Eastern Europe. These rights were extended to other minorities and incorporated by the Peace Conference into the treaties with a number of European countries. When the enlarged **Jewish Agency** for Palestine was organized in 1929, Louis Marshall was one of the leading non-Zionists to become a member of its executive body.

Louis Marshall. Courtesy James Marshall.

MARTINIQUE. One of the Windward Islands in the West Indies, ruled by **France** since 1635. The largest Jewish community Martinique has ever known is composed of 300 Brazilian exiles who settled there in 1654. They were expelled in 1683. Though refugees arrived from Europe during World War II, they were not allowed to establish themselves.

MARTYRS, TEN. After the unsuccessful revolt of **Bar Kokhba** from 132 to 135 against Roman rule, the Roman emperor Hadrian attempted the spiritual destruction of the Jewish people. Upon penalty of death, he forbade the study of the **Torah**. Jews were not permitted to practice the most fundamental laws of their religion. **Sabbath** observance, celebration of holidays, and **circumcision** were forbidden.

Jewish scholars were the major target of this persecution. However, they braved death rather than submit to Roman oppression. The story of their courageous stand and martyrdom became embodied in legend. The foremost scholars and leaders of their people defied the Roman decree and continued to teach the Torah to their students. Among these martyrs were Rabbi **Akiba** ben Joseph, Juda ben Bava, and Hananiah ben Teradion. While enduring a slow agonizing death, the martyrs proclaimed their faith in God. It is related that the executioner of Hananiah ben Teradion was so moved by the spirit of the sage that he did everything possible to spare his suffering. Moved to remorse by his victim's saintly bearing, the executioner leapt into the flames to atone for the cruel task he had been forced to perform. Thereafter, the heroic death of the ten scholars served as a symbol of martyrdom. Their faith and fortitude gave countless Jews the strength to sacrifice their lives "for the sanctification of the name of God."

MARX BROTHERS, THE. *See* **Stage and Screen.**

MARX, KARL (1818-1883). Economist, thinker, and founder of scientific socialism. Born to a German-Jewish family, Marx was destined to become one of the leading revolutionary thinkers of modern times. Exiled from **Germany** for political activity in 1845, he went to Paris where he joined revolutionary Socialist circles. There, in collaboration with Friedrich Engels, he wrote *The Communist Manifesto* in 1848, calling upon the workers to rise in violent revolution against their capitalist oppressors. Exiled from **France** and then again from Germany, Marx settled in **London** where he devoted his life to the development and exposition of his theories of history and society and to the organization of an international workers' movement.

Marx believed that labor was the source of all economic value and that the profits of an employer (a "capitalist") therefore constituted "theft." In Marx's theory, capitalism not only led to the worker's impoverishment, it also led to the perversion of human nature, which Marx believed to be essentially good. Because Marx held that all history and culture were determined by economic conditions, he favored a world revolution which would give labor its due and permit the "rehumanization" of people. *Das Kapital* (Capital), setting forth his economic theory, was his most important work, and later became the handbook of both the Socialist and Communist movements. Its assumptions were the basis for early economic policy in the Soviet Union.

Karl Marx on a Hungarian stamp.

Marx was baptized at the age of six, a practice common among German Jews with ambitions for their children, and in his future years he avoided involvement in Jewish life. Only one article, *Zur Judenfrage* (On the Jewish Question), dealt directly with Jewish affairs.

MARYLAND. Most of the state's 210,000 Jews live either in **Baltimore** (94,500) or in Montgomery and Prince George's counties (104,500), which constitute the Maryland suburbs of Washington, DC. After the Revolutionary War, there were few Jews in Maryland because of the requirement to espouse **Christianity**. But in 1826 a law was passed that allowed Jews to hold office. At the same time synagogues were founded in **Baltimore**, and Jewish communities in the state began to grow. Jews became active in the political and social life of the state, and during the Civil War Jews of the state—which supported the South—were divided in their loyalties between the two sides. In the late 19th and early 20th century, Baltimore became one of the leading Jewish communities in the U.S. Today, Maryland's two main Jewish communities, namely, Baltimore and the Washington, D.C. suburbs, have become models of organized Jewish life, served by Jewish Federations, JCCs, Jewish day schools, Jewish institutions of health, social welfare, retirement housing, and nursing homes.

MASADA. Ancient fortress in the Judean wilderness, famed for the last stand of the Zealots in the war against the Romans in 70 C.E. In recent years it has been the site of much archaeological activity. In 1965, Prof. Yigael **Yadin** of the **Hebrew University** reported that his expedition had discovered a large piece of scroll belonging to the long-lost Hebrew original of the Book of Jubilees, one of the most important of **Apocryphal** writings. (*See also* **Archeology**.)

MASHGIACH. Literally, supervisor. Someone familiar with **dietary laws** who is appointed to supervise the preparation of food in keeping with those laws.

MASORAH. Literally, tradition. Literary activity centering around the text of the **Bible**. This activity took place in **Tiberias** in Palestine during the 8th century, resulting in a standard Bible text.

The Massoretes, or scholars who devoted themselves to establishing the Masoretic text, divided the biblical books into chapters and verses which were lacking in the original text, and set down the correct pronunciation of biblical words which were often unclear because vowel and accent marks were unknown in early times. They compiled spelling lists and introduced a system of vowel and accent marks which enabled every Jew to read and study the Bible. The Masoretic activity was brought to a close at the beginning of the 10th century by the last of the Masorites, Aaron ben Asher.

MASSACHUSETTS. One of the major centers of Jewish life and culture in the U.S. With close to 280,000 Jews, 228,000 live in Greater **Boston**, 20,000 in Lynn, and 10,000 each in Springfield and Worcester. Smaller communities exist in Cape Cod, Fall River, Greenfield, Lowell, Pittsfield, and Taunton.

The zeal of the early Puritans in the state scared away Jews in the 17th century. A few Jewish merchants found their way there before the Revolution, but organized Jewish life did not begin until mid-19th century. In the 20th century, Massachusetts became one of the main centers of Jewish communal and cultural life in the U.S. (*See also* **Boston** *and* **Brandeis University**.)

MATRIARCHS. The collective name for the mothers of the people of Israel: Sarah, Rebecca, Leah, and Rachel. Their husbands constituent the three **patriarchs**: **Abraham, Isaac,** and **Jacob**. On **Sabbath** and holiday eves, it was customary for fathers to bless their daughters: "May the Lord make you like unto Sarah, Rebecca, Rachel, and Leah."

MATTATHIAS. *See* **Maccabees**.

MATTHAU, WALTER. *See* **Stage and Screen**.

MATZAH. Unleavened bread. *See* **Passover**.

MAUROIS, ANDRÉ (1885-1967). French author. He is noted for his biographies of **Disraeli**, Shelley, and Balzac. He was elected member of the Académie Française in 1938.

MEGGIDO. Ancient Palestinian city in Emek Jezreel at the foot of the Samarian hills. Strategically located on the ancient highway that links **Egypt** in the south of **Israel** to **Syria** and **Assyria** in the north, Meggido was the scene of many battles until the 4th century B.C.E, when the city was abandoned. **Joshua** subjugated the Canaanite king of Meggido (Joshua 12:21); later **Solomon** fortified the town and established a garrison of horsemen there. During the period of the Kings, ending with Josiah (II Kings 23:29), numerous battles were fought in and around the city. Meggido has become a Christian symbol of war, and it was believed that at the "end of days" the final war between Good and Evil, known as the Battle of Armaggedon, would be carried on there. During the World War I campaign for the Holy Land, General **Allenby** and his British forces defeated the Turks near this spot. The *tel*, or mound, all that remains of Meggido, has been the subject of archaeological diggings since 1903, the most significant being the Rockefeller expedition of 1926-1939. The excavations have exposed seven layers of ancient cities built one on top of the other, the earliest probably dating back to 3500 B.C.E. Early Canaanite altars and Solomon's stables may be seen in a remarkable state of preservation among the ruins of Meggido.

MEGILLAH. Literally, scroll. A book written on a single roll of parchment, different from a *sefer*, a larger book mounted on double rollers. The following five books of the Bible are each called a megillah: **Song of Songs, Ruth, Lamentations, Ecclesiastes,** and **Esther**; collectively they are known as the *megillot*. The proper noun *megillah* refers primarily to the Scroll of Esther. Written by hand in illuminated script and often decorated with colorful border designs, megillot were kept in cases of carved wood and figured on filigreed silver. Examples of megillot dating back to the 13th century are found in museums.

MEIR BAAL HA-NES (Meir the Miracle Worker). Name given to Rabbi Meir (2nd century), because of his reputation as a performer of miracles. Charity boxes in Jewish homes in the

Diaspora bearing his name were used to give charity to poor Jews in the Holy Land.

MEIR, GOLDA (1898-1979). Labor Zionist leader and Prime Minister of Israel from 1969 to 1974. She was born Gold Mabowitz to a carpenter in Kiev, Russia. The Mabowitz family came to the U.S. in 1906 and settled in Milwaukee where Meir grew up and taught school. A Zionist since youth, she married Morris Myerson on the condition that they go to Palestine to settle as pioneers. Arriving in Palestine in 1921, they joined the **kibbutz** *Merhavia*, where Golda Myerson trained to become its specialist in poultry raising.

Her public career began with her work as secretary of the Women's Labor Council. This work involved her in shuttling between Palestine and the U.S., and developed her remarkable skill as administrator, organizer, propagandist, and fund-raiser. These abilities were recognized by the **Histadrut**, the General Federation of Labor in Palestine, and Myerson was appointed to its executive committee. She served the Histadrut ably in a variety of executive posts, heading the Workers' Sick Fund and organizing the unemployment insurance system by persuading the workers to tax themselves for this purpose. Her versatility enabled her to raise single-handedly the capital to finance Nachshon, the Histadrut harbor installations in **Tel Aviv**. In retaliation for resistance to its immigration policy, the British arrested the top leaders of the Jewish community in Palestine on June 29, 1946. Myerson replaced the imprisoned Moshe **Sharett** as head of the **Jewish Agency** Political Department.

Golda Meir. Courtesy Israel Office of Information.

She was one of two women who signed Israel's Declaration of Independence in May 1948 and became Israel's first ambassador to **Russia**. She was enthusiastically welcomed by Russian Jews. Because of her experience in labor relations and in social insurance, she was recalled to Israel in 1949 to become Minister of Labor in Prime Minister **Ben-Gurion**'s first cabinet. Myerson served in this position until 1956 when, upon the resignation of Moshe Sharett, she assumed the office of Minister for Foreign Affairs. In keeping with the established practice that foreign service officials Hebraize their names, she changed her last name to Meir. Meir was succeeded as Minister of Foreign affairs by Abba **Eban** in 1965.

When the Mapai, Ahdut HaAvodah, and the Rafi parties officially merged early in 1968, Meir was elected secretary general of the new party. She held this office until 1969 when she succeeded Levi **Eshkol** as Prime Minister of Israel. As Prime Minister she paid several official visits to the U. S. as the guest of President Richard M. Nixon. In 1974, following the **Yom Kippur War**, she resigned from the government, and was succeeded by Yitzhak **Rabin**.

MEIR OF ROTHENBURG (1215-1293). Scholar and poet. Renowned rabbi in Western **Germany**. At age 66 he fled with his family from the persecutions of German rulers with the intention of going to the Holy Land, but was arrested on the way and returned as a prisoner to Germany. Emperor Rudolph of Hapsburg demanded from the Jews a large sum for the liberation of their beloved leader. Although the Jews were ready to pay, Rabbi Meir refused to be ransomed so as not to establish the precedent of redeeming imprisoned Jewish leaders. Rabbi Meir died in prison, and again the Emperor demanded a heavy ransom before relinquishing the rabbi's body for Jewish burial. Fourteen years later, a wealthy Jew ransomed the body on condition that he himself be buried beside the remains of the venerable rabbi. To this day, one can see in the Jewish cemetery of Worms the double grave with a single tombstone marking the resting place of the rabbi and his loyal follower.

MEIR, RABBI (2nd century C.E.). Greatest of Rabbi **Akiba**'s disciples, this 2nd-century Tanna figures prominently in the Mishnah. All laws in the Mishnah whose authorship is not specified are ascribed to Rabbi Meir. Although second only to the head of the **Sanhedrin** in scholarship and rank, Rabbi Meir earned a modest living by copying holy scrolls. He had a keen legal mind, and the imaginative side of his nature was expressed in legends, fables, and parables. It is said that he composed 300 fox fables; all except three have been lost.

Rabbi Meir was a pupil of **Elisha Ben Abuyah** who later strayed from Judaism. Unlike other sages who forsook this once revered teacher, Rabbi Meir continued to benefit from his learning and tried to bring Elisha Ben Abuyah back to Judaism. Rabbi Meir had an abiding, deep love for the land of Israel and for the Hebrew language. He said, "One who lives in the land of Israel and speaks the holy tongue is assured of his share in the world to come."

MEISELS, DOV BERISH (1798-1870). Chief Rabbi of **Warsaw** and Polish patriot. He took part in the Polish rebellion of 1863. A street in Warsaw is named after him.

MELCHETT, LORD (SIR ALFRED MOND) (1868-1930). English industrialist, chemist, and Zionist leader. He was the head of the Imperial Chemical Industries of **London**, one of the largest of its kind in the world. In his youth, Lord Melchett studied law and participated actively in the economic and political life of Britain. For 17 years he was a member of Parliament; during World War I he served as Minister of Health and Labor. In 1917, Lord Melchett was attracted to **Zionism** and worked closely with Louis D. **Brandeis** for the economic development of Palestine. He was at one time president of the English Zionist Federation and Joint Chairman of the Jewish Agency. A colony in Palestine, Tel-Mond, is named after him. His son, Lord Henry Melchett (1898-1949), was

Lord Melchett. Courtesy British Information Service.

president of the Maccabi World Union, and wrote several books, one of which, *Your Neighbor*, expounds the ideals of Judaism and Zionism.

MEM. Thirteenth letter of the Hebrew alphabet; numerically, forty.

MENASSEH. Older son of Joseph.

MENASSEH BEN ISRAEL (1604-1657). Rabbi and author. In 1655, when **England** was a Republic under the rule of Cromwell the Lord Protector, a strange figure with a strange case to plead appeared in **London.** He was Menasseh ben Israel, a Lisbon-born rabbi who had settled in **Amsterdam** and become famous throughout Europe for books on religious and other subjects. In 1650, he wrote *Esperanza de Israel* (Hope of Israel), a treatise arguing that the Messiah would not come until Jews had been scattered to the four corners of the earth. Convinced by the argument, Oliver Cromwell had invited Menasseh to discuss the return of Jews to England, from which they had been banished in 1290. Menasseh pleaded eloquently, but a Whitehall convention rejected his plan. Nonetheless, a Jewish community was founded in 1656. Menasseh died a year later in Middelburg, Holland. His face is known to us from a portrait by his friend **Rembrandt**, the greatest Dutch artist of the day.

Menasseh Ben Israel.

MENDELE MOCHER SEFARIM (ABRAMOWITZ, SHALOM JACOB) (1836-1917). Pioneer Hebrew and Yiddish writer, best known by his pen-name, Mendele Mocher Sefarim (Mendele the Bookseller). Born in a small town in White **Russia,** he received a traditional Jewish education, studying for a time at a Talmudical academy. At 17 he was persuaded to join an adventurous traveling beggar who promised the youth an exciting life in faraway places. His travels through the populous Jewish towns in southern Russia furnished the material for Mendele's realistic novel *Fishke der Krumer* and others. Abramowitz began his literary career during the **Haskalah**, or Enlightenment, period, and he successfully adapted a work on natural history from German into Hebrew. In 1857, he published articles urging the improvement of Jewish education. His Hebrew novel *Fathers and Sons* deals with the clash between generations, and completes the first cycle of his literary career. In his second period, Mendele chose to write in the vernacular, or spoken language, of the people, Yiddish. In his novels, *The Little Man*, *Meat Tax*, and *The Mare* he introduced the social reform motive, criticizing the community for exploiting the poor. In *The Travels of Benjamin the Third* and his other works, he revealed himself as a sharp satirist, ridiculing the pettiness, narrow-mindedness, and ignorance of small town inhabitants. In masterly fashion he described the stark poverty of the Jewish masses, mixing, as Dickens did, humor with compassion. Mendele created a new Hebrew and Yiddish literary style, making full use of the rich, hidden treasures of the language and contributing to its revival. His works present a vivid picture of Jewish life in the first half of the 19th century. Odessa, where Mendele had lived since 1881, became an important Hebrew literary center. Mendele's influence was far-reaching. **Bialik**, one of the foremost Hebrew poets, prided himself on being among Mendele's disciples.

Mendele Mocher Sefarim.

MENDELSSOHN, MOSES (1729-1786). Philosopher and founder of the German Jewish Enlightenment movement. Born in Dessau, the son of Mendel, a Torah scribe, young Mendelssohn received a traditional Jewish education in the **Bible** and **Talmud.** One of his early teachers introduced Moses to the study of **Maimonides.** This study influenced him deeply and formed his taste for philosophy. Coming to Berlin at age 14, he studied mathematics, Latin, Greek, and philosophy, and became a master of German prose. At a time when German Jews were still locked in their ghettos and required special permits to live in Berlin, Moses Mendelssohn became widely known as a German writer on philosophical subjects and on the theory of art. His home became the meeting place for many of the cultural leaders of his day, both Jewish and non-Jewish.

Mendlessohn tried to break down the walls of the ghetto from both the inside and outside. He wanted Jews to learn the German language as a gateway to the knowledge of the outside world. He wanted Jewish children to learn manual trades. With the help of wealthy friends, he opened a free school in Berlin where Jewish boys were trained in manual occupations and taught some German, in addition to the Bible and Talmud. Mendelssohn set for himself the task of translating the **Pentateuch** and the **Psalms** into German. Eventually, he published this German translation in Hebrew letters by the side of the original Hebrew text. The influence of this Bible translation was enormous. From it many Talmud students learned the German language and went on to the study of general European culture. The **Haskalah**, or Enlightenment, movement in Germany and Eastern Europe is often dated back to this translation.

Moses Mendelssohn.

To breach the walls of the ghetto from the outside, Mendelssohn wrote his *Jerusalem*. When published, some parts of this book were attacked by Christians and Jews alike. In *Jerusalem*, he outlined his ideals of religious and political toleration, separation of church and state, and equality of all citizens. At the same time he pleaded with Jews to hold on to their "particularism" and the absolute authority of Jewish laws. Mendelssohn used his literary friendships to prevent new restrictions from being placed upon Swiss Jews, and he tried to save the Jews of Dresden from expulsion. He induced Christian Wilhelm Dohm, a Prussian aristocrat, to write an essay urging that Jews be granted civil rights. Mendelssohn's devoted friendship with the famous author Gotthold Ephraim Lessing also contributed to the eventual emancipation of Jews in **Germany**. Lessing wrote a highly successful play *Nathan Der Weise* (*Nathan the Wise*), a portrait of his friend Moses Mendelssohn and a powerful plea for religious tolerance.

MENDELSSOHN-BARTHOLDY, FELIX (1809-1847). Composer, pianist, and conductor. His grandfather was Moses **Mendelssohn**, the Jewish philosopher whose work opened the period of emancipation in Jewish history. Felix's father, Abraham, wanted to spare his children from social and other forms of anti-Jewish discrimination, and therefore had them baptized as Lutherans. "That is the form of religion of most cultured men," said Abraham Mendelssohn. To further conceal his son's Jewish origin, he took the additional surname of Bartholdy. Felix often dropped the "Bartholdy" from his signature, and in the world of music his work is known simply as "Mendelssohn's." He retained a sincere and positive regard for Judaism, and there are many references in his correspondence to his Jewish identity.

A child prodigy, Mendelssohn began composing at the age of 11, and wrote some of his greatest work at 17. Some of his works—*Midsummer Night's Dream*, the Scotch and Italian symphonies, and the Hebrides and Meeresstille overtures—rank among the great musical masterpieces of the world. Mendelssohn's music is characterized by a fusion of classic and romantic styles. The religious element of his nature appears in his psalms, motets, and oratorios. His oratorio *Moses* was discovered only in recent years. Mendelssohn's inspired oratorio *Elijah* is as dramatic as an opera.

MENDES NASI, DONNA GRACIA (1510-1569). Financier, philanthropist, and patron of Jewish learning. She was born to a family of **Marranos**, or secret Jews, in **Portugal** and named Beatrice de Luna. She was only 25 when her husband, the banker Francisco Mendes of Lisbon, died. She became the head of the Mendes banking house with its widespread business interests, including an important branch in Antwerp.

When life for Marranos in Portugal became dangerous because of the **Inquisition**, she gathered up her family, including her daughter and her nephew Joao Miguez, and left for Antwerp, sailing in her own ship.

In Antwerp she joined her brother-in-law Diego Mendes in managing their business. The family had a high social position. Donna Gracia's responsibilities were great, and after the death of Diego in 1545, they became even greater. Her beautiful daughter Reyna was sought in marriage by many young nobles, and her firm refusals aroused justified suspicions that the Mendes family were secret Judaizers who would not intermarry with Christians. Before the authorities could act, Donna Gracia fled with her family to Venice, a way station to **Turkey** where they could practice Judaism openly. In Venice she was denounced to the authorities, who imprisoned her and confiscated her fortune. The king of **France**, in debt to the Mendes Bank, used his piety as a pretext for not paying his debt.

Her nephew Joao Miguez managed to obtain the help of the Turkish sultan Suleiman the Magnificent, and Donna Gracia was released. She was permitted to settle in Ferrara, a haven for Jews under the rule of the Dukes d'Este. Here Donna Gracia shed the disguise of Christianity and became Hannah Nasi, a devoted Jewess. In Ferrara she brought together a conference of Marrano notables to organize their flight to freedom, using her wealth to help finance this movement. She was interested in Jewish learning and became a patroness of Jewish scholars. When Abraham Usque of Ferrara published the first translation of the **Bible** into Spanish, a special edition was dedicated to Gracia. This edition became the Bible from which generations of Marranos relearned their Judaism. Finally, in 1552, the Nasi family was permitted to leave for **Turkey**. They settled in Constantinople where Gracia built her home, the Belvedere. She also built a synagogue and set up a Hebrew printing press in her home. The Belvedere became a haven for Jewish scholars, a respite continued by her daughter Reyna after Gracia's death.

Shortly after the family settled in Constantinople, Reyna married her cousin Joao Miguez, who had taken the name Joseph Nasi when the family returned to Judaism. After her husband's death Reyna continued to house the printing press which issued many important Hebrew books.

MENDES-FRANCE, PIERRE (1907-1982). French statesman. From an old Bordeaux Sephardi family, he served in Léon **Blum**'s government and fought under General De Gaulle. From 1954 to 1955 he served as Prime Minister of France, ended the war in Indo-China (the precursor of the Vietnam War), and produced a new economic plan. Mendes-France was a practicing Jew and a supporter of Israel.

MENDOZA, DANIEL. *See* **Sports**.

MENORAH. Candelabrum. There were seven branches in the original oil menorah used in the **Tabernacle** (Exo. 25:37) and later in **Solomon**'s **Temple**. It is this menorah that Titus is said to have carried away after the destruction of the Temple and that is

Menorah.

pictured in bas-relief on the **Arch of Titus** in Rome. On **Hanukkah** an eight-branched menorah (plus a *shammash*, or servant candle) is lit to commemorate the Maccabean victories. This menorah is frequently silver, bronze, or brass, and decorated with elaborate representations of animals and flowers.

MENUHIN, YEHUDI (1916-1999). American-born violinist. He made his debut as a child, and later became one of the world's leading violinists. He made his home in **England** and became a major organizer of concerts in Europe, while giving performances around the world. He is also known for his work with musically-gifted children. His sister, pianist Hephzibah Menuhin (1920-1981), provided him with musical accompani ment on many of his concerts.

MERON. Village in upper **Galilee**, mentioned in the Bible as the site of **Joshua**'s victory over the **Canaanite** kings. Rabbi Simeon ben Yohai took refuge in a cave at Meron to escape a death sentence imposed by the Romans during **Bar Kokhba**'s uprising in the 2nd century C.E. After Bar Kokhba's victory Rabbi Simeon founded an academy and synagogue there. When the **Kabbalists** began settling in nearby Safed during the 16th century, they instituted the custom of visiting his tomb on Lag b'Omer (*see* **Omer**). This custom has been revived in modern times. Today, thousands of pilgrims from all parts of **Israel** stream to Meron to celebrate the holiday with song and dance, as well as prayer and meditation. Bearded **Hasidim** in dark gabardines, Asian Jews in native costume, and tow-haired young Israelis join arms to dance around great bonfires in this most colorful of folk festivals.

MESSIANISM. The belief that Jewish people and all humanity would be led to a golden age of perfect justice and universal peace by a Messiah, an ideal king and a perfect man. The Hebrew *mashiah* means "one anointed with oil," the ancient way of dedicating a man to a special service or office. *Mashiah Adonai*, the Anointed of God, was a title of honor given in the **Bible** to the kings of **Israel**. The prophet **Samuel** anointed both **Saul** and **David** as kings. The high priest Zadok and the prophet Nathan anointed Solomon king of Israel at David's request. The prophets described the Messiah as a divinely appointed man, an ideal ruler who would lead the world in righteousness and in peace.

When the Persians would not permit a descendant of David to rule Judea, the people began to dream of a time when an anointed king from the House of David would again sit on the throne of Israel. The more Judea was oppressed, particularly by the Roman empire, the stronger the belief grew in the coming of the Messiah who would bring salvation and freedom to the Jewish people, while the Roman empire would be replaced by the Kingdom of God on earth.

When Judea fell in 70 C.E. and the **Temple** was destroyed, longing for the Messiah among the Jewish people intensified. In their last revolt against Rome from 132 to 135 C.E., they were led by Simeon, son of Koziba. The aged Rabbi **Akiba** called Simeon "God's Anointed," or Messiah, and changed his name from Bar Koziba to **Bar Kokhba**, "the son of a star." Defeated again, the people yearned for the Messiah more than ever, and his figure began to be surrounded with mystery. Instead of a human Messiah he became a divine deliverer and a being with supernatural powers. His coming would be announced by the prophet **Elijah**. A forerunner would appear first—the Messiah son of Joseph. The first Messiah would defeat Israel's enemies, Gog and Magog, and prepare the way for the Messiah, son of David. Then the dead would rise again, the Day of Judgment would begin, and the righteous would be rewarded.

During the long centuries of exile, the Jewish people continued to dream of the Messiah and the return to Israel. Many false Messiahs arose, mystics who really believed in themselves and impostors who took advantage of the people's despair. Each false Messiah brought suffering and disillusion in his wake, yet each new "Messiah" found many followers anxious to believe that the Return was at hand. (*For false Messiahs, see* **Alroy, David**; **Molkho, Solomon**; **Reubeni, David**; *and* **Sabbatai Zevi**.)

METHUSELAH. Longest living person in the **Bible** (Gen. 5:25-27). He lived 969 years, but all that is known about him is that he lived and he died.

METZENBAUM, HOWARD (1917-). Former U.S. Democratic Senator from Ohio. A lawyer and businessman from Cleveland, he supported liberal causes in the Senate.

MEXICO. Federated republic in North America. Early in the 16th century, Mexico was a center of activity for Spanish conquistadores intent on exploiting the wealth of Montezuma's empire. With them had come a group of **Marranos**, or secret Jews. The Marranos quickly prospered in commerce and thus aroused the hostility of their neighbors. As early as 1528, a Marrano shipbuilder was burned at the stake. But systematic persecution began only in 1570, with the establishment of an Office of the **Inquisition**. By 1820, when the Inquisition was abolished, the Marrano community had disappeared. Its only remaining traces are several thousand Indians who live in Mexico City and claim Marrano descent.

The modern community, composed chiefly of East European Jews, was founded in the 19th century. In 1998, there were about 40,000 Jews in Mexico, an increase of about 20,000 since 1940. Immigration has been limited since 1950. The vast majority of the Jewish population lives in Mexico City, but there are active

The Jewish Community and Sports Center in Mexico City. Photo Guillermo Zamora.

communities in Guadalajara, Monterey, and elsewhere. Mexican Jews, living in freedom and equality with their neighbors, have become shopkeepers, manufacturers, and artisans. A small number have entered the professions. They have formed several synagogues, Zionist organizations, local charity activities, **B'nai B'rith** lodges, and youth groups.

Mexico City is especially noted for its community center and Jewish schools, in which about 85% of the capital's Jewish children are enrolled. There are a number of all-day schools. The pride of the system is the Colegio Israelita de Mexico, where Spanish, Yiddish, and Hebrew are taught from the elementary school through the college levels. Its Faculty of Philosophy and Letters, founded in 1952, is affiliated with the National University of Mexico. The Albert Einstein School is a non-sectarian institution built by the Jewish community and presented to the government to aid its school construction program.

The Mexican Jewish press is also notable. There were three publications of Jewish interest: one in Yiddish, one in Spanish and Hebrew, and one in Spanish. The *Encyclopedia Judaica Castellana*, a Jewish encyclopedia in Spanish, with special emphasis on Latin American Jewry, was first published in 1952. (*See also* **Latin America**.)

Silver Mezuzah, by Judah Wolpert.

MEZUZAH. Literally, doorpost. Case containing a rolled parchment inscribed with several passages from Deuteronomy (6:4-9 and 11:13-21), affirming the unity of God and teaching the love of God. This case is attached to the right doorposts of the entrance and each room in Jewish homes in accordance with the biblical commandment, "And thou shalt write them on the doorposts of thy home" (Deut. 6:9). The parchments are kept in decorative cases which are slightly open to reveal the word *Shaddai*, or Almighty, written on the back of the parchment.

MICAH (ca. 730-705 B.C.E.). Sixth of the minor prophets. A peasant from tiny Moreshet in **Judah**, Micah cried out against the social corruption of the cities, the injustice of the rulers, and the wrongs done to the poor. He predicted the destruction of the **Temple** and the beloved city **Jerusalem**. Reminding the people of God's love for Israel, he pleaded with them to live with justice and kindness, and prophesied that in the "end of days" universal justice would emanate from Zion and fill the world.

MICHIGAN. Of Michigan's 107,000 Jews, 94,000 live in the Detroit area and 5,000 in Ann Arbor. There are smaller communities in Lansing, Flint, Grand Rapids, and Kalamazoo. Jews first arrived in the state as fur traders in the mid-18th century, and during the Revolutionary War there were a few Jews in Michigan. Organized religious life started in Ann Arbor in 1845, and by the late 18th century Jews began to arrive in Detroit, starting a major Jewish community. The Jewish Welfare Federation was organized in Detroit in 1926, and a Community Council was started in 1937 with more than 260 local organizations. The *Detroit Jewish News* was first issued in 1942. Today, Detroit has a well-organized Jewish community with an extensive Hebrew school system, a thriving Jewish Community Center, and active Jewish cultural life.

MIDLER, BETTE. *See* **Stage and Screen.**

MIDRASH. Literally, to search. A particular manner of interpreting the verses of the **Bible**, developed mainly in Judea during the period of the Second **Temple**. Jewish sages were convinced that the words of the Bible lent themselves to multiple interpretations, each intended for people of a particular level of understanding and culture, as well as for a particular age and circumstance. The sages contemplated and discussed some of the greatest and most profound ideas of humankind. They were anxious, moreover, to teach these exalted ideas to ordinary people of the towns and villages of Judea. On **Sabbaths** and holidays they would preach in the synagogues, using Bible verses as their text and revealing many profound interpretations of these verses. So that their ideas might be understood by the people, they used illustrative parables, imaginative stories, and poetic interpretations of the verses. In their sermons, the sages also discussed those problems that deeply troubled the people. After the burning of the Temple and the destruction of the Jewish state, the sages strove to heal the wounds of the people, raise their spirit, and restore their courage. They extolled the greatness and power of God, His abiding love for His people, His sympathy for their suffering, and His promise of a glorious future.

The sages preached on the weekly portion of the Torah, to which pertinent verses from other parts of the Bible were added. Most of their sermons were lost, but the finest of them were often repeated and zealously guarded in the memories of devoted students. Eventually, beginning with the 4th century, many of the sermons were collected and written down, as books of midrashim. Today, we possess more than 100, the most important of which are:

Midrash Rabbah (The Great Midrash), which consists of collections of midrashim on the Five Books of Moses and the Five Scrolls (**Song of Songs**, **Ruth**, **Lamentations**, **Ecclesiastes**, and **Esther**). Each collection was edited by a different man at a different time from the 6th to 12th century C.E.; they were the most popular collections of midrashim, widely read by Jews the world over.

Midrash Tanhuma, a more homogeneous collection of midrashim on the Five Books of Moses, in which the preachings of Rabbi Tanhuma, a sage of the 4th century, predominate.

Pesikhtot, two collections of lengthy sermons delivered on the special Sabbaths before **Passover** and the High Holy Days).

Yalkut Shimoni, a collection of midrashim on all the books of the Bible. This collection was edited in the 13th century and consists of material taken from many early collections of midrashim now lost to us.

A number of briefer midrashim, such as: Pirke D'Rabbi Eliezer on the first nine chapters of **Genesis**; Midrash Shohar Tov on Psalms; Midrash Mishle on Proverbs; Midrash Shemuel on the books of **Samuel**; and Midrash Lekah Tov on the third, fourth, and fifth Books of Moses and the Book of Ruth.

MIKVEH. Jewish ritual bath. The use of the mikveh is governed by Jewish ritual laws and forms an integral part of the Jewish religious living environment. Often it is built next to the synagogue. It is used for both physical and ritual purification, as in the case of post-menstrual women.

MIKVEH ISRAEL. Literally, Gathering of Israel. Agricultural school southeast of **Tel Aviv**. It is approached by an avenue of stately palms and surrounded by orange orchards, vineyards, vegetable gardens, and cornfields. It was the first, and for many years, the only agricultural school in Israel. It was originally open only to boys, established in 1870 by the **Alliance Israélite Universelle** in response to an appeal to help Jews in the Holy Land learn a productive occupation. The eucalyptus tree, which the Arabs called "the Jewish tree," was first introduced at this school. The **Bilu** settlers came to Mikveh Israel to learn how to handle the plough and the turia, or a mattock.

MILLER, ARTHUR (1915-). American playwright. Best known for his plays *Death of a Salesman* and *The Crucible*, he is considered one of the great American playwrights of the 20th century. While Miller exhibited little interest in Jewish life, film actress Marilyn Monroe converted to Judaism when she married him.

MILHAUD, DARIUS (1892-1974). French composer. A member of an old French Jewish family, he distinguished himself as a composer of operas and symphonies. His operas on Jewish themes include *Esther* and *David*. He also composed music for the Sabbath morning service.

MILSTEIN, NATHAN. *See* **Music.**

MINCHA. *See* **Prayer.**

MINHAG. *See* **Custom.**

MINNESOTA. Of Minnesota's 41,000 Jews, 31,500 live in Minneapolis and 9,200 in St. Paul. Jewish immigrants arrived in St. Paul in the mid-19th century and in Minneapolis in the late 1860's. In the beginning of the 20th century, Jews settled throughout the state, mainly for the purpose of farming. Today, there are few Jewish farmers in the state.

MINYAN. Quorum of ten adult Jewish males traditionally required for congregational services.

MIRACLES. The **Bible** tells that the universe is governed by established laws, yet **God**, or God's messengers, can perform acts known as miracles that break with such laws. After biblical times, the Jewish tradition no longer recognizes miracles (*nes* in Hebrew), which now pass from the realm of the divine to folk belief. Today, the belief in the literal truth of biblical miracles persists, while many maintain that they have to be viewed as myth rather than historical fact.

MIRIAM. **Moses**' sister. She helps save his life as an infant by entrusting him to the Pharaoh's daughter. After crossing of the Red Sea, she led the Israelite women in a victory song and dance. Later she rebelled against Moses and was temporarily punished. In Jewish tradition she is considered a prophet and righteous person.

MISHNAH. *See* **Talmud.**

MISSISSIPPI. With fewer than 2,000 Jews, of whom 550 live in Jackson, Mississippi has one of the smallest Jewish communities in the U.S. Jews were among the first settlers in the state who settled in

Biloxi and Natchez in 1699. The first synagogue was started in Natchez in 1840. Today, there are Reform congregations in Jackson, Greenville, Hattiesburg, and Cleveland, and a Conservative congregation in Biloxi.

MISSOURI. Of Missouri's 75,000 Jews, 54,000 live in St. Louis and 19,100 reside in Kansas City. Jews began to settle in the state in the early 19th century, while the first major influx began in the 1840's as German Jews began to arrive. In the early 20th century Jews settled throughout the state in 51 different communities.

MITZVAH. Literally, commandment. An obligation or duty taught by the Torah and rabbinic law; a good deed. Traditionally, there are 613 commandments contained in the Torah, 248 affirmative ("thou shalt") and 365 negative ("thou shalt not"). Jews regarded these as representing a desirable way of life and an opportunity for fulfilling one's duty to God and fellow humans. By performing a meritorious act, such as giving charity, a person is said to have "earned a mitzvah."

MIZRACH. Literally, the place where the sun rises; the east. Traditionally, Jews have always faced east toward **Jerusalem** when praying. Therefore, it was customary to hang a picture or ornament to mark the eastern wall in their home or synagogue. These illustrations of plants and animals mentioned in the **Bible** were often handsome examples of folk art.

MIZRACHI. Religious Zionist movement. Mizrachi's slogan is "The land of Israel for the people of Israel according to the Torah of Israel." Religious leaders wanting to work with secularists had been part of the Zionist movement since its inception in Basle in 1898. As a political party Religious Zionism made its initial appearance on the Zionist scene on March 4, 1902, when Rabbi **Isaac Jacob Reines** convened the Mizrachi conference in Vilna. In 1902, religious Jews took sharp exception to the Fifth Zionist Congress' proposal that the Zionist organization conduct a kind of secularist educational program. The Mizrachi rallied many religious Jews to its side and fought secularism within the Zionist movement.

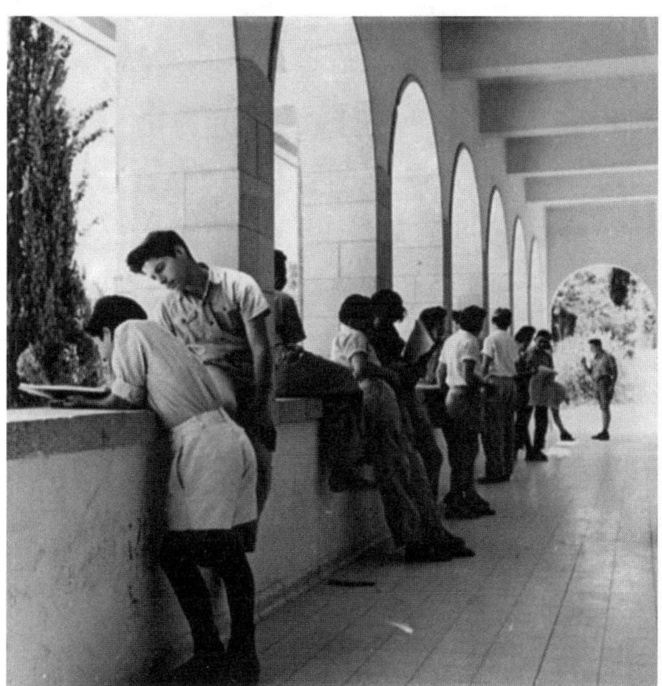

Students at the Bnei Akiva Yeshiva. Courtesy Religious Zionists of America.

The Mizrachi soon had active branches wherever Zionism took root, becoming particularly active in education. Mizrachi's network of religious schools eventually became part of the Israel government's religious school system. The Mizrachi Organization of America built and sponsored **Bar Ilan University**, the first religious institution of higher academic learning in Israel.

Mizrachi was formally organized in the U.S. after 1913, although groups existed even earlier. The first national convention was held in Cincinnati in 1914 following an intensive tour of the country by Rabbi Meyer **Bar Ilan**, who eventually became the president and leader of the world Mizrachi movement. Affiliated with the Mizrachi Organization of America are the Mizrachi Women, who have concentrated on education and child care, and B'nai Akiva, the Mizrachi Youth Organization.

Hapoel Hamizrachi, or the Mizrachi Worker, was founded in 1922, when religious young people began to arrive in Palestine in increasing numbers. They formulated a program based on the slogan of *Torah Ve-Avodah*, or Torah and Labor. Despite the hardships and discrimination it suffered because of its religious principles, the movement grew rapidly both in Israel and abroad. Hapoel Hamizrachi worked with the Mizrachi in the world Mizrachi movement. In 1955, it merged with Mizrachi to form one united religious party within Zionism. *Kibbutz Hadati*, Hapoel Hamizrachi's organization of religious collective settlements, played an important role in Israel's defense and growth. (*See also* **Israel, Government and Political Parties**.)

MODIGLIANI, AMEDEO. *See* **Art**.

MOHAMMED. *See* **Arab Influence in Jewish History**.

MOHEL. *See* **Circumcision**.

MOHILEVER, SAMUEL (1824-1898). Outstanding Russian rabbi; a founder and leader of the Zionist movement. He founded the first **Hoveve Zion** society in **Warsaw** in 1882, at a time when Orthodox opinion frowned on any active attempt to bring about the return to Zion. In 1891, Rabbi Mohilever visited Baron Maurice de **Hirsch** and successfully pleaded with him to found Jewish agricultural settlements in Palestine instead of **Argentina**. When Theodor **Herzl** began to work for political **Zionism**, Mohilever delivered a stirring message to the first **Zionist Congress** in 1897, supporting him.

Rabbi Samuel Mohilever.

MOLKHO, SOLOMON (ca. 1500-1532). False Messiah. Born in **Portugal** and died in Mantua, Italy, Molkho was born Diego Pires to Christian parents who were **Marranos**, or secret Jews. When David **Reubeni**, considered a forerunner of the Messiah, came to Portugal, Diego fell completely under his spell. He gave up a government post and returned openly to Judaism. He had himself circumcised and renamed Solomon Molkho; then he left Portugal secretly and went to Salonika, **Turkey**. He studied the **Kabbalah** and was drawn to **Safed**, a Kabbalist center in the Holy Land. Influenced greatly by Joseph **Karo** and the Safed Kabbalists, Molkho predicted that the Messiah would come in 1540.

Molkho was deeply mystical and came to believe in his mission as a Messiah, winning many followers. Italy, seat of the Pope, seemed to him the place to begin his mission. He came to Ancona in 1529, where despite opposition from some Jewish leaders, he preached to admiring congregations. Disguised as a beggar, he went to Rome, managed to see Pope Clement VII, and prophesied that the Tiber would flood its banks and that an earthquake would shake Portugal while comets showered from the sky. On October 8, 1530, the Tiber actually overflowed and on January 26, 1531, Portugal was indeed shaken by an earthquake and a comet appeared in the sky. The Pope was impressed by this visionary and protected Molkho even when some of his writings were found offensive to Christianity. He was condemned to death by the **Inquisition**, but the Pope helped him escape. Molkho joined Reubeni in Venice and went with him to Ratisbon in 1532. Carrying a banner inscribed with initials of the Hebrew words, "Who is like unto Thee, O Lord, among the mighty," they appeared before Charles V, Emperor of the Holy Roman Empire, to persuade him to call the Jews to arms against the Turks. The Emperor put them both in chains and had them sent to Italy. There, Molkho was immediately condemned by the **Inquisition** as a renegade from Catholicism and sentenced to burn at the stake. Molkho refused to return to the Church and died in the flames of an **auto-da-fe.** Charles V had Reubeni sent to Spain where he was turned over to the Inquisition. (*See also* **Messianism**.)

MONASH, SIR JOHN (1865-1931). General and engineer. Born in Melbourne, **Australia**, to Austrian Jewish immigrants, Monash earned degrees in arts, law, and engineering at the University of Melbourne. After a brilliant career in engineering, he enlisted in the Victoria militia through which he advanced rapidly. During World War I he was named commander of the Australian forces on the Western Front with the rank of lieutenant general. Thus, he became the first Jewish general in the English army. After the war, Monash was active in Australian Jewish life, and in 1928, was elected President of the Anzac Zionist Federation. His many foreign military honors include the U.S. Distinguished Service Medal.

MOND, SIR ALFRED. *See* **Melchett, Lord.**

MONOTHEISM. *See* **God**.

MONTANA. With fewer than 500 Jews, of whom 200 live in Billings and 100 in Butte, Montana has no established Jewish congregations. Jews, however, were among the first settlers of Montana, even before it became a state. In 1866, there was a Jewish congregation in Helena.

MONTEFIORE, SIR MOSES (1784-1885). English Jewish philanthropist and community worker. By age 37, he had amassed a fortune as a stockbroker and was able to retire. Henceforth, he devoted himself completely to Jewish affairs. The Jewish community in Palestine was foremost among his interests. Montefiore bought land for agricultural enterprises and encouraged Jewish settlement. He endowed hospitals, established the first girls' school in **Jerusalem**, helped to provide almshouses, and built synagogues. Montefiore visited **Russia** twice in 1846 and in 1872, intervening on behalf of oppressed Russian Jewry with the Tsar. He traveled to **Egypt** and Constantinople to intercede in the **Damascus affair**, and also undertook missions to Rome, **Morocco**, and **Romania**. He was the most beloved Jewish leader of his day, and his picture hung in Jewish homes around the world. Queen Victoria knighted him in 1837, the same year he was elected Sheriff of London. Montefiore remained devoutly Orthodox in belief and practice throughout his life. Many places and institutions bear his name, such as Zikhron Moshe near Jerusalem, Shkhunat Montefiore near **Tel Aviv**, and Montefiore Hospital in New York.

Sir Moses Montefiore.

MONTREAL. *See* **Canada**.

MORDECAI (5th century B.C.E.). Mentioned in the Book of **Esther**, he was a cousin and guardian of a young woman named Esther whom King Ahasuerus chose to be his queen. After the king's chief minister, Haman, received the king's permission to destroy the Jews, Mordecai enlisted Esther's help and succeeded in thwarting the plan and having Haman executed.

The Greatness of Mordecai, by Lucas Van der Leyden. Courtesy Metropolitan Museum of Art.

MORGENTHAU, HENRY SR. (1856-1946). Diplomat and financier. Brought to the U.S. from Germany in 1865, he studied law but made his fortune in real estate. A supporter of Woodrow Wilson, he was named Ambassador to **Turkey** in 1913. After World War I, he headed two U.S. commissions on refugee problems. His last years were devoted to writing; Morgenthau's works include *All in a Lifetime*, an autobiography.

MORGENTHAU, HENRY JR. (1891-1967). American statesman and agricultural expert. Son of Henry **Morgenthau, Sr.**, he was called to Washington by President Franklin D. Roosevelt to head the Farm Credit Board. He was soon named Undersecretary of the Treasury, then promoted to Secretary. He played a key role in the recovery of the U.S. from the economic depression of the 1930's, and in its mobilization for World War II. After his retirement from public office he became active in Zionist fund-raising. In 1947, he was named General Chairman of the **United Jewish Appeal**, and in 1951, became Chairman of the Board of Governors of the **Bonds for Israel** drive. In Israel, *Kibbutz Tal Shahar*, or Morning Dew, is named for Morgenthau.

Henry Morgenthau, Jr. Courtesy United Jewish Appeal.

MOROCCO. The Jewish community of Morocco dates back to the period before the destruction of the Second **Temple** in 70 C.E. Under Roman rule, Jews suffered continual harassment. This torment ended temporarily with the fall of the Roman Empire, when the Vandal King Generich permitted Moroccan Jews equal citizenship. They engaged in navigation, maritime commerce, vinegrowing, and agriculture, and flourished for a time. But the era of prosperity soon ended. Under Arab rule during the 10th century, there was an upsurge of Jewish cultural and religious life. Such famous Talmudic scholars as Isaac **Alfasi** and Moses **Maimonides** lived in Morocco. The notorious *mellahs*, or ghettos, whose cramped and twisted streets came to symbolize Moroccan Jewish degradation to second-class citizenship, were originally instituted in the 13th century to protect Jews from Muslim mob attacks. These ghettos have continued into the 20th century.

Jews' expulsion from **Spain** in 1492 brought a great influx of Jews to Morocco, where they introduced European traditions of art, culture, and commerce. The Jewish community witnessed another cultural resurgence in the 16th century, when Morocco became the home of many noted Jewish scholars. But Jews remained second-class citizens, always subject to Moslem violence. War with **France** and Spain in the 19th century further inflamed Moslem fanaticism, and the mellahs became the scene of brutal, unprovoked attacks. With French and Danish occupation of Morocco in 1912, conditions took a turn for the better. The worst abuses ended, corporal punishment was abolished, the observance of the **Sabbath** was recognized, and compulsory military service was ended.

A group of children at an Alliance school in Morocco.

General Arab antagonism to the State of **Israel** created a rising feeling of insecurity among Moroccan Jews. There was a large-scale shift of the Jewish population from villages and small towns to the larger cities which offered greater protection. In addition, since 1948, almost 300,000 Jews have emigrated to Israel.

In 1956, France and Spain relinquished their protectorate, and Morocco achieved its independence. In 1998, there were about 6,500 Jews in the country. Casablanca has the largest Jewish community of any Moslem city. Other important centers were Tangier, Meknes, Fez, and Tetuan. A number of welfare, religious, and educational institutions operate in Morocco, aided by the **American Jewish Joint Distribution Committee.**

MORTARA CASE. In 1858, church authorities kidnaped a six-year-old Jewish boy, Edgar Mortara, from his parents in Bologna, **Italy.** This became an international incident, and emperors Franz Joseph of Austria and Napoleon III of France sent personal messages to Pope Pius IX pleading that the child be returned to his parents. Their requests and all other protests were rejected, and Edgar Mortara was raised as a Catholic. The Church argued that Edgar's Catholic nurse had him secretly baptized when he was two years old, and baptism was irrevocable. The child was never given back to his parents, and when he grew up he entered the Church as a priest.

MOSES. In Hebrew, *Moshe Rabbenu*; literally, Moses our teacher, also known as "Father of the Prophets," the only prophet who knew God "face to face." He was the liberator and lawgiver of Israel, the one who turned a mob of slaves into a nation willing to receive the law of the Almighty and capable of conquering the promised land, setting themselves apart as "a kingdom of priests and a holy nation," to become "a light unto the nations!"

> *"And the angel of the Lord appeared to him in a flame of fire out of the midst of a bush."*
>
> — EXODUS 3:2

The details of Moses' career are vividly recorded in the pages of the **Bible**. Of the five books that bear his name, known as the Pentateuch, four recount the story of his leadership. He was the third child of Amram and Yocheved of the tribe of **Levi**; his birth in Egypt is surrounded by secrecy as is his death in the wilderness near Mt. Nebo, "no man knowing his burying place."

To escape the Pharaoh's cruel decree ordering every Hebrew male child cast into the Nile, Moses was hidden by his mother for three months after his birth, then placed onto an ark of bulrushes by the river's edge, with his sister **Miriam** keeping watch at a distance. There, he was discovered by the daughter of the Pharaoh who took pity on the child and, through the clever prompting of Moses' sister Miriam, engaged the child's mother to act as nurse. Brought up as an Egyptian prince in the palace of the Pharaoh, Moses never forgot his Hebrew origin, for his mother reared him in the faith and traditions of his people.

Moses' zeal for justice finds dramatic expression when he kills an Egyptian taskmaster for assaulting a Jew. When the news of this act reaches the Pharaoh, Moses flees for his life to Midian where he joins the household of Jethro the priest, whose daughter Zipporah he takes for a wife. She bears him two sons, Gershom and Eliezer.

While tending his father-in-law's flocks Moses received his first call from God from a burning bush. He is assigned the task of liberating the people and accepts it, though with some reluctance.

With his brother **Aaron** who acts as his spokesman (for Moses stammered), he appears before the Pharaoh, whom he orders to free the Children of Israel from bondage. The Pharaoh's consent comes only after the infliction of ten plagues. The hurried exodus of the Children of Israel from Egypt is followed by the miraculous crossing of the Red Sea. Free at last, the people of Israel now journey into the desert to receive the **Ten Commandments** at the foot of Mt. Sinai and to enter into an eternal covenant with God.

The prayer of Moses against Amalek, 18th century engraving.

The Burning Bush. From an old engraving.

But the habits of a long-enslaved people are not easily broken. In Moses' 40-day absence during his encounter with God in the craggy solitudes of Mt. Sinai, old superstitions and beliefs asserted themselves with the making of a golden calf. The trials of desert life demoralized the people. They lost faith in themselves and their leader Moses, and their constant murmurings soon turned into open rebellion, sealing their fate. They were condemned to wander in the desert for 40 years, by the end of which time a new generation grew up to undertake the conquest of the land of Canaan. Even Moses had to share this fate, dying at the desert's edge in sight of the promised land. On the seventh of Adar he ascended Mt. Nebo for a last look at the land, then, Jewish tradition has it, he died by "the kiss of God" at the age of 120 in the prime of his powers—"his eye was not dim, nor his natural force abated."

> *"But Moses' hands were heavy... and Aaron and Hur held up his hands."*
>
> — EXODUS 17:12

The towering personality of Moses impressed itself upon the Jewish people and shaped their character. The people learned to live by the laws of the Five Books of Moses. They revered the qualities of Moses' character, his loving kindness, strength and humility, wisdom and modesty. And they wove innumerable legends about his life. The people of the world share with Israel the reverence for Moses, the world's greatest liberator and giver of the Ten Commandments which provided a moral direction to the civilization of the West.

MOSES BEN MAIMON. *See* **Maimonides.**

MOSES BEN NAHMAN (1195-1270). Also known as Nahmanides or Ramban. Born in Gerona, **Spain**, he was one of the outstanding Talmudic scholars and **Bible** commentators of the Middle Ages. Nahmanides' fame rose when he brilliantly defended the Jewish faith in one of the forced religious disputes between Christians and Jews. The dispute took place at Barcelona, Spain, in 1263. Nahmanides was compelled to participate under order of King James I of Aragon. The question "Has the Messiah already arrived, or is he yet to appear and redeem the world from its state of misery and suffering?" was one of the central themes of the debate. The King conceded the success of the great Jewish scholar who presented winning arguments in support of the Jewish religion. This victory enraged his adversaries, the Dominican priests, who accused him of insulting the Christian faith. Forced to leave Spain, Nahmanides came to Palestine in 1267, settling first in **Jerusalem** and later in **Acre** where he founded a Talmudical academy. Finding few Jews in Palestine, Nahmanides issued a call to his brethren in other countries and urged them to come and settle in the Holy Land.

Nahmanides was recognized as the foremost authority on Jewish law. His commentary on the Bible continues to be highly regarded for its profound interpretations based on reason and deep knowledge. A physician by profession, Nahmanides also engaged in the study of mysticism, or Kabbalah, philosophy, and science.

MOSES, ROBERT (1888-1981). American civil servant. Moses played a major role in the development of New York City's parks and roads, and was in charge of the New York World's Fair.

MOSHAV. Form of cooperative agricultural settlement in Israel. Different from the **kibbutz**, each member of the moshav has a home and plot of land worked by himself and his family. However, all marketing of produce and purchase of supplies is done cooperatively, and some of the machinery is owned by the village as a whole. The Moshav Shitufi is run along lines midway between a kibbutz and a moshav.

MOURNING. *See* **Burial.**

MUNI, PAUL. *See* **Stage and Screen.**

MUSIC, JEWISH. Jewish music began when the Israelites were wandering tribes in the desert. They sang with joy when they discovered water and good grazing for their flocks. They beat rhythms on simple drums and tambourines. They blew their crude rams' horns when they were attacked by marauders or when they wanted to summon an assembly of the tribe. After settling in the land of Canaan, they sang songs of triumph, mourning, harvest, and love. They also had professional musicians and singers who knew how to play the more sophisticated instruments of the Middle East—strings, wind, and percussion, and who were trained to perform the elaborate music of the **Temple** service. King **David** played the lute and sang as he composed **Psalms** of praise and supplication.

An ancient Hebrew lute from an Egyptian engraving.

All of this ancient music has been lost. We can only attempt to reconstruct it by studying wall paintings and friezes which have remained from ancient times and by noting the names of instruments mentioned in the **Bible** and their derivations. The Bible, particularly **Psalms** and the **Song of Songs**, contains the words of many ancient songs.

After the destruction of the Second **Temple**, synagogue songs replaced Temple chants. Carried down from generation to generation into many faraway lands, the chant changed further. Still, similarities can be found in the chants of Jews as far apart geographically and culturally as **Germany**, North Africa, and **Yemen**. Probably the oldest music still in use in synagogues is the biblical chant, the melody in which the readings from the Torah, the Prophets, and the special scrolls are chanted on **Sabbaths** and Festivals in the synagogue.

In the early Middle Ages, these chants were written down for the Bible text in a primitive sort of musical sign language. The symbols are vague, so that people in different parts of the world sounded them differently. Besides, the same set of signs is sung differently in connection with the various sections of the Bible. In other words, even in the tradition of the East European Jews, for example, the melody of the Torah or Pentateuch chant sounds quite different from that of the prophetic chant; the Book of **Esther** and the **Song of Songs** are chanted still differently.

Another heritage from the distant past is the prayer chant, known as *nusach*, which is the basis of the **hazan**'s improvisations. The *hazan* is free to elaborate on the *nusach*. Some of these chants may indeed be descendants of Temple songs. Others are believed to have been composed by unknown composers in the Middle Ages, in the days of the troubadours and minnesingers of Europe.

In Germany and East Europe, biblical and prayer chants became part of the folk songs of the people. Conversely, wherever Jews lived, their folk songs took on the color of the country. Folk songs were usually sung in a vernacular, that is, in the language of everyday life. There are a number of such languages, usually a combination of Hebrew with the language of the country, for example, **Yiddish**, **Ladino**, and Judeo-Arabic. Sometimes Jews would borrow tunes from their neighbors and put their own words to them. The songs that lasted the longest were religious folk songs, that is, Sabbath table songs, or *zemirot*, wedding songs, and holiday songs.

The 18th century gave birth to **Hasidism**, a sect which considered singing a major conduit for communion with God. The Hasidim excelled in composing melodies that had become popular throughout the Jewish world. They created a genre known as Hasidic *niggun*, a melody that is either hummed, chanted, or sung, conveying deep feelings and often conducive to spontaneous and spirited dancing.

In the 19th century, as Jews began to participate in the non-Jewish cultures in which they lived, professionally composed music

The Israeli Philharmonic at the Mann Auditorium in Tel Aviv.

finally emerged. Solomon Sulzer and Louis Lewandowski were pioneers in writing music in four-part harmony for the synagogue for cantors and choirs. They and their immediate followers were so eager to make their music sound Western that they lost almost all the flavor of the traditional *nusach*. Later in the 19th century, however, with the development of **Yiddish** and the revival of **Hebrew**, interest was renewed in the traditional synagogue music. Folk songs and Jewish music in other parts of the world were studied intensively. As the 20th century dawned, a movement of young Jews in **Russia** attempted to create a "national" Jewish music. At the same time, a new folk music was growing up in the first Jewish settlements in Palestine. This folk music was at first much like that of Russia and **Poland**. At the same time, a beginning was made in the composition of new synagogue music in the U.S. Some of the composers of this music have come here from Europe, others are native born and trained. Much of the music, though written in a modern style, has its roots in the ancient chants.

Folk songs continue to be created in Israel, where the melodies of Eastern and Asian Jews have added an exotic flavor to the earlier Slavic tunes of the Land. In recent years, Israeli popular music has been greatly influenced by Middle Eastern and Mediterranean music, particularly Greek and Spanish, as well as American and Western popular music. The once soft music of the accordion or flute accompanying the singing has been replaced by boisterous rock bands which dominate today's musical scene. This is true of liturgical music in all its varieties, including Orthodox and Hasidic.

MUSIC, JEWS IN. Since the 19th century, Jews have made major contributions to Western music in general and to American music in particular. Perhaps the greatest composer of Jewish origin in the early 19th century was Felix **Mendelssohn**. Jacques **Offenbach** is another major example of that period. Gustav **Mahler**, a leading modern composer, represents the end of that century. In the 20th century the French Darius **Milhuad**, the Viennese Arnold **Schoenberg**, and the Americans George **Gershwin** and Aaron **Copland** set music trends.

Jews have also given the world some of the greatest violinists of the past hundred years, including the Europeans Jascha **Heifetz**, Yehudi **Menuhin**, David Oistrakh, and Nathan Milstein; the American Isaac **Stern**; and the Israelis Yitzhak **Perlman** and Pinchas Zuckerman. Among great Jewish pianists of our time are the Europeans Artur **Rubinstein**, Vladimir **Horowitz**, Rudolf Serkin, and Vladimir Ashkenazy; and the Israelis David Bar-Ilan and Daniel Barenboim, who was born in Argentina.

Another area where Jews have made an enormous musical contribution is orchestra conducting. Many of the great Jewish conductors were born in Europe, but a good number pursued their careers in the U.S. where they conducted major orchestras: George Szell (Cleveland), Eugene Ormandy (Philadephia), Andre Previn (Los Angeles), William Steinberg (Pittsburgh), Max Rudolf (Cincinnati), José Serebrier (Cleveland), George Solti (Chicago), Fritz Reiner (Pittsburgh), Erich Leinsdorf (Rochester), and Serge Koussevitzky (Boston). The first prominent American-born conductor was Leonard **Bernstein**, a major figure in American music.

Some Jewish conductors became great popularizers of both classic and popular music. Besides Bernstein, Mitch Miller and his television program "Sing Along with Mitch" were enormously popular. Andre Kostelanez recorded a wide range of music, and Arthur Fiedler won fame with the Boston Pops.

Among great 20th century opera singers in the U.S. were Richard Tucker, Robert Merrill, Roberta Peters, and Beverly Sills.

Jews in Popular Music. The Jewish contribution to music in the U.S. has not been limited to classical music. The American musical show, an original American art form, was greatly enriched by Jewish songwriters and composers, such as Jerome Kern (*Show Boat*), Gershwin (*Porgy and Bess*), and particularly Richard Rogers and Oscar Hammerstein (*Oklahoma!, South Pacific, Carousel*). More recently, Frederick Loewe's *My Fair Lady* (lyrics by Lerner) and the work of Stephen Sondheim (*Sunday in the Park with George*) have gained great popularity.

Al Jolson.

American Jews have also written many of the popular songs of our time. Irving **Berlin** may hold the record for the number of songs written (*God Bless America, White Christmas*); Bob Dylan (*Blowin' in the Wind*) and Paul Simon, with Art Garfunkel, *(Bridge Over Troubled Water*) won Grammys for their popular folk-rock music.

Al Jolson (*Swanee*), a cantor's son, was one of the leading American entertainers before World War II. Sophie Tucker (*Yiddishe Mamme*) was a musical comedy singer. Another great comedienne and singer of the time was Fanny Brice (*I'd Rather Be Blue*). More recently, singers Bette Midler (*The Rose*) and Barbra Streisand (*People, The Way We Were*), as well as singer-songwriters Neil Diamond (*You Don't Bring Me Flowers*) and Barry Manilow (*Mandy*) have become household names.

MYSTICISM. *See* **Kabbalah**.

NA'AMAT USA. Women's Labor Zionist Organization. Na'amat has branches in **Argentina, Australia, Belgium, Brazil, Canada, Chile, England, France, Mexico, Peru, Spain,** and **Uruguay.** Its largest constituency is in Israel, while the second largest is in the U.S.

Na'amat USA. Na'amat USA is a 50,000-member volunteer organization of clubs throughout the country which help support the work of Na'amat in Israel and who implement domestic programs, including advancing the rights and status of women. These programs build a better America, a more secure Israel, and a fuller life for women and children everywhere. Na'amat USA educates women on Israel's strategic alliance with the U.S.; advocates legislation on full employment and social security benefits for women; participates in allied campaigns for Israel; co-sponsors Youth Aliyah; supports Habonim/Dror, the Labor Zionist Youth movement, promotes Zionist educational programs; and aids Jewish, Yiddish, and Hebrew cultural institutions.

Na'amat in Israel. Founded in 1921, Na'amat became the largest women's organization in Israel. It is committed to a more equitable society for every Israeli citizens and to equal rights for women. To this end, Na'amat operates institutions for women, children, and young people to help narrow the existing social, educational, and cultural gaps.

Day Care. Nearly 33,000 children have been attending Na'amat's agricultural boarding high schools in Eron, Kanot, and Aynot.

Vocational Training. Na'amat's Timon vocational high schools offer courses, counseling, and job training to disadvantaged Jewish and Arab girls and boys, many of whom are potential drop-outs. Women who want to be employed or upgrade their current jobs can choose from hundreds of courses in fields where work is readily available. Na'amat services for Arabs and Druze women foster their personal development, helping them and their families become productive citizens.

Dina Spector, President of Na'amat USA.

Community Centers. At 65 centers located wherever social services are needed in small towns and major cities, most Na'amat activities are found under one roof.

Status of Women. In Israel, Na'amat has responded to every issue important to women, with free legal counsel, Centers for Problems of Violence in Family, pre-release workshops, and Women's Studies at Haifa University.

NACHMAN OF BRATZLAV (1770-1811). Hasidic leader, one of the most remarkable personalities produced by **Hasidism.** Grandson of the founder of the movement, **Israel Baal Shem Tov,** Nachman's unique gifts became evident in childhood. He was still young when followers began to flock to him to listen eagerly to his interpretation of Hasidic philosophy. He taught them to pray joyfully and devote time to contemplation. Aside from his Hasidic works, he created imaginative original fairy tales.

Unlike other Hasidic rabbis, Rabbi Nachman did not establish a dynasty. Followers of his teachings are to be found all over the world, especially in **Israel.** They revere his memory, marking the anniversaries of his death with special observance.

NAHAL. Literally, Fighting Pioneer Youth. A branch of the **Israel Defense Forces** formed by young men and women preparing for agricultural life. They spend part of their tour of duty living in frontier settlements.

NAHMANIDES. *See* **Moses Ben Nachman.**

NAHUM. Seventh of the minor prophets. The Book of Nahum in the **Bible** describes in poetic language the downfall of Nineveh and the Assyrian empire. Excavations of Nineveh make it evident that the prophet knew well the city whose destruction he painted so vividly.

NAHUM OF GIMZO. *See* **Tannaim.**

NAMES. Proper Names. In biblical times, a name expressed a thought or emotion. In the story of Creation, **Adam** named his wife **Eve,** or *Havah,* meaning "life" in Hebrew, because she was the "mother of all living." When **Rachel** bore her first son, she named him **Joseph,** Hebrew for "he will add," saying, "The Lord will add to me another son."

Sometimes a name was the compound of two related words. The Hebrew *Ab,* meaning "father," was combined with a variety of words: *Abishai,* Father-of-a-gift; *Abner,* Father-of-light; *Abraham,* Father-of-multitudes; and *Absalom,* Father-of-peace.

The Hebrew *Ah*, or "brother," was variously fused to make: *Ahijah*, Brother-of-God; *Ahinadab*, Brother-of-nobility; and *Ahitub*, Brother-of-goodness. *Ben*, Hebrew for "son," is part of *Benjamin*, Son-of-the-right-hand or Son-of-good-fortune, and *Reuben*, Behold-a-son; while *Bat*, or "daughter," is in *Bathsheba*, Daughter-of-the-oath. Often the divine names El, IAH, Jeho, and Shaddai were contained in proper names. *El* was combined to make *Eldad*, Beloved-of-God; *Elkanah*, God-created; *Bezalel*, In-the-shadow-of-God; and *Israel*, Warrior-of-God. Most familiar is the use of **Iah**, as in *Isaiah*, Help-of-God; and *Jeremiah*, Whom-God-raised-up. *Jeho* is found in the names *Jehoiadah*, Whom-God-favors; *Joab*, God-desired; and *Jonathan*, God-given. Finally, *Shaddai* was used to make *Ammishaddai*, Kindred-of-God; and *Zurishaddai*, God-protected.

People were also named after animals and plants: Arieh, Lion; Deborah, Bee; Jonah, Dove; Rachel, Ewe; Tamar, Palm Tree. The custom of naming children after deceased relatives, especially grandparents, was adopted after the Babylonian exile; later, among the **Hasidim** it was customary to name the boy after a deceased *tzaddik*, a Hasidic rabbi. Sephardic Jews name their children after living grandparents; among Reform Jews the son often bears the father's name with the addition of Junior, as among the Christians.

The use of foreign names first found in the later biblical period (e.g., **Esther** derived from Ishtar, **Mordecai** from Marduk) became more prevalent in Talmudic and medieval times. Some of the names in Jewish history that bear witness to contact with Greek and Roman civilizations are Antigonus, Symachus, Tarphon, Marcus, Justus, and Titus. The Greek name Alexander was shortened in time to Sander and Sender, while Phoebus became Feivel or Feivish, names that persist in Yiddish to this day. Beginning with the Greek-Hellenistic period, when the records show us Judah-Aristobulus, Salome-Alexandra, SimonPeter, and Saul-Paul, dual names, one Jewish and the other non-Jewish, became popular under the influence of foreign cultures.

Today, Jewish children as a rule receive one name typical of the country in which they live and one Yiddish or Hebrew name. The tendency is to retain a likeness in sound to the Jewish name: Arthur-Aaron, Hyman-Hayim, Bella-Beile, and Rose-Reizel. A boy's Hebrew name is usually bestowed at the circumcision ceremony, while a girl is named soon after birth. Among German Jews, the giving of the civic name was marked by the so-called *Hollekreisch* ceremony on the fourth Sabbath after birth. The first child is named after someone in the father's family; the second child after someone in the mother's. Sometimes a child is given two Hebrew or "Jewish" names to satisfy the wishes of both parents.

The influence of the **Kabbalah** is felt in the naming of children. People who have been dangerously ill are given additional names such as Hayim for men and Hayah for women. Hope for good health is expressed by the name Raphael, "God heals." Azriel, "God is my help," invokes divine aid, and Alter or Alte, "Old One," expresses the wish for a long life. Yiddish contains the largest variety of male and female names adopted from the Hebrew and European languages. Thus, the Hebrew Brakhah becomes Brokhe in Yiddish, Israel becomes Isser, Jacob, Koppel, Mordecai, Motel, Rebbeca, Rive, and Zipporah, Feiga (one Hebrew, the other Yiddish for bird). French and Spanish names also became Yiddishized: Belle becomes Beile, and Esperanza, Sprinze. The Italian name Angelo turns up as Anshel, and Benedetto, Bendet. A few German transformations are Braun to Bryna, Enoch to Henach, Hirsch to Hertz, Freude to Frade, Fradl, or Freidl. From Czech Bohdanka becomes Badane and Benes Beinish. The Russian Dobra becomes Dobre in Yiddish, Khvala, Khvoles, and Zlata, Zlate; the Polish Czarna becomes Charne.

Among **Yemenite** and other Arabic-speaking Jews, the influence of Arab names is apparent, e.g., Aminah, Asisah, Barhun, Dunash, Faradi, Gamilah, Hassan, Masudah, Nogema, Yahiah, and Yaish. Under the influence of **Zionism**, the use of biblical names has increased, and new Hebrew names have developed, particularly in the State of **Israel**. For boys, new names are *Amikam*, My-people-have-risen; *Arnon*, Torrent; *Eran*, Awakened; *Raanan*, Verdant; *Shaanan*, Peaceable; *Uzzi*, My-strength; and *Yigal*, God-will-redeem. New names for girls include *Adinah*, Delicate or Noble; *Aviva*, Spring; *Geulah*, Redemption; *Nitza*, Blossom; *Nurit*, Light; *Tikvah*, Hope; *Zahavah*, Goldie. Zionah and Galilah are adaptations of Israel place names.

In the 19th century laws prohibiting Jews to use non-Jewish names were in force in Prussia, Bohemia, and Tsarist **Russia**. A decree in Nazi **Germany**, published in August 1938, suggested the use of 276 typical Jewish names (185 for males and 91 for females) for Jewish children born after that date. Among these were such humiliating male names as Ahab and Ahasuerus, wicked biblical kings; Assur, the nation that defeated Israel; Chamor, Esau, Korah, Laban, and Lot, ignoble biblical personalities; Moab, another enemy of Israel; and Orev, a crow. Two wicked queens, Athalaiah, Jezebel, and the ludicrous Chinke and Driesel were Nazi-prescribed names for females. Under this decree, Jewish males and females were ordered to add the names Israel and Sarah, respectively, if their names did not proclaim their Jewish lineage.

Under the influence of the Bible, Christians borrowed many Hebrew names either in their pure biblical form (Aaron, Abner, Abigail, Adah, Beulah) or in a derivative form (Ann, Anna from Hannah, John from Yohanan, Elizabeth from Elisheba, Mary and Maria from Miriam).

Surnames. Jewish family names are of recent origin. Until 1800, the father's name would often be the family name; for example, Aaron *ben* (son of) Samuel was known as Aaron Samuel. In the early Middle Ages, Cohen, Levi, and their Hebrew abbreviations Katz (from the initials of *Kohen Zedek*, Priest of Justice) and Segal (from *S'gan Levi*, Levitical Head) are mentioned. Names such as Aaronson, Abramson, Hirschenson, and Jacobson (and their Slavic forms Aronovsky, Abramsky, Hirshovsky, Yakubovsky, or Aronovitsh, Abramovitsh, Hirshovitsh, and Yakubovitsh) originated from the use of the father's name. The elimination of "son" restored such names to their anglicized forms (Aaron, Abrahams, Hirsh, Jacobs), while the addition of "mann" to Hebrew or Yiddish proper names created surnames like Abermann (from Abraham), Heymann (Hayim), Koppelmann (Jacob), Mosesmann, Nachmann, Saulmann, and Urimann.

More than 60% of Jewish family names in Europe are of geographic derivation, the oldest being Spiro, Mintz, Horowitz, Liebshitz, and names ending in "burg" (Friedburg, Maidenburg, Ruttenburg, and Warburg). A small percentage denotes occupations (Buchbinder, Drucker, Goldschmidt, Hutmacher, Kirzhner, Lederer, Milner, Schneider, Tischler) or Jewish communal functions (Chazan, Cantor; Lehrer, Teacher; Magid, Preacher; Parnes, President; and Singer). Abbreviations are also common: Asch from Eisenstadt; Bach from Bayit Chadash, "Newhouse"; Bahrav from Ben Ha-rav, "Rabbi's Son"; Back from Ben Kedoshim, "Son-of-Saints"; Barash from Ben Rabbi Shimon, Son-of-Rabbi-Simon; Shatz from Sheliah Tzibur, "Public Pleader"; Zakheim from Zera Kodesh aim, "Seed-of-Holiness."

Among American Jews there is a tendency to anglicize the family name; a name such as Katzenelenbogen, one of the oldest among European Jews, may be changed to Katenel, Katzen, Katz, or Kat, ultimately to become Kay. In the State of Israel, the translation of a name into a Hebraized form is popular. Thus, Gutstein becomes Eventov; Lichtstein, Maor or Even-Ur; Goldberg, Har Zahav; Friedberg, Har Shalom; Friedman, Ish Shalom; Derbarimdiker, Rahman or Rahamim; Florentin, Perahiah; Diamant, Yahalom; Rosen, Shoshan; Stock, Sedan or Zmorah; Shertok, Sharett; and Treger, Amos.

Emblem of the tribe of Naphtali.

NAPHTALI. Literally, my struggle. Tenth son of **Jacob**. The tribe of Naphtali was war-like in its early days; it was allotted territory north and west of the Sea of **Galilee**.

NASI, JOSEPH (ca. 1510-1579). Jewish statesman, banker, and merchant. Born in **Portugal**, Joseph Nasi came from the historic Nasi-**Mendes** family of distinguished Spanish aristocrats. Some of them were among the refugees from **Spain** who settled in Portugal in 1492. Forced to adopt **Christianity** in 1497, they became **Marranos**, or secret Jews. Joseph's Marrano name was Joao Miguez. When he was about 15 years old, Joseph's widowed aunt, Donna Gracia de Mendesia, took him to Antwerp where there was less religious prejudice. In Antwerp, also, they came to be suspected of secretly observing Judaism, and fled to Venice. When Venice expelled all Marranos and arrested Donna Gracia, the powerful Nasi-Mendes banking and financial house brought its influence to **Turkey**. Joseph was therefore able to get the help of Sultan Suleiman the Magnificent in obtaining freedom for his aunt. When she was released, Donna Gracia, her daughter Reyna, and Joseph settled in Constantinople and threw off the disguise of Catholicism. Joseph married his beautiful cousin Reyna, and after Suleiman's death he entered the service of Sultan Selim. He was a favorite at the court, and his influence was greater than the Grand Vizier's. In gratitude for the success of his policies, Selim made Joseph Nasi Duke of Naxos and Prince of the Cyclades. He also gave him a grant of the city of **Tiberias** in Palestine. Joseph Nasi gathered up 200 Jewish refugees from the **Inquisition** in Italy and brought them to **Tiberias** in his ships. Into this colony he introduced mulberry trees for silk cultivation, although the results of this 16th-century experiment in agricultural settlement of the Holy Land are not recorded. One of Joseph Nasi's spectacular policies was dictated by his desire for revenge. He pressed the Sultan into declaring war on Venice; the result was the capture of Cyprus by the Turks.

NATIONAL CONFERENCE OF SYNAGOGUE YOUTH (NCSY). Organized by the **Union of Orthodox Jewish Congregations** in the 1950's, NCSY is a national youth movement open to all Jewish teenagers. It is organized in chapters affliated with twelve regions throughout the U.S. The NCSY conducts a large variety of programs in the U.S. and Israel, summer camps, an Israel summer program, leadership training, and a new program for Jewish children in Ukraine.

NATIONAL COUNCIL OF JEWISH WOMEN. The oldest major Jewish women's organization in the U.S., the National Council of Jewish Women has a history of pioneering advocacy and community service projects in the U.S. and Israel for more than 91 years. More than 100,000 members in 200 sections nationwide implement the mission of the organization, which in the spirit of Judaism is dedicated to furthering human welfare in Jewish and general communities, locally, nationally and internationally.

Currently, NCJW maintains five priorities: children and youth; women's issues; Israel; the elderly; and Jewish life. The organization offers a myriad of programs and projects in each priority. For example, NCJW's Court Appointed Special Advocate (CASA) project, implemented by its sections, provides volunteers as advocates for children in the foster care system. The NCJW Research Institute for Innovation in Education at the Hebrew University which promotes education and social welfare.

NATIONAL FEDERATION OF TEMPLE SISTERHOODS. The women's division of the **Union of American Hebrew Congregations**, the central organization of Reform Judaism in the U.S. Organized in 1913, the organization has a membership consists of members of more than 800 sisterhoods. Functioning groups are also found in **Canada**, the U.K., **Latin America**, **Australia**, and **South Africa**. Through program material, study courses, and projects, the Federation assists its members in serving the synagogue, gaining Jewish knowledge, and translating religious ideals into practical expression of concern for humanity. The Federation provide scholarships and aid to students at the **Hebrew Union College**. The Jewish Institute of Religion helps to promote and support the youth activities program of the Union of American Hebrew Congregations, and subsidizes institutes for religious school teachers and laypersons. It grants rabbinic fellowships to foreign students to enable them to serve congregations belonging to the World Union of Progressive Judaism after ordination and graduation. To further interfaith awareness and understanding, the sisterhoods conduct institutes on Judaism for Christian women to acquaint them with the traditions, ritual, and philosophy of Judaism.

NATIONAL FEDERATION OF TEMPLE YOUTH. The National Federation of Temple Youth (NIFTY) represents teenagers affiliated with Reform synagogues in the U.S. NIFTY is divided into regions. Members in the various regions are encouraged to attend conclaves, to participate in leadership institutes, and to help in NIFTY projects. The national organization seeks to exert a direct influence on the individual members through its Mitzvah Program. A Mitzvah Kit details the projects of the individual groups and forms the basis for the major part of teenage activity. The program includes various activities of NIFTY in Israel.

NAVON, YITZHAK (1921-). Israeli educator, public servant, and fifth president of the State of **Israel**. Born in **Jerusalem** to an old **Sephardic** family, he studied at the **Hebrew University**, then taught at elementary and secondary schools. He also served as director of the Arabic department of **Haganah**. In 1949, he joined Israel's foreign service. Later, he was political secretary first to Moshe **Sharett** and from 1952 to 1963 to Prime Minister David **Ben-Gurion**. In 1965, after serving two years with the Ministry of Education, he was elected to the **Knesset**. In 1978, he was elected president of the State of Israel, the first Sephardic Jew and native-born Israeli to hold that office. He has written books and stories on the folklore of Sephardic communities, one of which, *The Sephardic Orchard*, has become a popular musical in Israel.

NAZARETH. Israeli town of about 69,000 inhabitants. It is the main Arab city in Israel, mostly Christian with a Moslem minority. Nazareth nestles in a secluded glen in the hills of lower **Galilee** in the shadow of Mount Tabor, overlooking the great Plain of Jezreel. The home of Jesus as a child and young man, Nazareth has many beautiful churches, monasteries, and sacred sites, including the Fountain of the Virgin. Next to Nazareth is Natzrat Ilit, a new Jewish town of some 30,000 inhabitants.

NAZIRITE. One in biblical times who vowed to abstain from various pleasures for a limited period of time and dedicate himself to God. The Nazirite was not allowed to drink wine, go near a dead body, or cut his hair (Num. 6). **Samson** was a Nazirite and caused his own downfall by allowing Delilah to shave his head (Judges 16:19). The Nazirite assumed vows for a period of not fewer than thirty days, at the end of which he brought a sacrifice at the Temple. Although a section of the **Talmud** is devoted to the laws of the Nazirite, Jewish tradition discouraged people from placing personal restrictions on themselves and separating themselves from society.

NAZISM. *See* **Holocaust**.

NEBRASKA. Jews arrived when the territory was first organized in 1854. Mostly Central European traders and merchants, they settled in Omaha, Lincoln, Plattsmouth, Grand Island, and other towns. By the end of the century more Jews, mostly East European, arrived. Attempts to establish a Jewish agricultural settlement failed. In the 20th century Jews became active in the public life of the state, and several Jews served as mayors of their towns. Among the prominent Jews of Omaha were Aaron Cahn, who served in the state legislature in 1863, and Henry Monsky, a **B'nai B'rith** leader. Today, there are 7,500 Jews in the state, with 6,500 in Omaha and 800 in Lincoln. The *Jewish Press* is published in Omaha.

NEBUCHADNEZZAR. King of **Babylonia** from 605-562 B.C.E. He conquered the ancient Middle East, and when the kingdom of Judah rebelled against him in 586, he captured **Jerusalem**, destroyed the **Temple**, and exiled its people, thus ending the first commonwealth and starting the Babylonian exile.

NEGEV. Southern and still largely uninhabited part of **Israel**, more than 4,000 square miles in area. It has a desert climate, hot and dry by day, cold and humid by night. The Negev is the largest compact territorial block in Israel, made up of uplands and plateaus with elevations of up to 3,000 feet, as well as canyons and wide, dry river beds. For many centuries the Negev was a forsaken wasteland, although evidence of past life is shown in the ruins of cities and villages such as **Elat** and Haluza, Avdat and Shivta. Relics of terraces, dams, and pools date back to Nabatean, Roman, and Byzantine times. These were stations of the ancient trade routes and the mining cities of **Solomon**. Today, the dry lands of the Negev are slowly coming to life. New settlements are growing with newly arrived immigrants; sheep ranches are being established and crops are being cultivated with the aid of water piped from the Yarkon River. Underground water sources are being tapped, and copper mining has been resumed at the ancient sites. Minerals such as phosphates and kaolin are being successfully exploited.

NEHARDEIA. *See* **Babylonia**.

NEHEMIAH, BOOK OF. Eleventh book in the Ketuvim, or Writings, section of the **Bible**. It relates the history of Nehemiah, son of Hacaliah, who was the cup-bearer of Artaxerxes II, King of Persia (ca. 446 B.C.E.). When news of the poor condition of the returned exiles in **Jerusalem** reached Nehemiah in Susa, he obtained a commission from the King to return to Judea as its governor. One of Nehemiah's first tasks was to lead the people in rebuilding the walls of Jerusalem, as they defended themselves from attacks by the **Samaritans**.

Nehemiah inspired the builders to defend themselves as they worked, saying "one of his hands does the work and in the other he holds his weapon." Together with **Ezra the Scribe**, Nehemiah reinstituted festivals and observances which preserved the identity and continuity of the Jewish people.

NER TAMID. Literally, eternal light. Light kept on perpetually over the ark in the synagogue, as a symbol of God's presence.

NEILAH. Literally, closing. Final service of **Yom Kippur**. Traditionally, the recital of this prayer indicated that the gates of heaven were about to close and judgment would be passed on the fate of men and women for the coming year. The Neilah service dates back to the 3rd century, one of the most solemn portions of Jewish liturgy.

NETANYAHU, BENJAMIN (1950-). Chairman of the Likud Party since 1993, he was elected Prime Minister of **Israel** in May 1996 in the state's first direct election of Prime Minister. He served as Israel's Deputy Foreign Minister from 1988 to 1991 and as Deputy Minister in the Prime Minister's Office from 1991 to 1992.

Prime Minister Benjamin Netanyahu. Courtesy Embassy of Israel, Washington D.C.

The Portuguese Synagogue in Amsterdam. Engraving by Romain de Hooghe, 1675.

Netanyahu's previous posts were Israel's Ambassador to the UN (1984-88) and Deputy Chief of Mission to the U.S. (1982-84). In the 13th Knesset (1992-1996) he was a member of the Knesset Committees on Foreign Affairs and Security and on Constitution, Law, and Justice.

Before entering public life, Netanyahu, a graduate of the Massachusetts Institute of Technology, served as a soldier and officer in an elite anti-terror unit in the **Israel Defense Forces** (1967-1972). He is the editor of several books, including *Terrorism: How the West Can Win* (1986) and *International Terrorism: Challenge and Response* (1991). More recently, he wrote *A Place Among the Nations: Israel and the World* (1993) and *Fighting Terrorism: How Democracies Can Defeat Domestic and International Terrorism* (1995).

NETHERLANDS. Jews began to settle in Holland in 1322, but were driven out in the latter part of that century. However, late in the 15th century, as Jews and **Marranos** began to arrive from Spain, many Marranos returned openly to the Jewish faith. Many of the Jewish refugees had capital and initiative, and in time they attained positions of economic importance. In the 17th century, their ranks were swelled by **Ashkenazic** Jews arriving from Germany and Poland. The flourishing Dutch communities were strictly Orthodox and did not tolerate any act of reform or heresy. For this reason **Uriel Acosta** was excommunicated in 1618, as was Baruch **Spinoza** in 1655. Dutch Jewry enjoyed more political rights than did their fellow Jews in other European lands. Until the occupation of Holland by the Germans in 1940, local Jewry played a significant part in the economy, culture, and media of the Netherlands.

In 1942, the Germans herded all Dutch Jews into ghettos and concentration camps. The largest of the latter was Westerbork, from which 117,000 Jewish men, women, and children were transferred to **Auschwitz** and Sobibor in Poland, where they were exterminated in gas chambers. Their possessions, factories, and businesses were plundered by the Germans. About 25,000 Jews, some of them of mixed ancestry, and others concealed in special hiding places survived.

In 1998, the Jewish community in the Netherlands numbered 27,000, of whom about half lived in **Amsterdam**. The years following World War II were taken up with recuperation-efforts to recover property and assets, to restore a semblance of order to religious and social institutions, and to bring back Jewish children harbored by Christians and often brought up in the Christian faith. By the end of 1949, the remnants of Dutch Jewry had begun to take on the characteristics of a stable community. Economically, they were self-supporting and better off than the rest of Europe's Jewry. Synagogues and schools were reopened, and the work of restitution proceeded at a steady, if slow pace. The central Jewish welfare agency reported at the end of 1955 that it was affiliated with 28 religious and 37 private organizations.

NETHERLANDS ANTILLES (DUTCH WEST INDIES). Made up of Curaçao and Aruba, two Caribbean islands off the coast of Venezuela. They have a combined population of 175,000.

Curaçao is the home of one of the oldest permanent Jewish settlements in the New World. Jews from Holland and Brazil settled here during the 1650's and prospered in farming and trade. Their synagogue, built in 1732, is the oldest in the Western Hemisphere. The community flourished in the 18th century, some of its members rising to important positions in the administration of the island. Commercial decline in the 19th century led to a sharp drop in the Jewish population. The community in 1998, numbering 300, was composed chiefly of **Sephardic** Jews, with a small East European minority. It maintains a Jewish Relief Committee and a Hebrew School.

Aruba, an island 75 miles west of Curaçao, is home to about 100 Jews who arrived from Europe in the late 1930's and early 1940's. An old Jewish cemetery on the island indicates that a lost Jewish community existed in earlier times. The members of the present community are engaged in trade or employed by the Standard Oil Company.

NETTER, KARL (1826-1882). Entrepreneur in London and Paris. One of the founders of the **Alliance Israélite Universelle** in France, he helped persecuted Jews in Eastern Europe, traveling widely on rescue missions. Netter's outstanding achievement was the founding of the agricultural school at **Mikveh Israel** in Palestine, where he died in 1882.

NETURE KARTA. Literally, Guardians of the City. Group of Orthodox extremists who oppose the State of **Israel** because they believe that Israel can be redeemed only through the direct intervention of God and the advent of the Messiah. In 1935, a few hundred members of **Agudath Israel** under the leadership of Amram Blau objected strenuously to their organization's cooperation with other Zionist groups. They broke away and formed the Neture Karta, and have not hesitated to resort to violence in support of their beliefs. The organization is small but has supporters outside of Israel, particularly in the U.S.

NEUMANN, EMANUEL (1893-1980). American Zionist leader. Brought to the U.S. from **Lithuania** as an infant, he was a founder of **Young Judea** and served as president of the **Zionist Organization of America** from 1947 to 1949 and from 1956 to 1958. For more than half a century, he played an important role in the American Zionist movement as a speaker, author, and organizer, and was a member of the **Jewish Agency** Executive from 1951.

NEVADA. Of the 22,000 Jews in the state, 20,000 live in Las Vegas and 1,400 in Reno. Jews came mostly from California to Nevada in the mid-19th century in search of gold and silver. In 1862, a **B'nai B'rith** lodge was established in Virginia City, and in 1869, services were held in Carson City. In the first half of the 20th century there was little influx of Jews to the state, but as Las Vegas became a major entertainment and gambling center, the Jewish population grew rapidly, with many working in the hotel and tourist industry. There are two Conservative and two Reform congregations in Las Vegas, and one each in Reno. Las Vegas has two Jewish newspapers, the *Las Vegas Israelite* and the *Jewish Reporter*.

NEW HAMPSHIRE. The last of the 13 colonies to grant political equality to Jews, it was only in 1885 that the first Jewish community was organized in the state. Today, there are 9,500 Jews, with 4,000 in Manchester and the rest in Nashua, Dover, and Portsmouth. All of these towns have Reform congregations, with Conservative congregations only in Nashua and Portsmouth.

NEW JERSEY. The state's 435,000 Jews are scattered throughout the state in many communities, many of which are part of the Greater **New York** area, and in towns such as Trenton, Atlantic City, Morristown, and in smaller communities. Jewish communities began to grow in the state in the mid-19th century in towns such as Paterson, Newark, New Brunswick, and Trenton. At the turn of the century, communities grew in Jersey City, Elizabeth, Perth Amboy, Hoboken, East Orange, and Bayonne. Jewish farming, mostly chicken farming, flourished in southern New Jersey during the 1880's and well into the 20th century. Today, New Jersey is one of the main centers of Jewish life in the U.S., with a large number of congregations of the three major movements and a wide network of Hebrew schools and Jewish day schools.

NEW MEXICO. Of the 9,000 Jews in the state, 6,000 live in Albuquerque, the rest in Santa Fe and Las Cruces. Jewish organized life did not start until the mid-19th century in Santa Fe. The first Jewish organization was the B'nai B'rith lodge in Albuquerque. From 1930 to 1933, Arthur Seligman was governor of the state. There are a Conservative and a Reform synagogue in Albuquerque. Santa Fe and Las Cruces have each a Reform congregation.

NEW MOON. *See* **Rosh Hodesh**.

NEW YEAR. *See* **Rosh Ha-shanah**.

NEW YORK. With 1.65 million Jews, or about 9 percent of the total population, New York has by far the largest Jewish population of any state, with a much higher percentage in the general population than the national rate, where the Jews constitute fewer than 2%. **New York City** alone accounts for close to 1.5 million. Jews first arrived in New York in 1654, but communal life did not start until the 1830's, when Jewish communities began to appear outside New York City, first in Albany, then Syracuse, Buffalo, Rochester, and a dozen other cities. Today, there are 26,000 Jews in Buffalo, 22,500 in Rochester, 12,000 in Albany, and 9,000 in Syracuse. The Satmar Hasidic community of Kiryas Yoel has 10,000 Jews. Rockland County has 83,000 Jews. New York City remains the major center of Jewish life and culture in the state.

NEW YORK CITY. Jewish refugees fleeing persecution in Brazil arrived in New Amsterdam in 1654. In 1664, the British took the town from the Dutch and renamed it New York. Not until 1728 was the Jewish community permitted to build a synagogue. Two years later, Congregation **Shearith Israel** was dedicated. In 1731,

Dedication ceremony for the new building of Congregation Shearith Israel in New York City in September 1860.

New York's first Jewish school was founded. In 1740, when the English Parliament made Jews eligible for citizenship in the American colonies, most Jews took advantage of the privilege.

During the Revolutionary War, the community, which had grown to 300, was split between Loyalists and Rebels. Establishment of the United States brought no great change in the life of New York Jewry. At the time of the War of 1812, it is estimated that there were 400 Jews in the city. In the decades that followed, however, the community grew by leaps and bounds, its ranks swelled by immigrants from **Germany** and Central Europe. By 1840, the settlement numbered 13,000. Forty years later, it was 60,000. Founding synagogues, periodicals, schools, and charitable organizations, New York Jews formed a community which, by the 1870's, could begin to claim leadership in American Jewry. After 1881, New York became the thriving center of Jewish life that it is today.

Fleeing persecution in Eastern Europe, more than two million Jews came to the U.S. between 1881 and 1914; three-quarters of them lived at least for a time in New York's Lower East Side. Here they created their own Yiddish-speaking world with hundreds of synagogues, schools and **heders** (one-room schools), newspapers, theaters, clubs, political groups, fraternal orders, mutual-aid societies, and the like. By 1900, there were six Yiddish dailies and numerous weekly and monthly periodicals. With readers who knew only Yiddish, these publications were more than newspapers: they served as schools, libraries, and personal guidance bureaus for thousands of immigrants eager to find their place in a strange new world. Yiddish theater flourished as it never had in the "old country."

However, the golden days of the East Side were numbered. The East Side soon became a squalid slum. As soon as immigrants could afford to move to a better neighborhood, they did so. At first the majority of immigrants became peddlers or entered "sweatshops," usually clothing factories, where workers were "sweated" long hours for starvation wages. In time, many peddlers, after scrimping and saving, opened small shops or factories; workers began to organize in unions to demand better conditions and a living wage. While the first generation could not escape the ghetto, the second generally did. Parents struggled to educate their children, first in the high schools, then at college. Movement away from the East Side was movement up the social ladder.

By the end of the 1920's, New York Jewry had changed radically. After 1924, immigration laws stopped the flow of newcomers, and the center of population shifted from lower Manhattan to Brooklyn and the Bronx. By that time, too, a second generation whose mother tongue was English, not Yiddish, had grown up and mixed more freely with the older Jewish and non-Jewish communities. A relatively large proportion of the younger generation entered the professions. Those who remained in their parents' occupations did so under new and improved conditions. Immigrants had revolutionized the garment industry, introducing new mass-production techniques. Bolstered by national and state labor laws, the great "Jewish" union organizations, such as the International Ladies Garment Workers founded in 1900 and the Amalgamated Clothing Workers established in 1913, assured their members a decent return for their labor.

Before the gradual "Americanization" of immigrants and their integration into American life, the early immigrants had kept together, founding institutions to satisfy their immediate needs. But now it was necessary to educate a new generation and to organize a community which could sustain the traditions of Jewish life. Efforts to organize the sprawling mass of New York Jewry into a single comprehensive community organization, or **kehilla**, were

A Purim ball in New York City in 1879.

made early in the century; between 1909 and 1922 such a kehilla functioned under the chairmanship of Judah **Magnes**. Although the kehilla plan collapsed, areas of cooperation were found. A bureau of Jewish education, later absorbed by the Jewish Education Committee, continued to function after the kehilla's failure; so did the Federation of Jewish Philanthropies formed in Brooklyn in 1906 and a similar federation founded in Manhattan in 1917. In 1937, the two federations merged to form a single Greater New York Federation. Similarly, Zionist activities and the need to unite in defense against Nazi-fomented anti-Semitic groups in the 1930's required the participation of the entire community.

The Jewish community, as it emerged in the 1940's, tended to be organized around independent synagogues, community centers, *landsmanschaften* (organizations of people from the same town in Europe), and some independent Zionist organizations. In the 1950's ever-increasing numbers of Jews moved to the suburban areas of New York. The synagogue became the basic unit of affiliation, with community and nationwide organizations working through synagogue groups. But individual Jews also continued to belong to other communal organizations such as labor groups and fraternal orders.

At present New York is the home of about 1.5 million Jews in a total city population of about 8 million, undoubtedly the center of Jewish life in America. All national Jewish religious, national, and cultural organizations maintain offices in the city. There are many Jewish day schools at the elementary level and a large number of full-time high schools. A number of Hebrew high schools offer courses in Hebrew in the afternoons and Sundays, and many public high schools also teach Hebrew as a foreign language. A number of colleges in New York have departments of Jewish studies. Yiddish groups support a network of afternoon schools at the elementary and high school levels. The majority of children, however, receive their Jewish education in synagogue-affiliated afternoon and Sunday schools. New York's Jewish publications include a Yiddish weekly, two Hebrew weeklies, and dozens of English language weeklies and monthlies put out by various organizations and denominations. (*See also* **United States, History of Jews in the**.)

NEW ZEALAND. British dominion comprising two large and many small islands in the Pacific Ocean southeast of **Australia**. New Zealand has about 4,800 Jews in a total population of 3.5 million.

A few adventurous Jews settled in New Zealand a few years before British rule was established in 1840. The first group arrived with the first transports of immigrants from **England**. In 1843, they founded the dominion's first Jewish community at Wellington. A second community was established at Auckland in 1859 and a third at Dunedin in 1862.

The New Zealand Jewish community remained one of the smallest in the world until the discovery of gold in the Otago district in 1861 increased the settlement more than ten-fold. While there were 65 Jews in the country in 1851, 1,247 arrived in 1867 alone. Later growth of the community was restricted by the dominion's severe immigration policies.

The early settlers braved the backland wilds to trade with the aborigines. Others went into dairy and sheep farming or sought to exploit the gold fields. At present, however, close to 90% earn their living in commerce and industry, 9% in the professions, and 2% in agriculture.

Both Auckland and Wellington house two synagogues, while Dunedin and Christchurch each have one. The community is prosperous and has made considerable contributions to Israel.

From the beginning Jews played an important role in New Zealand's political and cultural life. Sir Julius Vogel served as prime minister from 1873 to 1876, then as New Zealand's general agent in London. Sir Michael Myers served as Chief Justice. Jews have filled a number of cabinet and administrative posts in government and have served in the Legislative Council.

NICHOLS, MIKE. *See* **Stage and Screen.**

NILI. *See* **Aaronsohn, Aaron.**

NINTH OF AV. *See* **Fast Days.**

NISAN. Seventh month of the Jewish civil calendar, considered as the first month of the religious year. *See* **Passover**.

NOAH. Literally, rest. According to the biblical account (Gen. 6:9-9), Noah's generation, the tenth since **Adam**, had become so corrupt that God decreed its destruction by a deluge. Because of his righteousness, Noah and his family were the only humans preserved from the flood. At God's command, Noah erected an ark aboard which he placed pairs of every living thing on earth. The flood poured down for 40 days; after another 150 days, every living creature had perished from the earth. Finally, the ark rested on Mount Ararat, and Noah came out, built an altar, and offered thanksgiving sacrifices to God.

NOAH, MORDECAI MANUEL (1785-1851). Born in Philadelphia, the son of a Revolutionary War patriot and soldier, Noah was a journalist, playwright, and visionary before entering politics. He held numerous posts, including surveyor of the Port of **New York**, sheriff, and judge. He was U.S. Consul in **Tunisia** when piracy and extortion were governmental policies in the Mediterranean world. In Tunisia, Noah studied the history and customs of the Tunisian Jewish community. In 1820, Noah petitioned the legislature of the State of New York for a grant of land to establish a Jewish colony in the U.S. Five years later, Grand Island on the Niagara River was surveyed and subdivided into farm lots. There, Noah planned to establish Ararat as a city of refuge for homeless and persecuted Jews. When this project failed, Noah began to advocate the Jewish resettlement of Palestine. Despite the fanfare and theatrics associated with Noah's Ararat venture, he may be viewed as a forerunner of **Zionism**.

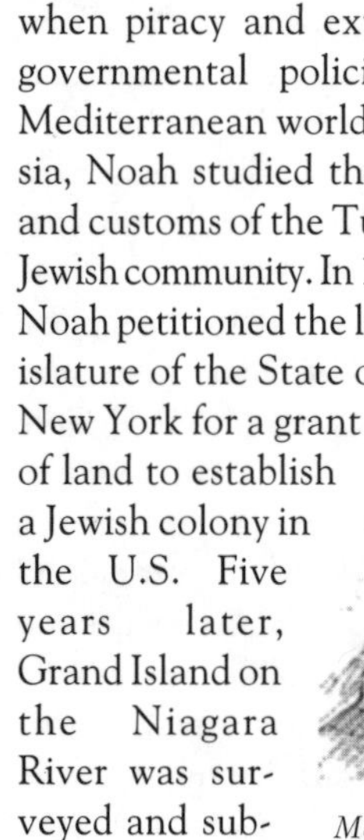

Mordecai Manuel Noah.

NOBEL PRIZE. The Nobel Prize has five categories, awarded annually since 1901 on an international basis from a fund established under the will of Alfred Nobel, Swedish chemist and inventor (1833-96) "to those who, during the preceding year, shall have conferred the greatest benefit on mankind" in the fields of physics, chemistry, physiology and medicine, literature, and in the promotion of international peace. Jews have won this prize in all categories, far beyond their numbers in the world population, and continue to win almost every year. (*See the following page for* **Jewish Nobel Prize Winners**.)

NORDAU, MAX (1849-1923). Writer, physician, Zionist leader, and social philosopher. Born in Budapest, **Hungary**, the son of a rabbi, Nordau studied medicine, traveled, then came to **Paris** and set up practice as a neurologist in 1880. At the same time, he wrote a whole series of books of social criticism. Of these, his *Conventional Lies of our Civilization* and *Paradoxes* were the most famous and controversial.

When Theodor **Herzl** came to him with the manuscript of **Judenstaat** (The Jewish State), Nordau accepted the idea immediately and became Herzl's first and most loyal colleague and closest advisor. His brilliant oratory and sharp pen were of enormous help to the young Zionist movement. Yet he steadily refused to hold any Zionist office, including that of president, offered to him after Herzl's death. The last years of his life were saddened by differences of opinion with the Zionist leadership. At the Zionist Conference in London in 1920, he pleaded for immediate mass immigration of half a million Jews to Palestine. He died in Paris in January 1923. Five years later, his body was brought to Palestine and buried in Tel Aviv.

NORTH CAROLINA. The Jewish population of 20,000 is divided as follows: Charlotte, 6,000; Raleigh, 5,500; Chapel Hill-Durham, 3,100; Greensboro, 2,500; Asheville, 1,300; and Wilmington, 1,200. North Carolina was among the first of the 13 colonies to welcome Jews. It was not until the second half of the 19th century, however, that German Jews began to arrive and establish communities and synagogues in the state. Today, there are two dozen synagogues in the state, mainly Reform and Conservative.

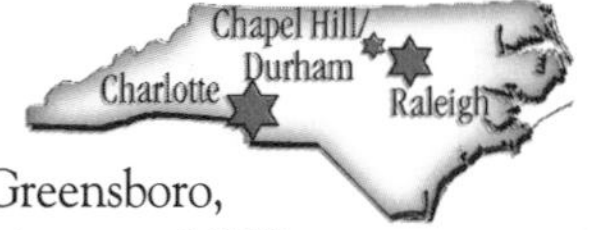

NORTH DAKOTA. Jews came to North Dakota in the late 19th century, mainly from **Russia**, to establish agricultural settlements around Bismarck. These settlements continued into the 20th century, but have since disappeared. Today, there are 500 Jews living in Fargo, and 150 in Grand Forks.

NORWAY. The earliest Jews in Norway were Sephardic. When the country came under Swedish rule in 1814, Jews were expelled, but were permitted to return in 1851. Full emancipation was granted in 1891.

At the time of the Nazi invasion, there were some 3,500 Jews in Norway. In 1998, there were about 1,500. Communal organizations exist in Oslo and Trondheim, the latter being the northernmost Jewish community in the world.

NUMBERS. Fourth book of the Pentateuch in the **Bible**. Its Hebrew name is *Bamidbar*, "In the Wilderness." The term Numbers, or Numeric, was chosen because of the two censuses of the Israelites reported in the book. The first numbering, or census, was taken at Sinai in the second year of the **Exodus**; the second was taken on the banks of the Jordan in the 40th year of the Exodus. The Book of Numbers contains laws given to Israel and tells the story of the 38 years the children of Israel spent wandering from Sinai to the Jordan near **Jericho**.

NUMERUS CLAUSUS. Literally, Jewish quota. A restriction on the number of Jews to be admitted to schools, universities, and the professions. The first form of numerus clausus is based on special legislation, and thus is openly admitted. The second, secret type uses devious ways to achieve the same practical results. The representative country for open discrimination was Tsarist **Russia**, where, after 1887, Jews could make up from only 3 to 6 percent of the students at higher institutions of learning. After the 1905 Revolution the quota was abandoned in Russia, but restored in 1908. A numerus clausus based on special legislation existed in Hungary after 1920.

The secret type of numerus clausus was used in **Germany** prior to the revolution of 1918 to limit the number of Jewish university teachers; numerus nullus, the total exclusion of Jews, was practiced in the officer corps. **Poland** and **Romania** followed a practice similar to the Germans'. The numerus clausus practice of the Polish and Romanian authorities was largely due to the anti-Semitic attitude of the non-Jewish students.

NUN. Fourteenth letter of the Hebrew alphabet; numerically, fifty.

NUREMBERG LAWS. Decreed in Nuremberg on September 15, 1935, at a rally of the Nationalist Socialist (Nazi) Party, these laws were the culmination of the anti-Jewish decrees enacted since the establishment of the Nazi government in **Germany**. By virtue of these highly discriminatory laws, Jews became second-class citizens as compared with Aryans and were denied the rights of citizenship. Under these laws, persons who had Jewish grandparents and persons who were married to Jews could not be classed as "Aryans." Jews were forbidden to marry Germans or persons of "Aryan" blood. Marriages of this kind were treated as null and void, and persons entering such marriages were severely punished. The Nuremberg laws practically created a Jewish **ghetto** in Germany. They were abolished by the Allies after the defeat of Germany in 1945.

JEWISH NOBEL PRIZE WINNERS

PHYSICS

Albert Abraham Michelson (1852-1931)	American	1907
Gabriel Lippman (1845-1921)	French	1908
Albert Einstein (1879-1955)	German	1921
Neils Bohr (1885-1962)	Danish	1925
Gustav Hertz (1887-1950)	German	1925
James Franck (1882-1964)	German	1925
Enrico Fermi (1901-1954)	Italian	1938
Otto Stern (1888-1969)	American	1944
Isidor Isaac Rabi (1898-1988)	American	1944
Felix Bloch (1905- 1983)	American	1952
Max Born (1882-1970)	German	1954
Emilio Segre (1905-1989)	American	1959
Robert Hofstadter (1915-1990)	American	1961
Lev D. Landau (1908-1968)	Russian	1962
Richard Phillips Feynman (1918-1988)	American	1965
Julian Schwinger (1918-)	American	1965
Hans Albrecht Bethe (1906-)	American	1967
Murray Gell-Mann (1929-)	American	1969
Denis Gabor (1900-1979)	English	1971
Brian David Josephson (1940-)	English	1973
Ben R. Mottelson	Danish	1975
Burton Richter(1931-)	American	1976
Aron Penzias (1905-)	American	1978
Piotr Kapitza (1894-1984)	Russian	1978
Sheldon Lee Glashow (1932-)	American	1979
Steven Weinberg (1933-)	American	1979
Leon M. Lederman (1922-)	American	1988
Melvin Schwartz (1932-)	American	1988
Jack Steinberger (1921-)	American	1988
Jerome Friedman (1930-)	American	1990
Joseph Rotblat (1908-)	English	1995
Martin Perl (1927-)	American	1995
Frederick Reines (1918-)	American	1995
Douglas Osheroff (1945-)	American	1996

CHEMISTRY

Adolf J.W.F. von Bayer (1835-1917)	German	1905
Otto Wallach (1847-1931)	German	1910
Richard Wilstaetter (1872-1942)	German	1915
Fritz Haber (1868-1934)	German	1918
George von Hevesy (1885-1966)	Hungarian	1943
Melvin Calvin (1911-)	American	1961
William Stein (1911-)	American	1972
Paul Berg (1926-)	American	1980
Walter Gilbert (1932-)	American	1980
Roald Hoffmann (1937-)	American	1981
Aaron Klug (1926-)	English	1982
Sidney Altman (1939-)	American	1989

LITERATURE

Paul J.L. von Heyse (1830-1914)	German	1910
Henri Louis Bergson (1859-1941)	French	1927
Boris Pasternak (1890-1960)	Russian	1958
Samuel Joseph Agnon (1888-1970)	Israeli	1966
Nelly Sachs (1891-1971)	Swedish	1966
Saul Bellow	American	1976
Isaac Bashevis Singer	American	1978
Elias Canetti	English	1981
Yosif Brodski		1987
Nadine Gordimer	South African	1991

MEDICINE AND PHYSIOLOGY

Elie Metchnikoff (1845-1916)	Russian	1908
Paul Ehrlich (1854-1918)	German	1908
Robert B. Bárány (1876-1936)	Austrian	1914
Otto Meyerhof (1884-1951)	German	1922
Karl Landsteiner (1868-1943)	American	1930
Otto Heinrich Warburg (1883-1938)	German	1931
Otto Loewi (1873-1961)	Austrian	1936
Joseph Erlanger (1874-1965)	American	1944
Ernst Boris Chain (1906-l979)	English	1945
Herman Joseph Muller (1890-1967)	American	1946
Tadeusz Reichstein (1897-1996)	Swiss	1950
Selman Abraham Waksman (1878-1973)	American	1952
Fritz Albert Lippmann (1899-1986)	American	1953
Sit Hans Adolf Krebs (1900-1981)	English	1953
Joshua Lederberg (1925-)	American	1958
Arthur Kornberg (1918-)	American	1959
Max F. Perutz (1914-)	English	1962
Konrad Bloch (1912-)	English	1962
Francois Jacob (1920-)	French	1965
Andre Lwolff (1902-)	French	1965
George Wald (1906-)	American	1967
Marshall W. Nirenberg (1927-)	American	1968
Salvatore E. Luria (1912-1991)	American	1969
Julius Axelrod (1912-)	American	1970
Sir Bernard Katz (1911-)	English	1970
Gerald Maurice Edelmen (1929-)	American	1972
David Baltimore	American	1975
Hard Martin Temin	American	1975
Baruch Blumberg	American	1976
Rosalyn Yalow	American	1977
Daniel Nathans	American	1978
Baruj Benacerraf (1920-)	American	1980
Cesar Milstein (1927-)	American	1984
Michael Stuart Brown (1941-)	American	1985
Joseph Leonard Goldstein	American	1985
Stanley Cohen (1922-)	American	1986
Rita Levi-Montalcini (1911-)	American	1986
Gertrude B. Elion	American	1988

ECONOMICS

Paul Samuelson (1915-)	American	1970
Simon Kuznets (1901-1985)	American	1971
Kenneth Arrow (1921-)	American	1972
Leonid Kaniorovich	Russian	1975
Milton Friedman	American	1976
Herbert A. Simon	American	1978
Lawrence Robert Klein (1920-)	American	1980
Franco Modigliani (1918-)	American	1986
Robert Solow (1924-)	American	1987
Harry Markowitz (1927-)	American	1990

PEACE

Tobias Michael Caret Asser (1838-1913)	Dutch	1911
Alfred Hermann Fried (1864-1921)	Austrian	1911
Rene Cassin (1887-1976)	French	1968
Henry Alfred Kissinger (1923-)	American	1973
Menachem Begin (1913-1992)	Israeli	1978
Elie Wiesel (1928-)	American	1986
Yitzhak Rabin (1922-1995)	Israeli	1994
Shimon Peres (1923-)	Israeli	1994

OBADIAH. Fourth of the minor prophets in the **Bible**. The Book of Obadiah, the shortest in the Bible, predicts the destruction of Edom and describes the reestablishment of the children of **Jacob** in their homeland.

OCHS, ADOLPH (1858-1935). Newspaper publisher. His father was an officer in the Union Army during the Civil War. Born in **Tennessee**, Ochs went to **New York** where he took over a failing newspaper called the *New York Times* and turned it into one of the world's leading newspapers. His son-in-law, Arthur Sulzberger, succeeded him as publisher of the *Times*.

ODESSA. City in **Ukraine**. Jews came to Odessa at the end of the 18th century from **Poland** and **Lithuania**. They participated in the rapid development of the city, engaging in commerce and various trades, as well as in the professions. The Enlightenment movement of the 19th century played an important role in the Odessa Jewish community. The first Russian-Jewish weekly was published here. The weekly Hebrew newspaper, *Ha-Melitz*, and a Yiddish weekly *Folksblat* made their appearance in Odessa. By the end of the 19th century, the town became a center of **Zionism**, **Hebrew**, and **Yiddish literature**. Some of the foremost Hebrew writers, among them **Mendele Mocher Sefarim,** Ahad **Ha-Am,** Chaim Nachman **Bialik**, and Joseph **Klausner** lived and wrote in Odessa. Here also was the seat of the central committee of **Hoveve Zion**, whose leaders were Leon **Pinsker** and, later, Menachem **Ussishkin**. During times of stress, waves of anti-Semitic attacks swept over the city. In the 1905 pogrom, thirty Jews were killed and many more injured. Odessa's Jewish youth joined in the self-defense movement, at that time an innovation in Jewish life. Odessa Jewry also suffered greatly during the civil war in 1918-1919. On the eve of World War II, Odessa's Jewish population neared 160,000. Most were killed by the Nazis and their collaborators from 1941 to 1943. The current Jewish population of the city is unknown.

OFFENBACH, JACQUES (1819-1880). German-born composer. Son of a cantor, he lived in **France** and became known for more than 100 lively and satirical operettas. His lyric opera, *Tales of Hoffmann*, continues to be produced throughout the world.

OHIO. With fewer than 130,000 Jews, the state's importance to Jewish life exceeds the size of its Jewish population. There are several reasons: one is the **Hebrew Union College** in Cincinnati, the other is the Jewish community of Cleveland. Hebrew Union College is the oldest American rabbinical school, housing the American Jewish Archives and one of the most important Jewish libraries in the world. As one of the model American Jewish communities, Cleveland has excelled in providing leadership to American and world Jewry, the best known example being Abba Hillel **Silver**, the rabbi and Zionist leader who played a crucial role in the establishment of **Israel**. Rabbi Solomon Goldman and Rabbi Arthur Lelyveld also served in Cleveland while providing leadership to world Jewry. Rabbi Eliezer Silver in Cincinnati was a world leader of Orthodox Jewry.

Jews first settled in Ohio in the early 19th century, but the first influx—which included Rabbi Isaac Mayer **Wise**, the main organizer of the Reform movement in the U.S.—came from **Germany** in the 1840's. Today, there are 65,000 Jews in Cleveland, 23,000 in Cincinnati, 15,600 in Columbus, 6,000 in Toledo, 5,500 in Akron, and 4,000 in Youngstown. Among the distinguished Jewish papers in the state are *The American Israelite* (Cincinnati), started by I.M. Wise, and *The Cleveland Jewish News*.

OISTRAKH, DAVID. *See* **Music, Jews in.**

OKLAHOMA. The 5,000 Jews in the state are equally divided between Oklahoma City and Tulsa. Each city has a Reform and a Conservative congregation. Jews first arrived in the state at the end of the 19th century. The *Southwest Jewish Chronicle* has been published in Oklahoma City since 1929.

OLAM HA-BAH. *See* **Heaven and Hell.**

OLD TESTAMENT. The name given to the Hebrew **Bible** distinguish it from Christianity's New Testament.

OMER. Literally, sheaf, or first sheaf of grain, cut during the barley harvest and offered in the **Temple** on the second day of **Passover**. No new grain could be eaten before that offering was made. The **Bible** commands Jews to count seven weeks from the day of the offering of the Omer, a custom which has been preserved to this day (*sefirat ha-omer*, or counting of the Omer). This 50-day period culminates in the Feast of Weeks (*Shavuot*, or Pentacost), commemorating the giving of the **Torah** at Mount Sinai.

Because of misfortunes that have overtaken the Jewish people during this time of year, it has come to be regarded as a period of mourning. For this reason, weddings and other festivities are not celebrated. Especially associated with the sefirah is a plague which broke out among the disciples of Rabbi **Akiva** during **Bar Kokhba**'s uprising which took place in the month of Nisan 135 C.E. Jewish legend tells that the plague subsided on Lag b'Omer ("the 33rd day of Omer"). Therefore marriages may be solemnized on that day which is celebrated outdoors and, in Israel, with pilgrimages to **Meron**, a town in **Galilee**.

ONEG SHABBAT. Literally, the enjoyment of the Sabbath. Originally, it referred to social and cultural activities on Saturday afternoon, related to the "third meal" (*see* **Sabbath**). In the U.S. today it is mostly known as Oneg, the social activity following a Friday night or Saturday morning service.

ONKELOS (Aquila). Author of the **Aramaic** translation of the **Bible**, believed to be a convert to Judaism and one of Rabbi **Akiva**'s students in the 2nd century. **Targum** Onkelos, or the Onkelos translation, occupies a prominent place in Jewish tradition. It is printed alongside the Hebrew text of the Bible and consulted by Jewish commentators in explaining obscure passages.

OPATOSHU, JOSEPH. *See* **Yiddish Literature.**

OPHIR. Land of **Solomon**'s gold, located somewhere between **India** and north central Africa. The Biblical account tells that King Solomon's ships left for Ophir from Ezion Geber on the Red Sea every three years, together with the ships of Phoenician King Hiram. The ships came home laden with gold and silver, peacocks, ivory, and apes (I Kings 9:28; 10:11).

OPPENHEIM, DAVID. *See* **Prague**.

OPPENHEIMER, J. ROBERT (1904-1967). One of America's leading nuclear physicists, Oppenheimer played a major role in the development of the atomic bomb. Head of the Los Alamos Scientific Laboratory from 1943 to 1945, he was Chairman of the General Advisory Committee of Atomic Scientists from 1946 to 1952 and a Professor of Physics at Princeton University's Institute of Advanced Studies.

ORAL LAW. *See* **Talmud**.

ORDINATION. Ceremonial transfer of authority. In Hebrew, *semikhah*, or the "laying on" of hands. The Bible tells how **Moses** ordained **Joshua** by laying hands upon him, and thus transferring the leadership to him (Num. 27:22-23). In the time of the Second **Temple**, the members of the **Sanhedrin**, the judicial and legislative body, were also ordained. The **Talmud** requires two rabbis to be present when the master lays his hands upon the head of his pupil as a sign that he is now qualified to teach. *Semikhah* traditionally refers to rabbinic ordination.

OREGON. The Jewish population of 19,500 is divided mainly among Portland (14,000), Eugene (3,000), and Medford (1,000). Jews first arrived in 1849, mainly from Germany, and in 1858, the first synagogue was founded in Portland. The city of Heppner is named after the first Jew who settled in the northeastern part of the state. Portland has Reform and Conservative congregations.

ORMANDY, EUGENE. *See* **Music, Jews in.**

ORT. The Organization for Rehabilitation through Training is a worldwide vocational training organization. Founded in **Russia** in 1880, it has since become a global movement in Jewish life. It now operates in 35 countries, with a student body of nearly 100,000 attending classes and workshops in more than 800 training units. Its institutions include vocational high schools, advanced technical courses and schools on the junior college level, apprenticeships and pre-apprenticeship courses, factory schools, and prevocational programs for adults.

ORT's largest program is ORT Israel with more than 70,000 students. It plays an important part in building Israel's economic strength and social structure. ORT is represented in the U.S. by the American ORT Federation (AOF), founded in 1922.

Women's American ORT members speak out at a national convention.

ORTHODOXY. *See* **Judaism**.

OSLO AGREEMENT. *See* **Israel, State of.**

OSTROPOLER, HERSHELE. Hasidic court jester of the 18th century in eastern Europe named Hirsch. He became a figure of Jewish folklore in many stories and jokes.

OZ, AMOS (1939-). Israeli novelist, considered the leading Israeli writer of his generation. A keen observer of Israeli society, he is best known for such novels as *My Michael* and *Black Box*. He is also a leader of the Israeli peace movement. In 1998, he received the Israel Prize, the highest honor in Israeli society.

PALE OF SETTLEMENT. In 1791, the Tsarist government of **Russia** designated certain districts in which Jews were allowed to reside. The pretext for this restriction was the need to "protect" the Russian people from Jewish influence. Until 1910, this policy of restricting Jewish rights of residence continued. Sometimes the Pale was enlarged; other times a given city or village was withdrawn from the Pale. Restrictions, changing from time to time, were placed on Jews living inside the Pale as well. They were forbidden to lease land or keep taverns in villages. They had to pay double taxes, and they were barred from higher education. Only after the overthrow of the Tsarist government in 1917 was the Pale of Settlement finally abolished.

PALESTINE. The area now occupied partly by the State of **Israel** and partly by the Palestinian Authority was called Palestine by the Greeks and Romans, after the **Philistines** who lived in the southern coastal region.

PALMACH. Acronym for *Plugot Mahatz*, or shock troops. Serving as the commando units of the **Haganah**, Palmach members were recruited mainly from the agricultural settlements and city high schools. Organized in 1939, they carried out daring missions. They rescued thousands of Jews from Nazi Europe, running the British

Two famous Palmach battles in Israel's War of Independence. Left, the Castel hilltop on the way to Jerusalem. Right, the Nebi Yusha fortress in the Galilee.

blockades of Palestine in the "death ships" of the "illegal immigration" period. During the chaotic period when the British were prepared to abandon Palestine, the Palmach guarded the settlements and highways. In the War of Independence its members bore the brunt of the Arab attack. A large proportion of them lost their lives in action. In 1949, Palmach was absorbed by the **Israel Defense Forces.** Many of its commanders, including Yigal **Allon**, Moshe **Dayan**, and Yitzhak **Rabin,** became leaders of Israel.

PANAMA. The first Jews to reach Panama were merchants, including Spanish and Portuguese Jews who first settled in the Caribbean Islands. Because of the unhealthy climate and poor living conditions, most of them fled the isthmus. The small permanent community which remained grew only when the U.S. began building the Panama Canal in 1904. In 1998, there were about 5,000 Jews in a total population of almost 3 million. They engage in trade and industries. The majority lives in Panama City, but there is a small community in Colon, the Pacific terminus of the Canal. Both communities maintain synagogues and are affiliated with the **World Jewish Congress**, The **Anti-Defamation League**, the **Jewish National Fund**, and **Women's International Zionist Organization** (WIZO). (*See also* **Delvalle, Arturo**.)

PALEY, GRACE (1922-). American short story writer and poet whose stories capture the idiosyncrasies and idiom of New Yorkers. Her *Collected Stories* appeared in 1994, her *Collected Poems* in 1992.

PALEY, WILLIAM S. (1901-1990). Founder of the Central Broadcasting System (CBS), a radio and television network. He revolutionized the television industry by taking the programming away from the advertising agencies and investing it in the network itself. During World War II, he served as deputy chief of U.S. war propaganda in Europe. His foundation supported the **Weizmann Institute of Science** in Israel as well as many other causes in Israel and the U.S.

PARADISE. *See* **Heaven and Hell.**

PARAGUAY. Republic in South America. Immigrants from **Turkey, Russia, Germany,** and **France** established a small Jewish community in Paraguay around 1900. Refugees from Nazi Europe swelled its ranks to 2,200 by 1940. Lack of economic opportunities led most of the refugees to emigrate after World War II. The Jewish community of Paraguay now numbers 900 out of a total population of 4.8 million. It maintains three synagogues, none of which has a rabbi, as well as Zionist and youth groups.

PARIS. Jews have lived in Paris since the 6th century. In the 12th and 13th centuries, the city was a center of Jewish learning and home of a famous Talmudic academy. By the 14th century repeated persecutions had weakened the community; it was finally banished with the rest of French Jewry in 1394, although Jews continued to live in Paris illegally. In 1791, they finally gained civil and residence rights. When Napoleon organized French Jews in centralized "consistories," Paris became the hub of French Jewry. As the community grew, synagogues, schools, and charitable organizations were established. At mid-century, the extensive

> *Zog nit keinmol az du geist dem letsten veg.*
> *Never say this is your last road.*
>
> — FROM THE SONG OF THE PARTISANS

banking and commercial activities of financiers like the **Rothschilds** and the Pereiras, as well as the political eminence of men like Adolphe **Crémieux** brought the community to the forefront of Parisian life. Establishment of the **Alliance Israélite Universelle** in 1860 strengthened cultural life. The Alliance also served as an instrument for cooperating with foreign Jewries and for rendering assistance to distressed brethren abroad.

Eastern European immigrants began to settle in Paris in fairly large numbers during the 1880's. They created a "little world" of their own, the colorful Jewish Quarter. They founded folk universities, libraries, schools, theaters, and an active Yiddish press which in 1939 published 14 periodicals, including two daily newspapers. Active in these undertakings were distinguished writers, scholars, and artists who continued the work they had begun in Eastern Europe. Paris was the artistic center of the world, and many immigrants rose to world fame in the arts. French critics often referred to them as the *École Juive*, or Jewish School, of art. Outstanding among them are Marc **Chagall**, Chaim Soutine, Moise Kisling, Amedeo Modigliani, Mane-Katz, and Jules Pascin.

When the Germans occupied Paris in 1940, many Jews fled to the south of France; the majority of others were deported to **Poland**. Many who fled became active in the French underground. After the war, many survivors returned. Their numbers were augmented by streams of Jews fleeing from all parts of the continent. In 1998, a large influx of refugees from North Africa brought the Jewish population of Paris to 310,000.

PARKER, DOROTHY (1893-1967). American poet and short story writer, noted for her quick and biting wit and sense of irony. A member of the famous Algonquin group, her most famous story is *Big Blonde*.

PARNAS. From Greek. The president and secular leader of a congregation. In Talmudic times a man of merit and scholarship was appointed parnas to administer congregational affairs. In later times, the office was given to men of wealth and influence. Beginning in the Middle Ages, some communities elected the parnas annually, even monthly.

PASCIN, JULES. *See* **Art**.

PARTISANS. In World War II, many resistance groups from different nationalities throughout Europe fought the Nazis. Among them were Jewish groups, who fought either on their own or as part of other national groups. Such groups began to operate in eastern Europe as early as 1941, mostly in the forests in White **Russia**, **Poland**, and **Lithuania**. Later, they were absorbed by the Russian partisans on the Soviet side, while in Poland they continued to operate on their own. In all, there were more than 20,000 Jewish partisans, many of whom showed great courage and resourcefulness in fighting under difficult conditions and with scant arms against the German war machine. The song of the Vilna partisans, *Shir Ha-partisanim*, is sung every year on Yom Ha-Shoah.

PASSOVER. In Hebrew, *Pesach*. Anniversary of Israel's liberation from Egyptian bondage. The holiday begins on the fourteenth day of **Nisan** and lasts for eight days. It reminds each Jew that if God had not freed his forefathers "he and his sons and the sons of his sons would still be slaves to Pharaoh in **Egypt**." Passover is also *Hag Ha-Aviv*, the Festival of Spring, the first of the three holidays when the agricultural population of Israel set out on a pilgrimage to the **Temple** in **Jerusalem**. They brought an offering of barley in thanksgiving for the spring harvest. (*See also* **Omer**.)

The *matzot*, or unleavened bread, which gives Passover the name *Hag Hamatzot*, the Feast of Unleavened Bread, is eaten in memory of the unleavened bread prepared by the Israelites during their hasty flight from Egypt, when they had no time to wait for the dough to rise. Since no leavened bread or food containing leaven may be eaten during Passover, special dishes and household utensils are used during the eight-day observance. Laws are prescribed for the cleaning or scalding in boiling water of utensils which are used throughout the year but also on this holiday.

On the eve of the 14th day of Nisan, the ceremony of *B'dikat Hametz*, the search for leaven and its removal from the house, is performed. Inspection for hametz is done by candlelight wherever food is usually kept or eaten. On the morning of the 14th day of Nisan, the hametz is burned as a special benediction is recited. This observance is called *Bi'ur Hametz*, the removal or burning of hametz. The day preceding Passover, the fast of the first-born takes place to commemorate the "passing over" of the Israelite homes by the Angel of Death on his way to slay the firstborn Egyptians. In ancient times, the paschal lamb was slaughtered to recall the fact that God spared the Israelites.

While the holiday is celebrated for eight days in the **Diaspora**, in **Israel** it is observed for seven days. The first and last two days of the holiday are more festive than the four intermediate days called *Hol Ha-Moed*, or half-holidays. On the first two nights of Passover, the Seder (literally, "order"), the central event of the holiday, is celebrated. On this occasion, the **Haggadah**, or narration, is chanted as the events of the **Exodus** from Egypt are told and Israel's gratitude to God for its redemption is expressed.

The Seder service is one of the most colorful and joyous occasions in Jewish life. It is adorned with ancient ceremonies and symbols which recall the days when the Children of Israel were liberated from Egypt. It also evokes hope that despite present trials and tribulations there is a brighter future for the Jewish people. The family gathers around the Seder table, on which are placed the traditional ceremonial objects. The Seder service begins with the **Kiddush**. The youngest son of the household asks the "Four Ques-

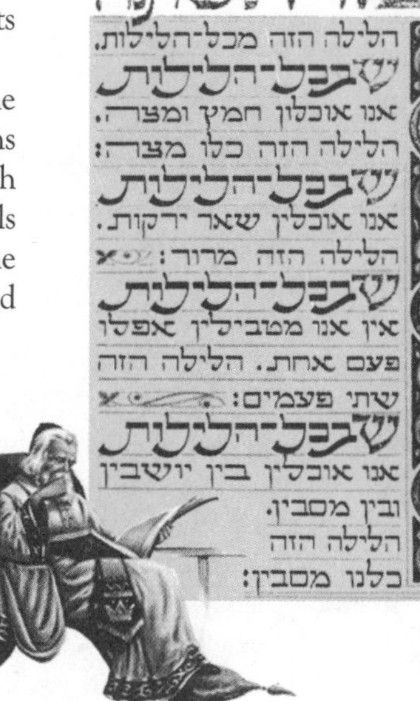

Ma Nishtana (The Four Questions). A page from the Rose family Haggadah, illuminated by Sol Nodel, commissioned by Mr. and Mrs. Rose, New York.

The First Plague. 17th century Dutch engraving. "And all the waters in the river turned into blood." — Exodus 7:20

tions," and all participants read the Haggadah in reply. During the Seder, traditional melodies are chanted and age-old ceremonies are performed. The Seder plate, or *ka'arah*, displays symbolic foods. Each one commemorates events connected with Passover. The roast egg stands for the festival offering at the time of the Temple; the roast shoulder bone, or *z'roa*, for the paschal lamb; bitter herbs, or *maror*, for the bitter lot of Jews under Egyptian bondage; *haroset*, a mixture of ground nuts, apples, cinnamon, and red wine, represents the clay with which Jews worked to make bricks; the parsley, or *karpas*, dipped in salt water was considered a delicacy in ancient times.

The three matzot which are placed on the table represent the three classes of Jews: **Kohen** (priest), **Levi**, and Israelite. The middle matzah is broken in two. One half called the *afikoman*, Greek for "dessert," is hidden until after the meal. It is customary for the children to steal the afikoman and ask a prize for its return. The "stealing" enlivens the Seder service. The afikoman is the last food eaten. During the seder each person drinks four cups of wine, representing the four expressions of redemption used in the Bible. A fifth cup of wine, representing *Vehayveiti*—"And I will bring you into the land..."—is the cup of **Elijah**, reserved for the prophet. According to tradition, Elijah visits every Jewish house on the Seder night to herald the coming of the Messiah. The chanting of *Shir Hashirim* (**Song of Songs**) adds a spring-like atmosphere at the end of the Seder service. Symbolically, it is a song of love between God and the people of Israel.

PATRIARCHS. Biblical ancestors of the people of Israel; **Abraham**, **Isaac**, and **Jacob** are known as the Patriachs. Their wives, **Sarah**, **Rebecca**, **Leah**, and **Rachel**, are the Matriarchs.

PAUKER, ANA (1890-1960). Daughter of a rabbi, Pauker became a communist leader. In 1947, she became foreign minister of **Romania**. In the 1952 purges she lost her government and party positions.

PAUL (died ca. 65 C.E.). Key figure in establishing **Christianity** as a world religion. St. Paul was born Saul of Tarsus, a Jew who persecuted the new sect known as Christians, then later converted to this religion. He played a critical role not only as an effective proselytizer, but also as a religious thinker who modified the teachings of the new sect to make them easier for the people of the Greek and Roman world to accept.

PE. Seventeenth letter of the Hebrew alphabet; numerically, eighty. With a dot it is sounds as *p*; without, it corresponds to *f*.

PEERCE, JAN. *See* **Music, Jews in.**

PEKI'IN. Village occupied by **Druzes** and Jews, northwest of Safed, Israel, near the hills of Upper **Galilee**. Unnoticed in their valley, Jewish farmers remained in Pekiin for centuries, successfully resisting the successive armies of Roman, Crusader, and Bedouin invaders. Rabbi Simeon ben Yohai and his son Eliezer are said to have taken refuge from the Romans in a cave in Peki'in. Recently, the Jewish community has developed into a well-equipped *moshav ovdim*, or smallholders' settlement.

PENNSYLVANIA. Of the 325,000 Jews in the state, 250,000 live in the **Philadelphia** area, and 40,000 live in Pittsburgh. Smaller communities exist in Harrisburg (7,000), Scranton and Wilkes-Barre (3,200 each), and Lancaster (2,500).

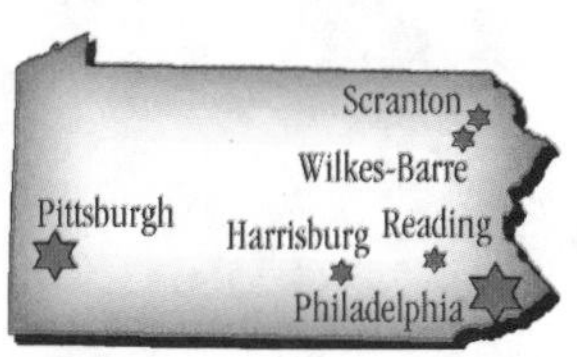

Jewish life started in Philadelphia in 1738 when Nathan Levy bought a burial plot. It started in Pittsburgh in 1760. Jews played an important part in the Revolutionary War. In the 1850's there was an influx of German Jews, and in the Civil War more than 500 Jews served in the Union Army. In the early years of the 20th century, close to 100,000 Jews arrived in the state from Eastern Europe, giving rise to today's large urban communities.

PENTACOST. *See* **Shavuot**.

PENTATEUCH. From Greek, literally, "five-fold." The Five Books of Moses. (*See also* **Bible**.)

PERES, SHIMON (1923-). Israel political leader and cabinet member. Brought to Palestine from his native **Poland** in 1934, he was a founder of **Kibbutz** Alumot, and from 1941 to 1945 was general secretary of the Labor Zionist Youth organization. During the War of Independence, he headed Israel's fledgling navy. In 1950, he joined the staff of the Ministry of Defense and in 1956 helped plan the **Sinai** Campaign. Eventually, he rose to the rank of Deputy Minister of Defense, a post he held from 1959 to 1965. During those years the Defense Ministry took over Israel's armaments industry, expanded the aircraft industry, and made headway in nuclear development and research. From 1974 to 1977, he was Minister of Defense and briefly served as acting Prime Minister between the resignation of Premier Yitzhak **Rabin** and the election which brought Menachem **Begin** to the premiership. In 1979 and 1984, Peres was elected as head of the Labor Alignment in the **Knesset**, and headed the opposition. From 1984 to 1986 he served as Prime Minister in the Labor-Liked government. Until 1990, he was Finance Minister under Yitzhak **Shamir.** In 1992 Labor returned to power with Rabin as Prime Minister and Peres as Foreign Minister. He was instrumental in bringing about the Oslo Agreement in 1993, which resulted in a peace process with the Palestinian Arabs, and for which he won the **Nobel Peace Prize.** In 1995 Rabin was assassinated, and Peres became Prime Minister. He was, however, defeated in the early elections which he called for in 1996. He resigned as leader of the Labor Alignment and was replaced by Ehud Barak.

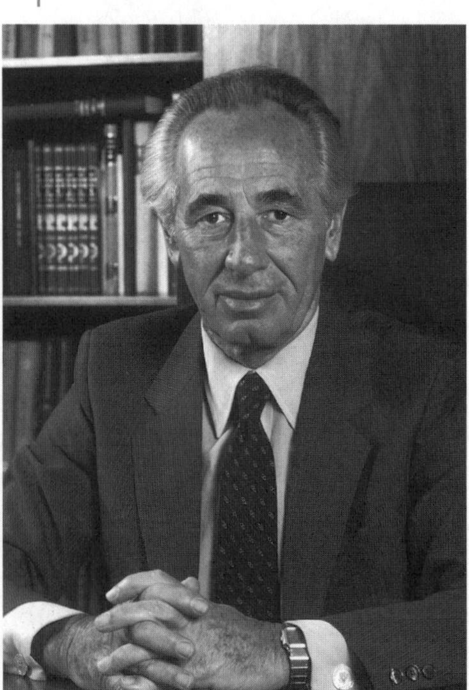

Shimon Peres. Courtesy Embassy of Israel, Washington D.C.

PERETZ, ISAAC LEIB (1852-1915). Yiddish and Hebrew writer. He is considered one of the founding fathers of both modern **Hebrew** and **Yiddish literature**. He was also one of the first major Jewish writers to find beauty, moral strength, and a new, happier approach to life in **Hasidism**. Peretz was influenced early by the **Haskalah**, or Enlightenment movement, and turned to secular studies. For some time he practiced law. In his sympathy with the plight of the poor suffering masses, he was attracted to socialist ideals. His sensitivity to injustice and the social evils of the world eventually found expression in his creative writing. His short stories brought Peretz lasting fame. They came to be considered among the classics of Yiddish literature. His tales of Hasidism and of the common people are gems of poetry and humor. In them, he glorified the heroism of humble folk and the unbounded faith of rich and poor, exalting the life of the righteous. Among the first to point a finger at social injustice, Peretz wrote *Bontche the Silent*, a folk tale of great delicacy and compassion. For sheer beauty, delicate humor, and forcefulness, Peretz's stories, such as *The Wondermaker*, *The Zaddik of Nemirov*, *The Treasure*, and *The Three Gifts*, have few equals. Many of his stories have been translated into English. Maurice Samuel's *Prince of the Ghetto* is a fascinating study of Peretz and his work.

I.L. Peretz, by I. Friedlander. Courtesy YIVO, New York.

PERLMAN, YITZHAK (1945-). One of the great violinists of the century, Perlman was born in **Tel Aviv** where he received his early training and continued to study in **New York**. Handicapped by polio, he nevertheless performs with great vigor and mastery, thrilling audiences around the world. He has special interest in Jewish music, which he has performed with **klezmer** bands.

PERSIA. *See* **Iran**.

PERU. In the 16th century, Lima, the capital of Peru, was the home of a wealthy and flourishing **Marrano** community. These Jews, who had converted to Catholicism to escape expulsion from **Spain** in 1492, had fled to the New World in the hope of finding greater freedom to practice Judaism. Their great wealth, amassed in international trade, soon aroused the envy of the Spanish rulers. In 1569, an Inquisitorial Office was founded to detect the heretics and confiscate their property. In the course of two centuries, after

34 public burnings of "heretics," the **Inquisition** succeeded in eradicating the entire Marrano community. In 1870, Alsatian Jews settled in Lima and quickly assimilated. Not until the 1920's did immigrants from **Argentina, Brazil, Turkey**, and Europe succeed in establishing a permanent Jewish community. They achieved considerable success in the manufacture and sale of furniture, furs, and knitted goods. During the 1930's, anti-Semitic propaganda spread by the German Embassy led the government to impose severe restrictions on immigration, restrictions which are still in effect. In 1998 there were about 3,000 Jews out of a total population of more than 22 million. More than 90% live in Lima, the rest in small cities.

PESACH. *See* **Passover**.

PETACH TIKVAH. Known as the "Mother of the Colonies," it was the first Jewish colony established in 1878 in Palestine by a handful of Orthodox Jews who left their shops in the Old City of **Jerusalem** to become farmers as a first step toward the Redemption. Lacking experience, they bought 900 acres of swampland near the Yarkon River. Malaria took a heavy toll and drove them back to Jerusalem. But reinforced by new immigrants, they returned to Petach Tikvah, built their houses at some distance from the river, planted eucalyptus trees to drain the swamps, and fought against Arab attacks. Baron Edmond de **Rothschild** and the **Hoveve Zion** movement gave them a helping hand. The success of Petach Tikvah encouraged other settlements and attracted many workers and settlers. Petach Tikvah was the first colony to introduce citriculture, or orange-growing, which became the economic mainstay of Israel. It became a municipality in 1937. In 1998, Petach Tikvah had a population of approximately 150,000, an industrial zone with numerous factories, and a large farming community.

PHARISEES. Literally, separatists. One of the three parties in Palestine during the 2nd and 1st centuries B.C.E. Most of Rabbinic law as it exists today originated with the Pharisees, who prized the study of Jewish law as it developed through the generations. They were opposed by the **Sadducees**, literalists who allowed no interpretation of the law beyond the letter of the Biblical text.

It is believed that the majority of the Jewish people supported the Pharisees. They instituted centers of learning and synagogues for worship. The Pharisees emphasized the importance of prayer independent of the **Temple** services. Through teachings that strengthened the Jewish religion and morality, the Pharisees prepared Jews to withstand the hardships that followed the destruction of the Temple and subsequent dispersion.

The Pharisees came into conflict with two of the rulers of the Hasmonean dynasty: Johanan **Hyrcanus** and **Alexander Jannaeus**. They were dissatisfied with Hyrcanus's preoccupation with wars of conquest and with the religious practices of Alexander Jannaeus. Their opposition led these kings, especially Jannaeus, to persecute the Pharisees, many of whom fled the country to escape his heavy hand.

In the New Testament the Pharisees are mentioned unfavorably. Apparently, a few Pharisees pursued their own selfish ends under the guise of piety. There is no doubt, however, that the majority of them were true to the high ideals of their great spiritual leaders.

PHILADELPHIA. Historically, one of the most important and, with 250,000 Jews, one of the largest American Jewish communities. Organized Jewish life began in the late 18th century. During the Revolutionary War, most Jews supported the cause and played an important part in supplying Washington's troops. A letter from President Washington to Jews in Philadelphia affirmed their full rights, the first time in the modern world such equality was granted to Jews.

In the 19th century, Philadelphia Jewry was the leading Jewish community in the U.S. While **New York City** had a much larger Jewish community, the Philadelphia community was more cohesive and provided national leaders to American Jewry. Some of these leaders were Sabato Morais who founded the **Jewish Theological Seminary**; Isaac **Leeser** who gave American Jewry its first English translation of the **Bible**; Hyman **Gratz** who made provisions in his will to establish **Gratz College**, the first Jewish teachers' college in America; and Cyrus **Adler** who co-founded the **Jewish Publication Society,** a leading publisher of Jewish books in the U.S.

Today, Philadelphia is home to the **Annenberg Research Institute**, the Reconstructionist Rabbinical Seminary, and the weekly *Jewish Exponent*.

PHILANTHROPY. *See* **Charity**.

PHILISTINES. Seafaring people from one of the islands on the shores of the northern Mediterranean who emigrated to the coast of **Canaan** in the 12th century B.C.E. The Philistines dominated the fertile southern coastal plain, which included five cities: Gat and Ekron in the interior, and the three ports of **Ashod, Ashkelon**, and Gaza. They were the implacable enemies of Israel and continued to harass their neighbors until **David** reduced them to a minor, mainly commercial role.

PHILO (30 B.C.E.-40 C.E.). Hellenistic philosopher and Biblical interpreter. Philo was a descendant of a distinguished Jewish family in **Alexandria, Egypt**. His brother was head of the Jewish community in Egypt. Philo dedicated his life to scholarship and acquired an extensive knowledge of literature, philosophy, and the sciences. He made a pilgrimage to **Jerusalem**, where he offered prayers and sacrifices in the **Temple**. Philo also led a delegation of Jews to the Roman emperor Caius Caligula to appeal against the anti-Jewish decrees of the Roman high commissioner, Flaccus of Egypt.

Philo's works include allegorical, or symbolic, commentaries on the **Bible** and *The Lives of Moses and the Patriarchs*. The latter work interprets Jewish teachings in philosophical terms in an attempt to reconcile the basic ideas of the Bible with Greek thought. Philo had great influence on Hellenized Jews who were steeped in Greek **philosophy** and knew little about Judaism. His idea of the Logos, or the Word, through which God influences the world, greatly influenced the Fathers of the Christian Church and indirectly Jewish mystical thought.

PHILOSOPHY. Judaism came to philosophy relatively late. While both religion and philosophy occupy themselves with the ultimate questions, religion starts with faith while philosophy starts with human knowledge. Starting in the Greek or Hellenistic period, many Jews came under the influence of Greek philosophy. Jewish scholars such as **Philo** began what became a centuries-long tradition of utilizing the philosophical thinking of such Greek philosophers as Aristotle and Plato to prove or disprove the validity of Jewish belief as embodied in the **Bible**. This kind of philosophical speculation and disputation was driven by the rivalry between Judaism and the two new monotheistic religions, **Christianity** and **Islam**. Under Islamic rule, Jews gave rise to philosophers like **Maimonides** and Yehudah **Ha-Levi**. The former incorporated Aristotelian thought into his teachings of Judaism, while the latter strongly rejected the validity of Islam and Christianity on philosophical grounds, affirming the exclusive validity of Judaism.

In our time, religious philosophers like **Buber, Rosenzweig,** and **Heschel** have espoused contemporary European philosophies such as existentialism to prove the validity and explore the message of Judaism.

Additionally, Jews contributed great philosophers after the Renaissance, the greatest being **Spinoza**, one of the world's most original and most important thinkers. A more recent example is the French philosopher **Bergson**.

PHOENICIANS. Sidonians of the **Bible**. They occupied the coast of **Canaan** from southern **Syria** through northern **Palestine** up to the hills of the region that separated them from Acco, or **Acre**. They were organized in city-states, two of which, Sidon and Tyre, are familiar to Bible readers. Seafarers, navigators, and traders, the Phoenicians were also skilled artisans and builders. By the time of kings **David** and **Solomon**, their power had waned, and they had become friendly allies of **Israel**. They supplied engineers and craftsmen and floated down "the cedars of **Lebanon**" in rafts for David's palace and for Solomon's **Temple**. Ancient empires contending for domination of that part of the world eventually swallowed up the Phoenician cities. The Phoenicians made valuable contributions to ancient civilization. Tyre taught the world how to make the famous purple dye, and Sidon introduced blown glass. From the Phoenician language, akin to **Hebrew**, the Greeks borrowed the **alphabet** which became the basis for European alphabets.

PHYLACTERIES. *See* **Tefilin**.

PICON, MOLLY. *See* **Stage and Screen**.

PIDYON HA-BEN. Literally, Redemption of the Firstborn. When they are thirty days old, firstborn sons pass through a festive ceremony known as *pidyon ha-ben*, based on the Biblical command that the firstborn male offspring of both man and beast be dedicated to the service of God. All children but those of priests, or *Kohanim*, must be "redeemed" or released from this dedication. In ancient times this was done by offering a special sacrifice; since the destruction of the **Temple** it has become customary to give money to charity instead.

PIKUACH NEFESH. *See* **Life, Sanctity of.**

PILPUL. From *palpel*, literally, to search or judge; possibly from *pilpel*, literally, pepper, indicating the sharpness of discussion. Pilpul is an analytic method used in Talmudic study, which explores all possible sides of an argument. It was first used in yeshivot in **Germany** and was introduced to **Poland** in the 16th century by the famous Talmudic scholar, Rabbi Jacob Pollack. The term pilpul is often associated with hair-splitting and unproductive argumentation.

PINSKER, LEO (1821-1891). Russian physician, writer, and Zionist leader. He studied medicine and settled in **Odessa.** In 1861, he began to publish articles favoring **assimilation** and internationalism as the only solution to the Jewish problem. The Odessa pogroms of 1871 shook his faith in **assimilation** though it was not until the great pogroms of 1881 that he completely abandoned his earlier convictions. The following year he published *Auto-Emancipation*, an extraordinary pamphlet in which he diagnosed **anti-Semitism** as a "disease" caused by fear of the alien, stateless Jew. He prescribed "the creation of a Jewish nationality… living on its own soil" as the only cure. At first Pinsker believed that a Jewish homeland might be established anywhere. After contact with the **Hoveve Zion**, or "Love of Zion" movement, however, he came to think of **Palestine** as the Zionist goal. Pinsker was chosen president of the Lovers of Zion societies at their conference in 1884, and served the movement until his death in 1891.

Leo Pinsker.

PINTER, HAROLD (1930-). British playwright. His plays *The Birthday Party* and *The Caretaker* earned him the reputation of being one of the more complex and psychologically challenging playwrights of our time. His plays have been performed in **England** and the U.S., and some were made into films.

PISSARRO, CAMILLE (1830-1903). Painter of Sephardic origin, he was born on a small island in the West Indies and as a young man emigrated to **France**. There he lived for many years in poverty, until toward the end of his life he became recognized as one of the outstanding landscape painters of his time. Having experienced misery himself, he often painted with warmth and sympathy peasants pushing wheelbarrows, digging potatoes, tending geese, or farm workers in coarse garments with backs bowed by labor and limbs gnarled by rheumatism. Pissarro had no spiritual links with Judaism though he was troubled by the rise of French **anti-Semitism** and the unjust condemnation of Captain **Dreyfus**.

PITTSBURGH. *See* **Pennsylvania**.

PIYYUT. Liturgical poetry. (*See also* **Hebrew Literature**.)

PLAGUES OF EGYPT. *See* **Passover**.

PLANTS OF ISRAEL. The **Bible** mentions about 100 names of plants, mostly in the land of Israel. Many of those plants have become symbolic of the various regions of Israel: the palm tree represents the desert; the myrtle is symbolic of the Judean mountains; the willow is the plant of the rivers; citrus trees represent the coast; cedars are the trees of the northern mountains.

The **Talmud** adds hundreds of plant names to those mentioned in the Bible. They are particularly numerous in the *Mishnah Zeraim*, which deals with agricultural laws. Plants play a central part in

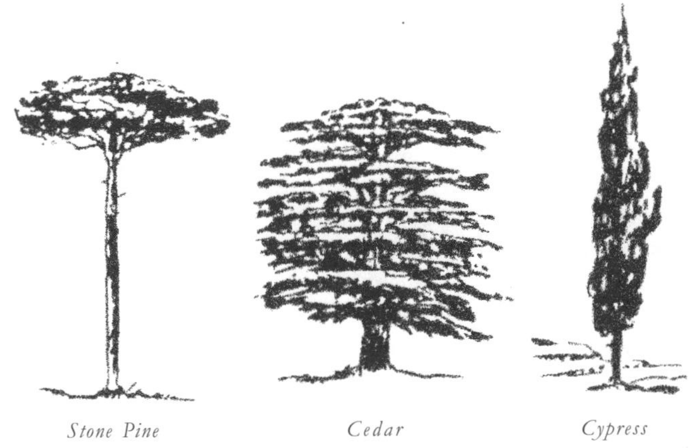

many Jewish holidays, and the Talmud even designates a special "New Year" day for plants. Both in antiquity and today, such holidays as **Sukkot**, **Shavuot**, and **Passover** have been observed with rituals connected with various plants, such as the **lulav** and **etrog** on Sukkot, the bringing of the harvest on Shavuot in modem Israel, and the vegetables of the Seder plate.

Jewish concern with ecology dates back to early Biblical times. One striking example is the *shemitah*, or sabbatical year, during which the land is made to rest so that it can regain its strength and grow better crops.

During the period of foreign rule over Israel, culminating with the Turkish rule of the 19th and early 20th centuries, much of Israel's flora were destroyed as the land was defoliated. Through the work of the **Jewish National Fund**, the land has been reclaimed, and much of the traditional flora of Israel were restored in the **Galilee**, the Valley, the Coast, the mountain ranges, and even parts of the desert.

The best-known traditional flora of Israel are the palm tree, cedar, fig tree, vine, citrus tree, myrtle, willow, pomegranate, lily of the valley, and olive tree. They appear on both ancient and modern Jewish coins, as well as in Jewish art and architecture.

POALE AGUDATH ISRAEL. Orthodox labor organization affiliated with **Agudath Israel**. Its aim is to help rebuild Israel in the spirit of traditional Judaism. The organization encourages preparation and education of pioneers for Israel and solicits funds for its institutions in Israel. It has been instrumental in the establishment of kibbutzim and villages in various parts of Israel. It maintains ten children's homes and two children's villages, housing more than 1,000 Israeli youngsters. It has taken an active part in the political life of the country, and has participate in government coalitions. It maintains educational institutions ranging from kindergartens to teachers' seminaries. Ezra, its youth movement, is dedicated to Orthodox education and training pioneers to live on collectives in Israel. Outside of Israel, the organization is active in the U.S., **Canada**, **England**, and other countries.

POALE ZION. *See* **Labor Zionism.**

POGROM. Russian. Literally, riot. In Russian Jewish history, particularly after 1881, the pogrom was a recurring phenomenon. All violent attacks against Jews have since become known as "pogroms." The Russian pogroms started a wave of mass migrations of Russian Jews to the U.S. and to other countries.

POLAND. During several centuries, Poland was central to Jewish history. The great-grandparents of the majority of today's Jews were born in territories that once formed part of Poland. The traditions of modern Jews, therefore, are deeply grounded in the history, culture, and customs of Polish Jews. The important cultural, social, and national movements of our time—**Hasidism**, **Haskalah**, and **Zionism**—came into full fruition and development in Poland.

Jews first came to Poland from Asia Minor and settled on the shores of the Black Sea at the beginning of the Common Era. From there they spread northward. In the 8th century they succeeded in converting the ruling classes of the **Khazars**, who dominated a large territory between the Volga and the Dnieper rivers, north of the Black Sea. When the Mongolians invaded Eastern Europe in 1240, many Jews (and many Khazars) fled to Poland and eventually settled there. Most of the Polish Jews, however, came later from **Germany**. They brought with them a German dialect mixed with Hebrew words which they had used for hundreds of years. This vernacular developed into **Yiddish**, the universal language of Polish Jewry.

Thus, a substantial, permanent settlement of Jews began in Poland at the end of the 12th century. Some of them became the mint-masters of Polish kings. Since apparently at that time Jews were the only merchants in Poland, these mint-masters stamped their coins with Hebrew inscriptions. Jews were useful in the Polish economy; therefore, the kings made a strong effort to attract large numbers to settle in Poland. In 1246, Boleslav the Pious issued a favorable charter offering privileges to Jews based on the Charter of

The Village, by S. Yudovin.

Wooden synagogue of 19th-century Polish countryside.

Privileges issued in 1244 by Duke Frederick of **Austria**. This charter, which became the cornerstone of Polish Jewish legislation, allowed Jews to organize themselves into autonomous communities and regulated the business relationships of Jews and Gentiles in a manner favorable to the former. The charter protected Jews against hostile Christian clergy, guaranteed the inviolability of their life and property, and assured their protection while transporting their merchandise and carrying on their business.

At the end of the 13th century, life became difficult for German Jews, and many migrated to Poland. In 1344, Casimir the Great reaffirmed the charter of Boleslav and extended further privileges to Jews in his kingdom. In the following years during the Black Plague, Poland became a refuge for Jews of **Germany** who were either massacred or driven out of the towns in which they resided. They began to stream into Poland in large numbers. Germany was practically emptied of its Jewish population, and Poland became the great center of Yiddish-speaking Jews.

In the late 14th century, when Jagello, Duke of **Lithuania**, married the heiress to the Polish throne, Lithuania became part of Poland. Jews who had settled about the same time in Lithuania and Poland were now united under one ruler. With few exceptions, the Polish kings treated Jews well and protected them against hostile clergy, German merchants, and artisans who had settled in the larger towns. Poland was an agricultural country, its land divided into large estates worked by serfs for the benefit of the nobility. Jews served the nobility as managers of their estates, buyers and distributors of their excess farm produce, financial agents, tax farmers, and suppliers of luxury articles. Although few Jews became rich, they lived comfortably, married young, reared large families, and devoted their time and energy to the study of **Torah** and **Talmud**.

Jews were organized into autonomous communities, each community having full jurisdiction over its members. The Polish government levied a single tax on all Jews of Poland. It was up to Jews to apportion this sum among the various communities. It became necessary to establish a council made up of outstanding rabbis and heads of important communities in order to represent them before the government. This council was charged with the task of negotiating the amount of the tax due to the government, collecting the tax from the various communities, and protecting the rights and interests of Polish Jewry. In the 16th century this representative body was known as the Council of the Three Lands, since it represented the Jews of Poland, Lithuania, and Polish Russia. In the 17th century a Council of the Four Lands, representing the Jews of Great Poland, Little Poland, Podolia (including Galicia), and Volhynia was established. The members of the council met twice yearly at the great fairs of Lublin and Jaroslav. In addition to managing communal affairs, the Council acted as the supreme court of the Jewish communities, settling disputes and enacting necessary ordinances. They also supervised elementary education and the *yeshivot*, or Talmudic academies.

Jewish learning flourished in Poland. There was hardly a home where the Talmud was not studied. Yeshivot were established in many important cities, and the world-famous Talmudic scholars who taught there attracted hundreds of students from far and wide. Among these scholars were Shalom Shakhna (1500-1558), who established the famous yeshiva of Lublin; Moses Isserles (1530-1572), whose notes on the **Shulhan Arukh** made it the accepted code of Jewish law for Polish Jewry; Solomon Luria (1510-1573), author of an important commentary on parts of the Talmud; Mordecai Jaffe (d. 1612), author of a great code of law; Joshua Falk (d. 1614), great commentator on the codes of Jacob ben Asher and Joseph **Karo**; Meir of Lublin (d. 1616); Samuel Edels (d. 1631); and Joel Sirkes (d. 1640).

Modern Period. In the second half of the 17th century, the Cossack uprisings led by Chmelnicki, and subsequent wars with **Sweden** and **Russia** had catastrophic effects on Polish Jews. Numerous communities were completely destroyed. Tens of thousands of Jews perished; many fled to neighboring countries. When order was restored, the remaining Jews, joined by returning refugees, re-established their communal life. Through legislation, King Jan Casimir helped to improve the economic status of the Jewish population in the devastated regions.

However, the recovery of Polish Jewry was not complete. They were constantly exposed to the accusations of the Church and the anger of the mob. The general anarchy which engulfed Poland in the 18th century further aggravated the Jewish position. Efforts of the Council of the Four Lands to reopen the once famous yeshivot were only partially successful. The suffering masses sought consolation in mysticism and in illusions of redemption. The Messianic movement led by Sabbatai Zevi stirred the imagination of considerable numbers of Polish Jews who believed that the day of deliverance was near. Even after they were disillusioned in the false Messiah, many Polish Jews remained in the grip of mysticism. Some followed the adventurer Jacob **Frank**, who proclaimed himself a successor to Sabbatai Zevi. In the middle of the 18th century the quest of Polish Jewry for spiritual fortitude and a glowing faith was realized in **Hasidism**. The movement at-

Polish Jews in the 16th century.

tracted many adherents. It preached contentment and cheerfulness and imparted a sense of importance to simple people who were scorned or ignored by scholars.

Throughout the 18th century, Jews of Poland, which included **Ukraine** and White Russia, were almost constantly terrorized by their Christian neighbors. Subjected to the hostility of the church and the whims of local rulers and landowners, the life of the Jew was at times intolerable. The frequent **blood accusations** and riots lasted until the final partition of Poland by Russia, Prussia, and **Austria** in 1795. In the rebellion against foreign rule led by Kosciusko, Berek Joselovic, heading a Jewish legion in 1794, fought on the side of the Poles. In 1807, Napoleon formed part of the country into the Duchy of Warsaw, a demarcation which lasted for eight years. The Jewish situation was only slightly changed during this period. The majority of Jews in the partitioned provinces of Poland became part of Austria and Russia, sharing the general lot of their brethren in these two countries. Jews of Galicia became, in 1782, subject to the Edict of Tolerance issued by the Austrian Emperor Joseph II. This edict endeavored to foster assimilationist tendencies among Jews. Although the Revolution of 1848 secured equal rights for the Jewish population, economic discrimination lasted until the outbreak of World War I.

A number of Jews living under Russian rule identified closely with the Polish cause. They participated in the revolt of 1830-31, forming a regiment which defended the city of **Warsaw** against Russian attacks. In 1863, led by Rabbi Dov Berish Meisels, head of the Jewish community in Warsaw, they took active part in an unsuccessful attempt to overthrow Russian rule.

Due to their devotion to the cause of Polish national liberation, Jews of Russian Poland fared poorly during the 19th century. They suffered at the hands of Russian oppressors and Polish oppressed alike. However, the difficult economic and political plight of Polish Jewry did not hamper its spiritual and cultural growth. In addition to being a stronghold of Talmudic scholarship and Hasidism, it became, in the late 19th century, fertile ground for the **Haskalah**, or Enlightenment, movement. Some of the best-known Hebrew writers and scholars were active in the Jewish centers of Poland, especially in Warsaw. These included Hayim Selig Slonimski, a scientist and inventor who edited *Ha-Tzefirah*, and Nahum **Sokolow**. Other scholars and writers were J.L. **Peretz**, David **Frischmann**, Sholom **Asch**, Simon Berenfeld, Samuel Abraham Poznanski, Moses Schorr, Meyer Balban, and Ignaz Schipper.

Attacks and persecution of Jews followed the establishment of Poland as an independent state after World War I. Minority rights for Polish Jews were secured in the peace treaty of **Versailles**. With the inclusion parts of White Russia and Galicia in the new Poland, the Jewish community became one of the largest in the world, numbering more than 3 million. The national, economic, and political rights of the Jewish population were rigorously pursued by Jewish representatives in the Polish *Sejm*, or Parliament. Despite vicious anti-Semitic propaganda, economic restrictions, and the often hostile government policy, Jewish national and cultural life in Poland flourished. All parties—the Zionists, the Jewish Socialist **Bund, Agudath Israel**, and **Mizrachi**—had a large following among Polish Jewry. Polish Jewry served as a main source for Palestinian pioneers. Jewish schools in which the language of instruction was either Hebrew, Yiddish, or Polish were opened in every Jewish community by various political and religious factions. The Yiddish press exerted great influence on the Jewish masses. There were Yiddish dailies, outstanding among them being *Haint* and *Moment*. There were close to 200 periodicals in Yiddish, Hebrew, and Polish, all devoted to Jewish affairs.

Polish Jews in the 19th century.

Rabbi Dov Beirish Meisels, Chief Rabbi of Warsaw, participated in the Polish uprising in 1863 against Tsarist occupation.

The most prominent Jewish political leaders were Isaac Gruenbaum, Joshua Thon, Leon Reich, Emil Sommerstein, and Ignaz Schwarzbart, the only Jewish representative in the Polish Government in Exile during World War II in London.

Just before World War II, the anti-Semitic movement in the country assumed a more threatening character. A new Polish party called O.N.R. openly advocated Nazi-style extermination of Jews. Attacks on Jews became a frequent occurrence. The government concurred with the economic boycott instituted against them. Nevertheless, Polish Jewry heroically defended its rights. Even during the first few years of the Nazi occupation of Poland, when Polish Jewry was reduced to complete enslavement, it gave evidence of vitality and spiritual fortitude. The extermination of more than 3 million Polish Jews from 1942 to 1945 is one of the greatest tragedies in Jewish history. Only a few hundred thousand survived the Nazi slaughter. The story of the revolt of the **Warsaw Ghetto** and the resistance of Jewish partisans and ghetto fighters in other parts of the country are heroic chapters in the annals of Jewish martyrdom and courage.

After the war, only about 60,000 Jews remained in Poland; thousands who survived Soviet exile and Nazi camps fled to Israel. Spurred by a renascence of **anti-Semitism** in the new Communist Poland, another exodus began late in 1956, and more than 35,000 Jews left, almost all of them for Israel. At the same time, about 19,000 Jews of Polish origin were repatriated from the Soviet Union. About two-thirds of them re-emigrated to Israel.

In 1982, there was a resurgence of anti-Semitism in Poland after the introduction of martial law. Jews were accused of being key leaders in Poland's anti-Soviet Solidarity movement. In 1998, there were approximately 4,000 Jews in all of Poland, although some sources claim that tens of thousands of Jews in Poland, born after World War II, have yet to come to terms with their Jewish identity.

Of the more than 900 Jewish cemeteries in Poland, the majority were destroyed and expropriated, mostly after the war. An international rabbinical group, under the leadership of Rabbi S. Halberstam of Bobov, has been active since 1978 in restoring and renovating at least some of them. Rabbi Chaskel O. Besser of New York was instrumental in these and other activities.

For the past few years, the Ronald S. Lauder Foundation has succeeded in bringing new life into Jewish activities in Poland, including a kindergarten in Warsaw, summer and winter camp programs for Jewish youth, religious and cultural activities, and the reestablishment of a rabbi in Warsaw.

POLLOCK, JACKSON. *See* **Art**.

POPULATION, WORLD JEWISH. Information on Jewish population, by continent and country, is hard to obtain. A variety of difficulties in obtaining accurate figures in some countries, as well as the extent of Jewish migrations, and the rise in mixed marriages during recent decades, result in figures which are in many cases an approximation rather than an accurate count.

COUNTRIES WITH THE LARGEST JEWISH POPULATION

1	*United States*	*5.8 million*
2	*Israel*	*4.6 million*
3	*France*	*525,000*
4	*Russia*	*360,000*
5	*Canada*	*360,000*
6	*Great Britain*	*300,000*
7	*Argentina*	*210,000*
8	*Ukraine*	*180,000*
9	*Brazil*	*100,000*
10	*South Africa*	*98,000*
11	*Australia*	*95,000*

PORTUGAL. The history of the Jewish community, founded in the 12th century, follows the same tragic pattern as that in **Spain**. Jews enjoyed many privileges and high offices in the state, until they were subjected to forced baptism and finally expulsion in 1496. Jews had complete charge of their affairs. They were governed by the chief rabbis, to whom the state delegated much authority. For this privilege they had to pay various taxes, including a degrading poll-tax. Among the notable Jews who served the king were Don Isaac **Abravanel** and the astronomer Abraham **Zacuto**, whose astrolabe, the forerunner of the modern sextant, was used by the explorer Vasco da Gama. With their expulsion from Spain in 1492, many Jews found refuge in Portugal. But here, too, tragedy would soon overtake them. King Manoel, though friendly at first, agreed to their expulsion as part of a marriage bargain he entered into with Ferdinand and Isabella of Spain. The Spanish rulers insisted that Manoel's marriage to their daughter be conditional on the expulsion of Jews from Portugal. The expulsion order, promulgated in 1496, permitted Jews to take all their property, but ordered the baptism of all young people. However, even the adults brought to Lisbon were not allowed to leave; they were offered the choice of being sold as slaves or baptized. Many who were baptized secretly clung to their faith as Marranos. In 1998 there were 400 Jews in Portugal. Engaged mainly in the textile trade, they are concentrated in Lisbon and Oporto.

POTOCKI, COUNT VALENTINE (d. 1749). Polish nobleman and convert to Judaism. In the early 18th century, European Jewry was degraded and oppressed. Nevertheless, Potocki was so deeply impressed by the Jewish faith that he embraced Judaism. Potocki went to **Paris** to complete his education, and there, the sight of an aged Jewish scholar studying the **Bible** aroused his interest in Judaism. He persuaded the old man to teach him the Bible and Hebrew. Potocki became a convert to the Jewish faith in **Amsterdam**, the only country in Europe where conversion was permitted. Later, he returned to his native **Poland** and lived with Jews in the **ghetto** of **Vilna**. When his identity was discovered, the Poles arrested him. Despite entreaties by his mother and his friends, he refused to return to his former faith. Instead, Potocki chose to accept a martyr's death and was burned at the stake in 1749. The memory of this *ger zedek*, or righteous convert, was long revered by Eastern European Jews.

POTOK, CHAIM (1929-). American novelist, Conservative rabbi, and former editor at the **Jewish Publication Society.** His first novel, *The Chosen,* introduced American readers to the closed world of the **Hasidim** in Brooklyn, where he grew up. Subsequent novels established him as one of the popular American Jewish writers of his time.

PRAGUE. Capital of the **Czech Republic** and home of one of the oldest and most important Jewish communities in Europe. Jews settled in Prague at the beginning of the 10th century. In 1096, at the time of the first Crusade, Jews suffered grievously. In the following centuries, Kings Sobeslav II and Ottokar issued laws which regulated relations between Christians and Jews. Early in the 13th century, Jews settled in the Altstadt, or Old City, where they built the famous Altneuschul synagogue, one of Prague's ancient and most celebrated landmarks. According to legend, this synagogue was partially built with stones from the destroyed **Temple** in **Jerusalem.** Despite protection from the Bohemian king, they were constantly persecuted. The worst attack on the **ghetto** took place in 1389, when 3,000 Jews were killed. The ghetto was again plundered in 1421, when Jews sided with the Hussites who were rebelling against the Catholic Church. The situation for Prague Jews improved slightly in the 15th century. In 1527, they were permitted to display the "Jew's flag" in processions. At the same time, however, restrictions and expulsions from the city continued, but did not deter Jewish economic and intellectual advancement. The community of Prague produced some outstanding rabbis and scholars, the most prominent being Judah **Loew,** known as the Maharal, and Yom Tov Lipman Heller (1579-1654), author of a commentary on the Mishnah, astronomer, and liturgical poet. David ben Solomon Gans (1541-1613) was a famous historian and astronomer who was a friend of the great astronomers Johannes Kepler and Tycho Brahe. David Oppenheim (1664-1736) was a famous collector of Hebrew books and manuscripts now a part of the Bodleian Library of Oxford, **England**.

At the end of the 17th century, two misfortunes befell the Jewish community: an epidemic and a raging fire which destroyed eleven synagogues and much property. As late as 1744, Empress Maria Theresa ordered the expulsion of 10,000 Jews from Prague. They were allowed to return a few years later only after paying a heavy tax. The **Haskalah**, or Enlightenment, movement at the end of the 18th century, made a deep impression on Prague's Jewry. Many Jews began to play an important role in the intellectual life of the city and the country. The Orthodox element was centered around Rabbi Ezekiel ben Judah Landau (1713-1783).

In 1848-1849, Prague's Jews were granted equality, and in the next century the community grew rapidly. Conditions improved further after the establishment of the Czechoslovak Republic in 1919. A number of Jewish writers in Prague achieved fame in German literature, among them Max Brod, Franz **Werfel**, and Franz **Kafka**.

Nazi occupation of Prague in 1939 spelled the doom of the thriving Jewish community of 35,000. In 1948, the Communist government of Czechoslovakia came to the support of the newly established state of **Israel** when it was attacked by its Arab neighbors. This cooperation was soon replaced by a violent anti-Semitic and anti-Zionist campaign, culminating in the infamous Slansky trial in Prague in 1953. The estimated Jewish population in 1998 was about 2,000.

JEWISH POPULATIONS AROUND THE WORLD

EUROPE

Austria	8,500
Azerbijan	12,000
Belarus	28 ,000
Belgium	32 ,000
Bulgaria	3,200
Croatia	1,300
Czech Republic	2,200
Denmark	6,500
Estonia	3,000
Finland	1,200
France	525,000
Georgia	10,000
Germany	60,000
Gibraltar	600
Great Britain	300,000
Greece	5,000
Hungary	55,000
Ireland	1,300
Italy	30,000
Kazakhstan	12,000
Latvia	15,000
Lithuania	6,000
Luxemburg	600
Moldova	10,000
Netherlands	27,000
Norway	1,500
Poland	4,000
Portugal	400
Romania	14,000
Russia	360,000
Slovakia	3,700
Spain	14,000
Sweden	15,000
Switzerland	18,000
Turkey	20,000
Ukraine	180,000
Uzbekistan	20,000
Yugoslavia	2,000

AFRICA

Egypt	200
Ethiopia	200
Morocco	6,500
South Africa	98,000
Tunisia	1,800
Zaire	320
Zambia	300
Zimbabwe	925

NORTH AMERICA

Canada	360,000
Mexico	40,700
United States	5.8 million

CENTRAL AMERICA

Bahamas	300
Costa Rica	2,500
Cuba	700
Dominican Republic	100
Guatemala	1,000
Jamaica	300
Netherlands Antilles	300
Panama	5,000
Puerto Rico	1,500

SOUTH AMERICA

Argentina	210,000
Bolivia	700
Brazil	100,000
Chile	21,000
Colombia	5,000
Ecuador	900
Paraguay	900
Peru	3,000
Suriname	200
Uruguay	24,000
Venezuela	20,000

ASIA

Hong Kong	900
India	4,400
Iran	14,000
Iraq	120
Israel	4.6 million
Japan	1,200
Lebanon	100
Philippines	150
Singapore	300
Syria	250
Thailand	250
Yemen	300

OCEANIA

Australia	95,000
New Zealand	4,800

PRAYER. The spiritual communion with God through prayer as an important form of worship has been part of Jewish religious experience from the beginning. In the Jewish religion, prayers may be individual or congregational, since organized religious services consisted in the offering of sacrifices. Some eloquent examples of individual prayers in the **Bible** are the prayers of praise and thanksgiving offered by **Moses** after the Israelites' deliverance from **Egypt** and the crossing of the Red Sea (Exod. 15:1-18); by **Deborah** after her victory over Sisera and his Canaanite hordes (Judges 5:2-31); by Hannah after the birth of her son **Samuel** (I Samuel 2:1-10); and by King **Solomon** after the construction of the Holy **Temple** (I Kings 8:23-53). Most psalms were also individual prayers.

Congregational services began in the period of the Babylonian exile from 586-536 B.C.E. When Jews returned to Judea, rebuilt the Temple, and organized community life under **Ezra**, **Nehemiah**, and the Men of the Great Assembly, an early form of congregational service developed. These services took place alongside sacrifices at the Temple, as well as in numerous synagogues throughout Palestine and **Babylonia**. However, with the destruction of the Second Temple in

An Israeli soldier at prayer at the Western Wall in Jerusalem.

70 C.E., the dispersion of the Jewish people, and the complete elimination of sacrifices, congregational services in the synagogue became the exclusive form of worship. Prayers were standardized by religious authorities and assembled into prayer books. In the course of centuries, new prayers were composed and incorporated into the prayer book.

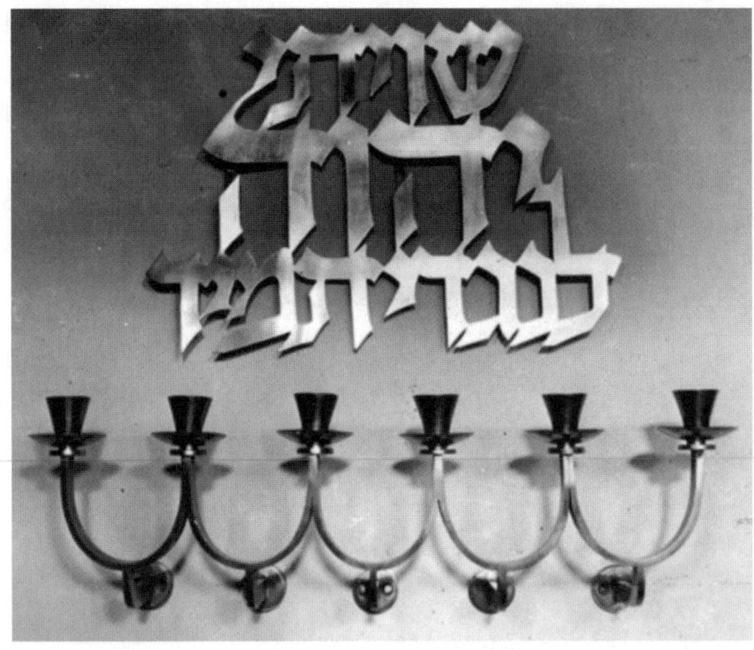

Synagogue ornament above the cantorial lecturn, by Judah Wolpert.

The traditional Jewish prayer book is known as the **siddur**, and the special holiday and festival prayer book is called the **mahzor**. The present prayer book consists of portions of the Bible, including approximately half of the **psalms**; selections from the **Talmud**; religious poems by medieval poets; **Maimonides**' Thirteen Principles of Faith and other prayers of benediction, petition, adoration, confession, and thanksgiving, originating in various ages.

Congregational prayers are grouped into the following services: *shaharit* (morning service), *minhah* (late afternoon service), and *maariv* (evening service). On **Sabbaths** and festivals, the *musaf* (additional service) follows the reading from the **Torah** after *shaharit*, and on **Yom Kippur**, the *neilah* (closing service) is added at the end of the *minhah*. The **Kiddush** (Sabbath and festival consecration service over wine), the *Havdalah* (separating the holy day from the weekdays), and the *Birkat Ha-mazon* (grace after meals) are examples of prayers in the home.

The most important daily synagogue prayers are the **Shema** (Deut. 6:4), which proclaims the unity and sovereignty of God; the *Shmone Esre* (or *Amidah*), consisting of eighteen basic benedictions which comprise the main portion of every service; the *Ashre* (Psalm 145) and the *Alenu*, both prayers of adoration repeated three times a day.

The great majority of prayers in the traditional prayer book are in **Hebrew**, the holy tongue of the Jew. A few are in **Aramaic**, a Semitic language akin to Hebrew, which the Jews spoke for many generations. (*See also* **Synagogue**.)

PRESS, JEWISH. More than 1,000 Jewish newspapers and periodicals in about 25 languages appear in all parts of the world today. Of these, about 40% are published in Israel. The U.S. ranks second in the number of Jewish newspapers published, about 25% of the total number.

Amsterdam was the birthplace of the first Jewish periodical in 1678. Named *Gazeta de Amsterdam*, it was printed in **Ladino,** a Spanish-Jewish dialect. Sporadic attempts were made to publish magazines for more than a century thereafter, but all were short-lived. In 1841, the first issue of a weekly *The Jewish Chronicle* made its appearance in **London**. It is today one of the oldest and most important Jewish periodicals. In the U.S., the earliest surviving weekly, *The American Israelite*, was founded in 1854 by Isaac Mayer **Wise.** The first Yiddish daily in the world, *Yiddishe Tageblatt*, began publication in 1885 in **New York**. It merged with the *Jewish Morning Journal* in 1928. The first Hebrew magazine, *Ha-Tzofeh Be-Eretz Ha-Hadasha* (The Observer in the New Land), edited by Zvi Hirsch Bernstein, was published in 1871.

In the latter 19th century, the Hebrew press in **Russia** made great strides. In 1856, the appearance of the first regular Hebrew weekly, *Ha-Maggid*, coincided with the growth of the Enlightenment movement. Thirty years later, the first Hebrew daily, *Ha-Yom* (The Day), began publication in St. Petersburg, Russia's capital at that time. The two other Hebrew weeklies, *Ha-Melitz* (The Advocate) and *Ha-Tzefirah* (Daybreak), turned into dailies. With the advancement of the Zionist and socialist movements and the development of Jewish public opinion in Eastern Europe and in particular in Russia and **Poland**, the Yiddish press reached widespread circulation and wielded great influence. Before World War II, there were Yiddish dailies in several large Jewish centers in Poland and **Lithuania** and three dailies in the Soviet Union. With the destruction of East European Jewry, only a few Yiddish periodicals continued publication in Poland, while in Russia only one is published in Birobidjan.

In the last two decades, the number of Jewish dailies has declined, while the number of weeklies, monthlies, and other periodicals is on the increase. In **Israel**, in addition to the Hebrew daily press, there are daily publications in Arabic, English, Russian, French, Hungarian, Yiddish, and German. This diversity of the Jewish press in Israel reflects the diversity of the country's languages and culture. Israel is the only country in the world where a vibrant and diverse daily Jewish press exists. Israel's oldest existing Hebrew daily, *Ha-Aretz*, founded in 1919, is a respected liberal newspaper. It advocates a policy of moderation in political and social affairs.

Masthead of the Hebrew daily Davar, announcing the establishment of the State of Israel.

Masthead of the first Hebrew journal in Palestine, Halbanon, which began publication in 1863.

Davar is the organ of the **Histadrut.** *Al Hamishmar* is the party organ of Mapam; *Hatzofe* and *Hamodi'ah* express the views of religious parties. The afternoon newspapers *Maariv* and *Yedioth Ahronoth* reflect all shades of opinion and are the most widely read in Israel. Israel's only English daily, *The Jerusalem Post*, is a prestigious paper widely read among Jews around the world. Almost all daily newspapers in Israel publish literary supplements and popular magazines on weekends.

Only a limited number of Yiddish dailies is published outside of Israel. The two American Hebrew weeklies, *Yisrael Shelanu* and *Hadoar*, are published in New York. The best-known Yiddish weeklies in the U.S. are the *Algemeiner Journal* and the *Forward*. The latter now appears in English. There are two Hebrew illustrated monthlies for young people, *Olam Chadash* and *Lamishpachah*. Other monthly magazines are *Bitzaron* (Hebrew) and *Zukunft* (Yiddish).

Of the Anglo-Jewish press in the U.S., among the most widely circulated are the weeklies, *The Jewish Week* and *The Jewish Press* in New York, *The Jewish Exponent* in Philadelphia, *The Jewish News* in Michigan, *The Jewish Advocate* in Boston, *B'nai B'rith Messenger* and *Sentinel* in Chicago; the monthlies *Commentary*, *Hadassah Magazine*, B'nai Brith's *National Jewish Monthly*, *Midstream*, *Moment* and *Tikkun;* the quarterlies *Judaism*, *Tradition*, and *Jewish Spectator*. The children's magazine, *Olomeinu*, is published by Torah Umesorah.

PREVIN, ANDRE. *See* **Music, Jews in.**

PRIEST. *See* **Kohen**.

PROPHETS. *See* **Bible** and the Biblical prophets.

PROTOCOLS OF THE ELDERS OF ZION. *See* **Anti-Semitism**.

PROUST, MARCEL (1871-1922). French novelist; one of the greatest novelists of all time. Deeply influenced by his mother—his one Jewish parent—he grew up among the upper class of French society of his time. Confined to his house by illness, he embarked on writing a multi-volume novel called *In Search of Lost Time*, in which he recalls his childhood in great detail and with deep psychological insight, recreating an entire era.

PROVERBS, BOOK OF. Written, according to tradition, by King **Solomon**, Proverbs, together with **Job** and **Ecclesiastes**, is part of the Wisdom Literature in the **Bible**. It is composed of a variety of sayings, teaching wise and moral conduct for everyday life.

PSALMS. From *Tehilim*, meaning praise or chants of praise. The first book in *Ketuvim* (Writings), the third division of the **Bible.** The Book of Psalms is itself divided into five books, like the Pentateuch. It contains 150 hymns, most of them ascribed to **David,** some to Asaph the Musician, others to the Sons of Korah. Some of the psalms are odes praising God, called Halleluyahs; others are poems of thanksgiving, pilgrim songs, and mournful elegies. They vary in length, structure, and subject matter. The confidence and joy of the 23rd Psalm (beginning with "The Lord is my shepherd") have comforted men and women since its creation. Psalm 104 is a nature poem that kindles the imagination with the majesty of all creation. Psalm 24, a stirring ode of praise, has been incorporated, like many other psalms, into the synagogue services. During all morning services, except those that fall on the **Sabbath,** this Psalm is chanted as the Torah scroll is returned to the Ark.

The psalms were knitted closely into the daily life of the Jewish people. In the synagogue, morning services end each day with a different Psalm. In each community, simple pious people who had been unable to acquire learning joined within a *Hevra Magide Tehilim*, a "band of Psalm chanters." They met daily at the synagogue and sought inspiration in reciting the Mizmor Shel Yom-the day's reading from the Book of Psalms until they had completed it on the Sabbath. In folklore there were stories about the "Psalm-Chanter," a folk hero who was the secret student of mystic lore, a modest saint who concealed his knowledge and joined the Psalm-chanters daily in the house of prayer. He also joined those gathered at the bedside of the dangerously ill and those at houses of mourning in their recital of the psalms, a distillation of piety and a plea of mercy to Heaven. The Book of Psalms has also been read by Christians since

FAMOUS PROVERBS

Fear of the Lord is the beginning of knowledge;
But fools despise wisdom and instruction.

Be not afraid of sudden fear,
Fear not the wicked,
For the Lord shall be your strength,
And shall keep you from stumbling.

A soft answer calms anger,
But harsh words stir it up.

The scorners take their delight in scorning,
And fools hate knowledge.

The merciful man does good to his own soul,
But he that is cruel troubles his own flesh.

The lip of truth will stand firm forever,
But only for a moment with tongue of falsehood.

At the fall of your enemy do not rejoice;
And at his stumbling let not your heart be glad.

The wicked flee when no man pursues;
But the righteous are bold as a lion.

If your enemy is hungry, give him bread to eat;
And if he is thirsty, give him water to drink.

the time of the Apostles. It has given comfort and inspiration during religious services and in private devotions.

PUERTO RICO. U.S. Commonwealth, occupying the easternmost island of the Greater Antilles. Puerto Rico was ruled by **Spain** until ceded to the U.S. in 1898. Jewish business persons and government officials arrived in the island after its occupation by the U.S. Most of them came in connection with American industrial plants set up in recent years. Until 1955, when an Orthodox congregation was founded under the leadership of a rabbi from the U.S., there was no organized Jewish community life on the island. Today, there are also Reform and Conservative congregations on the island, serving a community of 1,500.

PULITZER, JOSEPH (1847-1911). Half-Jewish immigrant from Hungary, he became one of the key personalities in the history of American journalism. He owned newspapers in St. Louis and **New York** and founded the Columbia School of Journalism. In his will he established the Pulitzer Prize for outstanding achievement in journalism, literature, and music, which has been awarded since 1917.

PUMBEDITHA. *See* **Babylonia.**

PURIM. The Feast of Lots. This holiday falls on the 14th of Adar, commemorating a day on which the Jews were saved from their oppressors. Read on the evening and morning of the holiday, the Book of **Esther** relates how Haman drew lots to determine when to put Jews of Persia to the sword. Fortunately, Haman's scheme was foiled by the faithful **Mordecai** and by Queen Esther.

Purim is celebrated with great merriment after the fashion of the Persian Jews who made their victory over Haman an occasion "for feasting and gladness." During the reading of the Book of Esther, children twirl noisemakers in derision at every mention of Haman's name. Some Asian Jewish communities even hang Haman in effigy. *Hamentaschen*, or ears of Haman, are eaten, and it is considered a "good deed" to drink wine. Comic plays, called *Purimspile*, are presented at the *seudah*, or feast, with which the holiday closes. Among the finest of Purim customs is *mishloah manot*, the practice of sending gifts of food to friends and gifts of food and money to the poor.

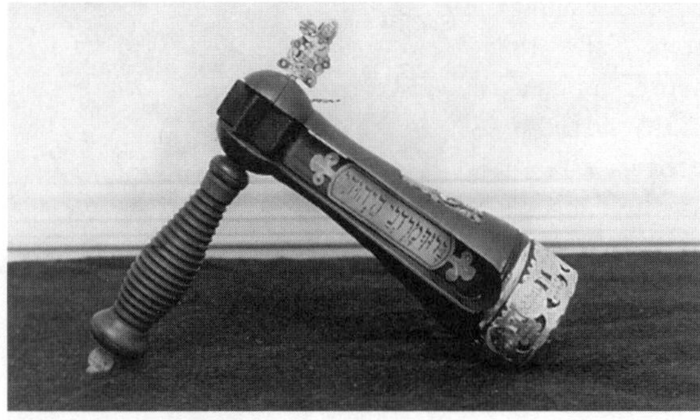

Purim grogger (noisemaker).

Mordecai and Haman. Woodcut by Ilya Schor.

The day after Purim is called *Shushan Purim*. This is so named because Jews of Shushan, the capital of Persia, fought their enemies for an additional day. Many other local Purims, established for later acts of deliverance, are observed, such as those celebrated in **Tiberia**, Israel, **Egypt,** Frankfurt, Germany, Saragossa, **Spain,** and other places. (*See also* **Esther, Scroll of.**)

PURITY LAWS. In addition to the dietary laws, which are partly hygienic in nature, there are ceremonies which have to do with ritual purity. The Jewish religion literally believed that "cleanliness is next to godliness." The **Bible** carefully defines types of personal and ritual uncleanliness and provides for exacting rituals of purification. These include the quarantining of persons with such diseases as leprosy and of those considered impure because of some contamination. Persons in a state of impurity had to leave the "camp" or community, and all objects with which they came into contact required cleansing or burning. After their recovery, "unclean" individuals had to bathe in clean, "living" (running) water. Further, the **Talmud** lists the *mikveh,* or ritual bath, as one of ten institutions which must be provided for wherever Jews live. Before private baths became common, regular visits to such public baths were the only assurance of personal cleanliness. Besides the visits to the mikveh, the washing of the hands before meals and of the feet before retiring was prescribed by Talmudic sages.

Judaism directly associates purity of body with purity of soul. The prophet **Isaiah** predicts that the sins of Israel, which have been red as crimson, shall be "washed" white as snow. Similarly, the granting of the **Torah** at Mount Sinai was preceded by three days of "purification." The white gowns, or kittels, worn in synagogue on the New Year and the Day of Atonement are associated with this idea. Also associated with it are the white tablecloths and clothing with which the Sabbath is received, and the white shrouds in which the dead are buried.

RABBI. Literally, my teacher. Title conferred upon a religious leader and teacher. According to historian Heinrich **Graetz**, the title was first used during the time of the destruction of the Second **Temple** in 70 C.E., probably introduced by the disciples of **Johnanan Ben Zakkai**. Today, a rabbi is ordained by the head or faculty of the rabbinical seminary from which he is graduated. The present functions of a rabbi consist of the religious leadership of his or her congregation; making decisions with regard to practical questions of Jewish law; conducting services and preaching on **Sabbaths**, holy days, and festivals; teaching Judaism, particularly to adult groups; officiating at important events in the life of congregants, such as **circumcision**, **marriage**, and burial. In some cases, the rabbi is also the educational head of the congregational school. Many rabbis have excelled as scholars and authors of important works on religion. A number have also distinguished themselves as gifted orators and leaders of the community or of Jewish national and world movements, such as **Zionism** and Hebrew culture.

RABBINICAL ASSEMBLY OF AMERICA. *See* **Jewish Theological Seminary of America.**

RABBINICAL COUNCIL OF AMERICA. *See* **Yeshiva University**.

RABIN, YITZHAK (1922-1995). Israeli soldier and Prime Minister. Born in **Jerusalem**, he was a member of the **Palmach** and took part in the Allied invasion of **Syria**, then under the control of Vichy **France**. During the War of Independence he commanded Israeli forces as they defended the outskirts of Jerusalem. In 1949, he took part in the Rhodes armistice negotiations. He became deputy chief of staff of the Israeli Army in 1960 and chief of staff in 1964. He was responsible for the strategy employed by the Israeli army during the **Six-Day War** of 1967. In 1968, he was appointed Israeli ambassador to the U.S. In 1974, he joined the Israeli cabinet as Minister of Labor and succeeded Golda **Meir** as Prime Minister, serving until 1977. He was reelected Prime Minister in 1992. In 1993, he signed the Oslo Agreement, recognizing Yasser Arafat as the leader of the Palestinian Arabs, and began working with him on establishing a Palestinian Authority in the Gaza Strip, **Jericho**, and parts of the **West Bank**. Soon after, he signed a peace treaty with Jordan. For his peace efforts he received the **Nobel Peace Prize**. In 1995, during a peace rally, he was assassinated by a right-wing Israeli who opposed the return of land to Arabs.

Yitzhak Rabin. Courtesy Embassy of Israel, Washington D.C.

RABINOWITZ, SHALOM. *See* **Shalom Aleichem**.

RACHEL. **Jacob**'s second and beloved wife; mother of **Joseph** and **Benjamin**. The prophet **Jeremiah** refers to her as the loving mother of the people of Israel who grieves for their exile and pleads for their return.

RACHEL (1890-1931). Pen name of Rachel Bluvstein, Hebrew poet. Few modern Hebrew poems have captured the hearts of the readers as Rachel. Her poetry is simple and sincere, yet it captures the spirit of **Israel** and expresses universal verities.

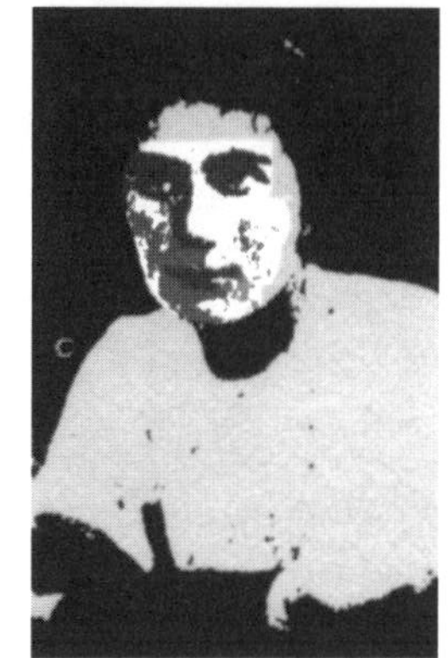

Rachel.

When Rachel came to Palestine from **Russia** at age 19, she worked as a farmhand at **kibbutz** Kinneret in the **Galilee.** When she arrived, she did not know a word of **Hebrew** or **Yiddish**, yet she mastered the Hebrew language. In 1913 she went to Europe to study agriculture and contracted tuberculosis. She returned to Palestine when World War I ended, but her illness disabled her for life. No longer able to till the land, her longing and loneliness poured out in such poems as the well-loved *Ve-ulai* (Perhaps).

RAMBAM. *See* **Maimonides**.

RASHI (1040-1105). Acronym of Rabbi Solomon Yitzhaki, a preeminent Biblical and Talmudic commentator. His commentaries are indispensable to the study of the **Bible** and the **Talmud.** He became a beloved figure in Jewish history and the subject of many

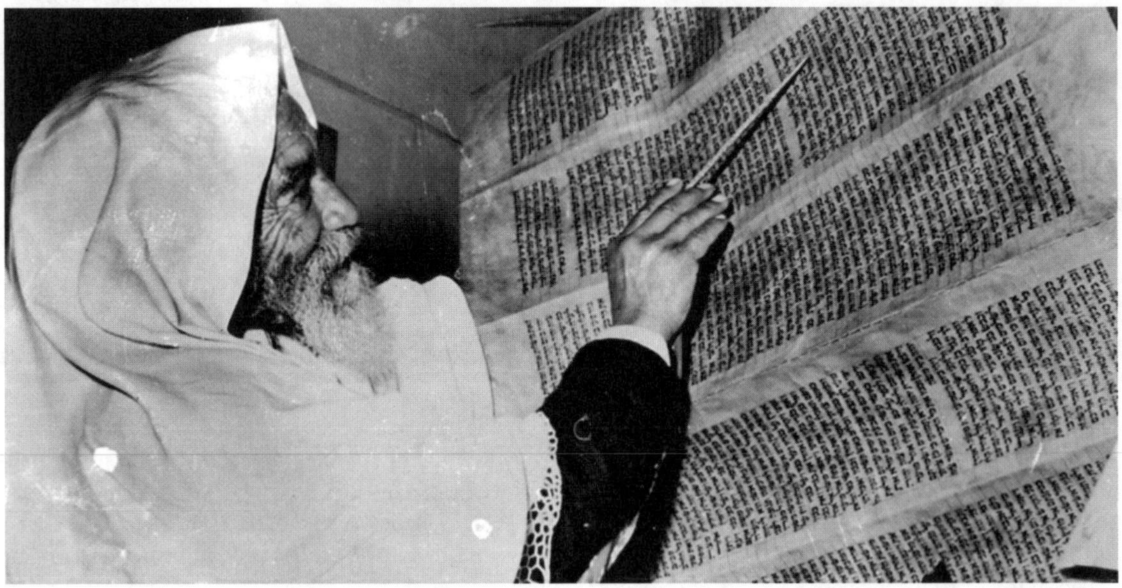

An aged Yemenite Jew had become accustomed to reading the Torah upside down because of book-sharing in Yemen.

legends about life, piety, and saintliness. Born in Troyes, **France**, Rashi spent a brief period of study in Worms, **Germany**, and on his return founded a Talmudic academy in his native land. The fame of this school grew rapidly, attracting students from far and wide. In teaching the Talmud, Rashi felt there was a lack of good commentaries to facilitate its study and undertook the task of providing one. Rashi's commentary became a standard guide for every student of the Talmud. Its explanations are clear and explicit, written in a lucid Hebrew style. His commentary on the Pentateuch and on most of the other Biblical books are invaluable for an understanding of the Bible along traditional lines. These commentaries, in which Rashi makes full use of **Midrashic** sources, have been widely used by both Jewish and Gentile scholars. They have been translated into Latin and other languages.

RATHENAU, WALTER (1867-1922). German industrialist and statesman; son of the engineer and industrialist Emil Rathenau. During World War I, he organized the supply of raw materials of great importance to the German war effort. In 1922, he became the German Foreign Secretary and concluded the famous agreement with Soviet **Russia** at Rapallo. He was assassinated by German ultra-nationalists.

RAV (ABBA ARIKHA). *See* **Babylonia**.

READING, RUFUS DANIEL ISAACS, FIRST MARQUESS OF (1860-1935). Broker, jurist, and public servant. Born in **London**, the son of a poor Jewish storekeeper, Rufus Isaacs, after a dazzling career at the bar and several terms in Parliament, was named chief justice of England, the first Jew to attain that distinction. The following year he was ennobled and, as the First Marquess of Reading, took a seat in the House of Lords. From 1921 to 1926 he served as viceroy of **India**, again the first Jew to hold the post. Long interested in Zionist affairs, Lord Reading joined U.S. Supreme Court Justice Louis D. **Brandeis** in drafting an economic plan for Palestine. This plan was presented to the Zionist Conference in London in 1920. Elected president of the Palestine Electric Corporation in 1926, he visited Palestine and joined in the protests to the British cabinet after the 1929 riots in Palestine.

READING, EVA VIOLET, MARCHIONESS (1895-1973). Chairwoman of the National Council of Women in Britain, and President of the British Section of the **World Jewish Congress**. Her father-in-law was the first Marquess of Reading, and Lord **Melchett** was her father.

READING OF THE LAW. In Hebrew, *K'riat Ha-Torah*. The reading of the Law is a distinct part of the prayer service, observed during the morning and afternoon assemblages on **Sabbaths**, holidays, and each Monday and Thursday. One portion of the Five Books of **Moses** is read each week, divided so that the entire Five Books are read each year. *Simhat Torah* (the Rejoicing of the Law) is the day on which the last portion of one year's cycle is read and the first portion of the following year is begun.

During the reading of the Law, the **Torah** scrolls, written on parchment by special scribes, are removed from the Ark of the Law. Originally, the portion was read by various members of the congregation, who were "called up to the Law." Later, it became customary for a special reader to chant the entire portion to a melody handed down from ancient times. The older practice, however, is preserved in the custom of "calling up" seven readers, each of whom chants a blessing before the reading of each section of the weekly portion. An eighth reader is "called up" for the reading of the **Haftorah**, the short passage from the Prophets which follows the weekly portion of the Law. Sabbaths and holidays are also the occasion for the reading of other portions of the Bible and other holy books. *Pirke Avot* (*see* **Ethics of the Fathers**), is read every Saturday afternoon during the summer, while one of the five *megillot*, or scrolls, is read on each of five holidays: the **Song of Songs** on **Passover**, **Ruth** on **Shavuot**, **Ecclesiastes** on **Sukkot**, **Esther** on **Purim**, and **Lamentations** on the Ninth of Ab.

In the synagogue, the reading of the regular portion of Law is often followed by a *derashah*, or sermon, delivered by the **rabbi** or some member of the congregation. Based on the portion of the week, it generally deals with some religious or ethical subject.

REBECCA. Wife of **Isaac** and second matriarch of **Israel**. Of her twins, **Esau** and **Jacob**, she favored Jacob and arranged for Isaac's blessing of the firstborn to go to the younger Jacob.

RECONSTRUCTIONISM. Religious movement which attempts to reinterpret Judaism in modern terms without abandoning its cultural values and usages. Reconstructionism began to emerge as a movement in 1934 under the leadership of Rabbi Mordecai M. **Kaplan** (1881-1983). Kaplan believed that Judaism is a "religious civilization" emerging from the language, history, customs, laws, religion, art, and folkways of the Jewish people. This civilization and the basic values it embodies can be perpetuated only through social institutions in which these entities continue to be meaningful to the individuals who participate in them. Reconstructionism has therefore striven for the organization of closely integrated Jewish communities in the U.S. Because it also believes that Jewish nationalism is a part of Judaism, it stresses the ties between the State of **Israel** and Jewish communities in the Diaspora. In religion, it is close to Reform Judaism in its call for a reexamination of religious beliefs and to Conservative Judaism in its desire to preserve as many forms of religious practice as possible. Its work has been conducted through the Reconstructionist Foundation formed in 1940. Its periodical, *The Reconstructionist*, has served the movement as a forum since 1935.

REDEMPTION. *Ge'ulah* in Hebrew. It is one of the key beliefs of Judaism, according to which the Jewish people will be rescued by a divinely-appointed leader and returned to their land. The Zionist movement adopted this concept to mean physical and political recovery of land and nationalism.

REFORM JUDAISM. *See* **Judaism.**

REFUSNIKS. *See* **Russia.**

REINER, FRITZ. *See* **Music, Jews in.**

REINES, ISAAC JACOB (1839-1915). Scholar, teacher, and founder of the religious Zionist movement **Mizrachi.** Born in **Russia**, Reines introduced a new method for the study of the **Talmud**, one in which reason and logic replaced drastically literal interpretation. To modernize traditional Jewish education, he founded the Yeshiva of Lida. He worked actively for the Zionist cause and, in 1884, participated in the **Hoveve Zion** conference at Kattowitz, where strategies for settling Jews in Palestine were considered. When Theodor **Herzl** issued a call for the establishment of a Jewish state, Reines became an ardent supporter. He was a fiery partisan of the rebuilding of the Jewish homeland and fought bitterly against the anti-Zionism of his contemporaries. In 1902, he founded the **Mizrachi** movement.

Isaac Jacob Reines.

REINHARDT, MAX (1873-1943). Austrian theater producer and director. He began his brilliant career as a minor actor in Berlin. By the mid-1920's, his *Grosses Schauspielhaus* (Great Theater) had become the theatrical center of **Germany**. Under his direction, it excelled in spectacular productions and the effective use of setting, design, and color. Reinhardt's films were as famous as his stage productions. Forced to flee Germany when the Nazis came to power, Reinhardt settled in the U.S. and was active in its theatrical life. He directed the Hollywood film version of his production of *A Midsummer Night's Dream*. Reinhardt is generally regarded as one of the leading influences on the development of both the European and American theater.

REMBRANDT HARMENSZOON VAN RIJN (1606-1669). This Dutch painter was the first master to show Jews not as caricatures, but as individuals endowed with human dignity. He was on friendly terms with the intellectual leaders of the Jewish quarter of **Amsterdam** where he lived for many years. His sitters included the famous physician Dr. Ephraim Bonus and Rabbi Saul Levi Morteira (who was **Spinoza**'s first teacher). In addition to the wealthy and educated Sephardic immigrants from **Portugal**, from whom he received commissions, he painted poor refugees from **Poland.** Reared in the Protestant faith, this great Dutchman was thoroughly familiar with Jewish life and lore, as indicated by his beautiful and accurate renderings of Old Testament episodes.

Mordecai, by Rembrandt.

REPENTANCE. *See* **Teshuvah.**

RESH. Twentieth letter of the Hebrew alphabet; numerically, 200.

RESH GALUTA. *See also* **Exilarch** *and* **Babylonia.**

RESPONSA. Answers to questions on Jewish law. A huge *responsa* literature by leading rabbis and scholars has developed in Judaism since post-Talmudic times. Many of the answers were collected in such codes of Jewish law as the **Shulhan Arukh,** but questions keep creeping up, and both Orthodox and non-Orthodox authorities continue to provide answers.

RESURRECTION. The belief in the physical revival of the dead is not biblical, but rather appears in Judaism after biblical times, as part of the belief in the **Messianic** era. The belief persists, but is not universally accepted. The Reform movement has replaced it with the belief in the immortality of the soul.

RETRIBUTION. *See* **Reward and Punishment.**

Emblem of the tribe of Reuben.

REUBEN. Literally, "Behold, a son." Firstborn of **Jacob** and **Leah**. In his blessing, Jacob characterized Reuben as "unstable as water" (Gen. 49:4). The tribe of Reuben were cattle- and sheep-raisers, permitted to settle on the east side of the **Jordan** on the condition that they help in the conquest of **Canaan**.

REUBENI, DAVID (ca. 1491-ca. 1535). False Messiah. He was born in Khaibar, Central Arabia, and died in **Spain**. Half-mystic, half-adventurer, David Reubeni created a great stir, and despite the warnings of level-headed leaders, many Jews saw him as a forerunner of the Messiah who would bring freedom to them and to the Holy Land. Reubeni arrived in **Rome** in 1524 and managed to get an audience with Pope Clement VII. He declared himself ambassador from his brother, King Joseph Reubeni, ruler over the descendants of the tribe of **Reuben**, one of the Ten **Lost Tribes** dwelling somewhere in Tatary. He promised the Pope to raise an army of Jews of the East to fight against the Turks in the Holy Land. Such were Reubeni's bearing and personality that the Pope believed him and gave him credentials to the kings of **Portugal** and Abyssinia. To secure the aid of these monarchs in freeing Palestine, wealthy members of the Roman Jewish community supplied Reubeni with money to travel in state. He came to Portugal in 1525, where King John III received him with high honors. The **Marranos** thought Reubeni was the Messiah and flocked around him. One of them, Diego Pires, openly returned to Judaism, took the name of Solomon **Molkho**, and joined Reubeni's followers. The Portuguese authorities became suspicious, and Reubeni found it necessary to leave Portugal. Continuing his fantastic career, he went to Venice where he offered the Senate an alliance with his king. The Venetian authorities had him investigated, and he was forced to leave empty-handed. In 1532, bearing a banner inscribed with initials of the Hebrew words "Who is like unto You, O Lord, among the mighty?" Reubeni together with Molkho appeared in Ratisbon before Charles V, Emperor of the Holy Roman Empire. Reubeni tried to persuade the Emperor to call the Jews to arms against the Turks. Charles V put both Reubeni and Molkho in chains; eventually, Reubeni was sent to **Spain** where he was placed in the hands of the **Inquisition**. The circumstances of his death are uncertain. Reubeni's diary is now in the Bodleian Library at Oxford University. (*See also* **Messianism**.)

REUCHLIN, JOHANN (1455-1522). Non-Jewish defender of Jews and Hebrew literature against many malicious attacks. He was an authority on Hebrew grammar and was fascinated by the mystical teachings of the **Kabbalah**. Perhaps the expulsion of Jews from **Spain** in 1492 stirred Reuchlin to uphold their cause in his native **Germany**. He thwarted the attempt by Johann Pfefferkorn, the Jewish convert to Christianity, to burn all the Hebrew books in Cologne and Frankfurt. Because of Reuchlin's influence with the Emperor Maximilian, which he exerted in favor of the Jews, he bore the brunt of the Catholic Church's attack, especially the Dominican order. Reuchlin was the first non-Jew to make Hebrew an official course of study at a university (Tubingen).

REVEL, BERNARD (1885-1940). First president of Yeshiva College (now **Yeshiva University**). Born in Kovno, **Lithuania**, he studied at the yeshiva of Telz, where he was ordained a **rabbi**. Revel came to the U.S. in 1906. He studied at the University of Pennsylvania, New York University, and **Dropsie College**, obtaining the degree of Doctor of Philosophy in 1911.

In 1915, Revel became president of the Rabbi Isaac Elhanan Theological Seminary. He founded the Talmudical Academy, and, in 1928, a Yeshiva College of Liberal Arts was established through his efforts. He contributed articles in the fields of Semitics and rabbinic literature. A department of the Graduate School at Yeshiva University is named in his memory.

REVISIONIST ZIONISM. Zionist party organized in 1925 by Vladimir **Jabotinsky**. It called itself "Revisionist" because it felt the need for revision of the official Zionist policy toward Great Britain as the mandatory government of Palestine. The program of Revisionism included the creation of a Jewish majority on both sides of the **Jordan**; unrestricted mass immigration of Jews into Palestine; encouragement of middle-class immigration and of private enterprise to increase the absorptive capacity of the country; the outlawing of strikes and the substitution of compulsory arbitration during the period of national upbuilding; and the restoration of the **Jewish Legion** as a distinct part of the British garrison in Palestine. **Brith Trumpeldor** (Betar), the Revisionist Youth Organization, was part of the Revisionist World Union. The Revisionist party was a part of the **World Zionist Organization** until the 19th **World Zionist Congress** held in 1935. At that time, the Revisionist party differed so sharply with the prevailing Zionist policies that it seceded and formed the New Zionist Organization. A small group of Revisionists broke off from the parent body and, calling itself the Jewish State Party, remained as a part of the World Zionist Organization. In 1946, the New Zionist organization merged with the State Party to form the United Zionist Revisionists and again became a constituent part of the World Zionist Organization. In Palestine a resistance group (against British restrictive policies and against Arab terror) grew out of Revisionism. This underground body, the *Irgun Z'vai L'umi* (National Military Organization), functioned until after the creation of the State of **Israel** when it merged with the Army of **Israel**. Many of its veterans joined the Herut party, which is the Israeli counterpart of the Revisionist party.

REWARD AND PUNISHMENT. In the **Bible** it is made clear that good is rewarded and evil is punished, yet no clear doctrine on this matter is enunciated. The prophet **Jeremiah** asks God why evil people prosper while good people suffer. In Talmudic times a new belief attributes reward and punishment to the next world (*see* **Heaven and Hell**), which helps explain why one is not always rewarded or punished in this life. To this day, however, this basic human question remains open in Judaism, as in other religions and philosophy.

RHODE ISLAND. Of the state's 16,000 Jews, 14,000 live in Providence. Jewish life started in the mid-17th century, when the first **Sephardic** Jews settled in Newport. That community prospered in the 18th century, and was recognized by George Washington (his letter of welcome still hangs in the synagogue). It later declined, and in the late 19th century Eastern European Jews settled in Providence, the main Jewish community in the state.

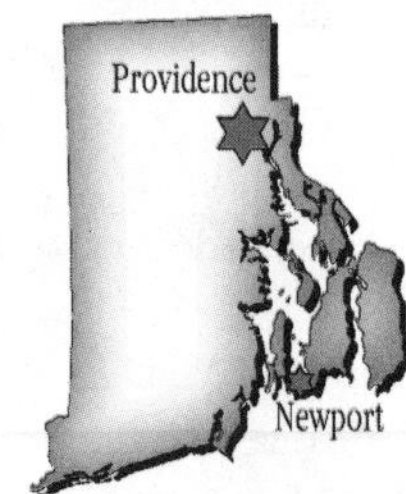

RIBICOFF, ABRAHAM A. (1910-1998). Political leader and attorney. Elected congressional representative from **Connecticut** in 1948 and 1950, Ribicoff served on the Foreign Affairs Committee. In 1954, he was elected Governor of Connecticut. He was Secretary of Health, Education, and Welfare from 1961 to 1962, serving under President John F. Kennedy. He served as Democratic Senator from Connecticut from 1962 to 1980.

Abraham Ribicoff.

RICARDO, DAVID (1772-1823). Political economist. Born in **London** to a family of wealthy Sephardic Jews, his marriage to a Quaker led to a breach with his family. Before he was 25, Ricardo had made a fortune in the stock market. *Principles of Political Economy and Taxation*, published in 1817, won him immediate fame. The following year, in 1818, Ricardo was elected to Parliament. There, despite his early breach with Jewish life, he spoke in favor of political emancipation for Jews.

RICHLER, MORDECAI (1931-). Canadian novelist. He is known for his biting humor in books like *The Apprenticeship of Dudley Krevitz* and *Joshua Then and Now*, both of which were made into movies.

RICKOVER, HYMAN G. (1900-1986). American nuclear energy expert who helped launch the first atomic submarine, for which he was promoted to the rank of admiral.

RIESSER, GABRIEL. *See* **Germany**.

RIGHTEOUS OF THE NATIONS. Jewish belief according to which some Gentiles achieve the high degree of righteousness to which Jews aspire. Such a person has been of exceptional help to Jews in their hour of need. **Yad Vashem** established a program for honoring righteous Gentiles who helped or saved Jews during the **Holocaust**. An "Avenue of the Righteous," with carob trees dedicated to their memory, leads to the official Israeli museum of the Holocaust.

RISHON-LE-ZION. Literally, First of Zion. A settlement founded in 1882 by members of the **Hoveve Zion** movement from **Russia** in the plain south of Jaffa. After a rocky start, the village was taken over by Baron Edmond de **Rothschild**, with whose aid it became a grape-growing center. In 1887, the Baron built the Rishon wine cellars, among the largest in the Mediterranean area. Later, many of the vineyards were converted into orange groves. Rishon-Le-Zion has developed rapidly and is presently a pleasant, tree-shaded town with about 165,000 inhabitants engaged mainly in the wine industry, citriculture, and various industrial enterprises.

RITUAL MURDER. *See* **Blood Accusation**.

ROBINSON, EDWARD G. *See* **Stage and Screen.**

RODGERS, RICHARD *See* **Music, Jews in.**

ROMANIA. Jewish history in Romania goes back to the 4th century. It is believed that Jews settled there in earliest times, even before the Roman conquest of Dacia, now Transylvania. In 397 C.E., the Roman emperor issued a decree granting protection to Jewish settlers and their synagogues in Dacia. Thereafter, the fate of the Jews in the region is unknown until the early Middle Ages, when, in the 8th and 9th centuries the **khazars** conquered the region. Some 300 years later, the famous traveler, **Benjamin of Tudela**, told of a Jewish colony in Wallachia. During the Middle Ages, the country was divided into small principalities. In most of them, Jews suffered bitter persecution. Yet they were pioneers in commerce and industry and were among the first to settle in the city of Bucharest. Some of the local rulers recognized the contribution of Jews to the welfare of the country, and occasionally even encouraged them to settle in their territories. Usually, however, treatment of Jews was inhuman and cruel. The Cossack uprising in 1648 spread from the **Ukraine** to Moldavia, causing suffering along the way. Nevertheless, the following century saw a rise in the Jewish population in both Romanian provinces of Wallachia and Moldavia.

After the tumultuous Turkish rule, the two provinces were united to form an independent state in 1859. This independence was recognized by the Congress of Berlin in 1878. According to the treaty signed at the Congress, Romania was obligated to grant full civil and political fights to all nationalities, including Jews. The government, however, failed to live up to the treaty. Economic as well as educational restrictions and attacks against Jews were frequent. At the end of the 19th century, constant persecution forced many to emigrate to the U.S. Some also settled in Palestine where they founded the colonies of Rosh Pinah and Zikhron Yaakov.

Following World War I, discrimination and anti-Semitic riots continued and spread to large Jewish communities in Bessarabia and Bukovina, which had been annexed by Romania. A strong anti-Semitic campaign was carried on by the Iron Guard party. During World War II, the anti-Jewish groups cooperated with the Nazis in the extermination of Jews. Only about half of Romanian Jewry survived the slaughter; some succeeded in fleeing the country and settled in Palestine. More than 200,000 Jews remained. In 1998, the Jewish population was estimated at fewer than 14,000. The community has produced outstanding people, such as scholars Moses Gaster and Solomon **Schechter** and the contemporary Yiddish poet Itzik Manger. Jews were permitted to emigrate to **Israel** in 1958-59, but Arab political pressure has slowed down the process.

ROME. The Jewish community of Rome is the oldest in Europe, dating back at least to 180 B.C.E., and is also the one in which Jews have lived most continuously (with minor interruptions) to this day. Their numbers, fairly large in Maccabean times, were increased in 70 C.E., when Titus and his Roman Legions defeated Judea and burned the Second **Temple**. He brought many Jewish captives to Rome, and in his train were King **Agrippa II**, Princess Berenice, and the historian **Josephus**. After the defeat of the **Bar Kokhba** rebellion in 135 C.E., captives and refugees again increased the Jewish population of Rome.

Judea may have been defeated, but Judaism was not. Conversions of Romans to Judaism must have been fairly widespread, because in 204 such conversions were prohibited by law. On the whole, Jews were persecuted less in Rome than elsewhere. About 212 to 217 C.E., Judaism was recognized as a *religio licita*, a legal religion. In 590, the Pope confirmed the Jewish rights. In 855, all Jews were ordered to leave **Italy**, but evidently this order was not strictly enforced, because three years later, special clothing was introduced to identify Jews. The ebb and flow of alternate persecution and protection of Jews continued through the centuries. In 1021, Jews were persecuted; but between 1058 and 1061, the Pope opposed their compulsory baptism. In 1215, Jews had to wear a special badge; only two decades later, a Papal decree gave Jews protection. In this same 13th century, the power of the **Inquisition** was extended, but within a few years, another Papal decree denounced **blood accusations** as false. During the first half of the 16th century, popes and cardinals befriended Jews, yet in 1555, forced them to live in a **ghetto** and wear the "Jewish badge" to distinguish them from non-Jews. Jews were also barred from many trades.

Through it all, Jewish life went on, and Roman Jewry produced its share of great scholars. In the 11th century, Nathan Ben Yechiel compiled the *Arukh*, an encyclopedic work on **Talmud** vocabulary. **Immanuel of Rome** (ca. 1270-1330), writing under the influence of Dante, left a colorful picture of Jewish life in 14th-century Italy. A Jewish printing press established in 1545 flourished. In 1581, the Inquisition was still active, and in 1784, a compulsory baptism ordinance was enforced.

In the 19th century, the Jews no longer submitted passively to persecution. When their rights as citizens, proclaimed in 1809, were later denied them again, they revolted and tore down the ghetto walls in 1829. Finally, in 1849, the Assembly granted them full civic rights. From then on, anti-Jewish manifestations diminished and the Jewish Ernesto Nathan became mayor of the city in 1907.

After World War I, when Mussolini's Fascist regime came to power, Jews remained undisturbed. However, under Nazi pressure, racist doctrines were adopted. When German troops occupied the country toward the end of World War II, Rome's Jewish community suffered, although they found some protection among their neighbors. In 1998, there were about 15,000 Jews in Rome. A new community center and school building show a renewed civic and educational effort, while an active Zionist organization is in close contact with the Jews of **Israel**.

ROSENFELD, FANNY. *See* **Sports**.

ROSENHEIM, JACOB. *See* **Agudath Israel**.

ROSENWALD. American Jewish family of philanthropists. Born of immigrant parents in Springfield, **Illinois**, Julius Rosenwald (1862-1932) began as a clothing merchant and came to head Sears, Roebuck, the world's largest mail-order firm. At his death it was estimated that he had distributed more than $70 million for philanthropic purposes. Black education and housing headed a list of causes to which he contributed. Other interests of Rosenwald 's included a program of Jewish colonization in **Russia**, to which he contributed $6 million, and an agricultural research station in Palestine and Jewish institutions in the U.S. His elder son, Lessing Julius, succeeded Julius as head of Sears, Roebuck. He is best known as the founder and first president of the anti-Zionist American Council for Judaism. William, Julius's second son, was active in business and in pro-Israel and communal fund-raising affairs. He served as chairman of the **United Jewish Appeal** for the New York district.

Julius Rosenwald. Courtesy the Rosenwald Family.

ROSENZWEIG, FRANZ (1886-1929). German philosopher. He was born to an assimilated family and was about to convert to Christianity when, stopping at a synagogue on **Yom Kippur**, he had a change of heart and returned to Judaism. In his book *Star of Redemption* he expounds his philosophy of Judaism. With Martin **Buber**, he translated the **Bible** into German. He remains an influential Jewish thinker.

ROSH HA-SHANAH. Literally, the New Year. The cycle of the High Holidays begins with Rosh Ha-Shanah. Falling on the first and second days of the month of **Tishri**, it introduces the Ten Days of Penitence, when Jews examine their souls and take stock of their actions. The season, beginning with the New Year on the first day of Tishri and ending with **Yom Kippur**, the Day of Atonement, on the tenth, is known as "Days of Awe." The tradition is that on Rosh Ha-Shanah God sits in judgment on humanity. Then the fate of every living creature is inscribed in the Book of Life or Death. These decisions may be revoked by prayer and repentance before the sealing of the books on Yom Kippur.

18th century Dutch Rosh Ha-Shanah plate used on the eve of the New Year for serving honey-dipped apples. Courtesy the Jewish Museum, New York City.

Also known as *Yom Teruah* (the Day of the Sounding of the Shofar), *Yom ha-Din* (the Day of Judgment), and *Yom ha-Zikkaron* (the Day of Remembrance), the holiday is highlighted by the blowing of the ram's horn (*see* **Shofar**). Sounded in the **Temple** on solemn occasions, on this day the shofar reminds the congregation of the gravity of the day and calls them to repent. It also brings to mind the sacrifice of **Isaac**, the story of whose rescue from death is an example of God's mercy.

On the eve of the holiday, Jews greet each other with the words *L'shanah tovah tikatevu*, May you be inscribed for a good year. Bread or apples are dipped in honey on the eve of the holiday to express hope for sweetness in the year ahead. To symbolize purity of heart, some men wear white robes in synagogue; these are the shrouds in which observant Jews are buried. On the afternoon of the first day, Jews go to a river or other body of water for the *Tashlikh*, or Casting Off, ceremony, in which each person symbolically casts his sins into the water.

ROSH HODESH. *See* **New Moon.**

ROSS, BARNEY. *See* **Sports**.

ROSSI, AZARIAH BEN MOSES DEI (1511-1578). Physician, linguist, scholar. Born in Mantua to an ancient Italian-Jewish family at the height of the Renaissance, Rossi was one of the first to apply scientific methods to the study of Jewish history. This he did in *Me'or Enayim* (Light of the Eyes), a scholarly work telling the history of the Jewish people from the destruction of the Temple onward. Jews and non-Jews thought it important, and parts of it were translated into Latin.

ROTH, CECIL (1899-1970). Jewish historian who taught at Oxford University in **England**. He wrote extensively on many subjects of Jewish history and culture, and was editor-in-chief of the *Encyclopedia Judaica.*

ROTH, PHILIP (1933-). American novelist. He wrote controversial stories and novels, often about Jews, and mostly using biting humor. His first literary success was the short story collection *Goodbye Columbus.* He drew much attention and criticism with *Portnoy's Complaint,* a satirical novel about a young Jew looking for his manhood in Gentile America. His later novels drew less attention than his early work.

ROTHSCHILD, HOUSE OF. Family of bankers and philanthropists. Meyer Amschel Rothschild (1743-1812) was the son of a German Jewish merchant. Meyer entered banking when he agreed to invest the fortune of an Austrian nobleman. He was so successful that he soon found himself in charge of the finances of several royal families. At his death, he bequeathed to his five sons a banking establishment with enormous assets and branches in several financial centers. The eldest son, Anselm Mayer (1773-1855), became the head of the Frankfort bank; Solomon Mayer (1774-1855) headed the Vienna establishment; Nathan Mayer (1777-1836), the **London** bank; Carl Mayer (1788-1855), the Naples Bank; Jacob (James) Mayer (1792-1868) founded and headed the **Paris** bank. Because of the extent of the Rothschild family enterprises, they came to be known as the financial kings of Europe. Their influence was enormous. By refusing loans to warlike governments they could help to prevent the outbreak of war; by extending credit, they helped launch educational systems in **France** and **Germany** and accelerated the industrial development of many European countries.

Baron Edmond de Rothschild.

Later generations of the Rothschild family gained prominence as patrons of the arts and philanthropists. Outstanding among them was Baron Edmond de Rothschild (1845-1934), one of the chief builders of modern Palestine. Anonymously at first, he poured millions into the support of the early agricultural settlements. In fact, from the early 1890's until 1905, most Jewish settlers were directly dependent on "the Baron" or "the well-known benefactor," as he was known.

RUBINSTEIN, ARTUR (1899-1982). This distinguished pianist was born in Lodz, the seventh child of a textile manufacturer. He began to play the piano at the age of three and made his debut in a Mozart concert at the age of seven. The promising child prodigy developed into a brilliant interpreter of classical and modern music. Rubinstein achieved great success on the European concert stage, coming to the U.S. for the first time in 1906. The recognition accorded him all over the world included many awards. He was elected to the French Legion of Honor and to the **Brazil** Academy of Music. His love of music and his prodigious energy often led him to give more than 100 concerts a year.

Artur Rubinstein. Courtesy Hurok Attractions.

RUBINSTEIN, HELENA (1871-1965). One of the leaders of the American cosmetics industry in the 20th century. She was born in **Poland** and came to the U.S. in 1914 where she developed a major beauty industry.

RUDOLF, MAX. *See* **Music, Jews in.**

RUSSIA. The earliest Jewish settlers in Russia were probably merchants from Byzantium, who arrived sometime during the 6th century C.E. In the course of the 8th century Jews arrived from the land of the **Khazars**, south of Russia, where Judaism had become the national religion. Jewish fugitives from the **Crusades** sought haven in Russia during the 12th century. Most of these immigrants hoped to reach Kiev, a large trading center that linked the Black Sea zone and Asia with western Europe. In the 13th century the Tatars conquered Russia, stunting the growth of its Jewish communities.

Since Christianity did not take hold of the Russian people until late in the history of Europe (about the 10th century), the clergy and the ruling classes remained highly suspicious of Jews and classed them with unbelievers and considered them a threat to the young Church. At the end of the 15th century, a strong movement of conversion to Judaism arose in Novgorod, from where it spread to some of the nobility in Moscow. This movement was ruthlessly suppressed in 1504. Thereafter, Jews became an even greater object of suspicion among the people of Russia, who saw them as enemies of Christianity.

From the time of Ivan the Terrible (1553-1584) the Tsars were in general fanatically anti-Semitic and either limited or prohibited the Jews' right to live in Russia (*see* **Pale of Settlement**). Toward the end of the 17th century, there were many Jews in Muscovy who practiced their religion in secret.

With the first partition of **Poland** during the reign of Catherine II (r. 1762-1796), 100,000 Jews from Poland and what is now White Russia came under Russian rule. Their numbers and importance in commerce necessitated a revision of the official policy. When Alexander I (r. 1801-1825) came to the throne, the Jewish community, or **Kahal**, had received official recognition. However, Jews were still subject to much discrimination, including excessive taxation and restricted living areas. During the Napoleonic wars, Jews gained in prestige by their opposition to Napoleon, whom they regarded as an enemy of religion.

With the accession to the throne of Nicholas I (r. 1825-1855), a reaction set in. He was responsible for the ordinance under which Jewish children were recruited for the army, sent to the most-distant regions of Russia, and forcibly converted to **Christianity** in the course of their military training (*see* **Cantonists**). This form of persecution ended with the rule of the new Tsar, the liberal Alexander II (r. 1855-1881), when the condition of the Jews generally improved. Together with the rest of the Russian population, they prospered culturally and economically, gained new privileges, and witnessed the abolition of abuses such as serfdom.

However, a new wave of anti-Jewish antagonism and suspicion developed during the end of the 19th century. One of numerous ritual murder trials on record in Russian-Jewish history occurred in 1878 (*see* **Blood Accusation**). In 1881, Alexander II was assassinated, and the highly anti-Semitic Alexander III came to the throne. He encouraged the popular notion that Jews had been responsible for his predecessor's death. A long series of **pogroms** began, fostered by court circles to divert the people from the developing revolutionary movement. In the winter of 1891, all Jews were expelled from Moscow. Numerous new discriminatory regulations were passed.

In 1906, as a result of a revolution in 1905, the Tsar convened the first Duma, or representative assembly, in Russian history. Jewish delegates were present, and Jewish problems discussed, but on the whole, the Duma was dominated by reactionary, anti-Semitic groups. The Russian government continued to follow a policy of social and economic restrictions against Jews. Continued persecution caused an increase in Jewish emigration. Close to one million Jews left Russia during the decade preceding World War I, most of them heading for the **U.S**. Despite its hardships, the Russian Jewish community before World War I was the most active and numerous in the world. In the 18th and 19th centuries, such highly important movements in Jewish history as **Hasidism**, **Haskalah**, and **Zionism**, and Jewish socialist bodies took root and flourished in Russia. World-renowned yeshivot existed in many towns. Russia was the center of Hebrew and Yiddish literary activity. **Mendele Mocher Sefarim**, **Sholom Aleichem**, **Peretz**, **Ahad Ha-am**, **Bialik**, and **Tschernichowsky** are a few of the great writers of the pre-Revolutionary period.

The Bolshevik Revolution of 1917 was followed by the most terrible **pogroms** since the Cossack uprising of 1648. Various opponents of the Bolsheviks—the counter-revolutionary leaders Denikin, Petliura, Kolchak, and others—accused Jews of sympathizing with the Communists. Their bands of soldiers and peasants attacked Jewish communities, murdering and pillaging the defenseless population. It is estimated that between 1917 and 1921,

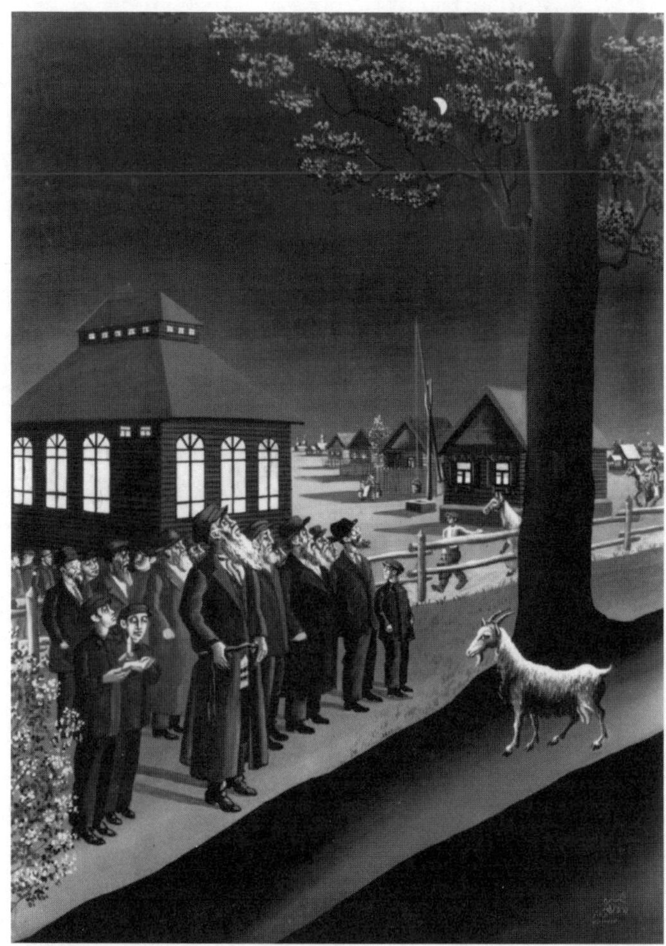

Blessing of the New Moon.

100,000 Jews lost their lives, most of them in the **Ukraine**. More than 900 communities suffered the ravages of pogroms and famine. Hundreds of thousands of children were orphaned and remained destitute.

> *"Wherever you go, I will go; wherever you lodge, I will lodge; your people shall be my people, and your God my God."*
>
> — RUTH 1:16

The Soviet government secured complete political and economic emancipation for Jews. However, their economic condition steadily deteriorated. The curtailing of private enterprise and trade severely crippled the economic position of the Jewish population. An exodus from the small towns to larger industrial centers, especially of Jewish youth, began. To alleviate the situation of unemployed Jews, the government encouraged their settlement in agricultural colonies. Aided by Jewish organizations from abroad, especially by the **American Joint Distribution Committee**, tens of thousands of Russian Jews settled in the Crimea and in agricultural areas in Ukraine and White Russia.

The Soviet government outlawed anti-Semitism, yet discrimination and anti-Jewish feeling prevailed. Recognized as a national group, Jews were allowed to form their own village and town soviets, or councils, wherever they constituted a majority of the population, for example, in parts of the Crimea and in **Birobidjan**. In 1934, Birobidjan became an autonomous Jewish district and was represented in the central government. **Yiddish** was the primary language of instruction in a number of educational institutions and of cultural expression in certain segments of the Jewish population. However, the Birobidjan experiment failed. Jewish religious life, like all religious life in Russia, was greatly restricted and officially ridiculed and proscribed. The government banned **Zionism** and the **Hebrew language** entirely. Many of the 3 million Jews living in Russia before 1941 assimilated rapidly into the general population.

With the outbreak of World War II, hundreds of thousands of Jews in Russian territory perished during the Nazi invasion. Facing a common enemy, world Jewry hoped Russian Jews would be able to draw close to the Jewish communities abroad. These hopes, encouraged by a more lenient policy in the Soviet government, were destined to be shattered when the victory in World War II made the need for a favorable world public opinion and a "united front" less crucial for Russia. Under a new policy toward Jewish culture, the Yiddish press, theater, and literature were all but destroyed. Many outstanding writers, artists and poets were killed or banished. Autonomous Jewish life in Russia ceased to exist. The spontaneous demonstration of Jewish national feeling after the establishment of the State of **Israel** was quickly suppressed by the Soviet authorities. In 1956, Jewish activity in Russia appeared to be limited to a small number of synagogues.

A dramatic change in the history of Soviet Jews took place in the late 1960's, when, for the first time, large numbers of Jews were allowed to leave the USSR. By 1983, some 260,000 Jews were permitted to leave, of whom 170,000 settled in Israel, the U.S., **Canada**, and elsewhere. In the mid-1980's, however, the flow was drastically reduced, and some 382,000 Jews wishing to emigrate entered a period of harassment and unemployment, acquiring the status of "Refuseniks."

The National Conference on Soviet Jewry was created in June 1971 in the U.S. by 37 national Jewish organizations and hundreds of Jewish community councils and federations as a unified effort to attain freedom and equality for Russian Jews. In 1970, a massive crackdown against some of the more activist Soviet Jews led to a series of trials in which death sentences were issued against Jews who allegedly attempted an escape from Russia. Afterward, American Jewish organizations realized that the critical nature of this problem required a coordinated effort on the part of American Jewry, and the National Conference for Soviet Jewry (NCSJ) was formed. The Conference, enjoying a broad base support of American Jewry and particularly American Jewish youth highly sensitive to the plight of Soviet Jewry, organized mass rallies and protest meetings and exerted influence on the American government, greatly contributing to the release of thousands of Jews from the Soviet Union.

Between 1989 and 1993, under the leadership of President Gorbachev, Jews were once again allowed to leave Russia. Since 1990, well over 500,000 Russian Jews arrived in Israel. At the same time, a growing number of Jews in Russia is returning to Jewish studies and the study of the Hebrew language. In 1998, the Jewish population in Russia was down to 360,000. The former USSR began to renew diplomatic relations with Israel.

RUTH, BOOK OF. Second of the five scrolls in the Bible. It is read in the synagogue on **Shavuot**, the Feast of Weeks. It tells of Elimelech and Naomi of Bethlehem in **Judah**, who in a time of famine take their two sons, Mahlon and Kilyon, and migrate to Moab. There Mahlon marries Ruth, and Kilyon marries Orpah. Elimelech dies, as do Mahlon and Kilyon, ten years later. The grieving Naomi prepares to return home to Bethlehem and tells her daughters-in-law to go back to their parents. Orpah obeys sadly, but Ruth refuses, saying, "Wherever you go, I will go; wherever you lodge, I will lodge; your people shall be my people, and your God my God." Ruth clings to Naomi and follows her loyally to Judah. Eventually, she marries Boaz, a rich farmer of Bethlehem, and they become the ancestors of King **David.** This charming idyll has been loved by countless generations.

Overleaf: First page of the Book of Ruth. Early 18th century, Italy. Courtesy The Jewish Museum, New York.

וַיְהִי בִּימֵי שְׁפֹט הַשֹּׁפְטִים וַיְהִי רָעָב בָּאָרֶץ וַיֵּלֶךְ
אִישׁ מִבֵּית לֶחֶם יְהוּדָה לָגוּר בִּשְׂדֵי מוֹאָב הוּא
אִשְׁתּוֹ וּשְׁנֵי בָנָיו : וְשֵׁם הָאִישׁ אֱלִימֶלֶךְ וְשֵׁם אִשְׁתּוֹ נָעֳמִי וְשֵׁם
שְׁנֵי בָנָיו מַחְלוֹן וְכִלְיוֹן אֶפְרָתִים מִבֵּית לֶחֶם יְהוּדָה וַיָּבֹאוּ שְׂדֵי
מוֹאָב וַיִּהְיוּ שָׁם : וַיָּמָת אֱלִימֶלֶךְ אִישׁ נָעֳמִי וַתִּשָּׁאֵר הִיא וּשְׁנֵי
בָנֶיהָ : וַיִּשְׂאוּ לָהֶם נָשִׁים מֹאֲבִיּוֹת שֵׁם הָאַחַת עָרְפָּה וְשֵׁם

SAADIAH GAON (892-942). First of the Jewish medieval philosophers. His fight against the **Karaite** sect, which broke away from traditional Judaism, was decisive in preserving the unity of historical Jewry. He was born at Fayyum, **Egypt**. At 20, he compiled a Hebrew dictionary. He also translated the **Bible** into Arabic and wrote a commentary on most of its books. At about the same time, he combated the Karaite attack on the Talmud, refuting all the arguments of their leader, **Anan Ben David**. Saadiah's brilliant defense of the **Talmud** spread his fame throughout the Jewish world. Saadiah left Egypt and spent some years in Palestine. At that time, **Babylonia** was still a great center of Jewish learning. The head of the Academy of Palestine, Ben Meir, disputed the right of the Babylonian scholars to compute the **calendar**. Saadiah sided with the Babylonian academies, and strengthened their authority.

When he arrived in Babylonia, he was invited to become head of the ancient Academy of Sura. Saadiah accepted the post, revitalized the Academy, and reestablished its fame. Unfortunately, a dispute arose between Saadiah and the **exilarch**, David ben Zakkai. The exilarch succeeded in bribing the Caliph to side with him, and the Gaon was forced to hide in Baghdad for seven years. During his forced exile, he produced his most important work, written in Arabic and called *Beliefs and Opinions*. His aim was to prove that the Jewish religion is based on reason and does not contradict philosophic thought. The book exerted great influence on Jewish thought, and is one of the standard works of Jewish religious philosophy. Five years before his death, Saadiah was reinstated as head of the Academy of Sura.

SABBATAI ZEVI (1626-1676). False Messiah, a native of Smyrna, **Turkey**. When Sabbatai Zevi was still a young and impressionable **Talmud** student, he became so deeply attracted by the **Kabbalah** that he devoted himself completely to its study. In Kabbalist circles, he learned that the year 1648 would bring the "end of days," when the Messiah would come to bring Israel back to the Holy Land. Exactly when he came to look upon himself as the Messiah is difficult to tell. It is known, however, that at the age of 20 he lived the life of a mystic, praying, fasting, and bathing in the sea, even in the winter. He saw mystic visions and began to interpret the messianic passages in the Kabbalah. Handsome and magnetic, Sabbatai was swiftly surrounded by a circle of followers, to whom he revealed openly for the first time in 1648, at age 22, his belief in himself as the Messiah. The Jewish community of Smyrna expelled Sabbatai, and he began the wanderings that spread his fame far and wide. The time was ripe for him. Everywhere, the Jewish people were suffering from poverty, degradation, and persecution. They longed with all their might for the coming of the Messiah who would save them, and almost everywhere there were people who believed Sabbatai was the Messiah. When Sabbatai Zevi came to Constantinople, Abraham Jachine, a self-proclaimed prophet, produced an "ancient document" prophesying Sabbatai's Messiahship.

Banished from Salonika, he went to Cairo. There, Rabbi Joseph Calaba, treasurer at the governor's court, honored him with his open support. In **Jerusalem** he was warmly received by the local Kabbalists. Sabbatai was now convinced he was the Messiah. He fasted and prayed, wept and chanted psalms through wakeful nights. Sent on a mission to Cairo, he heard of Sarah, a beautiful Jewish

Sabbatai Zevi, an 18th-century engraving.

maiden from **Poland** who believed that she was the predestined bride of the Messiah. His disciples sent for Sarah, and Sabbatai married her amid great rejoicing. "Prophets" continued to spring up and proclaim him the Messiah, and his fame grew so wide that he dared to return to his native Smyrna in 1655. There he came to the **synagogue**, and amid the blowing of trumpets and the shouting of "Long Live Our King, Our Anointed One!" Sabbatai proclaimed himself the Messiah.

His following grew everywhere, among **Marranos** in **Amsterdam**, among the communities of Hamburg and Venice, among Polish Jews stricken by the Cossack uprising, and in far-off **Morocco** as well. In Smyrna, all business stopped, and people prepared to follow the Messiah to the Holy Land. In 1666, Sabbatai Zevi set sail for Constantinople, in full expectation that Sultan Mohammed IV would give him a royal reception as the supreme king on earth. On landing, he was arrested and taken in chains to prison. Meantime, a rival "Messiah" from Poland, Nehemiah Cohen, became a Muslim and told the authorities that Sabbatai was plotting to overthrow the Ottoman rule. Sabbatai was brought before the Sultan and given the choice of becoming a Muslim or dying. Sabbatai chose to live, took off his Jewish head-covering, and put on the white turban of the Turkish Muslim. The Jewish Messiah was no more; he had assumed the name Mehemet Effendi. Sabbatai was banished to Dulcigno, a small Albanian town, where he lived until his death on the Day of Atonement in 1676. Neither his conversion nor even his death put an end to the Sabbataian movement. His imprisonment and conversion were accepted as preliminary, mystic suffering before the final glory. After his death, one false messiah after another followed Sabbatai's ways. Mystic dreamers as well as imposters continued to draw followers because of the people's hunger to return to the Holy Land and because of their great longing for redemption. (*See also* **Messianism**.)

SABBATH. The climax of the Jewish week is the Sabbath, the seventh day of the week. The holiness of the Sabbath is stressed in the fourth commandment (Ex. 20:8-11), "Remember the Sabbath Day to keep it holy. Six days shall you labor and do all thy work, but the seventh day is a Sabbath Day unto the Lord thy God." This commandment has been given deep symbolic meaning and great social significance. It is an everlasting sign between God and Israel: "For in six days the Lord made Heaven and Earth and on the seventh he ceased from work and rested" (Ex. 31:17). The Sabbath day also is a reminder of the liberation from Egyptian bondage. It has served as a lesson to all humankind, proclaiming the need of human beings for a day free from labor and devoted to spiritual matters.

Sabbath Symbols, by Raymond A. Katz.

The Jewish Sabbath, likened in song and story to a queen or a bride, has given a touch of royalty to the humblest home. Its joyful family observance is traditionally marked by special prayers, three festive meals, Sabbath songs, and study of the holy writings. Mourning ceases on the Sabbath, and except for **Yom Kippur,** no fast day disturbs this holy day. The house is cleaned and scoured beforehand and the family dresses in its Sabbath best. Even the poorest householder tries to provide some delicacy for the day. Fish, wine, and the twisted white loaves of bread (hallah) are part of the Sabbath meals.

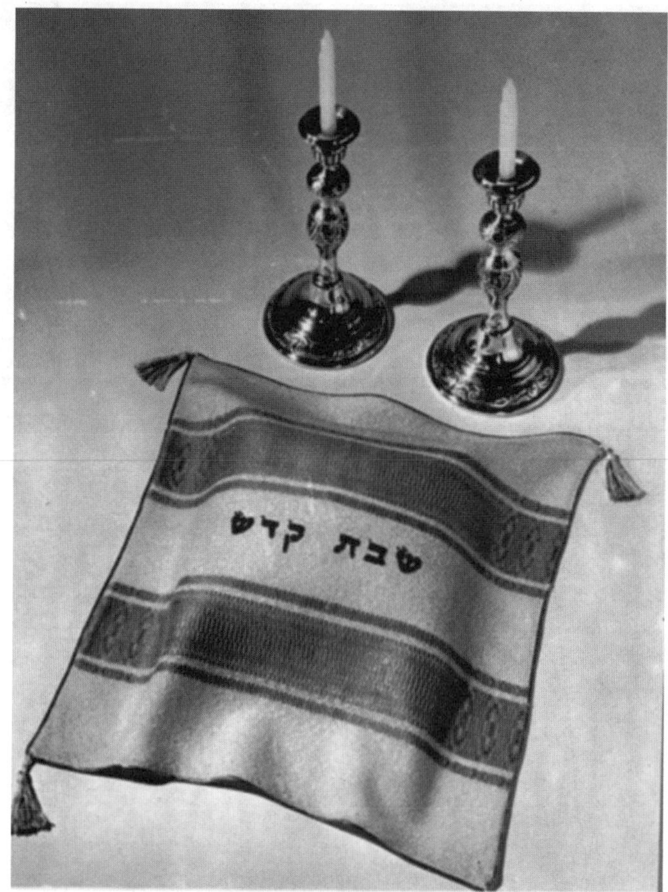

Sabbath candles and hallah cover. Textiles woven by Sidney Quitman and Evelyn Appelbaum, Philadelphia, Pa.

On Friday evening, the table is set with a white cloth. Two loaves of hallah are placed at one end and covered. Ornamental candlesticks grace the table. All preparations are completed before sundown, at which time the day is ushered into the home by the mistress of the house as she lights the candles and pronounces the proper blessing. In the synagogue, the 45th psalm, beginning "Come let us sing before the Lord," opens the services. *Lekhah Dodi*, song of welcome to the Sabbath Queen, composed about 1540 by Solomon **Alkabetz** follows. On his return to the home, the master of the house greets the two legendary Sabbath angels (who are said to accompany every worshiper from the synagogue) with the chant *Shalom Aleichem*, "Peace to you, ministering angels."

> *"For six days the Lord made Heaven and earth and on the seventh he ceased from work and rested."*
>
> — EXODUS 31:17

From the moment the candles are lit until the Sabbath is ushered out the next evening with the strains of Havdalah, all work is prohibited; cooking, cleaning, business transactions, carrying, excessive walking, traveling, writing, and kindling fires. An entire volume of the **Talmud** has been devoted to defining and explaining limitations set up in order to safeguard the sacredness of the day and the comfort and well-being of the individual. Despite stringent regulations, the Sabbath never was a burden to the Orthodox Jew. It has served as an endless reservoir of spiritual strength to Jews of all ages.

Spice box. Late 18th century Galicia.

Each Sabbath has its special section of the **Torah**, to be read during the morning service along with the appropriate **Haftarah**. *Shabbat Bereshit*, immediately after **Sukkot**, begins the annual cycle of Reading the Law. A number of other Sabbaths are given special designations for one reason or another. On *Shabbat Shira* in the winter months, the portion *Beshalah* (Ex. 13-17) containing the famous Song of **Moses** and the Children of Israel, thanking God for their deliverance from the Egyptians at the Red Sea, is read. *Shabbat Hagodol* is the Sabbath immediately preceding **Passover**. *Shabbat Hazon* (Sabbath of the Vision), read before the 9th of Av, and *Shabbat Nachamu* (Sabbath of Consolation), read directly after the 9th of Av, take their names from the Haftarah read on these Sabbaths. *Shabbat Shuvah* (Sabbath of Repentance) appropriately occurs between the New Year and Yom Kippur.

On Sabbath afternoon during the summer months, chapters from the **Ethics of the Fathers** (*Pirke Avot*) are studied and discussed. Similarly, a special group of psalms, beginning with *Borki Nafshi*, are recited in the winter time.

Havdalah plate. Courtesy the collection of Sidney L.Quitman.

SABIN, ALBERT (1906-1993). Medical researcher. Born in **Poland**, he settled in the U.S. in 1921 and started polio research in 1931. In 1959, he developed an oral vaccine for polio that was put into mass use around the world two years later, and ended the scourge of this paralyzing disease. From 1969 to 1972 he lived in **Israel** where he served as president of the **Weizmann Institute of Science.**

SABORAIM. Literally, clarifiers. Teachers and scholars who were active about the 6th century C.E. and succeeded the Amoriam (*see* **Amora**) in clarifying the laws of the Babylonian **Talmud**.

SACHS, NELLY (1891-1970). German-Jewish poet. Born in Berlin, she went to **Sweden** with her mother in 1940 as a refugee from Nazism. Her first published work, a volume of stories and legends, appeared in 1921. From 1929 to 1933 her verses were published in various German and German-Jewish newspapers. In Sweden she first earned her living by translating Swedish poetry into German. In her writings, all in German, she portrays in a mystical, descriptive style the sorrows of the Jewish people, its mission and its survival. In 1966, she shared the **Nobel Prize** for Literature with S.J. **Agnon**. In the award citation, her works were described as "a testimony to Jewish destiny in times that were inhuman....Her lyrics and plays are...works of forgiveness, deliverance, and peace."

SACRIFICES. Offerings to a deity. All ancient people offered sacrifices to their gods. Some sacrifices were tendered in thanksgiving for a rich harvest, for a victory in battle, or other happy events. Some were offered in times of trouble, to appease the deity when he was thought to be angry. Others symbolized the bond between a people, a tribe, or a clan and its god. The Israelites in biblical times offered up cattle, sheep, goats, doves, and farm products chiefly as a symbol of their loyalty to God. At first such offerings could be made anywhere. Later, they were permitted only at the Holy **Temple** in **Jerusalem**, where the priests ceremoniously slaughtered the sacrificial animals on behalf of the entire people. The ritual was prescribed in great detail. There were "regular" sacrifices offered each morning and evening, with "additional" offerings on **Sabbaths** and holidays. From these and the services accompanying them there evolved the daily morning, afternoon, evening, and holiday services that have been recited at synagogues since the destruction of the Temple. In addition, there were personal sacrifices, offered after a sin had been committed and expiated, as well as thanksgiving offerings after a vow had been fulfilled. Prophets like **Amos** and **Jeremiah** spoke out against the sacrificial cult. They were not opposed to the idea of sacrifices so much as to the fact that people thought they could fulfill their obligations to God through material offerings rather than through purity of heart and action. Although Jews have not offered sacrifices since the destruction of the Second Temple, Orthodox Jews have always prayed that sacrifices will be restored with the coming of the Messiah and the rebuilding of the Temple in Zion.

SADDUCEES. Second largest religious and political party in Palestine during the 2nd and 1st centuries B.C.E. Its members are believed to have been the followers of the high priests, descendants of the house of Zadok, the high priest under King **Solomon**. The Sadducees recognized the **Bible** as the only source of Jewish law and rejected most of the traditions and interpretations which had developed since **Ezra** the Scribe. They drew their followers from the rich and aristocratic, as well as military circles. Often, the Sadducees came into conflict with the **Pharisees** in religious and political matters. In opposition to the Pharisees, they supported the wars for expansion led by Johanan **Hyrcanus** and Alexander **Jannaeus**, as well as the policy of forcing conquered peoples to convert to Judaism. The Sadducees, as opposed to the Pharisees, did not believe in reward and punishment after death.

The numerous differences between the two parties often led to bloody clashes. Whenever the Sadducees were in power, they suppressed and persecuted the Pharisees. After the final war with the Romans, the Sadducees disappeared. The Jewish people henceforth followed the tradition of the Pharisees.

SAFDIE, MOSHE (1938-). Israeli-born Canadian architect who became world famous in 1967 with his Habitat 67 built for Expo '67 in Montreal. His bold experiment in modular prefab housing impacted on contemporary architecture, and later examples are his urban projects in Puerto Rico, Baltimore, and Jerusalem. In 1978, he became professor of urban design at Harvard.

SAFED. Capital of Upper Galilee. Kabbalists led by Rabbi Isaac Luria and Rabbi Joseph **Karo** settled there in the 15th century. Since then there has been a settled Jewish community in Safed. A substantial part of the city was destroyed by earthquakes and ensuing epidemics in mid-19th century. After heavy fighting in the 1948 War of Independence, the Arabs fled. With its beautiful mountain location Safed is today an art center and a popular resort city. Its population in 1998 was about 20,000.

SALANTER, RABBI ISRAEL (1810-1883). Founder of an ethical movement, known as Musar, which spread through many of the **yeshivot** of Eastern Europe. Born in a small town in **Lithuania**, Israel Lipkin spent his youth studying the **Talmud**. He was given to reflection and was deeply concerned with self-improvement. In his later years, he was recognized as a great Talmudic authority. His modesty was proverbial and so was his generosity. His ethical philosophy was in close agreement with that of **Maimonides**. Advocating participation in worldly matters, rather than isolation from them, he sought to win back to Judaism those yeshiva and university students who had been influenced by the Enlightenment movement. He hoped to have them return to the study of the **Torah** and observance of its laws. It is an interesting fact that Rabbi Salanter included the Hebrew translation of Benjamin Franklin's *Poor Richard's Almanac* among the list of ethical books recommended to his students.

SALINGER, J.D. (Jerome David) (1919-). American writer. Son to a Jewish father, he is known for his short stories and his popular 1951 novel *Catcher in the Rye*, about an adolescent turning his back on the phoney adult world. In the 1960's Salinger gave up writing and became a recluse, refusing to see anyone. His novel is still regarded a landmark in American literature.

SALK, JONAS EDWARD (1914-1995). American medical researcher and educator. In 1947, he joined the staff of the University of Pittsburgh as director of the Virus Research Laboratory of the School of Medicine. While continuing his work on influenza, he became interested in finding a way to prevent poliomyelitis. He developed the Salk vaccine, made by cultivating three strains of the polio virus separately in monkey tissue. Thanks in large measure to the Salk vaccine the dreaded "infantile paralysis" disease has largely become a thing of the past.

Jonas E. Salk. Courtesy University of Pittsburgh.

SALOME ALEXANDRA. Queen of Judea who ruled from 76 to 67 B.C.E. On his death bed, Salome's husband, the Hasmonean King Alexander **Jannaeus,** appointed her to succeed him on the throne. Salome Alexandra brought peace to Judea by reversing her husband's policy and favoring the **Pharisees**, who were the majority party in the country. Her brother, the learned Pharisee **Simeon ben Shetah,** served as president of the **Sanhedrin**, the legislative-judicial body of the people.

SALOMON, HAYM (ca. 1740-1785). American Revolutionary banker. Salomon, a native of **Poland**, described himself as "Broker to the Office of Finance"; he purchased and sold on commission bank stock and bills of exchange of European governments. During the American Revolution, he provisioned the troops of General Washington, often at personal cost. Salomon lent money to many impoverished members of the Continental Congress, including James Madison. He played an important role in the crucial years of the Revolutionary War, negotiating war subsidies from France and Holland. Salomon was captured as a spy and imprisoned by the British in New York, but managed to escape to Philadelphia, where his wife and child joined him.

SAMARIA. The capital of and another name for the northern Kingdom of Israel. (*See also* **Israel**.)

SAMARITANS. Possibly the smallest religious sect in the world. There are about 400 Samaritans, most of whom live in Nablus (Shechem), an Arab town in the **West Bank**; others are settled in the vicinity of **Tel Aviv-Jaffa**. The Samaritans are historically related to the Jewish people. When the Israelite kingdom Samaria fell in 722 B.C.E., the Assyrian conquerors exiled most of the Israelites to **Babylonia**. Samaria was then resettled by members of varied Semitic groups. The few remaining Israelites intermarried with the heathen settlers. Out of this union grew the new Samaritan sect. The Samaritans were anxious to join the Jewish group. However, conflict developed. Jews who returned to Palestine from Babylonian captivity in 537 B.C.E. refused to accept the offer of the Samaritans to help rebuild the **Temple** in

Jerusalem because of the differences in religious practice and belief between the two groups (the Samaritans strictly obeyed the laws of the Five Books of Moses, but rejected the Prophets and sacred traditions of the Babylonian exiles).

Hurt by this refusal of cooperation, the Samaritans informed the Persian King Artaxerxes I that the Jews were plotting a rebellion against him. In the days of **Nehemiah**, the Samaritans joined the "Arabians, Ammonites, and Ashdodites" in building a wall around Jerusalem.

Failing in their plans to join or harm the Jews, the Samaritans chose Mount Gerizim near Nablus as their holy place and later established a shrine there. Gerizim became the religious center of the sect. To the **Ten Commandments** the Samaritans added another, proclaiming the sanctity of Mount Gerizim.

During the reign of the **Maccabees**, the feud between Jews and Samaritans became intense. At the end of the 2nd century B.C.E., the Hasmonean king Johanan **Hyrcanus**, captured Samaria and destroyed its temple on Mount Gerizim. It was rebuilt in 56 B.C.E. by Gabinus, governor of **Syria**.

The Samaritans shared with Jews the painful conditions under the rule of the Roman emperors Vespasian (r. 79-81 C.E.) and Hadrian (r. 117-138 C.E.). When Palestine came under the rule of the Byzantine kings, persecutions continued. The Samaritan temple on Mount Gerizim was again destroyed. Twenty thousand Samaritans perished in a revolt against the Byzantine ruler Justinian I in 572. His successor deprived them of all rights and forced many of them to embrace the Christian faith. The Arab conquest of Palestine in the 7th century and the short reign of the **Crusaders** in the 11th and 12th centuries saw the further dwindling of their numbers. After 400 years of Turkish rule (1516-1917), the sect had disappeared almost completely. By the end of World War I, only 200 Samaritans remained.

To this day, the Samaritans adhere strictly to the ancient traditions of their religion. Their yearly **Passover** ceremony of the sacrifice of the Paschal lamb on Mount Gerizim is a colorful event reminiscent of an old Jewish custom practiced in Jerusalem. The

Samaritan High Priest Amram ben-Yitzhak Ha-Cohen, Israel.

Sacrifical lamb carried by a Samaritan. Courtesy Zionist Archives and Library, New York City.

Samaritan Bible is written in the old Hebrew script and differs slightly from the traditional Jewish version. Like Jews, the Samaritans recognize the 613 laws of the Five Books of Moses. They also accept the Book of **Joshua**, but they reject the writings of the prophets and the oral law known as the **Talmud**. The sanctity of Mount Gerizim is another point of departure from Jewish tradition. The Samaritans believe that the **patriarchs** are buried in this mountain and that the sacrifice of **Isaac** took place upon it. They also believe in the coming of the Messiah, who will rebuild the Temple on Mount Gerizim and proclaim the glory of the Shomrim, or "the observant," as the Samaritans call themselves.

The Samaritans possess a modest literature that includes a few works of biblical commentary, law, theology, and history. Some of their writings date back to the 4th century. At the head of the Samaritan community stands the High Priest, whom they believe to be a descendant of **Aaron**, brother of **Moses**. Yitzhak **Ben-Zvi**, Israel's second president, wrote extensively on the Samaritans. His studies are collected in *The Book of the Samaritans*.

SAMBATYON. Legendary river whose turbulent waters did not flow on the **Sabbath**. Jewish and non-Jewish writers have described similar rivers, which they have located variously in Ethiopia, **India**, and near the Caspian Sea. The Sambatyon, an actual river located in **Syria**, has been pointed to as possibly connected with the fabled stream. The most famous of the tales about the Sambatyon is that of the 9th-century traveler, Eldad Hadani. He tells of visiting the **Ten Lost Tribes** of Israel who dwelled on the banks of the river.

SAMSON. Son of Manoah of the tribe of **Dan**, and one of the **Judges** of Israel. Samson was marvelously strong, and three chapters of the biblical Book of **Judges** are full of his great deeds, his downfall, and heroic death. According to the **Bible**, Samson was a **Nazirite**, a consecrated man whose supernatural strength lay in his unshorn hair. Single-handed, he fought the **Philistines** until he was trapped by Delilah, a Philistine woman. Shorn of his hair and blinded, he was imprisoned in Gaza. During one of the festivals in honor of their fish-god Dagon, the Philistines had Samson brought into their temple to "make sport before them"

Samson's death, by Gustav Doré.

(Judges 16:25). By that time his hair had grown back, and with it, his strength had returned. Standing between two pillars that supported the roof of the temple, the blinded giant prayed, then, crying, "Let my soul perish with the Philistines!" he grasped the two pillars, bent them, and brought the roof crashing down upon himself and his tormentors.

SAMUEL (ca. 1100-1020 B.C.E.). Prophet and priest. He succeeded the **Judges** as a leader of the people. In his old age the people asked him to select a king to rule over them and to lead them in battle. Samuel warned them against a monarchy, which would limit their freedom. When the people insisted, he chose **Saul** and anointed him king. The two Books of Samuel in the Bible describe the founding of the Kingdom of Israel and the reigns of Saul and **David**.

SAMUEL HA-NAGID (993-1055). Statesman, poet, Talmudic scholar, and grammarian. Born in Cordova, **Spain**, he was forced by anti-Jewish persecution to flee to Malaga, where he studied both Jewish and secular subjects. Samuel's learning and wisdom attracted the attention of the vizier Abu-al-Kasim, who appointed Samuel his confidential secretary. On the vizier's death, Samuel became counselor and prime minister to the king of Granada. For thirty years, he had overseen the political, financial, and military affairs of the kingdom. The kingdom of Granada prospered, due largely to Samuel's discretion and sagacity. While holding high political office, Samuel was also the spiritual leader, or Nagid, of the Jewish community. He supported men of letters and institutions of learning, not only in Spain, but also in **Egypt**, **Babylonia**, and other Jewish settlements. He found the time to teach the **Talmud**, as well as to write works of grammar. Samuel Ha-Nagid opened the golden era of Hebrew poetry in Spain. He was the first to write secular poetry; his unique war poems describe military campaigns vividly.

SAMUEL, MAURICE (1895-1972). Author, translator, and lecturer. Born in Romania, he came to the U.S. in 1914. He wrote books on Israel including *What Happened in Palestine* and *Harvest in the Desert*. In *The Great Hatred* (1940) he reached the conclusion that Jews are hated because they taught the world a system of morality which humans have not been able to live up to.

In addition to a number of novels, Samuel produced many excellent translations from Yiddish, Hebrew, and German. These include most of the poetry of Chaim Nahman **Bialik** and several novels by Sholem **Asch**. His most popular books are *The World of Sholom Aleichem* and *Prince of the Ghetto*, which recreates the stories of the great Yiddish writer Y.L. **Peretz**.

SAMUEL, VISCOUNT HERBERT LOUIS (1870-1963). British statesman. Born in Liverpool and educated at Oxford, Samuel turned to politics as a profession. He was elected to Parliament in 1902, became a member of the British Cabinet in 1909, and became Secretary of State for Home Affairs in 1916. From 1931 to 1935, he served as leader of the Liberal Party in the House of Commons. He was knighted and, in 1937, he was made a viscount as a reward for his public services. Samuel's connection with **Zionism** began in the early stages of the World War I. He aided in the preliminary negotiations between Zionist leaders and the British government which resulted in the **Balfour Declaration.** In 1920, he was appointed first High Commissioner of Palestine under the British Mandate. During Samuel's five years in this office, his efforts to serve as an impartial British administrator failed to please the Arabs or Jews. He became member of the **Jewish Agency** for Palestine in 1929. Samuel was a member of the British Institute of Philosophy and the author of such books as *Philosophy and the Ordinary Man* and *Liberalism: Its Principles and Proposals*.

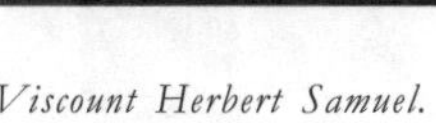

Viscount Herbert Samuel.

SANCTIFICATION OF THE NAME. *See* **Kiddush Ha-shem.**

SANHEDRIN. From Greek. Name applied to the higher courts of law which in the latter period of the Second **Temple** administered justice in Palestine according to the Mosaic law. It dealt with serious cases, both criminal and capital. Sanhedrin is also the name of a tractate of the **Talmud** which deals fully with the composition, powers, and functions of the court.

Two types of Sanhedrin existed side by side: the Great Sanhedrin with 71 members, and several lesser Sanhedrin with 23. According to tradition, both were instituted by **Moses**, but the first reference to a functioning Sanhedrin is from 57 B.C.E. Some scholars maintain there was also a Sanhedrin with more political powers. The president was called the *nasi*; his deputy, the *ab bet din*; and the expert or specialist on any given case, the *mufla*. The Great Sanhedrin met in the Chamber of Hewn Stone in the Temple of Jerusalem. Decisions required a majority of the votes to be valid. The Sanhedrin organized in **Yavneh** after the destruction of the Second Temple was purely religious in character.

SANHEDRIN, NAPOLEONIC. *See* **France**.

SAPIR, PINHAS (1909-1975). Israeli cabinet member and public official. Born in **Poland**, he came to Palestine in 1929 and early became active in the labor movement there. In February 1948, he was put in charge of the quartermaster general's branch of **Haganah**. Between 1948 and 1968, he served variously as Director General of the Ministry of Defense, Director General of the Ministry of Finance, Minister of Commerce and Industry, and Minister of Finance. In 1968, he became secretary general of the Mapai party while serving in the Cabinet as Minister without Portfolio. In 1974, he became chairman of the Executive of the **Jewish Agency**.

SARAH. Wife of the patriarch **Abraham** and mother of the patriarch **Isaac**. Sarah was barren for many years and finally at age 90 gave birth to Isaac.

SARNOFF, DAVID (1891-1971). American media leader. He was born in **Russia** and came to the U.S. as a child. Working as a wireless operator, he was the first to receive a message about the sinking of the *Titanic*. A pioneer in the radio industry, he headed RCA (Radio Corporation of America), and in 1953 became head of NBC (National Broadcasting Company).

SASSOON. Family of merchants, industrialists, and public servants. David Sassoon (1793-1864), founder of the "Sassoon dynasty," was descended from an old Baghdad Jewish family. Forced to flee his birthplace in 1829, David settled in Bombay, **India**, where he founded a textile firm which came to dominate the Indian cotton industry. With his eight sons he extended his trading empire to **China**, **Japan**, and Central Asia. David was a pillar of the Bombay Jewish community and fabled for both his charity and his piety. At David's death, Abdullah (later Albert) Sassoon (1817-1897), his eldest son, assumed control of the family business. After founding Bombay's first great textile mills, Albert moved the headquarters of the firm to **London**. There, together with his brothers, Reuben (1835-1905) and Arthur (1840-1912), Albert figured prominently in London society, becoming an intimate of the Prince of Wales (later Edward VII). In 1890, Albert was made first Baronet of Kensington-Gore.

Later generations of the Sassoons tended to loosen their ties with Judaism (except for one branch, which has remained strictly Orthodox), as well as to lose interest in the family business. The Sassoons achieved eminence in politics, the armed forces, and the arts. A number married into English nobility. Among the best known of the later Sassoons were Siegfried Sassoon (1886-1967), who gained a reputation as a poet before World War I; Rachel Sassoon Beer (1858-1927), who owned and edited two rival London newspapers at once; and Philip Sassoon (1888-1939), who rose to a high place in government.

> *"Then Samuel took the vial of oil and poured it upon his head."*
>
> — I SAMUEL 10:1

SATAN. In the Hebrew **Bible**, where he makes his first appearance (I Chron. 21:1), Satan, or the devil, is not the supreme evil force of the universe he became later in Jewish tradition and even more so in **Christianity**. Rather, he is part of the divine entourage of good and bad angels, and his function is to tempt people, as in the case of Job. Medieval Bible commentators, however, identify him as the snake in the story of the Garden of Eden, and ascribe him a much greater role in the divine plan. Today, Satan no longer occupies a position of prominence in most Jewish thinking, but his power is seen in the dark side of the human character which turns individuals into perpetrators of evil acts.

SAUL (11th century B.C.E.). First king of Israel. The youngest son of Kish the Benjaminite, Saul was a modest shepherd lad when the prophet **Samuel** anointed him as king. He defeated the Ammonites and fought successfully against the **Philistines**, Moabites, Arameans, and **Amalekites**. Saul's dispute with the prophet Samuel followed his defeat of the Amalekites. The prophet's public rebuke depressed the king and tragic melancholia—the biblical "evil spirit"—clouded his mind. **David**, the lad brought to soothe Saul with his music, aroused the king's suspicion and had to flee for his life. Saul's last battle was with the Philistines in the Plain of Jezreel. Badly defeated, his sons slain by the enemy, he fell upon his sword and killed himself (I Samuel 8-31). (*See also* **David**.)

SAVING REMNANT. *See* **Sheerit ha-pletah.**

SCHAPIRA, HERMANN (1840-1898). Mathematician and Zionist. Born in **Russia**, he taught mathematics at the University of

Samuel anointing Saul king of Israel.

Heidelberg, Germany, where he founded the first Zionist society in **Germany**. He is best remembered as the originator of the **Jewish National Fund** (*Keren Kayemet le-Israel*), based on a plan for the purchase of land in Palestine for Jews through small donations from the Jewish masses. He presented this proposal again at the first **Zionist Congress** in 1897, but it was not adopted until the 5th Congress in 1901, three years after Schapira's death. Another of his proposals that was made at the first Congress was adopted at the 11th in 1913, the last congress before World War I began; it was then decided to proceed immediately with the creation of a **Hebrew University** in **Jerusalem**. The poet Chaim **Bialik** reminded the delegates that this vision of a new house of learning in Zion came from the mind of the mathematician Hermann Schapira.

Hermann Schapira.

SCHATZ, BORIS (1866-1932). Painter and sculptor. Born in **Lithuania**, his works are found in many European and American museums. His statue of Mattathias, the Hasmonean, is his best known work in **Israel**. In **Paris**, he assisted the great Russian sculptor, Mark **Antokolsky**, and in Sofia he helped found the Academy of Fine Arts. Schatz's crowning achievement was founding the **Bezalel Museum** and School of Art in **Jerusalem** in 1906.

SCHECHTER, JODY. *See* **Sports.**

SCHECHTER, SOLOMON (1847-1915). Scholar and founder of American Conservative Judaism. Born in **Romania**, he studied in Vienna and Berlin and eventually came to **England**. There, the wealth of Hebrew manuscripts at the British Museum in **London** and at the Bodleian Library of Oxford absorbed him for years. He taught at Cambridge University, where he was elected Reader in Rabbinics. He became Professor of Hebrew at the University College of London in 1899. In 1896, Schechter came upon a large part of the original Hebrew of the Book of **Ben Sira**; this discovery led him to visit the Cairo **Genizah**, a literary "cemetery" for worn-out sacred books and manuscripts. He investigated the many thousands of fragments in the Genizah, brought them back to Cambridge, and spent years sorting and studying this great scholarly treasure. The writings he published as a result of these studies brought him worldwide fame among scholars. In 1902, Schechter came to the U.S. to serve as president of the **Jewish Theological Seminary of America.** During his presidency he reorganized the Seminary and enlarged its scope. His essays, particularly the three-volume *Studies in Judaism*, were widely read.

SCHIFF, JACOB HENRY (1847-1920). Financier and philanthropist. Schiff came to the U.S. from **Germany**, where his family had lived since the 14th century. He received his early business training in his father's Frankfurt brokerage house. In 1885, he became head of Kuhn, Loeb, and Co., which had a significant share in financing the expansion of railroads in the U.S. Deeply hostile to Tsarist **Russia** for mistreating its Jews, he consistently refused to help that country obtain loans, foregoing opportunities for great profit. He was one of the founders of the **American Jewish Committee** in 1906 and a leader in its successful effort in 1911 to have the U.S.-Russia commercial treaty abrogated because Russia discriminated against holders of U.S. passports. The range of his philanthropies, Jewish and nonsectarian, was immense. A Reform Jew, he retained much of the traditional piety he had learned in his childhood, and generously supported the religious, educational, and scholarly work of all branches of Judaism. He was opposed to **Zionism** insofar as it was nationalist and secularist, but he felt that Palestine was needed as a refuge and as a spiritual and cultural center. Schiff supported educational institutions in Palestine, donating $100,000 toward the founding of the **Technion** (the **Haifa** Institute of Technology).

Jacob H. Schiff.

SCHONBERG, ARNOLD (1874-1951). Composer. One of the masters of modern music, Schonberg gained international acclaim early in **Austria** and **Germany** with his *Verklarte Nacht* for strings and the *Gurrelieder*. In the years before World War I he evolved his controversial "twelve-tone principle," a theory of composition which abandoned the harmonic tonality of traditional western music. His compositions on Jewish themes include *Kol Nidre*, in the twelve-tone system; *A Survivor of the Warsaw Ghetto*, a cantata for solo, chorus, and orchestra; *Moses and Aaron*, an opera; and *Die Jakobsleiter*, an unfinished oratorio. Schonberg was a teacher of genius as well as a composer and conductor. Fleeing Nazi persecution in 1934, he settled in the U.S., and taught at the University of California until his death.

SCHINDLER, ALEXANDER (1925-2000). American Reform leader. Former president of the **Union of American Hebrew Congregations**, his leadership of the Reform movement saw a greater Reform involvement with the State of **Israel** and intiated some radical changes in Reform philosophy, such as ordained female rabbis and the acceptance of people with only a patrilineal tie to Judaism. He also advocated reaching out to the "unchurched," in other words, actively seeking converts to Judaism.

SCHINDLER, OSKAR (1908-1974). German businessman who worked for the Nazis during World War II in **Poland**, where he used Jewish slave labor. He seized upon the idea of preserving the lives of his Jewish workers by arguing that they were vital for the war effort. In this manner he ultimately saved the lives of some 1,200 Jews. **Yad Va-shem** honored him as a **Righteous of the Nations.** He is the subject of Steven Spielberg's widely acclaimed film *Schindler's List.*

SCHNITZLER, ARTHUR (1862-1931). Austrian playwright and novelist known for his acute psychological character analysis. His views of the role of the Jew in the modern world is expressed in his play *Professor Bernhardi.*

SCHOLEM, GERSHOM (1897-1982). Leading authority on Jewish mysticism. He was born in **Germany** and became a Zionist at an early age. In 1923, he became professor of Jewish mysticism at the **Hebrew University** and published major works on the **Kabbalah** and Jewish mysticism, including *Major Trends in Jewish Mysticism.*

SCHORSCH, ISMAR (1925-). German-born American scholar. He came to the U.S. in his youth and was ordained at the **Jewish Theological Seminary,** where he later taught History of German Jewry, and in 1986 became chancellor of the seminary.

SCHWARTZ, MAURICE. *See* **Stage and Screen.**

Solomon Schechter. Painting by C. Mielziner. Courtesy the Jewish Theological Seminary of America.

SCHWARZ-BART, ANDRÉ (1928-). French author. He lost his family in the **Holocaust**, and later wrote a novel, *The Last of the Just*, which is based on Jewish martyrdom and is still considered a key book about the Holocaust. In his later writing he turned away from Jewish themes.

SCOUTS. *See* **Tzofim.**

SCRIPTURE, SCRIPTURES. From Latin; literally, writing. The **Bible** is also known as the Sacred Scriptures.

SEDER. *See* **Passover.**

SEFIRAH. *See* **Omer.**

SEFIROT. *See* **Kabbalah.**

SEINFELD, JERRY. *See* **Stage and Screen.**

SELIHOT. Literally, forgiveness. Prayers requesting God to pardon sins and end suffering. Thousands of selihot were written mainly between the 7th and 17th centuries. Well-known writers such as Judah **Ha-Levi**, Solomon **Ibn-Gabirol**, and **Rashi**, as well as numerous anonymous poets, produced fervent selihot, many bearing acrostics with the author's name. Many of the selihot have been incorporated into the synagogue services, particularly those of the High Holy Days.

SELLERS, PETER. *See* **Stage and Screen.**

SEMIKHAH. Literally, laying on of hands. The act of **ordination** of a religious leader, originally performed by the ordainer's placing his hands upon the person to be ordained, probably in emulation of the manner in which **Moses** ordained **Joshua** (Num. 27: 22-23).

Gradually, the ceremony of the laying on of hands was abolished, and by the 2nd century B.C.E., religious leaders were ordained simply by being awarded the title "rabbi."

Any ordained rabbi is empowered to confer the rabbinate upon a worthy disciple by ordination. This practice has persisted in Orthodox Jewry to our day, although it has largely been replaced by institutional ordination, namely through the award of an ordination certificate by a recognized rabbinical school. In the United States today, one may be ordained as a rabbi in Orthodox Judaism by one of the numerous yeshivot, or theological colleges, or by **Yeshiva University**; in Conservative Judaism, by the **Jewish Theological Seminary**; and in Reform Judaism, by the **Hebrew Union College-Jewish Institute of Religion**.

A traditional Semikhah vests the ordained rabbi with the authority of rendering decisions in ritual matters and in monetary disputes.

SELZNICK, DAVID. *See* **Stage and Screen.**

SENESCH (SZENES), HANNAH (1921-1944). Poet. Born in Budapest, at age 18 she came to Palestine and studied at the Nahalal Agricultural School, then joined the Sdoth Yam kibbutz near **Caesarea.** In 1943, Senesch joined the band of parachutists from Palestine who jumped into Nazi-occupied Europe on rescue missions. She was the first to cross into **Hungary** from **Yugoslavia**, where she landed and fought with the partisans. She was captured, tortured, and executed at the age of 23. Her poem, *Blessed Is The Match*, which she wrote in Yugoslavia, has been set to music. Another poem, *Eli Eli*, has become one of Israel's most popular songs.

Hannah Senesch.

SEPHARDIM. Literally, Spaniards. Jews of Spanish and Portuguese origin. The customs, rituals, synagogue services, and Hebrew pronunciation of the Sephardim differ from those of the **Ashkenazim**, Jews of Germany and Eastern Europe. Expelled from **Spain** by the **Inquisition** of 1492, the Sephardim were scattered throughout the Mediterranean world, along the north coast of Africa, the Turkish Empire, and the Balkans. Wherever they went, they established the Sephardic ways and rituals. The **Marranos**, or secret Jews, transported their customs to the New World. When Zionists began to migrate to Palestine at the close of the 19th century, they adopted the Sephardic pronunciation of Hebrew for their daily use.

SEPHIROT. *See* **Kaballah**.

SEPTUAGINT. Latin, literally, seventy. Greek translation of the **Bible** made between 250 and 100 B.C.E. According to tradition, the translation was made in **Alexandria** at the request of the ruler, Ptolemy Philadelphus, by 72 scholars. Working individually, they are said to have produced identical translations in 72 days. The Septuagint was the first translation of the Bible, and it made the Scriptures accessible to large numbers of Jews and Gentiles alike. Because the Septuagint was translated from Hebrew texts now lost, biblical scholars have found it invaluable in comparing translations, as an aid in the recovery of a better Hebrew text and in interpreting difficult Hebrew passages.

SERENI, ENZO (1905-1944). Scholar, author, and pioneer. Born in **Rome**, son of the physician to King Victor Emmanuel III, Sereni abandoned a brilliant intellectual career to settle in Palestine in 1926. He was the founder and moving spirit of the settlement of Givat Brenner. During World War II, Sereni organized a group of Jewish parachutists to jump into enemy territories on Jewish rescue missions. Although nearly 40, he joined the group, was caught, and was executed in Dachau in 1944.

SERKIN, RUDOLF. *See* **Music**.

SHAATNEZ. Fabric mixture of wool and linen. The **Bible** (Lev. 19:19) forbids the wearing of garments made of such compositions although the material may be used for other purposes. This prohibition follows the general laws forbidding two other kinds of mixtures: the cross-breeding of different species of animals, and the planting together of different varieties of seeds.

SHABAZI, SHALOM (17th century). Yemenite poet and Kabbalist. He wrote close to 5,000 poems and songs in Hebrew and Arabic. Shabazi became almost a legendary figure, and is one of the most beloved poets of the Yemenite Jews. His poems are included in the festival and holiday liturgy of the Yemenites. A street in **Tel Aviv** is named in his honor.

SHADKHAN. Literally, mediator or go-between. The shadkhan was a matchmaker employed by parents to arrange their children's marriages. The shadkhan's profession attained importance in Jewish life in the early Middle Ages. His legal position was regulated by the rabbis, and he is already mentioned in the **Talmud**. Piety, modesty, and the early age of marriage among Jews tended to preserve the shadkhan as a go-between until recent times. In modern **Yiddish** and **Hebrew literature**, as well as in folk stories, he is usually pictured as a ne'er-do-well, sometimes funny, sometimes downright ridiculous.

SHAHN, BEN. *See* **Art**.

SHALOSH SEUDOT. *See* **Sabbath**.

SHAMIR, MOSHE. *See* **Hebrew Literature.**

SHAMIR, YITZHAK (1915-   ). Israel's seventh prime minister, minister of foreign affairs, and speaker of the Knesset. Born in Ruzinoy, **Poland**, Shamir immigrated to Palestine in 1935 and studied at the Hebrew University. He served in the **Irgun Z'vai L'umi** and the **Stern Group**, was arrested twice by the British but escaped. From 1955 to 1965, he served in the Mossad, Israel's intelligence service, and was active on behalf of Soviet Jewry. In 1970, Shamir joined the Herut movement and chaired its Executive Committee in 1975 and 1977. He has served on the committees for defense, foreign affairs, and state control. In 1980-1981 he was Foreign Minister and became Prime Minister in 1983, following Menachem **Begin**'s resignation. He served until 1984, then again from 1990 to 1992, when Labor came back to power under **Rabin**.

SHAMMAI. Talmudic scholar of the 1st century B.C.E. He was the contemporary and rival of **Hillel** and founder of a school named after him. Hillel was president of the **Sanhedrin**, and Shammai, the vice-president. The **Talmud** records a number of differences of opinion between Hillel and Shammai. In most instances, Shammai and his followers were more strict in their interpretation of the law. The opinions of the School of Hillel were accepted by the sages. The stories about Shammai reveal his inflexible personality. But Shammai also preached friendliness; one of his favorite sayings was: "Welcome every man with a friendly face." Shammai and Hillel were the last of the "pairs," or *zugot,* of scholars whose teachings formed the basis of the Talmud.

SHARETT, MOSHE (1894-1965). Zionist and Israeli leader. Moshe Shertok was brought by his family to Palestine in 1906. In 1913, he went to Istanbul, **Turkey**, to study law. Sharett mastered a number of languages, which later served him in good

Moshe Sharett, Prime Minister, and Moshe Dayan, Commander-in-Chief of the IDF, accompany Burma's Prime Minister U Nu, as they inspect an honor guard in Israel, 1955.

stead in his political work. Besides his mother tongue Hebrew, he spoke and wrote fluently in Arabic, Turkish, German, French, and English. During the World War I, Sharett served as an officer in the Turkish army. Between the two World Wars, he took part in Zionist political work. For five years he lived in **England**, where he continued with his studies and helped Chaim **Weizmann** as an expert in Arab affairs. During World War II he shared in the political work that led to the establishment of the **Jewish Brigade**, which fought the Nazis and played an important part in saving and bringing the remnants of the Nazi victims to Palestine. From 1946 until the establishment of Israel in 1948, Sharett did intensive work in the U.S. In the first Israel cabinet, Sharett became Minister of Foreign Affairs, and from 1954 to 1955, he served also as Prime Minister. He was one of the key figures in the early years of the state.

SHARON, ARIEL (1928-). Israeli soldier and politician, one of Israel's outstanding generals, who played a critical role in the Sinai Campaign in 1956, and in the **Yom Kippur War** in 1973. As **Begin**'s Minister of Defense, he was condemned for his conduct of the 1982 Lebanon War, and had to resign. He remained in the cabinet, and later became Minister of Housing, and played a major role in settling Russian immigrants. In early 2001 Sharon became prime minister of Israel after his predecessor, Ehud **Barak**, failed to conclude a peace treaty with the Palestinians.

Torah Crown, by Ludwig Y. Wolpert.

SHAS. Term applied to the **Talmud**, it is the abbreviation of *shishah sedarim* or six "orders," or divisions, of the Mishnah.

SHAVUOT. Also known as the Feast of Weeks, it falls on the sixth day of **Sivan**, just seven weeks after **Passover**. The three days before Shavuot are called the "Three Days of Limitation" or "Preparation," for the people of Israel had to purify themselves for a period of three days in order to be ready to receive the Law from Mount Sinai. One of the pilgrimage festivals, Shavuot is both *Hag ha-Bikkurim* (Holiday of the First Fruits) and *Zeman Motan Toratenu* (The Time of the Giving of Our Torah.) In biblical times, offerings of the first fruits of tree and field were brought to the **Temple**. Today, this aspect of the holiday is observed by decorating the **synagogue** with green boughs. In **Israel**, Shavuot is marked by the ceremonial offering of the first fruits to the **Jewish National Fund**, which hold the land in trust for the Jewish people. Because the Rabbis calculated that the Jews had received the Torah at Sinai on Shavout, it was considered appropriate for children to begin their Hebrew studies on this day. *Tikkun Shavuot*, a collection of passages from the **Bible** and other sacred books, is read on Shavout night, while the biblical Book of **Ruth** is read after the morning service.

Tradition has it that **David** was born and died on Shavuot. It is therefore customary to read **Psalms** on the second evening of Shavuot. In **Jerusalem**, many Jews make a pilgrimage to Mount Zion, on which, according to tradition, King David was buried. In some communities, Jews light 150 candles in the synagogue, the numbers of chapters in the Book of **Psalms** attributed to David. The custom is to prepare and eat dairy dishes on Shavuot. In recent times, Reform synagogues, as well as some Conservative and Orthodox congregations, have designated the day for the ceremony of **confirmation** for children past **Bar Mitzvah** age. The Shavuot service also includes the singing of a poem called Akdamut. This poem written in **Aramaic**, deals with the grandeur of God, the greatness of His deeds, and the rewards that await the righteous in the world to come. Written in the 11th century, Akdamut has a mystical theme, for which an inspiring melody has been composed.

SHAZAR, ZALMAN (1889-1974). Scholar, author, third President of **Israel** (1963-1973). Born in Mir, **Russia**, and raised in a Hasidic environment, he attended the Academy of Jewish Sciences at Leningrad as well as the Universities of Freiburg, Strasbourg, and Berlin. Shazar settled in Palestine in 1924. He served as editor of the daily *Davar* until 1948, and was a leading organizer of Israel's labor movement. As Israel's first Minister of Education, Shazar introduced general compulsory education. He also held educational posts in the **Jewish Agency** and **World Zionist Organization.** He was a man of widely varied interests and impressive scholarship. He was a gifted and persuasive speaker, and authored a number of scholarly works on biblical archeology and messianic figures.

The third paragraph of the Shema, with commentaries given above and below the verses, in the oldest Hebrew biblical manuscript, located at the Jewish National and University Library, Jerusalem.

SHEARITH ISRAEL CONGREGATION OF NEW YORK. Literally, remnant of Israel. Organized in 1654 by the first Jewish pilgrims to come to Nieuw Amsterdam. Its founders had escaped from the **Inquisition** in South America. The first Jewish congregation in what is now the U.S., it has had continuous history of more than three centuries as a **Sephardic** synagogue.

SHEERIT HAPLETAH. Literally, the remnant or the saving remnant. This concept dates back to biblical times, and refers to that part of the Jewish people left after a major calamity. The prophets often predict that a small portion of Jews will come back from exile and reestablish itself in its land. This, indeed, happened more than once in Jewish history. First, after the **Babylonian** exile in 586 B.C.E., and more recently in our time with the birth of the State of **Israel**.

SHEHITAH. The slaughter of ritually pure animals according to Jewish law. The laws which govern slaughtering grew out of a verse in the Bible (Deut. 12:21), and are contained in the tractate Hullin of the **Talmud**. The *shohet* (slaughterer) is required to follow a special course of study dealing with these laws, and is permitted to practice his profession only upon receiving a certificate known as a kabbalah. The *shohet* employs a special knife called hallaf, which must be applied to a specific spot on the animal's neck. Before slaughtering, the *shohet* must examine his blade for flaws. To avoid causing the animal unnecessary pain, the *shohet* must follow strictly the rules for slaughtering; if he fails, the animal is ruled a *nevelah* (carcass), forbidden as food. After the slaughter, the *shohet* must subject the animal's inner organs, particularly the lungs, to a minute examination. The discovery of the slightest sign of disease is sufficient cause to forbid the consumption of the animal. The shehitah laws were intended to safeguard the health of the individual, and to avoid pain to the animal as much as possible.

SHEKEL. Literally, weight. The measure against which pieces of silver and gold were weighed for use as money. When **Sarah** died, **Abraham** bought from Ephron the Hittite the Cave of **Machpelah** as a family burial ground. In payment, he "weighed out... 400 shekels of silver current with the merchant" (Gen. 23:12-16). When **Moses** took a census of the Children of Israel, God instructed that everyone was to give a tax of half a shekel as a "tribute unto the Lord" to use "for the service of the **Tabernacle**" (Ex. 30:1 3). It is thought that as a unit of weight the shekel came to equal a little over sixteen grams. In **Maccabean** times, the shekel was a silver coin bearing inscriptions of the current ruler. In modern times, the first Zionist **Congress** in 1897 established the payment of nominal dues called a "shekel." This payment, together with the acceptance of the Basle Program made any Jew or Jewess over eighteen years of age a member of the **World Zionist Organization**. By means of the shekel, (then about 25 cents) the Congress aimed to create a worldwide democratic Zionist association. Thereafter, only those who paid the shekel were entitled to vote for delegates to world Zionist congresses.

Shekel.

SHEKHINAH. Literally, indwelling. A term used to express **God**'s omnipresence. Though the Shekhinah is everywhere, it is the prophet and the righteous individual, the judge who pronounces true judgment, the charitable person, and the one who lives as well as believes his Judaism, are said to particularly attract the Divine Presence to themselves.

SHEMA. The declaration of faith in the unity of God, traditionally recited mornings and evenings: "Hear, O Israel, the Lord our God, the Lord is One" (Deut. 6:4-9). (*See also* **Prayer**.)

Shema, illuminated by Sol Nodel. Courtesy the private collection of the Goldbergs.

SHEMINI ATZERET. *See* **Sukkot**.

SHERIRA GAON (ca. 900-100 C.E.). Babylonian sage who claimed descent from King **David**. Sherira Gaon's scholarship commanded the respect of all Jewish communities. He headed the academy at Pumbeditha from 969 until his death. His letter to the Jewish scholars of Kairwan, North Africa, relates the origin of the Mishnah and enumerates in chronological order the scholars and leaders from the time of the Mishnah to his day. The work is a major source of information on because it is of utmost importance, 800 years of Jewish history.

SHIN. Twenty-first letter of the Hebrew alphabet; numerically, 300.

SHLONSKY, ABRAHAM (1900-1973). Hebrew poet. Born in **Ukraine**, educated at the **Tel Aviv Herzliah Gymnasium** and at the Sorbonne University in **Paris**. Shlonsky's experiences as a pioneer in Palestine are reflected in his poetry. He is a first-rate craftsman, whose poetry excels in rich imagery and mastery of language and style. He has translated into Hebrew a number of works from world literature.

SHMONEH ESREH. Eighteen Benedictions. (*See* **Prayer** *and* **Siddur**.)

SHNEERSON. Family of Hasidic rabbis. Shneour Zalman (1748-1812), founder of the dynasty, was born in Liozno, White **Russia**, where he received a traditional Talmudic education. Won over to **Hasidism**, he founded a movement known as Habad, which stressed Talmudic learning and the forms of Orthodox Judaism rather than the ecstatic mysticism of other types of Hasidism. Known as the Rabbi of Ladi, he drew many followers from among the conservative Jewish communities of **Lithuania** and White Russia. During his lifetime, Habad had more than 100,000 adherents. Leadership of the movement, which has survived into the present, has remained with the Shneerson family. It passed from Shneour to his son, Baer (1774-1812), and then to his grandson, Menachem Mendel (1786-1866), whose direct descendants have remained the spiritual guides of Habad. Menachem Mendel's son, Samuel (1834-1883), settled in the town of Lubavitch; followers of Habad consequently call themselves Lubavitch Hasidim. The leadership passed to Samuel's son, Sholom Baer (1861-1920), whose son, Joseph Isaac (1890-1950), founded the World Habad movement in 1934. In the tradition of his ancestors, who had fought assimilation in Tsarist Russia, Joseph Isaac refused to acquiesce to a Soviet order closing Jewish schools. For this refusal he was exiled from Greater Russia. In 1940, he settled in **New York** City; here he conducted Habad activities and supervised the establishment of Lubavitch academies throughout North and South America.

The late Lubavitcher Rebbe, Rabbi Menachem M. Shneerson.

The Lubavitcher movement's most recent rebbe, Rabbi Menachem Mendl Shneerson, died on June 12, 1994. He built a worldwide Habad network, sending young Lubavitch families as emissaries of Judaism to remote parts of the globe. Their primary purpose is to promote Jewish education in the spirit of Torah-true Judaism among all Jews, regardless of background, to establish contact with, and to retrieve alienated Jewish youth, and to promulgate the observance of the **Torah** as a daily experience among all Jews.

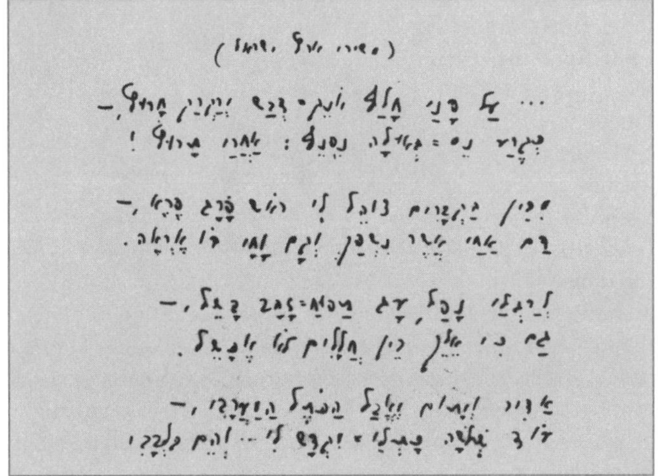

Facsimile of one of Shneur's poems in his handwriting.

SHNEUR, ZALMAN (1887-1959). Hebrew and Yiddish poet and novelist. Born in **Russia**, Shneur began to write when he was barely 14 years old. His creative talents were quick to develop, and as a youth of 20 he was already recognized as one of the most original and powerful poets in modern Jewish literature. His poetry appealed to the younger generation in its rebellion against convention. His novels, describing Jewish life in Eastern Europe, rank with the classic works of **Mendele Mocher Sefarim** and **Sholom Aleichem** in artistic achievement. His novel *Noah Pandre* appeared in an English translation in 1936.

SHOFAR. Literally, horn or trumpet. Traditionally the curved horn of a ram, the animal that **Abraham** sacrificed instead of his son, **Isaac**. In the **Bible**, the shofar is blown to announce all important occasions. The blast of the ram's horn proclaimed the **Jubilee** year, the beginning of the **Sabbath**, the festivals and the **New Moon**. The shofar is blown during the month of **Elul** preceeding the High Holy Days as a call to repentance. It is an essential part of the **Rosh ha-Shanah** services, and the **Yom Kippur** day of fasting and prayer ends with the sound of the shofar.

Shofar.

SHOLOM ALEICHEM (1859-1916). Pen name of the Yiddish writer and humorist Sholom Rabinowitz. Born in a small town in **Ukraine**, he displayed in his early childhood a remarkable talent for mimicry and caricature. Young Sholom was also endowed with keen sensitivity and an imaginative mind. While he liked best to play pranks on his elders, he nevertheless excelled in his studies. He was especially attracted to the **Bible**, most of which he learned by heart. Later, he attended a government high school, and at seventeen, he accepted a job as a private tutor. For some time he even served as a rabbinical functionary, and also engaged in business until he lost all his money.

Sholom Aleichem.

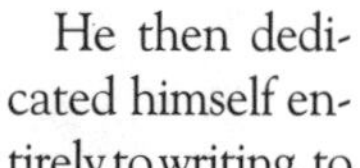

He then dedicated himself entirely to writing, to the great enrichment of Yiddish literature. In his hundreds of stories, novels, and plays, Sholom Aleichem mirrored Jewish life of the small towns in Eastern Europe. He reflected in his tales the wisdom and wit of his people and became their favorite writer. Universally admired, he was given rousing receptions on his visits to the Jewish centers in **Russia**. He came to America twice, the last time shortly before World War I broke out. It is said that a half million people came to his funeral when he died in **New York** in 1916.

Sholom Aleichem created unforgettable types: Tevyeh, the milkman, Menachem Mendel, the luckless broker, and Motel, the cantor's son, whose escapades are especially endearing to young readers. He has been compared to Charles Dickens and Mark Twain. Much of his work has been translated into English; Maurice **Samuel**'s *World of Sholom Aleichem* has distilled the flavor of the great humorist into one volume.

SHTADLAN. Literally, persuader. A representative chosen by the Jewish community, or self-appointed, to plead the Jewish cause before governments or rulers. He was usually appointed because of his wealth, eloquence, or good relations with important personalities. In 1315, five such shtadlanim were chosen to negotiate with Philip the Fair of **France** for the return of Jews who had been expelled from the country. During the 16th century, another Shtadlan, Josel of Rosheim, pleaded successfully with the nobility of Brandenburg, and Jews were not expelled from that German state. The Shtadlan, as an unofficial diplomat or lobbyist, continued to serve the Jewish people until he was replaced by modern professional organizations and democratically chosen communal leaders.

SHULHAN ARUKH. Authoritative code, prepared by Joseph **Karo**, containing all the traditional rules of Jewish conduct, based on Talmudic sources and later opinions or decisions of the great rabbis. Originally, the *Shulhan Arukh* was intended for young students who were not yet prepared to weigh the complex decisions of the authorities. However, the work suited so well the need for a methodical and easily accessible arrangement of the various laws that it became the most popular handbook for both scholars and laypersons.

The *Shulhan Arukh* is divided, like its predecessor, the *Arbaah Turim*, into four parts: one summarizing the laws pertaining to **prayers**, **Sabbath**, and holidays; a second, the **dietary laws**, laws of mourning and other ritual matters; a third, civil laws; and a fourth, the laws relating to **marriage**, divorce, and similar matters.

Title page of the Amsterdam edition of the Shulhan Arukh published in 1698.

The Code of Joseph **Karo** was accepted immediately by **Sephardic** Jewry. **Ashkenazic** scholars, chief among them Moses Isserles, amended, revised, and added many customs and practices current among the Ashkenazic Jewry. With the additions of Isserles and other commentaries, the Shulhan Arukh has been the most vital and influential book in Jewish religious life.

SHVADRON, SHOLOM MORDECAI BEN MOSES (Maharsham) (1835-1911). Rabbi in Galicia. He served as rabbi first in the town of Potok and then in Brezen. He is best known for his **responsa**, four volumes of which were published during his lifetime and three after his death. His rulings on Jewish law were widely accepted as authoritative and essential in coping with the practical problems of the time in which he was active. A modest and kindly man, he adhered stringently to the requirements of Jewish law but endeavored to reach as lenient decisions as possible in religious questions addressed to him.

SIDDUR. Literally, order or arrangement. The daily prayer book. Since **prayer** in a **synagogue** came to take the place of animal sacrifices after the destruction of the Second **Temple**, the prayers in the Siddur were arranged to follow closely the order of sacrifices in the Temple. The three daily services are included in all daily prayer books, though some editions contain numerous additions, such as the **Psalms** and the **Song of Songs**. Many editions of the daily prayer books include the **Sabbath** and Festival prayers, as well as *Pirke Avot* (The Ethics of the Fathers). The oldest of the prayers is the *Shema* (Hear, O Israel). The *Shemoneh Esreh*—the Eighteen Benedictions—recited standing up and therefore called the *Amidah*, was drawn up by the men of the Great Assembly some time between the 5th and 3rd centuries B.C.E. The *Amidah* is the most solemn of the daily prayers. Various confessions said by those who brought sacrifices to the Temple, and the Psalms chanted by the **Levites**, also went into the making of the Siddur. The prayer book as we know it today is based on the one compiled ca. 860 C.E. by Amram ben Sheshna, the Gaon of the Academy in Sura, **Babylonia**. There is a slight difference in arrangement and in types of prayers between the **Sephardic** version (*nusah*) and the **Ashkenazic**. Hymns and songs have been added to the Siddur over the years. Some of the most popular closing hymns of the Siddur are *Adon Olam* (Master of the Universe), *Aleinu* (Let Us Praise), and *Yigdal* (Magnify). (*See also* **Prayer** *and* **Mahzor**.)

SILLS, BEVERLY. *See* **Music**.

SILVER, ABBA HILLEL (1893-1963). Rabbi, author, and Zionist leader. Brought to the U.S. from **Lithuania** as a child, Silver rose to a position of leadership in American **Zionism** in the years of struggle that preceded the creation of a Jewish state. He prepared for the rabbinate at the **Hebrew Union College** in Cincinnati. In 1917 he took the pulpit of The Temple in Cleveland, **Ohio**, a post he held for the rest of his life. During the 1940's when Zionists were undecided whether to cooperate with **England** or to oppose it on the question of Jewish statehood in Palestine, Silver came to head the "activist" opposition faction. As chairman of the American Zionist Emergency Council from 1945 to 1948, and of the American Section of the **Jewish Agency** for Palestine, he led the campaign that gained U.S. support for a Jewish state. From 1946 to 1948, Silver was also president of the **Zionist Organization of America**. In 1956, he became chairman of the **Bonds for Israel**. Silver's extensive writings include *Messianic Speculation in Ancient Israel* (1927), *Religion in a Changing World* (1930), and *Vision and Victory* (1949), his report on the Zionist struggle.

Abba Hillel Silver visiting a maabara in Israel. Courtesy Zionist Archives and Library, New York.

SIMCHAT TORAH. *See* **Sukkot**.

Emblem of the tribe of Simeon.

SIMEON. Second son of **Jacob** and **Leah**. The tribe of Simeon settled in **Canaan** in the territory south of **Judah**. Eventually, the Simeonites merged with the dominant tribe of Judah.

SIMEON BEN SHETAH. President of the **Sanhedrin** during the 1st century B.C.E. For nine prosperous years, during the reign of his sister, Queen **Salome Alexandra**, Simeon was the leader of the **Pharisees**, the majority party of Judea. The Pharisees interpreted the Law according to traditions handed down over the generations. They were opposed by the aristocratic **Sadducees**, who insisted on a literal interpretation of the biblical law. As president of the Sanhedrin, Simeon rid this legislative and judicial council of its Sadducee members. The reforms he introduced gained him the title of "restorer of the Law." Simeon was also known for his personal integrity. One story that has come down relates that Simeon once received a donkey as a gift from his students. As he mounted the donkey, he found a valuable jewel hung around his neck. His students were exultant: Now their master would be able to retire from active life and devote himself to his studies. Simeon, however, ordered them to return the treasure to the Arab from whom they had bought the animal. The Arab, he said, had sold them a donkey, and not a jewel. The students protested, but Simeon insisted, and the jewel was returned.

SIMEON BEN YOHAI. *See* **Tannaim**.

SIMON, NEIL. *See* **Stage and Screen.**

SIMON, PAUL. *See* **Music.**

SINAI CAMPAIGN. *See* **Israel, State of** *and* **Sinai Peninsula.**

SINAI PENINSULA. Situated between the two continents of Asia and Africa, and between two seas: the Mediterranean and the Red Sea. Triangular in shape, the Peninsula is 11,200 square miles. The coastal route which runs through the Sinai, by way of el-Arish to Gaza, is one of the oldest in history. The Egyptians and Assyrians used it in ancient times, the former establishing military outposts along it. **Alexander the Great** traveled it, and, in modern times, Napoleon used it on his march to **Acre**. During World War I, the British Army, under the command of General **Allenby**, reached Gaza through this road.

The Sinai Peninsula is mainly desert, sparsely settled by wandering Bedouins. Few permanent settlements exist because of the lack of rain and the shifting sand dunes. The largest town, El-Arish, has a population of 20,000, most of which engages in trade and agriculture. The Peninsula is rich in natural resources, which were already exploited by the ancient Pharaohs. Their limited exploitation today is due to poor means of communication and lack of water.

The Peninsula is famous because the Children of Israel traveled through it when they came out of **Egypt** and made their way to the Holy Land. "In the third month after the Children of Israel went out of the land of Egypt, the same day they came into the wilderness of Sinai. And when they were departed from Rephidim,

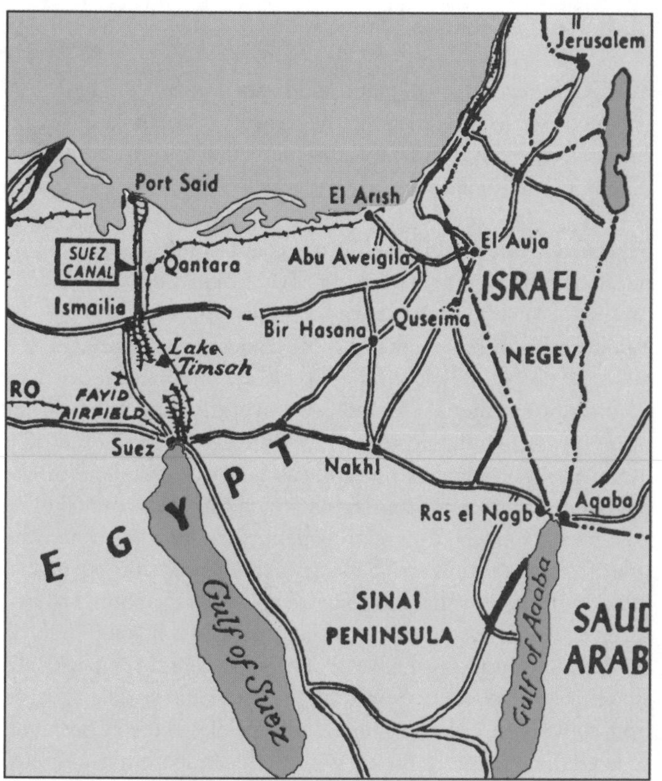

Sinai Peninsula.

and came to the wilderness of Sinai, they encamped in the wilderness, and there Israel encamped before the mount" (Ex. 19:1-2).

The location of Mount Sinai, also known as Horeb, is uncertain. According to Christian tradition, it lies close to the southern tip of the Peninsula, and its peak is known as Jebel Musa (Mountain of Moses). It is an awe-inspiring mountain, deserving the name of Mountain of God. Nearby is a place called Ein Musa, where, tradition has it, **Moses** watered Jethro's flocks. However, the biblical account of the routes taken by the Children of Israel through the desert does not support the claim that Jebel Musa is Mount Sinai. According to it, it is reasonable to identify Mount Sinai with Jebel Hilal, in the vicinity of Kadesh Barnea, in the northern part of the Peninsula. Jebel Hilal is only 890 feet tall, but it dominates the whole area. This region was the scene of the battle between the Israelites and **Amalek** in ancient times, Here, also, in the vicinity of Abu Aweigila, a pitched battle took place between the Israeli and Egyptian forces in the course of the four-day 1956 Sinai campaign. This battle ended with the occupation of the whole Peninsula by the Israeli army. However, Israel was forced to return the Peninsula to Egypt. In 1967, Egypt used the Peninsula as a staging area for a planned full-scale invasion of Israel, and in the **Six-Day War** Israeli forces once again recaptured it. Following the **Yom Kippur War**, part of the Peninsula was returned to Egypt and the rest of the Peninsula was returned to Egypt under the peace agreement signed between Israel and Egypt on March 26, 1979.

SINGER, AL. *See* **Sports.**

SINGER, ISAAC BASHEVIS (1904-1991). Yiddish novelist and journalist. The younger brother of Israel Joshua **Singer** (the brothers were sons and grandsons of Hasidic rabbis), he was born in **Poland** and in 1935 he settled in **New York,** where he joined the staff of the *Jewish Daily Forward*. Beginning in the 1950's, several novels, collections of short stories, volumes of memoirs, and children's books written by Singer in Yiddish have appeared in English translations. His stories deal mostly with mysticism, love, and the conflict between piety and enlightenment; their settings are in Eastern Europe and the U.S. His novels include *The Family Moskat, In My Father's Court, The Manor, The Estate*, and *Shosha*. His short story anthologies include *The Spinoza of Market Street, Short Friday*, and *A Crown of Feathers*. Among his children's books is *Zlateh the Goat*. His play, *Yentl*, was produced on Broadway in 1975. He was awarded the 1978 **Nobel Prize** for Literature.

SINGER, ISRAEL JOSHUA (1893-1944). Older brother of Isaac Bashevis **Singer**, he is best known for his play *Yoshe Kalb* and his epic novel *The Brothers Ashkenazi*.

SIVAN. Ninth month of the Hebrew calendar. **Shavuot** falls on the 6th of Sivan.

SIX-DAY WAR. Contrary to Israel's hopes and the assumptions of its allies, Israel's withdrawal from the **Sinai Peninsula** and the Gaza Strip after the Sinai Campaign of 1956 was not followed by the true peace. Emboldened by diplomatic and military support from the Soviet Union, Gamal Abdel Nasser, the president of **Egypt**, and his associates continued to declare their aim to destroy Israel. These threats were

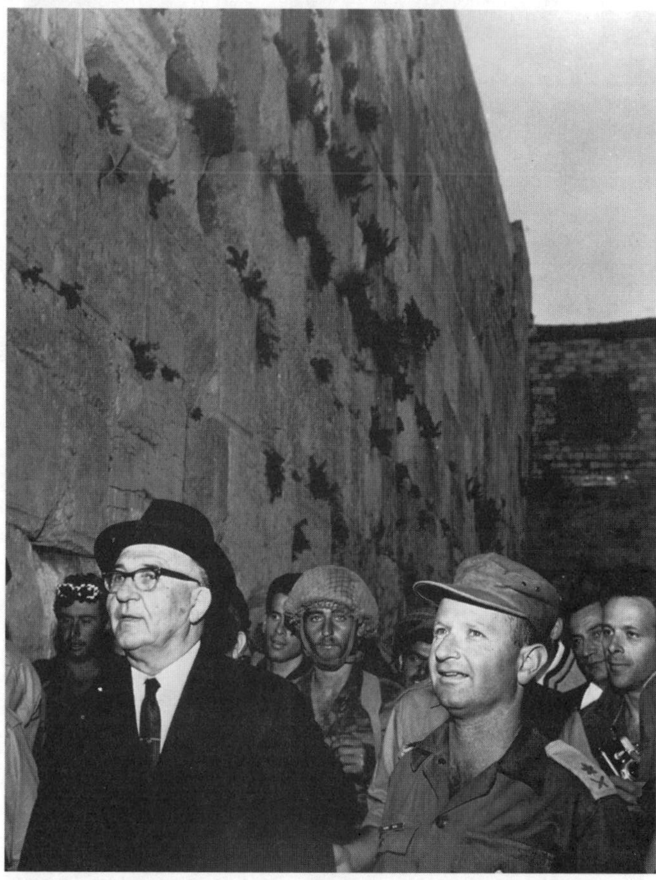

Prime Minister Levi Eshkol and General Uzi Narkiss, commander of the forces in the Jerusalem sector during the Six-Day War, view the liberated Western Wall for the first time.

accompanied by increasingly serious Arab incursions into Israel from **Syria**, **Lebanon**, and **Jordan**, and Israeli border villages were constantly shelled by Arab artillery. In the middle of May 1967, Nasser began to move Egyptian troops and Russian-supplied armor into the Sinai Peninsula for an all-out invasion of Israel and summarily evicted the UN Emergency Force which had been stationed in Sinai and in the Gaza Strip. Next, Egypt closed the Straits of Tiran to all Israeli shipping and cargoes. On May 30, Nasser signed an anti-Israel pact with the Kingdom of **Jordan** and on June 4 with **Iraq**. Surrounded by enemies and unable to obtain support from the UN and the friendly powers who had promised to guarantee her security, Israel had no other choice but to strike back at her enemies. On June 5, 1967, Israel destroyed most of Egypt's air force on the ground. With Egypt's air power neutralized, Israel's forces moved forward and by June 8 had reached the Suez Canal. In the meantime, Israeli troops had repulsed a Jordanian attack, and by June 7 had taken the sector of **Jerusalem** that had been occupied by Jordan in 1948. For the first time since 1948, Jews were able to worship at the **Western Wall**. Next, Israeli forces stormed and occupied the Syrian fortifications in the Golan Heights which had posed a constant threat to Israeli border settlements. By June 11, Egypt, Jordan and Syria had agreed to a cease-fire.

SIYYUM. The formal conclusion of the writing of a **Torah** Scroll or the completion of the study of a section of the **Bible** or **Talmud**; usually marked by a celebration. The custom is to hold a siyyum on the morning preceding the first day of **Passover**: the purpose is to release the firstborn male from the pre-Passover fast.

SMOLENSKIN, PERETZ (1842-1885). Hebrew novelist in **Russia**, and pioneer of Jewish national revival. His restless spirit led him in his early youth to wander through the Jewish towns of Eastern Europe, and he later described his experiences in the foremost Hebrew novel of the period, *The Wanderer on the Paths of Life,* which criticized the existing Jewish educational and communal system. It inspired young Jewish people to strive for radical changes in Jewish society. (*See also* **Hebrew Literature**.)

SOKOLOW, NAHUM (1859-1936). Zionist leader, Hebrew writer and editor in **Poland**, he came to **London** in 1915 to participate in the diplomatic negotiations that resulted in the issuing of the **Balfour Declaration.** During World War I, Sokolow traveled to **Italy** and the Vatican, and then to **France**, and secured the approval of the British, Italian, and French powers for the declaration before its publication. In 1919 he led the presentation of Zionist claims before the **Peace Conference at Versailles**. When the **Jewish Agency** for Palestine was created in 1929, Sokolow was elected its president. From 1931 to 1935 he was president of the **World Zionist Organization**. Sokolov was a man of vast learning, a prolific writer, and one of the great orators of the early Zionist movement.

SOLOMON. Third king of Israel, son of **David** and Bathsheba, builder of the **Temple**, poet and man of wisdom. His reign, like his name, was one of peace, and lasted about forty years (970-931 B.C.E.). Solomon secured peace on his southern borders by marrying Pharaoh's daughter, and kept the road to Ezion Gever with its copper mines safe and free. He used his alliance with King Hiram of Tyre, on his northwest border, to develop the arts of commerce and seafaring. Solomon was a great administrator and builder. He erected the **Temple** in **Jerusalem** and instituted its impressive services which were accompanied by singing and instrumental music. He built palaces, roads, aqueducts, and his wisdom became a byword in history and in countless legends. However, his marriages to the daughters of neighboring kings introduced into the splendor of his rule the seeds of disruption. The price of Solomon's luxury was high taxation. His peace was earned at the cost of unrest, political conflict and the idol worship by his foreign wives. Yet Solomon's glory and his wisdom echo through the ages in the **Song of Songs**, in **Proverbs** and in **Ecclesiastes**, the Scriptural works traditionally ascribed to him.

The Judgment of Solomon, by Gustav Doré.

SOLOVEICHIK FAMILY. Talmudic scholars. Joseph Baer Soloveichik (1820-1892) and his son, Hayim (1853-1919), were considered the greatest rabbinical authorities in **Russia**. The latter served for several years as head of the famous yeshiva, or Talmudical Academy, of Volozhin. Both held the position of rabbi in the city of Brest-Litovak (Brisk), Russia. Moses Soloveichik, son of Hayim, was dean of Talmudic studies, first at the Tahkemoni school in **Warsaw**, Poland, and later at **Yeshiva University** in **New York**. Joseph Baer Soloveichik (1903-1992), who arrived in the U.S. in 1932, occupied the chair previously filled by his father at Yeshiva University, and was one of the leading spirits in the religious Zionist movement in the U.S. Combining Talmudic scholarship with extensive secular knowledge (he received his doctorate in philosophy at the University of Berlin), he was considered one of the most brilliant and stimulating Orthodox teachers and lecturers. Rabbi Soloveichik was head of two congregations, one in **Boston** and one in New York. He served as chairman of the Law Commission of the Rabbinical Council, and contributed to scholarly and rabbinical journals.

SOLTI, SIR GEORGE. *See* **Music**.

SONCINO. Small Italian town in which Israel Nathan Soncino, a learned physician, set up his noted printing press in 1483. His descendants carried on his work. The name was adopted by the Soncino Gesellschaft in Berlin, 1925, and by the Soncino Press of **London**, publishers of the English **Talmud** and many other books of Jewish scholarly interest.

SONDHEIM, STEVEN. *See* **Music**.

SONG OF SONGS. The first of the five scrolls in the **Bible**, it is read in the synagogue service on **Passover**. According to tradition, King **Solomon** is the author of this series of beautiful love poems traditionally interpreted as describing symbolically God's love of Israel.

SOPHER (SCHREIBER), MOSES (1762-1839). The leading authority on Jewish law in his day, he was known as the *Hatam Sofer* because of his major six-volume work on Jewish law (mainly **responsa**). He bitterly opposed the Reform movement and resisted any innovation in Jewish practice.

SOUTH AFRICA, REPUBLIC OF. South Africa has 98,000 Jews in a general population numbering 43 million. The first Jews arrived in 1806 from St. Helena. In 1820, they were joined by a handful of coreligionists who came with 4,000 colonists sent by the English. South Africa then consisted only of the sparsely populated province of Capetown, and a vast, unexplored wilderness stretching into the heart of the Dark Continent. Inhabited by savage Zulu tribes and containing great untapped natural resources, it offered a promise of wealth and adventure to those who could face its dangers and survive. For a century, hardy pioneers hacked at its frontiers, carving for themselves private empires in mountain and veldt. Among them were enterprising Jews such as Aaron de Pass and his son Daniel, who prospered in the country's infant shipping, fishing and whaling industries, opened copper mines, founded sugar plantations, and established one of Natal's first industries. Nathaniel Isaacs and Benjamin Norden were active in the "Zulu trade"; the former was the partner and right-hand man of "empire-builder" Cecil Rhodes.

The turning point in South African history came with discovery, in the 1870's, of the world's richest gold and diamond mines, in Kimberly and the Transvaal. Bringing unprecedented wealth to the area, it drew immigrants from all over the world. These included East European Jews who migrated via **England**, Holland and other West European countries. The newcomers swelled the ranks of the community, going chiefly into small trade and establishing some of the country's earliest manufacturing plants. But it was the old-timers who exploited the mineral finds: Solomon Barnato Joel came to control huge copper fields in North Rhodesia; Barney I. Barnato, who started out as a busboy in **London**'s East End, became Kimberly's "diamond king."

With the outbreak of the Boer War in 1899, the growing Jewish community found itself fighting with distinction in two armies. The war was fought between the English, who wished to unite the country under their flag, and Dutch farmers (known as Boers) who had trekked northward at mid-century to preserve their independence. The Boers had founded the Orange Free State and the Transvaal, where Jewish farmers and traders had settled early. As in English Capetown and Natal, Jews played an important role in the commercial and political life of the provinces.

The war ended in 1902 with an English victory. Eight years later, Capetown, Natal, the Orange Free State and the Transvaal were joined in the Union of South Africa; two years after that (1912), the Jewish communities, scattered throughout the country, joined together to form a united Board of Deputies to represent them before the central authorities. In the national life of South Africa Jews continued to play an important role in politics, law, medicine, and the arts, as well as in the economic life. South Africa's most Popular writer of English in recent times was Sarah Millin, a Jewess, whose husband, Judge Philip Millin, was one of the country's leading jurists. Jews have sat in Parliament from the outset; they have also held government positions. Jewish patrons have founded the country's leading art museums. Artists such as Irma Stem are in the first rank of South African painters and sculptors. The country's best writers include such Jews as Dan Jacobson and Nadine **Gordimer**.

The wealth and earlier security of South Africa's Jews did not shield them from the serious threat of **anti-Semitism** during the 1930's and 1940's. Under the influence of Nazi propaganda, the Powerful Nationalist Party threatened to deprive Jews of economic and political rights. With the collapse of Nazism, this program was discarded, and the community has since been assured that discrimination will not be practiced.

South Africa's Jewry maintains strong ties with **Israel**. There has been a **Zionist** movement in the country since the 1890's, and today the Zionist Federation is the most active organization in the community. The government of the Union of South Africa has pursued a policy friendly to Zionism and Israel.

Jewish communal life is intensive. The first synagogue was founded in 1841, and during the 19th century both synagogues and Jewish schools were set up in all communities. Since 1928, a Board of Jewish Education has coordinated educational activities. Jewish education, however, is a problem with which the community is seriously concerned, as there is a shortage of both funds and adequately trained teachers. The small but flourishing Jewish press includes a number of weeklies, published mainly in Capetown and Johannesburg, the two largest communities, with a Jewish population of 25,650 and 57,500 respectively. The Hebrew Order of David, similar to **B'nai B'rith** in the U.S., is active in all Jewish communities.

The entire community is represented in governmental matters by the Jewish Board of Deputies. The Board is the community's **World Jewish Congress** affiliate, and is also linked with the **Board of Deputies** of English Jewry, and the U.S. B'nai B'rith, in the Coordinating Board of Jewish Organizations in the UN Economic and Social Council.

SOUTH AMERICA. *See* **Latin America**.

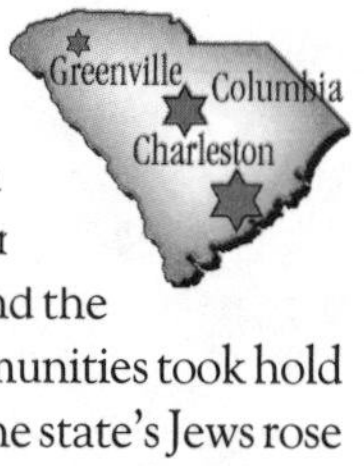

SOUTH CAROLINA. Most of the state's 8,000 Jews live in Charleston (3,500), Columbia (2,500), Greenville (1,200), and Myrtle Beach (425). Jewish life dates back to the 17th centur[illegible] when Sephardic Jews first arrived from Europe and the West Indies. In the late 18th century Jewish communities took hold in Charleston and in Columbia. The fortunes of the state's Jews rose and fell. At one point, Charleston was the leading Jewish community in North America. The state's Jews fought in the Civil War, but during Reconstruction many left. In the late 19th century an influx of Jews arrived from eastern Europe. Today, there are seven Reform and four Conservative synagogues in the state.

SOUTH DAKOTA. After the Civil War small numbers of Jews arrived in the state, mostly merchants. Others followed and tried farming, for the most part unsuccessfully. Today, there are about 300 Jews, with close to 200 living in Sioux Falls, where there is a Reform temple. Aberdeen has a Conservative congregation.

SOUTINE, CHAIM. *See* **Art.**

SPAIN. The first Jewish settlement in Spain is veiled by the mists of time. Did they come with the **Phoenicians** who had established trading stations in Andalusia? This might account for an ancient Jewish tradition that Jews settled in Spain in the time of King **Solomon.** However, it is evident that by the 1st century C.E., there were Jews in Spain, for the Christian apostle, Paul, spoke of visiting them there. During the unsettled times of the declining Roman empire, in which commerce and travel were very difficult, many Spanish Jews became farmers. They were held in respect by their neighbors, and Christian farmers sômetimes called a Jew to bless their crops, as was the custom of the time. This condition could not be pleasing to the Christian clergy, and beginning with their Council at Elvira, in 303, councils passed various resolutions designed to break such peaceful relationships with Jews.

Beginning with the 5th century, during the early Visigoth rule of Spain, there was mutual trust between the rulers and Jews, who were merchants in, the large cities and owners of large agricultural estates, as well as artisans and workmen of all kinds. In 589, when the Visigoth King Recared became a Roman Catholic, the bishops obtained power to prohibit Judaism. Jews were given the choice of becoming Catholics or of leaving the country. This edict was not strictly enforced until the ruthless reign of King Sisebut (612-621). For a century and a half, the Jewish struggle for survival continued. Some Jews escaped from the country; some were forcibly converted and practiced Judaism secretly until the welcome Muslim invasion in 711.

In the five centuries that followed, under the rule of the various Muslim dynasties, and even under some of the newly formed Christian kingdoms, Jews had a large measure of religious freedom. Many who had fled the country returned in numbers. They also grew in power and entered every major avenue of life. Discrimination and persecution were sporadic and not too severely applied. Accompanying the increasing economic opportunities and growth, was a Jewish cultural development so rich that the period became known as the Golden Age of Spain. The Moorish scholars of Spain became the leaders in the science, poetry and philosophy of the Mediterranean lands. Under their influence, Jewish scholars, physicians, and grammarians, philosophers, poets, and commentators entered a period of brilliant creativity. The storied cities of Cordova, Toledo, Granada, and others were the homes of these men and great centers of Jewish learning. Among the first of these writers was Hasdai **Ibn Shaprut**, Jewish scholar and a patron of Jewish scholarship. Court physician to Caliph Abd-al-Rahaman in 10th-century Cordova, Hasdai was also a linguist, and served the ruler as interpreter and unofficial advisor in the conduct of affairs with foreign diplomats at the court. There were the great grammarians, from Menachem ben Saruk to Jonah Ibn Jannah, who charted the course of the Hebrew language and ordered its ways. Greatest in a galaxy of poets, Solomon **Ibn Gabirol**, Judah **Ha-Levi**, and Moses **Ibn Ezra** distilled new beauties from the ancient Hebrew tongue. The roster of famous names that illuminates this period includes Samuel Ibn Naghdella, the grocer who became a diplomat, and Moses **Maimonides**, the philosopher and commentator who went into exile because persecutions had begun to tarnish the Golden Age.

After the Christians completed their reconquest of Spain, the power of the Church in general and of some religious orders in particular grew very great. Gradually, the Inquisition closed in upon the Jews, and under its pressures, the Jewish communities suffered. Their diminished creativity resulted in the 13th-century Silver Age of **Nahmanides**, the scholar who inclined to mysticism, Rabbi Solomon Ibn Adret, the religious teacher of Barcelona, and the codifier Rabbi Jacob ben Asher, who died in 1340. In 1480 the **Inquisition** was set up as a permanent religious court in charge of discovering, judging and handing over for punishment all religious offenders. The final triumph of the Inquisition was achieved by the monk Thomas de Torquemada. Under his influence, Queen Isabella and King Ferdinand expelled the Jews from Spain in 1492.

Thereafter, the history of Jews in Spain is the history of the **Marranos**, those who had publicly accepted **Christianity** and secretly practiced Judaism. For centuries, the Marranos were the legitimate prey of the Inquisition, until, for all intents and purposes, it was dissolved at the close of the 18th century. In 1858, the Spanish edict of expulsion was dissolved, but few Jews returned to settle there. By 1904, there were enough of them in Madrid to form a congregation. Yet even then, Jews were not permitted to use a public building as a synagogue. In 1998, the Jewish population in Spain was estimated at 14,000, concentrated mainly in Madrid, Barcelona, and Seville.

SPERTUS COLLEGE OF JEWISH STUDIES, CHICAGO. An institution of higher Jewish learning, founded in 1924 by the Chicago Board of Jewish Education. Reorganized in 1929 to suit the needs of a growing community it includes departments for advanced Hebrew studies, Hebrew teachers' training, general Jewish studies, Sunday School teachers' and cantors' training, and a Women's Institute of Jewish Study. Some courses are offered in cooperation with the University of Chicago. Graduate studies lead to degrees of Master of Hebrew Literature and Doctor of Hebrew Literature. Affiliated with the College are a Summer Camp Institute, founded in 1946, and the Leaf Library and Museum.

SPIELBERG, STEVEN. *See* **Stage and Screen.**

SPINOZA, BARUCH (Benedict) (1632-1677). Philosopher. He was born in **Amsterdam** to a family of Marrano refugees from the Portuguese **Inquisition.** Spinoza received a thorough education in **Bible** and **Talmud**, and wrote a grammar of the Hebrew language. After studying the philosophy of Descartes and Giordano Bruno, he developed views for which he was excommunicated (1655) from the Jewish community. He left Amsterdam, settled in The Hague, and became an optician, grinding lenses for a living. It was dangerous for him to publish his books, since his philosophy was unacceptable to Christian dogma. To keep his freedom of thought,

Baruch Spinoza.

he lived a lonely life, refusing a professorship at the University of Heidelberg, as well as a pension from Louis XIV of France.

In his first work, *A Theological Political Treatise*, Spinoza held that "in a free commonwealth it shall be lawful for every man to think and to speak what he thinks." He completed his masterpiece, *The Ethics*, in 1675, but it was not published until after his death. His philosophy, very important in Western thought, is based on the pantheistic idea: the idea that God is the universe, and everything in it is a manifestation of Him.

SPITZ, MARK. *See* **Sports**.

SPORTS. Jewish athletes have contributed their share to the history of sports all over the world, and have added to the legends of boxing, baseball, track and field, swimming, football, chess, and scores of other major and minor sports.

In ancient Israel, Jews did not show the kind of passion for sports which the ancient Greeks and Romans did, although some Jews were noted gladiators. Physical skills in biblical times were mainly associated with martial arts. In post-biblical times and almost until the 19th century, Jews did not have many opportunities to participate in sports. Beginning in the 19th century, however, Jews in Europe began to participate in sports and even organized such Jewish sports clubs as Ha-Koach of Vienna and the Maccabi clubs throughout Europe.

In the first Olympiad (Athens, 1896), a Hungarian Jew, Hache, won the 100 meter freestyle swimming contest. By the 1990's, Jews won more than 300 Olympic medals.

The following are some of the better known examples of Jews excelling in specific sports:

Boxing. While few Jews box today, in the past there have been more than twenty Jewish boxing champions. In fact, in the late 1700's, Daniel Mendoza of **England** was one of the greatest and earliest Jewish boxing kings, who contributed to the development of that sport. In the U.S., there have been equally outstanding Jewish prize fighters. Benny Leonard, who began to fight in 1912, was for nearly a decade the lightweight champion of the world, and ranks as perhaps the finest titleholder in the 135-pound class. There have been other notable Jewish lightweights, including Al Singer, Lew Tendler, and Jackie "Kid" Berg of England, who did much of his boxing on American shores. Barney Ross, who held both the lightweight and welterweight championships, also gained acclaim as one of boxing's immortals. Battling Levinsky (U.S.) was light heavyweight world champion, 1916-1920. Louis "Kid" Kaplan (U.S.) was featherweight world champion in 1925-1927. Max Baer (U.S.) was heavyweight world champion in 1934. Jackie Fields, at 16, was the youngest American to win an Olympic gold medal, for boxing (welterweight). As the social status of the Jew in America improved, fewer boys participated in boxing. Yet the records show that in one of the roughest sports in the world, Jews have done as well as the best.

Baseball. Fewer Jews have achieved excellence in baseball. As a game played mainly in small towns, it did not produced many Jewish stars. But those Jews who have excelled at baseball are among the top names in the game. Johnny Kling, who caught at the turn of the century and was the best receiver the Chicago Cubs ever had, is considered one of the three or four best catchers in baseball history. And, of course, Hank Greenberg, who played first base and the outfield for the Detroit Tigers in the 1930's and 1940's, is a member of baseball's Hall of Fame and was one of the most potent home-run hitters in the annals of the sport. He hit 58 homers in one year, a mark bettered by Babe Ruth and equaled only by one other man in the game. More recently, Al Rosen, who started at third base for the Cleveland Indians, became a baseball notable when he was voted the Most Valuable Player Award for 1953 in the American League by a unanimous vote, the first time any player had won such an accolade. One of the greatest Jewish baseball stars of contemporary times has been Sandy Koufax, a left-

Benny Leonard.

Sid Luckman.

Barney Ross.

handed pitcher for the Los Angeles Dodgers. Koufax pitched four no-hit, no-run games in his brilliant career, which was cut short at the age of 29 by a chronic arthritic elbow. But his diamond feats won him a place in baseball's Hall of Fame, even though he had a comparatively brief career. His four no-hitters, in consecutive seasons, was a record in itself. In 11 years on the mound, he won acclaim for his remarkable fast ball and his "unhittability." He won the Cy Young Award as the best pitcher of the year three times and the Most Valuable National League Player Award (rarely given to a pitcher) in 1963. He also won the National League Player of the Year Award of the Sporting News in 1963-1965. He established many strikeout records and shutout marks. He was the first pitcher to fan more than 300 batters in two consecutive years. Before that he was the first to strike out 200 men in two years in succession. Koufax also was extraordinarily effective in the World Series. He gained the record of most strikeouts in a four-game Series (23) and the most in a single game (15) against the New York Yankees in 1963. That same year he won 25 games and 26 in 1965.

Other Jewish baseball players have included: Andy Cohen, a N.Y. Giant second baseman, who succeeded the famous Rogers Hornsby; Buddy Myer, who won the American League batting title once; Harry Danning and Sid Gordon of the N.Y. Giants; Ken Holtzmann, a fine left-handed pitcher who twirled a no-hitter himself; Mike Epstein, a pretty good home-run batter; and Ron Blomberg, who showed promise of stardom with the Yankees.

Football, both amateur and professional, also has produced prominent Jewish gridiron stars. The best of them were quarterbacks, the men who called the plays and pitched the passes. Thus, Benny Friedman, great quarterback of the 1920's and later professional football player and coach at **Brandeis University**, Harry Newman of Michigan, and Sid Luckman of the Columbia Lions and the Chicago Bears, are among the football greats. Many other Jews have made All-American football teams, and are remembered by fans.

Basketball once was called "the Jewish game" because of the predominance of Jewish hoop stars. But today the players are extremely tall and no longer come exclusively from metropolitan areas. Still, the accomplishments of Jewish basketball players, in college and professional ranks, is impressive. Nat Holman, once known as "Mr. Basketball," star of the Celtics, a famous professional team, later was the coach of CCNY and led his clubs to many victories. The Long Island University teams, loaded with Jewish players, also won national fame. New York University and St. John's had Jewish stars and led their teams to prominence. Harry Boykoff was notable at St. John's and Adolph Schayes at NYU. Schayes went on to a highly successful pro career. Others who won recognition include Art Heyman, Sid Tanenbaum, Max Zaslofsky and, in more recent years, Neal Walk, the professional star, and Bob Kaufmann, who has made the National Basketball League All-Star team. More notably, Red Holtzman has been a brilliant coach with the New York Knicks, and Red Auerbach was coach and general manager of the Boston Celtics.

Above, Hank Greenberg. Courtesy Bloch Publishing Company. Below, a Sandy Koufax stamp from the island of St. Vincent. Bottom, Tal Brody, holding up the Europe Cup which Israel won in 1977. Courtesy Tal Brody.

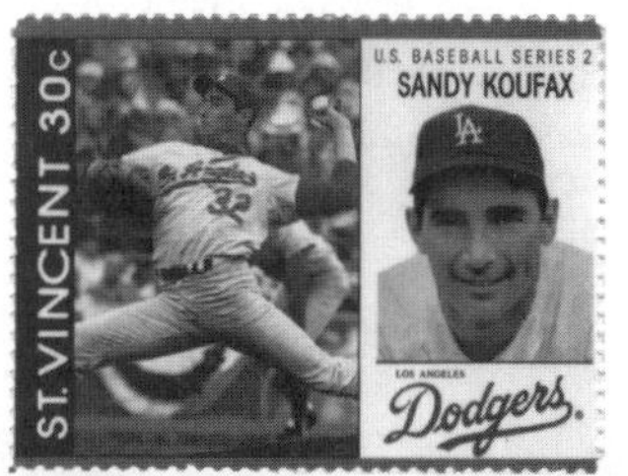

Tennis, once a "social" sport with few Jewish players of the top rank, has undergone major changes. The professional game is now a great deal more important than the amateur sport. Nonetheless, there are not many outstanding Jews in tennis. Dick Savitt won the Wimbledon championship. Herb Flam was a member of the U.S. Davis Cup team. Tom Okker of Holland was one of the top pros in the sport. More recently, Israeli champions Shlomo Glickstein and Amos Mansdorf reached the ranks of the world's best tennis players, and played with the best.

Swimming. Jews have produced some of the greatest swimmers of the 20th century. Johnny Weissmüller, known as the first and best Tarzan in the movies, was the first American to win five gold medals (in the 1920's), and was elected the greatest swimmer of the half-century. Eva Szekely of Hungary set 10 world records in swimming. One of the greatest Jewish names in sports, Mark Spitz, emerged as a result of what happened in the swimming competition in the 1972 Olympic Games in Munich. Spitz won 7 gold medals, the first time this feat has ever been accomplished in the long history of the Games. In 1968, Mark Spitz was considered to be a coming champion, but he was young and failed to do well. By 1972, he had become battle-hard, for he already had competed in the Maccabiah Games in Israel and was ready for top competition. His first championship race was for the 200-meter butterfly. He broke his own world record in this event and immediately placed his foes on the watch for his later achievements. That

Mark Spitz. Courtesy UPI/Corbis-Bettmann.

same evening he won his second gold medal, the 400-meter free-style relay. He was one of a group, but his own contribution was a record time race. The next evening, he took part in the 200-meter free-style. He had to come from behind with a burst of speed to win. But he did. That made it three gold medals and Spitz had become the talk of the Olympic Games. He won 5 gold medals in three days. More were to come. In the end, he had 7, was named the Male Athlete of the Year by the Associated Press, and entered sports history.

Track and Field. Here European and Canadian Jews have produced some of the best. Fanny Rosenfeld of **Canada** won Olympic gold in 400-meter relay in 1928, and was elected in 1950 Canada's best female athlete of the half-century. Harold Abraham of England won the 100 meter dash in the Paris Olympics, and became one of England's leading sprinters. Irena Kirszenstein-Szewinska of **Poland** is considered the greatest female track and field athlete of all time. In the Tokyo Olympics she won gold in the 400 meter relay and silver in the 200 meter. In **Mexico** she won gold in the 200 meter, totaling seven Olympic medals.

Stamp commemorating the 11 Israeli Olympic athletes killed in Munich in 1972.

Gymnastics have seen many Jewish athletes excel. Agnes Kelety of Hungary, saved by Raoul **Wallenberg** during the **Holocaust**, won 5 gold and a total of 11 Olympic medals in the 1940's and 1950's, in gymnastics. She settled in Israel in 1957, and became a member of the Jewish Sports Hall of Fame.

Golf. Here not too many Jews have excelled, but one of the best female golfers of our time is Amy Alcott, who won the U.S. Women's Open in 1980.

Bullfighting. One would hardly ever think to associate Jews with bullfighting, yet **Spain** did produce Jewish bullfighters, and one of the better known bullfighters of the 20th century is Brooklyn-born Sidney Franklin.

Chess, which is considered a sport, has seen scores of Jewish chess masters all over the world, as well as in the U.S. William Steinitz and Emmanuel Lasker held the world title successively for 57 years. Mikhail Botvinnik and Mikhail Tal, both Soviet chess masters, also where world champions. Samuel Reshevsky and Bobby **Fischer** held many American championships and have ranked high on the world scene.

Stamp commemorating the Third Maccabiah.

Sports in Israel. Israelis are avid sports fans who are primarily interested in soccer and in basketball, including American basketball. Military service, which prevents young men during the ages of 18 to 21 from training when they are in their physical prime, accounts for the fact that Israel has not produced more sports champions. However, Israel sends athletes to the Olympic and the Asian Games. Since 1932, the finest amateur Jewish athletes have been competing in Israel in the Maccabiah, a kind of Jewish Olympics.

At the Munich Olympics in August, 1972, Arab terrorists entered the Israeli quarters at the Olympic Village and held members of the Israeli Olympic team as hostages, demanding the release of fellow Arab terrorists jailed in Israel. The Israeli government refused to meet their demand, and after nightfall the German police took the terrorists and their hostages to a nearby airfield from where they expected to fly out of **Germany**. The police opened fire on the terrorists in an attempt to release the prisoners. Eleven Israeli athletes perished in the melee. The entire Olympiad came to a halt with a memorial in honor of the victims, after which the games were resumed.

Yael Arad, the first Israeli to win an Olympic medal.

In the Barcelona Olympics in 1992, a young Israeli woman, Yael Arad, finally brought an Olympic medal back to her country, when she won the silver in judo. In recent years, some of the former Soviet Union athletes and coaches have immigrated to Israel, and have been training Israeli athletes, hence it is to be expected that in the next Olympics in the year 2000 the Israelis will take home a few medals.

STAGE AND SCREEN. Jews have made a vast contribution to the American and the world's entertainment industry, encompassing such areas as vaudeville, comedy, singing, drama, musical stage, radio, motion pictures, and television. Historically, Jews did not cultivate drama and other forms of audiovisual entertainment to the same extent such cultures as the Greek or Roman did. Nevertheless, there is great drama in the **Bible** and in Jewish culture in general, and the emotional aspect in Judaism is well developed. Beginning in the 19th century, Jews in Europe began to take an active part in the theater, both as playwrights, producers, and actors. Rachel Felix and Sarah **Bernhardt** dominated the French stage during the 19th century. Sir Arthur Wing Pinero played a major role in shaping British drama. Many Jews wrote for the stage in **Germany**, including Arthur **Schnitzler** and Hugo von Hoffmannsthal. Max **Reinhardt** achieved prominence as theatrical producer and director.

Rachel Felix.

At the start of the 20th century, as large waves of Jewish immigrants arrived in the U.S., Yiddish theater, which had started to develop in Europe, found a home in **New York**, under the direction of playwrights like Abraham **Goldfaden** and actors like Maurice Schwartz. During the first half of the century, the American Yiddish theater was not only a major source of culture and entertainment for Yiddish-speaking Jews, but also a major source of talent for the American entertainment industry as a whole. Many highly talented performers who got their professional start on the Yiddish stage or in the Yiddish-speaking environment, made the transition to Broadway and to Hollywood, as well as to radio and later television. Early examples were Paul Muni, Al Jolson, Eddie Kantor, Sophie Tucker, Molly Picon, and Fanny Brice. Those were followed by screen greats like Edward G. Robinson, Danny Kaye, Lauren Bacall, Shelly Winters, Esther Williams, Johnny Weissmüller, Kirk Douglas, the Marx Brothers, Jerry Lewis, Zero Mostel, Walter Matthau, and Mel Brooks in the U.S., and Claire Bloom and Peter Sellers in England. The next, fully Americanized generation includes Woody Allen, Billy Crystal, Debra Winger, Dustin Hoffman, Barbra Streisand, and Bette Midler. One could add to the list many Jewish comedians such as George Jessel, Sam Levenson, Milton Berle, George Burns, or, more recently, Paul Reiser and Jerry Seinfeld. Interestingly, the prevalence of Jewish entertainers in the U.S. brought many Yiddish expressions into American English.

Danny Kaye.

Many Jews have written for the American stage and screen. Those include Elmer Rice, George S. Kaufman, Moss Hart, Lilian Hellman, Sidney Kingsley, S.N. Behrman, Clifford Odets, Arthur Miller, Woody Allen, and Neil Simon.

The American motion picture industry in particular is largely the result of the efforts of several Jewish entrepreneurs who created the big studios and made Hollywood the dream factory of the world. Paramount was created by Adolf Zukor; Universal, by Carl Laemmie; Warner Brothers, by Sam, Albert, Harry, and Jack Warner; Metro Goldwyn Mayer, by Louis B. Mayer; 20th Century Fox, by William Fox; and Columbia by Harry Cohn. One of the early movie producers was David Selznick (*Gone with the Wind*), and among the outstanding movie-makers today are Mike Nichols and Steven Spielberg. Motion pictures have been the most popular and universal form of entertainment of the 20th century, and even in the age of television they remain highly popular with old and young.

Barbra Streisand. Courtesy Reuters/Corbis-Bettmann.

STAMPS. Stamp collecting, one of the world's most popular hobbies, reached a high peak of interest among Jews with the establishment of **Israel** and that nation's issuance of attractive postage stamps, but it was not until Israel undertook to print stamps reflecting Jewish and Israeli history, religion, and traditions, that the theme of Jews on stamps became internationally popular.

Countries all over the world have not hesitated to honor prominent Jewish scientists, writers, statesmen, political leaders and other noted personalities on their stamps. The U.S., for example, has issued a stamp in tribute to Samuel **Gompers** the labor leader; another to four chaplains who died heroically during World War II, one of whom, Alexander D. Goode, was a rabbi; a third to Joseph **Pulitzer**, the half-Jewish newspaper publisher. The former Soviet Union has commemoratives for Isaac Levitan, the painter, and Anton Rubinstein, the musician. Ludwig **Zamenhof**, the creator of the international language Esperanto, has been honored on stamps by the Soviet Union, **Brazil**, **Austria**, the **Netherlands**, **Yugoslavia**, and **Bulgaria**. The actress Sarah **Bernhardt** is on a French stamp. Walter **Rathenau**, the statesman assassinated by

Early Israeli stamps.

Germans in **Germany** also has had a stamp issued in his memory by West Germany. **Hungary** has recognized David Schwarz as the inventor of the zeppelin, and West Germany has similarly honored the scientist Paul **Ehrlich**. **Poland**, too, has recalled a tragic but glorious moment in Jewish history by issuing a stamp commemorating the **Warsaw Ghetto** uprising, when trapped Jews chose to fight with small arms against the mechanized might of the German army.

Nearly all the Israeli stamps are, naturally, more directly concerned with Jewish history and tradition. Today, it is a Jewish education in miniature to know the background of each stamp issued by the State of Israel. Many of the symbols and themes reproduced on the stamps were resurrected from Israel's proud and valiant past. Some of the stamps, which commemorate individuals, offer the collector a chance to study the lives of the great scholars and idealists who did so much to influence the course of Jewish history. There are, for example, stamps of Albert **Einstein**, of **Maimonides**, of Chaim **Weizmann**, of Theodor **Herzl**, and of Baron Edmond de **Rothschild**.

The story of the development of the Jewish state can also be studied from the stamps of Israel. There are stamps marking the birth of various **kibbutzim**, or settlements; there is a stamp of **Tel Aviv**, and one of **Jerusalem**, another stamp pays tribute to the **Hebrew** linguists who helped bring about a rebirth of Hebrew as a modern, living tongue. And, of course, many of Israel's remarkable institutions (the **Hebrew University**, the **Haifa Technion**, the **Red Magen David**, (the Israel Red Cross) are commemorated in stamps. Some of the decisive battles against the Arab invaders during the Israel War of Independence are marked in stamps released for each Independence Day; one dedicated to the parachutists who helped save Jewish lives during World War II has been especially popular. Some stamps celebrate the Jewish holidays, taking their inspiration from the **Bible** and from Jewish festivals. To collect stamps of Jewish interest, particularly those from Israel, is to absorb something of the spirit of the Jewish people.

STAR OF DAVID. *See* **Magen David.**

Einstein on a Polish stamp.

Heinrich Heine on a Russian stamp.

Samuel Gompers on an American stamp.

The Warsaw Ghetto fighters on a Polish stamp.

Ludwig Zamenhof on a Hungarian stamp.

Hebrew alphabet on a stamp from Monaco.

STEIN, GERTRUDE (1874-1946). American writer who lived in **Paris**, where she interacted with and influenced American expatriate writers like Hemingway. She wrote in a highly individualized and idiosyncratic style, and is still considered a key figure in the development of 20th century American literature.

STEINBERG, MILTON (1903-1950). American Conservative rabbi who served Park Synagogue in Manhattan from 1933 until his untimely death. Steinberg's insights into modern Jewish life are reflected in his widely read book *Basic Judaism.* He also wrote a historical novel about **Elisha ben Abuyah**, *As a Driven Leaf*.

STEINSALTZ, ADIN (1937-). Israeli Talmudic scholar and writer on traditional Jewish subjects. He has issued a new edition of the Babylonian **Talmud**, with a Hebrew translation. His other books include *The Essential Talmud*, and retelling of Hasidic stories.

STERN COLLEGE FOR WOMEN. *See* **Yeshiva University**.

STERN GROUP. Also known as LEHI, Hebrew acronym for Fighters for the Freedom of Israel. Extremist splinter faction which split off from the **Irgun Z'vai L'umi** in 1940. It was formed by Abraham (Yair) Stern, who was killed by the British in 1942. Believing that the Irgun was not sufficiently aggressive in its fight against British rule in Palestine, the Stern Group resorted to terror tactics, including assassinations, to drive the British out of the country. It dissolved after the establishment of the Jewish state. Some of its leaders have become prominent in Menachem **Begin**'s Herut party (*see* **Revisionist Zionism**). One of them. Yitzhak **Shamir**, was speaker of the Knesset during the period of Israel's peace negotiations with Egypt, and served as Prime Minister of Israel.

STERN, ISAAC. *See* **Music, Jews in.**

STRAUS, NATHAN (1848-1931). Merchant and philanthropist. Born in **Germany**, Straus served as president of the **New York City** Board of Health in 1898. He came to hold this office out of a deep interest in public health. In 1890, he had established a system for the sterilization and distribution of milk to the poor of New York. He installed his own laboratory and distributed pasteurized milk in many cities in the U.S. and abroad. During the panic of 1893-1894, he started a chain of groceries to distribute coal and groceries to the needy. Straus retired from R.H. Macy and Co. in 1914; during World War I, he became a one-man society to relieve the suffering of people all over the world. Deeply interested in Palestine, he joined the Zionist movement, repeatedly visited Palestine, and founded the Nathan and Lina Straus Health Centers of **Hadassah**, in **Tel Aviv** and **Jerusalem**. His self-sacrifice and generosity won him the love and respect of millions.

STRAUS, OSCAR (1870-1954). Composer. Oscar Straus studied music in his native Vienna and Berlin, and began his musical career as a conductor in theaters and cabarets. Although he wrote serious music as well, Straus made his mark as a master of light opera. He composed the music for over fifty operettas, including the much-produced *Waltz Dream* (1907) and *Chocolate Soldier*. Fleeing Nazism, he settled first in France and then in the U.S. in 1940.

Abraham (Yair) Stern.

STRAUS, OSCAR SOLOMON (1850-1926). Diplomat and philanthropist. A brother of Nathan **Straus** he became active in the business enterprises run by his family. He served as U.S. Minister (later Ambassador) to **Turkey** from 1887 to 1890, 1898 to 1900, and again from 1909 to 1910. From 1906 to 1909 he served as U.S. Secretary of Commerce and Labor, the first Jew to hold a position in the U.S. Cabinet. He was active also in Jewish communal affairs and had contacts with Zionist leaders.

STREISAND, BARBRA. *See* **Stage and Screen**.

SUKKOT. The Feast of Booths. Five days after **Yom Kippur**, Jews observe Sukkot, the Feast of Booths, or Tabernacles. This holiday is celebrated for seven days in Palestine and eight days in the Diaspora. During the festival the family gathers for meals in booths erected for the occasion. Beautifully decorated and covered with greenery which permits the stars to shine through, the booths recall the times when Israel wandered in the wilderness after the **Exodus** from **Egypt**. Sukkot is also the Harvest Festival, recalling the days when Israelite farmers went to the fields and lived in lean-tos until the harvest was in. Also associated with the harvest are the lulav, a palm branch flanked with sprigs of willow and myrtle and the **etrog**, or citron. Together, these are the biblical four species, over which a blessing is recited daily during the holiday. They are also carried during Hakafot, a ceremonial march around the synagogue.

Blessing of the Etrog. Painting by Leopold Pilichowski.

Sukkot is one of the *shalosh regalim*, the three Pilgrimage festivals observed in ancient times with Pilgrimages to **Jerusalem**. (The other two are **Passover** and **Shavuot**, the Feast of Weeks, which, like Sukkot, were also harvest festivals.) In olden days, in the Temple, the high point of the Sukkot festivities was *simhat bet ha-Shoevah* (the ceremony of water drawings). The importance of this ceremony was seasonal, for Sukkot comes in the fall, after the long dry summer and just before the rainy season in Israel. Therefore, prayers of thanksgiving were offered for the rains which had made the year's crops grow.

On Shemini Atzeret, which immediately follows Sukkot, prayers for rain during the coming season are chanted. The preceding day is known as Hoshana Rabba, after the prayers beginning with Hoshana, which means "Save us." Many such prayers are said, because it is believed that on Hoshana Rabba the Books of Judgment, sealed on Yom Kippur, are put away until the following year. During the Hoshana Rabba service, willow branches are beaten until all the leaves have fallen off. This is associated both with the rituals of penitence and the seasonal festivities. The beaten willows symbolize the suffering man inflicts upon himself in the search for forgiveness. They also represent the hope that after the trees and plants lose their greenery God will provide new warmth and moisture for the renewal of nature, as well as for man's strength and his trust in God.

Sukkah, Germany, early 19th century. The Israel Museum, Jerusalem.

Shemini Atzeret and Simhat Torah are associated with Sukkot, but are not properly part of that festival. The former dates from biblical times. Because it was the occasion of the crucial prayers for rain, it was marked with great solemnity. Simhat Torah (The Rejoicing of the Law) is a joyous holiday. It arose after the Rabbis instituted the practice of reading through the entire **Torah** (Five Books of Moses) in the synagogue each year. On Simhat Torah the last portion of one year's cycle is read, and a new cycle is begun with the reading of the first portion of **Genesis**. Hakafot, an "encircling" procession with Torah scrolls, is the special mark of the day. Special attention is paid to children, who join in the Hakafot with flags and singing.

Simchat Torah, Livorno, Italy, 1841. Courtesy the Jewish Museum, New York.

SULZBERGER FAMILY. Distinguished American Jewish family, originating in Salzburg in southern **Germany**. Four branches of the family emigrate to the U.S. in the 19th century.

Mayer Sulzberger (1843-1923), brought to **Philadelphia** in 1849, became one of that city's leading judges. He was a scholar of Jewish history, publishing studies on the legal and political institutions of ancient Judea. Cyrus Leo Sulzberger (1858-1932), his cousin, settled in **New York** and prospered in the textile trade. Entering municipal politics as a liberal, he maintained a lifelong interest in Jewish communal affairs, serving as president of the Jewish Agricultural and Industrial Aid Society and of the United Hebrew Charities. Although opposed to Jewish nationalism, he was vice-president of the Federation of American Zionists. Cyrus's son, Arthur Hays Sulzberger, studied at Columbia University, and joined *The New York Times* in 1919. He became its publisher in 1935. A supporter of the New Deal, he campaigned for active U.S. participation in world affairs. Other well-known Sulzbergers include Cyrus L., foreign correspondent, and Marion B., leading dermatologist.

SURA. *See* **Babylonia**.

SURINAM (DUTCH GUIANA). Dutch possession on the northeastern coast of South America. Surinam is the home of the Jewish community with the longest continuous history in the Western Hemisphere. Established in 1630, it was augmented in the 1650's and 1660's by Jews from **Brazil** and **England**. In 1665, the English, who held the territory for a time, granted full religious freedom to "the Hebrew Nation" residing there. The Dutch confirmed this freedom when Surinam was returned to them two years later. In 1682, the Brazilian Jews, who had prospered in the cultivation of sugar, founded a colony at Woden Savanne (Savannah of the Jews). This community survived until 1832, when fire destroyed the village. Most if its inhabitants moved to Paramaribo, where German Jews had settled in the 18th century. The present Jewish community, numbering about 200, is concentrated in the

Early synagogue in Surinam

capital. Some of its members are refugees who arrived from Europe during World War II. The community is organized in **Sephardic** and **Ashkenazic** congregations, both of which are represented in the Central Committee for Jewish Affairs.

SWEDEN. One of the Scandinavian countries. Few Jews lived there until the late 18th century. Jews have since played an important part in the life of the country, especially in the arts, and the old residents are well integrated in Swedish life. The rate of intermarriage is probably higher in Sweden than in any other country in Europe. Sweden received a large number of refugees from the **Holocaust**. In 1998, the Jewish population of 15,000 was more than double that of 1933. About 6,000 live in Stockholm and vicinity, 2,000 each in Goteborg and Malmo, 350 in Boras, and 250 in Narrkoping. There is a central Council of Mosaic Communities. The Jewish community as a whole, including the "Vikings," as the old families are called, are keenly interested in **Israel**.

SWITZERLAND. Located between **Germany**, **Italy,** and **France**. It had some Jewish inhabitants during the Middle Ages. At the time of the Black Death, Jews were viciously massacred, and 1622 the Swiss Diet expelled all Jews. There was a gradual return, beginning in the late 17th century. The federal constitution of 1874 finally abolished Jewish disabilities.

During World War II, Switzerland gave shelter to a limited number of refugees, some of whom have remained. In 1996 there were about 18,000 Jews in Switzerland of whom about 6,800 were in Zurich, 4,400 in Geneva and 2600 in Basle, with the rest scattered in other communities.

SYNAGOGUE. From Greek, meaning assembly. In Hebrew, *Bet Knesset,* or House of Meeting. The synagogue can be traced back to the period following the destruction of the First **Temple** in 586 B.C.E. The exiled Jews in **Babylonia** gathered at first in private homes, later in special buildings, to read from the Scriptures and to observe holidays. Even when the Temple was rebuilt in 537 B.C.E., the number of houses of worship continued to increase. Following the destruction of the Second Temple in 70 C.E., the synagogue assumed a central place in Jewish religious and communal life. Wherever Jews settled, they established a place of worship and study. During the Middle Ages, the synagogue was the hub from which the religious, educational, social and charitable spokes of community life radiated. Wherever the Jewish communities moved, the synagogue moved with them and flourished.

The structure and magnificence of the synagogue varied depending upon the degree of religious freedom. In countries where Jews were oppressed their building was often restricted. But where Jews were permitted some measure of freedom, especially in the ancient East, beautiful structures were erected. Excavations in Dura Europos (**Syria**), Capernaum, and Bet Alpha in Palestine have uncovered the remains of highly ornate houses of prayer.

Traditionally, the worshipers in the synagogue face east, toward **Jerusalem**. Into the eastern wall of the structure is built the Holy **Ark**, where the **Torah** Scrolls are kept. This Ark is often lavishly decorated and ornamented with symbolic paintings of lions, eagles, and ceremonial objects such as the ram's horn, **Menorah**, and musical instruments. The two tablets of the covenant inscribed with the **Ten Commandments** and surmounted by the Torah crown are generally placed above the Ark. A richly embroidered velvet or satin curtain is draped before the Ark. Suspended from the ceiling nearby hangs the Ner Tamid, the eternal light, which, as the name suggests, must never be extinguished. Traditionally, the Bimah, or pulpit, is located in the center of the house of prayer. The Amud, or reader's stand, which is directly in front of the Ark, is decorated by a tall seven-branched candelabrum. In Orthodox synagogues, a separate seating section is provided for the women.

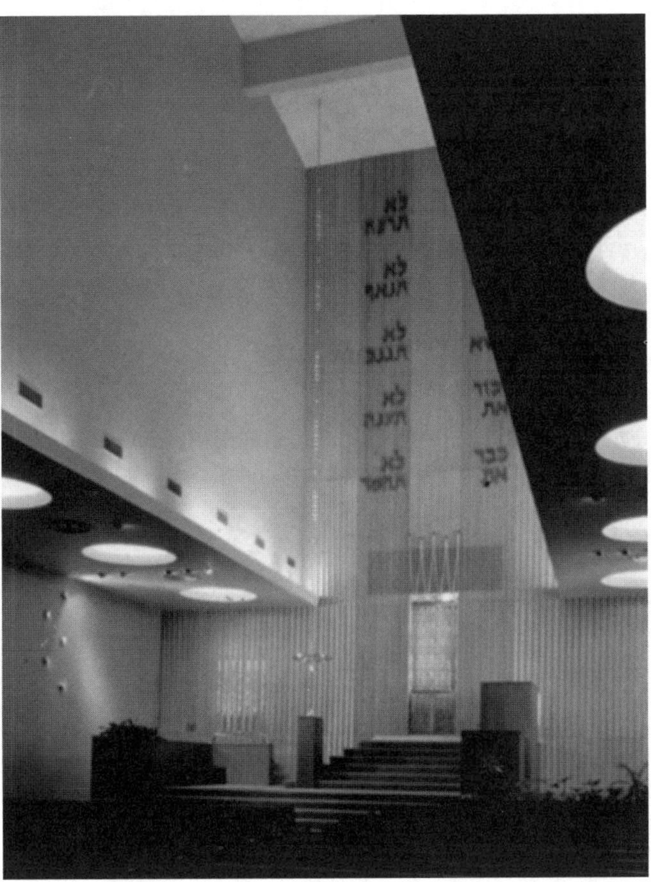

Mount Zion Temple, St. Paul, Minnesota. Eric Mendelsohn, Architect.

SYRIA. The Aram of the Old Testament, called Syria in the **Septuagint**. It became a free Arab republic in 1946, and, with **Lebanon**, covers most of the northwest horn of the Fertile Crescent. During the Hellenistic period, particularly in the time of **Herod** the Great (36-4 B.C.E.), a considerable Jewish community gathered in Syria. Jews were accorded equal rights, but in the course of the wars in Israel many were massacred. With the advance of **Christianity** many Jews were forcibly baptized. The invasion of the Arabs in the 7th century brought Jews greater religious tolerance but placed them in an inferior status. Jews congregated mainly in the large cities, Damascus, the capital, Aleppo, and Tripoli, largely as traders and craftsmen. They numbered about 18,000 but never became a strong cultural community. In 1840, the Syrian Jews suffered the effects of the **Damascus** blood libel. World Jewry intervened, and rescued the Damascus Jews from mob violence.

Since the **Six-Day War**, Syrian Jews have suffered constant harassment and persecution officially sponsored by the government and carried out by the police, as a result of which a worldwide movement has been established to help reduce the number of

Syrian Jews and bring them out of Syria. As of 1998, hopes that Syria would enter into peace negotiations with Israel have not materialized. In 1982, Israel's Operation Peace for Galilee sought to challenge and defeat Syria's pro-PLO military base in Lebanon. Despite a resounding defeat, the Syrians were rearmed by the USSR and were influential in forcing the abrogation of the Israel-Lebanese peace treaty concluded in 1983. In 1984, an unprecedented exchange of Syrian and Israeli prisoners of war occurred when 291 Syrian soldiers and officers were exchanged for six Israelis (three soldiers and three civilians). In 1992 the Syrian government allowed some Jews to leave. By 1998, only 250 Jews remained in Syria.

SYRKIN, NACHMAN (1867-1924). Labor Zionist leader. As a boy in **Russia**, he was active in the **Hibbat Zion** movement. He saw Socialist Zionism as a modern expression of the Hebrew prophets' teachings of justice for all men. Syrkin became one of the earliest founders of the Labor Zionist party (*see* **Labor Zionism**). Returning to Russia, he took part in the 1905 revolution against the oppressive, corrupt Tsarist government. He came to America in 1908, where he continued his Zionist work, and also became active in the **American Jewish Congress**. After World War I, he helped organize the Jewish delegation to the **Versailles Peace Conference**, and served as one of its delegates. A biography of Syrkin was published in 1960 by his daughter Marie Syrkin, a noted Zionist writer.

Henrietta Szold.

SZEKELY, EVA. *See* **Sports.**

SZELL, GEORGE. *See* **Music, Jews in.**

SZOLD, HENRIETTA (1860-1945). Founder of **Hadassah**. She was born in **Baltimore**, the eldest of Rabbi Benjamin Szold, a scholar and leader of Conservative Judaism. Rabbi Szold guided his daughter's education, and from early youth, Henrietta Szold became a companion and an assistant to her father in his complex tasks. Broad sympathy and understanding for all manner of human beings were a part of her environment. In her home she became acquainted with work for the liberation of the former slaves. When the flood of Jewish immigration from Eastern Europe poured into America, the Szold home gave shelter, aid, and guidance to all within its reach. Henrietta Szold, teaching at the time at a fashionable girls' school, founded, managed, and taught in one of the first night schools for immigrants in the United States.

Henrietta Szold had shared in her father's scholarly interests and had written articles for periodicals since she was 17. When the **Jewish Publication Society of America** (JPS) was organized in 1888, she became a volunteer member of its publication committee, and from 1893 to 1916 was its paid literary secretary. In this capacity, her translation labors included editing a five-volume translation of **Graetz**'s *History of the Jews*. She also translated and edited the seven-volume *Legends of the Jews* by Louis **Ginzberg**. In addition, she edited, together with Cyrus **Adler**, the *American Jewish Year Book*.

Szold's **Zionism** was a natural development. It grew out of the home atmosphere, and was nourished by her scholarly preoccupation with Jewish history and literature. In 1895 Szold made her first Zionist speech before the Baltimore section of the **National Council of Jewish Women**. In 1909, she went to Europe with her mother. The trip included a visit to Palestine from where she wrote: "If not Zionism, then nothing," and, "there are heroic men and women here doing valiant work. If only they could be more intelligently supported by the European and American Jews." What she saw of disease and suffering in Palestine, and her own dislike of holding theories without translating them into action, bore fruit in 1912. The Hadassah Study Circle, to which Henrietta Szold had belonged since 1907, was transformed into a national women's organization that undertook the practical task of fund raising for health work in Palestine. Its first goal, a system of visiting began modestly in 1913 with the arrival of two American-trained nurses who set up a small welfare station in **Jerusalem**.

> *If not Zionism, then nothing.*
>
> — HENRIETTA SZOLD

That same year, Szold began a series of tours of the **United States** for Hadassah; Hadassah grew in strength and membership. During World War I, Supreme Court Justice Louis D. **Brandeis**, head of the Provisional Zionist Committee, entrusted Henrietta Szold with the responsibility for organizing the American Zionist Medical Unit for Palestine. In the autumn of 1918, equipment for a 50-bed hospital and a group of 44 doctors, nurses, dentists, sanitary engineers and administrators arrived in Palestine. Szold joined them in 1920, and from then until 1927, she divided her time between Hadassah's work in Palestine and in the U.S. Even after she had settled permanently in Palestine and undertook other major responsibilities, she remained dedicated to Hadassah's work. She was elected honorary president of Hadassah in 1926. In 1933, Szold laid the foundation stone for the Rothschild Hadassah University Hospital. When World War II broke out, she served on the Hadassah Emergency Committee that was engaged in solving the problems created by the war. As a result of her survey and recommendations, Hadassah established the Alice Seligsberg Trade School for Girls in Jerusalem.

In 1927, Szold had been elected one of the three members of the Palestine Executive Committee of the **World Zionist Organization**, the first woman ever to serve in this capacity. Her portfolios were education and health. Since, however, the other two members of the Executive (Harry Sacher and Colonel Frederick Kisch) were frequently abroad for long periods, the task of political work and of negotiations with the Palestine government in behalf of the Yishuv fell upon her. The prevailing attitude toward women added to the delicacy of the task. The Yishuv had to learn how to accept guidance from a woman. How successful she was may be seen in her election in 1930 to serve on the Vaad Leumi, the National Council of Jews in Palestine, which entrusted her with the responsibility for social welfare. She trained social workers for the whole country, and in 1941 initiated an educational and correctional system for young offenders.

At age 73, she wanted to return to America "to be coddled by my sisters," but her deep sense of responsibility made her shoulder a new undertaking. In 1933, Nazism had come to power in Germany, and German Jews began to migrate to Palestine. The year before had seen the onset of a youth immigration into Palestine. Inevitably, Szold assumed the task of developing the Youth Aliyah movement initiated by Recha **Freier**. As organizer and leader of Youth Aliyah, she first worked out a program of education that would give individual attention to each child. Afterward, she guided the immigration, reeducation, and resettlement of these children, straining to establish a personal contact at some point with each child.

In 1942, her concern for the problem of Arab-Jewish relations led her to join the Ihud (Unity) movement, an organization for the promotion of good relations between Arabs and Jews and for the formation of a binational Arab-Jewish state in Palestine. Henrietta Szold received many honors from Jews and non-Jews alike. Not the least of these was the enduring deep regard of her close associates and coworkers for the astonishing variety of her endeavors to help humanity.

SZYK, ARTHUR (1894-1951). Artist. Born in **Poland**, he studied in **Paris** and came to America in 1940. Noted for his book illuminations, including the **Passover Haggadah** and the U.S. and Israel Declarations of Independence.

Overleaf: Passover plate, silver. Vienna, Austria, 1815. Courtesy Marsh Photo.

TABERNACLE. In Hebrew, *ohel moed*, literally, "tent of meeting." Also called *mishkan*, the sanctuary which was a symbol of God's presence among the Children of Israel. According to the **Bible**, the Tabernacle was built by the Israelites in the wilderness after their exodus from **Egypt** (Ex. 25-27). It became the first sanctuary where sacrifices were offered and services were conducted by priests and **Levites**. Bezalel and Oholiab were the principal artists in charge of building and decorating it. The Tabernacle, a square portable tent, stood on the western side of its forecourt, pointed in the direction of the Promised Land. The forecourt was enclosed by wooden columns draped with blue, purple, and scarlet hangings. At the entrance to the Tabernacle stood the laver, a copper basin where the priests washed before they brought the sacrifices on the altar. The acacia-wood altar was overlaid with copper and had four horns. Within the Tabernacle in the Holy Place stood the gold overlaid wooden table holding the twelve shewbreads. There, too, was the seven-branched candelabra, accessible by stairs. The gilded incense altar was centered in front of the veil that hung from four gilded pillars and hid the Holy of Holies. The Holy of Holies held the **Ark of the Covenant** and the stone tablets of the **Ten Commandments**. By day a dark cloud and by night a fiery cloud rested upon the Tabernacle. It was located in the center of the camp, and, forming a living square around it, the twelve tribes of Israel marched on their 40-year journey to the Promised Land.

When the Children of Israel settled in **Canaan**, the Tabernacle rested at Shiloh, almost in the center of the Land. In the time of King **David**, the service in the sanctuary took on a new significance as the favored center of worship. After an overwhelming victory over the **Philistines**, the king built a splendid new Tabernacle on Mt. Zion. Then, dancing at the head of a procession of Levites who played musical instruments, David brought the Holy Ark to its new sanctuary in the capital, and **Jerusalem** became the holy city in Israel. Until King **Solomon** built the Temple, the Tabernacle on Mt. Zion was the place of worship for the nation.

TABERNACLES, FEAST OF. *See* **Sukkot.**

TABLETS OF THE LAW. *See* **Moses** *and* **Ten Commandments**.

TAF. Twenty-second letter of the Hebrew, alphabet; numerically, 400.

TALLIT. Prayer shawl, usually of silk or wool, sometimes banded with silver or gold thread, and fringed at each of the four corners in accordance with biblical law (Num. 15:38). The wearing of the tallit at worship is obligatory only for married men, but it is customarily worn also by males of **Bar Mitzvah** age and older. Occasionally it is spread over the marriage canopy or used as a burial shroud. In recent years, some women have begun to wear tallits.

TALMID HAKHAM. Literally, disciple of the wise. Any scholar or authority on the Talmud. For many centuries, the Talmid Hakham was respected as the social aristocrat of the Jewish community. Conversely, at the opposite end of the social ladder was the **Am Ha-Aretz**, or ignoramus. During the Middle Ages, the Talmid Hakham was consulted as an authority on worldly and religious affairs, even when he held no official position in the community.

Numerous pithy savings in the Talmud reflect the position of the scholar in Jewish life. Perhaps the most typical and most frequently quoted is, "*Talmidei Hakhamim* increase peace in the world." Another frequent quotation mirroring the same attitude is the biblical proverb, "The learning of the wise man is a source of life" (Prov. 13:14).

TALMUD. Literally, study or teaching. Legal code whose compilation spans almost 1,000 years. Based on the teachings of the **Bible**, the Talmud interprets biblical laws and commandments, branching out into many fields of knowledge. Although dealing primarily with law, the Talmud also contains a rich store of historic facts and traditions. In its pages are found scientific discussions, ethical teachings, legends, and profound observations on all phases of human experience.

Young Talmud student in a Jerusalem yeshiva.

The Talmud is composed of two basic divisions: the Mishnah and the Gemarah. The Mishnah is the interpretation of the biblical law as handed down over time as the "Oral Tradition." The Gemarah represents a commentary on the Mishnah by a group of later scholars, the **Amoraim**.

The Mishnah has its origin in the period following the return of the Jews from Babylonian captivity (515 B.C.E.). **Ezra the Scribe** is believed to have founded the Great Assembly, a supreme Jewish religious and legislative authority. The distinguished scholars of this learned body set certain basic rules for the interpretation of Jewish law. They instituted the prayer of *Shmoneh Esreh*, or The Eighteen Benedictions, and edited some of the books of the Bible. Out of the Great Assembly arose the Scribes, who represented the official copyists of the Bible and taught its laws. They were followed by the **Tannaim**, sages who continued for several generations to develop methods of interpreting the laws contained in the Bible. As life progressed, new problems and situations arose that demanded a broader and clearer defining of biblical law. The schools of the Tannaim dealt with the urgent legal needs of their time. The discussions, arguments, ordinances, and interpretations of the Tannaim are known as the Oral Tradition, as distinguished from the Written Law, that is, the Bible itself.

The oral traditions of the Tannaim, from the days of the great scholars **Hillel** and **Shammai**, needed classification and editing. Some of the laws were systematized by the great scholars Rabbi **Akiba** and his pupil Rabbi Meir. The major task of arranging the *halachot*, or laws, fell to **Judah the Prince** (Yehudah Hanasi). He was head of the **Sanhedrin**, the highest court of Jewish law (about 200 C.E.).

The final form of the Mishnah consists of six sections, or orders, which include all the laws and customs which govern traditional Jewish religious life to this present day. The six sections are divided into 63 tractates, or treatises; each tractate is subdivided into chapters, and each chapter is further divided into paragraphs.

ב ברכות פרק ראשון מאימתי

First page of the Talmud. The text of the Mishnah and the Gemarah, found in the center, is surrounded by commentaries.

The following are the six sections of the Mishnah:

First, *Zeraim* (Seeds) contains laws relating to agriculture. The first treatise in this section, *Berachot*, deals mainly with prayers.

Second, *Moed* (Appointed Time) refers to laws involving the Sabbath, festivals, feasts, and fast days. A separate treatise is devoted to each important festival: Rosh ha-Shanah, Sukkot, Passover, and others.

Third, *Nashim* (Women) deals with laws concerning family life.

Fourth, *Nezikim* (Damages), the section studied most often, discusses civil and criminal laws. This section includes the treatise *Avot* (**Ethics of the Fathers**), a collection of moral teachings, epigrams, and acute observations on human conduct.

Fifth, *Kodashim* (Holy Objects), concerned mainly with sacrificial rites, laws dealing with **shehitah**, or ritual slaughter and kosher and non-kosher foods. (*See also* **Dietary Laws**.)

Last, *Tahorot* (Purity) states all the laws of cleanliness and uncleanliness, known as ritual purity (*see* **Purity Laws**).

The Mishnah is written in Hebrew. Its style is expressive, forceful, exact, and terse. It is a development of the biblical Hebrew, enriched by new words and forms, assimilating **Aramaic** and some Greek and Latin terms.

The opinions of the Tannaim which were not included in the Mishnah are called *baraitot*, or external traditions. These opinions were assembled separately and are quoted in the text of the Gemarah. Similarly, the *Tosefta* (literally, additions) contains discussions of the laws by the Tannaim and is written in the style of the Mishnah.

Actually, there are two Talmuds: one Palestinian and one Babylonian. Some time after the Mishnah was edited in its final form, called the canon, the **Amoraim**, scholars in **Palestine** and **Babylonia**, began an intensive study of the Mishnah. In the course of interpreting and discussing the laws and decisions of their predecessors, the Tannaim, they often found obscure passages and contradictory opinions in the Mishnah. The Amoraim sought to reconcile the varying opinions and draw clear conclusions from the mass of conflicting material. From around 200 to 500, after the completion of the Mishnah, this intellectual activity continued. The commentaries on the Mishnah by the Amoraim are known as the *Gemarah*, Hebrew for "completed."

Among the foremost Amoraim was Johanan bar Napaha, the son of a blacksmith. He rose to fame as the head of a famous academy and as a teacher of scholars. His brother-in-law, Simeon bar Lakish (or Reish Lakish), was once a gladiator and a highwayman. Rabbi Johanan convinced him to the study of the Law, and bar Lakish became a brilliant Talmudic scholar.

The editing of the Palestinian Talmud took place during the period when **Christianity** was becoming entrenched in the Roman Empire. Jews of Palestine were forced to escape to Babylonia by Roman persecutions. Centers of Jewish learning in Palestine deteriorated. The scholars who remained, concerned with the decline in the study of the Law, compiled the work of the Palestinian Amoraim. Of their interpretations of the Mishnah only four sections have survived: Zeraim, Moed, Nashim, and Nezikin. The Palestinian, or Jerusalem Talmud, although rich in legal, moral, and **aggadic** material, bears the mark of incompleteness. It is written in the Aramaic mixed with Hebrew that was spoken in Palestine at that time.

Like the Palestinian Talmud, the Babylonian Talmud, the work of the Babylonian Amoraim, consists of the Mishnah and its commentary, the Gemarah. It is much wider in scope, embracing the religious, communal, and social Jewish life for many centuries. As the source-book of Jewish law, it became the most important guide and companion of Jews throughout the ages. The Babylonian Talmud is also an encyclopedic work, embodying all that was known of medicine, agriculture, history, geography, and astronomy at the time of its creation.

The Babylonian Talmud is the monumental work of approximately 2,000 scholars. Among the foremost Amoraim were Rav and Samuel. Rav was born in Babylonia and studied at the academy of Judah ha-Nasi in Palestine. When he returned to Babylonia, in about 220 C.E., he established the famous academy of Sura. A great scholar of the Law, he was also the author of masterly liturgical poems, legends, and parables. Rav's comrade Samuel was also a pupil of Judah ha-Nasi. Upon his return to Babylonia, he too became head of another famous academy in Nehardea. Thoroughly learned in medicine, astronomy, and the natural sciences, Samuel's opinions were decisive in all laws involving monetary matters.

Six generations of Amoraim contributed to the interpretation and clarification of the law. The last of the Amoraim, Rav Ashi, who revived the Academy of Sura, assembled all the works of his predecessors dealing with law, ethics, religious thought, legends, and the general knowledge of the day. He systematized the vast accumulation of material, accomplishing a task equal to that of Judah ha-Nasi, editor of the Mishnah. The work of Rav Ashi, who died in 427 C.E., was continued by Rabbina and Jose. They completed the final editing of the Babylonian Gemarah in the year 500. The **Saboraim**, scholars who lived in the beginning of the 6th century, clarified further the text of the Talmud and helped to give it the form which it has retained to this day.

Studying the Talmud. Woodcut by Joseph Budko.

The Babylonian Talmud follows the order arrangement of the Mishnah. However, only 36 treatises of the 63 contained in the Mishnah are supplemented by the comments of the Amoraim, or the Gemarah.

The two fundamental elements of the Talmud are **Halakhah**,

Learning is a life-long pursuit for this old Jew.

composed of legal discussions, and **Aggadah**, consisting of legends, tales, and fables. They are almost always poetic and moving; the aggadot attempt to teach a moral lesson.

Among the great codifiers of Talmudic law were Issac **Alfasi** and **Maimonides**. The aggadic part of the Talmud was compiled and published separately by Rabbi Jacob Haviv (1460-1516) under the name En Yaakov.

It can be safely said that the Talmud served as the greatest force in preserving the unity and integrity of Jews in the Diaspora. Jewish religious life revolved around it. The Talmud regulated every act and every hour of the day. Its lofty moral teachings sustained the Jewish spirit in the dark days of persecution. As soon as Jewish children had some grounding in the Bible and its commentaries, especially **Rashi**, they dived into the "Sea of Talmud." Many emerged eventually as scholars of Jewish law, fortified by the high ideals and wisdom of the sages. The Talmud and its commentaries are a most fascinating and significant product of the Jewish religious genius.

TAM, RABBENU (Jacob ben Meir) (1100-1171). Talmudic scholar. Grandson of the famous commentator, **Rashi**, he was the head of a school of Talmudists whose works are called *Tosafot*, or additions. These scholars, or Tosafists, analyzed the opinions in the **Talmud**. Their comments and discussions are characterized by keen and critical examination of' Talmudic law. They also dealt with problems arising in their time and rendered important decisions which influenced Jewish life and institutions throughout the Middle Ages.

Rabbenu Tam, whose surname "Tam" means perfect, was rich and influential, as well as modest and forthright. On the festival of **Shavuot** in 1147, he was nearly killed by Crusaders. He was saved by a knight who took him under his protection. From his native town of Rameru, he moved to Troyes, where he opened an important Talmudic academy. Rabbenu Tam became the spiritual leader of all the Jewish communities of **France**. He called for assemblies of rabbis to discuss new decisions. As many as 150 rabbis participated in these assemblies, which helped strengthen Jewish unit and regulate religious life for many generations.

TAMMUZ. Tenth month of the Jewish calendar. The 17th of Tammuz is a fast day commemorating the beginning of the fall of Jerusalem in 586 B.C.E.

TANNAIM. From Aramaic, literally, "those who repeat." Teachers and scholars of the first two centuries C.E. who set down the laws of the **Talmud**. They were called Tannaim because they were teachers who taught their students to rehearse the Oral Tradition, based on the Written Law of the Bible, for the purpose of memorization. The group of laws taught by a Tanna was called his Mishnah, or repetition. Among the nearly 300 Tannaim were the famous rabbis Johanan ben **Zakkai**, **Akiba**, Meir, Joshua ben Hananyah, Nahum of Gimzo, Eliezer ben Hyracanus, Eleazor ben Azaryah, and **Judah the Prince**. (*See also* **Talmud**.)

TANYA. Classic book about **Hasidism** by Shneor Zalman of Lyady, the founder of the Habad movement.

TARBUT. Literally, culture. After the first Russian revolution in 1917, Hebrew culture flourished among Russian Jews. An organization called Tarbut was founded and established cultural institutions, teacher's seminaries, and schools. Tarbut published Hebrew newspapers for adults and children and contributed to the revival of Hebrew as a spoken language. However, the Tarbut movement was short-lived. As soon as the Soviet regime was established, it banned all of the widespread Tarbut activities. Tarbut organizations then sprang up in other Eastern European

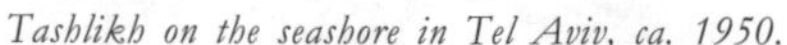

Tashlikh on the seashore in Tel Aviv, ca. 1950.

Technion City on the slopes of Mount Carmel.

countries, especially in **Poland** and **Lithuania**. They made an important contribution to modern Hebrew education. On the eve of World War II, 70,000 pupils were enrolled in Tarbut schools. These were destroyed by the Nazis, together with the vast majority of Eastern European Jewry.

TARGUM. Literally, translation. Usually applied to the **Aramaic** translation of the Bible, of which the best known is **Targum Onkelos**. An Aramaic translation was necessary to make the Bible understandable to the large number of Jews who spoke Aramaic for many generations during and following the period of the Second **Temple**. Targum Onkelos is an excellent, almost literal translation. To this day, many editions of the Bible carry the Targum Onkelos, which in many instances enables us to interpret more correctly the original Hebrew text. (*See also* **Onkelos**.)

TASHLIKH. The ceremony of casting one's sins into the sea, observed on the first day of the New Year near a body of water. (*See* **Rosh Ha-shanah**.)

TECHNION, ISRAEL INSTITUTE OF TECHNOLOGY IN HAIFA. The Technion is the oldest educational institution of university rank in **Israel**. It was founded in 1912 by a group of far-sighted men from around the world, including K.Z. Wissotsky of Moscow, Jacob H. **Schiff** of **New York**, Julius **Rosenwald** of **Chicago**, and Dr. Paul Nathan of Berlin. The outbreak of World War II delayed the opening of the Technion until 1924. Since then its graduates have supplied more than half of the technically trained manpower for the scientific and industrial development programs of Israel.

The original institute was built at the foot of Mt. Carmel, intended to accommodate about 300 students. Today close to 9,000 students are enrolled in the Technion, the affiliated Junior Technical College, and Technical High School. A new campus, Technion City, consisting of 300 acres on the slopes of Mt. Carmel, was deeded to the school by the Government of Israel. The campus, still growing, currently consists of more than 20 buildings which include aeronautical, hydraulics, building research, soil research, and other laboratories; classroom, library and workshop buildings; and dormitories.

The Technion's College of Engineering, with its faculties of civil, mechanical, chemical, agricultural, and aeronautical engineering and departments of architecture and town planning, currently supplies Israel with engineers, applied scientists, and high-level technicians. Its various research laboratories are engaged in solving some of the manifold problems of Israel's pioneering economy. Since 1940, the American Technion Society has been aiding the Technion with funds and scholarships, making it possible for select graduates to come to the U.S. for a year of practical experience in American industrial plants.

TEFILLIN (PHYLACTERIES). Two prayer boxes with leather straps worn on the forehead and the left arm. The boxes contain four selections from the Bible (Ex. 13:1-10, 11-16 and Deut. 6:4-9, 11:13-21), inscribed on parchment, which proclaim the existence and unity of God and serve as a reminder of the liberation from Egypt. They are worn during the morning prayers on each weekday and the afternoon service on the Ninth of Ab. by Jewish males who have reached the age of bar mitzvah. Since Sabbaths and festivals are themselves "signs," no phylacteries are worn on these days.

Tefillin cases. Poland, 19th century, engraved silver. Courtesy Jewish Museum, New York.

TEL AVIV. Largest city in Israel. In 1998, it and its twin city **Jaffa** had a population of more than 380,000 (more than a million in the Greater Tel Aviv area). Tel Aviv was founded in 1909, when a

Cancer research at the Department of Microbiology at Tel Aviv University.

group of Jewish residents of Jaffa bought two stretches of sand dunes and built a garden suburb which they called Tel Aviv, after **Herzl**'s Jewish utopia *Altneuland*. By 1914, this all-Jewish town had 1,416 inhabitants. Most of them were expelled by the Turks as "enemy aliens" during World War I. After the British occupation of the country in 1918, Tel Aviv grew swiftly. Twenty years after its founding, Tel Aviv had a population of 40,000, and was becoming the cultural and industrial leader of the country. But its expansion was greatest in the 1930's when German immigrants arrived. Houses and streets multiplied rapidly. It became consolidated as a dynamic urban center, the heart of the country's trade and light industry. During the chaos and terror that marked the end of the British Mandate, Tel Aviv was the center of underground activities and the defense movement operated by **Haganah**. In 1948, the independence of Israel was declared in Tel Aviv's Museum, as **Jerusalem** was under siege. During the latter 20th century, Tel Aviv became Israel's metropolis, a center of an intense cultural life with a considerable tourist industry. It houses Israel's leading theaters, including **Habimah**, the Israeli Philharmonic Orchestra, the new Israeli opera, and the campus of **Tel Aviv University** (founded in 1956), which houses the **Diaspora Museum**.

TEL AVIV UNIVERSITY. Founded in 1956, it has an enrollment of 27,000 and a faculty of 1,800. It is housed in an American-style campus in the Ramat Aviv suburb of **Tel Aviv**. One of its main attractions is the **Diaspora Museum**, which covers the history of the Jewish people. Its renowned research institutes engage in advanced study of cancer, heart, and 16 other medical specialties, as well as urban studies, Middle Eastern and African Studies, petroleum, space and planetary science, nature preservation, labor studies, and Russian studies. The American Friends of Tel Aviv University maintain an office in **New York City**.

A view of Tel Aviv around 1959. Inset, new buildings in contemporary Tel Aviv.

Model of Solomon's Temple, by Joseph Doctorwitz, based on the biblical text. Courtesy Jewish Museum, New York.

TEMPLE, FIRST AND SECOND. The First Temple was planned by King **David** and erected by King **Solomon** (970-931 B.C.E.). It took seven years to build the sanctuary: its walls were made of huge blocks of granite, quarried, dressed, and dovetailed in the hills surrounding **Jerusalem**. On the Temple site itself, no iron tools were used because implements of war were made of iron, and the Temple was a symbol of peace (I Kings 6:7). Solomon imported Phoenician craftsmen to build it. For the Temple roof, cedars and cypresses were hewn in the forests of **Lebanon**, floated down in rafts from **Phoenicia** to Joppa (**Jaffa**), and then borne up, log by log, to the heights of Jerusalem. The Temple was surrounded by courts and auxiliary buildings. It had three divisions: the vestibule before which were freestanding pillars, Jahin and Boaz; the holy place containing the altar of incense, the table of the shewbread and the seven branched **Menorah**; and the Holy of Holies, which held only the **Ark of the Covenant** and the **Ten Commandments**. The altar for the sacrifices was in the Temple court. The services in the Temple were impressive and accompanied by singing and instrumental music. For 380 years, this shrine was the heart of the nation. To it the people went up in pilgrimage three times a year on the festivals of **Pesach**, **Shavuot**, and **Sukkot**. The Temple was destroyed on the ninth day of Av in 586 B.C.E., by Nebuchadnezzer, King of **Babylonia**, who deported the people of Judah and made it a Babylonian colony.

The Second Temple was completed 70 years later by the people who had returned from the Babylonian exile. Many of the original Temple vessels, plundered by the conqueror, had disappeared. The Ark of the Covenant was gone, and the Holy of Holies stood quite empty. When the sacredness of the Temple was defiled in 168 B.C.E. at the command of the Syrian King Antiochus, the people revolted. After the Maccabean victory, the Temple was restored, but did not reach its full magnificence until **Herod** rebuilt it in 20-19 B.C.E. Ninety years later, the Roman legions under Titus set fire to the Temple, again on the ninth day of Ab, and left it a heap of ruins in 70 C.E. Since then, the day of the destruction has been remembered by Jews with fasting and prayer. Historic events are mentioned as having occurred "in the days of the First Temple" or "in the time of the Second Temple."

TEN COMMANDMENTS. According to the **Bible**, the divine laws, in Greek known as Decalogue, spoken by God to **Moses** and written on two tablets of stone (Ex. 20:2-14and Deut. 5:6-18). They are the highest laws in Judaism and the source of all Jewish law and ethics. **Christianity** and **Islam** also have accepted them. The Ten Commandments cover the whole religious and moral life of humanity. They teach the unity of God and prescribe the fundamental ways of behavior among people.

TEN LOST TRIBES. *See* **Lost Tribes**.

TEN MARTYRS. *See* **Martyrs, Ten**.

TENNESSEE. With close to 20,000 Jews, 8,500 live in Memphis, 5,750 in Nashville, 1,650 in Knoxville, and 1,350 in Chattanooga. There are Jewish congregations in those cities, as well as in Jackson, Johnson City, and Oak Ridge. Organized Jewish life began in the state in 1845, first organized in Nashville and Memphis.

TESHUVAH. Literally, return, turning away from sin and back to God's teachings. In the **Bible**, the prophets urge the people to return to God. In the **Talmud**, *teshuvah* becomes a central Jewish concept, beginning with repentance and culminating in divine forgiveness. The ten days between **Rosh Ha-shanah** and **Yom Kippur** are called the Ten Days of Repentance.

TESTAMENT, OLD. *See* **Old Testament**.

TET. Ninth letter of the Hebrew alphabet; numerically, nine.

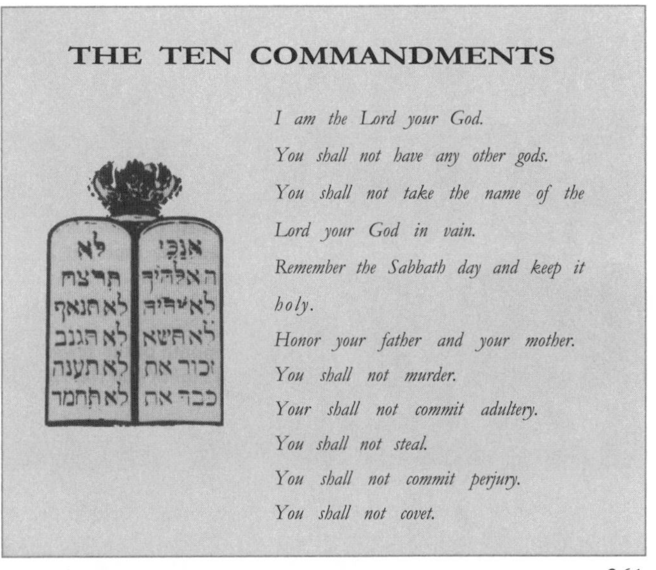

THE TEN COMMANDMENTS

I am the Lord your God.

You shall not have any other gods.

You shall not take the name of the Lord your God in vain.

Remember the Sabbath day and keep it holy.

Honor your father and your mother.

You shall not murder.

Your shall not commit adultery.

You shall not steal.

You shall not commit perjury.

You shall not covet.

Temple Emanu El, Houston, Texas.

TEXAS. Of the 100,000 Jews who live in the state, 42,000 live in Houston, 35,000 in Dallas, 10,000 in San Antonio, 6,400 in Austin, 4,900 in El Paso, 5,000 in Ft. Worth, with smaller communities in the rest of the state. The first known settler was Samuel Isaacs, who went to Austin in 1821. Later, Jews settled in Galveston, and by the 1850's German Jews had settled in Houston. Reform Judaism became the popular movement in the state, with Conservative Judaism in second place. Jews have been active in state affairs.

THIRTEEN ATTRIBUTES OF MERCY. According to the **Bible** (Exod. 34:6-7), God has several attributes of mercy and forgiveness, which rabbinic tradition considers to be thirteen, although the logic for this number is not clearly explained.

Tomb of Rabbi Meir Baal Hanes in Tiberias. Courtesy Zionist Archives and Library, New York.

THIRTEEN PRINCIPLES OF FAITH. According to **Maimonides**, Jewish faith consists of 13 principles, as follows: God's existence; God is one; God has no physical appearance; God is eternal; God is the only one to be worshiped; God's word was revealed through the biblical prophets; Moses is the chief prophet; God's law was given at Mount Sinai; the Torah is eternal and irreplaceable; God is aware of human action; God rewards good and punishes evil; God will send a messiah; the dead will come back to life.

TIBERIAS. City on the Sea of Galilee (Kineret), famous for its healing hot springs. It was built by Herod Antipas in 18 B.C.E. in honor of the reigning Roman emperor, Tiberius Caesar. Notwithstanding its pagan origin and alien style of architecture, it soon became Judaized. In the 2nd century C.E., after the failure of **Bar Kokhba**'s revolt, the **Sanhedrin** moved to Tiberias, where the Mishnah and **Masorah** were edited. During the following centuries, Tiberias attracted many pilgrims and scholars as one of the four Holy Cities and as the burial place of Rabbi Meir Baal Hanes and **Maimonides**. In 1560, Don Joseph **Nasi**, a **Marrano** from **Spain**, received permission from the Turkish sultan to rebuild Tiberias as a Jewish agricultural and industrial center. His project failed, however, and Tiberias lay in ruins until 1740, when the Bedouin sheikh Daher el Omer restored the city with the help of Rabbi Aboulafia of Izmir. Today, as in ancient times, it is the economic center and metropolis of Lower Galilee and Israel's principal health resort and spa.

TISHRI. First month of the Jewish civil calendar. It is during this month that the High Holidays occur.

TORAH. Literally, teaching. Though originally *Torah* may have applied only to the Ten Commandments and later to the **Pentateuch**, it was from an early period employed as a general term to cover all Jewish law, including the vast mass of teachings recorded in the **Talmud** and other rabbinical works. This latter literature was called Oral Torah, or Tradition, as opposed to Written Torah, or Written Law. To the pious Jew, both Torahs are sacred and inviolable. The Torah guided God in the creation of the world, says the Talmud, and if people were not to observe it, the universe would cease to exist.

TORAH UMESORAH. Orthodox Jewish educational agency whose aim is to found

Torah dressed with mantle, crown, breastplate, and pointer.

A Torah scribe (sofer) in Israel carrying on the ancient art of inscribing the Pentateuch on parchment.

yeshivot, or Hebrew day schools. These yeshivot provide religious and secular studies under the same auspices in the Jewish communities of the U.S., particularly in small towns and suburban communities. It was founded in 1944 by Rabbi Feivel Mendlowitz. At that time only seven of the 33 day schools in the U.S. were situated outside of New York.

In the 1980's there were 516 Hebrew day schools located in 37 states and five Canadian provinces. Of these, 254 were located outside of the New York Metropolitan area. In the New York area there were 209 schools. There were 150 high schools functioning in the U.S.

Torah Umesorah tries to maintain high standards in existing yeshivot through curriculum study and evaluation, supervisory visits by staff members, and regular consultation with principals and boards of education. It also carries on a program of teacher placement and interviews. Other activities include publication of textbooks coordinated with the school program, including the children's magazine, *Olomeinu* (Our World), and the organization and maintenance of a network of parent-teacher groups affiliated with the National Association of Hebrew Day School Parent-Teacher Associations.

During the past few years, Torah Umesorah has been concentrating upon the training of teachers. It conducts such programs in five major seminaries, and has its own teacher-training program called *Aish Dos*, the "Fire of Faith."

TOSAFOT. *See* **Tam, Rabbenu**.

TOSEFTA. *See* **Talmud**.

TOURO COLLEGE: Chartered in 1970, Touro College opened in 1971 with an enrollment of 35 students. Under the direction of its founder and president, Dr. Bernard Lander, Touro developed into a major institution which includes the College of Liberal Arts and Sciences, the Graduate School of Jewish Studies, the Graduate School of Education and Psychology; the School of Health Sciences; the School for Lifelong Education, and the Touro Law School. Touro College offers separate Men's and Women's Divisions with campuses in Manhattan and Brooklyn.

TOURO, JUDAH (1775-1854). Philanthropist. Born in Newport, R.I., where his father was a cantor, Touro was educated in **Boston** by his uncle, Moses Michael Hays. Touro prospered as a merchant in New Orleans, amassing a huge fortune which was distributed at his death to causes in the U.S. and **Jerusalem**. When a Universalist church was foreclosed and sold at auction, Touro bought the property and returned it to its congregation. His name is honored in many places, notably in the Touro Synagogue at Newport, which was named a national religious shrine in 1947.

TOWER OF BABEL *See* **Babel, Tower of.**

TRANSJORDAN. *See* **Jordan, Hashemite Kingdom of** *and* **Zionism**.

TREE OF LIFE. One of two trees specified in the story of the Garden of Eden in **Genesis**. Eating its fruit resulted in eternal life.

TRUMPELDOR, JOSEPH (1880-1920). Zionist pioneer leader, soldier, and founder of the pioneer movement Hechalutz. He was born in **Russia** and had little contact with Jewish life. He fought in the Russo-Japanese War in 1904 where he lost his left arm in the siege of Port Arthur, and was decorated four times for conspicuous bravery. He emerged from the army with the unheard of distinction of being the only Jewish officer in the Tsar's forces. However, the wave of pogroms against Russian Jewry turned him into a Zionist, and he went to Palestine as a pioneer. With one arm he learned to till the soil in the settlement of **Degania**.

At the outbreak of World War I, he organized the Zion Mule Corps to fight on the side of the British against the Turks. He served as captain in the Gallipoli Expeditionary Force. The record of bravery of the Corps was helpful in organizing the **Jewish Legion** in 1917. Meanwhile, when the Tsarist government fell, Trumpeldor returned to Russia hoping to organize an army of 10,000 Jews to lead over the Caucasus and Anatolia to Palestine. The Bolshevik Revolution broke out, and his plan failed. Instead, he organized the young Zionists of Russia in the Hechalutz pioneer movement and succeeded in getting a group of them out of Russia. Back in Palestine he turned to self-defense work. At the end of World War I, the borderline between **Syria** and Palestine was unsettled. Three small Jewish settlements were in this disputed area. The British and French forces had withdrawn, and Metulla, Ayelet Hashachar, and Tel Hai lay exposed to the bands of hostile Bedouins. Trumpeldor realized the importance of defending these settlements and holding them within the boundaries of Palestine. With a small band of men and women, Trumpeldor defended the area and was killed in battle. The area he fought for remained part of Israel. In the history of the State of **Israel**, he was the first Jewish hero of modern times, a model for the new generations of Jews willing to risk their lives for their land.

Joseph Trumpeldor.

TSCHERNICHOWSKY, SAUL (1875-1943). Hebrew poet. Together with Chaim N. **Bialik**, he was one of the two leading modern Hebrew poets. Tschernichowsky's education did not include Talmudic training, but the Bible left a deep impression upon him, as did Greek philosophy and culture. He became a practicing physician in St. Petersburg and continued this work after he settled in Palestine.

Saul Tschernichowsky.

Tschernichowsky's poetry is distinguished by a vigorous sense of beauty and a closeness to nature. His idylls, or pastoral poems, possess wonderful charm and humor. They reflect the wholesome and happier phases of Eastern European Jewish traditional life. His sonnets are works of art, skillfully designed and executed.

Tschernichowsky identified himself with the Jewish national revival. He wrote some of his first poems on the Palestine landscape and its historical themes. In addition to his original works, he made a great contribution to Hebrew letters by outstanding translations of Homer, Sophocles, Shakespeare, Goethe, Longfellow (*Evangeline* and *Hiawatha*), and many other great writers.

TU BISHEVAT. Literally, the 15th day of Shevat, known as the "New Year of Trees." It marks the end of winter and the beginning of spring, and in ancient times people thought of it as the day in which sap begins to flow again in the trees. Before the Jews were driven from their land, it was celebrated with the festive planting of saplings. This custom has been revived in modern **Israel**, and is joyously observed in a land that centuries of neglect have denuded of green things. In the Diaspora, Tu Bishevat was also celebrated by eating such Israel fruits as figs, dates, and "boxer," the fruit of the carob tree.

TUCKER, RICHARD. *See* **Music**.

TUCKER, SOPHIE. *See* **Music**.

TUNISIA. The Jewish community of Tunisia dates back to the destruction of the Second **Temple**. Since that time the settlement has felt the yoke of both Muslim and Christian domination in a history marked by alternating periods of peaceful development and bitter persecution. Tunisian Jews knew their darkest days under Spanish domination from 1535 to 1575, but they also felt the lash under Moslem leaders. Despite their hardships, Tunisian Jewry maintained the Jewish tradition intact. During the 18th century, Tunisia became an important seat of Talmudic learning. A bright era began in 1881, when **France** assumed the protectorate over the country. Jews received equal citizenship rights along with Muslims and, for the first time, were permitted to enter the fields of commerce and industry. The **Alliance Israélite Universelle** then organized schools which are still in operation. In 1956, Tunisia gained its independence from France. Jews of Tunisia had been perhaps the most secure Jewish community in all the Muslim lands. Their religious, cultural, and communal life was close-knit, active, and well-organized. But recent Tunisian participation in the Arab League has led to increasing wariness about their future. Emigration since 1947, mainly to Israel and France, left in 1998 a Jewish population of about 1,800, a number which is still decreasing. Communications between Tunisia and Israel have been severed.

Tu Bishevat celebration in Ramat Gan, Israel.

> *A person is nothing but*
> *A small parcel of land;*
> *A person is nothing but*
> *A reflection of his native ground.*
>
> — SAUL TSCHERNICHOWSKY

TURKEY. When the Ottoman Empire replaced the Byzantine Empire in the 14th century, it found Jewish communities with origins dating back to Roman times. The Turkish Jews welcomed the Ottoman invasion for their situation had been hard under Christian Byzantine rule. Under the rule of **Islam**, they were granted religious liberty, security against attack, and the right to own land. This period of prosperity and calm lasted several centuries as Turkey became a haven for persecuted Jews throughout Europe. Jews played an important role in the courts of the sultans as ministers, scholars, and physicians; often, they were able to intervene on behalf of their less fortunate brethren in other countries.

In 1453, Sultan Mohammed II conquered Constantinople, and that city became a center of Jewish cultural and political life. In 1492, Sultan Bayazid II welcomed Jews who had been expelled from **Spain** and **Portugal**. Many of these settled in **Palestine**, which fell under Turkish rule from 1516 until the end of World War I. A great influx of **Sephardic** Jews with their highly developed cultural tradition, as well as many of Europe's foremost scholars and physicians, enriched Turkey. The great Sephardic spiritual centers at Salonica and Smyrna flowered in the 16th and 17th centuries. Turkish

Turkish Jew, 16th century.

Jews attained their greatest prominence during the reigns of Suleiman the Magnificent (r. 1520-1556) and Selim II (r. 1556-1574). Don Joseph Nasi, a former **Marrano**, became Sultan Selim's chief adviser and exerted great influence over European affairs. During the 16th century, Turkey became a center of Talmudic and Kabbalistic teaching. The works of Joseph **Karo**, Isaac Luria, and Hayyim Vital had great influence on Jewish learning and mysticism. **Sabbatai Zevi**, the messianic pretender, attracted a fanatical following among thousands of Jews in Turkey and Europe.

The end of Salim II's reign saw the beginning Turkey's decline as an important power and the disappearance of Jewish fortunes. Later sultans enacted discriminatory measures against Jews. At the end of the 19th century, Turkey played a crucial role in the history of political **Zionism**. In 1899, Theodor **Herzl** tried to obtain a colonization charter from the Turkish Sultan which would allow unlimited immigration to Palestine. His efforts were unsuccessful due to the Turkish suspicions of Zionist political aims. After World War I, the government of Kemal Pasha began a policy of Ottomanization of Turkey. Jewish autonomy was weakened in 1923 when Turkish became the only language of instruction permissible in Jewish schools. More restrictions followed. With the outbreak of World War II, however, Turkey was firm in its refusal to return Jewish refugees to **Germany**. Since 1947, about 45,000 Turkish Jews left for Israel, and an estimated 25,000 Jews remain. They are concentrated in the three major cities, Istanbul, Ismir, and Ankara. The Turkish government has been friendly to Israel, and in 1997, **Israel** sold military aircraft to Turkey and started joint military exercises.

TWELVE TRIBES. Descended from Jacob's sons: **Reuben, Simeon, Levi, Judah, Issachar, Zebulun, Gad, Asher, Dan, Naphtali, Joseph,** and **Benjamin**. While the tribe of Levi was set apart to serve in the Holy **Temple**, the sons of Joseph, **Ephraim** and **Manasseh**, were each given the status of an independent tribe at the time of the possession and distribution of the land of Israel.

TZADE. Eighteenth letter of Hebrew alphabet; numerically, ninety.

TZADDIK. Righteous person; Hasidic saint. (*See* **Hasidism**.)

TZEDAKAH. *See* **Charity**.

TZENAH U-REENAH. Compilation of Torah commentaries and stories written in Yiddish in the late 16th century. It became popular with Jewish women in Eastern Europe, who took it to the synagogue and read it silently during the service, since they did not participate in the formal prayers and since many of them did not read Hebrew.

TZIMTZUM. *See* **Kabbalah**.

TZITZIT. Ritual fringes on the **Tallit**.

TZOFIM. Israeli youth organization, equivalent to the Boy and Girl Scouts, first started in **England** by Baden-Powell. Unlike other scouting programs, the Tzofim is coed, and besides camping, sports activities, and community service, they followed the pattern of other Israeli youth organizations and prepared their members for farming and settling on the frontier. The Tzofim have formed several **kibbutzim**. There are both Jewish and Arab scouts in **Israel** today, belonging to the Israel Boy and Girl Scout Federation.

• *Overleaf: Torah silver case, France, 1860. The Scroll is from Spain, 17th century. Courtesy The Jewish Museum, New York.*

UKRAINE. Now an independent country, about half of the former USSR's three million Jews lived there before World War II. The Jewish population has been quickly dwindling, most leaving for Israel and the U.S.

Jewish-Khazarian settlement in Kiev can be traced to the 10th century; the Russian-speaking community was later absorbed by Yiddish-speaking immigrants from Central Europe. In the 17th century, Jews suffered from the Chmielnicki uprising against the Polish gentry, and thousands lost their lives. Despite 19th century restrictions, Jews played a prominent role in the development of commerce and industry and in the growth of major cities such as Kiev, Odessa, and Kharkov.

Ukraine was the venue of some of the worst pogroms of Tzarist Russian rule. In the Civil War and during the struggle for an independent Ukraine, about 100,000 Jews were slaughtered in 1919-1920. With the collapse of the Ukrainian state in 1920, plans for Jewish National Autonomy were ended. Yiddish culture flourished until the Stalinist regime liquidated most Jewish institutions. Religious and Zionist activity was forced underground, and most of the leaders arrested.

Four autonomous Jewish districts were established in the southern part of the republic and in the Crimea, which lasted until World War II when the Germans overran the communities and murdered the occupants. More than half of the Jews living in the Ukraine were wiped out, with the worst slaughter taking place at Babi Yar. Many Ukrainians were active in the murder and despoliation of their Jewish neighbors. After the war, returning Jews were met with hostility; repression of Jewish cultural and spiritual life was severe.

The collapse of Communism and the creation of an independent Ukraine set the stage for the revitalization of Jewish life. There are 78 Jewish schools in the country in 45 cities, including Chernovtsy, Dnepropetrovsk, Kharkov, Kiev, Lvov, Odessa, Vinnitsa, and Zapozoshye. In 1998, the Jewish population was 180,000 out of a general population of 53 million.

ULPAN. Literally, house of learning. Israeli adult education program to give newcomers an accelerated, intensive course in the **Hebrew language** and Israeli lifestyle. Ulpanim, using the same intensive method for study of the Hebrew language, have been set up in other countries as well.

UNION OF AMERICAN HEBREW CONGREGATIONS (UAHC). Association of Reform or Liberal congregations in the Western Hemisphere. It was founded in 1873 by Rabbi Isaac Mayer **Wise** whose primary purpose was to establish a seminary for the training of American rabbis; this was accomplished two years later with the founding of the **Hebrew Union College** in Cincinnati. The UAHC maintained its headquarters in Cincinnati until 1951, when the Berg Memorial House of Living Judaism in **New York** was opened as headquarters for the organization and all its affiliates.

The UAHC maintained the Board of Delegates of American Israelites from 1878 until 1925 when it ceased to exist. The Board published the first Jewish census in the U.S. in 1880. It concerned itself throughout with the rights of Jews in foreign countries.

The primary purpose of the UAHC and its affiliates is to service the constituent synagogues and temples. Currently there are more than 800 congregations with a total membership of about 1.4 million.

The chief legislative authority of the UAHC is its Biennial General Assembly. Between assemblies, the executive board of 120 persons and the administrative committee of that board carry on policy-making functions. Various commissions deal with such programs as Jewish education, synagogue activities, and interfaith activities.

The UAHC has organized three national affiliates: the National Federation of Temple Sisterhoods, founded in 1913, the National Federation of Temple Brotherhoods, founded in 1916, and the National Federation of Temple Youth, founded in 1939. Each carries on a full program of religious, cultural, educational, and social activities. In addition, the UAHC has been affiliated with the National Association of Temple Secretaries, founded in 1943, an organization of professional temple executives, and the National Association of Temple Educators, founded in 1955. The UAHC publications include the periodical *American Judaism*.

UNION OF ORTHODOX JEWISH CONGREGATIONS. On June 8, 1898, representatives of fifty Orthodox congregations met in **New York** to organize the Union of Orthodox Jewish Congregations of America. The affiliate synagogues of the UOJCA list approximately 500,000 individuals on their membership rolls. The Union also serves as a representative body for an additional 250,000 Orthodox Jews who comprise other elements of Orthodoxy.

The UOJCA holds a biennial general convention, setting the policies of the organization and discussing the status and problems of Orthodox Judaism. The day-to-day work is carried on by national commissions, including Armed Forces, communal relations, community activities, education, Israel and overseas, *Orthodox Jewish Life* monthly magazine, kashruth, law and legislation, Orthodox Union Association, public relations, religious standards, synagogue relations, and youth activities. By far the most famous and wide-spread activity of the UOJCA is its kashruth program.

UNION OF ORTHODOX JEWISH CONGREGATIONS OF AMERICA, WOMEN'S BRANCH. National organization representing the women affiliated with Orthodox synagogues in the U.S. It was organized in 1923 to spread the understanding and observance of Orthodoxy, to instill an appreciation of traditional Judaism in young people, and to help Jewish women realize their roles as Jews, mothers, and members of the community. The Women's Branch formed a kashruth committee, which sought to make kosher products available to the public. The Women's Branch helped raise funds for dormitories at **Yeshiva University** and established the Hebrew Teachers Training School for Girls, now housed in the Stern College for Women of Yeshiva University.

UNION OF SOVIET SOCIALIST REPUBLICS. *See* **Russia**.

UNITED HIAS SERVICE. The Hebrew Sheltering Society and the Hebrew Immigrant Aid Society, established to meet the needs of Jewish immigrants to the U.S., united in 1909 to form HIAS, the Hebrew Sheltering and Immigrant Aid Society. In 1954, HIAS, the United Service for New Americans, and the migration services of the **American Jewish Joint Distribution Committee** consolidated into a single international migration agency, United Hias Service. United Hias Service is funded by Federations, welfare funds, membership, and individual contributions.

The Service locates friends and relatives through its global network of offices. It assists immigrants at every step of the journey, preparing documents and arranging transportation, offering a personal welcome and shelter upon arrival, and providing a plan for resettlement. It further helps the newcomer comply with government regulations and naturalization procedures. The Service intervenes with government authorities in cases of unjustified detention and deportation, and presses constantly for relaxation of immigration barriers all over the world.

UNITED JEWISH APPEAL. Organization which raises money in the U.S. for the resettlement and rehabilitation of Jews in **Israel** and throughout the world and for humanitarian programs benefitting needy and troubled Jews in Israel and 33 other countries. Since its founding in 1939, the UJA has contributed to the rescue and resettlement of more than 4 million people, about half of them immigrants brought to Israel. To accomplish this, since its inception the UJA has collected more than $12 billion and distributed it to its beneficiary agencies.

Through United Jewish Appeal Inc., the UJA supports the Jewish Agency's programs of immigrant absorption and human support services designed to improve the quality of life in Israel. These include initial resettlement services to new immigrants, such as Hebrew-language instruction, vocational training, and subsidized housing; special programs for disadvantaged youth; support of pre-school and higher education; health and welfare aid; the establishment of **kibbutzim** and **moshavim**, and their support to the point of self-sufficiency. In 1979, the Jewish Agency also began a program called Project Renewal for the physical and social rehabilitation of the lives of immigrant families in distressed urban neighborhoods.

Stamp of United Jewish Appeal.

Recent UJA leaders: left, National Chairperson Joel Tauber; center, Executive Vice President Rabbi Brian L. Lurie; right, President Marvin Lender.

Operation Exodus is UJA's special campaign to take Jews out of the former Soviet Union and settle them in Israel with freedom and dignity. Since 1990, more than 500,000 Soviet Jews came to Israel.

Another UJA beneficiary is the **American Joint Distribution Committee** (JDC), which operates in Israel and 33 other countries throughout the world. In Israel, it provides services for the physically and mentally handicapped and supports extensive programs on behalf of the elderly, as well as special day-care programs for infants and toddlers. Its life-support services among Jewish communities in other countries include food and clothing parcels, kosher meals, medical care, nursery and day schools, centers for senior citizens, and relief-in-transit for Jewish migrants from distressed areas. It also supports worldwide vocational training for Jewish youth through the Organization for Rehabilitation through Training (ORT).

In American Jewish communities, the annual fund raising campaigns support local and national programs as well as UJA-funded overseas services. Local programs include Jewish day schools, day-care centers, Y's and community centers, vocational workshops, medical care, family counseling, youth guidance, home and institutional care for the elderly, aid to the indigent, and a full range of resettlement services for the incoming Jewish immigrants. Some 500 communities throughout the U.S. conduct annual fund-raising campaigns on behalf of the UJA. A portion of the money is used for local need, and a portion goes to support the UJA's overseas services.

UNITED KINGDOM. *See* **England**.

UNITED STATES. American Jewish history has its roots in the work of the scientists and explorers of the 15th century. Individual Jews landed in what is now the U.S. between the years 1621, when Elias Legardo came to **Virginia**, and 1654, when Jacob Barsimson came to New Amsterdam from Holland, and scattered along the Atlantic seaboard region of North America. By common consent, however, American Jewish history began in September 1654, when a group of 23 Jewish refugees from **Brazil**,

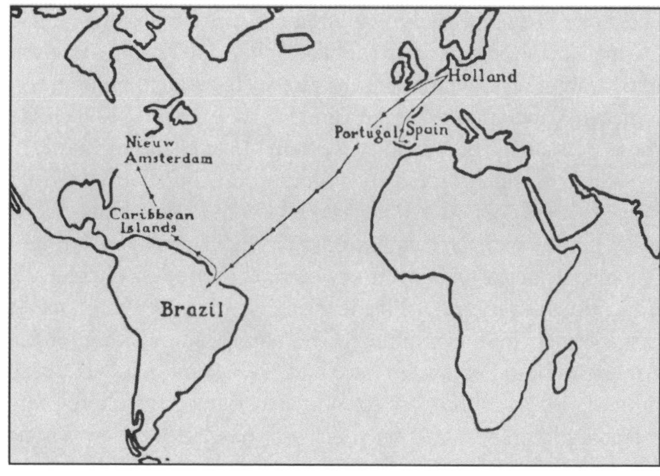

Since the 17th century, the New World has been the "shores of hope" for European Jews. From An Old Faith in a New World *by David and Tamar de Sola Pool. Courtesy Columbia University Press.*

pursued by the **Inquisition**, arrived in New Amsterdam. They were destitute, their belongings sold to pay for their passage, and three of them were thrown in jail while they awaited financial help from Jews in Holland. Faced with official hostility and every hardship known to a pioneering community, these refugees in New Amsterdam courageously fought for their rights. The Dutch governor, Peter Stuyvesant, and his officials barred them from the obligations and civil rights of the New Amsterdam citizens. These obligations included the duty of standing guard for the protection of the town. Asser **Levy** fought for and secured this right. Jews also won from Stuyvesant the privilege of laying out a cemetery for the new Jewish community. The struggle continued until 1664, when the English assumed control of New Amsterdam and recognized the right of public worship for all creeds. As this right spread among the colonies, Jewish community life became normalized. In 1729, the **New York** Congregation **Shearith Israel**, after many years of worshiping in private or rented dwellings, built a synagogue.

First synagogue erected in North America. Drawn from contemporary illustrations by Esther H. Oppenheim.

For the next century, Jews filtered into other seaboard settlements. Among the colonies in New England, **Rhode Island** provided a most congenial climate for Jewish settlers. Under the guiding genius of Roger Williams, this colony secured a charter in 1663 that provided full religious freedom. As a result, a thriving Jewish community flourished in Newport more than 100 years before the American Revolution. In **Pennsylvania**, **South Carolina**, and **Georgia**, freedom-loving people pressed for religious toleration, and Jews came and settled in these colonies. In 1750, there were enough Jews in Charleston, S.C., to organize a religious community. In Georgia, Jews in Savannah established a congregation in 1734, two years after the colony was settled by Oglethorpe. By the Revolutionary War, Jews, concentrated chiefly in a half-dozen seaboard centers, were deeply rooted in their adopted land. When the colonies revolted against England, launching the American Revolution, Jews threw themselves into the cause of the revolution wholeheartedly. Jewish patriots served in the armed forces and helped finance and provision the armies. In New York, outspoken patriot members of Congregation Shearith Israel, led by their hazzan, Gershom Mendes Seixas, fled the city

Grace Seixas Nathan (1752-1831) and Simon Nathan (1746-1822) were prominent citizens of New York.

rather than fall into Tory hands. In **Philadelphia** Haym **Salomon** worked ceaselessly to help finance the revolutionary cause. Jews were sent as confidential messengers to European governments, and their names in the lists of the prisoners, the dead, and the wounded tell the story of their involvement in this period of American history.

Throughout this period, culminating in the establishment of the Republic and in the adoption of the American constitution in 1789, the Jewish population was no more than 2,000 to 3,000 Jews. Among these were a number of German Jews and even a sprinkling of East European Jews. An overwhelming majority, however, were descendants of **Sephardic** exiles from the Mediterranean area. With Asser Levy's act of wresting from Peter Stuyvesant the right to stand guard duty, the Sephardim established the pattern characteristic of American Jewry: integration into American political life by achieving civic, political, and economic equality without assimilating.

Because they had fought to create the new nation, American Jews were grateful for their rights and ever vigilant in resisting encroachments or violations of them. The Virginia constitution establishing religious liberty was widely followed, and it was reflected in the Northwest Ordinance, in the constitutions of

Touro Synagogue, Newport, Rhode Island. The oldest synagogue in the U.S., dedicated in 1763. It was designated as a national monument in 1946.

Pennsylvania, New York, and finally in the U.S. Constitution. Disabilities remained and had to be removed by legal action. In **Maryland**, Thomas Kennedy led the fight for extending equal rights to Jews and finally won in 1826. **North Carolina** lagged in this respect until 1868. The Board of Delegates of American Israelites (1865-1878) labored to obtain the removal of the remaining relics of legal discrimination against Jews from several state constitutions. They were equally watchful in calling attention to the infringement of Jewish rights abroad. During the Civil War, when more than 700 Jews fought with both Confederate and Union armies, after persistent effort rabbis were permitted to serve as chaplains.

The regional history of Jews in the U.S. followed the general pattern of development. As the westward movement followed the water and overland routes to the Mississippi River and as it opened up the verdant valleys to settlers, individual Jews moved westward. They became landowners and traded with the Indians. Jewish peddlers, known as "hawkers and walkers," brought much-needed goods to the most distant pioneer outposts. At first they went as solitary travelers, but gradually families moved westward, and congregations began to dot the land.

The 19th century brought many changes. A period of expansion unique in the annals of history opened in the U.S. This growth was paralleled in the Jewish community as well. During the two decades preceding the Civil War, about 200,000 German Jews settled in the U.S. Some of them settled on the Atlantic coast, establishing the first German Jewish congregation in Philadelphia in 1802. Others moved into the interior, founding or developing such Jewish communities in **Chicago**, Cincinnati, Memphis, and St. Paul. From 1840 to 1880, these German Jewish immigrants assumed leadership and founded the religious, philanthropic, and fraternal organizations that are still basic to Jewish communal life in the U.S. In Philadelphia, Rabbi Isaac **Leeser** pioneered by introducing the English sermon as a regular part of the synagogue service and by founding the Hebrew Education Society and institutions of higher Jewish education. At first German Jews encountered the patronizing attitude of the American-born Sephardim, who had by this time achieved social prominence, wealth, and considerable influence. There were religious differences among them as well. German Jews, Isaac Mayer **Wise** outstanding among them, introduced the Reform movement in the U.S., while the Sephardim clung largely to strict observance and to their synagogue ritual. Soon, however, the German Jews who had started out as peddlers with packs on their backs opened retail stores and went on to establish great merchandising firms and became quickly absorbed in the American middle class. When mass Jewish immigration from Eastern Europe began in the 1880's, the German Jewish element in turn felt superior to the new immigrants, poverty-stricken and foreign in their ways of life. Nevertheless, German Jews established philanthropic organizations to aid and assist their brethren.

For the third time, Jewish immigrants repeated the cycle of economic, political, and social adjustment in the U.S. Between 1880 and 1920, two million Jews came to the U.S. from Eastern Europe. They came out of a Tsarist **Russia** that had inaugurated pogroms and persecution as instruments of government; they came out of Galician poverty and Romanian oppression. They took to peddling and poured into sweat shops until gradually they established themselves in this country and made their contributions to its economy and culture. They created trade unions in the garment industries and emerged from the sweat shops. They established light industries and businesses in the large cities, took to education in large numbers, and entered the professions. Within their communities they created secular organizations. Out of their need for self-help, comfort, and well-being in their new environment, they organized landsmannschaften and various social and cultural Jewish movements and labor organizations. They established a vital Zionist movement. The **Yiddish literature**, press, and theater were their creation, as were Hebrew and Jewish literature in English. They built up religious institutions and a complex Jewish educational system culminating in great yeshivot and seminaries. Under the leadership of Solomon **Schechter** the Conservative movement took root and developed. **Reconstruction** was fathered by Mordecai M. **Kaplan**.

Eleanor Roosevelt on an Israeli stamp.

Jewish life in the U.S. is largely urban. Because Jews came mainly from lands that deprived them of equality, American Jews have prized citizenship deeply, and their participation in American political life has been marked by an awareness of major issues. They have been not merely voters, but also candidates for office. They have been members of Congress and have held state offices, including governor. They have held important diplomatic posts; for example, Henry **Kissinger** was secretary of state. On the Supreme Court, the figures of **Brandeis, Cardozo,** and **Frankfurter** are outstanding by any measure. Throughout American history, Jews' identification with their adopted country has run deep.

Rabbi A.H. Silver on an Israeli stamp.

Since 1920, a number of changes have taken place in the American Jewish community. The process of integration into all phases of American life has been greatly accelerated. With immigration restricted by the quota system, American Jewry has become largely native-born. Before World War I, the majority of American Jews were laborers. Since then, the occupational pattern has changed, and most Jews have become middle class professional and business persons. A more affirmative attitude toward religious observance and Jewish identification has become generally evident in education and in religious and cultural activity. Since the Nazi destruction of six million Jews in Europe, American Jewry has become the largest Jewish body in the world, and has correspondingly accepted great responsibilities. Rescue, relief, and reconstruction are shouldered by American Jews under the leadership of such organizations as the **United Jewish Appeal,** the **American Jewish Joint Distribution Committee**, the Organization for Rehabilitation through Training (**ORT**), and the United **HIAS** Service. Dedicated to safeguarding Jewish rights at home and abroad are the **American Jewish Congress**, **B'nai B'rith**, and the **American Jewish Committee**. Before and since the establishment of the State of **Israel**, the **Zionist Organization of America** and **Hadassah**, the Women's Zionist Organization of America, have lent assistance to Israel in absorbing a million Jewish newcomers onto its soil and into its industry.

President Harry S. Truman on a Brazilian stamp.

Rabbi Bernard Revel, first president of Yeshiva University in New York City on a U.S. stamp.

American Jewish leaders such as Abba Hillel **Silver** played a decisive role in bringing about the creation of the State of Israel, as did President Harry Truman, who recognized the new state and laid the groundwork for the close relations between the tow democracies. Over the years, most U.S. presidents of both parties were strongly supportive of Israel. Jimmy Carter mediated the peace between **Egypt** and Israel, Ronald Reagan formed a strategic partnership with Israel, and Bill Clinton facilitated the peace initiative between Israel and the Palestinian Arabs, as well as the peace agreement between Israel and Jordan.

At the close of the 20th century, Jews remain 2% the total U.S. population (5.8 million out of 269 million), yet their contributions to American society and to the Jewish world far exceed their numbers. This is true in particular in all areas of social, business, scholarly, scientific, and artistic endeavor (*see* **Art**; **Music**; **Stage and Screen**). More than half of American Jewry is affiliated with a synagogue, a truly impressive rate in an open and highly mobile society. On the other hand, more than half of the marriages at century's end are mixed marriages, creating serious questions about Jewish continuity.

Rarely in history have Jews been more accepted in a non-Jewish society than they are in the U.S. today, a fact which raises the question whether the various forms of Jewish religious and cultural expression in the U.S. can continue to keep large numbers of Jews within the fold in the next century, rather than losing them to the general culture.

UNITED STATES HOLOCAUST MUSEUM. The U.S. Holocaust Memorial Museum was chartered by an Act of Congress in 1980, and was formally dedicated on April 22,1993, on the newly-renamed Raul Wallenberg Place SW, Washington, D.C.

The Museum is dedicated to presenting the history of the persecution and murder of six million Jews and millions of other victims of Nazi tyranny from 1933 to 1945. The Museum's primary mission is to inform Americans about this tragedy, to remember those who suffered, and to inspire visitors to contemplate the moral implications of their choices and responsibilities as citizens in an interdependent world.

The Museum has amassed a collection of artifacts and oral histories for the Permanent Exhibition which authenticate the tragic and heroic story of the Holocaust. The Children's Wall consists of thousands of tiles hand painted by American schoolchildren to record their impressions of the Holocaust. The Wall is dedicated to the 1.5 million innocent children who were murdered by Hitler's Third Reich. The Education Department at the Museum creates a variety of learning experiences for children and youth groups. Educational materials and curriculum units are available for use outside the Museum. The museum attracts millions of people annually, and has become one of Washington's most visited places.

UNITED SYNAGOGUE OF CONSERVATIVE JUDAISM. Organization of Conservative synagogues in the U.S. and Canada. The United Synagogue was founded in 1913 by a group of rabbis and educators under the leadership of Solomon **Schechter**. Through a series of departments and commissions it aids affiliated congregations in solving religious, educational, cultural, and administrative problems. These institutions include the department of education, the department of youth activities, the National Academy for Adult Jewish Studies, the department of regional activities, the department of programs, the Commission on

U.S. Holocaust Museum in Washington, D.C.

Social Action, the National Ramah Commission, and the department of synagogue administration.

Some 800 congregations, serving more than 1.5 million people, are affiliated with the United Synagogue. As the representative of Conservative Jewry in the U.S., it participates with delegates of Orthodox and Reform organizations in the Synagogue Council of America. The United Synagogue is closely associated with the **Jewish Theological Seminary of America** and the Rabbinical Assembly of America. Close to fifty synagogues and groups belong to the Conservative, or Masorti, movement in Israel. Worldwide, conservative congregations are affiliated with the World Council of Synagogues.

The **Women's League for Conservative Judaism** is the organization of Conservative synagogue sisterhoods.

The United Synagogue Youth is the national organization of teenagers (ages 13 through 17) affiliated with Conservative congregations, launched in December 1951. It presently consists of more than 500 chapters and seventeen regions. United Synagogue Youth sponsors twenty regional conferences, ten local summer camps, leadership training institutes, and a national convention annually. A two-month Israel Pilgrimage is conducted each summer.

United Synagogue Youth's purpose is to provide high school youth with "an awareness of the essential harmony between the ideals and traditions of Judaism and American democracy," as expressed by the Conservative movement.

The National Youth Commission of the United Synagogue of America guides and supervises United Synagogue Youth activity.

UNITED SYNAGOGUE YOUTH (USY). *See* **United Synagogue of Conservative Judaism**.

UNVEILING. *See* **Burial** *and* **Mourning**.

URIS, LEON (1924-). American novelist; one of the best-selling writers of the post-World War II era. His novel *Exodus* depicts the birth of Israel; *Mila 18* tells the story of the Warsaw Ghetto uprising, while *QB7* deals with Nazi atrocities during the war.

URUGUAY. Located on the Atlantic coast, between **Brazil** and **Argentina**, Uruguay is the smallest of the South American republics. Its Jewish community, however, is the third largest and one of the most highly organized in Latin America. In 1998, it numbered about 24,000 in a total population of 3.3 million. The majority live in Montevideo, where they are engaged in the manufacture and sale of furs, furniture, clothing, and oil.

The Jewish community achieved its high degree of organization during World War II. At that time **Germany** was interested in gaining control of Uruguay, and Nazi agents began to spread effective anti-Semitic propaganda in the country. Jews were forced to unite in order to combat this menace. Uruguay's break with Germany in 1943 put a stop to the anti-Semitic agitation, and the peaceful conditions of this most democratic of South American republics were restored. Uruguayan Jewry did not relax, however, and its energies were channeled to work within the community. One of the results of its efforts was an extensive educational system, which included eleven schools in Montevideo and three in the provinces. More than 1,000 Jewish children attended those institutions. Zionist activity, too, was vigorous. Montevideo's Jewish press was widely read. Two Yiddish dailies, as well as periodicals of Jewish interest, in Spanish and German, have been published. Two of these, in Spanish, were for younger readers. Many organizations maintained libraries and arranged cultural activities. A Jewish daily radio program and a weekly program devoted to Jewish scholars, writers, and artists were broadcast. All sectors were represented in the Central Jewish Community of Uruguay. The Central Committee has been the government-recognized spokesperson for Uruguayan Jewry.

USSISHKIN, MENACHEM MENDEL (1863-1941). Zionist leader. In 1920, he settled in Palestine, and as chief of the Zionist Commission, he forced the purchase of the Emek, or Valley, of Jezreel swamp lands, now lush farms and orchards. This lifelong fixed interest in agricultural settlement of the Land of Israel became Ussishkin's duty in 1923, as president of the Keren Kayemet, the **Jewish National Fund**. Until his death, eighteen years later, the Keren Kayemet, under his guidance, raised large sums of money and bought large tracts of land in Israel, now teeming with life.

UTAH. Most of Utah's 3,000 Jews live in Salt Lake City. Jews first arrived in 1854, among those who went west looking for gold. The first non-Mormon governor of Utah was a Jew, Simon Bamberger. Salt Lake City has a Jewish Council, a Jewish Welfare Fund, one Reform congregation, and one Conservative congregation.

VAV. Sixth letter of the Hebrew alphabet; numerically, six.

VENEZUELA. Republic, the northernmost state in South America. Italian Jews who wandered from Cayenne to Curaçao finally settled at Tucaca in Venezuela in 1693. Since the 19th century, the commercially prosperous Jewish community has been concentrated in Caracas, the capital, numbering about 20,000 in a total population of about 20 million. The Jewish community is made up of an old **Sephardic** settlement and more recent Eastern European immigrants. The latter predominate. Zionist organizations are active within the community, and religious education is increasing. In 1947, the Escuela General Herzl-Bialik, a day school combining general and Jewish studies, was established. Nearly 90% of Jewish youth attended Jewish schools.

VERMONT. Of the state's 4,000 Jews, close to 3,000 live in Burlington, with 500 each in Montpelier-Barre and Rutland. Jewish life began after the Civil War. Burlington has a congregation that has been in existence since 1880. Rutland's community started around 1900. There are four Reform and two Conservative congregations in the state.

VERSAILLES PEACE CONFERENCE (1919). After World War I, representatives of the nations met at Versailles, France, to work out the terms of peace. A Jewish delegation made up of representatives of the European and American Jewish communities came to the peace conference to present the Zionist claims on Palestine, and the claims for minority rights for the Jews of **Poland**, **Rumania**, **Bulgaria**, and **Yugoslavia**. On February 27, 1919, Nahum **Sokolow**, Menachem **Ussishkin**, Chaim **Weizmann**, and Andre Spire presented the Zionist claims. At a later session, another committee headed by Louis **Marshall** presented the claims for Jewish minority rights. The peace conference accepted the validity of these claims, extended them to other groups, and wrote them into the peace treaties. These stated that minority rights "shall be recognized as fundamental law and shall be placed under the guarantee of the League of Nations."

Members of the Committee of Jewish Delegations from Europe, the U.S., and Palestine at the Versailles Peace Conference. Courtesy Dr. Joseph Tenebaum.

VIENNA. *See* **Austria**.

VILNA. City in **Lithuania**, famous as a center of Talmudic learning, cultural institutions, and traditional Judaism. It was the cradle of modern **Hebrew** and **Yiddish literature**, and a stronghold of **Zionism** and Jewish socialism from the 19th century on.

Jews settled in Vilna in the 14th and 15th centuries and were, for the most part, traders. In the beginning they were on good terms with their Christian neighbors. As the Jewish community grew and prospered, the Gentile population became hostile. Jews of Vilna suffered great losses at the hands of the invading Cossacks in 1654. The remaining Jews were expelled by the Russian King Alexis a year later, but returned once more after the victory of the Polish army in 1661. Early in the 17th century, Vilna again changed hands. It was occupied in turn by the Russian and Swedish armies. During this time, 4,000 Jews perished from famine.

Known as the "Jerusalem of Lithuania," the Jewish community of Vilna rose to prominence through its renowned scholars, the most famous being **Elijah, Gaon of Vilna**. It was also one of the centers of the Enlightenment (**Haskalah**) movement. In the early 1860's, the scholar Samuel Joseph Finn published the Hebrew periodical **Ha-Carmel** in Vilna. Vilna was the seat of the well-known Romm Publishing house, printer of the **Talmud**.

Between the two World Wars, the Jewish population of Vilna was close to 60,000. The city had many yeshivot, Hebrew and Yiddish teachers' training schools, and numerous newspapers. It housed the famous Strashun Library and the **YIVO** Yiddish Scientific Institute.

During World War II, Vilna was occupied first by Soviet Russia and later, in 1941, by the Nazis. The extermination of the Jews extended through 1942 and 1943. All the historic landmarks and institutions were destroyed. Only a few of Vilna's Jews managed to escape the Nazi slaughter, among them several hundred who fought as partisans in nearby forests. In 1998, it was estimated that several thousand Jews were living in Vilna.

Old synagogue in Vilna.

VIRGIN ISLANDS. Group of islands in the eastern Caribbean Sea. The three largest, St. Thomas, St. John, and St. Croix, are inhabited. These islands, formerly the Danish West Indies, were purchased by the U.S. from **Denmark** in 1917.

In 1998, there were more than 250 Jewish families in the Virgin Islands. St. Thomas has had a Jewish population since 1764. The Jewish settlers, mainly sailors and merchants, came from the nearby island of St. Eustatius, one of the Dutch West Indies. By 1850, about 500 Jews lived in St. Thomas. The flourishing commercial and maritime settlement built a number of synagogues successively, Orthodox-Sephardic in character except for a brief period of Reform. The economic decline, resulting from the abolition of slavery in 1848 and the removal of the Royal Mail Steamship Company in 1855 to Barbados, led many Jews to leave the island. Jews figured prominently in the public life of the Virgin Islands. Among important Americans descended from Jewish families of the Virgin Islands was Judah P. Benjamin, distinguished lawyer and Secretary of State for the Southern Confederacy.

VIRGINIA. Of Virginia's 70,000 Jews, 35,000 live in Alexandria (outside D.C.), 19,000 in Norfolk, 12,000 in Richmond, about 2,000 each in Newport News and Portsmouth, and 1,000 in Roanoke. Jewish life began in Virginia in the mid-17th century. A congregation was organized in Richmond in 1789. The Jewish population grew significantly after 1880, and by 1900 there were 13 established Jewish communities. Today, there are 12 Reform and 10 Conserv congregation in the state, with Northern Virginia (Greater Washington, D.C.) having the most thriving Jewish communities.

VITAL, HAYIM. *See* **Kabbalah**.

VOLOZHIN, YESHIVA. **Lithuania** was the cradle of the yeshiva movement, and the Yeshiva of Volozhin was the first and most influential of the Lithuanian yeshivot. Under the influence of its founder, Rabbi Haim of Volozhin, the Yeshiva took over the teaching method of the beloved Rabbi **Elijah, Gaon of Vilna**, who had been Rabbi Haim's rabbi and teacher. The method, briefly, consisted of intensifying and broadening, while at the same time simplifying, the study of the **Talmud**. The heads of the Yeshiva, including Rabbi Naphtali Zvi Berlin, Rabbi Joseph Baer **Soloveichik**, and his son Rabbi Hayim Soloveichik of Brest-Litovsk, were among the most revered Talmudists of their time. Their students later founded yeshivot patterned after the Yeshiva of Volozhin throughout Lithuania.

The history of the Yeshiva of Volozin was a stormy one. Founded in 1803, it was closed by Russian edict in 1824, to be reopened later. In 1858, its doors were once again barred, but again it was reopened for study. In 1892, it was closed for the last time; there was no appealing the decision. But "illegal" study continued until World War I. Volozhin left its mark on all the great yeshivot of Lithuania and has strongly influenced the development of present systems of study in the U.S. and Israel.

WAKSMAN, SELMAN ABRAHAM (1883-1973). Scientist, educator, author. Born in **Ukraine**, Waksman came to the U.S. in 1910. By 1938, he was recognized as one of the world's authorities on soil microbiology. With the outbreak of World War II, Waksman's interest shifted from soil study to disease causes in humans and animals, and began intensive work on the development of antibiotics, substances which destroy or arrest the growth of certain disease-causing microbes. In 1952, Waksman was awarded the **Nobel Prize** in Physiology and Medicine for his work in antibiotics and for the development of streptomycin, an invaluable antibiotic for fighting tuberculosis. He donated all royalties from his discoveries to Rutgers University for the creation of the Institute of Microbiology, of which he was director. He was the holder of a number of honorary degrees. In 1952, Waksman traveled to **Israel** on the invitation of the government, to advise upon the construction of a new antibiotic center there.

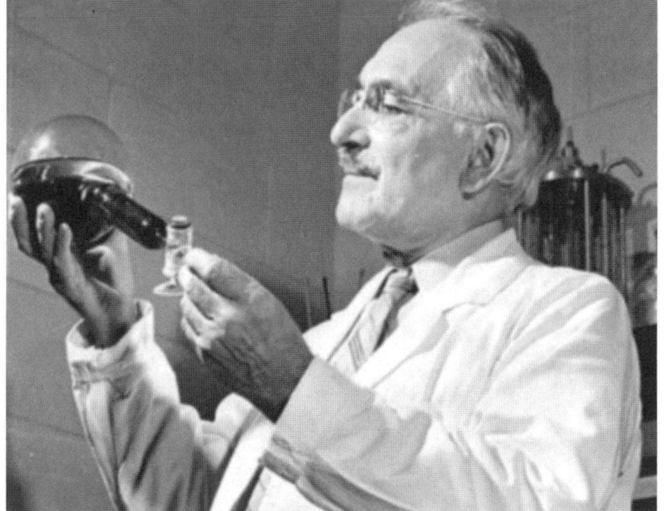

Dr. Selman A. Waksman. Courtesy Rutgers University, New Jersey.

WALD, LILLIAN D. (1867-1940). Social worker. A native of Cincinnati, **Ohio**, she left a sheltered existence to enter the field of nursing and organized the first city school nursing program in the world. Moved by the appalling conditions on **New York**'s Lower East Side, she became a pioneer social worker and founded the Henry Street Settlement in 1893. In 1908, she organized the Federal Children's Bureau, and her labors in behalf of the underprivileged earned her gratitude and an enduring place in the history of American social service. Her book describing the nurses' Settlement, *The House on Henry Street*, was published in 1915.

WALLENBERG, RAOUL (1912-ca. 1947). Swedish diplomat. During World War II he served in Hungary, and as Jews were being deported to the death camps by the Nazis, he forged papers and engaged in other clandestine activities which helped save thousands of Jewish lives. When the Russians occupied Hungary after the war they took him to Russia. For years, attempts were made to discover what had happened to him, but to no avail. Today, there is a street in Washington, DC named after him, where the **United States Holocaust Museum** is located.

WANDERING JEW. A medieval Christian legend, according to which Jews were punished for the death of **Jesus** by becoming homeless wanderers of the earth. The statelessness of Jews was seen as a validation of this belief. Once the State of **Israel** was born, the legend lost much of its validity.

WAR OF INDEPENDENCE. *See* **Israel, State of.**

WARBURG, FELIX M. (1871-1937). Banker, philanthropist, and communal leader. Born in Hamburg, Germany, to a noted banking family, Warburg settled in **New York City** in 1895, and joined one of the city's leading brokerage firms. From the time of his arrival he took an active interest in local charities, especially those caring for immigrants. Concerned with education, he made important contributions to educational institutions, both general and Jewish. He served as chairman of the Young Men's Hebrew Association in New York for many years, and was chairman of the **American Jewish Joint Distribution Committee** from its establishment in 1914 to 1932. In 1917, Warburg was instrumental in forming the Federation of Jewish Philanthro-

Felix Warburg. Courtesy the Jewish Theological Seminary.

pies in New York. Although opposed to Jewish nationalism, he supported agencies concerned with the economic development of Jews in Palestine, and mobilized support for the **Hebrew University** in **Jerusalem**. As a non-Zionist, he participated in the Jewish Agency for Palestine and took part in the political struggle against British anti-Zionist policy. He was the son-in-law of Jacob H. **Schiff**.

WARSAW. The oldest records that mention the presence of Jews in Warsaw date to the 14th century, when this city was the capital of Mazovia, a principality later united with **Poland**. After 1453, Jews were known to have been banished by official decree. When Warsaw became the capital of the Polish Kingdom at the close of the 16th century, Jews were brought into the city by the senators and delegates to the Polish parliament. In the 18th century, many Jews were permitted to settle in Warsaw on the condition that they pay a special tax. Two small Jewish towns were founded on the outskirts of Warsaw by the Poles Potocki and Sulkowski. However, the existence of these towns was challenged by the native Polish population, and they were destroyed in 1775. Jews finally received full permission to settle in Warsaw in 1788. They were not popularly accepted, however, and suffered intermittently from the hostile outbursts of their Christian compatriots. Nevertheless, Jews helped defend the city against the Russians in 1794 and organized a regiment of light cavalry. Three years later Jews were compelled to adopt surnames and pay a poll tax.

During the time of Napoleon, a Duchy of Warsaw was set up and chartered by a constitution that included full civil and political rights for Jews. In 1808, these rights were suspended by the Duke of Warsaw upon the instigation of anti-Semitic noblemen. In the course of the 19th century, Jews of Warsaw gradually received greater official acceptance. In 1863, many Jews participated in the Polish uprising against the Russians.

Detail of the monument of the Warsaw Ghetto Uprising.

The famous Warsaw Synagogue, destroyed by the Nazis during the uprising of the Warsaw ghetto.

Pogroms drove thousands of Russian Jews to Warsaw at the close of the 19th century. At the same time, **anti-Semitism** in Poland, and especially in Warsaw, began to grow as the new Polish middle class found itself in competition with Jewish merchants and industrial workers. When the Russian government convened the Dumas, or legislatures, at the beginning of the 20th century, Jews of Warsaw supported liberal labor candidates in opposition to the reactionary and anti-Semitic candidates of the National Democratic Party. The resulting anti-Jewish agitation in Warsaw was great.

By the time of World War I, Warsaw had become a spiritual, economic, and political center for Jews of Eastern Europe. Jews had built a compact community, which included Orthodox, assimilationist, **Zionist**, and **Bundist** (socialist) sectors. When Poland received its independence in 1919, Warsaw contained the headquarters of all these Jewish "parties," as well as commercial and cultural organizations, yeshivot, and seminaries. A flourishing and influential Jewish press had appeared: there were seven Yiddish daily newspapers and numerous periodicals. There were also two Jewish dailies in the Polish language and, intermittently, one in Hebrew. In addition, the Jewish community in Warsaw produced and supported numerous prosperous publishing houses, theaters, art exhibits, and professional organizations. In the political sphere, Jews of Warsaw saw many of their numbers elected to the Polish parliament. Nevertheless, anti-Semitism never completely abated, and economic discriminations against Jews continued to exist up to the outbreak of World War II.

At the time of the Nazi invasion in 1939, there were approximately 330,000 Jews in Warsaw, or 10 percent of the total

Jewish population of Poland. By October 1940, the Germans had herded the entire Jewish population of Warsaw into a ghetto the size of about 100 square city blocks, surrounded by walls and barbed wire. Until July 1942, the Germans were content to make life difficult for Jews by keeping them on starvation rations and denying them medical care. Then the Nazis began systematically deporting Jews from the Warsaw ghetto; told that they were being taken to labor camps, Jews actually were sent to death camps where millions of Jews perished. In spring 1943, the leaders of the Jewish underground of Warsaw rose up against the Germans, much to the latter's surprise. By April 1943, the Germans had ordered the complete evacuation of the ghetto. Only lightly armed, the remaining Jews of the ghetto put up a gallant struggle against the heavily armed Germans sent to destroy them. The Jewish resistance, led by the young commander-in-chief Mordecai **Anielewicz** fought to the last, until September 1943. Two uprising leaders who survived were Yitzhak Cukerman and Zivia Lubetkin, who settled in Israel.

The postwar period saw the return of a small number of Jews to Warsaw—survivors of the concentration camps and death camps, as well as those who had somehow managed to hide under the protection of non-Jewish friends. Conditions for Jewish development in Warsaw were unfavorable in the country where, under Communist domination, the official policy was anti-religious and anti-Zionist. An estimated 2,000 Jews lived in Warsaw in the 1990's, maintaining one synagogue and a Yiddish theater.

WASHINGTON. Of the state's 32,000 Jews, 29,300 live in Seattle and about 1,000 in both Spokane and Tacoma. Jews first arrived in the 1850's. In 1870, the state had its first Jewish governor, Edward S. Solomon. The Jewish community grew in Spokane and Tacoma in the late 19th century. Today, there are eight Reform and six Conservative congregations in the state.

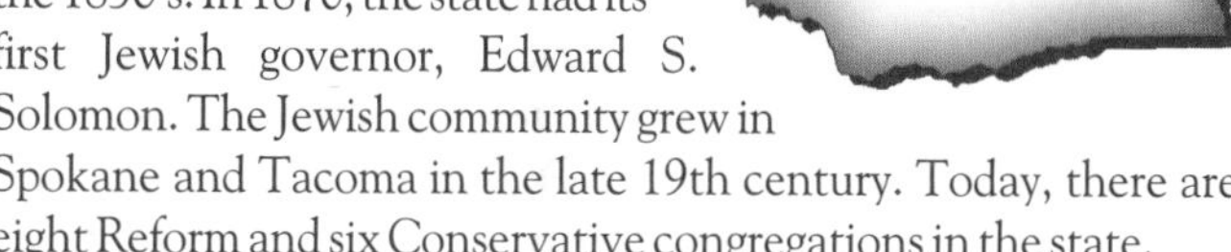

WASSERMANN, AUGUST VON (1866-1925). German Jewish scientist. He did important research into immunity and in the field of bacteriology. In 1906, he found serodiagnosis in syphilis (the so-called "Wasserman Reaction"), a discovery which made him famous. Wasserman was much interested in Jewish affairs, and was president of the Jewish Academy of Science in Berlin.

WASSERMANN, JAKOB (1873-1934). Novelist. A writer of international repute, he strove all his life to reconcile his Jewishness with his love for German culture. Opposed both to **assimilation** and to Jewish nationalism, he sought to fuse the two cultures. Disillusionment with his quest was expressed in *My Way as a German and a Jew*, written in 1921. His stories often deal with Jewish characters; his chief works are *The Jews of Zirndorf*, *Casper Hauser*, *The Gooseman*, and *The Maurizius Case*.

WEBER, MAX (1881-1961). American artist. Born in **Russia**, his abstract style at first angered critics, but eventually he came to be recognized as one of America's most vigorous artists. In 1954, he was elected to membership in the National Institute of Arts and Letters. Among contemporary American artists, none has struck his roots more deeply into the spiritual soil of Judaism than he. His best works are those which deal with Jewish topics. Favorite subjects are the Talmudists Weber saw in downtown Manhattan and Brooklyn; he has painted them sitting around the table, using their eloquent hands to underline an argument. He often elongates and even distorts their faces and figures, to indicate the highest pitch of emotional and spiritual experience.

WEEKS, FEAST OF. *See* **Shavuot**.

WEIL, SIMONE (1909-1943). French philosopher. She lived a tormented life, experiencing the life of the hard- working poor in France and later in the U.S. She rejected Judaism but did not quite embrace Roman Catholicism, which appealed to her in theory but not in the example of the Church. Her search for God is articulated in her book *Waiting for God*.

WEILL, KURT (1900-1950). German composer. His great success in pre-Nazi Germany was his music for Brecht's *Three Penny Opera*. Fleeing the Nazis, he came to **New York** where he wrote scores for plays and films. He was also active in the **Irgun**'s struggle for the birth of **Israel**.

WEISSMÜLLER, JOHNNY. *See* **Sports**.

Still Life, by Max Weber.

WEIZMANN, CHAIM (1874-1952). Scientist, Zionist statesman, first President of **Israel**. Born in **Russia**, he joined the Hibbat Zion movement. His twin passions for science and **Zionism** were all-absorbing. At 18, he went to **Germany** and studied at German and Swiss universities. While still young, he made an important discovery in the chemistry of dyes, and in 1904, he became instructor in chemistry at the University of Manchester in **England**. During World War I, Weizmann served as the head of the British Admiralty Laboratories and developed a process for manufacturing acetone out of starches, a vital link in the production of the explosives needed in the war effort. Lloyd George records in his memoirs that, when asked how the British government might repay him, Weizmann answered, "There is only one thing I want—a national home for my people."

Weizmann's international Zionist role began in 1901 at the 5th Zionist Congress. Influenced by Ahad **Ha-am**, the philosopher of cultural Zionism, he led a group that demanded that the Zionist Organization, in addition to its political work, set up a program of cultural work in Palestine and among the Jewish masses throughout the world. In 1903, Weizmann opposed Theodor **Herzl**'s idea of founding a Jewish home in Uganda (since Palestine was under Turkish rule, and thus unattainable). At the Zionist Congress in 1907, Weizmann pleaded for uniting the political work for obtaining Palestine as a Jewish homeland with the practical work of immediate colonization. Throughout his Zionist career, Weizmann strove to join political, cultural, and practical Zionism in one effort.

His greatest triumph came in the midst of World War I. The good will he had gained through his scientific achievements and his war efforts helped bring about the **Balfour Declaration**, supporting the establishment of a Jewish National Home in Palestine. In 1918, as head of a Zionist commission to Palestine, Weizmann visited Emir Feisal of Transjordan and discussed with him the idea of peaceful relations between Jews in Palestine and the Arab world. The same year he began the realization of an old Zionist dream when he laid the cornerstone for the **Hebrew University** on **Jerusalem**'s Mt. Scopus. In 1919, Weizmann appeared before the **Versailles Peace Conference** together with other Zionist leaders to ask endorsement of a Jewish National Home. He was elected president of the **World Zionist Organization** in 1920. Anxious to obtain wide support for Zionism, Weizmann proposed, in 1923, that the World Zionist Executive be enlarged to include non-Zionists. This idea was opposed vigorously for fear of weakening the Zionist movement. By 1929, however, Weizmann had won, and the enlarged **Jewish Agency** came into being, with Weizmann as its president. Weizmann headed the Zionist movement as president, continuously except for the break between 1931-1935, until the British mandate began to crumble in 1946, two years before the birth of the State of Israel. Meanwhile, his scientific interests continued without interruption. He served the Hebrew University in Jerusalem (inaugurated in 1925) as chairman of the board of governors and later as honorary president. He was instrumental in the establishment of the Daniel Sieff Research Institute, which later developed into the **Weizmann Institute of Science**. During World War II, he was invited by President Roosevelt to come to the U.S. to work on developing synthetic rubber needed for the vast war effort.

The last years of Weizmann's life were spent in two battles. On the political front he fought for a Jewish State before the various commissions investigating Palestine and before the United Nations. His other struggle was with growing blindness and failing health. The first battle was successful. The UN voted to partition Palestine into an Arab and a Jewish state, and on the day that the British left Palestine, the State of Israel was proclaimed. Weizmann lived to witness Israel's victory over the Arab invaders and to open the first session of the Knesset, Israel's parliament, on February 14, 1949. Two days later, the Knesset elected Chaim Weizmann the first president of the reborn State of Israel. At his death he was honored by the world and mourned by his people.

Chaim Weizmann.

WEIZMAN, EZER (1924-). Israeli soldier and public servant. A native Israeli, he is a nephew of Chaim **Weizmann**. Known as the Father of Israel's Air Force, he served as chief of operations of the IDF's general staff during the **Six-Day War** of 1967. He was Minister of Transport from 1969 to 1970 and was appointed Minister of Defense in 1977 in the **Begin** government. He played a key role in Israel's negotiations with Egypt after Anwar el-Sadat's visit to Israel in November 1977, and took part in the Camp David peace talks between Israel and Egypt. In 1993, Weizman was elected as the sixth president of the State of Israel, succeeding Chaim Herzog. He was re-elected in 1998.

Ezer Weizman.

WEIZMANN INSTITUTE OF SCIENCE. Located in Rehovot, Israel, the Institute is a city of science with 19 departments, under five faculties: Mathematics; Physics; Chemistry; Biophysics-Biochemistry; Biology, devoted to fundamental research in the natural sciences related to human welfare. Its primary task is the discovery of knowledge and the training of new generations of scientists. It was first conceived in 1944 in honor of the 70th birthday of Chaim **Weizmann**.

Relevance of Science Research. Engaged in some several hundred research projects, Weizmann Institute scientists are studying the elements which constitute the life forces of humans, animals, and their environs to fathom how they function, and thereby to learn how birth, congenital defects, disease, aging can be controlled, and how the energies of the earth, of the ocean tides, and the atmosphere can be deflected from destruction and harnessed for humankind's welfare.

Status of Institute. It is in the forefront of research in the life sciences (cell biology, experimental biology, biological ultrastructure, biodynamics, biophysics, genetics, plant genetics, chemical immunology, biochemistry, polymer research), in physics, in chemistry, and in mathematics. It has become an important scientific resource, not only for Israel, but for the world.

Contributions to the State of Israel. Institute scientists are principal advisors to the Israeli government on science, new resources, water economy, industry, education, population of and development of the desert, agriculture, new food potentials, mineral exploitation, and the like.

Aid to Science Education. The Weizmann Institute is serving the educational and scientific manpower needs of Israel on two levels: the graduate student through the Feinberg Graduate School, and the high school student through its Science Teaching Department.

The Feinberg Graduate School is a multidisciplinary school for the training of independent researchers both in the natural sciences and in modern science technology. It is accredited as an American school abroad by charter from the New York State University Regents. In 1968, the Institute set up a Science Teaching Department, the first of its kind in Israel.

As a further stimulus to science learning, the Institute sponsors an Annual Science Fair, a Mathematics Olympiad, science clubs, special courses for gifted children, and a Summer Science Youth Camp.

In May 1973, a Weizmann Institute scientist, Professor Ephraim Katchalsky-**Katzir**, world renowned authority on protein research, was inaugurated as the fourth President of Israel. Founder and head of the Institute's Biophysics Department for 25 years, President Katzir continued his research while in office.

Israeli paratroopers gazing at the newly-liberated Western Wall in June 1967.

The Weizmann Institute has been ranked by Nobel Laureate Dr. Arthur Kornberg as among the top ten research institutes in the world.

WERFEL, FRANZ (1890-1945). One of leading poets of the German expressionist movement. Born in **Prague**, Werfel was one of the most versatile writers in the German language before World War II. He wrote plays which attracted international attention, including *Jacobowski and the Colonel*, later made into a movie with Danny Kaye, titled *The Colonel and I*; his novels included *The Forty Days of Musa Dagh*, an epic story of the genocide committed by the Turks against the Armenians.

WEST BANK. Area west of the **Jordan** river, part of Palestine. Assigned in 1947 by the United Nations as a separate Arab state, it was annexed by the Hashemite Kingdom of Jordan in 1948 and occupied by Israel in 1967. It is the biblical land of Judea and Samaria.

WEST VIRGINIA. Of the state's 2,000 Jews, 950 live in Charleston, 300 in Huntington, and 300 in Wheeling. Jewish life in the state began in the 1840's. The first congregation was organized in Wheeling in 1849. An influx of Jewish settlers arrived after 1880. Jews in the state have engaged in commerce and in the milling, pottery, and tobacco industries. There are three Reform and two Conservative congregations in the state.

WESTERN WALL. Last relic of the western defense wall of the First and Second **Temples** in **Jerusalem**. The Western Wall is holy to Jews, who have prayed and wept over its stones since the destruction of Jerusalem in 70 C.E. almost continuously, except during periods when this was prohibited on pain of death. Since the fall of the Old City of Jerusalem to the Arab forces of **Jordan** in 1948, it had been inaccessible to Jews. On June 7, 1967, during the **Six-Day War**, the Israeli Army recaptured the Old City of Jerusalem, and since then Jews have had free access to the Wall. Since then, it has been officially referred to as the Western Wall, or in Hebrew, *Kotel Ma'aravi*. Shortly after the area was liberated, the Government of Israel started extensive archaeological excavations in the vicinity of the Wall. The Wall is about 54 feet high and 85 feet long, and has about 24 layers of immense uncut gray stones. This section of the wall belongs to the Second Temple, however, buried beneath the surface are almost as many layers of stones which are the remains of the First Temple. Prayers are recited at the Wall day and night, but pilgrimages usually take place on Tisha B'av, the anniversary of the razing of the temple.

WIESEL, ELIE (1928-). Novelist and journalist. Born in **Romania** and raised in a Hasidic environment, he was deported by the Nazis and was in the death camps of Birkenau, **Auschwitz**, Buna, and **Buchenwald**. For several years following World War II he lived in **Paris**; later, he settled in **New York**. His novels, which

Elie Wiesel.

he originally wrote in French and which were subsequently translated into English, brought him fame not only as a writer on Jewish themes, but also as a major French novelist. Most of his novels are concerned with the **Holocaust**. Among his best-known works are *Night*, *The Town Beyond the Wall*, *The Gates of the Forest*, *Legends of Our Time*, *The Jews of Silence* (an eyewitness report of the plight of Soviet Jewry), *A Beggar in Jerusalem*, *One Generation After*, and *Souls on Fire*. Wiesel played a major role in bringing the Holocaust to the conscience of the world, not only as a novelist but also as an active spokesman for Holocaust survivors. He also spoke out effectively on other issues, both Jewish and general, and in 1986, he won the **Nobel** Peace Prize in recognition for his advocacy.

WIESENTHAL, SIMON (1908-). A **Holocaust** survivor, Wiesenthal settled in Vienna, **Austria** after the war, where he opened a Jewish Historical Documentation Center, dedicated to hunting Nazi war criminals. Over the years, his center has played a major role in bringing Nazi criminals to justice. His books include *The Murderers Among Us.*

WINCHELL, WALTER (1897-1972). American journalist. His gossip columns and radio and television programs had a large audience beginning in 1929, making him one of the most influential media personalities in the country.

WINGATE, MAJOR GENERAL ORDE CHARLES (1903-1944). Wingate is renowned as the creator of the long-range penetration tactics by which his Burma campaign (1943-44) saved **India** from the Japanese in World War II. Earlier, in 1941, he used similar tactics to drive the Italians out of Abyssinia and restore Haile Selassie to his throne in Addis Ababa. But it was in Palestine that Wingate achieved his early fame. Under his training, special night squads broke the grip of the Arab terror in 1938. And, throughout his later career, his heart was set on returning to the Holy Land.

Major General Orde Charles Wingate.

The deeply idealistic and fiercely individualist personality of Orde Charles Wingate, a non-Jew, was shaped by the twin influences of the **Bible** and of military service. He came to Palestine in 1936 as an intelligence officer to the British Forces stationed there. His lifelong absorption in the Bible made Wingate feel at home in the Holy Land. He traveled to all the Holy Places, learned Hebrew, sought out Jews in **Haifa** where he was stationed, and got to know the Jewish leaders in **Jerusalem** and the young **halutzim** in the **kibbutzim**.

The Arab terror that had broken out in 1936 was aided by German and Italian subsidies and was making life difficult in Palestine. Arab guerrillas infiltrated from **Syria**, **Lebanon**, and Transjordan. They attacked settlements and road traffic, and instigated the local Arabs to join them in looting, killing, and sabotaging the oil pipelines that led from **Iraq** to the British-controlled refineries in Haifa. Wingate found that the British police and troops were ineffectual in controlling the situation because of their tradition-bound methods, and because of the prevailing anti-Zionist policy. The British administration drove the Jewish self-defense militia underground and actually arrested those caught defending Jewish settlements with arms.

Wingate obtained official permission to investigate the ways and methods of Arab infiltrators; unofficially, he got assistance from members of the **Haganah** in carrying out this task. His report to General Wavell included a plan for wiping out the Arab terrorists and a request for permission to carry it out. Despite considerable official opposition, Wingate was granted permission and set up headquarters at En Harod, a kibbutz in the shadow of Mount Gilboa. In the same countryside where **Gideon** had chosen his warriors, Wingate chose and trained his special night squads. They were composed mainly of 400 selected members of the kibbutzim, including Moshe **Dayan** and Yigal **Allon**, with about 200 equally handpicked British soldiers. Within three months, Wingate had a highly trained commando force. These he led in swift nightly attacks on Arab rebel centers and points of infiltration. In six months, the back of the Arab terror was broken. Wingate's achievement brought him the Distinguished Service Order but the intense dislike of the local anti-Jewish British officials.

Moreover, the Palestine administration did not like to see military skills developed in Jews, and shortly after his success in 1938, Wingate was recalled to London.

Wingate's brilliant contributions to Allied victories in World War II ended tragically while he was touring his forward bases in the Burma jungle. During a severe storm, his plane crashed against a Mountainside and Wingate died at age 41. In Israel, Wingate has become a legend. He is remembered gratefully in many ways. A Wingate Forest was planted near En Harod on the southern slopes of Mt. Gilboa. A school for physical training has been named for him, and Yemin Orde, a **Youth Aliyah** village on the slopes of his well-loved Carmel, was established as a living memorial to him.

WINGER, DEBRA. *See* **Stage and Screen.**

WINTERS, SHELLEY. *See* **Stage and Screen.**

WISCONSIN. Of the 35,000 Jews in the state, 29,000 live in Milwaukee and 4,500 in Madison. Jewish peddlers and traders first arrived in the state in 1792, but the first community was organized in Milwaukee in 1836, where a congregation was formed in 1847. By that time an influx of German Jews arrived in the state, and Jewish merchants began to reach such towns as Madison, La Crosse, Green Bay, Racine, and Fond du Lac. The Jewish population further grew at the turn of the century with the arrival of East European Jews. There are nine Reform and Seven Conservative congregations in the state. The *Wisconsin Jewish Chronicle* is published in Milwaukee.

WISE, ISAAC MAYER (1819-1900). Main organizer of the Reform movement in the U.S. Rabbi Wise left his native Bohemia in 1846 and came to the U.S., where he took an Orthodox pulpit and began to reform the service. In 1854, he settled in Cincinnati where he proceeded to lay the groundwork for Reform Judaism in the U.S. He founded an English weekly called *The American*

Israelite, the oldest Anglo-Jewish newspaper in the U.S. In 1873, he organized the **Union of American Hebrew Congregations**, the organization of Reform congregation in the U.S., and two years later the **Hebrew Union College**, the Reform rabbinical seminary, the oldest rabbinical seminary in the U.S. In 1889, he organized the **Central Conference of American Rabbis**, the organization of American Reform rabbis. These accomplishments not only ensured the vigorous growth of the Reform movement, but also served as a model for organized Jewish life in the U.S., emulated by other religious movements and by social and cultural organizations.

WISE, STEPHEN SAMUEL (1874-1949). Rabbi, author, and Zionist leader. Born in Budapest and brought to the U.S. as an infant, Stephen Wise was educated in **New York City**, where he studied at City College and Columbia University and prepared privately for the rabbinate. He took his first pulpit at 19, and from 1900 to 1906 served in Portland, **Oregon**. In 1907, Wise returned to New York and founded the Free Synagogue, which he led to the end of his life. Fifteen years later he established the Jewish Institute of Religion, a rabbinical seminary dedicated to the liberal ideals Wise embodied as rabbi and citizen. In 1950 this institution merged with the **Hebrew Union College.**

Wise's brilliant gifts as orator and administrator early gained him a distinguished position in the two areas that were to preoccupy him throughout his career: social reform and Zionist affairs. While still in Portland, he spoke out on behalf of labor reform. Later, he became a prominent advocate of civil rights, labor legislation, and Franklin D. Roosevelt's New Deal program. An early Zionist, he was a founder of the Federation of American Zionists in 1898, the year of the second Zionist Congress. During the half-century that followed, he worked passionately within the community to gain adherents for the movement. But Zionism was only one facet of Wise's concern with Jewish life. To provide democratic representation for American Jewry as a body, he joined with Justice Louis **Brandeis** and Felix **Frankfurter** in founding the **American Jewish Congress** in 1917, whose interests, as well as those of **Zionism**, he represented at the **Versailles Peace Conference** in 1919. In 1936, to provide an agency for contact between Jewish communities the world over, he organized the **World Jewish Congress**. During World War II, Wise made many attempts to influence President Roosevelt to do more to help rescue European Jews from the Nazis, but found out that the war effort precluded such action.

Stephen S. Wise.

WIZO. Women's International Zionist Organization, founded in 1920. Wizo developed from the Federation of Women Zionists in Great Britain in 1920 as a welfare organization for the care of women and children in Eretz Israel. With headquarters in **Tel Aviv**, it has branches in 54 countries with a total membership of about 220,000. Some 13,000 children are in the care of 197 Wizo child welfare institutions in Israel, ranging from homes for babies through pre-school day centers to clubs and playgrounds for schoolchildren. In the field of education, Wizo maintains six agricultural and vocational training schools in Israel with a total of 3,000 pupils. The services for women and families maintained by Wizo in Israel number 260 and range from mending and sewing courses to a mobile library. Wizo activity in Israel is not centralized but covers social services for women and children from the cradle to the grave, in the whole area from Dan to **Elat**, wherever there are underprivileged in need of help.

WOLFSON, SIR ISAAC (1897-1991). British businessman and philanthropist. Born in Glasgow, Scotland, of Eastern European immigrant parents, he has worked since age 14 and now heads a chain of 2,600 retail stores in Great Britain, **Canada**, and **South Africa**; he controls the largest mail-order enterprise outside the U.S. Wolfson is active in innumerable Jewish organizations, and has contributed more than $1 million to the **Weizmann Institute of Science**, as well as considerable funds to Youth Aliyah and other institutions. Heichal Shlomo, a religious center in **Jerusalem**, was built by him as a memorial to his father. In 1955, he set up the Isaac Wolfson Foundation which has since donated more than $15 million to worthy British causes. He was created a baronet in 1962 "for philanthropic services." Wolfson was an observant Jew and served as president of the United Synagogue. In March 1963, Sir Isaac made a contribution of rare munificence in the sum of $2 million to help develop community projects in **Acre**, Israel. The unparalleled extent and variety of his benefactions places him in the foremost ranks of philanthropists in Jewish history.

WOMEN'S AMERICAN ORT. *See* **ORT**.

WOMEN'S LEAGUE FOR CONSERVATIVE JUDAISM. Previously known as National Women's League of the United Synagogue of America. An organization of women belonging to sisterhoods of the Conservative synagogues throughout the United States and Canada. Founded in 1917 by the wife of Solomon **Schechter**, the organization totals more than 800 sisterhoods with a membership of more than 200,000 women affiliated with the **Jewish Theological Seminary of America**.

The goal of Women's League is to bring the ideas of Conservative Judaism to the attention of the American Jewish woman. For this purpose, the organization fosters study courses, Judaism-in-the-home Institutes, and synagogue libraries. It publishes books for children, education and program kits, a magazine called *The Outlook*. The organization sponsors a comprehensive Leadership Training Program to prepare leaders for local sisterhoods. Its Social Actions Committee seeks to give American Jewish women a better understanding of their civic responsibilities. The League helps to support the

Jewish Theological Seminary of America through the Torah Fund. It is one of the sponsors of the United Synagogue Youth and cooperates with other organizations in civic welfare and Israel projects.

WORKMEN'S CIRCLE. Jewish fraternal order organized in 1892 to protect working immigrants in the U.S. and assist them in times of illness or unemployment. These arrivals, mainly in **New York**'s East Side, who became needle workers, carpenters, painters, laundryman, and cleaners, were immediate beneficiaries of the new order. In 1984, there was a membership throughout the U.S. and **Canada** of 50,000, in more than 280 functioning branches. The Circle operated a system of medical aid, hospitalization, and various forms of insurance and direct benefits. It had summer camps, women's clubs, homes for the aged, burial grounds, high schools and teachers' seminaries, educational publications, and other periodicals in English and Yiddish. Aid has been extended to Yiddish schools in South America and other centers. Notably, the Circle supported Jewish and non-Jewish victims of need and discrimination in the Americas and abroad.

WORLD FEDERATION OF BERGEN BELSEN ASSOCIATIONS. Organization dedicated to perpetuating the memory of the martyrs exterminated at Bergen **Belsen** and all other concentration camps in Europe by creating and maintaining public movements and memorial libraries throughout the free world, and publishing materials and preserving books, artifacts, and other memorabilia relating to the **Holocaust**. The federation sponsors the International Remembrance Award for Excellence and Distinction in the Literature of the Holocaust, and allocates grants to universities for research projects in the history of the Holocaust. The founder and first president of the federation was the late Joseph Rosensaft.

WORLD JEWISH CONGRESS. Founded at Geneva in August 1936, the World Jewish Congress (WJC) assumed responsibility for consultations on behalf of persecuted Jews in various countries and in the councils of the League of Nations. It was active in the planning of the Evian Conference on Refugees in 1938. Following the failure of that conference, it continued to work to save Jews from the clutches of the Nazis and their allies. At the end of World War II, the WJC worked with and on behalf of the survivors of Nazi terror, the Jewish displaced persons all over Europe and Africa. During the Nuremberg war crimes trials the WJC served in a consultative capacity, supplying factual dossiers from its files. The WJC has also consistently helped Israel.

Representatives of the WJC attended the founding conference of the United Nations at San Francisco in 1945. They worked for the inclusion of rights planks in the UN charter and for the most democratic structure possible for the UN. The WJC serves as a consulting organization for the UN and its specialized agencies, concerning itself with such matters as human rights, genocide, and cultural affairs.

The WJC was active in the negotiations which resulted in the agreements by **Germany** and **Austria** to pay collective restitution to Jews for damages done by the Nazis. It is a member of the Conference on Jewish Material Claims Against Germany.

WJC offices in various countries represent Jews individually and Jewish communities collectively in negotiations with governments with regard 10 various political and related problems.

Sixty-six countries have affiliates of the WJC. There were regional councils in the Americas and Europe. Full Congress meetings were held at Montreux, **Switzerland**, in 1948 and in Geneva in 1953.

In recent years the WJC was active in uncovering the war crimes of Kurt Waldheim, who, while becoming president of **Austria**, also was proclaimed a *persona non grata* in the U.S. It also became involved in claims against Swiss banks which kept accounts deposited by former Nazis, consisting of funds stolen from Jewish victims of the Holocaust.

The official aims of the World Jewish Congress are coordination of the efforts of its affiliated organizations in respect to the political, economic, social, and cultural problems of the Jewish people; securing and defending the rights, status, and interests of Jews and Jewish communities throughout the world; assisting their creative development; and representing and acting on their behalf before governmental, inter-governmental, and international authorities.

WORLD ZIONIST ORGANIZATION. Organized in 1897, the 204 delegates to the first Congress represented many Zionist societies in 17 countries. The Congress elected Theodor **Herzl** as the first president of the World Zionist Organization and worked out a constitution with the Basle Program as its basic plank. The constitution provided that any Jew could become a member of the World Zionist Organization by subscribing to the Basle Program and by paving the minimal dues, called a **shekel**. The Zionists of each country elected one delegate to the Zionist Congress for each unit of 1,500 shekel holders. The Congress in session served as the governing body of the Zionist movement. Each Congress elected two bodies: the general council, or actions committee, to determine Zionist policy between sessions, and the executive, to carry on day-to-day Zionist affairs. As the movement grew, right- and left-wing parties developed programs reflecting the times, conditions, and the thinking of the various groups within the Jewish communities. These parties, advocating their particular programs for the upbuilding of Palestine, became constituent organizations, elected delegates to the Congress, and were represented on the Actions Committee and on the Executive. (*See also* **General Zionism, Mizrachi, and Labor Zionism**.)

WOUK, HERMAN (1915-). American novelist. He became known mainly as a chronicler of U.S. involvement in World War II, beginning with his novel *The Caine Mutiny*, and later with *Winds of War* and *War and Remembrance.* An observant Jew, he wrote about his Jewish faith in *This Is My God.*

WYOMING. Of the state's 450 Jews, 230 live in Cheyenne. Jewish settlement dates back to the 1860's, when Jewish peddlers and traders began to arrive in the state. The first congregation did not get organized until 1915.

YADIN, YIGAEL (1917-1984). Soldier and archeologist. Son of the late Eliezer I. Sukenik, a professor of Archaeology in the **Hebrew University** of **Jerusalem**, he shared his father's love for rediscovering the secrets of the past. Brilliant in military tactics, he applied his knowledge of ancient battle strategy effectively to defeat the superior Egyptian forces in the Negev during the Israel War of Independence in 1948.

As soon as he could be relieved from his military duties, Yadin returned to his first love, archeology. Yadin's gift for deciphering the past led him to the study of the famous **Dead Sea Scrolls**. His introduction and commentary to *The Scroll of the War of the Sons of Light Against the Sons of Darkness* won him the Israel Prize for scholarly achievement. In 1965, he reported a number of significant archeological finds in **Masada**. A founder and the leader of the middle-of-the-road Democratic Movement for Change (DASH) in Israel, he became Israel's deputy prime minister in 1977.

YAD VASHEM. Literally, Monument and Memorial. Israel's memorial to the Jewish communities and people who perished in the **Holocaust**. Located on the Mount of Remembrance near **Jerusalem**, the Yad VaShem building includes a library, an archives building, exhibits, and a memorial chamber. Foreign diplomats visiting **Israel** are taken to visit Yad VaShem, and schools organize regular visits so that the new generation born and raised in Israel learns about one of the most tragic episodes in the history of their people.

YAHRZEIT. *See* **Burial and Mourning**.

YAVNEH. Jamnia in Greek. Old Palestinian city on the Mediterranean coast between **Jaffa** and old **Ashdod**. At the time of the Second **Temple**, Yavneh was a well-populated, well-fortified city. During the Roman siege of **Jerusalem**, it is said that Rabbi **Johanan Ben Zakkai** escaped the city and made his way to the camp of the Roman general Vespasian. He told Vespasian that he would soon become Emperor of **Rome**, which indeed happened. After the fall of Jerusalem, Vespasian, in gratitude, granted Ben Zakkai's request to let him gather a small community of sages and organize a school. The **Sanhedrin** was reestablished at Yavneh, and Ben Zakkai became its head. Yavneh remained the seat of scholarship and culture until the **Bar Kokhba** revolt in 132-135 C.E., when the Sanhedrin was disbanded, and many of the Jewish inhabitants of the city fled. In 1948, Yavneh was an Arab market-town known as Yebneh. In 1979, there was a religious **kibbutz** near the abandoned site of the old Yavneh. Recently the inhabitants of the kibbutz built a **yeshiva**, and the tradition of scholarship for which ancient Yavneh was famed is now carried on by modern settlers.

YEHOASH (1871-1927). Solomon Bloomgarden, Yiddish poet. Born in **Lithuania**, he came to the U.S. in 1890. Yehoash contributed to the modernization of **Yiddish literature** in the U.S. and cultivated in his readers a taste for the best in world literature through his Yiddish translations. His major achievement was his masterly translation of the **Bible** into Yiddish. This work combines a deep scholarly understanding of the original Hebrew with poetic skill. Yehoash's translation of the Bible became one of the most popular works in Yiddish literature.

YELLIN, DAVID (1864-1942). Hebrew scholar. Born in **Jerusalem**, he became one of the first active supporters of Eliezer **Ben Yehudah** in his efforts to revive Hebrew as a spoken language. Yellin helped found the Hebrew Language Academy and wrote important works on **Maimonides**, Hebrew poetry of the Middle Ages, and Hebrew grammar. He established a Teachers' Institute in Jerusalem, and in his later years taught at the **Hebrew University** of **Jerusalem**.

YEMEN. Muslim kingdom in the southwest corner of the Arabian peninsula, made up of plateaus and hills rising to 10,000 feet. This altitude gives Yemen enough rain to supply a population of about 7 million with corn, vegetables, fruit, and wheat, and enough of its famous mocha coffee to export. In ancient times, Yemen traded with Africa and the Far East, but since adopting **Islam** in 628, the country has been fearful of strangers, isolated, and poor. The Jewish community of Yemen is thought to be the oldest in the world, dating back to **Solomon**'s time. In the 5th century C.E., Jewish influence was so great that the Himyaritic kings adopted Judaism; however, the Ethiopian invasions ended this dynasty. When Yemen adopted Islam, Jews were made second-class citizens; they were not, for example, permitted to walk on the pavement or ride on a donkey, lest a Jew look down upon a Muslim pedestrian. Jewish orphans were forcibly converted to Islam. Nevertheless, through centuries of oppression, the Yemenite Jews preserved their traditional religion. In 1172, **Maimonides** wrote his famous *Epistle to the Yemenites*, in which he expressed his sympathy for Jews of Yemen in their martyrdom and exhorted them to remain true to their faith. Their yearning for Zion led the Yemenite Jews to place their faith in a number of false Messiahs, a danger Maimonides had warned against. Despite their isolation, Yemenite Jews were in

Yemenite Jew.

contact with Jewish spiritual and creative life during the Middle Ages. **Kabbalah** was a popular study among them, and they had Kabbalist writers, poets, and scholars. In 1517, Yemen became a part of the Ottoman (Turkish) empire. Periodic clashes between Arab and Turk followed; the Turks were driven out of Yemen, but returned to reoccupy the country. Each change worsened the position of Jews. This situation and their ancient love of the Holy Land induced them to begin migration to **Israel** in 1881. This migration reached its climax after the establishment of the State of Israel, when the entire community of 40,000 Yemenite Jews was transported by plane within about a year. To Yemenite Jews, these flights were the "eagle's wings" in the prophecy of redemption. In 1998, there were about 300 Jews still in the country.

YESHIVA. Yeshivot, plural; literally, academy. Traditional Orthodox institution where young men devote themselves to the study of Talmudic law. Some graduates receive rabbinic ordination; others remain for varying periods and then leave to enter a secular vocation. Some yeshivot have *kollelim*, schools of advanced Talmudic study where married students receive support for their families while they concentrate on their studies. More recently, the term has been used also for all-day Orthodox schools where both Jewish and secular subjects are taught. *Yeshiva Ketanah*, or little yeshiva, is an Orthodox all-day school on the elementary level.

YESHIVA UNIVERSITY. First founded in **New York** in 1886 as a small Talmudical school named *Yeshiva Etz Chaim*. Ten years later, another Yeshiva was founded and named after the great Lithuanian rabbi, Rabbi Isaac Elchanan **Spector**. In 1915, the two institutions merged, under the head of a leading scholar, Bernard **Revel**. Recognizing the need for combined religious and secular training, the Yeshiva opened the Talmudical Academy, the first academic high school under Jewish auspices in the U.S. In 1921, a Teachers' Institute, originally founded in 1917 by the **Mizrachi Organization of America**, was added to the Yeshiva. The Teachers' Institute has provided hundreds of principals and teachers for Hebrew schools throughout the country. Yeshiva University's rabbinical graduates are organized in the Rabbinical Council of America.

In 1928, the first college of liberal arts and sciences in America under Jewish auspices, Yeshiva College, opened its doors. Under the name "Rabbi Isaac Elchanan Theological Seminary and Yeshiva College," the expanding institution moved the following year to the present Main Center, Amsterdam Avenue and 186th Street, in New York's Washington Heights. Since 1977, it has been headed by Dr. Norman Lamm. In 1945, the institution attained university status.

Above, Dr. Bernard Revel, first president of Yeshiva University. Below, Dr. Norman Lamm, President of Yeshiva University.

In addition to its rabbinical seminary, Yeshiva University has a total of 18 schools and divisions, including four high schools (for boys and girls), Stern College for Women, Albert Einstein College of Medicine, Wurzweiler School of Social Work, Ferkauf Graduate School of Humanities and Social Sciences, and Belfer

Graduate School of Science. In addition, the University maintained 24 special programs and services, among them the Community Service Division, Israel Rogosin Center for Ethics and Human Values, Information Retrieval Center on the Disadvantaged, Inservice Institute in Science and Mathematics for Secondary School Teachers, and Albert Einstein College Hospital.

YETZER HA-RAH. Literally, evil inclination. The internal impulse to do wrong. Judaism believes that the impulse to do evil is part of human nature, just as is the impulse to do good, *Yetzer Ha-tov*. However, one is not born to do evil, and through willpower one can conquer the Yetzer Ha-Rah. The rabbis suggested the study of **Torah** as one way of conquering the evil impulse.

YIDDISH. Language spoken by East European Jewry, approximately 1,000 years old. Jews have always spoken the language of the land in which they lived. Babylonian Jews spoke **Aramaic**; Jews who lived under Arab dominion spoke Arabic; and those of **France** spoke French in their daily lives. The language of Jewish religious life was **Hebrew**. Yiddish began to develop when French Jews settled along the Rhine, and their vocabulary was augmented by many words from the various medieval German dialects of their new neighbors.

Expulsions and persecutions forced the Jews to move from place to place, increasing the difference between their speech and that of the surrounding population. When the German Jews migrated to Bohemia, **Poland**, and **Lithuania**, they took their medieval German dialect with them, at the same time adapting more Hebrew and Slavic words. Jews in the ghetto were alienated from the cultural life of the surrounding people; this isolation, added to the special Jewish way of life, was also a basic factor in the development of the Yiddish language. Also, Yiddish reflects the East European Jews' concentration in cities and consequent separation from nature; few terms for flowers and trees, birds, animals and fishes exist in Yiddish. On the other hand, Yiddish may be pungent, colorful, and even sentimental, but it is rarely pompous (there was little room for sham in the **ghetto**). Jews continued to move eastward, and Ukrainian, White Russian, and Russian elements entered the Yiddish language. When Yiddish-speaking immigrants moved westward, to the New World, Yiddish vocabulary expanded to include English terms in the U.S. and Spanish words in **Argentina**, all of which has enriched the language. In all, Yiddish has a vocabulary of approximately 150,000 words.

Yiddish is the creation of **Ashkenazic** Jewry. Even before 1500, Yiddish was spoken in Ashkenazic communities. Beginning with the 13th century, as the role of Ashkenazic Jews in Jewish history became more prominent, the Yiddish language gained in importance. From the 16th through the 18th century, it was the spoken language of Ashkenazic Jews everywhere. Yiddish is still the language of communication among Jews in the various centers of the world. It is heard wherever Jews from diverse countries meet, for example, at Zionist Congresses. There are approximately 130 Yiddish periodicals internationally.

For many generations, Yiddish was the language of Jewish education. In the **heder**, the **Bible** was interpreted in Yiddish; in the **yeshiva**, Yiddish was used to study the **Talmud**. The 20th century saw the development of secular Yiddish schools. In North America, Yiddish afternoon schools have functioned since 1910. There are Yiddish day schools in **Canada**, **Mexico**, and other countries. In the U.S., Yiddish is taught at several colleges and universities.

It is estimated that before World War II, between 10 and 11 million Jews spoke Yiddish. Of the six million Jews who perished in the **Holocaust**, at least five and a half million spoke Yiddish. To this loss must be added the linguistic **assimilation** in the U.S. and other countries. It is difficult to estimate the number of Jews who speak Yiddish today.

YIDDISH LITERATURE. The history of Yiddish literature may conveniently be divided into five periods: from the beginning to approximately 1500; the flourishing years of the 16th and early 17th centuries; the period of stagnation from 1650 to 1750; the era of **Hasidism** and **Haskalah** (1750 to 1864); modern Yiddish literature since 1864.

Before 1500, Yiddish literature was based on Jewish folklore, religious Hebrew literature, and the secular literary output of the European peoples among whom Jews lived. There were three types of professionals making this literature popular: copyists, who prepared anthologies and who were themselves frequently anonymous authors; minstrels, who sang or recited ballads and poems at public gatherings; and jesters, who gave brief performances. The best known work of this first period is the *Shmuel-Bukh* (Samuel Book), which describes the life of King **David** in poetic form. In this early period, Yiddish literature already served as a medium of entertainment and education for all segments of Jewish people, particularly for women and the uneducated. The 16th century saw a dramatic upsurge in Yiddish literature, similar to that which took place in a number of European literatures. Printing became widespread, and since Jews were the most literate people in Europe, Yiddish books could be mass-produced. At the beginning of the 16th century the *Bova Bukh*, a romantic adventure novel, became tremendously popular. However, the most widely read book appeared at the close of the 16th century: *Tsena Urena*, a retelling of the **Pentateuch**, was interwoven with various legends, stories, and parables. For 300 years Jewish women read from this book every **Sabbath**.

In this period, Yiddish literature made use of all the narrative and a large part of the poetic materials of the earlier centuries in the history of the Jewish people. The popular *Maase Bukh* in 1602 contained a number of interesting stories from various periods of Jewish history. At this time there was close contact between readers of Yiddish in Eastern Europe and the Germanic countries. Yiddish books and authors circulated from east to west and from west to east. Yiddish literature made possible close contact among all **Ashkenazic** Jews. **Prague** and other Eastern European communities became centers of Yiddish literature.

The Thirty Years War in Western Europe, and the bloody persecutions of Jews in the **Ukraine** and **Poland** in 1648 and 1649 ushered in a period of intellectual stagnation. No new important works appeared. Many books were published in Amsterdam and there was a great demand for Yiddish books, but the spirit of the times was not conducive to the appearance of talented new writers.

The advent of **Hasidism** in the middle of the 18th century brought with it a spiritual revival among the masses of Jewish people in Eastern Europe. At the same time the **Haskalah**, or Enlightenment, movement developed in **Germany**, and a generation or two later, in Galicia, Ukraine, and **Lithuania**. These two opposing movements were represented in the renewed literary

Distinguished Yiddish writers in the United States. First row, l. to r.: S. Niger, H. Leivick, J. Opatoshu, H. Raisin, A. Glantz, P. Schwartz, and H. Novak. Second row, l. to r.: J. Patt, H. Poupko, and S. Tabachinsky. Courtesy A. Glantz.

activity of this period. The Enlighteners utilized Yiddish literature to write satiric works criticizing the negative aspects of rigid Judaism; the Hasidim created legends and stories dealing with the great achievements of the rabbis. Many of the Hasidim were talented narrators, poets, and writers of parables. The most interesting of these was Rabbi Nahman of **Bratzlav**. In Eastern Europe the Enlighteners included a number of able writers, the most important of whom were Shlomo Ettinger, a poet and dramatist, and the popular writer of the mid-19th century, and Isaac Meyer Dick, whose hundreds of stories were published in thousands of copies.

Modern Yiddish Literature. Modern Yiddish Literature is about 150 years old, dating back to 1864, the year when **Mendele Mocher Sefarim** published his first book. His works reflect the whole Jewish way of life in his time. Mendele was a realist and created a literary framework for narrative Yiddish prose. He had a number of followers and imitators, his greatest disciple the famous humorist **Sholom Aleichem**. The latter, with Mendele and J.L. **Peretz**, are known as the three classic writers of modern Yiddish literature. Peretz, in turn, influenced a group of younger writers; some of them later became outstanding: for example, the novelist Sholom **Asch** and the poet and short story writer Abraham **Reisen**. The classic period in Yiddish literature lasted from 1864 to 1914. The 1880's saw the beginnings of the Yiddish theater, pioneered by Abraham **Goldfaden**. This was the period of large-scale immigration to the U.S., and Yiddish literature developed there as well. Of the American Yiddish writers of that time, Morris **Rosenfeld**, the poet who described and protested against the life of the sweatshop worker, is outstanding. In the twenty years between the two World Wars there were distinct centers of Yiddish literary activity: **Warsaw**, Moscow, and **New York**. The Russian center was, of course, out of contact with the others; its greatest writers were the novelist David Bergelson and the poet Peretz Markish. In Poland, the classic tradition was followed; there was also a good deal of experimentation with various literary forms and trends. A number of the Yiddish writers from Poland emigrated to the U.S. Almost all of those who remained in Eastern Europe perished in the Holocaust. In 1948, Yiddish literature was liquidated in the **Soviet Union**; the most prominent writers were arrested and later executed.

Since 1914, New York has been the most important Yiddish literary center. There, Abraham Liesin, the editor of the magazine *Zukunft*, wrote his nationalistic poetry; and **Yehoash** produced an excellent Yiddish translation of the Bible. There were many fine poets, such as M.L. Halperin, Mani Leib, and I.J. Schwartz. The best Yiddish novelists (Zalman **Shneur**, Isaac B. **Singer**) were published in the New York Yiddish dailies. Here, the novelist J. **Opatoshu** spent all of his creative years. The greatest living Yiddish poet, H. **Leivick**, has written many poems and dramas in both symbolic and realistic styles. After World War II, the Rumanian-Polish master of the ballad, Itzik Manger, and the Lithuanian poet Chaim Grade migrated to New York with other poets and writers. Yiddish literary criticism, which had peaked in Eastern Europe in the writings of Baal Makhshovess, became significant in New York, largely because of the influence of Shmuel Niger. There is now a lively literary center in Buenos Aires and in Montreal. There is an active group of Yiddish writers in Israel, of whom the most important is A. Sutzkever, the editor of *Di Goidene Keyt*.

During the last ninety years there has been a considerable development in essay writing, scientific prose, children's literature, and other branches of creative writing. Modern Yiddish literature reflects all aspects of Jewish life and all facets of the Jewish personality. Most recently, Yiddish literature has concentrated on the description and commemoration of the destruction of Eastern European Jewry. In all, there are approximately 2,000 Yiddish poets and prose writers.

YISHUV. Literally, settlement. Term used for the Jewish community of **Palestine** before the founding of the State of **Israel**.

YIVO INSTITUTE OF JEWISH RESEARCH. Founded in **Vilna** in 1925 for the purpose of studying Yiddish language and literature, Jewish folklore and history (particularly the history of East European Jewry), contemporary Jewish social problems, Jewish

YIDDISH EXPRESSIONS COMMONLY USED IN AMERICAN ENGLISH

aha! (Hoo-ha!) *Eureka!; I see!; Now you understand.*
alrightnik *A boasting successful man; nouveau riche.*
A.K. *Alte kocker; a frail old man.*
Ashkenazi *Jews from Germany, Poland, or Russia.*

bagel *A boiled and baked doughnut-shaped roll.*
balabusteh *An exemplary home-maker and hostess.*
Bar Mitzvah *Jewish confirmation of a thirteen-year-old boy.*
Bat (or Bas) Mitzvah *Jewish confirmation of a thirteen-year-old girl.*
bialy *A floured onion roll.*
blintz *A cheese-filled crepe.*
borscht *Beet soup.*
boychik *A young boy.*
bris *Circumcision ceremony.*
bubaleh *Little grandmother or an affectionate term for a child.*

cabbalah *A Jewish mystic movement of Rabbinic origin.*
challah *A braided white egg bread.*
cholent *A bean and meat dish similar to a French Cassoulet.*
Chanukah *Festival of Lights (also spelled Hanukkah).*
chutzpah *Extreme nerve; unmitigated gall.*

dreck *Crap; trash; usually used figuratively.*
dybbuk *An evil spirit claiming the body of a living person.*

feh! *An exclamation of disgust.*
finif (Fin) *A five-dollar bill.*

gefilte fish *A fish loaf made of chopped fish.*
gelt *Money.*
gesundheit! *To your health! (Often used after one sneezes).*
glick *(Good) luck.*
golem *A robot; lifeless figure.*
goniff *Thief.*
goy *A non-Jew.*
gut yontiff *Happy holiday.*
gut shabbos *Good Sabbath.*

halvah *Candy made of sesame seeds and honey.*
Hamantash *A three-cornered poppyseed cake.*
Hanukkah *(See Chanukah.)*
hassid *Member of a pious Jewish religious sect.*
Hatikvah *Israel's national anthem.*

kaddish *A prayer for the dead.*
kasha *Cooked cereal; groats.*
kibitz *To offer unwanted advice while watching a game or listening to an argument.*
kibbutz *A co-op farm.*
kichel *A small, plain cookie.*
kinder *Children.*
kineh horah *Without the evil eye.*
kishka *Stuffed derma.*
klutz *A clumsy bungler.*
knish *A small dumpling, normally filled with potatoes.*
kosher *Ritually clean; acceptable; legal.*
kreplach *A triangular dumpling filled with cheese or meat.*
kugel *Potato or noodle pudding.*
kurveh *(also curveh) A prostitute.*
kvell *To gloat; show great pride and pleasure.*
kvetch *To intensely gripe or complain.*

latkes *Potato pancakes*
l'chaim! *To your health! To life! (A drinking toast).*
loshen horah *The evil tongue; gossip.*

matzoh *Unleavened bread.*
mavin *A real expert; a connoisseur.*
mazel *Good luck.*
mazel tov! *Congratulations.*
medinah *Country or state.*
megillah *An overly long story with too many details.*
mench *A decent human being.*
menorah *A candelabrum with seven or eight branches.*
meshuggeh *Crazy; wild.*
mezuzah *A small box containing a scrolled Biblical passage, usually mounted on the home entrance.*
mikvah *A ritual bath.*
mishpocheh *Family.*
mohel *A circumciser.*
momzer *A bastard; a shrewd person.*

naches *Extreme pride and pleasure from a child.*
no-goodnick *An unethical person; a bum.*
nu? *Well? What's cooking?*
nudnik *A pest; a real nuisance.*

oy! (Oy-oy-oy! Oy veh!) *An all-purpose word expressing worry, horror, dismay, surprise, etc.*

parnoseh *Livelihood.*
Pesach *The feast of Passover.*
pisher *A pisser; a young squirt.*
putz *A jerk; simpleton; fool.*

rebbe *A learned rabbi.*
Rosh Hashanah *Jewish New Year.*
Seder *Passover banquet and religious service.*
Sephardi *Jews from Spain, Portugal, and the Middle East.*

(Note: most of the following words beginning with "sh" are often spelled with "sch")

shalom *Peace; hello; good-bye.*
shamus *Synagogue sexton; a "private eye."*
schav *Sorrel or spinach soup.*
shaygetz *A non-Jewish male.*
shikker *Drunk.*
shiksa *A non-Jewish female.*
shlemiel *A fool; a social misfit.*
shlepp *To drag or pull behind.*
shlimazel *A hard luck person.*
shlock *Shoddy, cheaply made.*
shloomp *Stupid; dishevelled.*
shmaltz *Chicken fat; excessive sentimentality; bathos.*
shmatte *Rag; a cheap dress.*
shmeck *A taste.*
shmeer *To smear or to bribe.*
shmegeggy *Stupid person.*
shmo *A boob; a clumsy jerk.*
shmooze *Friendly talk or gossip.*
shmuck *Contemptuous term for a nasty dope or jerk.*
shnorrer *A beggar or a chiseler.*
shnook *A pathetic but likeable "sad sack."*
shnoz (shnozzle) *A nose, usually very big.*
shofar *A ram's horn trumpet.*
shpritz *A touch of; a spray.*
shtarker *A strong person.*
shtetl *A small town.*
shtik *A piece; a devious trick; contrived act or device.*
shtunk *An ungrateful person; a mean stinker.*
shtup *To push or press; to have sex or fornicate.*
shul *A synogogue.*
shvitzer *A braggart; a show-off.*

talis *Prayer shawl.*
Torah *The first five books of the Old Testament.*
tsimmes *Candied carrots; a big deal.*
tsuris *Trouble.*
tummler *Entertainer; inciter.*
tzaddik *A righteous person.*

yarmulke *A skullcap.*
yenta *A gossip; a shrew.*
yeshiva *A Rabbinical Seminary.*
yid *An offensive term for a Jew.*
Yom Kippur *The Day of Atonement; highest Jewish holiday.*

zaftig *Juicy, well-rounded, buxom.*

For a representative list of Hebrew words commonly used in English, see **Hebrew**.

psychology, education, and related subjects. Since 1940, the main office of YIVO, with branches in many countries, has been located in **New York**. YIVO has a library of approximately 170,000 volumes in all areas of Jewish knowledge and the largest Jewish archives in the world. The archives contain at least two million documents. Much of the YIVO library and archives was rescued from the Nazi-pillaged Vilna collection with the aid of the U.S. government. YIVO has published such Yiddish periodicals as *Yivo-Bletter*, *Yiddishe Shprakh*, *Yiddisher Folklore*, and the English language *Yivo Annual*. YIVO'S branch in **Argentina** publishes *Argentiner Yivo Bletter*. Recently, YIVO has been concentrating on an intensive study of Jewish life in the U.S.

YIZKOR. Memorial prayer for the dead recited at the synagogue on major Jewish holidays.

YOD. Tenth letter of the Hebrew alphabet; numerically, ten.

YOM KIPPUR. Literally, Day of Atonement. Regarded as the holiest day in the year and known as "the Sabbath of Sabbaths," *Shabbat Shabbaton*. A day of appeal for the forgiveness of sins, it is marked by fasting from sundown of the ninth to sunset of the tenth of **Tishri**. Because the rituals of repentance can absolve one only of sins committed against God and His law, the eve of the holiday is the appropriate time for asking the forgiveness of those whom one has offended. It is also customary among traditional Jews to offer *kapparot*, or atonement, on the eve of the fast. In the past, this was a colorful ceremony in which a live rooster or hen was swung around the head of each member of the family to recall the ancient sin-offerings. Today, a special money gift to charity is more common. During the ceremony, the head of the house recites the words, "This is my atonement, this is my forgiveness."

The Yom Kippur service is the longest in the Jewish liturgy. It begins with the chanting of the mournful Kol Nidre just before sunset on the eve of the holiday. This prayer, composed before the 9th century C.E., asks for release from vows or promises made that cannot be kept.

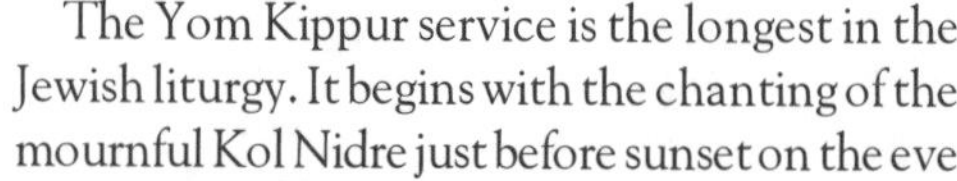

Prayers continue throughout the next day. Famous portions of the service include the *Viddui*, or confession of sins, and the *Seder Avodah*, or Order of Worship, attributed to the poet Yosi ben Yosi of Palestine, during the 4th or 5th century C.E. This long narrative describes the Yom Kippur service in the **Temple**. It reaches its climax with the entrance of the High Priest to the Holy of Holies to beg forgiveness for his own sins and those of the entire people. The Yom Kippur service concludes with the *Neilah*, or closing, so called because it refers to the closing of the gates of heaven at the end of the day. A single **shofar** blast and the words "Next year in **Jerusalem**!" terminate the fast.

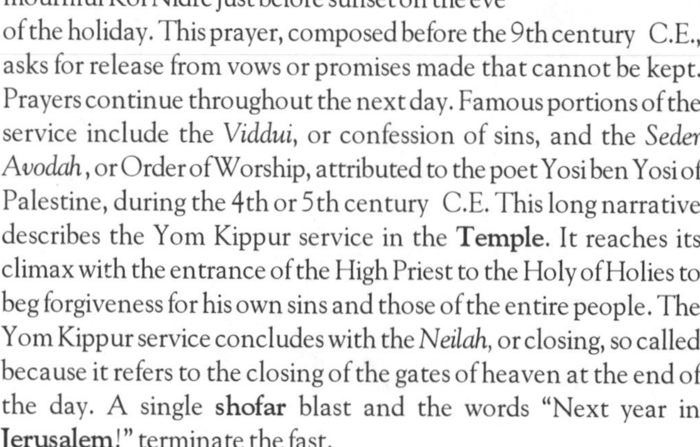

YOM KIPPUR WAR. Despite **Israel**'s overwhelming victory in the **Six-Day War** of 1967 and its oft-repeated offers of peace, its Arab neighbors refused to enter into negotiations with Israel or even to recognize its existence. On Yom Kippur 5734 (October 6, 1973), Egyptian and Syrian armies crossed the 1967 cease-fire lines on the Suez Canal and the Golan Heights, respectively. Israel was caught off guard, since it had not expected its neighbors to launch an all-out war at that time. Also, in contrast to the situation in 1967, Israel's air force was greatly hampered by new, highly effective anti-aircraft missiles with which **Russia** had supplied both **Egypt** and **Syria** gradually since the Six-Day War. Egypt succeeded in establishing bridgeheads east of the Canal, and Syria captured Mt. Hermon and the city of Kuneitra. Until Israel was able to mobilize its reserves, the outcome of the war was in doubt. On October 12, however, the tide began to turn in Israel's favor. Israeli forces recaptured all the territory taken by Syria, pushed the Syrian armies behind the 1967 cease-fire lines and eventually advanced to positions about 20 miles away from **Damascus**. On October 17, the Israelis crossed the Suez Canal, eventually coming within about 50 miles of Cairo. All the while, Russia had been constantly sending arms shipments to Syria and Egypt to replace the vast quantities of airplanes and tanks they had lost. Under the circumstances, and in view of Israel's heavy losses, particularly of airplanes, the U.S. began a massive airlift of weapons to Israel.

As long as the Arabs appeared to be winning the war, Russia did not seek an end to the fighting. But as Israel gained the upper hand, Russia summoned Secretary of State Henry **Kissinger** to Moscow and began to press for a cease-fire. On October 24, finally, all fighting ceased. Israel had lost almost 3,000 soldiers; Arab losses were close to 20,000. On November 11, 1973, Israel and Egypt signed a cease-fire agreement at Kilometer 101 on the Suez-Cairo highway, and four days later, the two sides began to exchange prisoners of war.

Yom Kippur service, by Maurice Gottlieb.

On May 29, 1974, Syria, the most implacable of Israel's enemies, agreed to sign a disengagement pact with Israel under terms to those agreed upon by Israel and Egypt. One June 5, 1974, the agreement between Israel and Syria was signed in Geneva.

Although fighting had officially ceased on Israel's northern and southern fronts, it was still, as of 1979, harassed by attacks from Palestinian guerillas who crossed into Israel from neighboring **Lebanon**. In the summer of 1979, the Palestinian Liberation Organization, whose charter calls for dismantling of the Jewish state, was clamoring for a voice in the peace conferences that were being planned between Israel and its Arab neighbors.

YOUNG ISRAEL. In 1912, a group of fifteen young men and women in **New York City** established the first Young Israel organization. Their purpose was to make traditional Judaism attractive to Jewish youth and to increase their Jewish education and awareness. In 1915, Young Israel opened its first model synagogue. The new synagogue featured decorum during services, a sermon in English, and congregational participation and singing. By 1998, Young Israel had some 200 affiliated branches in the **U.S.**, **Canada**, the **Netherlands**, and **Israel**, serving about 25,000 member families. Each Young Israel branch conducts services in its own synagogue, in strict conformance with traditional requirements. All branches offer an educational program for all age groups, placing particular emphasis on traditional Judaism. The National Council of Young Israel maintains the Young Israel Institute for Jewish Studies. Its youth department trains future leaders of the movement and sponsors the Young Israel Boy Scout Troop. Its employment bureau specializes in securing positions for Sabbath observers and part-time or vacation jobs for youngsters in school. Its armed forces division extends material and spiritual aid to Orthodox boys in the U.S. armed services. Young Israel supports major Jewish relief agencies throughout the world and the rebuilding of Israel. The official publication of the organization is the *Young Israel Viewpoint*.

YOUNG JUDEA. Organized in 1909 to help young American Jews develop healthy attitudes toward themselves, the Jewish people, and Israel. Its first president was Israel Friedlaender and such prominent Zionists as Henrietta **Szold** and Emanuel Newmann have been leaders. Under the auspices of Hadassah Zionist Youth Commission, Young Judea is provided with funds and administration, as well as with supervision and guidance. Young Judea provides cultural, religious, and recreational programs for Jewish young people up to age 18. It supports a youth farm in **Israel** for the benefit of Jewish scouts and those young Judeans who visit Israel. Young Judea maintains Tel Yehuda, a camp for high school youngsters which offers training in leadership. Young Judea sponsors both a summer-in-Israel course for seniors and a more intensive year-in-Israel course.

YOUNG MEN'S AND YOUNG WOMEN'S HEBREW ASSOCIATION. Popularly known as Y.M.H.A. and Y.W.H.A., a recreational and cultural Jewish institution throughout the U.S. The first Y.M.H.A. was established in **New York** in 1874, modeled after the Young Men's Christian Association and geared to serve the social and recreational needs of the individual. At the height of Jewish mass immigration into the U.S., the "Y" movement grew swiftly and devoted much of its program to Americanization work. Some of its tendencies were assimilationist during this period.

In 1913, the Y.M.H.A. and kindred organizations united to form one national association. Eight years later, this association merged with the **National Jewish Welfare Board**, which has guided the work of the movement since then. In the last few decades, the nature of the Y.M.H.A. has changed, becoming dedicated to family rather than the individual. This change is also reflected in the name and program of the affiliated institutions. A large proportion of them are called Jewish Community Centers, and Jewish cultural and educational programs are an integral part of their work. In the U.S. and **Canada**, 352 such centers are currently affiliated with the National Jewish Welfare Board.

YOUTH ALIYAH. Literally, youth immigration. Organization for the resettlement, education, and rehabilitation of Jewish youth in **Israel**. Youth Aliyah was founded in 1934, the year after Hitler's seizure of power in **Germany**, was to save German Jewish youth from imminent doom under the Nazi system. In the desperate days of 1932, the idea for youth immigration from Germany to Palestine came to Recha **Freier** in Berlin. She presented this idea to a gathering of children about to complete their elementary education, and the response was tremendous. The youth themselves organized *Juedische Jugendhilfe*, or Jewish Youth Aid, which was soon joined by *Ahava*, or Love, an orphanage in Berlin. For years Ahava had been transferring children to Ben Shemen, a children's village in Palestine. Under the leadership of Henrietta **Szold**, these spontaneous beginnings were organized into the Youth Aliyah movement. Selected adolescents were brought to Israel. There, in groups of 20 to 30, they were given two years of intensive training to enable them to settle on the land. During World War II, when communication with Europe was cut off, Youth Aliyah agents worked behind enemy lines, endangering their lives to bring children out of Europe to Palestine. The greatest challenge, however, came after the war. At that time thousands of children, wandering parentless over the face of a war-ravaged continent, had to be given homes and security. After the establishment of the State of Israel in 1948 and the beginning of mass immigration, the number of young people needing training and care increased further. Many of them came from Far Eastern countries and had to be helped to bridge the thousand-year gap between the lives they had led in their lands of origin and the lives they were about to lead in modern, westernized Israel. In time, other problems arose. While at first Youth Aliyah cared for youths separated from their parents, in recent years they have had to aid youngsters living with their families in underprivileged surroundings. It has undertaken a program of vocational training for immigrant youth and is founding clubs and youth centers in immigrant settlements. It has also taken under its wing underprivileged Israel-born youth; among its latest projects is an agricultural training course for Israeli Arabs. At the same time, Youth Aliyah is continuing to receive hundreds of youngsters each month in the 270 settlements throughout Israel; there, full-time educational programs are conducted under the guidance of specially trained counselors, many of whom are Youth Aliyah "graduates." Special centers are maintained for disturbed children and those needing medical treatment. The organization has cared for more than 160,000 Jewish youths from 80 different countries in its 45 years of existence. The majority of youth Aliyah wards have gone into agriculture, making a sizeable contribution to the farm community of Israel. There is at present scarcely an agricultural settlement without its Youth Aliyah graduates. Others have become skilled craftsmen, teachers, soldiers, artists, and social workers.

The Youth Aliyah program is conducted and partly financed by the **Jewish Agency**. **Hadassah**, which has taken a special interest in the project from its inception is the official representative of Youth Aliyah in the **U.S.**, and provides about 35% of its funds.

YUGOSLAVIA. Located in southeast Europe, this former republic, established in 1918, split in 1993 into three separate countries: Serbia, Bosnia-Herzegovina, and Croatia. Jews settled there in early Roman times, and after the Spanish expulsion in 1492, many more came to Belgrade and Sarajevo, preserving Sephardic traditions. Although for many years they were ill-treated, the stipulations of the new Serbia of 1878 carried out stipulations of the Berlin Treaty regarding religious liberty. After World War II, only 10,500 of the country's 72,900 Jews remained. Before the outbreak of the current fighting, 4,500 Jews lived there. Since then, hundreds of Jewish children have been brought to Israel, many followed by their parents and grandparents.

ZACUTO, ABRAHAM BEN SAMUEL (ca. 1450-ca. 1510). Astronomer, scientist, professor, and rabbinical scholar. A native of **Spain**, Zacuto lived in **Portugal** after the expulsion of the Jews from Spain in 1492. Fleeing the **Inquisition**, he left Portugal for Tunis and **Turkey**. Zacuto perfected the astrolabe, the forerunner of the sextant, used by Vasco da Gama. He was the author of the Almanach Perpetuum, nautical tables, and works on astronomy.

ZACUTO, MOSES. *See* **Hebrew Literature**.

ZAMENHOF, LAZARUS LUDWIG (1859-1917). Linguist. Born in Bialystok, he practiced medicine in Warsaw. Intent on solving the problem of national conflicts, he thought that a simple international language might hasten the solution. He created an auxiliary language called Esperanto (literally, hopeful). Esperanto, which brought its creator world fame, uses all the letters of the Roman alphabet, except Q, W, X, and Y. It is spelled as pronounced, its rules have no exceptions, and its guiding principle is to use roots common to the main languages of Europe. More than 10,000 publications have appeared in Esperanto; more than 100 Esperanto periodicals are regularly published.

ZANGWILL, ISRAEL (1864-1926). Writer, satirist, and founder of the Jewish Territorialist Organization. He was born and raised in **London**'s East End, amid the struggles of the East European Jewish immigrants to adjust to new surroundings. He understood the ghetto folk and saw their sorrow when the children left their parents' way of life for the new ways of modern London. In his *Children of the Ghetto* (1892), he brought these people to life with realism, sympathy, and humor. His journalistic essays were cruelly witty; his non-Jewish novels brought him passing success. *Children of the Ghetto* was Zangwill's first claim on lasting fame, followed closely by the *King of Schnorrers* and *Dreamers of the Ghetto*.

Israel Zangwill.

Theodor **Herzl** won Zangwill over to **Zionism** in 1895, and for a number of years he worked actively for the cause. When the Zionist movement rejected Uganda in British East Africa as a "temporary asylum" for the persecuted Jews of **Russia**, Zangwill left the Zionist organization. He wanted to rind a land in which the Jews could settle immediately and have their own state. For this purpose he founded the Jewish Territorialist Organization (JTO), which searched for a Jewish homeland in other countries, from Africa to **Australia**. After the **Balfour Declaration**, which promised "the establishment in Palestine of a national home for the Jewish people," Zangwill returned to the Zionist fold and worked for Zionism until the end of his life.

ZAYIN. Seventh letter of the Hebrew alphabet; numerically, seven.

ZEBULUN. Literally, he dwelled. Sixth son of Jacob and Leah. Zebulun was the only tribe to settle near the coast, its land a sliver in the center of Canaan.

Emblem of the tribe of Zebulun.

ZECHARIAH (ca. 520 B.C.E.). Eleventh of the Minor Prophets. Like his contemporary the prophet Haggai, Zechariah lived and preached in **Jerusalem** after the return from the Babylonian exile. He too urged the rebuilding of the **Temple** and prophesied the coming of the Messiah. His visions are mystic revelations replete with symbolic figures: horses, craftsmen, a golden candlestick, a flying scroll, and Satan in the role of an accusing angel.

ZEITLIN, HILLEL (1872-1942). Hebrew and Yiddish writer and thinker. Born in a small town in White **Russia**, his early youth was steeped in the study of the **Talmud** and **Hasidism**. He later contributed to the Hebrew and Yiddish press and became editor of a Yiddish daily, *Moment*, in **Warsaw**, **Poland**. In his books and numerous articles, Zeitlin dealt with the philosophical problems of good and evil; he also wrote extensively on the **Kabbalah** and on Hasidism. Deeply religious, his fine poetic essays expressed his love of nature, its harmony, and beauty.

Zeitlin died a martyr's death at the hands of the Nazis in the **Warsaw** ghetto while absorbed in prayer. His son Aaron Zeitlin became a Hebrew and Yiddish poet and essayist.

ZELOPHEHAD. Member of the tribe of Menasseh during the wanderings in the wilderness in the time of **Moses**. He had five daughters and no sons, and when he died his daughters approached Moses and laid claim to his estate. Special legislation had to be issued to allow daughters to inherit in the absence of sons, provided they married a member of their tribe. This appears to be the first time in Jewish history that women claimed their rights and were successful.

ZEPHANIAH, BOOK OF. Zephaniah, ninth of the Minor Prophets, lived toward the end of the 7th century B.C.E., and prophesied the downfall of Nineveh and the Assyrian empire. He warned the people that "a great and dreadful day of the Lord, a day of darkness and obscurity" would come upon them and they would be punished for evil-doing. After this punishment, salvation would come to Israel and to all the world.

ZERUBBABEL. Last King of Judea. Princely descendant of the House of **David**, who governed **Judea** in the 6th century B.C.E., Zerubbabel, grandson of Jehoiachin, ended his life a captive in **Babylonia**. Cyrus, the Median prince, having conquered Babylonia in 539 B.C.E., permitted Zerubbabel to lead a group of returning exiles back to Judea. With the aid of the high priest Joshua, Zerubbabel set up an altar, restored the celebration of the holidays, and began the rebuilding of the city walls and the Temple. Internal difficulties and hostile neighbors interrupted this work. About 520 B.C.E., Zerubbabel was appointed governor of Judea and, encouraged by the prophets **Haggai** and **Zechariah**, resumed the labor of reconstruction.

ZHIDLOVSKY, CHAIM (1865-1943). Socialist writer in **Russia** who founded the Jewish Section of the Socialist Revolution Party in 1885. He advocated Jewish national self-determination under socialism, and considered **Yiddish** the national Jewish language. In 1908, he settled in New York where he edited a Yiddish periodical and pursued his Jewish socialist teachings. To Jews before World War II who did not consider **Zionism** the national solution to Jewish life, but rather espoused socialism and Yiddishism, Zhidlovsky was an ideological leader.

ZIONISM. Modern political movement for the return of the Jewish people to Zion, the old prophetic name for Palestine. This movement began in the 19th century with the thinking and writings of a number of men in various parts of Europe, and was followed by the founding of several Jewish agricultural settlements in Palestine. Zionism received its political form from the work of Theodor **Herzl**, and its clearly defined program at the first Zionist **Congress**, held in Basel, **Switzerland**, in 1897.

History. Although the term Zionism did not come into use until the 1890's, the desire to reunite the Jewish people with their ancient homeland began eighteen centuries earlier, when the might of Rome destroyed Judea and exiled the Jews from Palestine. At that movement, Jews turned passionately to the vision of their prophets that a Messiah, an anointed son of the House of **David**, would appear "at the end of days" and lead them home to Zion. The mystical longing for the Messiah and the Return entered the people's dreams and prayers. It was so intense that, from time to time, persons who felt themselves to be either the "messiah" or his forerunner would appear, and announce themselves as such. Always these "messiahs" found followers, whom they sometimes led to open rebellion against their rulers. Some "messiahs" who started out as mystic believers ended up as crude impostors. The tragic, dangerous trail of **Messianism** runs through Jewish history, from the 8th-century warlike tailor Abu Isa of Persia to the 18th-century mystic poet Moses Hayim **Luzzato** of **Italy**.

The love of Zion expressed itself in the people's daily life and in its literature.

> *By the rivers of Babylon, there we sat,*
> *Yea we wept when we remembered Zion.*
>
> — PSALM OF THE FIRST EXILE

When they were given the opportunity, they left Babylon and returned to their homeland. They were exiled from Palestine a second time 600 years later and scattered across the continents. Life became difficult and survival uncertain; yet the Jewish people continued to turn in the direction of Zion thrice daily when they prayed. A thousand years after the second dispersion, the great poet Judah **Ha-Levi** sang in majestic poems of his love of Zion and his longing for Zion's restoration. Pious pilgrims made their way to the Holy Land throughout the centuries of exile, some to live there, and some to die and be buried in its sacred soil.

Forerunner of Modem Zionism. In the 19th century, when European nations were achieving their independence, Jews felt that the time was ripe to resettle in their ancient homeland. Yehuda **Alkalai** agitated for colonization among the **Hasidim** in Europe and among the pious recipients of **Halukkah** in Palestine. In 1862, Rabbi Z'vi Hirsch **Kalischer** published a book, *The Quest for Zion*, that urged people to help themselves by forming a settlement society for the purpose of buying land in Palestine and settling on it. At about the same time, Moses **Hess**, a German Jewish Socialist living in **Paris**, published a booklet called *Rome and Jerusalem* which discussed the Jewish problem, emancipation, **anti-Semitism**, and the Reform movement. The Jewish people, said Hess, would never lose its special character. Humankind was made up of many nations and peoples, like Jews, each of whom had something special to contribute to world civilization. The only way to solve the Jewish problem was "through the creation of a national center in Palestine" under the protection of some European power.

When *The Quest for Zion* and *Rome and Jerusalem* were published, few people accepted their ideas. For at that time many Jews thought to solve the problems of discrimination and anti-Semitism by becoming "enlightened," that is, by obtaining a modern education and adopting the language and manners of their non-Jewish compatriots. This was the Enlightenment, or **Haskalah,** movement, which absorbed the energies and thought of the Jewish intellectual leaders. Among the first to turn the Haskalah movement away from **assimilation** and toward a Jewish national revival was novelist Peretz **Smolenskin.** Smolenskin inspired the forming of the Kadimah Zionist students' societies in Vienna. In his book, *Am Olam* (1872), Smolenskin called the Jewish people an "eternal people" that must keep the eternal idea of Zion before it. According to Smolenskin, only the eternal Hebrew language embodied the Zionist ideal; and only by settlement on the soil of Palestine could the Jewish people maintain its uniqueness.

Another voice called the Jewish people to action. An **Odessa** physician, Leo **Pinsker**, had lost his faith in the struggle for Jewish emancipation in Russia under Tsarist persecution and **pogroms**. Pinsker diagnosed anti-Semitism as an incurable disease and prescribed the treatment for it in an essay called "Auto-Emancipation," or setting one's self free. Published in 1882, "Auto-Emancipation" diagnosed the Jewish sickness as homelessness: "The world sees in the Jewish people a ghost, a corpse that walks among the living. This ghost of a people without unity or organization, without a land of its own...is yet walking about among the living." Because the "living peoples of the world cannot understand this walking-ghost of the Jewish people, they fear and hate it. The nations of the world never have to deal with the Jews as another nation, but only as individuals, hence they cannot respect us." To achieve this respect, Pinsker claimed, "We must have a home, a land, a territory." "Now or never!" was his cry, and he called for a congress of Jewish leaders.

The Lovers of Zion. Pinsker's call was heard by the **Hoveve Zion** , or Lovers of Zion, a movement of scattered societies that sprung up in the 1860's. These groups got together at a conference in Kattowitz, Silesia, in November 1884, formed a federation, and elected Pinsker as its president. Their aim was to restore Jewish national life by settling Palestine. About two years earlier, a group of young university students who belonged to the Hoveve Zion had gotten together and had emigrated to Palestine. They called themselves **BILU**, from the Hebrew initials of the Biblical verse "O House of Jacob, come let us go!" The BILU group was determined to work only on the land as a cooperative body. City bred, they came to Palestine and heroically struggled to settle on the soil despite the hostility of Turkish rulers and Arab neighbors, overcoming the hardships of swampy valleys, stony hillsides, and burning sand. Such pioneering, which came to be known as "practical Zionism," was performed by idealists too impractical to recognize the impossible. The BILU were the vanguard of the First **Aliyah**, or migration. They were to be followed in time by the famous Second Aliyah from 1904-1914, whose principles set a lasting pattern for pioneering on the land of Israel. In the meantime, the example of the First Aliyah and the influence of the writings of Kalischer, Hess, Smolenskin, and Pinsker were the indispensable preliminaries for the political Zionism which appeared in 1896.

Theodor Herzl and Political Zionism. Theodor **Herzl**, the founder of political Zionism, knew nothing of the early Zionist movement or its literature. He was a successful Viennese journalist and playwright who apparently thought of his Jewishness only now and again when he was disturbed by anti-Semitism. In **Paris**, as correspondent of the famous *Neue Freie Presse*, Herzl was aroused by the **Dreyfus** case and deeply shocked by its effect on the French people. In a spiritual turmoil, he grappled with the Jewish problem and arrived at a solution: the Jewish people must have a Jewish State. A "charter" for such a state in Palestine must be obtained from **Turkey**. A Jewish society must be formed to engineer the mass movement of the Jewish people to Palestine.

Nordau greets Herzl at the first Zionist Congress in Basel, 1897.

In 1896, Herzl published his program in his book *Judenstaat* (The Jewish State) and began to search for a leader to translate his ideas into action. The philanthropist Baron Maurice de Hirsch, already engaged in Jewish settlement projects in **Argentina**, refused to assume leadership. Albert **Rothschild** of Vienna did not even answer Herzl's letter. The ultra-Orthodox Jews saw in his scheme an interference with the will of the Almighty, who, according to the traditional view, would send the Messiah to restore Jews to their land. The leaders of the Reform movement opposed Zionism because, they claimed, Jews represented only a religion, not a nation. Socialists said that the Jewish problem would be solved only when the world became one utopian classless society.

In January 1897, Herzl issued a call for a congress, and on August 27, the first Zionist Congress met in Basel, Switzerland. Herzl appeared before the delegates, a magnetic, majestic figure. He caught their imagination and held it as long as he lived and long afterwards. The first Zionist Congress formulated the **Basel Program**, which announced to the world that "Zionism aims to create for the Jewish people a home in Palestine secured by public law." In subsequent Congresses, the **World Zionist Organization** was given form and function. Herzl established *Die Welt*, a publication to speak for the Zionist movement. In 1899, the Zionist bank, called the Jewish Colonial Trust, was founded in **London**. A commission to further the colonization work in Palestine was set up, and the Keren Kayemet, or **Jewish National Fund,** was organized to purchase land in Palestine. People and ideas matured as the issues were debated at the various Congresses. From the beginning, physician and writer Max **Nordau** was Herzl's closest supporter and the master orator who gave winged words to the Zionist movement. Herzl's tireless negotiations with European governments for a charter to Palestine were not successful during his short life, but they did prepare the way for the future. In 1902, Great Britain offered to open up first the **Sinai peninsula** for Jewish settlement and then the territory of Uganda in East Africa for autonomous Jewish settlement. The 6th and 7th Zionist Congresses debated the Uganda project and rejected it, even though Herzl pleaded for its acceptance as a temporary asylum for the hard-pressed Russian Jews.

The death of Herzl in 1904 at age 44 was a severe blow to the Zionist movement. For a while the work slowed down, but did not halt. Disagreement arose between two Zionist schools of thought. The followers of Herzl, the "political Zionists," believed that Zionist energy must be concentrated on the political work of obtaining a charter to establish a Jewish state in Palestine. They held that the practical work of mass settlement would come after this legal guarantee for the colonizers had been achieved. On the other hand, "practical Zionists" supported by the old Lovers of Zion, were convinced that settlement must go on, since a larger Jewish settlement in Palestine would lend greater weight to the political efforts of the Zionist movement. A rising young leader, Chaim **Weizmann**, tried for years to convince the two factions that a combination of both approaches would benefit Zionism most.

Cultural Zionism. Still another important school urged Zionists to take yet a different road to their goal. This school was headed by the writer and philosopher, Ahad **Ha-Am** (Asher Ginzberg). The course he charted was "cultural Zionism." The cultural Zionists maintained that it was not enough for the driven and harassed among the Jewish people to find a national home in Palestine. Palestine had to be restored as a spiritual center for the whole Jewish people. Such a center, wrote Ahad Ha-am, could be accomplished gradually only by those who were imbued with the Hebrew prophetic ideals. The cultural Zionists feared that concentration on political and practical Zionism might overlook the spiritual and cultural starvation among the Jewish people, and the results would be disastrous.

Theodor Herzl and Chaim Weizmann, the two key figures of Zionism.

World War I put an end to these debates and opened a new chapter in Jewish history. Zionism was faced with the splitting of its forces between the hostile powers of Germany and Austria on one side, and Britain, France and Russia on the other. The World Zionists Organization, therefore, adopted a policy of neutrality and opened a central office in neutral Copenhagen. An important result of this policy came when the German government influenced the Turkish administration to soften to some extent its cruel treatment of the Jewish community in Palestine. The Turks were particularly suspicious of Palestinian Jews who had come from Russia. (Russia fought on the side of the Allies, while Turkey was leagued with Germany.) Since they were in danger of imprisonment by the Turks as enemy aliens, a large number of Jewish refugees fled from Palestine to Alexandria, Egypt. Their pressure in Egypt complemented Zionist political activity among the Allies. Joseph **Trumpeldor** and Vladimir **Jabotinsky** urged British military authorities in Alexandria and Cairo for permission to organize a **Jewish Legion** to fight on the side of the Allies. At first sharply opposed, the British at last relented somewhat and permitted Trumpeldor to form a transport unit, the Zion Mule Corps, which served with the British in the Gallipoli Expeditionary Force. By June 1917, Jabotinsky had succeeded in breaking down British resistance, and the Jewish Legion was finally formed; it fought with the British forces for the liberation of Palestine from the Turks.

The Balfour Declaration. Beginning in 1915, Chaim Weizmann, together with other leaders of British Jewry, began negotiations with the British government to obtain the charter that Herzl had vainly sought. For nearly three years these negotiations inched forward. Nahum **Sokolow** became Zionism's roving ambassador to the war-locked capitals of the Allies, returning again and again until their consent was won. When the **U.S.** entered the war in 1917, Justice Louis D. **Brandeis** led the drive to obtain President Woodrow Wilson's backing for Zionist aims. Finally, on November 2, 1917, the Balfour Declaration was issued in a letter to Lord Lionel Walter Rothschild, president of the British Zionist Federation. The declaration stated in part that "His Majesty's Government view with favor the establishment in Palestine of a national home for the Jewish people."

A few weeks after the Balfour Declaration, British troops entered Jerusalem. A few months later, a commission headed by Weizmann came to Palestine. Major W. Ormsby-Gore, representing the British government, was attached to the commission, whose responsibility it was to find out how the promise of the declaration could best be fulfilled. While in Palestine, Weizmann went to Amman to visit Prince Feisal, son of King Hussein of Hedjaz, and discussed the idea of peaceful relations between Jews in Palestine and the Arab world. This discussion resulted in an agreement signed by Feisal and Weizmann in London in January 1919, backing the Balfour Declaration and safeguarding the rights of the Arabs in Palestine. In the U.S. President Wilson expressed his approval of the Balfour Declaration and said that he was "persuaded...our own Government and people, are agreed that in Palestine shall be laid the foundation of a Jewish Commonwealth." On February 27, 1919, a Zionist delegation consisting of Weizmann, Sokolow, **Ussishkin**, and Andre Spire appeared before the **Versailles Peace Conference** and presented the Zionist claims based on the "historic claims of the Jewish people to Palestine." The Peace Conference accepted the Balfour Declaration and entrusted the mandate for Palestine to England. The Allied Supreme Council meeting at San Remo in April 1920, included the Declaration in its treaty with Turkey, and two years later, the League of Nations affirmed the British mandate for Palestine. Finally, President Warren Harding and the U.S. Congress approved the Balfour Declaration on September 21, 1922.

Retreat from the Mandate. But while international approval was making the Jewish National Home in Palestine legally more secure, the British government was doing the opposite. The British systematically stalled on and blocked the execution of their mandate. Thus, they gave away a tract of state lands to Bedouin nomads who did not cultivate it, and by numerous similar actions they administered Palestine in a manner intended primarily to hinder the development of a Jewish national home. The rivalry between Britain and France for control in the Near East, budding Arab nationalism, and the rival ambitions of Arab leaders all served to arouse Arab unrest and incite violence. In 1920 and again in 1921, there were Arab attacks on Jewish agricultural settlements and on Jews of Jerusalem, Jaffa, and **Tel Aviv.** The British administration in Palestine hampered Jewish self-defense, arresting defenders and attackers alike. The mandate was further weakened by the Churchill White Paper of 1922. The first of the white papers on the mandate, it diminished the area of Jewish Palestine by removing Transjordan and making it a separate Arab territory. The political activity to counter these British actions in which the Zionist movement engaged led to lasting internal divisions. (*See* **Revisionist Zionism.**)

Internal Difficulties. Other difficulties developed. In 1921, at the first Zionist Congress held after World War I, the Keren Hayesod, or Palestine Foundation Fund, was created to finance the development of Palestine. The Keren Hayesod was entrusted with the task of obtaining from world Jewry donations, as well as investments to develop industry and agriculture, to bring immigrants to Palestine, and to care for their health and education. Supreme Court Justice Louis D. Brandeis and his followers among American Zionists differed from the Zionists under Weizmann's leadership on whether it was advisable to use this method to finance the work in Palestine. Brandeis objected to setting up the Keren Hayesod as an umbrella fund to accept both investments and donations; he stressed the need to stimulate and to rely on large-scale private investment. When his point of view was not accepted, Justice Brandeis retired from the leadership of American Zionism. (*See also* **Zionist Organization of America.**) In 1924, the movement to create an enlarged **Jewish Agency**, within which non-Zionists would serve together with the Zionists, led to still other divisions of opinion. These were not settled until August 1929, when the enlarged Jewish Agency came into being at the 16th Zionist Congress held in Zurich.

This Congress marked a decade of Zionist growth since the end of World War I. World Zionism had reached out for support and membership to every corner of the globe. In Palestine the growth of Zionist settlements on the land and in the cities was remarkable, despite the economic crisis between 1925 and 1928. The Jewish National Fund had purchased the Emek and the Haifa Bay area. The Palestine Foundation Fund had provided the credit and the various other forms of assistance needed by the pioneers of the Second and Third Aliyot. The Arab riot of 1929, which took many Jewish lives and destroyed much Jewish property, failed to wipe out the Jewish settlement of Palestine or to deter the Zionist effort.

Arab Riots, White Paper Commissions, and Partition Proposal. The Arab riots did, however, lead the British to renew their efforts to nullify the Balfour Declaration. The major provisions of the Passfield White Paper, issued in October 1930, aimed to reduce Jewish immigration to a trickle and to stop altogether the purchase of agricultural lands by Jews. On the day this White Paper was published, Chaim Weizmann resigned his presidency of the World Zionist Organization and the Jewish Agency for Palestine in protest. His was the first in a series of protests and cries of indignation uttered by Jews and non-Jews alike. The result was a full-dress debate in the British parliament during which the government was severely attacked. In its wake, Prime Minister Ramsay MacDonald wrote a letter to Weizmann modifying the worst features of the White Paper.

The Arabs in Palestine quieted down, and there were no more serious disturbances until 1936. Yet the situation was not radically changed. As Hitler and the Nazis rose to power in Germany, persecutions sent a stream of German Jews to Palestine. The Arabs reacted with new riots. From 1936 to 1938, terrorist attacks on Jewish settlements, the setting of fire to fields and forests, and the murder and intimidation of Arabs friendly to Jews, went unchecked. British action to eradicate the terror was neither consistent nor forceful enough to accomplish its aim. But Britain did pursue vigorously another form of action. In November 1936, a new British Royal Commission headed by Lord William Robert Peel came to Palestine to investigate the causes of the Arab terror. The Peel Commission stayed until January 1937; it reported that the mandate had become unworkable, recommended further restriction of Jewish immigration and land purchase, and the partition of Palestine into an Arab state and a tiny Jewish state. The Arabs flatly rejected partition; the Zionist Congress held in August 1937 offered a compromise. The Zionist Executive was authorized to negotiate with the British to find out "the precise terms of his Majesty's Government for the proposed establishment of a Jewish State."

Balfour Declaration Scrapped. In 1938, a British commission went to Palestine to work out the partition boundaries. The report of this commission was negative. It found no boundaries possible which might make practical "the establishment of self-supporting Arab and Jewish states." Another White Paper announced that the partition plan had been abandoned as unrealistic. The British then called a round table conference of Jews and Arabs in London to find another solution to the Palestine problem. This conference failed, because the Arab delegation refused to sit down at the same table with the Jews, and insisted on the termination of the mandate. In May 1939, the final White paper appeared. It scrapped the Balfour Declaration with its promise of a Jewish National Home. To freeze the Jewish population as a permanent minority in Palestine, it limited Jewish immigration to 75,000 over a period of five years. The sale of land to Jews was severely restricted. Finally, the White Paper proposed that in ten years Palestine be made into an independent Arab state allied to Britain. This White Paper appeared at the time when Nazi Germany occupied **Czechoslovakia** and the Hitler regime began to murder Jewish victims, whose numbers were to mount into the millions in the next few years. The Zionist Congress met to act on this new British policy on the eve of World War II. Rejecting the White Paper unanimously, the Congress pledged its full support to the democracies in their fight against Nazism.

World War II and Jewish Brigade. Immediately after their return from the Congress, Zionist leaders began strenuous efforts to rescue European Jewry. During the years of World War II, the World Zionist Organization protested vehemently against British policy in Palestine and made every effort to mobilize public opinion against it. At the same time Weizmann pressed the British government to accept his offer to establish a fighting force of Palestine Jews for service with the British Army. For two years he met with no success. Then the dangerous situation in the Mediterranean campaign brought partial agreement. Selected Jewish units totaling 33,000 were permitted to serve with the British Forces in the Near and Middle East and elsewhere. In 1944, the British finally agreed to the formation of a **Jewish**

Vladimir Jabotinsky and David Ben-Gurion, leaders of the Zionist Right and the Zionist Left, respectively.

Brigade. When the victorious Allied armies swept into Austria and Germany, the Jewish Brigade under its own blue-white flag was a part of these Forces.

The Blockade and "Illegal Immigration." At the end of World War II, it was discovered that six million Jews, one-third of all the Jewish people in the world, had been destroyed by Hitler. It seemed only just that the pitiful survivors of Nazi concentration camps should be admitted freely to Palestine to be cared for by their own people. But the British government disagreed. The British White

Leaders of American Zionism after World War I. Seated, l. to r.: Henrietta Szold, Stephen Wise, Jacob de Hass, R. Kesselman, Louis Lipsky, Charles Cowen, Shmaryahu Levin, Rabbi Meir Berlin (Bar-Ilan).

Paper and the British fleet blockaded the Jewish National Home. The "illegal immigration" begun before the war by Palestine Jewry was, therefore, resumed and increased. In London and Washington, Zionist leaders used every form of pressure acceptable in democratic countries to change British policy and open the doors of Palestine to Jewish immigration. In April 1946, an Anglo-American Committee of Inquiry visited Palestine and the concentration camps in Europe. On its return, the Committee recommended that 100,000 survivors should be admitted to Palestine immediately. U.S. President Harry S. Truman gave this proposal his emphatic support. Nevertheless, the new Labor government in England vetoed this recommendation. The tiny Jewish community of Palestine increased its defiant resistance to the British Empire. In this unequal battle, the world Zionist movement acted to enlist public opinion and to increase its own strength. The disaster that wiped out European Jewry and the passionate struggle against British policy in Palestine brought hundreds of thousands of new members into Zionist ranks. Millions of dollars for reconstruction were poured into Palestine.

Meanwhile, the most powerful political and resistance weapon of the Palestine Jewish community, "illegal immigration," continued to bring in shiploads of refugees who preferred to run the British blockade rather than remain in the displaced persons camps of Germany. Many ships were caught by the British Navy, and thousands of refugees were deported to detention camps in Cyprus. Public opinion was outraged; finally, Foreign Minister Ernest Bevin in London gave up and, in February 1947, announced to the House of Commons his intention to refer the problem to the United Nations (UN).

"Palestine Problem" before the United Nations. On April 28, 1947, the UN Assembly met in special session to consider the situation in Palestine and to find a solution for it. A series of passionate and bitter debates began. The Arab side was represented by the delegates of six member states and by the members of the Arab Higher Committee. The Jewish side was presented by the leaders of the Jewish Agency: Abba Hillel **Silver**, head of its American section, Moshe Shertok (**Sharett**), head of its political department, and David **Ben-Gurion**, its chairman. When debate was completed, the UN Assembly appointed an eleven-member Special Committee of Inquiry on Palestine (UNSCOP) "to investigate all questions and issues relevant to the problem of Palestine." UNSCOP was instructed to bring back its report to the regular session of the assembly in September 1947.

UNSCOP visited Beirut and listened to the representatives of the Arab states; they went to Jerusalem and listened to all parties of the Yishuv, the Jewish community of Palestine. They went to Europe and visited the survivors of Hitler's horror, who were still fenced in camps and waiting for a home and freedom. The UNSCOP members were all deeply moved by these pitiful victims; two of them, Jorge Garcia Granados of **Guatemala** and Enrique Fabregat of **Uruguay**, became ardent Zionists. The UNSCOP report, published on August 31, 1947, recommended unanimously the termination of the mandate, the preservation of economic unity of Palestine, and the safeguarding of the Holy Places. On the political future of the country UNSCOP was divided. The majority suggested the partition of Palestine into a Jewish state, an Arab state, and an international authority for governing Jerusalem. A minority of three recommended a Federal Arab-Jewish state.

Partition Voted by U.N. For two months this report was debated by the UN Assembly. On November 29, 1947, the final vote was taken, and the partition resolution based on the UNSCOP majority report was approved by a UN majority. Political Zionism had reached its goal of a publicly recognized, legally secured Jewish state in Palestine, and a wave of joy spread over all the Jewish communities of the world.

Five months later, the British withdrew from Palestine, and the State of **Israel** was proclaimed. Zionism shouldered the new task of supporting the infant state that was immediately attacked by its Arab neighbors. (*See* **Israel**.) But the need for economic support continued after the Arabs had been repelled; for Israel opened its doors and absorbed about a million Jewish refugees from Europe and the Arab countries.

ZIONIST ORGANIZATION OF AMERICA. The history of the Zionist movement in the U.S. begins in the early 1880's when **Hoveve Zion,** or Lovers of Zion, societies were formed by Russian immigrants in **New York, Baltimore,** and **Chicago.** Dr. Joseph Bluestone, who practiced medicine and wrote poetry, was the founder of the New York Lovers of Zion group. Bluestone believed that **Zionism** should serve a spiritual purpose and safeguard American Jewry against **assimilation.** In 1897, the two-year-old Zion Society of Chicago was the only such group to send a delegate to the First Zionist Congress held in Basel.

Stimulated by the reports from this Congress, the Federation of American Zionists was organized in 1898 at a national conference in New York. Professor Richard **Gottheil** was the first president of the federation, and Rabbi Stephen S. **Wise** its first secretary. The following year, a young journalist, Louis **Lipsky,** founded the *Maccabean,* the monthly that became the official Zionist publication. The periodical later changed its name to *The New Palestine* and finally to *The American Zionist.* By 1900, there were more than 100 societies all over the country. In addition to those already mentioned, a brilliant group of men including Harry Friedenwald and Benjamin Szold of Baltimore and Judah L. **Magnes** of New York were the leaders of the infant movement. Yet, until World War I, its growth was rather slow. **Young Judea** was organized in 1907 as the youth department of the federation, and **Hadassah,** the Women's Zionist Organization of America, was founded in 1912. When World War I broke out in 1914, the role of American Zionism assumed new importance. The American Zionists were practically cut off from the European Zionist headquarters. Louis Lipsky, then chairman of the Zionist Federation, and Shmaryahu Levin, a member of the World Zionist Executive then visiting in the U.S., called an extraordinary conference to cope with the emergency. This conference established the Provisional Committee for Zionist Affairs under the chairmanship of Louis D. **Brandeis.** In its Berlin headquarters, the World Zionist Executive acted to avoid the splitting of Zionist forces between the contending hostile powers of the war by transferring its authority to the Provisional Committee. The Committee functioned until 1918, managing the Zionist institutions in Palestine and financing Zionist political activities in various war zones. Most important were the negotiations conducted by Brandeis and the Committee which contributed so largely to the issuance of the **Balfour Declaration,** and were so responsible for obtaining American backing for it.

In 1917, the **Mizrachi** and Poale Zion groups, representing the religious and **Labor Zionists,** withdrew from the Provisional Committee, and all the **General Zionist** groups united to form the Zionist Organization of America, replacing the Provisional Committee. The following year, the Zionist Organization met at a conference in Pittsburgh. There it adopted what came to be called the Pittsburgh Program which was liberal and appealed strongly to the Jewish love for social justice. Brandeis, appointed to the U.S. Supreme Court, withdrew from public Zionist leadership. He became the honorary president of the Zionist Organization of America, while Judge Julian W. Mack was elected president. At the Cleveland Zionist Convention in 1921, the Brandeis program stressed private initiative in preference to the use of public funds in the economic development of Palestine. This brought about a serious difference of opinion between the followers of Brandeis and Mack and the followers of Chaim **Weizmann,** president of the World Zionist Organization. Finally, Brandeis and his colleagues withdrew from active Zionist responsibility. Louis Lipsky and the men who led the opposition to the Brandeis group were entrusted with the leadership. Until 1931, Lipsky served as president of the Zionist Organization of America.

The **Keren Hayesod** was established as the principal agency to support the development of Palestine. The Zionist Organization began to grow in membership, particularly after President Harding and the U.S. Congress approved the Balfour Declaration on

Delegates of the ZOA to the 30th Zionist Congress in Jerusalem.

September 21, 1922. Eventually, the breach between the two factions in American Zionism was healed, and most of the members of the Brandeis group, including Judge Mack, Stephen S. Wise, and Abba Hillel **Silver**, returned to active leadership. Between 1921 and 1929, approximately $10 million was raised for the Keren Hayesod. The Arab riots in Palestine in 1929 and the world economic depression set back Zionist activity. However, the rising tide of Nazism in **Germany** was followed by a wave of **anti-Semitism** in the U.S.; the result was an increase in Zionist membership.

When World War II broke out in 1939, representatives of the Zionist Organization, Hadassah, Mizrachi, and the Labor Zionist movement came together in the American Emergency Committee for Zionist Affairs to meet the crisis facing the Jewish communities of Europe and Palestine.

Since 1948, with the rebirth of Israel, the Zionist Organization established and supports the ZOA House in Tel Aviv, Kfar Silver, and the technical high school in Ashkelon which trains more than 750 Israeli, American, and foreign high school youth.

Within the Jewish community, ZOA is committed to work vigorously on behalf of education and **Aliyah**. To contribute to these efforts. ZOA established four Institutes in the 1980's. They are the Jacob Goodman Institute for Middle East Relations and Information, The Ivan J. Novick Institute for Israel-Diaspora Relations, The George Rothman Institute on U.S. Foreign Policy in the Middle East, and the Greenwald-Tarnepol Foundation for the Advancement of Zionism.

ZOA's Masada movement is the second largest Zionist youth movement in the U.S. Through Masada, ZOA's Women's Division, Young Zionist Leadership Groups and Regions and Districts, public affairs programs, ZOA remains a strong and vital Zionist institution in the U.S.

ZOHAR. Literally, light or splendor. The holiest book of the **Kabbalah**, actually called the "Holy Zohar." Written in **Aramaic**, the Zohar first appeared in the 13th century when it was published by Moses de Leon. De Leon attributed the Zohar to Rabbi Simeon Ben Yohai who lived in the 2nd century and together with his son Eliezer hid for thirteen years in caves to escape Roman persecution. During this time, the Kabbalists believe, Ben Yohai occupied himself with composing mystical interpretations of the Bible.

The Zohar dwells on the mystery of **Creation** and explains the stories and events in the Bible in a symbolic manner. It finds hidden meanings in common statements of facts. The Zohar describes God as "the Infinite One." God makes himself known to the world through ten "spheres of emanation." The Zohar also contains wonderful stories, discourses by the ancient masters, ethical pronouncements, and some moving prayers.

The Zohar has exerted a profound influence on the religious thought of large groups of Jews, including the **Hasidim**.

ZOLA, EMILE (1840-1902). French novelist and founder of the naturalistic school of writing. During the **Dreyfus** affair, he published his famous pamphlet *J'Accuse* in 1901, and was an important champion of this Jewish army officer falsely accused of selling French secret documents to the German government. In addition to *J'Accuse*, Zola wrote a parable on the Dreyfus affair in his book *Verité*.

Emile Zola.

ZUCKERMAN, PINCHAS (1948-). Violinist. Born in Israel, Zuckerman studied in the U.S. and became one of the world's leading violinists.

ZUNZ, LEOPOLD (1794-1886). Jewish scholar in Germany, founder of the Jewish *Wissenschaft* movement, which introduced scientific methods of research to the study of the Jewish classics and influences Jewish scholarship to this day. Zunz studies in Midrash, liturgy, and medieval religious poetry are still essential for Jewish scholarship in those fields (*See also* **Midrash, Prayer,** *and* **Hebrew Literature**.)

ZWEIG, STEFAN (1881-1942). Critic, biographer, and dramatist. Best known for his play *Jeremiah*, and a biography of Marie Antoinette. He brought to his subjects great learning and a talent for breathing life into far-off places, persons, and times. An impassioned pacifist as well as a Jew, Zweig was forced to leave his native Austria when Hitler came to power. Although they had become British subjects, he and his wife fled to the New World during World War II. Overwhelmed by despair at the triumph of Nazism, Zweig and his wife committed suicide in **Brazil** in 1942.

THE BOOKS THAT SHAPED JEWISH HISTORY

(Note: This list is not exhaustive but rather representative)

The Bible *(1800 B.C.E.-300 B.C.E.)*
Contains the "Written Law" of Judaism, the early history of the Jewish people, ethical teachings of the prophets, poetry, prayers, and wisdom literature.

The Talmud *(300 B.C.E.-500)*
Known as the "Oral Law," it contains the Hebrew Mishnah, *or rabbinic code of law completed around 200, and the Aramaic* Gemara, *which expands the Jewish law, or Halakhah, and adds Jewish lore, or Aggadah.*

Midrash *(300 B.C.E.-1400)*
Collections of Jewish ethics, lore, beliefs, wisdom and instruction.

Beliefs and Opinions by Saadia Gaon *(940)*
Early Jewish philosophical work, reconciling Jewish faith with reason.

Rashi's Commentaries on the Bible and the Talmud *(1100)*
The greatest biblical commentator of all time.

Kuzari and Poetry by Judah Ha-Levi *(1140)*
The Kuzari *explains Judaism philosophically, while the poetry represents one of the high points of Hebrew expression and faith.*

Guide for the Perplexed and the Mishneh Torah by Maimonides *(1200)*
The first provides an explanation of the principles of Judaism, while the second explains Jewish law.

Zohar *(1280)*
The main book of Jewish mysticism, source of the teachings of the Kabbalah.

Shulhan Arukh *(1564)*
The code of Jewish law and religious practice which has been followed for over 400 years.

Hasidic Writings and Teachings *(18th-19th centuries)*
Best known are the stories of the Baal Shem Tov and the early Masters, particularly the stories of Nachman of Bratzlav, and Habad's Tanya. *Hasidic stories, ideas and songs have had a pervasive influence on the Jewish people.*

Mendelssohn's Bible Translation *(1780)*
Moses Mendelssohn's translation of the Hebrew Bible into German opened the door for the Jews in Europe to European culture and started the Jewish Enlightenment and modernization movement.

Zionist Literature *(1862)*
Beginning with Hess's Rome and Jerusalem, *and culminating in Herzl's* The Jewish State *and Ahad Ha-Am's* At the Crossroads, *these writings laid the groundwork for the Zionist movement and eventually for the reestablishment of the State of Israel.*

Early Hebrew Literature *(1853-1890)*
Beginning with Abraham Mapu's first modern Hebrew novel, Love of Zion, *and continuing with the poetry of J. L. Gordon and the novels of Mendele Mocher Sefarim, these writings ushered the beginning of modern Hebrew literature.*

Sholom Aleichem's Stories *(1900)*
The most popular of Yiddish writers, his stories represent an entire Jewish civilization, most of which had been destroyed by the Holocaust.

Modern Hebrew Poetry *(1900-1998)*
Perhaps the most important modern Hebrew poem was Bialik's In the City of Slaughter *(1903), which impelled young Jews for the first time to organize self-defense, laying the groundwork for the future Israel Defense Force. Influential poetry was also written by Tschernichwsky, Alterman, Shlonsky, Greenberg, and others.*

Jewish Religious Thinkers *(20th century)*
Among religious thinkers who have had a deep impact on Jewish life in the 20th century are Abraham Isaac Kook, Solomon Schechter, Martin Buber, Franz Rosenzweig, Leo Baeck, Mordecai Kaplan, Abraham Joshua Heschel, Joseph Soloveichik, and Rabbi Shneerson, the Lubavitcher Rebbe.

Holocaust Literature *(1945-1998)*
There is an enormous, ever-growing body of Holocaust literature. The books that stand out are Anne Frank's Diary, *Elie Wiesel's* Night, *and the novels of Aharon Appelfeld. Ultimately, the most important legacy of the Holocaust is not literature but the literally millions of documents which are being collected and preserved for future generations.*

Books by and about the Founders of Israel *(1948-1998)*
These include such historical figures as Chaim Weizmann, David Ben-Gurion, Golda Meir, Menachem Begin and others, whose lives and accomplishments embody the miracle of the rebirth of Israel.

GREAT JEWISH WOMEN

(Note: This list is not exhaustive but rather representative)

BIBLICAL TIMES

Sarah *The mother of the Jewish people. Left her native home to start a new nation.*

Rebecca *Helped her son Jacob fulfill his destiny as the father of the tribes of Israel.*

Leah *Married Jacob and gave rise to most of Israel's tribes.*

Rachel *Jacob's first love. She became the symbol of the loving and grieving mother of the Jewish people.*

Miriam *Moses' sister, called the prophetess, who rescued him as a newborn and accompanied him in the exodus.*

The Daughters of Zelophehad *The first women in Jewish history who, during the exodus from Egypt, claimed and obtained equal rights for women.*

Deborah *The great judge and prophet who rescued the tribes of Israel from their enemies.*

Hannah *Mother of the prophet Samuel, who overcame adversity and gave Israel a leader who started the monarchy.*

Ruth *One of the first converts to Judaism, a symbol of devotion, and an ancestor of King David.*

Esther *The courageous Jewish queen of Persia, who defied Haman and rescued the Jewish people.*

MACCABEAN PERIOD

Hannah *Mother of seven sons, who refused to eat pork and bow to Greek idols, and preferred martyrdom for herself and her sons.*

Salome Alexandra *Hasmonean queen, who helped Judaism overcome pagan threats.*

TALMUDIC PERIOD

Rachel *Wife of Rabbi Akiva, who helped him educate himself to become one of the greatest scholars and leaders of Israel.*

Bruriah *Wife of Rabbi Meir, herself a scholarly authority and a woman of uncommon courage.*

MIDDLE AGES

Rachel *Rashi's daughter. She wrote legal decisions for her father.*

16th-17th CENTURY

Gracia Mendes Nasi *Marrano Jew who returned to Judaism, defended the Marranos, and became a Jewish leader in Turkey.*

Glückel of Hameln *German Jew who recorded her memoirs and preserved the Jewish history of her period.*

19th CENTURY

Maid of Ludomir *Hannah Rachel, the only woman in Hasidic history who had a following as a teacher and leader.*

Rebecca Graetz *Early Jewish educator in the U.S. and one of the most celebrated Jewish women of her time.*

Emma Lazarus *American poet, author of* The New Colossus, *inscribed on the Satute of Liberty in New York.*

Sarah Bernhardt *French actress, considered the greatest actress in the world in her time.*

20th CENTURY

Henrietta Szold *Founder of Hadassah and early leader of Zionism in the U.S.*

Lillian Wald *Pioneer of U.S. social work and public health care.*

Rebekah Kohut *Jewish communal worker who served as president of the first World Congress of Jewish Women.*

Rosa Luxemburg *German revolutionary and founder of the Polish Socialist party.*

Lily Montagu *Founder of Liberal Judaism in England.*

Ana Pauker *Foreign Minister of Romania during the communist period.*

Rachel *Early Hebrew poet in the Land of Israel.*

Anna Freud *Eminent child psychologist, daughter of Sigmund Freud.*

Zivia Lubetkin *A leader of the Warsaw Ghetto Uprising.*

Anne Frank *Diarist and Holocaust victim.*

Hannah Senesch *Poet, pioneer of Israel, and paratrooper martyred by the Nazis.*

Geulah Cohen *Israeli underground fighter, member of LEHI, later Israeli political leader.*

Golda Meir *Russian-born, U.S.-raised first woman prime minister of Israel.*

Hannah Arendt *German-American political thinker.*

Simone Weil *French Jewish philosopher.*

Dahlia Rabikovitch *Leading Israeli poet.*

Nelly Sachs *German-born Jewish Noble Prize-winning poet.*

Nadine Gordimer *South African activist and Nobel Prize-winning novelist.*

Anita Brookner *English novelist and art historian.*

Irena Kirszenstein-Szewinska *Polish athlete, considered the greastest female track and field athlete of all time.*

Yael Arad *First Israeli Olympic medalist.*

Betty Friedan *A founder of the modern U.S. women's movement.*

Bella Abzug *U.S. Congresswoman and women's rights activist.*

Diane Feinstein *U.S. Senator from California.*

Barbara Boxer *U.S. Senator from California.*

Ruth Bader Ginsburg *U.S. Supreme Court Justice.*

Barbra Streisand *Singer, actress, Jewish activist.*

Cynthia Ozick *American Jewish fiction writer and essayist*

MAP OF ISRAEL'S MAIN CITIES AND TOWNS

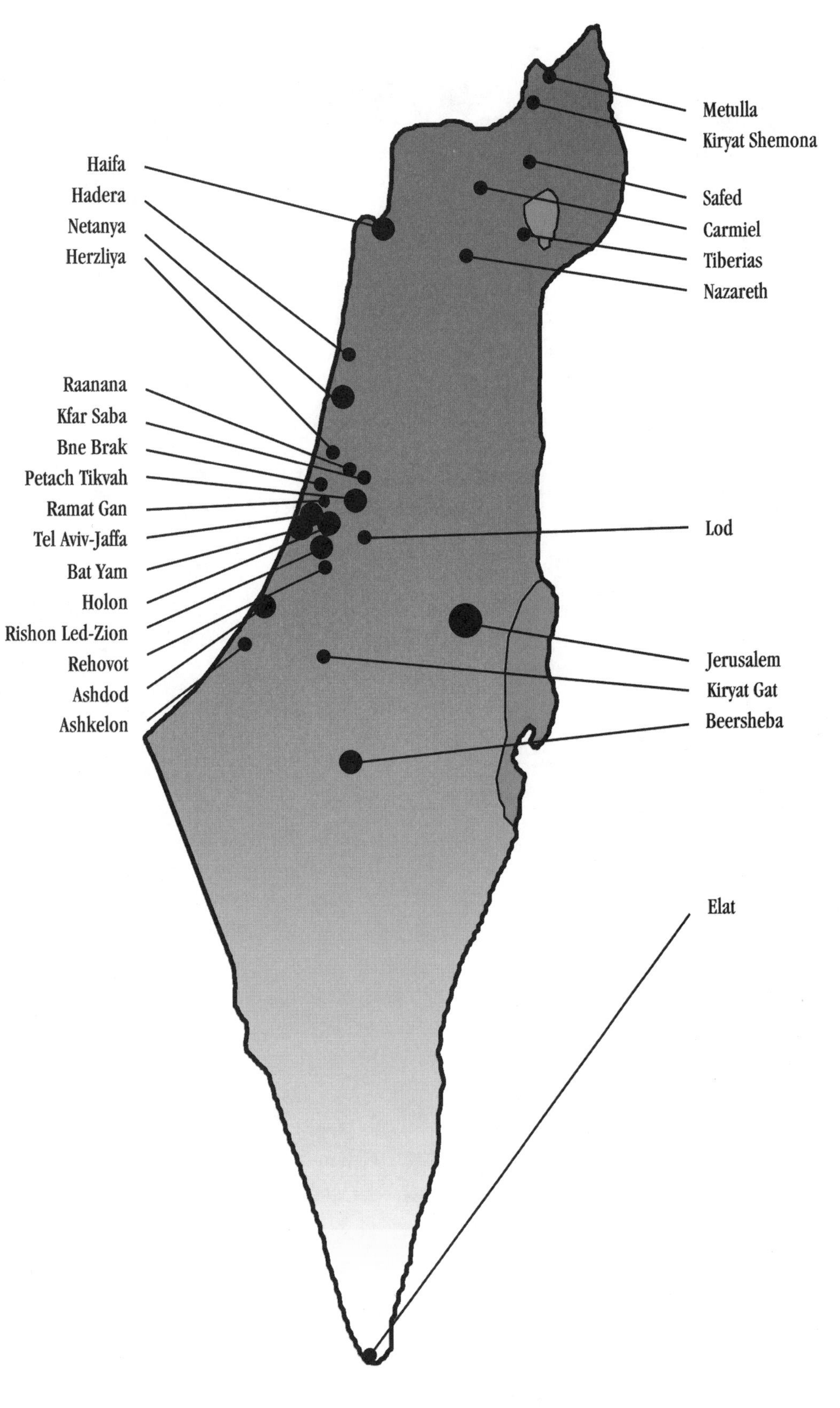

MAJOR WORLD JEWISH

NORTH AMERICA			SOUTH AMERICA			
Canada 360,000	Cuba 700		Argentina 210,000	Suriname 200	Zaire 320
Mexico 40,700	Dominican Republic 100		Bolivia 700	Uruguay 24,000	Zambia 300
United States 5.8 million	Guatemala 1,000		Brazil 100,000	Venezuela 20,000	Zimbabwe 925
	Jamaica 300		Chile 21,000		
CENTRAL AMERICA	Netherlands Antilles 300		Colombia 5,000	**AFRICA**	**OCEANIA**
Bahamas 300	Panama 5,000		Ecuador 900	Egypt 200	Australia 95,000
Costa Rica 2,500	Puerto Rico 1,500		Paraguay 900	Ethiopia 200	New Zealand 4,800
			Peru 3,000	Morocco 6,500	
				South Africa 98,000	
				Tunisia 1,800	

POPULATION CENTERS

EUROPE									
Austria	8,500	Finland	1,200	Latvia	15,000	Spain	14,000	Iran	14,000
Azerbijan	12,000	France	525,000	Lithuania	6,000	Sweden	15,000	Iraq	120
Belarus	28,000	Georgia	10,000	Luxemburg	600	Switzerland	18,000	Israel	4.6 million
Belgium	32,000	Germany	60,000	Moldova	10,000	Turkey	20,000	Japan	1,200
Bulgaria	3,200	Gibraltar	600	Netherlands	27,000	Ukraine	180,000	Lebanon	100
Croatia	1,300	Great Britain	300,000	Norway	1,500	Uzbekistan	20,000	Philippines	150
Czech Republic	2,200	Greece	5,000	Poland	4,000	Yugoslavia	2,000	Singapore	300
Denmark	6,500	Hungary	55,000	Portugal	400	**ASIA**		Syria	250
Estonia	3,000	Ireland	1,300	Romania	14,000	Hong Kong	900	Thailand	250
		Italy	30,000	Russia	360,000	India	4,400	Yemen	300
		Kazakhstan	12,000	Slovakia	3,700				

TIMELINE OF JEWISH

C.E.					
JEWISH HISTORY	*Pale of Settlement in Russia*	*French Sanhedrin under Napolean*	*Emancipation in Prussia*	*I.M. Wise arrives in the U.S.*	*Alliance Israélite Universelle founded*
	1791	1807	1812	1846	1860
	1793	1812	1823	1848	1860
WORLD HISTORY	*Second partition of Poland*	*Napolean retreats from Moscow*	*Monroe Doctrine*	*Revolutions in Europe*	*Garbaldi in Italy*

C.E.					
JEWISH HISTORY	*Mendel Beilis trial in Russia*	*Brandeis appointed to U.S. Supreme Court*	*Balfour Declaration*	*Arab riots in Jaffa*	*Hebrew University founded*
	1911	1916	1917	1921	1925
	1914-1918	1917	1917	1921	1929
WORLD HISTORY	*World War I*	*Russian Revolution*	*British capture Jerusalem; Mandate starts*	*U.S. limits immigration*	*Wall Street crash; Great Depression*

C.E.					
JEWISH HISTORY	*Brandeis University founded*	*Israel's War of Independence*	*Ben-Gurion made Israel's first prime minister*	*Sinai Campaign; Israel invades Egypt*	*Eichmann trial in Jerusalem*
	1946	1948	1949	1956	1962
	1947	1950	1953	1956	1961
WORLD HISTORY	*UN decides the partition Palestine*	*Korean War*	*Stalin dies*	*England and France invade Egypt*	*Kennedy elected U.S. President*

C.E.					
JEWISH HISTORY	*Mass exodus of Jews from former USSR*	*Oslo Agreement with Arafat*	*Rabin's assassination*	*Netanyahu elected prime minister*	*Israel celebrates 50th anniversary*
	1990	1993	1995	1996	1998
	1991	1993	1994		
WORLD HISTORY	*Gulf War against Iraq's Hussein*	*Rabin and Arafat greeted by President Clinton*	*Jordan signs peace with Israel*		